Standard Catalogue of British Coins

COINS OF ENGLAND

& THE UNITED KINGDOM
Decimal Issues

10th Edition

SPINK
LONDON

A Catalogue of the Decimal Coins of
Great Britain and Ireland

Standard Catalogue of British Coins
Coins of England and the United Kingdom
10th edition, 2024

© Spink & Son Ltd, 2023
69 Southampton Row, Bloomsbury
London WC1B 4ET
www.spinkbooks.com

www.spink.com

Typeset by Design to Print UK Ltd,
9 & 10 Riverview Business Park, Forest Row, East Sussex RH18 5FS
www.designtoprintuk.com
Printed and bound in Malta by
Gutenberg Press Ltd.

Cover design: Russell Whittle
Email: uk47@me.com

ISBN 978-1-912667-96-3

CONTENTS

CONTENTS BY CATALOGUE LETTER

ACKNOWLEDGMENTS

We wish to acknowledge the valuable contribution of the following who have submitted information and provided photographs which have greatly enhanced this edition.

David Bayford
Kevin Clancy, Royal Mint
Paul Davies
Jamie Howells, Royal Mint
Geoff Kitchen
London Coin Auctions
Mark Ray
Token Publishing Ltd

Also the collectors who have written in to point out errors or omissions.

Welcome to the tenth edition of the *Coins of England & the United Kingdom Decimal Issues*. Shortly before the previous edition went to press we received the sad news that Her Majesty Queen Elizabeth II had died. A new portrait of His Majesty King Charles III was speedily approved and a first series of coins commemorating the life and legacy of the late Queen was issued, brief details of which appeared in the previous edition. Unusually, proposed mintage figures were not announced for many of these coins and the number produced was equal to the number ordered by 31st December, 2022. Actual sales figures have recently been announced and are recorded in this edition.

A few coins bearing the portrait of the late Queen have been added and a number of anticipated issues have been deleted and transferred to the Charles III section. Two issues released late in 2022 but with 2023 date and bearing the late Queen's portrait were withdrawn from sale at very short notice on 31st December 2022 including the 2023 Chinese new year coins even though that new year did not commence until 22nd January. Illogically, some 2023 dated bullion coins bearing the late Queen's portrait were released in early 2023.

One major re-arrangement has occurred in this new edition. Most of the £5 cupro-nickel crowns previously scattered within the later sections have now been brought forward and listed within the main £5 commemorative crown section. Given the huge popularity of the crown size coin we hope this will be a supported change, although for convenience we have left the £5 Olympic coins in their section. This move has, of course, resulted in a number of catalogue number alterations and these are summarised at the end of the Elizabethan section. We see no further need to make any major amendments to the listing of the Elizabeth era coins.

We had hoped to be able to record actual sales figures of 2020 dated coins but these were received too late for publication. The Royal Mint has recently announced that all coins bearing the portrait of the late Queen will be withdrawn from sale on 31st December 2023. We therefore hope that sales figures for the 2021 and 2022 issues will be available in time for us to include in the next edition.

The change of monarch has caused a pause in the market for decimal issues. What is going to happen is the big question. Will collectors of decimal issues cease collecting or will the issue of new coins with a new monarch result in an upsurge of new collectors? Time will tell but in the meantime there are very few price alterations in this edition.

As previously mentioned, the range of coins has grown enormously in recent years and it is quite likely that if one was starting this catalogue today from scratch, it would not appear in this format. This presents a challenge as to how the coins of King Charles III's new reign are to be listed. We have continued to list the currency, maundy, and sovereign issues in the same style with catalogue numbers continuing. The remaining commemorative issues all with what we refer to as Britannia specifications have just been summarised at this stage with the listings ending with the bullion issues. The number of new coin issues and range of topics has not slowed since the Accession which, if there is no pause, will inevitably lead to the need for a separate volume for the new reign thus enabling a new editor to decide on the style of listing and allocation of catalogue numbers once a clear pattern of coin issues has been established. We will be pleased to hear the views from readers as to how the future new issues should be listed in order to provide consistency, clarity and completeness.

Happy collecting

David Fletcher
Editor, Decimal Issues.

INTRODUCTION

The decision to adopt a decimal currency in place of the £sd system was announced in March 1966 and the first of the new designs entered circulation in 1968, being five and ten pence pieces with the same specification as the old shilling and florin whose pedigree dates back to 1816 and 1849 respectively. In 1969 the fifty pence coin was introduced to replace the ten shilling banknote, thus presenting a gentle introduction to the decimal system prior to Decimal Day in February 1971.

Since that time other denominations have followed – the twenty pence in 1982, the one pound in 1983 and finally the two pound in 1997 though delayed until 1998. In the 1990s owing to higher metal costs and inflation the size of the 5p, 10p and 50p coins was reduced.

One fairly recent policy development either by the mint or the government is that some versions of 50p and £2 commemorative currency coins are not placed into circulation and therefore only available to collectors in brilliant uncirculated condition at a premium. This will surely discourage younger collectors especially those who have collectors' card packs with spaces for such coins. One has to question how the continued issue of commemorative £2 coins can be justified if there is no possibility of any of them entering circulation. An announcement in 2020 indicated that the Royal Mint had sufficient stocks of 2p and £2 coins to fulfil demand well into the 2020s so it was unlikely that circulation strikes of these two denominations would be made for some years although 2021 dated 2ps have subsequently appeared together with small numbers of 2021 and 2022 £2.

Arrangement

Each part of this catalogue has the uniformity of commencing the listing with the lowest denomination and concluding with the highest. The first section lists the currency coins commencing with the lowest 1/2p up to the £2. This is followed by the crowns (which used to be currency pieces) – 25p and £5 – , followed by the Maundy sets and ending with a listing of the uncirculated and proof sets that contain currency type coins.

One of the most popular British coins is the crown – originally a pre-decimal 5/- with a specification of .925 silver, 38.61mm diameter and 28.28grs weight dating back to 1816 and from 1971 becoming a decimal 25p, though uprated to £5 from 1990. But since 2013 there is also a crown size coin with 31.10grs (1oz) of .999 silver with only a face value of £2. And since 2016 there are slightly larger £5 coins but with 2oz .999 silver. So the crown series has become rather confusing with the result that such coins appear in various sections of this catalogue with most of the traditional pieces appearing first within the currency coins section.

The gold sovereign range, with specifications dating back to 1816, then follows with the relevant gold sets listed at the end of that section. Sales figures of the gold proofs are tabulated thus presenting a more accurate record of how many coins were sold singly and how many in sets.

The introduction of Britannia bullion coins in 1987 brought a totally different range of coin specifications to the UK market mainly based on the ounce and its fractions. The sections that follow the Britannia listings mainly comprise coins with Britannia based specifications with many of them issued as bullion pieces for investors as well as proof and BU pieces for collectors, but some sections also include coins with traditional currency specifications. It is not always straightforward to decide exactly where in the catalogue a new coin should be listed and we are prepared to reconsider listing decisions. Within the Britannia and some later sections coins are listed in denomination order within their metal sub groups.

Illustration Sizes
All coins from 1/2p to £5 are depicted actual size. Higher value coins are generally depicted with reduced size so readers should refer to the specification tables for accurate diameter.

Issue Numbers
The number of coins of both definitive and commemorative types isued into circulation can be found in tables immediately after the listing of the currency sets, and this is up to August 2023. Numbers issued of precious metal coins are noted within the coin listings where known.

Most commemorative coins are issued as single pieces but some are issued both as singles and included within a set. Sometimes the set will have a separate authorised mintage from the single coin and other times the issue limit for the coins in the set will be taken from the issue limit for the single coin. As a result of this, the issue limits printed on certificates can sometimes be confusing and it is not always obvious exactly how many pieces of an individual coin might have been made.

In the 20th century the Royal Mint would take coins off sale by 30th June the following year and then in the Spring of the next year the numbers sold would appear in their quarterly Bulletins although there were some gaps. More recently the Mint posts sales figures on their website but as they sometimes retain coins on sale for several years there is a longer time lag in obtaining accurate numbers. The Mint is also not consistent in their method of presentation with the result that we cannot always publish exact sales details of every product. There are some instances where the description of a product within their sales list is not clear and yet a few other instances where the published sales figure is higher than their previously advised issue limit. We hope that over time these anomalies can be cleared.

Coin numbering
Initially the catalogue numbers for the decimal coins started where the £sd coins in the pre-decimal volume ended which was 4159. The increase in the range of coins in subsequent years made it impractical to continue with this numbering sequence so a new numbering sequence commencing with A1 for the lowest denomination of 1/2p was commenced and this has now been extended to all sections. The prefix letter for each denomination or group is shown in the Contents table.

Multi Country Sets
Occasionally a national mint either independently or jointly with the Royal Mint will market a multi nation commemorative set containing a UK coin, and sometimes the UK coin may only be located in such set, which is noted in the catalogue listings. Consideration will be given to listing these sets in a future edition once full details of all of them are available.

Philatelic Numismatic Covers (PNCs)
The Royal Mint and the British Post Office have been issuing first day covers containing coins for much of the decimal period. Initially these covers contained only base metal coins and the numbers issued did not affect the availability of the basic

coins. In more recent years the range of PNCs has included some with gold and silver coins although these are not always announced at the launch of a new issue, but as their sales are now often included in the Royal Mint's published sales figures, we have started to include them and this listing will extend next year.

Definitions
Edition: The number quoted refers to the authorised mintage.
Issued: The number quoted refers to the published sales figure.
Uncirculated, Unc: Coins struck to normal standard for circulation but removed from circulation at an early stage without any wear thus preserving them in mint condition. There is a range of lower grades but there are very few coins in this catalogue with prices quoted for lower grades as the vast majority which are not unc are only worth face value.
Brilliant uncirculated, BU: Coins struck to a higher standard than those minted for release into general circulation.
Proof: Carefully struck coin from special dies with a mirror-like or matt surface, thus creating the highest minting standard.
Piedfort: The word comes from the French and can be translated as 'heavy measure'. Piedfort coins are double the weight of their proof counterparts.
FDC: From the French *Fleur de Coin* to reflect the highest standard of production
O, Obv, Obverse: That side of the coin which normally shows the monarch's head.
R, Rev, Reverse: The side opposite to the obverse, the 'Tails'.
Exergue: That part of the coin below the reverse design, usually separated by a horizontal line, and normally occupied by the date.
Mule: A coin with a current design on one side and an incorrect design on the other side.

Bullion Prices
The prices of some coins reflect the market price of precious metals, and at the time of preparing this edition Gold was £1500 and Platinum £800 per ounce.

Royal Mint Experience
In 2016 the Royal Mint opened the Royal Mint Experience at the Mint which not only offers exhibitions and tours to visitors but also has a range of fun events on offer including the opportunity for visitors to strike their own coin. We believe that some of these coins may differ from those in circulation or available for purchase but we have not had the opportunity to examine such coins to see whether they are standard uncirculated or BU quality. We will seek more information but in the meantime check your change to see what might turn up! We may consider that catalogue status for any 'odd-ball' coins is not appropriate.

Comments from readers will be welcomed about any aspect of this catalogue to *books@spink.com*.

Specifications of currency coins

Denomination	Diameter	Metal	Weight	Metal	Weight	Metal	Weight
½p	17.14 mm	bronze	1.78 g				
1p	20.32 mm	bronze	3.56 g	.925 silver	3.56 g	.916 gold	6.98 g
1p	20.32 mm	Copper-plated steel	3.56 g				
2p	25.91 mm	bronze	7.12 g	.925 silver	7.12 g	.916 gold	13.96 g
2p	25.91 mm	Copper-plated steel	7.12 g				
5p	23.59 mm	cupro-nickel	5.65 g	.925 silver	5.65 g		
5p from 1990	18.00 mm	cupro-nickel	3.25 g	.925 silver	3.25 g	.916 gold	6.32 g
6p	19.41 mm			.925 silver	3.35 g	.916 gold / .999 gold	5.59 g / 6.19 g
10p	28.50 mm	cupro-nickel	11.31 g	.925 silver	11.31 g		
10p from 1992	24.50 mm	cupro-nickel	6.50 g	.925 silver	6.50 g	.916 gold	12.65 g
20p	21.40 mm	cupro-nickel	5.00 g	.925 silver	5.00 g	.916 gold	9.74 g
25p Crown	38.61 mm	cupro-nickel	28.28 g	.925 silver	28.28 g		
50p	30.00 mm	cupro-nickel	13.50 g	.925 silver	13.50 g	.916 gold	26.32 g
50p from 1997	27.30 mm	cupro-nickel	8.00 g	.925 silver	8.00 g	.916 gold	15.58 g
£1	22.50 mm	nickel-brass	9.50 g	.925 silver	9.50 g	.916 gold	19.61 g
£1 from 2016 J39	23.03 mm	bi metal	8.75 g	.925 silver	10.47 g	.916 gold	17.72 g
£2	28.40 mm	nickel-brass	15.98 g	.925 silver	15.98 g	.916 gold	15.97 g
£2 bi-metal	28.40 mm	c-n/n-b	12.00 g	.925 silver	12.00 g	.916 gold	15.97 g
£5 Crown	38.61 mm	cupro-nickel	28.28 g	.925 silver	28.28 g	.916 gold	39.94 g

Maundy

Denomination	Diameter	Metal	Weight	Metal	Weight
4p	17.63 mm	.925 silver	1.88 g	.916 gold	3.16 g
3p	16.26 mm	.925 silver	1.41 g	.916 gold	2.37 g
2p	13.44 mm	.925 silver	0.94 g	.916 gold	1.58 g
1p	11.15 mm	.925 silver	0.47 g	.916 gold	0.79 g

Precious metal coins - Platinum

Denomination	Diameter	Metal	Weight
1p	20.32 mm	.9995 platinum	8.600 g
2p	25.91 mm	—	17.200 g
5p	18.00 mm	—	7.798 g
10p	24.50 mm	—	15.597 g
20p	21.40 mm	—	12.012 g
50p from 1997	27.30 mm	—	19.097 g
£1	22.50 mm	—	19.590 g
£1 from 2016	23.03 mm	—	21.560 g
£2 bi-metal	28.40 mm	—	30.000 g
£5	38.61 mm	—	94.200 g

For Specifications of Gold Sovereign coins, Britannia silver, Britannia gold and Britannia platinum, see pages 166 and 199.

The first section of the catalogue lists the various versions of all the currency coins from the ½p to £5 and ending with the sets containing these coins. The recently issued 6p is included for convenience together with the Maundy coins, although none have been issued for circulation. The ½p coin was demonetised and withdrawn from circulation in December 1984.

BRONZE

HALF PENNY COINS
Obverse portrait by Arnold Machin

A1   A2

A1 **Half new penny.** R. The Royal Crown and the inscription '1/2 NEW PENNY'.
(Reverse design: Christopher Ironside.)

1971............................£1	1975 ....£1	1979...............................£1
— Proof *FDC** £2	— Proof *FDC** £2	— Proof *FDC**.......... £2
1972 Proof *FDC** £6	1976................................£1	1980................................£1
1973............................£1	— Proof *FDC** £2	— Proof *FDC**...........£2
— Proof *FDC**...... £2	1977 ....£1	1981................................£1
1974............................£1	— Proof *FDC** £2	— Proof *FDC** £2
— Proof *FDC**...... £2	1978 ....£1	
	— Proof *FDC** £2	

A2 **Half penny.** R. As A1 with inscription 'HALF PENNY'.

1982............................£1	1983 ....£1	1984........Unc £2; BU* £6
— Proof *FDC**...... £2	— Proof *FDC** £3	— Proof *FDC**..........£6

ONE PENNY COINS
Obverse portrait by Arnold Machin

B1   B2   B3

B1 **One new penny.** R. A portcullis with chains royally crossed, being the badge of Henry VII and his successors, and the inscription 'NEW PENNY' above and the figure '1' below. (Design: Christopher Ironside.)

1971............................£1	1975 ....£1	1979...............................£1
— Proof *FDC**...... £2	— Proof *FDC** £2	— Proof *FDC**...........£2
1972 Proof *FDC** £6	1976................................£1	1980...............................£1
1973............................£1	— Proof *FDC** £2	— Proof *FDC**...........£2
— Proof *FDC** £3	1977 ....£1	1981...............................£1
1974............................£1	— Proof *FDC** £2	— Proof *FDC** £2
— Proof *FDC** £2	1978 ....£1	
	— Proof *FDC** £2	

B2 **One penny.** R. As B1 with inscription 'ONE PENNY'.

1982............................£1	1983 ....£1	1984........Unc £1; BU* £2
— Proof *FDC**....... £2	— *FDC** £2	— Proof *FDC**...........£2

Obverse portrait by Raphael Maklouf

B3   One penny. R. As B2.

1985......Unc £1; BU* £2	1988......... Unc £1; BU* £2	1991.........Unc £1; BU* £2
— Proof *FDC*...... £2	— Proof *FDC*............£2	— Proof *FDC*...........£2
1986......Unc £1; BU* £2	1989......... Unc £1; BU* £2	1992.........Unc £1; BU* £2
— Proof *FDC*...... £2	— Proof *FDC*............£2	— Proof *FDC*...........£2
1987......Unc £1; BU* £2	1990......... Unc £1; BU* £2	
— Proof *FDC*...... £2	— Proof *FDC*............£2	

COPPER PLATED STEEL

B4   One penny R. As B2.

1992..............Unc £1; BU* £2	1996...........................Unc £1; BU* £2
1993........................ Unc £1; BU* £2	— Proof *FDC*........................... £2
— Proof *FDC*................. £2	— Proof in silver *FDC*
1994..............Unc £1; BU* £2	(see PSS09)*....................... £15
— Proof *FDC*........................... £2	1997...........................Unc £1; BU* £2
1995........................ Unc £1; BU* £2	— Proof *FDC*.......................... £2
— Proof *FDC*.......................... £2	

Obverse portrait by Ian Rank-Broadley

B5

B5   One penny. R. As B2.

1998........................... Unc £1; BU* £2	2005...........................Unc £1; BU* £2
— Proof *FDC*...........................£3	— Proof *FDC*...........................£3
1999.............................. Unc £1	2006...........................Unc £1; BU* £2
2000...........................Unc £1; BU* £2	— Proof *FDC*...........................£3
— Proof *FDC*...........................£3	— Proof in silver *FDC* (see PSS26)*£10
— Proof in silver *FDC* (see PSS16)*£10	2007...........................Unc £1; BU* £2
2001...........................Unc £1; BU* £2	— Proof *FDC*...........................£3
— Proof *FDC*...........................£3	2008...........................Unc £1; BU* £2
2002...........................Unc £1; BU* £2	— Proof *FDC*...........................£3
— Proof *FDC*...........................£3	— Proof in silver *FDC* (see PSS38)*£10
— Proof in gold *FDC*	— Proof in gold *FDC*
(see PGCS02)*.........................£350	(see PGCS06)*......................£350
2003...........................Unc £1; BU* £2	— Proof in platinum *FDC*
— Proof *FDC*...........................£3	(see PPLS1)*.........................£300
2004...........................Unc £1; BU* £2	
— Proof *FDC*...........................£3	

BRONZE

B5A   One penny.

1999 BU*.. £3

— Proof *FDC*...£4

* Coins marked thus were originally issued in Royal Mint sets.

COPPER PLATED STEEL

B6

B6 **One penny.** R. A section of Our Royal Arms showing elements of the first and third quartering accompanied by the words 'ONE PENNY'. (Reverse design: Matthew Dent.)

2008 .... Unc £1; BU* £2
— Proof *FDC* (in 2008 set, see PS96)* £3
— Proof in silver *FDC* (in 2008 set, see PSS39)* £10
— Proof piedfort in silver *FDC* (in 2008 set, see PSS40)* £15
— Proof in gold *FDC* (in 2008 set, see PGCS07)* £350
— Proof in platinum *FDC* (in 2008 set, see PPLS2)* £300
2009 .... Unc £1; BU* £2
— Proof *FDC* (in 2009 set, see PS97)* £3
— BU in silver (issued: 8,467)...£15
— Proof in silver *FDC* (in 2009 set, see PSS46)* £15
2010 .... Unc £1; BU* £2
— Proof *FDC* (in 2010 set, see PS101)* £3
— BU in silver (issued: 9,701)...£15
— Proof in silver *FDC* (in 2010 set, see PSS50)* £15
2011 .... Unc £1; BU* £2
— Proof *FDC* (in 2011 set, see PS104) * £3
— BU in silver..£15
— Proof in silver *FDC* (in 2011 set, see PSS53)* £15
2012 .... Unc £1; BU* £2
— Proof *FDC* (in 2012 set, see PS107) * £3
— BU in silver (issued: 5,548)...£15
— Proof in silver *FDC* (see PSS56)* £15
— Proof in silver with selected gold plating *FDC* (Edition: 2,012) (see PSS57)* £15
— Proof in gold *FDC* (see PGCS11)* £400
2013 .... Unc £1; BU* £2
— Proof *FDC* (in 2013 set, see PS109)* £5
— BU in silver (Issued: 10,599) £10
— Proof in silver *FDC* (see PSS58)*..£25
— Proof in gold *FDC* (see PGCS13)* £400
2014 .... Unc £1; BU* £2
— Proof *FDC* (in 2014 set, see PS112)*
— BU in silver (Issued: 6,809) £10
— Proof in silver *FDC* (see PSS66)* £20
2015 .... Unc £1; BU* £2
— Proof *FDC* (in 2015 set, see PS115) * £5
— BU in silver..£10
— Proof in silver *FDC* (see PSS73)*..£25
— Proof in gold *FDC* (see PGCS18) * £350
— Proof in platinum *FDC* (see PPLS3) * £450

* Coins marked thus were originally issued in Royal Mint sets.

Obverse portrait by Jody Clark

B7

B7   **One penny.** R. As B6 above.

2015 ....Unc £1; BU* £2	
— Proof *FDC* (see PS116)* £5	
— BU in silver £10	
— Proof in silver *FDC* (see PSS74)* £20	
— Proof in gold *FDC* (see PGCS19) * £350	
— Proof in platinum *FDC* (see PPLS3) * £450	
2016 ....Unc £1; BU* £2	
— Proof *FDC* (see PS119)* £8	
— BU in silver (Issued: 3,291) £10	
— Proof in silver *FDC* (see PSS75)* £20	
2017 ....Unc £1; BU* £2	
— Proof *FDC* (see PS122)* £7	
— BU in silver £10	
— Proof in silver *FDC* (see PSS79)* £20	
— Proof in gold *FDC* (see PCGS25)* £400	
2018 BU* £5	
— BU in presentation pack £5	
— Proof *FDC* (see PS125)* £10	
— Proof in silver *FDC* (see PSS83)* £20	
2019 BU* £5	
— BU in silver (Issued: 3,687) £15	
— Proof *FDC* (see PS128)* £10	
— Proof in silver *FDC* (see PSS88)* £20	
2020 ....Unc £1; BU* £3	
— Proof *FDC* (see PS132)* £10	
— Proof in silver *FDC* (see PSS94)* £20	
2021 ....Unc £1; BU* £3	
— Proof *FDC* (in 2021 set, see PS134)* £10	
— Proof in silver *FDC* (in 2021 set, see PSS96)* £20	
2022 ....Unc £1; BU* £3	
— Proof (in 2022 set, see PS136/7)* £10	
— Proof in silver *FDC* (in 2022 set, see PSS98)* £20	

B8   **One penny.** R. As B5 above.

2018 BU in silver £15

Initially issued in a choice of blue or pink wallets, later coins were cased with a certificate celebrating the birth of Prince Louis.

* Coins marked thus were originally issued in Royal Mint sets.

B9   B10

B9   **One penny.** Ṟ. As B5 above but with date in exergue.
2019 BU in silver £15
2020 BU in silver £15
2021 BU in silver £15
 —   BU in silver with Windmill privy mark in folder £20
2022 BU in silver £15
 —   BU in silver with Windmill privy mark in folder £20

B10   **One penny.** O. As B7 but with privy mark displaying Her Majesty's birth year and
the year of her passing. Ṟ. As B7.
2022 BU* £5
 —   Proof in silver *FDC** £25
 —   Proof in gold *FDC** £350
 —   Proof in platinum *FDC** £450

BRONZE

TWO PENCE COINS
Obverse portrait by Arnold Machin

C1   C2

C1   **Two new pence.** Ṟ. The badge of the Prince of Wales, being three ostrich feathers
enfiling a coronet of cross pattee and fleur de lys, with the motto 'ICH DIEN', and the
inscription '2 NEW PENCE'. (Reverse design: Christopher Ironside.)

1971 .... £1	1976 ....£1	1979 ....£1
— Proof *FDC** £2	— Proof *FDC** £2	— Proof *FDC** £2
1972 Proof *FDC** £5	1977 ....£1	1980 ....£1
1973 Proof *FDC** £6	— Proof *FDC** £2	— Proof *FDC** £2
1974 Proof *FDC** £5	1978 ....£1	1981 ....£2
1975 .... £1	— Proof *FDC** £2	— Proof *FDC** £3
— Proof *FDC** £2		

C2   **Two pence.** Ṟ. As C1 with inscription 'TWO PENCE'.

1982* £2	1983* £1	1984 BU* £2
— Proof *FDC** £3	— Proof *FDC** £3	— Proof *FDC** £3

C2A   **— Error reverse.** The word 'new' was dropped from the reverse of the currency
issues in 1982 but a number of 2 pence coins were struck in 1983 with the incorrect
reverse die, similar to coins listed as C1. Reports suggest that the error coins, or
'Mules' were contained in some sets packed by the Royal Mint for Martini and
Heinz issued in 1983 ....£1500

Obverse portrait by Raphael Maklouf

C3

C3   Two pence. R. As C2.

1985...... Unc £1; BU* £2	1988..........Unc £1; BU* £2	1991.........Unc £1; BU* £2
— Proof *FDC*........ £3	— Proof *FDC*............. £3	— Proof *FDC*...........£3
1986...... Unc £1; BU* £2	1989...........Unc £1; BU* £2	1992.........Unc £1; BU* £2
— Proof *FDC*........ £3	— Proof *FDC*............. £3	— Proof *FDC*...........£3
1987...... Unc £1; BU* £2	1990...........Unc £1; BU* £2	
— Proof *FDC*........ £3	— Proof *FDC*............. £3	

COPPER PLATED STEEL

C4   Two pence R. As C2.

1992...............................Unc £1; BU* £2	1996.............................Unc £1; BU* £2
1993...............................Unc £1; BU* £2	— Proof *FDC*................................£3
— Proof *FDC* £3	— Proof in silver *FDC*
1994...............................Unc £1; BU* £2	(see PSS09) £15
— Proof *FDC*................................£3	1997...............................Unc £1; BU* £2
1995...............................Unc £1; BU* £2	— Proof *FDC* £3
— Proof *FDC* £3	

Obverse portrait by Ian Rank-Broadley

C5

C5   Two pence. R. As C2

1998..Unc £1; BU* £2
— Proof *FDC*..£3
1999...£1
2000..Unc £1; BU* £2
— Proof *FDC*..£3
— Proof in silver *FDC* (see PSS16)* £10
2001..Unc £1; BU* £2
— Proof *FDC*..£3
2002..Unc £1; BU* £2
— Proof *FDC*..£3
— Proof in gold *FDC* (see PGCS02)* £700

* Coins marked thus were originally issued in Royal Mint sets.

2003 ....Unc £1; BU* £2
— Proof *FDC** £3
2004 ....Unc £1; BU* £2
— Proof *FDC** £3
2005 ....Unc £1; BU* £2
— Proof *FDC** £3
2006 ....Unc £1; BU* £2
— Proof *FDC** £3
— Proof in silver *FDC* (see PSS26)* £10
2007 ....Unc £1; BU* £2
— Proof *FDC** £3
2008 ....Unc £1; BU* £2
— Proof *FDC** £3
— Proof in silver *FDC* (see PSS38)* £10
— Proof in gold *FDC* (see PGCS06)* £700
— Proof in platinum *FDC* (see PPLS2)* £650

BRONZE

C5A **Two pence.** ℞. As C2.
1998 ....£3
1999 BU* £3
— Proof *FDC** £3

COPPER PLATED STEEL

C6

C6 **Two pence.** ℞. A section of Our Royal Arms showing elements of the second quartering
accompanied by the words 'TWO PENCE'. (Reverse design: Matthew Dent.)
2008 .... Unc £1; BU* £2
— Proof *FDC* (in 2008 set, see PS96)* £3
— Proof in silver *FDC* (in 2008 set, see PSS39)* £10
— Proof piedfort in silver *FDC* (in 2008 set, see PSS40)* £20
— Proof in gold *FDC* (in 2008 set, see PGCS07)* £700
— Proof in platinum *FDC* (in 2008 set, see PPLS2)* £650
2009 .... Unc £1; BU* £2
— Proof *FDC* (in 2009 set, see PS97)* £1
— Proof in silver *FDC* (in 2009 set, see PSS 46)* £10
2010 ....Unc £1; BU* £2
— Proof *FDC* (in 2010 set, see PS101)* £3
— Proof in silver *FDC* (in 2010 set, see PSS50)* £10
2011 ....Unc £1; BU* £2
— Proof *FDC* (in 2011 set, see PS104)* £3
— Proof in silver *FDC* (in 2011 set, see PSS53)* £15

* *Coins marked thus were originally issued in Royal Mint sets*

2012 .... Unc £1; BU* £2
— Proof *FDC* (in 2012 set, see PS107)* £3
— Proof in silver *FDC* (see PSS56)*.. £25
— Proof in silver with selected gold plating *FDC* (Edition: 2,012) (see PSS57)* £25
— Proof in gold *FDC* (see PGCS11)* £700
2013 .... Unc £1; BU* £2
— Proof *FDC* (in 2013 set, see PS110)* £5
— Proof in silver *FDC* (see PSS58)*.. £25
— Proof in gold *FDC* (see PGCAS)* £750
2014 .... Unc £1; BU* £2
— Proof *FDC* (in 2014 set, see PS112)* £5
— Proof in silver *FDC* (see PSS66)*.. £25
2015 .... Unc £1; BU* £2
— Proof *FDC* (in 2015 set, see PS115)* £5
— Proof in silver *FDC* (see PSS73)*.. £25
— Proof in gold *FDC* (see PGCS18)* £700
— Proof in platinum *FDC* (issued: 10) (see PPLS3)* £800

Obverse portrait by Jody Clark

C7

C7   **Two pence.** R. As C6.
2015 .... Unc £1; BU* £2
— Proof *FDC* (in 2015 set, see PS116)* £5
— Proof in silver *FDC* (see PSS74)*.. £25
— Proof in gold *FDC* (see PGCS19)* £700
— Proof in platinum *FDC* (issued: 10) (see PPLS3)* £800
2016 .... Unc £1; BU* £2
— Proof *FDC* (in 2016 set, see PS119)* £5
— Proof in silver *FDC* (see PSS75)*.. £25
2017 .... Unc £1; BU* £2
— Proof *FDC* (in 2017 set, see PS122)* £5
— Proof in silver *FDC* (see PSS79)*.. £25
— Proof in gold *FDC* (see PCGS25)* £750
2018 BU* £5
— Proof *FDC* (in 2018 set, see PS125)* £5
— Proof in silver *FDC* (see PSS83)*.. £25
2019 BU* £4
— Proof *FDC* (in 2019 set, see PS128)* £5
— Proof in silver *FDC* (see PSS88)*.. £25
2020 BU* £4
— Proof *FDC* (in 2020 set, see PS132)* £5
— Proof in silver *FDC* (see PSS94)*.. £25

* *Coins marked thus were originally issued in Royal Mint sets.*

2021 ....:..........................Unc £1; BU* £3
— Proof *FDC* (in 2021 set, see PS134)* £8
— Proof in silver *FDC* (in 2021 set, see PSS96)* £20
2022 BU* £3
— Proof (in 2022 set, see PS136/7)* £8
— Proof in silver *FDC* (in 2022 set, see PSS98)* £20
C8   **Two pence.** O. As C7 but with privy mark (see B10) displaying Her Majesty's
birth year and the year of her passing. R. As C7.
2022 BU* £4
— Proof in silver *FDC* £25
— Proof in gold *FDC* £700
— Proof in platinum *FDC* £800

CUPRO-NICKEL

FIVE PENCE COINS
Obverse portrait by Arnold Machin

D1

D1   **Five new pence.** R. A thistle royally crowned, being the badge of Scotland, and the
inscription '5 NEW PENCE'. (Reverse design: Christopher Ironside.)

1968 ....£1		1976 Proof *FDC** £5	
1969 ....£1		1977 ....£1	
1970 ....£1		— Proof *FDC** £3	
1971 ....£1		1978 .... £1	
— Proof *FDC** £4		— Proof *FDC** £3	
1972 Proof *FDC** £5		1979 ....£1	
1973 Proof *FDC** £6		— Proof *FDC** £3	
1974 Proof *FDC** £5		1980 ....£1	
1975 ....£1		— Proof *FDC** £2	
— Proof *FDC** £5		1981 Proof *FDC** £4	

D2

D2   **Five pence.** R. As D1 with inscription 'FIVE PENCE'.

1982* £4	1983* £4	1984 BU* £4
— Proof *FDC** £5	— Proof *FDC* £5	— Proof *FDC** £5

* Coins marked thus were originally issued in Royal Mint sets.

Obverse portrait by Raphael Maklouf

D3

D3 Five pence. R̶. As D2.

1985 BU*................. £4	1988.........Unc £2; BU* £2	1990 BU*.....................£4
— Proof FDC*........£5	— Proof FDC*.............£3	— Proof FDC*...........£5
1986 BU*...................... £4	1989...........Unc £2; BU* £2	— Proof in silver FDC* £10
— Proof FDC*........£5	— Proof FDC*.............£3	
1987......Unc £2; BU* £2		
— Proof FDC* £3		

D4

D4 Five pence. R̶. As D2 but with reduced diameter of 18 mm.

1990............................Unc £2; BU* £2	1994............................Unc £2; BU* £2
— Proof FDC*.............................£4	— Proof FDC*.............................£4
— Proof in silver FDC*..............£10	1995............................Unc £2; BU* £2
— Proof piedfort in silver	— Proof FDC*.............................£4
FDC (Issued:20,000)...............£20	1996............................Unc £2; BU* £2
1991............................Unc £2; BU* £2	— Proof FDC*.............................£4
— Proof FDC*.............................£4	— Proof in silver FDC*
1992............................Unc £2; BU* £2	(see PSS09)............................£15
— Proof FDC*.............................£4	1997...£2
1993*..£4	— Proof FDC*.............................£4
— Proof FDC*.............................£6	

PSS03 - 1990 5p (D3 and D4) silver proofs (2) (Issued: 35,000) £25

Obverse portrait by Ian Rank-Broadley

D5

D5 Five pence. R̶. As D4.

1998...Unc £1; BU* £2
— Proof FDC *...£3
1999 ....Unc £1; BU* £2
— Proof FDC *...£3

* Coins marked thus were originally issued in Royal Mint sets.

2000 .... Unc £1; BU* £2
— Proof *FDC* * £3
— Proof in silver *FDC* (see PSS16)* £12
2001 .... Unc £1; BU* £2
— Proof *FDC* * £3
2002 .... Unc £1; BU* £2
— Proof *FDC* * £3
— Proof in gold *FDC* (see PGCS02) £325
2003 .... Unc £1; BU* £2
— Proof *FDC* * £3
2004 .... Unc £1; BU* £2
— Proof *FDC** £3
2005 .... Unc £1; BU* £2
— Proof *FDC** £3
2006 .... Unc £1; BU* £2
— Proof *FDC** £3
— Proof in silver *FDC* (see PSS26)* £12
2007 .... Unc £1; BU* £2
— Proof *FDC** £3
2008 .... Unc £1; BU* £2
— Proof *FDC* * £3
— Proof in silver *FDC* (see PSS38)* £12
— Proof in gold *FDC* (see PGCS06)* £325
— Proof in platinum *FDC* (see PPLS1)* £250

D6

D6   Five pence. R. A section of Our Royal Arms showing elements of all four quarterings
accompanied by the words 'FIVE PENCE'. (Reverse design: Matthew Dent.)
2008 .... Unc £1; BU* £2
— Proof *FDC* (in 2008 set, see PS96)* £3
— Proof in silver *FDC* (in 2008 set, see PSS39)* £12
— Proof piedfort in silver *FDC* (in 2008 set, see PSS40)* £25
— Proof in gold *FDC* (in 2008 set, see PGCS07)* £325
— Proof in platinum *FDC* (in 2008 set, see PPLS2)* £250
2009 .... Unc £1; BU* £2
— Proof *FDC* (in 2009 set, see PS97)* £3
— Proof in silver *FDC* (in 2009 set, see PSS46)* £12
2010 .... Unc £1; BU* £2
— Proof *FDC* (in 2010 set, see PS101)* £3
— Proof in silver *FDC* (in 2010 set, see PSS50)* £12

* Coins marked thus were originally issued in Royal Mint sets.

NICKEL PLATED STEEL

D7 **Five pence.** R. As D6.

2011 .... Unc £1; BU* £2
— Proof *FDC* (in 2011 set, see PS104)* £3
— Proof in silver *FDC* (in 2011 set, Edition: 2,500) (see PSS53)* £12
2012 ....Unc £1; BU* £2
— Proof *FDC* (in 2012 set, see PS107)* £5
— Proof in silver *FDC* (see PSS56)* £30
— Proof in silver with selected gold plating *FDC* (Edition: 2,012) (see PSS57)* £30
— Proof in gold *FDC* (see PGCS11)* £325
2013 .... Unc £1; BU* £2
— Proof *FDC* (in 2013 set, see PS109)* £5
— Proof in silver *FDC* (see PSS58)* £30
— Proof in gold *FDC* (see PGCS13)* £350
2014 .... Unc £1; BU* £2
— Proof *FDC* (in 2014 set, see PS112)* £5
— Proof in silver *FDC* (see PSS66)* £30
2015 ....Unc £1; BU* £2
— Proof *FDC* (in 2015 set, see PS115)* £5
— Proof in silver *FDC* (see PSS73)* £30
— Proof in gold *FDC* (see PGCS18)* £325
— Proof in platinum *FDC* (see PPLS3)* £450

Obverse portrait by Jody Clark

D8

D8 **Five pence.** R. As D6.

2015 ....Unc £1; BU* £3
— Proof *FDC* (in 2015 set, see PS116)* £5
— Proof in silver *FDC* (see PSS74)* £20
— Proof in gold *FDC* (see PGC5P)* £325
— Proof in platinum *FDC* (see PPLS3)* £450
2016 .... Unc £1; BU* £3
— Proof *FDC* (in 2016 set, see PS119)* £5
— Proof in silver *FDC* (see PSS75)* £30
2017 ....Unc £1; BU* £3
— Proof *FDC* (in 2017 set, see PS122)* £5
— Proof in silver *FDC* (see PSS79)* £30
— Proof in gold *FDC* (see PCGS25)* £350
2018 BU* £5
— Proof *FDC* (in 2018 set, see PS125)* £7
— Proof in silver *FDC* (see PSS83)* £30
2019 BU* £4
— Proof *FDC* (in 2019 set, see PS128)* £6
— Proof in silver *FDC* (see PSS88)* £25
2020 .... Unc £1; BU* £3
— Proof *FDC* (in 2020 set, see PS132)* £6
— Proof in silver *FDC* (see PSS94)* £25

* Coins marked thus were originally issued in Royal Mint sets.

2021 ....Unc £1; BU* £3
— Proof *FDC* (in 2021 set, see PS134)*...£5
— Proof in silver *FDC* (in 2021 set, see PSS96)* £25
2022 ....Unc £1; BU* £3
— Proof (in 2022 set, see PS136/7)* £5
— Proof in silver *FDC* (in 2022 set, see PSS98)* £25

D9 **Five pence.** O. As D8 but with privy mark (see B10) displaying Her Majesty's
birth year and the year of her passing. R. As D8.
2022 BU*...£4
— Proof in silver *FDC*...£20
— Proof in gold *FDC*...£325
— Proof in platinum *FDC*...£450

SIX PENCE COIN

E1

E1 **Six pence.** (0.925 silver). R. A design of Our Royal Cypher surrounded by a floral motif
with the inscription SIXPENCE' accompanied by the date of the year. (Reverse design:
John Bergdahl.)
2016 BU in presentation box (Issued: 4,825)..£30
2017 BU in presentation box...£30
2018 BU in folder..£20
2019 BU in presentation box...£30
2020 BU in presentation box...£30
2021 BU in presentation pack £32
— BU in presentation box with George V 6d £50
— Proof *FDC* in .916 rose gold £475
— Proof *FDC* in .999 yellow gold..£500
2022 BU in presentation pack £32
— Proof *FDC* in .916 rose gold £475

* Coins marked thus were originally issued in Royal Mint sets.

TEN PENCE COINS
Obverse portrait by Arnold Machin

F1   F2

F1   Ten new pence. R. Lion passant guardant being royally crowned, being part of the crest
of England, and the inscription '10 NEW PENCE'. (Reverse design: Christopher Ironside.)

1968.......................... £2	1974 .... £2	1978 Proof *FDC**..........£6
1969.......................... £2	— Proof *FDC** £3	1979................................£2
1970.......................... £3	1975 .... £2	— Proof *FDC*........... £3
1971.......................... £3	— Proof *FDC** £3	1980................................£2
— Proof *FDC** £4	1976 .... £2	— Proof *FDC** £3
1972 Proof *FDC** £5	— Proof *FDC** £3	1981................................£5
1973.......................... £2	1977 .... £2	— Proof *FDC** £5
— Proof *FDC** £3	— Proof *FDC** £3	

* Coins marked thus were originally issued in Royal Mint sets.

F2   Ten pence. R. As F1 with inscription 'TEN PENCE'.

1982*.......................... £4	1983* £4	1984 BU* £4
— Proof *FDC** £4	— Proof *FDC** £5	— Proof *FDC** £5

Obverse portrait by Raphael Maklouf

F3

F3   Ten pence. R. As F2.

1985 BU* £4	1988 BU* £4	1991 BU* £4
— Proof *FDC* * £5	— Proof *FDC** £5	— Proof *FDC** £5
1986 BU* £4	1989 BU* £4	1992 BU* £5
— Proof *FDC** £5	— Proof *FDC** £5	— Proof *FDC** £6
1987 BU* £4	1990 BU* £4	— Proof in silver *FDC** £14
— Proof *FDC** £5	— Proof *FDC** £5	

* Coins marked thus were originally issued in Royal Mint sets.

F4

F4   **Ten pence. R.** As F2 but with reduced diameter of 24.5 mm.

1992............................Unc £1; BU* £3	1995............................Unc £1; BU* £2
— Proof *FDC*................................£3	— Proof *FDC*................................£3
— Proof in silver *FDC*..............£10	1996............................Unc £1; BU* £2
— Proof piedfort in silver *FDC*	— Proof *FDC*................................£3
(Issued: 14,167).........................£30	— Proof in silver *FDC*
1993 BU*.......................................£4	(see PSS09).............................£15
— Proof *FDC*................................£4	1997............................Unc £1; BU* £2
1994 BU*.......................................£4	— Proof *FDC*................................£3
— Proof *FDC*................................£4	

PSS05 - 1992 10p (F3 and F4) silver proofs (2)...£30

Obverse portrait by Ian Rank-Broadley

          F5   F6

F5   **Ten pence. R.** As F4.

1998 BU*...£5	2005............................Unc £1; BU* £2
— Proof *FDC*................................£5	— Proof *FDC*................................£3
1999 BU*...£5	2006............................Unc £1; BU* £2
— Proof *FDC*................................£5	— Proof *FDC*................................£3
2000............................Unc £1; BU* £2	— Proof in silver *FDC*
— Proof *FDC*................................£3	(see PSS26)*.........................£15
— Proof in silver *FDC*	2007............................Unc £1; BU* £2
(see PSS16)*......................... £15	— Proof *FDC*.............................. £3
2001............................Unc £1; BU* £2	2008............................Unc £1; BU* £3
— Proof *FDC*................................£3	— Proof *FDC*................................£3
2002............................Unc £1; BU* £2	— Proof in silver *FDC*
— Proof *FDC*................................£3	(see PSS38)*......................... £15
— Proof in gold *FDC*	— Proof in gold *FDC*
(see PGCS02)*.....................£650	(see PGCS06)*..................... £650
2003............................Unc £1; BU* £2	— Proof in platinum *FDC*
— Proof *FDC*................................£3	(see PPLS1)*......................... £550
2004............................Unc £1; BU* £2	
— Proof *FDC*................................£3	

F6 **Ten pence.** ℞. A section of Our Royal Arms showing elements of the first quartering accompanied by the words 'TEN PENCE'. (Reverse design: Matthew Dent.)

2008 .... Unc £1; BU* £2
— Proof *FDC* (in 2008 set, see PS96)* £3
— Proof in silver *FDC* (in 2008 set, see PSS39)* £15
— Proof piedfort in silver *FDC* (in 2008 set, see PSS40)* £25
— Proof in gold *FDC* (in 2008 set, see PGCS07)* £650
— Proof in platinum *FDC* (in 2008 set, see PPLS2)* £550
2009 .... Unc £1; BU* £2
— Proof *FDC* (in 2009 set, see PS97)* £3
— Proof in silver *FDC* (in 2009 set, see PSS46)* £15
2010 .... Unc £1; BU* £2
— Proof *FDC* (in 2010 set, see PS101)* £3
— Proof in silver *FDC* (in 2010 set, see PSS50)* £15

NICKEL PLATED STEEL

F7 **Ten pence.** ℞. As F6.

2011 .... Unc £1; BU* £2
— Proof *FDC* (in 2011 set, see PS104)* £3
— Proof in silver *FDC* (in 2011 set, see PSS53)* £15
2012 .... Unc £1; BU* £2
— Proof *FDC* (in 2012 set, see PS107)* £3
— Proof in silver *FDC* (see PSS56)* £30
— Proof in silver with selected gold plating *FDC* (see PSS57)* £30
— Proof in gold *FDC* (see PGCS11)* £650
2013 .... Unc £1; BU* £2
— Proof *FDC* (in 2013 set, see PS109)* £5
— Proof in silver *FDC* (see PSS58)* £30
— Proof in gold *FDC* (see PGCS13)* £700
2014 .... Unc £1; BU* £2
— Proof *FDC* (in 2014 set, see PS112)* £5
— Proof in silver *FDC* (see PSS66)* £30
2015 .... Unc £1; BU* £2
— Proof *FDC* (in 2015 set, see PS115)* £5
— Proof in silver *FDC* (see PSS73)* £30
— Proof in gold *FDC* (see PGCS18)* £650
— Proof in platinum *FDC* (see PPLS3)* £800

* Coins marked thus were originally issued in Royal Mint sets.

Obverse portrait by Jody Clark

F8

F8   **Ten pence. R̶. As F6.**

2015 .... Unc £1; BU* £2
— Proof *FDC* (in 2015 set, see PS116)* £5
— Proof in silver *FDC* (see PSS74) £30
— Proof in gold *FDC* (see PGCS19)* £650
— Proof in platinum *FDC* (see PPLS3)* £800
2016 .... Unc £1; BU* £2
— Proof *FDC* (in 2016 set, see PS119)* £5
— Proof in silver *FDC* (see PSS75)* £30
2017 .... Unc £1; BU* £2
— Proof *FDC* (in 2017 set, see PS122)* £6
— Proof in silver *FDC* (see PSS79)* £30
— Proof in gold *FDC* (see PCGS25)* £700
2018 ....BU* £4
— Proof *FDC* (in 2018 set, see PS125)* £6
— Proof in silver *FDC* (see PSS83)* £30
2019 ....BU* £5
— Proof *FDC* (in 2019 set, see PS128)* £6
— Proof in silver *FDC* (see PSS88)* £30
2020 .... Unc £1; BU* £4
— Proof *FDC* (in 2020 set, see PS132)* £6
— Proof in silver *FDC* (see PSS94)* £30
2021 .... Unc £1; BU* £3
— Proof *FDC* (in 2021 set, see PS134)* £5
— Proof in silver *FDC* (in 2021 set, see PSS96)* £25
2022 .... Unc £1; BU* £3
--- Proof (in 2022 set, see PS136/7)* £5
--- Proof in silver FDC (in 2022 set, see PSS98)* £25

* Coins marked thus were originally issued in Royal Mint sets.

F9   F10

The Great British Coin Hunt – a series of 26 coins depicting the letters of the alphabet from A to Z. (Reverse designs: The Royal Mint Team.)

F9   **Ten pence.** Alphabet – A. ℞. Angel of the North.
2018 unc (Issued: 220,000) £6
— Unc on card (Issued: 118,712 plus 37,992 in US63A).............................£8
— Proof in silver *FDC* (Issued: 3,403 plus 200 in PSS87) £35
— Proof in silver *FDC* in acrylic block (Issued: included with above)....................£45
2019 unc (Issued: 97,044)..£10
— Unc on card (Issued: 1,204 plus15,660 in US67A) £14

F10 **Ten pence.** Alphabet – B. ℞ James Bond.
2018 unc (Issued: 220,000) £4
— Unc on card (Issued: 122,386 plus 37,992 in US63A) £7
— Proof in silver *FDC* (Issued: 6,178 plus 200 in PSS87) £35
— Proof in silver *FDC* in acrylic block (Issued: included with above)....................£45
2019 unc (Issued: 96,187)..£4
— Unc on card (Issued: 1,158 plus15,660 in US67A) £7

F11   F12

F11 **Ten pence.** Alphabet – C. ℞ Cricket.
2018 unc (Issued: 220,000) £2
— Unc on card (Issued: 105,371 plus 37,992 in US63A) £3
— Proof in silver *FDC* (Issued: 2,500 plus 200 in PSS87) £20
— Proof in silver *FDC* in acrylic block (Issued: included with above)....................£45
2019 unc (Issued: 97,045)..£4
— Unc on card (Issued: 1,074 plus15,660 in US67A) £6
— Proof in gold *FDC* (Edition: 256) £700
The gold coin was issued to commemorate the England victory in the Cricket World Cup Final.

F12 **Ten pence.** Alphabet – D. ℞ Double decker bus.
2018 unc (Issued: 220,000) £2
— Unc on card (Issued: 99,483 plus 37,992 in US63A) £3
— Proof in silver *FDC* (Issued: 2,466 plus 200 in PSS87) £20
— Proof in silver *FDC* in acrylic block (Issued: included with above)....................£45
2019 unc (Issued: 95,352)..£4
— Unc on card (Issued: 675 plus15,660 in US67A) £6

F13 F14

F13 **Ten pence.** Alphabet – E. Ŗ. English breakfast.
2018 unc (Issued: 220,000) £2
— Unc on card (Issued: 110,272 plus 37,992 in US63A)...........................£3
— Proof in silver *FDC* (Issued: 2,652 plus 200 in PSS87) £20
— Proof in silver *FDC* in acrylic block (Issued: included with above)...................£45
2019 unc (Issued: 96,844) £3
— Unc on card (Issued: 772 plus15,660 in US67A) £5

F14 **Ten pence.** Alphabet – F. Ŗ. Fish and chips.
2018 unc (Issued: 220,000)..£2
— Unc on card (Issued: 96,056 plus 37,992 in US63A) £3
— Proof in silver *FDC* (Issued: 2,236 plus 200 in PSS87) £20
— Proof in silver *FDC* in acrylic block (Issued: included with above)...................£45
2019 unc (Issued: 93,916)..£3
— Unc on card (Issued: 715 plus15,660 in US67A) £5

F15 F16

F15 **Ten pence.** Alphabet – G. Ŗ. Greenwich Mean Time.
2018 unc (Issued: 220,000) £2
— Unc on card (Issued: 93,141 plus 37,992 in US63A) £3
— Proof in silver *FDC* (Issued: 2,337 plus 200 in PSS87) £20
— Proof in silver *FDC* in acrylic block (Issued: included with above)...................£45
2019 unc (Issued: 93,844) £3
— Unc on card (Issued: 456 plus15,660 in US67A) £5

F16 **Ten pence.** 844 – H. Ŗ. Houses of Parliament.
2018 unc (Issued: 220,000) £2
— Unc on card (Issued: 97,941 plus 37,992 in US63A) £3
— Proof in silver *FDC* (Issued: 2,373 plus 200 in PSS87) £20
— Proof in silver *FDC* in acrylic block (Issued: included with above)...................£45
2019 unc (Issued: 95,149) £3
— Unc on card (Issued: 495 plus15,660 in US67A) £5

F17   F18

F17   **Ten pence.** Alphabet – I. Ṟ. Ice cream.

2018 unc (Issued: 220,000) £2
— Unc on card (Issued: 109,513 plus 37,992 in US63A) £3
— Proof in silver *FDC* (Issued: 2,347 plus 200 in PSS87) £20
— Proof in silver *FDC* in acrylic block (Issued: included with above)....£45
2019 unc (Issued: 95,537)..£3
— Unc on card (Issued: 502 plus15,660 in US67A) £5

F18   **Ten pence.** Alphabet – J. Ṟ. Jubilee.

2018 unc (Issued: 220,000)..£2
— Unc on card (Issued: 94,700 plus 37,992 in US63A) £3
— Proof in silver *FDC* (Issued: 3,469 plus 200 in PSS87) £20
— Proof in silver *FDC* in acrylic block (Issued: included with above)....£45
2019 unc (Issued: 94,660) £3
— Unc on card (Issued: 806 plus15,660 in US67A) £5

F19   F20

F19   **Ten pence.** Alphabet – K. Ṟ. King Arthur.

2018 unc (Issued: 220,000) £2
— Unc on card (Issued: 98,300 plus 37,992 in US63A) £3
— Proof in silver *FDC* (Issued: 2,598 plus 200 in PSS87) £20
— Proof in silver *FDC* in acrylic block (Issued: included with above £45
2019 unc (Issued: 94,123)..£3
— Unc on card (Issued: 536 plus15,660 in US67A) £5

F20   **Ten pence.** Alphabet – L. Ṟ. Loch Ness monster.

2018 unc (Issued: 220,000 ....£2
— Unc on card (Issued: 108,703 plus 37,992 in US63A) £3
— Proof in silver *FDC* (Issued: 2,832 plus 200 in PSS87) £20
— Proof in silver *FDC* in acrylic block (Issued: included with above)....£45
2019 unc (Issued: 97,080)..£3
— Unc on card (Issued: 731 plus15,660 in US67A) £5

F21 F22

F21 **Ten pence.** Alphabet – M. R. Mackintosh.
2018 unc (Issued: 220,000) £2
— Unc on card (Issued: 101,262 plus 37,992 in US63A) £3
— Proof in silver *FDC* (Issued: 2,471 plus 200 in PSS87) £20
— Proof in silver *FDC* in acrylic block (Issued: included with above).....................£45
2019 unc (Issued: 95,230) £3
— Unc on card (Issued: 537 plus15,660 in US67A) £5

F22 **Ten pence.** Alphabet – N. R. NHS.
2018 unc (Issued: 220,000) £3
— Unc on card (Issued: 110,977 plus 37,992 in US63A)...........................£5
— Proof in silver *FDC* (Issued: 3,357 plus 200 in PSS87) £20
— Proof in silver *FDC* in acrylic block (Issued: included with above).....................£45
2019 unc (Issued: 97,053) £5
— Unc on card (Issued: 906 plus15,660 in US67A) £7

F23 F24

F23 **Ten pence.** Alphabet – O. R. Oak tree.
2018 unc (Issued: 220,000) £2
— Unc on card (Issued: 101,520 plus 37,992 in US63A) £3
— Proof in silver *FDC* (Issued: 2,290 plus 200 in PSS87) £20
— Proof in silver *FDC* in acrylic block (Issued: included with above).....................£45
2019 unc (Issued: 95,097) £3
— Unc on card (Issued: 433 plus15,660 in US67A) £5

F24 **Ten pence.** Alphabet – P. R. Post box.
2018 unc (Issued: 220,000) £2
— Unc on card (Issued: 96,277 plus 37,992 in US63A) £3
— Proof in silver *FDC* (Issued: 2,331 plus 200 in PSS87) £20
— Proof in silver *FDC* in acrylic block (Issued: included with above).....................£45
2019 unc (Issued: 93,831) £3
— Unc on card (Issued: 468 plus15,660 in US67A) £5

F25   F26

F25 **Ten pence.** Alphabet –Q. R̩. Queue.
2018 unc (Issued: 220,000) £2
— Unc on card (Issued: 87,776 plus 37,992 in US63A) £3
— Proof in silver *FDC* (Issued: 2,082 plus 200 in PSS87) £20
— Proof in silver *FDC* in acrylic block (Issued: included with above)...................£45
2019 unc (Issued: 92,853) £3
— Unc on card (Issued: 274 plus15,660 in US67A) £5

F26 **Ten pence.** Alphabet –R. R̩. Robin.
2018 unc (Issued: 220,000) £2
— Unc on card (Issued: 110.935 plus 37,992 in US63A)...............................£3
— Proof in silver *FDC* (Issued: 2,937 plus 200 in PSS87) £20
— Proof in silver *FDC* in acrylic block (Issued: included with above)...................£45
2019 unc (Issued: 76,264) £8
— Unc on card (Issued: 1,249 plus15,660 in US67A) £12

F27   F28

F27 **Ten pence.** Alphabet – S. R̩. Stonehenge.
2018 unc (Issued: 220,000) £2
— Unc on card (Issued: 107,365 plus 37,992 in US63A) £3
— Proof in silver *FDC* (Issued: 2,796 plus 200 in PSS87) £20
— Proof in silver *FDC* in acrylic block (Issued: included with above)...................£45
2019 unc (Issued: 95,824) £3
— Unc on card (Issued: 854 plus15,660 in US67A) £5

F28 **Ten pence.** Alphabet – T. R̩. Tea.
2018 unc (Issued: 220,000) £2
— Unc on card (Issued: 97,262 plus 37,992 in US63A) £3
— Proof in silver *FDC* (Issued: 2,380 plus 200 in PSS87) £20
— Proof in silver *FDC* in acrylic block (Issued: included with above)...................£45
2019 unc (Issued: 95,128) £3
— Unc on card (Issued: 1,317 plus15,660 in US67A) £5

F29　　　　　　　　F30

F29 **Ten pence.** Alphabet – U. R. Union flag.
2018 unc (Issued: 220,000) £2
— Unc on card (Issued: 96,343 plus 37,992 in US63A) £3
— Proof in silver *FDC* (Issued: 2,658 plus 200 in PSS87) £20
— Proof in silver *FDC* in acrylic block (Issued: included with above)....................£45
2019 unc (Issued: 95,037) £3
— Unc on card (Issued: 290 plus15,660 in US67A) £5

F30 **Ten pence.** Alphabet – V. R. Villages.
2018 unc (Issued: 220,000) £2
— Unc on card (Issued: 94,244 plus 37,992 in US63A) £3
— Proof in silver *FDC* (Issued: 2,048 plus 200 in PSS87) £20
— Proof in silver *FDC* in acrylic block (Issued: included with above)....................£45
2019 unc (Issued: 93,722) £3
— Unc on card (Issued: 313 plus15,660 in US67A) £5

F31　　　　　　　　F32

F31 **Ten pence.** Alphabet – W. R. World Wide Web.
2018 unc (Issued: 220,000) £2
— Unc on card (Issued: 95,135 plus 37,992 in US63A) £3
— Proof in silver *FDC* (Issued: 2,186 plus 200 in PSS87) £20
— Proof in silver *FDC* in acrylic block (Issued: included with above)....................£45
2019 unc (Issued: 72,649) £7
— Unc on card (Issued: 1,191 plus15,660 in US67A) £10

F32 **Ten pence.** Alphabet – X. R. X marks the spot.
2018 unc (Issued: 220,000) £2
— Unc on card (Issued: 91,125 plus 37,992 in US63A) £3
— Proof in silver *FDC* (Issued: 2,066 plus 200 in PSS87) £20
— Proof in silver *FDC* in acrylic block (Issued: included with above)....................£45
2019 unc (Issued: 94,119) £2
— Unc on card (Issued: 279 plus15,660 in US67A) £4

F33   F34

F33   Ten pence. Alphabet – Y. R. Yeoman Warder.
2018 unc (Issued: 220,000) £2
— Unc on card (Issued: 95,394 plus 37,992 in US63A) £3
— Proof in silver *FDC* (Issued: 2,110 plus 200 in PSS87)............................£35
— Proof in silver *FDC* in acrylic block (Issued: included with above).....................£45
2019 unc (Issued: 74,095) £7
— Unc on card (Issued: 1,248 plus15,660 in US67A) £10

F34   Ten pence. Alphabet – Z. R. Zebra crossing.
2018 unc (Issued: 220,000) £2
— Unc on card (Issued: 92,759 plus 37,992 in US63A) £3
— Proof in silver *FDC* (Issued: 2,091 plus 200 in PSS87) £35
— Proof in silver *FDC* in acrylic block (Issued: included with above).....................£45
2019 unc (Issued: 73,278) £7
— Unc on card (Issued: 1,138 plus15,660 in US67A) £10

US63A - 2018 10p Alphabet A-Z (26) (Issued: 37,992) £75
US67A - 2019 10p Alphabet A-Z (26) (Issued: 15,660)..£75
PSS87 - 2018 10p Alphabet A-Z silver proofs (26) (Issued: 200)........................£900

F35   Ten pence. O. As F8 but with privy mark (see B10) displaying Her Majesty's
birth year and the year of her passing. R. As F8.
2022 BU* £4
— Proof in silver *FDC** £25
— Proof in gold *FDC** £650
— Proof in platinum *FDC** £800

CUPRO-NICKEL

TWENTY PENCE COINS

The 20p coin was issued on 9th June 1982. Whilst it was a first in the decimal series, a pre-decimal equivalent of 4/- was issued between 1887 and 1890. The new 20p proved very popular which resulted in an immediate lower demand for 50p coins.

Obverse portrait by Arnold Machin

G1

G1   Twenty pence. R. The Royal Badge of the Rose of England represented as a double rose barbed and seeded, slipped and leaved and ensigned by a Royal Crown and the date of the year with the inscription 'TWENTY PENCE' and the figure '20' superimposed on the stem of the rose. (Reverse design: William Gardner.)

1982 ....£2
— Proof *FDC** £3
— Proof piedfort in silver *FDC* (Issued: 10,000) £30
— Proof *FDC** £3
1983 ....£1
— Proof *FDC** £3
1984 ....Unc £1; BU* £2
— Proof *FDC** £3

Obverse portrait by Raphael Maklouf

G2

G2   Twenty pence. R. Crowned double rose.

1985 .... Unc £1; BU* £2	1989 .... Unc £1; BU* £2
— Proof *FDC** £3	— Proof *FDC** £3
1986 BU* £5	1990 .... Unc £1; BU* £2
— Proof *FDC** £6	— Proof *FDC** £3
1987 ....Unc £1; BU* £2	1991 .... Unc £1; BU* £2
— Proof *FDC** £3	— Proof *FDC** £3
1988 ....Unc £1; BU* £2	
— Proof *FDC** £3	

* Coins marked thus were originally issued in Royal Mint sets.

G2A

G2A   Twenty pence. Enhanced royal portrait.

1992......................................Unc £1; BU* £2
  — Proof *FDC*.................................£3
1993...........................Unc £1; BU* £2
  — Proof *FDC*.................................£3
1994...........................Unc £1; BU* £2
  — Proof *FDC*.................................£3
1995...........................Unc £1; BU* £2
  — Proof *FDC*.................................£3

1996...........................Unc £1; BU* £2
  — Proof *FDC*.................................£3
  — Proof in silver *FDC*............ £18
     (see PSS09)
1997...........................Unc £1; BU* £2
  — Proof *FDC*.................................£3

Obverse portrait by Ian Rank-Broadley

G3   G4

G3   Twenty pence. ℞. As G2.

1998...........................Unc £1; BU* £2
  — Proof *FDC*............................. £3
1999...........................Unc £1; BU* £2
  — Proof *FDC*............................. £3
2000...........................Unc £1; BU* £2
  — Proof *FDC*............................. £3
  — Proof in silver *FDC* (see PSS08) *£20
2001.......................Unc £1; BU* £2
  — Proof *FDC*............................. £3
2002...........................Unc £1; BU* £2
  — Proof *FDC*............................. £3
  — Proof in gold *FDC*
     (see PGCS02)*..........................£500
2003...........................Unc £1; BU* £2
  — Proof *FDC*............................. £3

2004 ....Unc £1; BU* £2
  — Proof *FDC* £3
2005 ....Unc £1; BU* £2
  — Proof *FDC* £3
2006 ....Unc £1; BU* £2
  — Proof *FDC* £3
  — Proof in silver *FDC* (see PSS26)* £20
2007 ....Unc £1; BU* £2
  — Proof *FDC* £3
2008 ....Unc £1; BU* £2
  — Proof *FDC* £3
  — Proof in silver *FDC* (see PSS38)* £20
  — Proof in gold *FDC* (see PGCS06)* .£500
  — Proof in platinum *FDC*
     (see PPLS1)* £450

G4   Twenty pence. ℞. A section of Our Royal Arms showing elements of the second and forth quartering accompanied by the words 'TWENTY PENCE'. (Reverse design: Matthew Dent.)

2008.. Unc £1; BU* £2
  — Proof *FDC* (in 2008 set, see PS96)* £4
  — Proof in silver *FDC* (in 2008 set, see PSS39)* £20
  — Proof piedfort in silver *FDC* (in 2008 set, see PSS40)* £40
  — Proof in gold *FDC* (in 2008 set, see PGCS07)* £500
  — Proof in platinum *FDC* (in 2008 set, see PPLS2)* £450

* Coins marked thus were originally issued in Royal Mint sets.

2009...Unc £1; BU* £2
— Proof *FDC* (in 2009 set, see PS97)*...£6
— Proof in silver *FDC* (in 2009 set, see PSS46)*...................................£20
2010...Unc £1; BU* £2
— Proof *FDC* (in 2010 set, see PS101)*...£6
— Proof in silver *FDC* (in 2010 set, see PSS 50)*.................................£20
2011...Unc £1; BU* £2
— Proof *FDC* (in 2011 set, see PS104) *..£3
— Proof in silver *FDC* (in 2011 set, see PSS53)*..................................£15
2012...Unc £1; BU* £2
— Proof *FDC* (in 2012 set, see PS107)*...£3
— Proof in silver *FDC* (see PSS56)*..£30
— Proof in silver with selected gold plating *FDC* (see PSS57)*............£30
— Proof in gold *FDC* (see PGCS11)*..£500
2013...Unc £1; BU* £2
— Proof *FDC* (in 2013 set, see PS109)*...£5
— Proof in silver *FDC* (see PSS58)*..£30
— Proof in gold *FDC* (see PGCS13)*..£550
2014...Unc £1; BU* £2
— Proof *FDC* (in 2014 set, see PS112)*...£5
— Proof in silver *FDC* (see PSS66)*..£30
2015...Unc £1; BU* £2
— Proof *FDC* (in 2015 set, see PS115)*...£5
— Proof in silver *FDC* (see PSS73)*..£30
— Proof in gold *FDC* (see PGCS18)*..£500
— Proof in platinum *FDC* (see PPLS3)*...£700

G4A – 2008 Error obverse – The new reverse design does not include the year date. This should appear on the obverse but a number of coins were struck using the previous undated obverse as G3 thus creating what is known as a mule.
VF...£45
UNC..£75

Obverse portrait by Jody Clark

G5

G5   Twenty pence. R̟. As G4.
2015...Unc £1; BU* £2
— Proof *FDC* (in 2015 set, see PS116)*...£5
— Proof in silver *FDC* (see PSS74)*..£30
— Proof in gold *FDC* (see PGCS19)*..£500
— Proof in platinum *FDC* (see PPLS3)*...£700
2016...Unc £1; BU* £2
— Proof *FDC* (in 2016 set, see PS119)*...£5
— Proof in silver *FDC* (see PSS75)*..£30
2017 BU*..£6
— Proof *FDC* (in 2017 set, see PS122)*...£10
— Proof in silver *FDC* (see PSS79)*..£30
— Proof in gold *FDC* (see PCGS25)*..£600

* Coins marked thus were originally issued in Royal Mint sets.

```
2018 BU* ...................................................................................................................... £6
 — Proof FDC (in 2018 set, see PS125)* ................................................................ £10
 — Proof in silver FDC (see PSS83)* .................................................................... £30
2019 ............................................................................................... Unc £1; BU* £4
 — Proof FDC (in 2019 set, see PS128)* ................................................................ £10
 — Proof in silver FDC (see PSS88)* .................................................................... £30
2020 .................................................................................................. Unc £1; BU* £4
 — Proof FDC (in 2020 set, see PS132)* ................................................................. £6
 — Proof in silver FDC (see PSS94)* .................................................................... £30
2021 .................................................................................................. Unc £1; BU* £3
 — Proof FDC (in 2021 set, see PS134)* ................................................................. £5
 — Proof in silver FDC (in 2021 set, see PSS96)* ................................................ £30
2022 ............................................................................................... Unc £1; BU* £3
 — BU with 40 privy mark on obverse (Edition: 2,022) ........................................ £15
 — Proof (in 2022 set, see PS136/7)* ................................................................... £5
 — Proof in silver FDC (in 2022 set, see PSS98)* ............................................... £30
```

The 2022 coin with privy mark was issued in a folder with a 1982 dated coin and specimens with Raphael Maklouf & Ian Rank-Broadley portraits all taken from circulation. The privy mark commemorates the 40th anniversary of the 20p coin.

G6   Twenty pence. O. As G5 but with privy mark (see B10) displaying Her Majesty's birth year and the year of her passing. R. As G5.

```
2022 BU* ....................................................................................................... £4
--- Proof in silver FDC* ................................................................................. £30
--- Proof in gold FDC* .................................................................................. £500
--- Proof in platinum FDC* ........................................................................... £700
```

FIFTY PENCE COINS
Obverse portrait by Arnold Machin

H1

H1   Fifty new pence (seven-sided). R. A figure of Britannia seated beside a lion, with a shield resting against her right side, holding a trident in her right hand and an olive branch in her left hand; and the inscription '50 NEW PENCE'. (Reverse design: Christopher Ironside.)

1969	£4	1976	£4	1979	£4
1970	£6	— Proof FDC*	£5	— Proof FDC*	£4
1971 Proof FDC*	£12	1977	£4	1980	£4
1972 Proof FDC*	£15	— Proof FDC*	£4	— Proof FDC*	£4
1974 Proof FDC*	£12	1978	£4	1981	£4
1975 Proof FDC*	£12	— Proof FDC*	£4	— Proof FDC*	£4

*For coins dated 2009 and 2019 see **H20** and **H62**.*

* Coins marked thus were originally issued in Royal Mint sets

H2   H3

H2   **Fifty pence.** Accession to European Economic Community. R. The inscription '50
PENCE' and the date of the year, surrounded by nine hands, symbolizing the nine
members of the community, clasping one another in a mutual gesture of trust, assistance
and friendship. (Reverse design: David Wynne.)
1973..£3
—   Proof *FDC***...£6

H2A   —Design as H2 above, but struck in very small numbers in silver on thicker blank.
Sometimes referred to as a piedfort but not twice the weight of the regular cupro-nickel
currency issue. The pieces were presented to EEC Finance Ministers and possibly
senior officials on the occasion of the United Kingdom joining the European Economic
Community..£3500

*For coins dated 2009 see **H21**.*

H3   **Fifty pence.** R. As H1 with inscription 'FIFTY PENCE'.
1982........................... £4   1983 ....£4   1984 BU* £5
—   Proof *FDC** .... £6   —   Proof *FDC** ....£8   —   Proof *FDC**.........£10

Obverse portrait by Raphael Maklouf

H4

H4   **Fifty pence.** R. As H3.

1985.....Unc £4; BU* £6	1990 BU*........................£6	1996 BU* £6
— Proof *FDC** £8	— Proof *FDC** £8	— Proof *FDC**...........£8
1986 BU* £6	1991 BU*......................£6	— Proof in silver *FDC**
— Proof *FDC** £8	— Proof *FDC** £8	(see PSS09)...........£20
1987 BU* £6	1992 BU*......................£6	1997 BU* £6
— Proof *FDC** £8	— Proof *FDC**..............£12	— Proof *FDC**.........£10
1988 BU* £6	1993 BU*........................£6	— Proof in silver *FDC**£20
— Proof *FDC** £8	— Proof *FDC** £8	
1989 BU* £6	1995 BU*........................£6	
— Proof *FDC** £8	— Proof *FDC** £8	

* *Coins marked thus were originally issued in Royal Mint sets*
** *Issued as an individual proof coin and in the year set*

H5

H5 **Fifty pence** Presidency of the Council of European Community Ministers and completion
of the Single Market. R A representation of a table on which are placed twelve stars, linked
by a network of lines to each other and also to twelve chairs, around the table, on one of
which appear the letters 'UK', and with the dates '1992' and '1993' above and the value
'50 PENCE' below. (Reverse design: Mary Milner Dickens.)
1992-1993 .... VF £30; Unc £50; BU* £75
— Proof *FDC** £80
— Proof in silver *FDC* (Issued: 26,890) £75
— Proof piedfort in silver *FDC* (Issued: 10,993) £90
— Proof in gold *FDC* (Issued: 1,864) £1500

*For coins dated 2009 see **H22**.*

US13 - 1992 50p (H4 and H5) BU in folder (2) £75

H6

H6 **Fifty pence** 50th Anniversary of the Normandy Landings on D-Day. R: A design
representing the Allied invasion force of the D-Day landings heading for Normandy and
filling the sea and sky, together with the value '50 PENCE'. (Reverse design: John Mills.)
1994 .... Unc £4; BU* £4
— BU in presentation folder £5
— Proof *FDC** £6
— Proof in silver *FDC* (Issued: 40,000) £35
— Proof piedfort in silver *FDC* (Issued: 10,000) £60
— Proof in gold *FDC* (Issued: 1,877) £1600

*For coins dated 2009 and 2019 see **H23** and **H67**.*

H7 **Fifty pence** R. As H3 but with reduced diameter of 27.3mm
1997 .... Unc £2; BU* £4
— Proof *FDC** £6
— Proof in silver *FDC* (Issued: 1,632) £25
— Proof piedfort in silver *FDC* (Issued: 7,192) £40

PSS06 - 1997 50p (H4 and H7) silver proofs (2) (Issued: 10,304) £45

* Coins marked thus were originally issued in Royal Mint sets

Obverse portrait by Ian Rank-Broadley

H8   H9

H8 **Fifty pence.** R. As H7.

1998 .... Unc £2; BU* £3
— Proof *FDC** £5
1999 .... Unc £2; BU* £3
— Proof *FDC** £5
2000 .... Unc £2; BU* £3
— Proof *FDC** £3
— Proof in silver *FDC* (see PSS16)* £25
2001 .... Unc £2; BU* £3
— Proof *FDC** £3
2002 .... Unc £2; BU* £4
— Proof *FDC** £4
— Proof in gold *FDC* (see PGCS02)* £750
2003 .... Unc £2; BU* £4
— Proof *FDC** £4
2004 .... Unc £3; BU* £4
— Proof *FDC** £3
2005 .... Unc £2; BU* £3
— Proof *FDC** £3
2006 .... Unc £3
— Proof *FDC** £3
— Proof in silver *FDC* (see PSS26)* £25
2007 .... Unc £3
— Proof *FDC** £3
2008 .... Unc £2; BU* £4
— Proof *FDC** £4
— Proof in silver *FDC* (see PSS38)* £30
— Proof in gold *FDC* (see PGCS06)* £750
— Proof in platinum *FDC* (see PPLS1)* £650

*For coins dated 2009 and see **H24**.*

H9 **Fifty pence.** 25th Anniversary of the United Kingdom's Membership of the European
Union and Presidency of the Council of Ministers.O. As H8. R. Celebratory pattern of
twelve stars reflecting the European flag with the dates 1973 and 1998. (Reverse design:
John Mills.)

1998 .... Unc £2; BU* £5
— Proof *FDC** £5
— Proof in silver *FDC* (Issued: 8,859) £30
— Proof piedfort in silver *FDC* (Issued: 8,440) £50
— Proof in gold *FDC* (Issued: 1,177) £900

*For coins dated 2009 see **H25**.*

US20 - 1998 50p (H8 and H9) BU in folder (2) £12

* Coins marked thus were originally issued in Royal Mint sets.

H10   H11   H12

H10 Fifty pence. 50th Anniversary of the National Health Service.O. As H8. ℞. A pair of hands
set against a pattern of radiating lines with the words 'FIFTIETH ANNIVERSARY' and
the value '50 PENCE' accompanied by the initials 'NHS' which appear five times on the
outer border. (Reverse design: David Cornell.)

1998..£3
— BU in presentation folder..£10
— Proof in silver *FDC* (Issued: 9,032)...£30
— Proof piedfort in silver *FDC* (Issued: 5,117) £50
— Proof in gold *FDC* (Issued: 651)...£1000

For coins dated 2009 see **H26.**

PSS14 - 1998 50p (H9 and H10) silver proofs (2) £60

H11 Fifty pence. 150th Anniversary of the Public Libraries Act. O. As H8. ℞. The turning
pages of a book above the dates '1850 – 2000'and the value '50 PENCE', all above
a classical library building on which the words 'PUBLIC LIBRARY' and, within the
pediment, representations of compact discs. (Reverse design: Mary Milner Dickens.)

2000.. Unc £2; BU* £5
— BU in presentation folder..£10
— Proof *FDC** (Issued: 10,205)...£5
— Proof in silver *FDC* (Issued: 7,634)...£28
— Proof piedfort in silver *FDC* (Issued: 5,721) £50
— Proof in gold *FDC* (Issued: 710)...£850

For coins dated 2009 see **H27.**

H12 Fifty pence. Centenary of the Suffragette Movement. O. As H8. ℞. The figure of a
suffragette chained to railings and holding a banner on which appear the letters 'WSPU',
to the right a ballot paper marked with a cross and the words 'GIVE WOMEN THE
VOTE', to the left the value '50 PENCE' and below and to the far right the dates '1903'
and '2003'. (Reverse design: Mary Milner Dickens.)

2003.. Unc £5; BU* £10
— BU in presentation folder (Issued: 9,582) £12
— Proof *FDC* (in 2003 set, see PS78)* £10
— Proof in silver *FDC* (Issued: 6,267) £28
— Proof piedfort in silver *FDC* (Issued: 6,795 including coins in PSS21)..................£50
— Proof in gold *FDC* (Issued: 942)...£850

For coins dated 2009 see **H28.**

* *Coins marked thus were originally issued in Royal Mint sets.*

H13 H14 H15

H13 **Fifty pence.** 50th Anniversary of the First Sub Four-minute Mile by Roger Bannister. O. As H8. R. The legs of a running athlete with a stylised stopwatch in the background and, below, the value '50 PENCE'. (Reverse design: James Butler.)

2004..Unc £2; BU* £7
— BU in presentation folder (Issued: 10,371)..£9
— Proof *FDC* (in 2004 set, see PS81)*...£7
— Proof in silver *FDC* (Issued: 4,924)..£28
— Proof piedfort in silver *FDC* (Issued: 4,054)...£60
— Proof in gold *FDC* (Issued: 644)...£850

For coins dated 2009 and 2019 see **H29** *and* **H63**.

H14 **Fifty pence**. 250th Anniversary of the Publication of Samuel Johnson's Dictionary of the English Language. O. As H8. R. Entries from Samuel Johnson's Dictionary of the English Language for the words 'FIFTY' and 'PENCE', with the figure '50' above, and the inscription 'JOHNSON'S DICTIONARY 1755' below. (Reverse design: Tom Phillips.)

2005 ....Unc £2; BU* £5
— Proof *FDC* (in 2005 set, see PS84)*...£8
— Proof in silver *FDC* (Issued: 4,029)..£28
— Proof piedfort in silver *FDC* (Issued: 3,808)...£60
— Proof in gold *FDC* (Issued: 584)...£850

For coins dated 2009 see **H30**.

H15 **Fifty pence.** 150th Anniversary of the Institution of the Victoria Cross. O. As H8. R. A depiction of the obverse and reverse of a Victoria Cross with the date '29. JAN 1856' in the centre of the reverse of the Cross, the letters 'VC' to the right and the value 'FIFTY PENCE'. (Reverse design: Claire Aldridge.)

2006 ....Unc £2; BU* £7
— Proof *FDC* (in 2006 set, see PS87)*...£8
— Proof in silver *FDC* (Issued: 6,310 including coins sold in sets)........................£30
— Proof piedfort in silver *FDC* (Issued: 3,532 including coins sold in sets).............£60
— Proof in gold *FDC* (Issued: 866 including coins sold in sets)..........................£900

For coins dated 2009 and 2019 see **H31** *and* **H69**.

* Coins marked thus were originally issued in Royal Mint sets.

H16   H17

H16 **Fifty pence.** 150th Anniversary of the Institution of the Victoria Cross. O. As H8.
R. A Depiction of a soldier carrying a wounded comrade with an outline of the
Victoria Cross surrounded by a sunburst effect in the background and the value
'FIFTY PENCE'. (Reverse design: Clive Duncan.)
2006 ....Unc £2; BU* £6
— Proof *FDC* (in 2006 set, see PS87)* £7
— Proof in silver *FDC* (Issued: 6,872 including coins sold in sets)..........................£30
— Proof piedfort in silver *FDC* (Issued: 3,415 including coins sold in sets) £60
— Proof in gold *FDC* (Issued: 804 including coins sold in sets) £900

For coins dated 2009 and 2019 see **H32** *and* **H70.**

US34 - 2006 50p (H15 and H16) BU in folder (2) (Issued: 31,266) £15
PSS30 - 2006 50p (H15 and H16) silver proofs (2) £65
PSS31 - 2006 50p (H15 and H16) silver piedfort proofs (2)..£115
PGCS04 - 2006 50p (H15 and H16) gold proofs (2) £1800

H17 **Fifty pence.** Centenary of the Founding of the Scouting Movement. O. As H8.
R. A Fleur-de-lis superimposed over a globe and surrounded by the inscription 'BE
PREPARED', and the dates '1907' and '2007' and the denomination 'FIFTY PENCE'.
(Reverse design: Kerry Jones.)
2007 ....Unc £2; BU* £5
— BU in presentation folder (Issued: 46,632) £10
— Proof *FDC* (in 2007 set, see PS90)* £5
— Proof in silver *FDC* (Issued: 10,895) £30
— Proof piedfort in silver *FDC* (Issued; 1,555)* £60
— Proof in gold *FDC* (Issued: 1,250) £850

For coins dated 2009 and 2019 see **H33** *and* **H64.**

* *Coins marked thus were originally issued in Royal Mint sets.*

H18

H18   Fifty pence. R. A section of Our Royal Arms showing elements of the third and fourth quarterings accompanied by the words 'FIFTY PENCE'. (Reverse design: Matthew Dent.)

2008 ....Unc £2; BU* £6	
— Proof *FDC* (in 2008 set, see PS96)* £10	
— Proof in silver *FDC* (in 2008 set, see PSS39)* £30	
— Proof piedfort in silver *FDC* (in 2008 set, see PSS40)* £60	
— Proof in gold *FDC* (in 2008 set, see PGCS07)* £750	
— Proof in platinum *FDC* (in 2008 set, see PPLS2)* £650	
2009 (in 2009 set, see US39) BU* £45	
— Proof *FDC* (in 2009 set, see PS97 & 100)* £45	
— Proof in silver *FDC* (in 2009 set, see PSS46, 47 & 49)* £45	
— Proof in gold *FDC* (in 2009 set, see PGCS09)* £800	
— Proof piedfort in gold *FDC* (Issued: 40) (see PGCS10)* £1750	
2010 BU* £40	
— Proof *FDC* (in 2010 set, see PS101)* £40	
— Proof in silver *FDC* (in 2010 set) (see PSS50)* £30	
2011 BU* £40	
— Proof *FDC* (in 2010 set, see PS104)* £40	
— Proof in silver *FDC* (in 2011 set) (see PSS53) * £30	
2012 ....Unc £2; BU* £7	
— Proof *FDC* (in 2012 set, see PS107)* £7	
— Proof in silver *FDC* (see PSS56)* £30	
— Proof in silver with selected gold plating *FDC* (see PSS57) £35	
— Proof in gold *FDC* (see PGCS11)* £800	
2013 .... Unc £2; BU* £15	
— Proof *FDC* (in 2013 set, see PS109) * £15	
— Proof in silver *FDC* (see PSS58)* £30	
— Proof in gold *FDC* (see PGCS13)* £850	
2014 ....Unc £2; BU* £10	
— Proof *FDC* (in 2014 set, see PS112)* £20	
— Proof in silver *FDC* (see PSS66)* £30	
2015 ....Unc £2; BU* £5	
— Proof *FDC* (in 2015 set, see PS115) * £7	
— Proof in silver *FDC* (see PSS73)* £30	
— Proof in gold *FDC* (see PGCS18) * £800	
— Proof in platinum *FDC* (see PPLS3) * £1000	

* Coins marked thus were originally issued in Royal Mint sets.

H19

H19 **Fifty pence.** 250th Anniversary of the Foundation of the Royal Botanical Gardens, Kew.
R. A design showing the pagoda, a building associated with the Royal Botanical Gardens
at Kew, encircled by a vine and accompanied by the dates '1759' and '2009', with the
word 'KEW' at the base of the pagoda. (Reverse design: Christopher Le Brun.)
2009 .... VF £125; BU £225
— BU in presentation pack (Issued: 128,364) £225
— Proof *FDC* (in 2009 set, see PS100)* £240
— Proof in silver *FDC* (Issued: 3,663 including PSS47 plus 2,749 in PSS46
and 1,163 in PSS49)...£100
— Proof piedfort in silver *FDC* (Issued: 467 plus 2,500 in PSS48).........................£150
— Proof in gold *FDC* (Issued: 629)...£3500
— Proof piedfort in gold *FDC* (Issued: 40) (see PGCS10)* £7500

*For coins dated 2019 see **H66**.*

2009 40th Anniversary of the Introduction of the 50p coin.
H20– Sets comprising 16 proof coins all with the Ian Rank-Broadley obverse in various metals
H33 were issued depicting all the reverse designs that had been used on 50p coins since 1969
with all of them in the reduced 27.3mm diameter. The sets included the 2009 Royal
Arms (H18) and Kew Gardens (H19) designs and the remaining 14 coins featured are
2009 dated versions of the following:

H20	Britannia - 50 new pence (as H1)
H21	Accession to the EEC (as H2)
H22	Presidency of the EU (as H5)
H23	50th Anniversary of D-Day (as H6)
H24	Britannia - 50 pence (as H8)
H25	25th Anniversary of Membership of EU (as H9)
H26	50th Anniversary of the National Health Service (as H10)
H27	150th Anniversary of Public Libraries (as H11)
H28	Centenary of the Suffragette Movement (as H12)
H29	50th Anniversary of the 1st sub Four Minute Mile (as H13)
H30	250th Anniversary of Samuel Johnson's Dictionary (as H14)
H31	150th Anniversary of the Victoria Cross – Award (as H15)
H32	150th Anniversary of the Victoria Cross – Heroic Act (as H16)
H33	Centenary of the Boy Scout Movement (as H17)

Single coins are priced from:
Proof *FDC** £15
Proof in silver *FDC** £30
Proof in gold *FDC** £850
Proof piedfort in gold *FDC** £2000
PS100 - 2009 50p (H18-H33) proofs (16) (Issued: 1,039)................................... £240
PSS49 - 2009 50p (H18-H33) proofs in silver FDC (16) (Issued: 1,168)........................... £450
PGCS09 - 2009 50p (H18-H33) proofs in gold FDC (16) (Issued: 70)........................... £15000
PGCS10 - 2009 50p (H18-H33) proof piedforts in gold FDC (16) (Issued: 40) £30000

* Coins marked thus were originally issued in Royal Mint sets.

H34   H35

H34 **Fifty pence.** 100th Anniversary of Girl Guides. O. As H8. R. A design which depicts a repeating pattern of the current identity of Girl Guiding, UK, accompanied by the inscription 'CELEBRATING ONE HUNDRED YEARS OF GIRLGUIDING UK' and the denomination 'FIFTY PENCE'. (Reverse design: Jonathan Evans and Donna Hainan.)
2010 ....Unc £2; BU* £4
 — BU on presentation card (Issued: 99,075, combined with below) £10
 — BU in presentation folder £12
 — Proof *FDC* (in 2010 set, see PS101)* £7
 — Proof in silver *FDC* (Issued: 4030, including PSS51, plus 1,241 in PSS50).........£30
 — Proof piedfort in silver *FDC* (Issued: 1,298 plus 1,581 in PSS52).......................£55
 — Proof in gold *FDC* (Issued: 355)..£900

For coins dated 2019 see **H65**.

H35 **Fifty pence.** Fiftieth Anniversary of the World Wildlife Fund. O. As H19. R. A design which features 50 different icons symbolising projects and programmes that the World Wildlife Fund has supported over the course of the last 50 years, with the Panda logo of the organisation in the centre and the date '2011' below. (Reverse design: Matthew Dent.)
2011 ....Unc £3; BU* £6
 — BU in presentation folder (Issued: 67,299) £18
 — Proof *FDC* (in 2011 set, see PS104)*..£10
 — Proof in silver *FDC* (Issued: 24,870 including coins in PSS53 & 54)..................£40
 — Proof piedfort in silver *FDC* (Issued: 2,244 including coins in PSS55) £65
 — Proof in gold *FDC* (Issued: 243) £1500

H36

H36 **Fifty pence.** O. As H8. R. A version of the Royal Arms with the inscription 'FIFTY PENCE' above and the denomination '50' below. (Reverse design: Christopher Ironside.)
2013 ....Unc £3; BU* £30
 — BU in presentation folder £60
 — Proof *FDC* (in 2013 set, see PS109)*..£30
 — Proof silver *FDC* (Issued: 1,823 plus 985 coins in PSS58)..................................£55
 — Proof piedfort in silver *FDC* (Issued: 816 plus 486 coins in PSS59).................£100
 — Proof in gold *FDC* (Issued: 198 plus 59 coins in PGCS13) £1200

* Coins marked thus were originally issued in Royal Mint sets.

H37

H37 Fifty pence. Centenary of the Birth of Benjamin Britten. ℞. In the centre the name
'BENJAMIN BRITTEN' superimposed over musical staves with the inscription
'BLOW BUGLE BLOW' above and 'SET THE WILD ECHOES FLYING' below.
(Reverse design: Tom Phillips.)
2013 ....Unc £3; BU £30
— BU in presentation folder £50
— Proof silver *FDC* (Issued: 717) £45
— Proof piedfort in silver *FDC* (Issued: 515)...£90
— Proof in gold *FDC* (Issued: 70) £2000

H38   H39

H38 Fifty pence. Commonwealth Games. O. As H19. ℞. A design of a cyclist and a sprinter
with the Scottish Saltire bisecting the coin and the inscription 'XX COMMONWEALTH
GAMES GLASGOW' and the date'2014'. (Reverse design: Alex Loudon with
Dan Flashman.)
2014 ....Unc £3; BU* £10
— BU in presentation folder (Issued: 14,581) £12
— Proof *FDC* (in 2014 set, see PS112)*..£15
— Proof silver *FDC* (Issued: 2,610 plus 368 coins in PSS66 & 283 in PSS67).........£45
— Proof piedfort in silver *FDC* (Issued: 992 plus 487 coins in PSS68)....................£90
— Proof in gold *FDC* (Issued: 271 plus 75 coins in PGCS17)..............................£1100

H39 Fifty pence. 75th Anniversary of the Battle of Britain. O. As H8. ℞. A design showing
airmen running to their planes with enemy aircraft overhead with the inscription
'THE BATTLE OF BRITAIN 1940'. (Reverse design: Gary Breeze.) N.B. With no
denomination.
2015 BU*..£15
— BU in presentation folder (Issued: 35,199) £25
— Proof *FDC* (in 2015 set, see PS116)*..£20
— Proof in silver *FDC* (Issued: 664, only in PSS70 & 71)* £50
— Proof piedfort in silver *FDC* (Issued: 434, only in PSS72)*............................£100
— Proof in gold *FDC* (Issued: 99, only in PGCS20)*...£1200

* Coins marked thus were originally issued in Royal Mint sets.

Obverse portrait by Jody Clark

H39A H39B H40

H39A Fifty pence. 75th Anniversary of the Battle of Britain. O. As H39A above. R.As H39.
2015 Unc (Issued: 5,960,000)...£2
H39B Fifty pence. 75th Anniversary of the Battle of Britain. O. As H39B above. R.As H39
— Proof in silver *FDC* (Issued: 2,839) £50
— Proof piedfort in silver *FDC* (Issued: 1,422)..£100
— Proof in gold *FDC* (Issued: 389) £1100
For coins dated 2019 see **H68.**

H40 Fifty pence. R. As H18.
2015 ....Unc £2; BU* £5
— Proof *FDC* (in 2015 set, see PS116)*...£15
— Proof in silver *FDC* (see PSS74)*...£30
— Proof in gold *FDC* (see PGCS19)*..£800
— Proof in platinum *FDC* (see PPLS3)*..£1000
2016 BU*...£30
— Proof *FDC* (in 2016 set, see PS119)*...£50
— Proof in silver *FDC* (see PSS75)*...£30
2017 ....Unc £3; BU* £3
— Proof *FDC* (in 2017 set, see PS122)*...£10
— Proof in silver *FDC* (see PSS79)*..£30
— Proof in gold *FDC* (see PCGS25)* £1000
2018 BU*...£25
— Proof *FDC* (in 2018 set, see PS125)*...£25
— Proof in silver *FDC* (see PSS81)*...£30
2019 ....Unc £2; BU* £3
— BU (Issued: 10,000 plus coins in US64/65) £3
— Proof *FDC* (in 2019 set, see PS128)*...£19
— Proof in silver *FDC* (see PSS88)*...£35
2020 ....Unc £2; BU* £3
— Proof *FDC* (in 2020 set, see PS132)*...£15
— Proof in silver *FDC* (see PSS94)*...£35
2021 BU*... £6
— Proof *FDC* (in 2021 set, see PS134)*...£15
— Proof in silver *FDC* (in 2021 set, see PSS96)* £35
The 2021 50p proof was also issued in a pouch for the Tooth Fairy
2022 ....Unc £2; BU* £6
— Proof *FDC* (in 2022 set, see PS136/7) £15
— Proof in silver *FDC* (in 2022 set, see PSS98)* £35

H40A Fifty pence. R. As H18 but with Star mint mark at 4 o'clock.
2022 BU in pouch...£15
Tooth Fairy My Lost Tooth Celebration set.

* *Coins marked thus were originally issued in Royal Mint sets.*

H41

H41 **Fifty pence.** Nine hundred and fiftieth anniversary of the Battle of Hastings. Ŗ. A design showing the scene from the Bayeux tapestry depicting King Harold with an arrow in his eye accompanied by the inscription 'BATTLE OF HASTINGS 1066'and the date of the year. (Reverse design John Bergdahl.)

2016 Unc...£3
— BU (Issued: 5,139 plus coins in sets) £4
— BU in presentation pack (Issued: 21,738) £10
— BU in PNC (Issued: 7,877)..£10
— Proof *FDC* (in PS119)* £15
— Proof in silver *FDC* (Issued: 2,338 plus 1,041 in PSS75 & 76)...........................£50
— Proof piedfort in silver *FDC* (Issued: 1,469 plus 456 in PS77) £100
— Proof in gold *FDC* (Issued: 237 plus 82 in PGCS23) £850

For coins dated 2019 see **H71.**

H42

H42 **Fifty pence.** One hundred and fiftieth anniversary of the birth of Beatrix Potter. O. As H39A. Ŗ. A silhouette of Beatrix Potter accompanied by an image of Peter Rabbit surrounded by a floral motif with the inscription 'BEATRIX POTTER 1866 1943'. (Reverse design: Emma Noble.)

2016 Unc (Issued 6,900,000)...£3
— BU (Issued: 48,650)...£4
— BU in presentation folder (Issued: 61,658) £12
— Proof in silver *FDC* (Issued: 7,471) £200
— Proof piedfort in silver *FDC* (Issued : 2,486)..£300
— Proof in gold *FDC* (Issued: 732) £1400

* Coins marked thus were originally issued in Royal Mint sets.

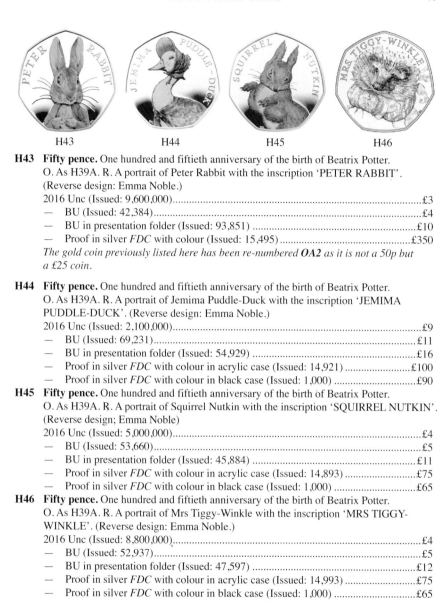

H43   H44   H45   H46

H43   **Fifty pence.** One hundred and fiftieth anniversary of the birth of Beatrix Potter.
O. As H39A. R. A portrait of Peter Rabbit with the inscription 'PETER RABBIT'.
(Reverse design: Emma Noble.)
2016 Unc (Issued: 9,600,000)..£3
— BU (Issued: 42,384)...£4
— BU in presentation folder (Issued: 93,851) £10
— Proof in silver *FDC* with colour (Issued: 15,495)...£350
*The gold coin previously listed here has been re-numbered **OA2** as it is not a 50p but
a £25 coin.*

H44   **Fifty pence.** One hundred and fiftieth anniversary of the birth of Beatrix Potter.
O. As H39A. R. A portrait of Jemima Puddle-Duck with the inscription 'JEMIMA
PUDDLE-DUCK'. (Reverse design: Emma Noble.)
2016 Unc (Issued: 2,100,000)..£9
— BU (Issued: 69,231)...£11
— BU in presentation folder (Issued: 54,929) £16
— Proof in silver *FDC* with colour in acrylic case (Issued: 14,921) £100
— Proof in silver *FDC* with colour in black case (Issued: 1,000) £90

H45   **Fifty pence.** One hundred and fiftieth anniversary of the birth of Beatrix Potter.
O. As H39A. R. A portrait of Squirrel Nutkin with the inscription 'SQUIRREL NUTKIN'.
(Reverse design; Emma Noble)
2016 Unc (Issued: 5,000,000)..£4
— BU (Issued: 53,660)...£5
— BU in presentation folder (Issued: 45,884) £11
— Proof in silver *FDC* with colour in acrylic case (Issued: 14,893) £75
— Proof in silver *FDC* with colour in black case (Issued: 1,000) £65

H46   **Fifty pence.** One hundred and fiftieth anniversary of the birth of Beatrix Potter.
O. As H39A. R. A portrait of Mrs Tiggy-Winkle with the inscription 'MRS TIGGY-
WINKLE'. (Reverse design: Emma Noble.)
2016 Unc (Issued: 8,800,000)..£4
— BU (Issued: 52,937)...£5
— BU in presentation folder (Issued: 47,597) £12
— Proof in silver *FDC* with colour in acrylic case (Issued: 14,993) £75
— Proof in silver *FDC* with colour in black case (Issued: 1,000) £65

US59 - 2016 50p (H42-H46) BU in boxed presentation folders (5) (Issued: 14,777)..............£50

Colour Coins - *Some 50p silver proof coins are issued with colour and this is noted in the
catalogue text. Uncirculated pieces of some issues are available in the market with colour
but these are private productions so are not listed in this catalogue.*

H47					H48

H47 **Fifty pence.** Team GB. O. As H39A. R̥. A depiction of a swimmer with the Team GB logo, the Olympic rings and the inscription 'TEAM GB'. (Reverse design: Consultancy Uniform.)

2016 BU (Issued 8,484)..Unc £2; BU* £5
— BU in presentation folder (Issued: 34,162) £8
— Proof in silver *FDC* (Issued: 4,456) £50
— Proof piedfort in silver *FDC* ((Issued: 1,296) £100
— Proof in gold *FDC* (Issued: 302) £1250

H48 **Fifty pence.** Sir Isaac Newton. O. As H40. R̥. An interpretation of elements of Newton's Proposition 11 from Book One of Principia Mathematica, accompanied by the inscription 'SIR ISAAC NEWTON' and the denomination 'FIFTY PENCE'. (Reverse design: Aaron West.)

2017 ....Unc £4; BU* £6
— BU in presentation folder (Issued: 64,859) £12
— Proof *FDC* (Issued: 706 plus coins in PSS122/123)* £20
— Proof in silver *FDC* (Issued: 3,926 plus 615 coins in PSS79 & 342 in PSS80).....£50
— Proof piedfort in silver *FDC* (Issued: 1,985 plus 364 coins in PSS81)..................£95
— Proof in gold *FDC* (Issued: 287 plus 34 in PGCS25 & 99 in PGCS26) £1000

H49					H50

H49 **Fifty pence.** Commemorating the life and work of Beatrix Potter. R̥. O. As H39A. A portrait of Benjamin Bunny with the inscription 'BENJAMIN BUNNY'. (Reverse design: Emma Noble.)

2017 Unc (Issued: 25,000,000)...£2
— BU...£3
— BU in presentation folder (Issued: 160,040) £9
— Proof in silver *FDC* with colour in black case (Issued: 4,893) £30
— Proof in silver *FDC* with colour in acrylic case (Issued: 29,801) £40
— Proof in silver *FDC* with colour in book gift set (Issued: 1,607)............£75

H50 **Fifty pence.** Commemorating the life and work of Beatrix Potter. O. As H39A. R̥. A portrait of Mr Jeremy Fisher with the inscription 'MR JEREMY FISHER'. (Reverse design: Emma Noble.)

2017 Unc (Issued: 9,900,000)..£3
— BU...£4
— BU in presentation folder (Issued: 167,160) £11
— Proof in silver *FDC* with colour in black case (Issued: 5,149)...............£30
— Proof in silver *FDC* with colour in acrylic case (Issued: 29,245) £50
— Proof in silver *FDC* with colour in book gift set (Issued: 1,355)............£75

* Coins marked thus were originally issued in Royal Mint sets.

H51   H52   H53   H54

H51 **Fifty pence.** Commemorating the life and work of Beatrix Potter. O. As H39A.
R̶. A portrait of Tom Kitten with the inscription 'TOM KITTEN'. (Reverse design:
Emma Noble.)
2017 Unc (Issued: 9,500,000)...£3
— BU..£4
— BU in presentation folder (Issued: 160,496) £10
— Proof in silver *FDC* with colour in black case (Issued: 5,070) £30
— Proof in silver *FDC* with colour in acrylic case (Issued: 27,955) £40
— Proof in silver *FDC* with colour in book gift set (Issued: 1,427).........................£75

H52 **Fifty pence.** Commemorating the life and work of Beatrix Potter. O. As H39A.
R̶. A portrait of Peter Rabbit running with the inscription 'THE TALE OF PETER
RABBIT'. (Reverse design: Emma Noble.)
2017 Unc (Issued: 19,900,000)..£2
— BU..£3
— BU in presentation folder (Issued: 223,661) £10
— Proof in silver *FDC* with colour in black case (Issued: 7,696) £30
— Proof in silver *FDC* with colour in acrylic case (Issued: 29,885) £40
— Proof in silver *FDC* with colour in book gift set (Issued: 2,623).........................£75
— Proof in gold *FDC* (Issued: 48) £1400
— Proof in gold *FDC* in book gift set (Issued: 377) £1400

H53 **Fifty pence.** Commemorating the life and work of Beatrix Potter. O. As H39A.
R̶. A depiction of Peter Rabbit with the inscription 'PETER RABBIT'. (Reverse design:
Emma Noble.)
2018 Unc (Issued: 1,400,000)..£3
— BU (Issued: 115,174)..£5
— BU in presentation folder (Issued: 48,229) £11
— Proof in silver *FDC* with colour in black case (Issued: 4,799) £30
— Proof in silver *FDC* with colour in acrylic case (Issued: 34,681) £40
— Proof in silver *FDC* with colour in book gift set (Issued: 2,700).........................£75
— Proof in gold *FDC* (Issued: 299) £1100
— Proof in gold *FDC* in book gift set (Issued: 262) £1400

H54 **Fifty pence.** Commemorating the life and work of Beatrix Potter. O. As H39A.
R̶. A depiction of Flopsy Bunny with the inscription 'FLOPSY BUNNY. (Reverse
design: Emma Noble).
2018 Unc (Issued: 1,400,000)..£3
— BU (Issued: 102,830)..£5
— BU in presentation folder (Issued: 29,929) £11
— Proof in silver *FDC* with colour in black case (Issued: 2,100) £30
— Proof in silver *FDC* with colour in acrylic case (Issued: 33,963) £40
— Proof in silver *FDC* with colour in book gift set (Issued: 1,729).........................£75

H55   H56

H55   **Fifty pence.** Commemorating the life and work of Beatrix Potter. O. As H39A.
R. A depiction of Mrs Tittlemouse with the inscription. 'MRS TITTLEMOUSE'.
(Reverse design: Emma Noble.)

2018 Unc (Issued: 1,700,000)..£3
—   BU (Issued: 102,888)...£4
—   BU in presentation folder (Issued: 27,497) £10
—   Proof in silver *FDC* with colour in black case (Issued: 2,744) £30
—   Proof in silver *FDC* with colour in acrylic case (Issued: 27,081) £40
—   Proof in silver *FDC* with colour in book gift set (Issued: 885).............................£75

H56   **Fifty pence.** Commemorating the life and work of Beatrix Potter. O. As H39A.
R. A depiction of the Tailor of Gloucester with the inscription 'THE TAILOR OF
GLOUCESTER'. (Reverse design: Emma Noble.)

2018 Unc (Issued: 3,900,000)..£3
—   BU (Issued: 109,278)...£4
—   BU in presentation folder (Issued: 27,079) £10
—   Proof in silver *FDC* with colour in black case (Issued: 3,018) £30
—   Proof in silver *FDC* with colour in acrylic case (Issued: 26,955) £40
—   Proof in silver *FDC* with colour in book gift set (Issued: 970).............................£75

H53-H56   In addition to the recorded sales above of the silver proof coins, a further 950 coins
were sold in a set of four to a trade customer.

H57

H57   **Fifty pence.** 100th Anniversary of the Representation of the People Act.
O. As H39A. R. A depiction of a line of people accompanied by the inscription '1918
REPRESENTATION OF THE PEOPLE ACT'. (Reverse design: Stephen Taylor.)

2018 Unc £2
—   BU (Issued: 38,614 plus coins in US62) £4
—   BU in presentation folder (Issued: 12,311) £10
—   BU in PNC (Issued: 1,303) £10
—   Proof *FDC* (in 2018 set, see PS125)* £15
—   Proof in silver *FDC* (Issue: 1,773 plus 612 in PSS83 and 368 in PSS84) £40
—   Proof piedfort in silver *FDC* (Issued: 984 plus 338 in PSS85)..............................£80
—   Proof in gold *FDC* (Issued: 139 plus 139 in PGCS29) £1000

* Coins marked thus were originally issued in Royal Mint sets.

H58   H59

H58 **Fifty pence.** 60th Anniversary of *A Bear called Paddington* by Michael Bond - I.
O. As H39A. R. Paddington Bear sitting on a suitcase inside Paddington Station.
(Reverse design: David Knapton.)
2018 Unc £2
—   BU (Issued: 117,340) £3
—   BU in presentation folder (Issued: 57,206) £11
—   Proof in silver *FDC* with colour (Issued: 39,481)...............................£30
—   Proof in gold *FDC* (Issued: 592)...£900

H59 Fifty pence. 60th Anniversary of *A Bear called Paddington* by Michael Bond - II.
O. As H39A. R. Paddington Bear waving a Union Flag outside Buckingham Palace.
(Reverse design: David Knapton.)
2018 Unc £2
—   BU (Issued: 104,298) £3
—   BU in presentation folder (Issued: 45,543) £10
—   Proof in silver *FDC* with colour (Issued: 33,369)...............................£30
—   Proof in silver *FDC* with colour in book gift set (Issued: 208)............................£50
—   Proof in gold *FDC* (Issued: 667)...£900
—   Proof in gold *FDC* with colour in book gift set (Issued: 71) £1000

*There are no prices given for some 50p coins in uncirculated condition from 2018 onwards as
none were issued for circulation so base metal pieces are only available in BU packs or year
sets. Loose coins can be found of some issues where the Royal Mint has supplied distributors
with BU coins at a premium.*

H60

H60 **Fifty pence.** 40th Anniversary of *The Snowman* by Raymond Biggs. R. O. As H39A.
The snowman and the little boy soar through the sky. (Reverse design: Natasha Radcliffe.)
2018 BU (Issued 103,061) £8
—   BU in folder (Issued: 67,644)..£14
—   Proof in silver *FDC* with colour in acrylic case (Issued: 20,831) £70
—   Proof in gold *FDC* (Issued: 400) £1100

H61

H61   **Fifty pence.** 160th Anniversary of the Birth of Sir Arthur Conan Doyle. O. As H40.
R. Profile of Sherlock Holmes against a background of the titles of the most popular
books that feature his adventures with the inscription 'SHERLOCK HOLMES' and '50
PENCE'. (Reverse design: Stephen Raw.)

2019 ....Unc £2; BU* £3
—   BU in folder (Issued: 30,349) £10
—   Proof *FDC* * £15
—   Proof in Silver *FDC* set (Issued: 5,805 plus 406 in PSS88) £60
—   Proof piedfort in silver *FDC* (Issued: 2,485 plus 282 in PSS89) £100
—   Proof in gold *FDC* set (Issued: 398 plus 88 in PGCS36) £900

2019 50th Anniversary of the Introduction of the 50p coin.
Two sets comprising 5 coins each all with the Jody Clarke obverse in various metals were issued
depicting reverse designs from previously issued commemoratives and all dated 2019.

H62–   **Fifty pence.** British Culture.
H66   **H62** Britannia (O. As H39A. R As H1) (Issued: BU 53,438)
         H63 1st sub Four Minute Mile (O. As H40. R As H13) (Issued: BU 53,435)
         H64 Boy Scout Movement (O. As H40. R As H17) (Issued: BU 53,431)
         H65 Girl Guide Movement (O. As H40. R As H134) (Issued: BU 53,436)
         H66 Kew Gardens (O. As H39A. R As H19) (Issued: BU 53,431)
         Single coins are priced from:
            BU* £5
            Proof *FDC* * £20
            Proof in silver *FDC* * £35
            Proof piedfort in silver *FDC* * £60
            Proof in gold *FDC* * £1000
            Proof piedfort in gold *FDC* * £1750

US66 -   2019 50p (H62-H66) British Culture (5) (Issued: 31,250) £75
PS130 -   2019 50p (H62-H66) British Culture proofs (5) (Issued: 3,531) £140
PSS90 -   2019 50p (H62-H66) British Culture proofs in silver *FDC* (5) (Issued: 1,933) £250
PSS91 -   2019 50p (H62-H66) British Culture proof piedforts in silver *FDC* (5)
            (Issued: 569) £350
PGCS32 -   2019 50p (H62-H66) British Culture proofs in gold *FDC* (5) (Issued: 71) £6000
PGCS33 -   2019 50p (H62-H66) British Culture proof piedforts in gold *FDC* (5)
            (Issued: 50) £9000

* Coins marked thus were originally issued in Royal Mint sets.

H67– Fifty pence. Military.
H71   H67 50th Anniversary of D-Day (O. As H40. Ŗ As H6) (Issued: BU 22,500)
         H68 Battle of Britain (O. As H39A. Ŗ As H39A) (Issued: BU 22,500)
         H69 Victoria Cross – Award (O. As H40. Ŗ As H15) (Issued: BU 22,500)
         H70 Victoria Cross – Heroic Act (O. As H40. Ŗ As H16) (Issued: BU 22,500)
         H71 Battle of Hastings (O. As H39A. Ŗ As H41) (Issued: BU 22,500)
         Single coins are priced from:
            BU* £6
            Proof *FDC* £20
            Proof in silver *FDC* £35
            Proof piedfort in silver *FDC* £60
            Proof in gold *FDC* £1000
            Proof piedfort in gold *FDC* £1750

US66 - 2019 50p (H67-H71) Military (5) (Issued: 9,902)......................................£45
PS131 - 2019 50p (H67-H71) Military proofs (5) (Issued: 3,144)...........................£120
PSS92 - 2019 50p (H67-H71) Military proofs in silver *FDC* (5) (Issued: 1,934)..................£200
PSS93 - 2019 50p (H67-H71) Military proof piedforts in silver *FDC* (5) (Issued: 333).......£300
PGCS34 - 2019 50p (H67-H71) Military proofs in gold *FDC* (5) (Issued: 75)..................£5500
PGCS35 - 2019 50p (H67-H71) Military proof piedforts in gold *FDC* (5) (Issued: 44).....£9000

H62A   H72

H62A Fifty pence. 50th Anniversary of the Introduction of the 50p coin. O. As H39A.
       R. As H62 but with a Privy Mark and on the outer rim, the letters A to G appear on each
       point and are joined by arced crossing lines.
       2019 BU (Issued: 49,992) £6
       — BU in folder (Issued: 10,990)...£10
       — Proof in silver *FDC* (Issued: 3,479) £40
       — Proof piedfort in silver *FDC* (Issued: 1,962) £65
       — Proof in gold *FDC* (Issued:299)...£1000
       — Proof piedfort in gold *FDC* (Issued: 144) £2000
H72   Fifty pence. The 20th Anniversary of *The Gruffalo* by Julia Donaldson - I.
       O. As H39A. Ŗ. The Gruffalo with inscription. (Reverse design: Magic Light Pictures.)
       2019 BU (Issued: 128,538) £5
       — BU in folder (Issued: 108,014)..£10
       — BU in PNC (Issued: 2,486) £10
       — Proof in silver *FDC* with colour (Issued: 26,064)..................................£35
       — Proof in silver *FDC* in PNC (Issued: 356) £35
       — Proof in gold *FDC* (Issued: 599)...£900

* Coins marked thus were originally issued in Royal Mint sets.

H73   H74

H73 **Fifty pence**. Celebrating the Life of Stephen Hawking. O. As H39A. R. A stylized
depiction of a black hole with the inscription 'STEPHEN HAWKING' and the entropy
equation. (Reverse design: Edwina Ellis.)
2019 BU (Issued: 105,000) £7
—   BU in folder (Issued: 107,209)...£14
—   Proof in silver *FDC* (Issued: 5,465) £40
—   Proof piedfort in silver *FDC* (Issued: 2,481) £90
—   Proof in gold *FDC* (Issued: 396)...£1400
This is the first coin in the Innovation in Science series

H74 Fifty pence. Peter Rabbit. O. As H39A. R. Peter Rabbit in his trademark blue jacket.
(Reverse design: Emma Noble.)
2019 BU (Issued: 78,133) £6
—   BU in folder (Issued: 47,527)..£11
—   Proof in silver *FDC* with colour (Issued: 27,953)...£45
—   Proof in gold *FDC* ((Issued: 497) ....:..£1000

H75   H76

H75 **Fifty pence**. 60th Anniversary of *A Bear called Paddington* by Michael Bond - III.
O. As H39A. R. Paddington Bear at the Tower of London. (Reverse design: David
Knapton.)
2019 Unc (Issued: 9,001,000) £2
—   BU (Issued: 55,500) £4
—   BU in folder (Issued: 32,465)..£10
—   Proof in silver *FDC* with colour (Issued: 17,027)...£45
—   Proof in gold *FDC* (Issued: 596)...£900

H76 **Fifty pence**. The 60th Anniversary of *A Bear called Paddington* by Michael Bond - IV.
O. As H39A. R. Paddington Bear at St Paul's Cathedral. (Reverse design: David Knapton.)
2019 Unc (Issued: 9,001,000) £2
—   BU (Issued: 55,499) £4
—   BU in folder (Issued: 28,219)..£10
—   Proof in silver *FDC* with colour (Issued: 14,017)...£45
—   Proof in gold *FDC* (Issued: 556)...£900

H77   H78   H79

H77 **Fifty pence.** 20th Anniversary of *The Gruffalo* by Julia Donaldson - II. O. As H39A.
R. The Gruffalo confronting a mouse in a wood with inscription. (Reverse design:
Magic Light Pictures.)
2019 BU (Issued: 60,250) £7
— BU in folder (Issued: 37,994)..£11
— Proof in silver *FDC* with colour (Issued: 12,635)..................................£40
— Proof in silver *FDC* with colour in book gift set (Issued: 988)............£45
— Proof in gold *FDC* (Issued: 443)...£900

H78 **Fifty pence.** 30th Anniversary of *Wallace and Gromit* by Nick Park. O. As H39A.
R. Wallace and Gromit with the inscriptions 'CASEUS PRAESTANS' (cracking cheese)
and 'WALLACE GROMIT'. (Reverse design: Nick Park.)
2019 BU (Issued: 60,499) £10
— BU in folder (Issued: 42,251)..£15
— Proof in silver *FDC* with colour (Issued: 15,085)..................................£50
— Proof in gold *FDC* (Issued: 624)..£900

H79 **Fifty pence.** Snowman II. O. As H39A. R. The snowman with James. (Reverse design:
Snowman Enterprises.)
2019 BU (Issued: 76,291) £8
— BU in folder (Issued: 41,959) £12
— Proof in silver *FDC* in acrylic case with colour (Issued: 12,652) £65
— Proof in gold *FDC* (Issued: 315) £1100

H80

H80 **Fifty pence.** Team GB 2020. O. As H39A. R. Symbols of medal winning sports,
the Team GB logo and date '2020'. (Reverse design: David Knapton.)
2020 BU*..£26
— Proof *FDC* (Edition: 5,000)*...£45
— Proof in silver *FDC* (Edition: 500)*...£80
— Proof piedfort in silver *FDC* (Edition: 300)* £200
— Proof in gold *FDC* (Edition: 75)*..£2500
2021 BU £7
— BU in folder...£10
— BU with colour in folder (Edition: 12,021) £20
— Proof in silver *FDC* with colour (Edition: 5,510) £65
— Proof piedfort in silver *FDC* with colour (Edition: 1,510)................£100
— Proof in gold *FDC* (Edition: 260)..£1250

* Coins marked thus were originally issued in Royal Mint sets.

H81

H81 **Fifty pence.** Brexit, the UK's withdrawal from the European Union. O. As H39A.
R. 'Peace, prosperity and friendship with all nations' and the date '31 January 2020'.
(Reverse design: The Royal Mint.)
2020 .... Unc £2
— BU..£6
— BU in folder..£10
— Proof in silver *FDC* (Edition:47,000)...£40
— Proof in gold *FDC* (Edition: 1,500)..£1250
— Proof piedfort in gold *FDC* (Edition: 1,000)...............................£2250

H82   H83   H84

H82 **Fifty pence.** Dinosaurs - I. O. As H39A. R. Megalosaurus with the inscription
'BUCKLAND 1824' (the name of the discover). (Reverse design: Robert Nicholls.)
2020 BU in folder £10
— BU with colour in folder (Edition: 50,000) £20
— Proof in silver *FDC* (Edition: 3,000).....................................£45
— Proof in silver *FDC* with colour (Edition: 7,000) £60
— Proof in gold *FDC* (Edition: 350)..£1000

H83 **Fifty pence.** Dinosaurs - II. O. As H39A. R. Iguanodon with the inscription
'MANTELL 1825' (the name of the discover). (Reverse design: Robert Nicholls.)
2020 BU in folder £10
— BU with colour in folder (Edition: 50,000) £20
— Proof in silver *FDC* (Edition: 3,000).....................................£40
— Proof in silver *FDC* with colour (Edition: 7,000) £50
— Proof in gold *FDC* (Edition: 350)..£1000

H84 **Fifty pence.** Dinosaurs - III. O. As H39A. R. Hylaeosaurus with the inscription
'MANTELL 1833' (the name of the discover). (Reverse design: Robert Nicholls.)
2020 BU in folder £10
— BU with colour in folder (Edition: 50,000) £20
— Proof in silver *FDC* (Edition: 3,000).....................................£40
— Proof in silver *FDC* with colour (Edition: 7,000) £50
— Proof in gold *FDC* (Edition: 350)..£1000

H85   H86

H85 **Fifty pence.** Peter Rabbit. O. As H39A. Ɍ. Peter Rabbit in his trademark blue jacket sneaking under the gate in search of lettuces. (Reverse design: Emma Noble.)
2020 BU in folder £10
—   Proof in silver *FDC* with colour in acrylic case (Edition: 15,000).......................£85
—   Proof in gold *FDC* (Edition: 500)..£1000

H86 **Fifty pence.** Centenary of Birth of Rosalind Franklin. O. As H39A. Ɍ. Depictions of printing techniques from the 1950s with a graphic representation of photograph 51 – one of the most important images in biological science demonstrating the double helix structure of DNA. (Reverse design: David Knapton.)
2020 BU in folder £10
—   Proof in silver *FDC* (Edition: 3,500)...£55
—   Proof piedfort in silver *FDC* (Edition: 1,500) £95
—   Proof in gold *FDC* (Edition: 250)..£1100
This is the second coin in the Innovation in Science series

H87   H88   H89

H87 **Fifty pence.** Characters from A. A. Milne 'Winnie-the-Pooh' books - I. O. As H39A.
Ɍ. Winnie-the-Pooh. (Reverse design: The Walt Disney Company.)
2020 BU in folder £10
—   BU in folder with colour (Edition: 45,000) £20
—   Proof in silver *FDC* with colour (Edition: 18,010) £68
—   Proof in gold *FDC* (Edition: 535).. £1200
—   Proof piedfort in gold FDC (Edition: 110) £2000

H88 **Fifty pence.** Characters from A. A. Milne's 'Winnie-the-Pooh' books - II. O. As H39A.
Ɍ. Christopher Robin coming down the stairs, bear in hand. (Reverse design:
The Walt Disney Company.)
2020 BU in folder..£10
—   BU in folder with colour (Edition: 45,000)..£20
—   Proof in silver *FDC* (Edition: 18,000) £68
—   Proof in gold *FDC* (Edition: 525) £1200

H89 **Fifty pence.** Characters from A. A. Milne's 'Winnie-the-Pooh' books - III. O. As H39A.
Ɍ. Piglet with a dandelion. (Reverse design: The Walt Disney Company.)
2020 BU in folder..£10
—   BU in folder with colour (Edition: 45,000)..£20
—   Proof in silver *FDC* with colour (Edition: 18,000) £68
—   Proof in gold *FDC* (Edition: 525) £1125

H90   H91   H92

H90 **Fifty pence.** Celebration of Diversity. O. As H39A. ℞. A depiction of a web symbolising the connections between communities across the country and the inscription 'DIVERSITY BUILT BRITAIN'. (Reverse design: Dominique Evans.)
2020...Unc £2, BU £6
— BU in folder...£9
— Proof in silver *FDC* (Edition: 25,000) £40
— Proof piedfort in silver *FDC* (Edition: 2,500)....................................£60
— Proof in gold *FDC* (Edition: 950) £1100
— Proof piedfort in gold *FDC* (Edition: 200) £2000

H91 **Fifty pence.** The Snowman - III. O. As H39A. ℞. The Snowman hugging the little boy. (Reverse design: Robin Shaw.)
2020 BU on Greetings card...£10
— BU with colour in folder (Edition: 15,000)...£20
— Proof in silver *FDC* with colour (Edition: 7,010) £68
— Proof in gold *FDC* (Edition: 285) £1150

H92 **Fifty pence.** 50th Anniversary of Decimal Day, 1971. O. As H39A. ℞. The inscription '1971 DECIMAL DAY' accompanied by a range of pre-decimal coins. (Reverse design: Dominique Evans.)
2021 BU in folder..£10
— Proof in silver *FDC* (Edition: 6,710) £58
— Proof piedfort in silver *FDC* (Edition: 2,510)...................................£100
— Proof in gold *FDC* (Edition: 474) £1150
— Proof in gold *FDC* with selected frosting (Edition: 700) Struck on
   15 February 2021 ....£1250
— Proof piedfort in gold *FDC* (Edition: 205) £2250

Obverse portrait by Arnold Machin

H92A

H92A **Fifty pence.** 50th Anniversary of Decimal Day, 1971. ℞. As H92.
2021 BU * £15
— Proof (Edition: 9,500) * £25
— Proof in silver *FDC* (Edition: 550)* £65
— Proof piedfort in silver *FDC* (Edition: 300)*....................................£110
— Proof in gold *FDC* (Edition: 95)* £1400

All versions of the above coin are only available in the year sets.

Obverse portrait by Jody Clark

H93

H93   **Fifty pence.** 75th Anniversary of the death of John Logie Baird. O. As H39A. R. The
inscription 'JOHN LOGIE BAIRD TELEVISION PIONEER' accompanied by a depiction
of a television mast emitting circular radio waves with a range of dates relating to John
Logie Baird and the dates '1888'and '1946' aside the mast. (Reverse design: Osborne Ross.)
2021 BU* £6
— BU in folder..£10
— Proof*...£18
— Proof in silver *FDC* [Edition: 5,010] £55
— Proof piedfort in silver *FDC* [Edition: 2,200]...£100
— Proof in gold *FDC* (Edition: 405) £1100
This is the third coin in the Innovation in Science series.

H94   H95   H96

H94   **Fifty pence.** Dinosaurs - IV. O. As H39A. R. Temnodontosaurus with the inscription
'MARY ANNING 1811' (the name of the discoverer). (Reverse design: Robert Nicholls.)
2021 BU in folder...£10
— BU with colour in folder (Edition: 50,000)..£20
— Proof in silver *FDC* (Edition: 3,010) £63
— Proof in silver *FDC* with colour (Edition: 7,410) £68
— Proof in gold *FDC* (Edition: 260) £1100

H95   **Fifty pence.** Dinosaurs - V. O. As H39A. R. Plesiosaurus with the inscription 'MARY
ANNING 1823' (the name of the discoverer). (Reverse design: Robert Nicholls.)
2021 BU in folder...£10
— BU with colour in folder (Edition: 50,000)..£20
— Proof in silver *FDC* (Edition: 3,010) £63
— Proof in silver *FDC* with colour (Edition: 7,410) £68
— Proof in gold *FDC* (Edition: 260) £1100

H96   **Fifty pence.** Dinosaurs - VI. O. As H39A. R. Dimorphodon with the inscription 'MARY
ANNING 1828' (the name of the discoverer). (Reverse design: Robert Nicholls.)
2021 BU in folder...£10
— BU with colour in folder (Edition: 50,000)..£20
— Proof in silver *FDC* (Edition: 3,010) £63
— Proof in silver *FDC* with colour (Edition: 7,410) £68
— Proof in gold *FDC* (Edition: 260) £1100

H97   H98

H97 **Fifty pence.** Characters from A. A. Milne's 'Winnie-the-Pooh' books - IV. O. As H39A.
R̃. Characters from the children's book with the inscription 'WINNIE THE POOH'.
(Reverse design: The Walt Disney Company.)
2021 BU in folder..£10
—   BU in folder with colour (Edition: 45,000)...£20
—   Proof in silver *FDC* (Edition: 19,095) £68
—   Proof in gold *FDC* (Edition: 630) £1100

H98 **Fifty pence.** 150th Anniversary of the death of Charles Babbage. O. As H39A. R̃. The
inscription 'CHARLES BABBAGE' accompanied by numbers representing the name
Babbage in numerical code. (Reverse design: Nigel Tudman and Jas Bhamra)
2021 BU in folder..£10
—   Proof in silver *FDC* (Edition: 4,000) £60
—   Proof piedfort in silver *FDC* (Edition: 1,510)....................................£100
—   Proof in gold *FDC* (Edition: 260) £1100
This is the fourth coin in the Innovation in Science series.

H99   H100

H99 **Fifty pence.** Centenary of the Discovery of Insulin. O. As H39A. R̃. A depiction of insulin
molecules and the chemical formula for insulin. (Reverse design: Iris De La Torre)
2021 BU in folder..£10
—   Proof in silver *FDC* (Edition: 3,710) £58
—   Proof in piedfort in silver *FDC* (Edition: 1,510)................................£100
—   Proof in gold *FDC* (Edition: 260) £1200
This is the fifth coin in the Innovation in Science series.

H100 **Fifty pence.** Characters from A. A. Milne's 'Winnie-the-Pooh' books V. O. As H39A.
R̃. Owl. (Reverse design: The Walt Disney Company.)
2021 BU in folder..£10
—   BU in folder with colour (Edition: 45,000)...£20
—   Proof in silver *FDC* (Edition: 18,000) £68
—   Proof in gold *FDC* (Edition: 535) £1100

H101   H102   H103

H101 Fifty pence. The Snowman - IV. O. As H39A. Ɍ. The little boy drawing a smile
on the face of his new friend. (Reverse design: Robin Shaw.)
2021 BU on Greetings card...£10
— BU with colour in folder (Edition: 11,510)..£20
— Proof in silver *FDC* with colour (Edition: 8,010).................................£68
— Proof in silver *FDC* with colour in book gift set (Edition: 1,000).......... £95
— Proof in gold *FDC* (Edition: 310) £1150

H102 Fifty pence. Characters from A. A. Milne's 'Winnie-the-Pooh' books VI.
O. As H39A. Ɍ. Tigger. (Reverse design: The Walt Disney Company.)
2021 BU in folder...£10
— BU in folder with colour (Edition: 45,000)..£20
— Proof in silver *FDC* (Edition: 18,000) £68
— Proof in gold *FDC* (Edition: 535) £1100
— Proof in piedfort in gold *FDC* (Edition: 110) £2000

H103 Fifty pence. Platinum Jubilee. O. Her Majesty the Queen on horseback with the
inscription 'ELIZABETH II • D • G • REG • F• D • 50 PENCE' accompanied by
the Garter Belt with the inscription 'HONI • SOIT • QUI • MAL • Y• PENSE •'
and the date of the year. Ɍ. The number '70' and the Royal Cypher surrounded
with the dates '1952-2022'. (Reverse design: Osborne Ross.)
2022 BU £6
— BU in folder...£10
— Proof in silver *FDC* (Edition: 7,605) £58
— Proof piedfort in silver *FDC* (Edition: 2,510)....................................£100
— Proof in gold *FDC* (Edition: 580) £1200
— Proof piedfort in gold *FDC* (Edition: 80) £2500
— Proof in platinum *FDC* (Edition: 150) £2000

H103A Fifty pence. Platinum Jubilee. O. As H39A. Ɍ. As H103.
2022 Unc £2
— BU (see US72/3)*..£6
— Proof (see PS136/7)*...£20
— Proof in silver *FDC* (see PSS98) (Edition: 1250)*...............................£65
— Proof piedfort in silver *FDC* (see PSS99) (Edition: 370)* £120
— Proof in gold *FDC* (see PGCS39) (Edition: 170)* £1250
— Proof in platinum *FDC* (see PPLS4) (Edition: 30)* £2200

All versions of the above coin except for the UNC are only available in the year sets.

US74 - 2022 50p (H103 and H103A) BU in folder (Edition: 1,952) £30
PSS100 - 2022 50p (H103 and H103A) proofs in silver (2) (Edition: 700)...........£130
PGCS40 - 2022 50p (H103 & H103A proofs in gold (2) *FDC* (Edition: 70) £2000

H104   H105   H106   H107

H104 **Fifty pence.** Commonwealth Games. O. As H39A. R̥. The symbol of Commonwealth
Sport and the inscription 'BIRMINGHAM 2022 COMMONWEALTH GAMES'.
(Reverse design: Natasha Preece.)

2022 BU £6
— BU in folder...£10
— BU with colour and Team England privy mark in England folder (Edition: 7,510).£18
— BU with colour and Team Wales privy mark in Wales folder (Edition: 5,010) £18
— BU with colour and Team Scotland privy mark in Scotland folder (Edition: 5,010) .£18
— BU with colour and Team Northern Ireland privy mark in Northern Ireland
folder (Edition: 5,010)..£18
— Proof (see PS136/7)*..£20
— Proof in silver *FDC* (See PSS98)*..£58
— Proof in silver with colour *FDC* (Edition: 4,760) £68
— Proof piedfort in silver *FDC* (See PSS99)* £100
— Proof piedfort in silver with colour *FDC* (Edition: 1,250) £113
— Proof in gold *FDC* (Edition: 410) £1200
— Proof in platinum *FDC* (see PPLS4) (Edition: 30)* £2000

H105 **Fifty pence.** Characters from A. A. Milne's 'Winnie-the-Pooh' books VII. O. As H39A.
R̥. Eeyore accompanied by the inscription 'EEYORE'. (Reverse design: Daniel Thorne.)

2022 BU £6
— BU in folder...£10
— BU in folder with colour (Edition: 12,500)..£20
— Proof in silver with colour *FDC* (Edition: 6,010) £68
— Proof in gold *FDC* (Edition: 160) £1150
— Proof piedfort in gold *FDC* (Edition:) £2200

H106 **Fifty pence.** Characters from A. A. Milne's 'Winnie-the-Pooh' books VIII. O. As H39A.
R̥. Kanga and Roo accompanied by the inscription 'KANGA & ROO'. (Reverse design:
The Walt Disney Company.)

2022 BU £6
— BU in folder...£10
— BU in folder with colour (Edition: 12,500)..£20
— Proof in silver with colour *FDC* (Edition: 6,010) £68
— Proof in gold *FDC* (Edition: 160) £1150

H107 **Fifty pence.** 50th Anniversary of Pride. O. As H39A. R̥. A design depicting elements of
the Pride flag accompanied by the inscription 'PRIDE PROTEST VISIBILITY UNITY
EQUALITY' and '50'. (Reverse design: Dominique Holmes.)

2022 Unc (Issued: 5,000,000) £1
— BU in folder...£10
— BU in folder with colour (Edition: 15,000)..£18
— Proof in silver with colour *FDC* (Edition: 4,955) £68
— Proof piedfort in silver with colour *FDC* (Edition: 1,510) £113
— Proof in gold *FDC* (Edition: 260) £1250
— Proof piedfort in gold *FDC* (Edition: 60) £2500

   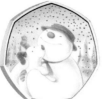

H108   H109   H110   H111

H108 Fifty pence. Alan Turing, O. As H39A. ℞. A cogwheel with the inscription 'ALAN
TURING' set against a background of letters. (Reverse design: Matt Dent and
Christian Davies.)

2022 BU £6
— BU in folder..£10
— Proof in silver *FDC* (Edition: 3,210) £58
— Proof piedfort in silver *FDC* (Edition: 1,510)...............................£100
— Proof in gold *FDC* (Edition: 210) £1150

This is the sixth and final coin in the Innovation in Science series.

H109 Fifty pence. Characters from A. A. Milne's 'Winnie-the-Pooh' books IX. O. As H39A.
℞. Winnie the Pooh and friends accompanied by the inscription 'WINNIE THE POOH'.
(Reverse design: The Walt Disney Company.)

2022 BU £6
— BU in folder..£11
— BU in folder with colour (Edition: 12,500)...£20
— Proof in silver with colour *FDC* (Edition: 6,010) £70
— Proof in gold *FDC* (Edition: 160) £1250

H110 Fifty pence. Centenary of the BBC. O. As H39A. ℞. A design depicting a globe with
transmitter waves accompanied by the inscription '1922-2022 100 YEARS OF OUR
BBC INFORM EDUCATE ENTERTAIN'. (Reverse design: Henry Gray.)

2022 BU £6
— BU in folder..£11
— Proof in silver *FDC* (Edition: 3,510) £60
— Proof piedfort in silver *FDC* (Edition: 1,110)...............................£110
— Proof in gold *FDC* (Edition: 360) £1250

100 gold proof were marketed in a set with a 1922 sovereign.

H111 Fifty pence. The Snowman - V. O. As H39A. ℞. A depiction of the Snowman and the
Snowdog. (Reverse design: Robin Shaw.)

2022 BU £11
— BU with colour in folder (Edition: 8,500)..£20
— BU with colour in Advent calendar (Edition: 2,500) £25
— Proof in silver *FDC* with colour (Edition: 5,010) £70
— Proof in gold *FDC* (Edition: 135) £1250

H112   H113

H112 Fifty pence. Harry Potter – I. O. As H39A. ℞. A depiction of Harry Potter with the inscription 'HARRY POTTER 25 YEARS OF MAGIC' with a latent feature that displays a lightning bolt and the number '25'. (Reverse design: Ffion Gwillim from illustration by Jim Kay.)

2022 BU £6
— BU in folder..£11
— BU in folder with colour £20
— Proof in silver *FDC* with colour (Edition: 15,010) £80
— Proof in gold *FDC* (Edition: 310) £1250

H113 Fifty pence. Harry Potter – II. O. As H39A. ℞. A depiction of the Hogwarts Express and the figure of Harry Potter with the inscription 'HOGWARTS EXPRESS 25 YEARS OF MAGIC' with a latent feature that displays a lightning bolt and the number '25'. (Reverse design: Ffion Gwillim from illustration by Jim Kay.)

2022 BU £6
— BU in folder..£11
— BU in folder with colour £20
— Proof in silver *FDC* with colour (Edition: 15,010) £80
— Proof in gold *FDC* (Edition: 310) £1250

H114 Fifty pence. O. As H40 but with privy mark (see B10) displaying Her Majesty's birth year and the year of her passing. ℞. As H40.

2022 BU* £8
--- Proof in silver *FDC*...£55
--- Proof in gold *FDC*..£1000
--- Proof in platinum *FDC*..£1000

NICKEL-BRASS

ONE POUND COINS

The first base metal £1 coin was issued on 21st April 1983 and it replaced the £1 note that was eventually withdrawn from circulation in 1988. A range of reverse designs was issued until it was replaced on 28th March 2017 by a bi-metal 12-sided coin.

Obverse portrait by Arnold Machin

J1   J2

J1 **One pound.** R. The Ensigns Armorial of Our United Kingdom of Great Britain and Northern Ireland with the value 'ONE POUND' below. Edge inscription 'DECUS ET TUTAMEN'. (Reverse design: Eric Sewell.)

1983 ....£3
—   Unc in presentation folder (Issued: 484,900) £5
—   Proof *FDC* (in 1983 set, see PS33)* £5
—   Proof in silver *FDC* (Issued: 50,000) £25
—   Proof piedfort in silver *FDC* (Issued: 10,000) £100

J2 **One pound.** (Scotland.) R. A thistle eradicated enfiling a representation of Our Royal Diadem with the value 'ONE POUND' below. Edge inscription 'NEMO ME IMPUNE LACESSIT'. (Reverse design: Leslie Durbin.)

1984 ....Unc £3; BU* £4
—   BU in presentation folder (Issued: 27,960) £5
—   Proof *FDC* (in 1984 set, see PS34)* £5
—   Proof in silver *FDC* (Issued: 44,855) £20
—   Proof piedfort in silver *FDC* (Issued: 15,000) £30

Obverse portrait by Raphael Maklouf

J3

J3 **One pound.** (Wales.) R. A leek eradicated enfiling a representation of Our Royal Diadem with the value 'ONE POUND' below. Edge inscription 'PLEIDIOL WYF I'M GWLAD'. (Reverse design: Leslie Durbin.)

1985 ....Unc £2; BU* £3
—   BU in presentation folder (Issued: 24,850) £4
—   Proof *FDC* (in 1985 set, see PS35)* £5
—   Proof in silver *FDC* (Issued: 50,000) £20
—   Proof piedfort in silver *FDC* (Issued: 15,000) £30
1990 ....Unc £2; BU* £3
—   Proof *FDC* (in 1990 set, see PS45)* £6
—   Proof in silver *FDC* (Issued: 23,277) £20

* Coins marked thus were originally issued in Royal Mint sets.

J4 J5 J6

J4 **One pound.** (Ireland.) R. A flax plant eradicated enfiling a representation of Our Royal
Diadem with value 'ONE POUND' below. Edge inscription 'DECUS ET TUTAMEN'.
(Reverse design: Leslie Durbin.)
1986..Unc £2; BU* £4
— BU in presentation folder (Issued: 19,908)..£5
— Proof *FDC* (in 1986 set, see PS37)*..£6
— Proof in silver *FDC* (Issued: 37,958)...£20
— Proof piedfort in silver *FDC* (Issued: 15,000) £30
1991..Unc £2; BU* £5
— Proof *FDC* (in 1991 set, see PS47)*..£6
— Proof in silver *FDC* (Issued: 22,922)...£20

J5 **One pound.** (England.) R. An oak tree enfiling a representation of Our Royal Diadem
with the value 'ONE POUND' below. Edge inscription 'DECUS ET TUTAMEN'.
(Reverse design: Leslie Durbin.)
1987..Unc £2; BU* £3
— BU in presentation folder (Issued: 72,607)..£4
— Proof *FDC* (in 1987 set, see PS39)*..£6
— Proof in silver *FDC* (Issued: 50,000)...£20
— Proof piedfort in silver *FDC* (Issued: 15,000) £30
1992..Unc £2; BU* £3
— Proof *FDC* (in 1992 set, see PS49)*..£6
— Proof in silver *FDC* (Issued: 13,065)...£20

J6 **One pound.** (Crowned Royal Shield.) R. A Crowned Shield of Our Royal Arms
ensigned by a representation of Our Royal Crown with the value 'ONE POUND' below.
Edge inscription 'DECUS ET TUTAMEN'. (Reverse design: Derek Gorringe.)
1988..Unc £4; BU* £5
— BU in presentation folder (Issued: 29,550)..£6
— Proof *FDC* (in 1988 set, see PS41)*..£6
— Proof in silver *FDC* (Issued: 50,000)...£20
— Proof piedfort in silver *FDC* (Issued: 10,000) £30

J7 **One pound.** (Scotland.) R. As J2.
1989..Unc £2; BU* £3
— Proof *FDC* (in 1989 set, see PS43)*..£6
— Proof in silver *FDC* (Issued: 22,275)...£20
— Proof piedfort in silver *FDC* (Issued: 10,000) £30

J8 **One pound.** (Royal Arms.) R. As J1.
1993..Unc £2; BU* £3
— Proof *FDC* (in 1993 set, see PS51)*..£6
— Proof in silver *FDC* (Issued: 16,526)...£20
— Proof piedfort in silver *FDC* (Issued: 12,500) £30

* Coins marked thus were originally issued in Royal Mint sets.

J9   J10   J11   J12

J9   **One pound.** (Scotland.) R. A Lion rampant within a double tressure flory counter-flory, being that quartering of Our Royal Arms known heraldically as Scotland with the value 'ONE POUND' below. Edge inscription 'NEMO ME IMPUNE LACESSIT'. (Reverse design: Norman Sillman.)

1994 ....Unc £2; BU* £3
— BU in presentation folder £5
— Proof *FDC* (in 1994 set, see PS53)* £6
— Proof in silver *FDC* (Issued: 25,000) £20
— Proof piedfort in silver *FDC* (Issued: 11,722) £30

J10 **One pound.** (Wales.) R. A dragon passant, being Our badge for Wales with the value 'ONE POUND' below. Edge inscription 'PLEIDIOL WYF I'M GWLAD'. (Reverse design: Norman Sillman.)

1995 ....Unc £2; BU* £3
— BU in presentation folder, English version £5
— BU in presentation folder, Welsh version..£10
— Proof *FDC* (in 1995 set, see PS55)* £5
— Proof in silver *FDC* (Issued: 27,445) £20
— Proof piedfort in silver *FDC* (Issued: 8,458) £30

J11 **One pound.** (Northern Ireland.) R. A Celtic cross charged at the centre with an Annulet therein a Pimpernel flower and overall an ancient Torque, symbolizing that part of Our Kingdom known as Northern Ireland with the value 'ONE POUND' below.
Edge inscription 'DECUS ET TUTAMEN'. (Reverse design: Norman Sillman.)

1996 ....Unc £2; BU* £3
— BU in presentation folder £6
— Proof *FDC* (in 1996 set, see PS57)* £6
— Proof in silver *FDC* (Issued: 25,000 including coins in PSS09)..........£20
— Proof piedfort in silver *FDC* (Issued: 10,000) £30

J12 **One pound.** (England.) R. Three lions passant guardant, being that quartering of Our Royal Arms known heraldically as England, with the value 'ONE POUND' below. Edge inscription 'DECUS ET TUTAMEN. (Reverse design: Norman Sillman.)

1997 ....Unc £2; BU* £3
— BU in presentation folder (Issued 56,996) £5
— Proof *FDC* (in 1997 set, see PS59)* £5
— Proof in silver *FDC* (Issued: 20,137) £20
— Proof piedfort in silver *FDC* (Issued: 10,000) £30

* Coins marked thus were originally issued in Royal Mint sets.

Obverse portrait by Ian Rank-Broadley

J13

J13   **One pound.** (Royal Arms design.) R. As J1.

1998 BU* £15
— Proof *FDC* (in 1998 set, see PS61)* £15
— Proof in silver *FDC* (Issued: 13,863) £25
— Proof piedfort in silver *FDC* (Issued: 7,894) £30
2003 ....Unc £2; BU* £3
— BU in presentation folder (Issued: 23,760) £5
— Proof *FDC* (in 2003 set, see PS78)* £6
— Proof in silver *FDC* (Issued: 15,830) £20
— Proof piedfort in silver *FDC* (Issued: 9,871 including coins in PSS21) £30
2008 ....Unc £2; BU* £3
— BU in presentation folder (Issued: 18,336) £7
— Proof *FDC* (in 2008 set, see PS93)* £6
— Proof in silver *FDC* (Issued: 9,134 plus 9,350 in PSS36 & 38) £20
— Proof in gold *FDC* (Issued: 674 plus 730 in PGCS06 & 08)..............................£950
— Proof in platinum *FDC* (Issued: 250 in PPLS1)* £750
2013 Proof in silver *FDC* (Issued: 1,311 in PSS65)* £60
— Proof in gold *FDC* (Issued: 17 in PGCS16)*..£1250

J13A   2008 Proof in silver with selected gold plating on reverse *FDC*
(Issued: 2,966 plus 2,005 in PSS41) £40

J14   **One pound.** (Scotland). R. As J9.

1999 BU* £15
— BU in presentation folder £20
— Proof *FDC* (in 1999 set, see PS63)* £15
— Proof in silver *FDC* (Issued: 16,328) £25
— Proof piedfort in silver *FDC* (Issued: 9,975) £30
2008
— Proof in gold *FDC* (in 2008 set, see PGCS08)* £950

J14A   1999
— Proof in silver *FDC*, with reverse frosting, (Issued: 1,994)* £50

J14B   2008
— Proof in silver with selected gold plating on reverse *FDC*
(Issued 2,862 plus 2,005 in PSS41) £40

J15   **One pound.** (Wales.) R. As J10.

2000 ....Unc £2; BU* £3
— Proof *FDC* (in 2000 set, see PS65)* £6
— Proof in silver *FDC* (Issued: 15,913 plus 13,180 in set PSS16) £20
— Proof piedfort in silver *FDC* (Issued: 9,994) £30
2008
— Proof in gold *FDC* (in 2008 set, see PGCS08)* £950

* Coins marked thus were originally issued in Royal Mint sets.

J15A 2000
— Proof in silver *FDC*, with reverse frosting, (Issued: 1,994)* £50

PSS07A - 1999-2000 £1 (J14A and J15A) silver proofs with reverse frosting (2)
(Issued: 1,994)..£75

J15B 2008
— Proof in silver with selected gold plating on reverse *FDC*
(Issued: 2,850 plus 2005 in PSS41)..£40
J16 One pound. (Northern Ireland.) R. As J11.
2001..Unc £2; BU* £3
— Proof *FDC* (in 2001 set, see PS68)* £6
— Proof in silver *FDC* (Issued: 11,697) £30
— Proof piedfort in silver *FDC* (Issued: 8,464) £60
2008
— Proof in gold *FDC* (in 2008 set, see PGCS08)* £950
J16A 2001
— Proof in silver *FDC*, with reverse frosting, (Issued: 1,540)* £60
J16B 2008
— Proof in silver with selected gold plating on reverse *FDC*
(Issued 2,855 plus 2,005 in PSS41)..£40
J17 One pound. (England.) R. As J12.
2002..Unc £2; BU* £3
— Proof *FDC* (in 2002 set, see PS72)* £6
— Proof in silver *FDC* (Issued: 17,693)..£20
— Proof piedfort in silver *FDC* (Issued: 6,599) £30
— Proof in gold *FDC* (in 2002 set, see PGCS02)* £950
2008
— Proof in gold *FDC* (in 2008 set, see PGCS08)* £950
J17A 2002
— Proof in silver *FDC*, with reverse frosting, (Issued: 1,540)* £60

PSS10A - 1999-2002 £1 (J14A - J17A) silver proofs with reverse frosting (4)
(Issued: 1,540) £150
*Purchasers of PSS07A were given the opportunity to purchase J16A and J17A
in a 4 coin case.*

J17B 2008
— Proof in silver with selected gold plating on reverse *FDC*
(Issued 2,858, plus 2,005 in PSS41)..£40

* *Coins marked thus were originally issued in Royal Mint sets.*

J18 J19 J20

J18 **One pound.** (Scotland.) ℞. A representation of the Forth Railway Bridge with a border
of railway tracks and beneath, the value 'ONE POUND' and an incuse decorative feature
on the edge symbolising bridges and pathways. (Reverse design: Edwina Ellis.)
2004 ....Unc £2; BU* £3
— BU in presentation folder (Issued: 24,014) £5
— Proof *FDC* (in 2004 set, see PS81)* £6
— Proof in silver *FDC* (Issued: 11,470) £23
— Proof piedfort in silver *FDC* (Issued: 7,013) £60
— Proof in gold *FDC* (Issued: 2,618)...£950
2008
— Proof in gold *FDC* (in 2008 set, see PGCS08)* £950
J18A 2008 Proof in silver with selected gold plating on reverse *FDC*
(Issued 2,815 plus 2,005 in PSS41) £40
J19 **One pound.** (Wales.) ℞. A representation of the Menai Straits Bridge with a border of
railings and stanchions, the value 'ONE POUND' and an incuse decorative feature on
the edge symbolising bridges and pathways. (Reverse design: Edwina Ellis.)
2005 ....Unc £2; BU* £3
— BU in presentation folder (Issued: 24,802) £6
— Proof *FDC* (in 2005 set, see PS84)* £6
— Proof in silver *FDC* (Issued: 8,371) £20
— Proof piedfort in silver *FDC* (Issued: 6,007) £40
— Proof in gold *FDC* (Issued: 1,195)...£950
2008
— Proof in gold *FDC* (in 2008 set, see PGCS08)* £950
J19A 2008 Proof in silver with selected gold plating on reverse *FDC*
(Issued 2,808 plus 2,005 in PSS41)*...£40
J20 **One pound.** (Northern Ireland.) ℞. A representation of the Egyptian Arch Railway
Bridge in County Down with a border of railway station canopy dags, the value
'ONE POUND' and an incuse decorative feature on the edge symbolising bridges
and pathways. (Reverse design: Edwina Ellis.)
2006 ....Unc £2; BU* £3
— BU in presentation folder (Issued: 23,856) £6
— Proof *FDC* (in 2006 set, see PS87)* £8
— Proof in silver *FDC* (Issued: 8,371 plus 6,394 in PSS26)...................................£25
— Proof piedfort in silver *FDC* (Issued: 5,129) £40
— Proof in gold *FDC* (Issued: 728)... £950
2008
— Proof in gold *FDC* (in 2008 set, see PGCS08)* £950
J20A 2008 Proof in silver with selected gold plating on rev. *FDC*
(Issued: 2,810 plus 2005 in PSS41)* £40

* Coins marked thus were originally issued in Royal Mint sets.

J21

J21   One pound. (England.) R. A representation of the Gateshead Millennium Bridge with
a border of struts, the value 'ONE POUND' and an incuse decorative feature on the
edge symbolising bridges and pathways. (Reverse design: Edwina Ellis.)

2007 ....Unc £2; BU* £3
— BU in presentation folder (Issued: 5,326) £7
— Proof *FDC** (in 2007 set, see PS90) £8
— Proof in silver *FDC* (Issued: 10,110) £25
— Proof piedfort in silver *FDC* (Issued: 5,739) £40
— Proof in gold *FDC* (Issued: 1,112)..£950
2008
— Proof in gold *FDC* (in 2008 set, see PGCS08)* £950
J21A 2008 Proof in silver as J21 with selected gold plating on reverse *FDC*
(Issued 2,816 plus 2005 in PSS41)* £40

2008 25th Anniversary of the Introduction of the £1 coin.
Sets of 14 coins in silver with selected gold plating and in gold were issued for this anniversary
depicting all the reverse designs used on the £1 coin between 1983 and 2007.
J22   One pound. (Scotland.) R. As J2.
2008 Proof in silver with selected gold plating on reverse *FDC*
(Issued: 3,069 plus 2,005 in PSS41)..£40
— Proof in gold *FDC* (see PGCS08)*..£950
J23   One pound. (Wales.) R. As J3.
2008 Proof in silver with selected gold plating on reverse *FDC*
(Issued: 2,931 plus 2,005 in PSS41) £40
— Proof in gold *FDC* (see PGCS08)*..£950
J24   One pound. (Northern Ireland.) R. As J4.
2008 Proof in silver with selected gold plating on reverse *FDC*
(Issued: 2,930 plus 2,005 in PSS41)..£40
— Proof in gold *FDC* (see PGCS08)*..£950
J25   One pound. (England.) R. As J5
2008 Proof in silver with selected gold plating on reverse *FDC*
(Issued: 2,889 plus 2,005 in PSS41) £40
— Proof in gold *FDC* (see PGCS08)*..£950
J26   One pound. (Crowned Royal Shield.) R. As J6
2008 Proof in silver with selected gold plating on reverse *FDC*
(Issued: 2,787 plus 2,005 in PSS41)..£40
— Proof in gold *FDC* (see PGCS08)*..£950
2013 Proof in silver FDC (Issued: 1,311 in PSS65)* £60
— ....Proof in gold FDC (Issued: 17 in PGCS16)*.....................................£1250
PSS41 - 2008 £1 (J13A, J14B-J17B, J18A-J21A, J22-J26) Proofs in silver *FDC*
with selected gold plating on reverse (14) (Issued: 2,005) £395
PGCS08 - 2008 £1 (J13-J26) Proofs in gold *FDC* (14) (Issued: 150) £13500
*PSS31-34 were previously listed here but we have no evidence that these four planned Regional
3 coin sets exist. They will be re-listed as PSS42-45 if required.*

* *Coins marked thus were originally issued in Royal Mint sets.*

J27

J27 **One pound.** R. A shield of Our Royal Arms with the words 'ONE' to the left and
'POUND' to the right. Edge inscription 'DECUS ET TUTAMEN'. (Reverse design:
Matthew Dent.)

2008 ....Unc £2; BU* £3
— Proof *FDC* (in 2008 set, see PS96)* £10
— Proof in silver *FDC* (Issued: 5,000 plus 10,000 in PSS39)...............................£30
— Proof piedfort in silver *FDC* (Issued: 2,456 plus 4,746 in PSS37 & 40)...............£50
— Proof in gold *FDC* (Issued: 860 plus 886 in PGCS07) £950
— Proof in platinum *FDC* (in 2008 set, see PPLS2)* £750
2009 ....Unc £2; BU* £3
— BU in presentation folder (Edition: 15,000)..£7
— Proof *FDC* (in 2009 set, see PS97)* £5
— BU in silver (Issued: 359) £30
— Proof in silver *FDC* (Issued: 5,759 including PSS47, plus 2,749 in PSS46).........£35
— Proof in gold *FDC* (Issued: 540)..£950
2010 ....Unc £2; BU* £3
— Proof *FDC* (in 2010 set, see PS101)* £5
— BU in silver (Issued: 1,551) £30
— Proof in silver *FDC* (Issued: 1,241 in PSS50) £35
2011 ....Unc £2; BU* £3
— Proof *FDC* (in 2011 set, see PS104) * £5
— BU in silver...£30
— Proof in silver *FDC* (Edition: 2,500) (in 2011 set, see PSS53)* £35
2012 ....Unc £2; BU* £3
— Proof *FDC* (in 2012 set, see PS107)* £5
— BU in silver (Issued: 1,234) £25
— Proof in silver with selected gold plating *FDC* (Edition: 2,012) (see PSS57)* £40
— Proof in gold *FDC* (Edition: 150) (see PGCS11)* £950
2013 .... Unc £2; BU* £3
— Proof *FDC* (in 2013 set, see PS109)* £7
— BU in silver (Issued: 4,414) £25
— Proof in silver *FDC* (Issued: 985 in PSS58 & 1,311 in PSS65)* £40
— Proof in gold *FDC* (Issued: 59 in PGCS13 & 17 in PGCS16)* £1100
2014 ....Unc £2; BU* £3
— Proof *FDC* (in 2014 set, see PS112)* £5
— BU in silver (Issued 750) £25
— Proof in silver *FDC* (Issued 368 in PSS66)* £35
2015 ....Unc £2; BU* £3
— Proof *FDC* (in 2015 set, see PS115)* £5
— Proof in silver *FDC* (Issued: 298 in PSS70 & 1,241 in PSS73)* £35
— Proof in gold *FDC* (Issued: 209 in PGCS18)*...£950
— Proof in platinum *FDC* (Issued: 10) (see PPLS3)*..£1800

2013 30th Anniversary of the Introduction of the £1 coin.
PSS65 – 2013 J13, J26 & J27 silver proofs (3) (Issued: 1,311) £150
PGCS16 – 2013 J13, J26 & J27 gold proofs (3) (Issued: 17) £3600

* Coins marked thus were originally issued in Royal Mint sets.

J28   J29   J30   J31

J28 – One pound. (London.) R. A design which depicts the official badges of the capital
cities of the United Kingdom, with the badge of London being the principal focus,
accompanied by the name 'LONDON' and the denomination 'ONE POUND'. Edge
inscription 'DOMINE DIRIGE NOS'. (Reverse design: Stuart Devlin.)
2010 ....Unc £3; BU* £5
— BU on presentation card (Issued: 66,313) £6
— Proof *FDC* (in 2010 set, see PS101)* £6
— Proof in silver *FDC* (Issued: 6,452 including PSS51, plus 1,241 in PSS50).........£35
— Proof piedfort in silver *FDC* (Issued: 2,101 plus 1,581 in PSS52) £55
— Proof in gold *FDC* (Issued: 950)..£1000

J29 – One pound. (Belfast.) R. A design which depicts the official badges of the capital
cities of the United Kingdom, with the badge of Belfast being the principal focus,
accompanied by the name 'BELFAST' and the denomination 'ONE POUND'. Edge
inscription 'PRO TANTO QUID RETRIBUAMUS'. (Reverse design: Stuart Devlin.)
2010 ....Unc £3; BU* £5
— BU on presentation card (Issued: 64,461) £6
— Proof *FDC* (in 2010 set, see PS101)* £5
— Proof in silver *FDC* (Issued: 4,564 including PSS51, plus 1,241 in PSS50).........£35
— Proof piedfort in silver *FDC* (Issued: 1,922 plus 1,581 in PSS52) £55
— Proof in gold *FDC* (Issued: 585)..£1000

US44 - 2010 £1 (J28 and J29) BU in folder (2) (Edition: 10,000) £20

J30   **One pound.** (Edinburgh.) R. A design which depicts the official badges of the capital
cities of the United Kingdom, with the badge of Edinburgh being the principal focus,
accompanied by the name 'EDINBURGH' and the denomination 'ONE POUND'.
Edge inscription 'NISI DOMINUS'. (Reverse design: Stuart Devlin.)
2011 ....Unc £5; BU* £15
— Proof *FDC* (in 2011 set, see PS104)*..£15
— Proof in silver *FDC* (Issued: 4,973 including coins in PSS53 & 54).....................£45
— Proof piedfort in silver *FDC* (Issued: 2,696 including coins in PSS55) £78
— Proof in gold *FDC* (Issued: 499) £1000

J31   **One pound.** (Cardiff.) R. A design which depicts the official badges of the capital
cities of the United Kingdom, with the badge of Cardiff being the principal focus,
accompanied by the name 'CARDIFF' and the denomination 'ONE POUND'. Edge
inscription 'Y DDRAIG GOCH DDYRY CYCHWYN'. (Reverse design: Stuart Devlin.)
2011 ....Unc £3; BU* £5
— Proof *FDC* (in 2011 set, see PS104) * £8
— Proof in silver *FDC* (Issued: 5,553 including coins in PSS53 & 54).....................£45
— Proof piedfort in silver *FDC* (Issued: 1,615 including coins in PSS55) £78
— Proof in gold *FDC* (Issued: 524) £1000

US47 - 2011 £1 (J30 and J31) BU in folder (2) (Edition: 10,000) £30

* Coins marked thus were originally issued in Royal Mint sets.

J32   J33

J32   **One pound.** (England.) ℞. Depicts an oak branch paired with a Tudor-inspired rose with
the denomination 'ONE POUND' below. Edge inscription 'DECUS ET TUTAMEN'.
(Reverse design: Timothy Noad.)
2013 ....Unc £3; BU* £5
— Proof *FDC* (in 2013 set, see PS109) *..£7
— Proof in silver *FDC* (Issued: 1,858 plus 985 coins in PSS58 & 1,476 in PSS64)...£50
— Proof piedfort in silver *FDC* (Issued: 1,071 plus 486 coins in PSS59).................£100
— Proof in gold *FDC* (Issued: 284 plus 59 coins in PGCS13)..............................£1250

J33   **One pound.** (Wales.) ℞. Depicts a leek and a daffodil with their leaves entwined
and the denomination 'ONE POUND' below. Edge inscription 'PLEIDIOL WYF I'M
GWLAD'. (Reverse design: Timothy Noad.)
2013 ....Unc £3; BU* £5
— Proof *FDC* (in 2013 set, see PS109) *..£7
— Proof in silver *FDC* (Issued: 1,618 plus 985 coins in PSS58 & 1,476 in PSS64)...£50
— Proof piedfort in silver *FDC* (Issued: 860 plus 486 coins in PSS59)...................£100
— Proof in gold *FDC* (Issued: 274 plus 59 coins in PGCS13)..............................£1250

US51A - 2013 £1 (J32 and J33) BU in folder (2) (Issued: 6,112)............................£18
PSS64 - 2013 £1 (J32 and J33) silver proofs (2) (Issued: 1,476).........................£100

J34   J35

J34   **One pound.** (Northern Ireland.) ℞. Depicts a flax and shamrock being the principle
focus for Northern Ireland accompanied by the denomination 'ONE POUND'. Edge
inscription 'DECUS ET TUTANEM' (Reverse design: Timothy Noad.)
2014 ....Unc £3; BU* £6
— Proof *FDC* (in 2014 set, see PS112)*..£7
— Proof in silver *FDC* (Issued: 1,502 plus 368 coins in PSS66 & 283 in PSS67)......£50
— Proof piedfort in silver *FDC* (Issued: 788 plus 487 coins in PSS68)...................£100
— Proof in gold *FDC* (Edition: 166 plus 75 coins in PGCS17) £1250

J35   **One pound.** (Scotland.) ℞. Depicts the thistle and bluebell being the principle focus
for Scotland accompanied by the denomination 'ONE POUND'. Edge inscription
'NEMO ME IMPUNE LACESSIT'. (Reverse design: Timothy Noad.)
2014 ....Unc £3; BU* £6
— Proof *FDC* (in 2014 set, see PS112)*..£7
— Proof in silver *FDC* (Issued: 1,540 plus 368 coins in PSS66 & 283 in PSS67)......£50
— Proof piedfort in silver *FDC* (Issued: ?? plus 487 coins in PSS68) £100
— Proof in gold *FDC* (Issued: 154 plus 75 coins in PGCS17)..............................£1250

US53A - 2014 £1 (J34 and J35) BU in folder (2) (Issued: 3,832)............................£18

* Coins marked thus were originally issued in Royal Mint sets.

Obverse portrait by Jody Clark

J36

J36   One pound. R. A shield of Our Royal Arms (as J27).

2015 BU*...£4

— Proof *FDC* (in 2015 set, see PS116)*..£5

— Proof in silver *FDC* (Issued: 1,876 in PSS74)*...£50

— Proof in gold *FDC* (Issued: 245 in PGCS19)*...£950

— Proof in platinum FDC (Issued: 10) (see PPLS3)* £1800

2016

— BU (in 2016 set, see US57)..£20

— Proof *FDC* (in 2016 set, see PS119)*..£30

— Proof in silver *FDC* (Issued: 383 in sets, see PSS75)*.......................................£50

J37   J38

J37   One Pound. R. A depiction of Our Royal Arms accompanied by the inscription 'ONE
POUND' below. Edge inscription 'DECUS ET TUTAMEN'. (Reverse design:
Timothy Noad.)

2015 ....Unc £3; BU £5

— BU in presentation pack £10

— Proof in silver *FDC* (Edition: 3,500)..£50

— Proof piedfort in silver *FDC* (Edition: 2,000) £100

— Proof in gold *FDC* (Edition: 500)..£1000

J38   One Pound. R. A design depicting a lion, unicorn, stag and dragon surrounding a
crown accompanied by the denomination 'ONE POUND'. Edge inscription 'DECUS
ET TUTAMEN'. (Reverse design: Gregory Cameron.)

2016 BU (Issued: 68,537)...£25

— BU in presentation folder (Issued: 96,089) £30

— Proof *FDC* (in 2016 set, see PS119)*...£30

— Proof in silver *FDC* (Issued: 7,491) £50

— Proof piedfort in silver *FDC* (Issued: 2,993).....................................£100

— Proof in gold *FDC* (Issued: 499) £1250

* Coins marked thus were originally issued in Royal Mint sets.

Pattern Proof £1 coins

Pattern proof sets were issued in 2003 & 2004 containing 4 coins each. The 2003 sets comprised the designs that were actually introduced on the circulation coins between 2004 and 2007. The designs of the 2004 sets depicted unadopted designs by Timothy Noad featuring an animal's head – (England) Lion, (Scotland) Unicorn, (Wales) Dragon, (Northern Ireland) Stag, All pieces have a plain edge with a hallmark with the description 'PATTERN'.

PPS1 - 2003 Proof set in silver *FDC* (4) (Edition: 7,500)..£75
PPS2 - 2003 Proof set in gold *FDC* (4) (Edition: 3,000) £3800
PPS3 - 2004 Proof set in silver *FDC* (4) (Edition: 5,000)..£75
PPS4 - 2004 Proof set in gold *FDC* (4) (Edition: 2,250) £3800
Single coins are priced from:
    Proof in silver *FDC** £25
    Proof in gold *FDC** £950

J39

J39 **One Pound.** (Bimetallic.) Nations of the Crown. R. A design depicting a rose, leek, thistle and shamrock encircled by and emerging from a crown with the denomination 'ONE POUND' below. (Reverse design: David Pearce.)
    2016 ....£2
    2017 ....Unc £2; BU* £3
    —   Specimen in presentation folder (Issued: 91,461) £8
    —   Proof *FDC* (in 2017 set, see PS122)...£10
    —   Proof in silver *FDC* (Issued: 12,649) £75
    —   Proof piedfort in silver *FDC* (Issued : 4,484)...£130
    —   Proof in gold *FDC* (Issued: 2,011 plus 24 in PGCS25) £900
    —   Proof in platinum *FDC* (Issued: 242)..£1500
    2018 ....Unc £2; BU* £4
    —   Proof *FDC* (in 2018 set, see PS125)...£10
    —   Proof in silver *FDC* (in 2018 set, see PSS81) £35
    2019 ....Unc £2; BU* £4
    —   Proof *FDC* (in 2019 set, see PS128)*..£10
    —   Proof in silver *FDC* (Edition: 1,000) (see PSS88) £35

* *Coins marked thus were originally issued in Royal Mint sets.*

2020 ....Unc £2; BU* £4
— Proof *FDC* (in 2020 set, see PS132)*...£10
— Proof in silver *FDC* (Edition: 500) (see PSS94) £35
2021 ....Unc £2; BU* £5
— Proof *FDC* (in 2021 set, see PS134)*...£10
— Proof in silver *FDC* (in 2021 set, see PSS96)) £35
2022 ....Unc £2; BU* £5
— Proof (in 2022 set, see PS136/7)* £10
— Proof in silver *FDC* (in 2022 set, see PSS98)* £35

PGCS28 - MD £1 (J38 and J39) gold proofs (2) (Issued: 100).......................................£2150

J39A One pound. With 'Cross Crosslet' mint mark (see below).
2016 BU*..£55

US59 - 2016 £1 (J38 and J39A) BU in folder (2) (Issued: 9,714)............................£60

J40   One pound. O. As J39 but with privy mark (see B10) displaying Her Majesty's
birth year and the year of her passing. R. As J39.
2022 BU*...£8
— Proof in silver *FDC* £60
— Proof in gold *FDC* £1250
— Proof in platinum *FDC* £1800

NICKEL-BRASS

TWO POUND COINS
The £2 nickel-brass coins issued from 1986 were all commemoratives and although not actively in circulation they were widely available within the UK except that K3 was only issued in Scotland. They ceased to be issued after the successor bi-metal coin became a main circulation piece from 1998 – delayed from 1997, hence the existence of coins with the earlier date. Bi-metal commemoratives have been issued into circulation in addition to the two definitive types but regrettably after 2016 the commemoratives have only been available in collectors' versions. Even the second definitive type depicting Britannia issued in 2015 is rarely seen in change as the banks have adequate stocks of earlier types.

Obverse portrait by Raphael Maklouf

K1

K1   Two pounds. R. St. Andrew's cross with a crown of laurel leaves and surmounted by a thistle of Scotland with date '1986' above. Edge inscription 'XIII COMMONWEALTH GAMES SCOTLAND'. (Reverse design: Norman Sillman.)
1986...Unc £4; BU* £5
— BU in presentation folder £8
— Proof *FDC** (in 1986 set, see PS37)* £10
— 0.500 silver (Issued: 58,881) £18
— Proof in silver *FDC* (Issued: 59,779) £35
— Proof in gold *FDC* (Issued: 3,277 plus 12,500 in sets) £900

* Coins marked thus were originally issued in Royal Mint sets.

K2   K3   K4

K2   **Two pounds.** 300th Anniversary of Bill of Rights. Ṟ. Cypher of W&M (King William
       III and Queen Mary II) interlaced surmounting a horizontal Parliamentary mace and
       a representation of the Royal Crown above and the dates '1689'and '1989' below, all
       within the inscription 'TERCENTENARY OF THE BILL OF RIGHTS'. .(Reverse
       design: John Lobban.)

       1989 ....Unc £4; BU* £5
       — BU in presentation folder £8
       — Proof *FDC* (in 1989 set, see PS43)* £10
       — Proof in silver *FDC* (Issued: 25,000) £35
       — Proof piedfort in silver *FDC* (in 1989 set, seePSS01)* £60

K3   **Two pounds.** (Scotland.) 300th Anniversary of Claim of Right. Ṟ. As K2, but with
       Crown of Scotland and the inscription 'TERCENTENARY OF THE CLAIM OF
       RIGHT'. (Reverse design: John Lobban.)

       1989 ....Unc £25; BU* £30
       — BU in presentation folder £35
       — Proof *FDC* (in 1989 set, see PS43)* £35
       — Proof in silver *FDC* (Issued: 24,852) £40
       — Proof piedfort in silver *FDC* (in 1989 set, seePSS01)* £60

US09 - 1989 £2 (K2 and K3) BU in folder (2) £45
PSS02 - 1989 £2 (K2 and K3) silver proofs (2) £65
PSS01 - 1989 £2 (K2 and K3) silver piedfort proofs (2) (Issued: 10,000) £85

K4   **Two pounds.** 300th Anniversary of the Bank of England. Ṟ. Bank's original Corporate
       Seal, with Crown & Cyphers of William III & Mary II and the dates '1694' and '1994'.
       Edge inscription 'SIC VOS NON VOBIS'on the silver and base metal versions.
       (Reverse design: Leslie Durbin.)

       1994 ....Unc £5; BU* £10
       — BU in presentation folder £12
       — Proof *FDC* (in 1994 set, see PS53)* £12
       — Proof in silver *FDC* (Issued: 27, 957) £35
       — Proof piedfort in silver *FDC* (Issued: 9,569) £60
       — Proof in gold *FDC* (Issued: 1,000) £900

K4A **— Error gold obverse – known as a Mule coin.** £3000
       The obverse of K4 is as shown for K1 which shows the denomination 'TWO POUNDS'.
       In error the Royal Mint struck some of the gold coins using the Sovereign series obverse
       of SD4 which does not show the denomination. It is not known how many exist.

* Coins marked thus were originally issued in Royal Mint sets.

K5   K6

K5 **Two pounds.** 50th Anniversary of the End of World War II. R. A stylised representation
of a dove as the symbol of Peace. Edge inscription '1945 IN PEACE GOODWILL
1995'. (Reverse design: John Mills.)

1995 ....Unc £5; BU* £8
— BU in presentation folder £10
— Proof *FDC* (in 1995 set, see PS55)* £12
— Proof in silver *FDC* (Issued: 35,751) £35
— Proof piedfort in silver *FDC* (Edition: 10,000) £60
— Proof in gold *FDC* (Issued: 2,500) £900

K6 **Two pounds.** 50th Anniversary of the Establishment of the United Nations. R. 50th
Anniversary symbol and a fanning pattern of flags with the inscription 'NATIONS
UNITED FOR PEACE' above and the dates '1945-1995' below. (Reverse design:
Michael Rizzello.)

1995... Unc £5; BU* £8
— BU in presentation folder...£12
— BU in card (issued as part of multi country United Nations Collection).................£12
— Proof in silver *FDC* (Edition: 175,000) £35
— Proof piedfort in silver *FDC* (Edition: 10,000)....................................£60
— Proof in gold *FDC* (Edition: 17,500) £900

K7

K7 **Two pounds.** European Football Championships. R. A stylised representation of a
football with the date '1996' centrally placed and surrounded by sixteen small rings.
Edge inscription 'TENTH EUROPEAN CHAMPIONSHIP'. The gold versions have a
plain edge with no inscription. (Reverse design: John Mills.)

1996... Unc £5; BU* £8
— BU in presentation folder...£10
— Proof *FDC* (in 1996 set, see PS57)* £12
— Proof in silver *FDC* (Issued: 25,163)..£35
— Proof piedfort in silver *FDC* (Issued: 7,634) £60
— Proof in gold *FDC* (Issued: 2,098)..£900

K7A **Incorrect blank.** When struck the coins have a dished appearance on both the obverse
and reverse but several pieces in gold have been reported where the surface of the coins
is flat. £1500

Coins marked thus were originally issued in Royal Mint sets.

Bimetallic issues

K8

K8 **Two pounds.** Bimetallic currency issue. R. Four concentric circles representing the
Iron Age, 18th Century industrial development, silicon chip, and Internet. Edge inscription
'STANDING ON THE SHOULDERS OF GIANTS'. (Reverse design: Bruce Rushin.)
1997 .... Unc £4; BU* £5
— BU in presentation folder £8
— Proof *FDC* (in 1997 set, see PS59)* £10
— Proof in silver *FDC* (Issued: 29,910) £32
— Proof piedfort in silver *FDC* (Issued: 10,000) £60
— Proof in gold *FDC* (Issued: 2,482) £900

Obverse portrait by Ian Rank-Broadley

K9

K9 **Two pounds.** Bimetallic currency issue. R. Four concentric circles, representing the
Iron Age, 18th Century industrial development, silicon chip and Internet. Edge
inscription 'STANDING ON THE SHOULDERS OF GIANTS'.
1998 .... Unc £4; BU* £5
— Proof *FDC* (in 1998 set, see PS61)* £10
— Proof in silver *FDC* (Issued: 19,978) £32
— Proof piedfort in silver *FDC* (Issued: 7,646) £60
1999 .... £8
2000 .... Unc £4; BU* £5
— Proof *FDC* (in 2000 set, see PS65)* £10
— Proof in silver *FDC* (see PSS16)* £35
2001 .... Unc £4; BU* £5
— Proof *FDC* (see PS68)* £10
2002 .... Unc £4; BU* £5
— Proof *FDC* (in 2002 set, see PS72)* £10
— Proof in gold *FDC* (in 2002 set, see PGCS02)* £950
2003 .... Unc £4; BU* £5
— Proof *FDC* (see PS78)* £10
2004 .... Unc £4; BU* £5
— Proof *FDC* (in 2004 set, see PS81)* £10
2005 .... Unc £4; BU* £5
— Proof *FDC* (see PS84)* £10
2006 .... Unc £5
— Proof *FDC* (in 2006 set, see PS87)* £10
— Proof in silver *FDC* (in 2006 set, see PSS26)* £35

2007 .... Unc £5
—   Proof *FDC* (in 2007 set, see PS90)* £10
2008 ....Unc £4; BU* £5
—   Proof *FDC* (in 2008 set, see PS93)* £10
2009 ....Unc £4; BU* £7
—   Proof *FDC* (in 2009 set, see PS97)* £10
—   Proof in silver *FDC* (Issued: 2,749 in PSS46)* £35
2010 ....Unc £4; BU* £5
—   Proof *FDC* (in 2010 set, see PS101)* £10
—   Proof in silver *FDC* (Issued: 1,241 in PSS50)* £35
2011 ....Unc £4; BU* £5
—   Proof *FDC* (in 2010 set, see PS104)* £10
—   Proof in silver *FDC* (in 2010 set, see PSS53)* £35
2012 ....Unc £4; BU* £10
—   Proof *FDC* (in 2012 set, see PS107)* £10
—   Proof in silver *FDC* (Edition: 2,012) (see PSS57)* £30
—   Proof in gold *FDC* (Edition: 150 (see PGGCS11)* £950
2013 ....Unc £4; BU* £15
—   Proof *FDC* (in 2013 set, see PS109)* £15
—   Proof in silver *FDC* (see PSS58)* £30
—   Proof in gold *FDC* (see PGCS13)* £1250
2014 ....Unc £4; BU* £10
—   Proof *FDC* (in 2014 set, see PS112)* £15
—   Proof in silver *FDC* (see PSS65)* £30
2015 ....Unc £4; BU* £5
—   Proof *FDC* (in 2015 set, see PS115)* £10
—   Proof in silver *FDC* (see PSS73)* £30
—   Proof in gold *FDC* (see PGCS18)* £900
—   Proof in platinum *FDC* (see PPLS3)* £3000

PSS13 - 1998 £2 (K8 and K9) silver proofs (2) £60

K10   K10A

K10   **Two pounds.** Rugby World Cup.O. As K9. R. In the centre a rugby ball and goal posts surrounded by a stylised stadium with the denomination 'TWO POUNDS' and the date '1999'. Edge inscription 'RUGBY WORLD CUP 1999'. (Reverse design: Ron Dutton.)
1999 ....Unc £4; BU* £6
—   BU in presentation folder £10
—   Proof *FDC* (in 1999 set, see PS63)* £10
—   Proof in silver *FDC* (Issued: 9,665) £40
—   Proof in gold *FDC* (Issued: 311) £1000
K10A —   Proof piedfort in silver with coloured hologram on reverse *FDC* (Issued: 10,000) £150

* Coins marked thus were originally issued in Royal Mint sets.

K11

K11   Two pounds. The centenary of Guglielmo Marconi's first wireless transmission across
the Atlantic. O. As K9. ℞. Decorative radio waves emanating from a spark of electricity
linking the zeros of the date to represent the generation of the signal that crossed the
Atlantic with the date '2001' and the denomination 'TWO POUNDS'. Edge inscription
'WIRELESS BRIDGES THE ATLANTIC MARCONI 1901'.
(Reverse design: Robert Evans.)

2001 ....Unc £4; BU* £8
— BU in presentation folder £12
— Proof *FDC* (in 2001 set, see PS68)* £12
— Proof in silver *FDC* (Issued: 11,488) £35
— Proof in silver *FDC*, with reverse frosting. (Issued: 4,803 in a 2-coin set
  with a Canadian $5 Marconi silver proof) £60
— Proof piedfort in silver *FDC* (Issued: 6,759) £60
— Proof in gold *FDC* (Issued: 1,658 plus 1,891 in sets PGS34 & 35)....................£900

K12   K13

K12   Two pounds. (England.) Commonwealth Games commemorative. O. As K9.
℞. A moving figure of an athlete holding a banner, the top of which being divided into
lines to symbolise lanes of a running track or swimming pool with a cameo of the
English flag and the inscription 'XVII COMMONWEALTH GAMES 2002' and the
denomination '£2'. Edge inscription 'SPIRIT OF FRIENDSHIP. MANCHESTER 2002'.
(Reverse design: Matthew Bonaccorsi.)

2002..Unc £10; BU* £20
— BU (in Presentation set, see US25)* £20
— Proof *FDC* (in set, see PS76)* £30
— Proof in silver *FDC* (in set, see PSS17)* £50
— Proof in gold *FDC* (in set, see PCGS1)* £1000
K12A As above but with colour added to the flag and parts of the banner.
— Proof piedfort in silver *FDC* (see PSS18)* £100

* Coins marked thus were originally issued in Royal Mint sets.

K13 **Two pounds.** (Northern Ireland.) Commonwealth Games commemorative. O. As K9.
R. As above but with a cameo of the Northern Ireland flag. Edge inscription 'SPIRIT
OF FRIENDSHIP. MANCHESTER 2002'. (Reverse design: Matthew Bonaccorsi.)
2002 ....Unc £20.; BU* £50
— BU (in Presentation set, see US25)* £50
— Proof *FDC* (in set, see PS76)* £60
— Proof in silver *FDC* (in set, see PSS17)* £50
— Proof in gold *FDC* (in set, see PCGS1)* £1000
K13A As above but with colour added to the flag and parts of the banner.
— Proof piedfort in silver *FDC* (see PSS18)* £100

K14   K15

K14 **Two pounds.** (Scotland.) Commonwealth Games commemorative. O. As K9.
R. As above but with a cameo of the Scottish flag. Edge inscription 'SPIRIT OF
FRIENDSHIP. MANCHESTER 2002'. (Reverse design: Matthew Bonaccorsi.)
2002 ....Unc £10; BU* £20
— BU (in Presentation set, see US25)* £20
— Proof *FDC* (in set, see PS76)* £30
— Proof in silver *FDC* (in set, see PSS17)* £50
— Proof in gold *FDC* (in set, see PCGS1)* £1000
K14A As above but with colour added to the flag and parts of the banner.
— Proof piedfort in silver *FDC* (see PSS18)* £100

K15 **Two pounds.** (Wales.) Commonwealth Games commemorative. O. As K9.
R. As above but with a cameo of the Welsh flag. Edge inscription 'SPIRIT OF
FRIENDSHIP. MANCHESTER 2002'. (Reverse design: Matthew Bonaccorsi.)
2002..Unc £10; BU* £25
— BU (in Presentation set, see US25)* £25
— Proof *FDC* (in set, see PS76)* £30
— Proof in silver *FDC* (in set, see PSS17)* £50
— Proof in gold *FDC* (in set, see PCGS1)* £1000
K15A As above but with colour added to the flag and parts of the banner.
— Proof piedfort in silver *FDC* (see PSS18)* £100

US25 - 2002 £2 (K12-K15) BU in folder (4) £120
PS76 - 2002 £2 (K12-K15) proofs (4) (Issued: 3358) £150
PS77 - 2002 £2 (K12-K15) proofs in display type case (4) (Issued: 673) £150
PSS17 - 2002 £2 (K12-K15) silver proofs (4) (Issued: 2553)..£250
PSS18 - 2002 £2 (K12A-K15A) silver proof piedfort (4) (Issued: 3497) £350
PGCS01 - 2002 £2 (K12-K15) gold proofs (4) (Issued: 315)...£4000

* Coins marked thus were originally issued in Royal Mint sets.

K16   K17

K16 **Two pounds.** 50th Anniversaryof the Discovery of the Structure of DNA. O. As K9.
R. In the centre the spiralling double helix structure of DNA with the inscription 'DNA
DOUBLE HELIX' and the dates '1953' and '2003' separated by the denomination 'TWO
POUNDS'. Edge inscription 'DEOXYRIBONUCLEIC ACID'. (Reverse design: John
Mills.)
2003 .... Unc £4; BU* £8
— BU in presentation folder (Issued: 41,568) £15
— Proof *FDC* (in set, see PS78)* £12
— Proof in silver *FDC* (Issued: 11,204) £35
— Proof piedfort in silver *FDC* (Issued: 8,728 including coins in PSS21) £60
— Proof in gold *FDC* (Issued: 1,500 plus 1,737 in PGS39) £900

K17 **Two pounds.** 200th Anniversary of the First Steam Locomotive. O. As K9. R. In the
centre a depiction of Trevithick's Locomotive Penydarren and the denomination 'TWO
POUNDS' surrounded by a cog representing the Industrial Revolution and the inscription
'R.TREVITHICK 1804 INVENTION INDUSTRY PROGRESS 2004'. Patterned edge.
(Reverse design: Robert Lowe.)
2004 .... Unc £4; BU* £8
— BU in presentation folder (Issued: 56,871) £15
— BU in silver (Issued: 1,923) £25
— Proof *FDC* (in 2004 set, see PS81)* £12
— Proof in silver *FDC* (Issued: 10,233) £35
— Proof piedfort in silver *FDC* (Issued: 5,303 including coins in PSS23) ....£ 65
— Proof in gold *FDC* (Issued: 1,500 plus 761 in PGS41) £950

* Coins marked thus were originally issued in Royal Mint sets.

K18 K19 K20

K18 **Two pounds.** 400th Anniversary of the Gunpowder Plot. O. As K9. ℞. An arrangement of crosiers, maces and swords, surrounded by stars, with the dates '1605' and '2005' above, and the denomination 'TWO POUNDS' below. Edge inscription 'REMEMBER REMEMBER THE FIFTH OF NOVEMBER'. (Reverse design: Peter Forster.)

2005 ....Unc £4; BU* £8
— BU in presentation folder (Issued: 12,044) £12
— Proof *FDC* (in 2005 set, see PS84)* £12
— Proof in silver *FDC* (Issued: 4,394) £40
— Proof piedfort in silver *FDC* (Issued: 4,584) £65
— Proof in gold *FDC* (Issued: 914)..£1000

K19 **Two pounds.** 60th Anniversary of the End of World War II. O. As K9. ℞. In the centre a depiction of the front of St. Paul's Cathedral in full floodlights with the denomination 'TWO POUNDS' and the dates '1945 - 2005'. Edge inscription 'IN VICTORY MAGNANIMITY IN PEACE GOODWILL'. (Reverse design: Robert Elderton.)

2005 ....Unc £4; BU* £8
— BU in presentation folder with medal (Issued: 53,686) £12
— Proof in silver *FDC* (Issued: 21,734) £35
— Proof piedfort in silver *FDC* (Issued: 4,798 including coins in PSS25) £65
— Proof in gold *FDC* (Issued: 1,578 single coins & 1,346 in a multi-country set).. £1000

K20 **Two pounds.** 200th Anniversary of the Birth of Isambard Brunel. O. As K9. ℞. In the centre a portrait of the engineer with segments of a wheel and bridge in the background surrounded by links of a heavy chain and the date '2006' and the denomination 'TWO POUNDS'. Edge inscription '1806 - 1859 ISAMBARD KINGDOM BRUNEL ENGINEER'. (Reverse design: Rod Kelly.)

2006 ....Unc £4; BU* £8
— Proof *FDC* (in 2006 set, see PS87)* £12
— Proof in silver *FDC* (Issued: 7,251) £35
— Proof piedfort in silver *FDC* (Issued: 3,199) (see PSS29)* £65
— Proof in gold *FDC* (Issued: 1,071)...£1000

K20A — **Edge Error.** Edge inscription as K18 ....£

* Coins marked thus were originally issued in Royal Mint sets.

K21   K22

K21 **Two pounds.** 200th Anniversary of the Birth of Isambard Brunel. O. As K9. R. In the
centre a section of the roof of Paddington Station with 'BRUNEL' below and the date
'2006' and the denomination 'TWO POUNDS'. Edge inscription 'SO MANY IRONS IN
THE FIRE'. (Reverse design: Robert Evans.)
2006 ....Unc £4; BU* £8
— Proof *FDC* (in 2006 set, see PS87)* £12
— Proof in silver *FDC* (Issued: 5,375) £35
— Proof piedfort in silver *FDC* (Issued: 3,018) (see PSS29)* £65
— Proof in gold *FDC* (Issued: 746) £1000

US33 - 2006 £2 (K20 and K21) BU in folder (Issued: 12,694)...£24
PSS28 - 2006 £2 (K20 and K21) silver proofs (2) £70
PSS29 - 2006 £2 (K20 and K21) silver piedfort proofs (2)..130
PGCS03 - 2006 £2 (K20 and K21) gold proofs (2) £2000

K22 **Two pounds.** Tercentenary of the Act of Union between England and Scotland. O. As K9.
R. A design dividing the coin into four quarters, with a rose and a thistle occupying two
of the quarters, and a portcullis in each of the other two quarters. The whole is overlaid
with a linking jigsaw motif and surrounded by the dates '1707' and '2007' and the
denomination 'TWO POUNDS'. Edge inscription 'UNITED INTO ONE KINGDOM'.
(Reverse design: Yvonne Holton.)
2007 ....Unc £4; BU* £7
— BU in presentation folder (Issued: 8,863) £15
— Proof *FDC* (in 2007 set, see PS90)* £10
— Proof in silver *FDC* (Issued: 8,310 including coins in PSS32).............................£35
— Proof piedfort in silver *FDC* (Issued: 4,000 including coins in PSS33) £60
— Proof in gold *FDC* (Issued: 750)...£1000

K22A — **Error edge.** The obverse and reverse designs of the Act of Union silver proof
combined with the edge inscription of the Abolition of Slave Trade issue (K23 below).
The edge inscription is impressed on the blanks prior to the striking of the obverse and
reverse designs and whilst one example has been reported, and confirmed as genuine
by the Royal Mint, it seems possible that a small batch may have been produced and
other pieces have yet to be detected. £1000

* Coins marked thus were originally issued in Royal Mint sets.

K23

K23 **Two pounds.** Bicentenary of the Abolition of the Slave Trade in the British Empire. ℞. The date '1807' with the '0' depicted as a broken chain link, surrounded by the inscription 'AN ACT FOR THE ABOLITION OF THE SLAVE TRADE', and the date '2007'. Edge inscription 'AM I NOT A MAN, AND A BROTHER'. (Reverse design: David Gentleman.) The designer's initials DG apppear below and to the right of the 7 in 1807 on all coins except those issued for circulation.

2007 ....Unc £4; BU* £15
— BU in presentation folder (Issued: 8,688) £20
— Proof *FDC* (in 2007 set, see PS90)* £20
— Proof in silver *FDC* (Issued: 7,095 including coins in PSS32)............£35
— Proof piedfort in silver *FDC* (Issued: 3,990 including coins in PSS33)* £60
— Proof in gold *FDC* (Issued: 1,000)...£1000

2008 £2 Olympic Centenary. *See LO30 in London 2012 Olympic section.*

2008 £2 Beijing Olympic Handover. *See LO31 in London 2012 Olympic section.*

K24

K24 **Two pounds.** 250th Anniversary of the Birth of Robert Burns. ℞. A design featuring a quote from the song *Auld Lang Syne* 'WE'LL TAK A CUP A' KINDNESS YET, FOR AULD LANG SYNE', the calligraphy of which is based on the handwriting of Robert Burns with the inscription '1759 ROBERT BURNS 1796' and the denomination 'TWO POUNDS'. Edge inscription 'SHOULD AULD ACQUAINTANCE BE FORGOT'. (Reverse design: Royal Mint Engraving Team.)

2009 ....Unc £4; BU* £12
— BU in celebration card (Issued: 120,223)..£15
— BU in presentation folder (Edition: 50,000)...£15
— Proof *FDC* (in 2009 set, see PS97)* £10
— Proof in silver *FDC* (Issued: 6,439 including PSS47, plus 2,749 in PSS46).........£35
— Proof piedfort in silver *FDC* (Issued: 1,000 plus 2,500 in PSS48).......................£60
— Proof in gold *FDC* (Issued: 1,000)...£1000

* Coins marked thus were originally issued in Royal Mint sets.

K25   K26   K27

K25 **Two pounds.** 200th Anniversary of the Birth of Charles Darwin.O. As K9. R. A design
showing a portrait of Charles Darwin facing an ape surrounded by the inscription '1809
DARWIN 2009' and the denomination 'TWO POUNDS'. Edge inscription 'ON THE
ORIGIN OF SPECIES 1859'. (Reverse design: Suzie Zamit.)
2009 ....Unc £4; BU* £15
— BU in presentation folder (Issued: 119,713) £20
— Proof *FDC* (in 2009 set, see PS97)* £20
— Proof in silver *FDC* (Issued: 6,608 including PSS47, plus 2,749 in PSS46)) £35
— Proof piedfort in silver *FDC* (Issued: 782 plus 2,500 in PSS48) £60
— Proof in gold *FDC* (Issued: 1,000)..£1000
K25A — **Edge error.** Edge inscription as K24. BU* ....£
K26 **Two pounds.** The Centenary of the Death of Florence Nightingale and the 150th
Anniversary of the Publication of *NOTES ON NURSING*. O. As K24. R. A design
depicting the pulse of a patient being taken, surrounded by the inscription 'FLORENCE
NIGHTINGALE – 1910' and the denomination 'TWO POUNDS'. The design being
set against a background texture of lines symbolising rays of light from a lamp. Edge
inscription '150 YEARS OF NURSING' on the precious metal versions. (Reverse
design: Gordon Summers.)
2010 ....Unc £4; BU* £7
— BU on presentation card (Issued: 73,160 combined with below) £10
— BU in presentation folder £12
— Proof *FDC* (in 2010 set, see PS101)* £10
— Proof in silver *FDC* (Issued: 3,876 including PSS51, plus 1,241 in PSS50).........£35
— Proof piedfort in silver *FDC* (Issued: 1,189 plus 1,581 in PSS52) £60
— Proof in gold *FDC* (Issued: 472)..£1200
K27 **Two pounds.** 500th Anniversary of the Launch of the Mary Rose. O. As K24. R. A
depiction of the ship based on a contemporary painting, surrounded by a cartouche
bearing the inscription 'THE MARY ROSE' above, the denomination 'TWO POUNDS'
below, and a rose to the left and right. The lettering on the reverse is rendered in
the Lombardic style employed on the coins of Henry VII. Edge inscription 'YOUR
NOBLEST SHIPPE 1511'. (Reverse design: John Bergdahl.)
2011 ....Unc £8; BU* £20
— BU in presentation folder (Edition: 20,000)...£25
— Proof *FDC* (in 2011 set, see PS104)*..£25
— Proof in silver *FDC* (Issued: 6,618 including coins in PSS53 & 54)....................£50
— Proof piedfort in silver *FDC* (Issued: 2,680 including coins in PSS55) £88
— Proof in gold *FDC* (Issued: 692) £1000

* Coins marked thus were originally issued in Royal Mint sets.

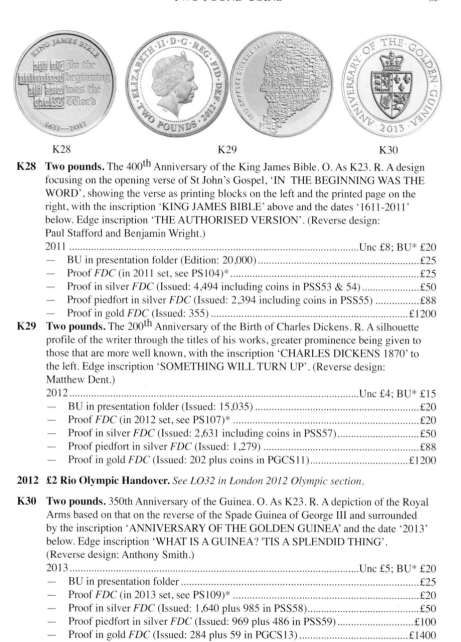

K28   K29   K30

K28 **Two pounds.** The 400th Anniversary of the King James Bible. O. As K23. R. A design focusing on the opening verse of St John's Gospel, 'IN THE BEGINNING WAS THE WORD', showing the verse as printing blocks on the left and the printed page on the right, with the inscription 'KING JAMES BIBLE' above and the dates '1611-2011' below. Edge inscription 'THE AUTHORISED VERSION'. (Reverse design: Paul Stafford and Benjamin Wright.)

2011 ....Unc £8; BU* £20
— BU in presentation folder (Edition: 20,000) £25
— Proof *FDC* (in 2011 set, see PS104)* £25
— Proof in silver *FDC* (Issued: 4,494 including coins in PSS53 & 54) £50
— Proof piedfort in silver *FDC* (Issued: 2,394 including coins in PSS55) £88
— Proof in gold *FDC* (Issued: 355) £1200

K29 **Two pounds.** The 200th Anniversary of the Birth of Charles Dickens. R. A silhouette profile of the writer through the titles of his works, greater prominence being given to those that are more well known, with the inscription 'CHARLES DICKENS 1870' to the left. Edge inscription 'SOMETHING WILL TURN UP'. (Reverse design: Matthew Dent.)

2012 ....Unc £4; BU* £15
— BU in presentation folder (Issued: 15,035) £20
— Proof *FDC* (in 2012 set, see PS107)* £20
— Proof in silver *FDC* (Issued: 2,631 including coins in PSS57) £50
— Proof piedfort in silver *FDC* (Issued: 1,279) £88
— Proof in gold *FDC* (Issued: 202 plus coins in PGCS11) £1200

2012 **£2 Rio Olympic Handover.** *See LO32 in London 2012 Olympic section.*

K30 **Two pounds.** 350th Anniversary of the Guinea. O. As K23. R. A depiction of the Royal Arms based on that on the reverse of the Spade Guinea of George III and surrounded by the inscription 'ANNIVERSARY OF THE GOLDEN GUINEA' and the date '2013' below. Edge inscription 'WHAT IS A GUINEA? 'TIS A SPLENDID THING'. (Reverse design: Anthony Smith.)

2013 ....Unc £5; BU* £20
— BU in presentation folder £25
— Proof *FDC* (in 2013 set, see PS109)* £20
— Proof in silver *FDC* (Issued: 1,640 plus 985 in PSS58).............................£50
— Proof piedfort in silver *FDC* (Issued: 969 plus 486 in PSS59).........................£100
— Proof in gold *FDC* (Issued: 284 plus 59 in PGCS13) £1400

* Coins marked thus were originally issued in Royal Mint sets.

K31   K32   K33

K31 **Two pounds.** 150th Anniversary of the London Underground. O. As K23. R.The
Roundel logo of the London underground system with the dates '1863' above and
'2013' below. Edge inscription 'MIND THE GAP'. (Reverse design: Edwina Ellis.)
2013 ....Unc £5; BU* £15
— Proof *FDC* (in 2013 set, see PS109)* £20
— Proof in silver *FDC* (Issued: 1,185 plus 985 coins in PSS58 & 2,204 in PSS64) £50
— Proof piedfort in silver *FDC* (Issued: 162 plus 486 coins in PSS59) £100
— Proof in gold *FDC* (Issued: 21 plus 59 coins in PGCS13 & 111 in PGCS14)...£1500

K32 **Two pounds.** 150th Anniversary of the London Underground. O. As K23. R. Depicts
a train emerging from a tunnel with the date '1863' to the left and the inscription
'LONDON UNDERGROUND' and the date '2013' to the right. Patterned edge
inspired by the map of the underground network. (Reverse design: Edward Barber and
Jay Osgerby.)
2013 ....Unc £5; BU* £15
— Proof *FDC* (in 2013 set, see PS109)* £20
— Proof in silver *FDC* (Issued: 2,042 plus 985 coins in PSS58 & 2,204 in PSS64).... £50
— Proof piedfort in silver *FDC* (Issued: 186 plus 486 coins in PSS59) £100
— Proof in gold *FDC* (Issued: 29 plus 59 coins in PGCS13 & 111 in PGCS14)...£1500

US518 - 2013 £2 (K31 and K32) BU in folder (2) (Issued: 11,647) £40
PSS62 - 2013 £2 (K31 and K32) silver proofs (2) (Issued: 2204) £100
PSS63 - 2013 £2 (K31 and K32) silver proof piedforts (2)...£200
PGCS14 - 2013 £2 (K31 and K32) gold proofs (2) (Issued: 111)......................................£3000

K33 **Two pounds.** 500th Anniversary of Trinity House. O. As K9. R. A depiction of a
lighthouse lens, surrounded by the inscription 'TRINITY HOUSE' and the dates '1514'
and '2014' with the denomination 'TWO POUNDS'. Edge inscription 'SERVING THE
MARINER'. (Reverse design: Joe Whitlock Blundell with David Eccles.)
2014 ....Unc £4; BU* £15
— BU in presentation folder (Issued: 10,521) £20
— Proof *FDC* (in 2014 set, see PS112)* £10
— Proof in silver *FDC* (Issued: 1,285 plus 368 coins in PSS66 & 283 in PSS67)........£50
— Proof piedfort in silver *FDC* (Issued: 652 plus 487 coins in PSS68) £100
— Proof in gold *FDC* (Issued: 204 plus 75 coins in PGCS17)..............................£1200

* Coins marked thus were originally issued in Royal Mint sets.

K34   K35

K34 Two pounds. World War I. O. As K23. Ṛ. A depiction of Lord Kitchener pointing, with
the inscription 'YOUR COUNTRY NEEDS YOU' below the effigy of Lord Kitchener,
and the inscription 'THE FIRST WORLD WAR 1914-1918' and the date '2014'. Edge
inscription 'THE LAMPS ARE GOING OUT ALL OVER EUROPE'. (Reverse design:
John Bergdahl.)

2014 ....Unc £4; BU* £15
— BU in presentation folder (Issued: 40,357) £18
— Proof *FDC* (in 2014 set, see PS112)* £25
— Proof in silver *FDC* (Issued: 5,483 plus 368 coins in PSS66 & 283 in PSS67) ...£50
— Proof piedfort in silver *FDC* (Issued: 2,496 plus 487 coins in PSS68) £100
— Proof in gold *FDC* (Issued: 751 plus 75 coins in PGCS17)............................£1200

K34A Obverse mule error. Obverse K33 used in error so no denomination shown.
One specimen reported in VF... £650

K35 Two pounds. World War 1, The Royal Navy. O. As K23. Ṛ. The designs shows a
dreadnought at sea with the inscription 'THE FIRST WORLD WAR 1914 – 1918'
and the date of the year below. Edge inscription 'THE SURE SHIELD OF BRITAIN'.
(Reverse design: David Rowlands.)

2015 BU* £10*
— BU in presentation pack £15
— Proof *FDC* (see PS117) * £15
— Proof in silver *FDC* (Issued 3,030 plus 664 coins in PSS70 & 71) £50
— Proof piedfort in silver *FDC* (Issued: 1,512 plus 434 coins in PSS72) £100
— Proof in gold *FDC* (Issued: 406 plus 99 coins in PGCS20)............................£1200

Obverse portrait by Jody Clark

K35A

K35A Two pounds. World War I, The Royal Navy. Ṛ. As K35

2015 ....£10

* Coins marked thus were originally issued in Royal Mint sets.

Obverse portrait by Ian Rank-Broadley

K36

K36 Two pounds. 800th Anniversary of the Signing of Magna Carta. O. As K29. R. The
design shows King John flanked by figures representing the clergy on one side and the
barons on the other with the inscription 'MAGNA CARTA' and '1215 – 2015'. Edge
inscription 'FOUNDATION OF LIBERTY'. (Reverse design: John Bergdahl).
2015 BU...£12
— BU in presentation pack (Issued: 32,818) £15
— Proof *FDC* (in 2015 set, see PS117) *...£15
— Proof in silver *FDC* (Issued: 298 in PSS70 & 366 in PSS71)*.............................£50
— Proof piedfort in silver *FDC* (Issued 434 in PSS72)* £100
— Proof in gold *FDC* (Issued: 99 in PGCS20)* £1500

Obverse portrait by Jody Clark

K36A

K36A Two pounds. 800th Anniversary of the Signing of Magna Carta. R. As K36.
2015 ....£8
— Proof in silver *FDC* (Issued: 2,995) £60
— Proof piedfort in silver *FDC* (Issued: 1,988) £100
— Proof in gold *FDC* (Issued: 399)..£1250

* Coins marked thus were originally issued in Royal Mint sets.

K37

K37 **Two pounds.** ℞. A depiction of Britannia holding a shield and trident with the inscription 'TWO POUNDS'. Edge inscription 'QUATUOR MARIA VINDICO'. (Reverse design: Antony Dufort.)

2015	Unc £5; BU* £10
— BU in presentation pack (Issued: 15,597)	£12
— Proof *FDC* (in 2015 set, see PS116)*	£15
— Proof in silver *FDC* (Issued: 2,971 plus 1,876 coins in PSS74)	£50
— Proof piedfort in silver *FDC* (Issued: 1,911)	£100
— Proof in gold *FDC* (Issued: 424 plus 245 coins in PGCS19)*	£1000
— Proof in platinum *FDC* (Issued:10) (see PPLS3)*	£2500
2016	Unc £5; BU* £10
— Proof *FDC* (in 2016 set, see PS119)*	£15
— Proof in silver *FDC* (Edition: 7,500) (see PSS75)*	£50
2017 BU*	£25
— Proof *FDC* (in 2017 set, see PS122)	£25
— Proof in silver *FDC* (see PSS79)	£50
— Proof in gold *FDC* (see PGCS25)*	£1250
2018 BU*	£25
— Proof *FDC* (in 2018 set, see PS125)*	£25
— Proof in silver *FDC* (see PSS83*	£50
2019 BU*	£20
— Proof *FDC* (in 2019 set, see PS128)*	£20
— Proof in silver *FDC* (see PSS88)*	£50
2020 BU*	£10
— Proof *FDC* (in 2020 set, see PS132)*	£20
— Proof in silver *FDC* (see PSS94)*	£50
2021	Unc £3; BU* £10
— Proof *FDC* (in 2021 set, see PS134)*	£18
— Proof in silver *FDC* (in 2021 set, see PSS96)*	£50
2022	Unc £3; BU* £10
— Proof (in 2022 set, see PS136/7)*	£18
— Proof in silver *FDC* (in 2022 set, see PSS98)*	£50

The £2 Britannia K37 became the definitive £2 for circulation from 2015 but very few have been issued as banks have adequate stocks of other types.

* Coins marked thus were originally issued in Royal Mint sets.

　　　　K38　　　　　　　　　K39　　　　　　　　　K40

K38 **Two pounds.** 400th Anniversary of the Death of William Shakespeare - I Comedy.
O. As K35A. R. A cap and bells with a Jester's stick accompanied by the inscription
'WILLIAM SHAKESPEARE 2016'. Edge inscription 'ALL THE WORLD'S A STAGE'.
(Reverse design: John Bergdahl.)

2016 ....£4
— BU (Issued: 3,500 plus coins in sets) £10
— Proof *FDC* (in 2016 set, see PS119)* £20
— Proof in silver *FDC* (Issued: 951 plus 383 in PSS75 & 658 in PSS76)...............£60
— Proof piedfort in silver *FDC* (Issued: 533 plus 456 in PSS77).........................£100
— Proof in gold *FDC* (Issued: 152 plus 82 in PGCS23).....................................£1250

K39 **Two pounds.** 400th Anniversary of the Death of William Shakespeare - II History.
O. As K35A. R. A dagger through a crown accompanied by the inscription 'WILLIAM
SHAKESPEARE 2016'. Edge inscription 'THE HOLLOW CROWN'. (Reverse design:
John Bergdahl.)

2016 ....£4
— BU (Issued: 6,341 plus coins in sets) £10
— Proof *FDC* (in 2016 set, see PS119)* £20
— Proof in silver *FDC* (Issued: 965 plus 383 in PSS75 & 658 in PSS76)...............£60
— Proof piedfort in silver *FDC* (Issued: 624 plus 456 in PSS77).........................£100
— Proof in gold *FDC* (Issued: 156 plus 82 in PGCS23) £1250

K40 **Two pounds.** 400th Anniversary of the Death of William Shakespeare - III Tragedy.
O. As K35A. R. A skull next to a rose accompanied by the inscription 'WILLIAM
SHAKESPEARE 2016'. Edge inscription 'WHAT A PIECE OF WORK IS A MAN'.
(Reverse design John Bergdahl.)

2016 ....£4
— BU (Issued: 6,550 plus coins in sets) £10
— Proof *FDC* (in 2016 set, see PS119)* £20
— Proof in silver *FDC* (Issued 1,004 plus 383 in PSS75 & 658 in PSS76)..............£60
— Proof piedfort in silver *FDC* (Issued: 769 plus 456 in PSS77))........................£100
— Proof in gold *FDC* (Issued: 209 plus 82 in PGCS23) £1250

K40A — **Edge error.** Edge inscription as K41. ....£50

US59A - 2016 £2 (K38-K40) BU in folder (3) (Issued: 22,060)..£28

* Coins marked thus were originally issued in Royal Mint sets.

K41

K41 **Two pounds.** World War 1, The Army. O. As K35A. R. A stylised silhouette of the heads of three soldiers and references the English cubism movement prevalent around the time of the First World War with the inscription 'THE FIRST WORLD WAR 1914 – 1918', and the date of the year. Edge inscription 'FOR KING AND COUNTRY'. (Reverse design: John Bergdahl.)

2016 ....Unc £4; BU* £10
— BU in presentation folder (Issued: 19,066) £15
— Proof *FDC* (in 2016 set, see PS119)* £20
— Proof in silver *FDC* (Issued: 1,703 plus 383 in PSS75 & 658 in PSS76)........... £60
— Proof piedfort in silver *FDC* (Issued: 931 plus 456 in PSS77) £100
— Proof in gold *FDC* (Issued: 279 plus 82 in PGCS23) £1200

K41A — **Edge error.** Edge inscription as K42. BU ....£

K42

K42 **Two pounds.** 350th Anniversary of the Great Fire of London. R. A view across the River Thames of the City of London in flames with boats fleeing the burning city with the inscription '1666 THE GREAT FIRE OF LONDON 2016'. Edge inscription 'THE WHOLE CITY IN DREADFUL FLAMES'. (Reverse design: Aaron West.)

2016 Unc £5
— BU (Issued: 4,857 plus coins in sets) £12
— BU in presentation folder (Issued: 23,215) £15
— Proof *FDC* (in 2016 set, see PS119)* £20
— Proof in silver *FDC* (Issued: 1,649 plus 383 in PSS75 & 658 in PSS76)... £60
— Proof piedfort in silver *FDC* (Issued: 1,356 plus 456 in PSS77) £100
— Proof in gold *FDC* (Issued: 259 plus 82 in PGCS23) £1200

K43 **Re-listed as NB2.**

No commemorative £2s have been issued into circulation since 2016. Base metal coins are only available in BU packs or year sets.

* Coins marked thus were originally issued in Royal Mint sets

K44

K44 **Two pounds.** World War 1, The Air Force. ℞. A First World War aircraft engaged in reconnaissance with the inscription '1914 - 1918' and 'THE WAR IN THE AIR'. Edge inscription 'THE SKY RAINED HEROES'. (Reverse design: Dan Flashman, Tangerine Design Agency.)

2017 BU £10
— BU in presentation folder (Issued: 54,159) £15
— BU in PNC (Issued: 8,289) £15
— Proof *FDC* (Issued: 520 plus coins in PSS122/123)* £20
— Proof in silver *FDC* (Issued: 2,924 plus 615 coins in PSS79 & 342 in PSS80) £68
— Proof in silver *FDC* in PNC (Issued: 440) £68
— Proof piedfort in silver *FDC* (Issued: 1,535 plus 364 coins in PSS81) £110
— Proof in gold *FDC* (Issued: 302 plus 34 coins in PCGS25 & 99 in PGCS26) ... £1200
— Proof in gold *FDC* in PNC (Issued: 20) £1200

K45

K45 **Two pounds.** Bicentenary of the Birth of Jane Austen. O. As K37. ℞. A depiction of a regency style silhouette of Jane Austen accompanied by her signature and the inscription 'JANE AUSTEN 1817 - 2017' with the denomination 'TWO POUNDS'. Edge inscription 'THERE IS NO DOING WITHOUT MONEY'. (Reverse design: Dominique Evans.)

2017 BU £14
— BU in presentation folder (Issued: 56,718) £17
— Proof *FDC* (in 2017 set, see PS122)* £20
— Proof in silver *FDC* (Issued: 3,531 plus 615 coins in PSS79 & 342 in PSS80) £68
— Proof piedfort in silver *FDC* (Issued: 2,155 plus 364 coins in PSS81) £110
— Proof in gold *FDC* (Issued: 347 plus 34 coins in PCGS25 & 99 in PGCS26) ... £1200

* Coins marked thus were originally issued in Royal Mint sets

K47   K48   K49

K47 **Two pounds.** 200th Anniversary of Mary Shelley's Frankenstein. O. As K35A.
R. The inscription 'FRANKENSTEIN' accompanied with 'BICENTENARY OF MARY
SHELLEYS' and '1818 – THE MODERN PROMETHEUS - 2018'. Edge inscription
'A SPARK OF BEING'. (Reverse design: Thomas Docherty.)
2018 BU (Issued: 17,479 plus coins in US62)..£14
— BU in presentation folder (Issued: 17,280)...£17
— Proof *FDC* (in 2018 set, see PS125)*...£20
— Proof in silver *FDC* (Issued: 2,198 plus 612 coins in PSS83 & 388 in PSS84).....£68
— Proof piedfort in silver *FDC* (Issued: 1,041 plus 338 in PSS85)........................£110
— Proof in gold *FDC* (Issued: 115 plus 139 in PGCS29)....................................£1200

K48 **Two pounds.** 250th Anniversary of Captain Cook's Voyage of Discovery - I. O.
As K35A. R. The hull of the ship Endeavour over a map of Plymouth Sound, Captain
Cook's signature and '250', accompanied with the inscription 'CAPTAIN JAMES COOK
1768 – 2018'. Edge inscription 'OCEANI INVESTIGATOR ACERRMVS'. (Reverse
design: Garry Breeze.)
2018 BU (Issued: 24,249) £20
— BU in presentation folder (Issued: 24,660)...£30
— BU in PNC (Issued 1,276) £20
— Proof in silver *FDC* (Issued: 4,778)..£68
— Proof in gold *FDC* (Issued: 339)..£1200

K49 **Two pounds.** World War I. 100th Anniversary of 1918 Armistice. O. As K37. R. The
inscription 'THE TRUTH UNTOLD THE PITY OF WAR' accompanied with 'THE FIRST
WORLD WAR • ARMISTICE • 1918'. Edge inscription 'WILFRED OWEN KILLED IN
ACTION 4 NOV 1918'. (Reverse design: Stephen Raw.)
2018 BU (Issued: 29,121 plus coins in US62) £15
— BU in presentation folder (Issued: 19,615)..£20
— BU in PNC (Issued: 641) £20
— Proof *FDC* (in 2018 set, see PS125)*...£25
— Proof in silver *FDC* (Issued: 3,426 plus 612 coins in PSS83 & 388 in PSS84)...............£68
— Proof in silver *FDC* in PNC (Issued: 183)..£68
— Proof piedfort in silver *FDC* (Issued: 1,172 plus 338 coins in PSS85) £110
— Proof in gold *FDC* (Issued: 254 plus 139 in PGCS29)..£1200
— Proof in gold *FDC* in PNC (Issued: 10)..£1200

* Coins marked thus were originally issued in Royal Mint sets.

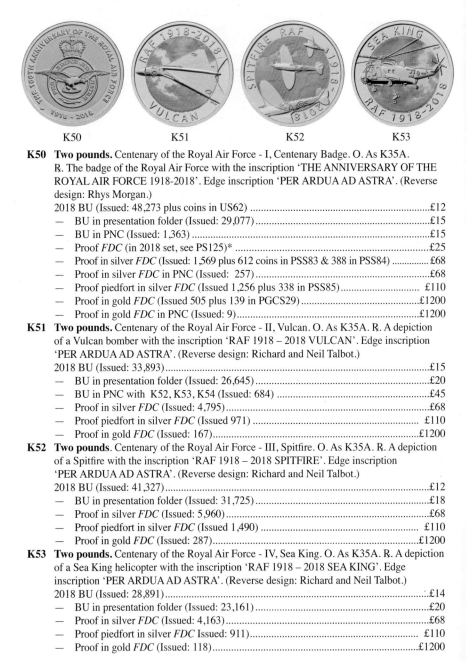

| K50 | K51 | K52 | K53 |

K50 **Two pounds.** Centenary of the Royal Air Force - I, Centenary Badge. O. As K35A.
R. The badge of the Royal Air Force with the inscription 'THE ANNIVERSARY OF THE
ROYAL AIR FORCE 1918-2018'. Edge inscription 'PER ARDUA AD ASTRA'. (Reverse
design: Rhys Morgan.)
2018 BU (Issued: 48,273 plus coins in US62) £12
— BU in presentation folder (Issued: 29,077) £15
— BU in PNC (Issued: 1,363) £15
— Proof *FDC* (in 2018 set, see PS125)* £25
— Proof in silver *FDC* (Issued: 1,569 plus 612 coins in PSS83 & 388 in PSS84) £68
— Proof in silver *FDC* in PNC (Issued: 257) £68
— Proof piedfort in silver *FDC* (Issued 1,256 plus 338 in PSS85)............................ £110
— Proof in gold *FDC* (Issued 505 plus 139 in PGCS29)...£1200
— Proof in gold *FDC* in PNC (Issued: 9)...£1200

K51 **Two pounds.** Centenary of the Royal Air Force - II, Vulcan. O. As K35A. R. A depiction
of a Vulcan bomber with the inscription 'RAF 1918 – 2018 VULCAN'. Edge inscription
'PER ARDUA AD ASTRA'. (Reverse design: Richard and Neil Talbot.)
2018 BU (Issued: 33,893)...£15
— BU in presentation folder (Issued: 26,645) £20
— BU in PNC with K52, K53, K54 (Issued: 684) £45
— Proof in silver *FDC* (Issued: 4,795) £68
— Proof piedfort in silver *FDC* (Issued 971) £110
— Proof in gold *FDC* (Issued: 167)...£1200

K52 **Two pounds.** Centenary of the Royal Air Force - III, Spitfire. O. As K35A. R. A depiction
of a Spitfire with the inscription 'RAF 1918 – 2018 SPITFIRE'. Edge inscription
'PER ARDUA AD ASTRA'. (Reverse design: Richard and Neil Talbot.)
2018 BU (Issued: 41,327)...£12
— BU in presentation folder (Issued: 31,725) £18
— Proof in silver *FDC* (Issued: 5,960) £68
— Proof piedfort in silver *FDC* (Issued 1,490) £110
— Proof in gold *FDC* (Issued: 287)...£1200

K53 **Two pounds.** Centenary of the Royal Air Force - IV, Sea King. O. As K35A. R. A depiction
of a Sea King helicopter with the inscription 'RAF 1918 – 2018 SEA KING'. Edge
inscription 'PER ARDUA AD ASTRA'. (Reverse design: Richard and Neil Talbot.)
2018 BU (Issued: 28,891)...£14
— BU in presentation folder (Issued: 23,161) £20
— Proof in silver *FDC* (Issued: 4,163) £68
— Proof piedfort in silver *FDC* Issued: 911).. £110
— Proof in gold *FDC* (Issued: 118)...£1200

* Coins marked thus were originally issued in Royal Mint sets.

K54 K55 K56

K54 Two pounds. Centenary of the Royal Air Force - V, Lightning II. O. As K35A.
R. A depiction of a Lightning II jet fighter with the inscription 'RAF 1918 – 2018
LIGHTNING II'. Edge inscription 'PER ARDUA AD ASTRA'. (Reverse design:
Richard and Neil Talbot.)
2018 BU (Issued: 28,891) £15
— BU in presentation folder (Issued 20,532) £25
— Proof in silver *FDC* (Issued: 4,072)..£68
— Proof piedfort in silver *FDC* (Issued: 786) £110
— Proof in gold *FDC* (Issued: 120)..£1200

K55 Two pounds. 75th Anniversary of D-Day. O. As K35A. R. Map of Normandy beaches
with arrows, named with the beach codes, pointing to the five landing sites with
inscription 'D-DAY 75TH ANNIVERSARY 2019'. Edge inscription 'THE LONGEST
DAY'. (Reverse design: Stephen Taylor)
2019 BU (Issued: 49,032) £9
— BU in folder (Issued: 25,935) £10
— BU in PNC (Issued: 1,167) £10
— Proof *FDC*...£15
— Proof in silver *FDC* (Issued: 5,900 plus 406 in PSS88) £68
— Proof in silver *FDC* with Newspaper History book (Issued: 191)..........£70
— Proof piedfort in silver (Issued: 1,594 plus 282 in PSS89)...................£110
— Proof in gold *FDC* (Issued: 450 plus 88 in PGCS36)..........................£1200
— Proof in gold *FDC* with Newspaper History book (Issued: 20) £1200

K56 Two pounds. 260th Anniversary of the Foundation of Wedgwood. O. As K35A.
R. A design depicting a Wedgwood vase and the inscription 'WEDGWOOD
1759-2019'. Edge inscription 'EVERYTHING GIVES WAY TO EXPERIMENT'.
(Reverse design: Wedgwood Design Team.)
2019 BU (Issued: 17,476) £12
— BU in folder (Issued: 15,529) £14
— Proof *FDC*...£17
— Proof in silver *FDC* (Issued: 1.951 plus 406 in PSS88) £65
— Proof piedfort in silver (Issued: 968 plus 282 in PSS89)....................£110
— Proof in gold *FDC* (Issued: 142 plus 88 in PGCS36)..........................£1200

* Coins marked thus were originally issued in Royal Mint sets.

K57   K58   K59

K57 Two pounds. 350th Anniversary of the Closing of Pepys's Diary. O. As K35A.
R. A depiction of Samuel Pepys's handwriting on the last page of his diary with the
inscription 'SAMUEL PEPYS DIARIST'. Edge inscription 'THE GOOD GOD
PREPARE ME'. (Reverse design: Gary Breeze.)
2019 BU (Issued: 17,476) £12
— BU in folder (Issued: 14,278) £14
— Proof *FDC**...£17
— Proof in silver *FDC* (Issued: 1,873 plus 406 in PSS88) £65
— Proof piedfort in silver *FDC* (Issued: 841 plus 282 in PSS89)..........................£110
— Proof in gold *FDC* (Issued: 138 plus 88 in PGCS36)......................................£1200

K58 Two pounds. 250th Anniversary of Captain Cook's Voyage of Discovery - II.
O. As K35A. R. The mast of Cook's ship, 'HM Bark Endeavour', below a celestial
image of the Transit of Venus with the inscription '1769 • 2019 CAPTAIN JAMES
COOK' and the number '250' to mark the anniversary of his time in Tahiti. Edge
inscription 'OCEANI INVESTIGATOR ACERRIMVS'. (Reverse design:
Gary Breeze.)
2019 BU £15
— BU in folder £20
— Silver proof *FDC* (Edition: 5,000) £65
— Gold proof *FDC* (Edition: 350) £1200

K59 Two pounds. 75th Anniversary of VE Day. O. As K35A. R. Joyful people symbolising
the first steps towards peace and recovery with dates '1945 2020' and inscription
'VICTORY IN EUROPE'. Edge inscription 'JUST TRIUMPH & PROUD SORROW'.
(Reverse design: Dominique Evans)
2020 BU* £8
— BU in folder £10
— Proof *FDC**...£15
— Proof in silver *FDC* (Edition: 4,750 plus coins in sets) £68
— Proof piedfort in silver *FDC* (Edition: 1,635 plus coins in sets) £110
— Proof in gold *FDC* (Edition: 475 plus coins in sets)..£1200

* *Coins marked thus were originally issued in Royal Mint sets.*

K60   K61   K62

K60 **Two pounds.** 400th Anniversary of 'The Mayflower' voyage to the New World.
O. As K35A. Ŗ. The Mayflower bursting out of the frame as it sails through the
rough seas with inscription '1620 MAYFLOWER 2020'. Edge lettering
'UNDERTAKEN FOR THE GLORY OF GOD'. (Reverse design: Chris Costello.)
2020 BU* £8
— BU in folder £10
— Proof *FDC** £15
— Proof in silver *FDC* (Edition: 4,000 plus coins in sets) £68
— Proof piedfort in silver *FDC* (Edition: 2,000 plus coins in sets) £110
— Proof in gold *FDC* (Edition: 400 plus coins in sets)..£1200

K61 **Two pounds.** Centenary of Agatha Christie's publication of first novel. O. As K35A.
Ŗ. Agatha Christie signature and monogram logo with inscription '1920 100 YEARS
OF MYSTERY 2020'. Edge inscription 'LITTLE GREY CELLS'. (Reverse design:
David Lawrence.)
2020 BU* £8
— BU in folder £10
— Proof *FDC** £15
— Proof in silver *FDC*(Edition: 2,250 plus coins in sets) £68
—· Proof piedfort in silver *FDC* (Edition: 800 plus coins in sets) £110
— Proof in gold *FDC* (Edition: 250 plus coins in sets)..£1200

K62 **Two pounds.** 250th Anniversary of Captain Cook's Voyage of Discovery - III.
O. As K35A. Ŗ. A Maori canoe in close proximity to the bow of HM Bark
'Endeavour'. Edge inscription 'OCEANI INVESTIGATOR ACERRIMVS'.
(Reverse design:
Garry Breeze.)
2020 BU £8
— BU in folder £10
— Proof in silver *FDC* (Edition: 4,795) £68
— Proof in gold *FDC* (Edition: 340) £1200

PGCS37A - 2018 £2 (K47), 2019 £2 (K58), 2020 £2 (K62) gold proofs (3) £3500

* *Coins marked thus were originally issued in Royal Mint sets.*

K63   K64   K65

K63 Two pounds. H G Wells O. As K35A. R̟. A depiction of the Invisible Man and a
Martian encircled by clock numerals accompanied by the inscription 'H G WELLS'
and the date of the year. Edge inscription 'GOOD BOOKS ARE THE WAREHOUSES
OF IDEAS'. (Reverse design: Chris Costello.)
    2021 BU* £8
    — BU in folder...£10
    — BU in PNC (Edition: 10,000)...£10
    — Proof* £15
    — Proof in silver *FDC* (Edition: 1,575 plus coins in sets) £68
    — Proof in silver *FDC* in PNC (Edition: 750)..£68
    — Proof piedfort in silver *FDC* (Edition: 675 plus coins in sets)............................£110
    — Proof in gold *FDC* (Edition: 175 plus coins in sets) £1200
    — Proof in gold *FDC* in PNC (Edition: 50) £1200

K64 Two pounds. 250th Anniversary of the birth of Sir Walter Scott. O. As K35A.
R̟. A depiction of Sir Walter Scott accompanied by the inscription 'SIR WALTER
SCOTT NOVELIST HISTORIAN POET' encircled by the inscription '250TH
ANNIVERSARY OF HIS BIRTH' and the date of the year. Edge inscription 'THE
WILL TO DO, THE SOUL TO DARE'. (Reverse design: Stephen Raw.)
    2021 BU* £8
    — BU in folder £10
    — Proof*...£15
    — Proof in silver *FDC* (Edition: 1,771 plus coins in sets) £68
    — Proof piedfort in silver *FDC* (Edition: 771 plus coins in sets) £110
    — Proof in gold *FDC* (Edition: 175 plus coins in sets)...£1200

K65 Two pounds. The life and legacy of Dame Vera Lynn. O. As K44. R̟. A portrait of
Dame Vera Lynn with the inscription 'DAME VERA LYNN 1917-2020' and an edge
inscription 'WE'LL MEET AGAIN'. (Reverse design: Royal Mint design team.)
    2022 BU £8
    — BU in folder £10
    — Proof * £15
    — Proof in silver *FDC* (Edition: 4,560) £73
    — Proof piedfort in silver *FDC* (Edition: 1,175 plus coins in sets) £118
    — Proof in gold *FDC* (Edition: 350 plus coins in sets)..£1200
    — Proof in platinum *FDC* (Edition: 30)* £1500

* Coins marked thus were originally issued in Royal Mint sets.

K66   K67

K66 **Two pounds.** The 150th Anniversary of the FA Cup. O. As K44. R. A depiction of
the FA Cup with the inscription 'CELEBRATING 150 YEARS OF THE FA CUP'
and an edge inscription of 'FOOTBALL'S GREATEST CUP COMPETITION'.
(Reverse design: Matt Dent & Christian Davies.)

2022 BU £8
— BU in folder £10
— Proof in silver FDC (Edition: 5,660) £73
— Proof piedfort in silver FDC (Edition: 1,160) (Edition: 360) £1200

K67 **Two pounds.** Centenary of the Death of Alexander Graham Bell. O. As K44.
R. A depiction of a numbered telephone keypad and the dates '1847' and '1922'
with the inscription 'ALEXANDER GRAHAM BELL' and an edge inscription
'INNOVATION IN SCIENCE • BELL'. (Reverse design: Henry Gray.)

2022 BU £8
— BU in folder £10
— Proof * £15
— Proof in silver FDC (Edition: 2,500 plus coins in sets) £68
— Proof piedfort in silver FDC (Edition: 1,000 plus coins in sets).........£110
— Proof in gold FDC (Edition: 125 Plus coins in sets)...........................£1200
— Proof in platinum FDC (Edition: 30)* £1500

K68 **Two pounds.** 25th Anniversary of the £2 bi-metal coin. O. As K44 with Iron Age
privy mark. R. As K8.

2022 BU £8
— BU in folder...£12
— Proof in silver FDC (Edition: 2,535)..£75
— Proof piedfort in silver FDC (Edition: 1,435) £125
— Proof in gold FDC (Edition: 285) £1225

K69 **Two pounds.** O. As K37 but with privy mark (see B10) displaying Her Majesty's
birth year and the year of her passing. R. As K37.

2022 BU* £10
— Proof in silver FDC* £70
— Proof in gold FDC* £1500
— Proof in platinum FDC* £2250

* Coins marked thus were originally issued in Royal Mint sets.

CUPRO-NICKEL

The collecting of crown size coins is one of the most popular pursuits among new and established coin collectors. Before decimalisation in 1971, crowns had a nominal denomination of five shillings and this was then changed to twenty five pence in 1972 when the Silver Wedding commemorative was issued. Over time with increasing metal, manufacturing and distribution costs, the production of coins with such a low face value was not economic and the decision was taken to change to a higher value that would last for many years. The first of the five pound crowns was issued in 1990 to mark the ninetieth birthday of The Queen Mother. It seems sensible to group all of the crown size coins together and therefore the earlier twenty five pence issues are not listed between the twenty pence and fifty pence denominations but appear below.

£5 crowns were issued from 2009 for the 2012 London Olympics and these are listed later within that section. Similarly other £5 crowns can be found listed in other sections alongside other denominations of the same topic and further details of these can be found at the end of this crown section.

TWENTY FIVE PENCE COINS

Obverse portrait by Arnold Machin

LL1

LL1   Twenty-five pence. (Crown.) Silver Wedding Commemorative. ℞. The initials E P on a background of foliage, figure of Eros above the Royal Crown with the inscription 'ELIZABETH AND PHILIP' above and the dates '20 NOVEMBER 1947 – 1972' below. (Reverse design: Arnold Machin.)

1972 ....£2
—   Proof *FDC* (in 1972 Set, See PS22)* £5
—   Silver proof *FDC* (Issued: 100,000) £35

* Coins marked thus were originally issued in Royal Mint sets.

LL2

LL2 **Twenty-five pence.** (Crown.) Silver Jubilee Commemorative. ℞. The Ampulla and Anointing Spoon encircled by a floral border and above a Royal Crown. (Obverse and reverse design: Arnold Machin.)

1977 ....£1
— Unc in presentation folder £2
— Proof *FDC* (in 1977 Set, See PS27)* £5
— Silver proof *FDC* (Issued: 377,000)..£30

LL3   LL4

LL3 **Twenty-Five pence.** (Crown.) Queen Mother's 80th Birthday Commemorative.
O. As LL1. ℞. In the centre a portrait of The Queen Mother surrounded by bows and lions with the inscription 'QUEEN ELIZABETH THE QUEEN MOTHER AUGUST 4th 1980'. Reverse design: Richard Guyatt.)

1980 ....£2
— Unc in presentation folder £3
— Silver proof *FDC* (Issued: 83,672).. £35

LL4 **Twenty-five pence.** (Crown.) Royal Wedding Commemorative. O. As LL1. ℞. .Portrait of the Prince of Wales and Lady Diana Spencer with the inscription 'HRH THE PRINCE OF WALES AND LADY DIANA SPENCER 1981'. (Reverse design: Philip Nathan.)

1981 ....£2
— Unc in presentation folder £4
— Silver proof *FDC* (Issued: 218,142)..£35

* *Coins marked thus were originally issued in Royal Mint sets.*

FIVE POUND COINS

Obverse portrait by Raphael Maklouf

L1

L1   **Five pounds.** (Crown.) Queen Mother's 90th Birthday Commemorative. R̥. A
Cypher in the letter E in duplicate above a Royal Crown flanked by a rose and a
thistle all within the inscription 'QUEEN ELIZABETH THE QUEEN MOTHER'
and the dates '1900 – 1990'. (Reverse design: Leslie Durbin.)
1990 ....Unc £7; BU £8
— BU in presentation folder (Issued: 45,250) £10
— Proof in silver *FDC* (Issued: 56,102) £35
— Proof in gold *FDC* (Issued: 2,500)...£2500

L2

L2   **Five pounds.** (Crown.) 40th Anniversary of the Coronation. R̥. St Edward's Crown
encircled by forty trumpets all within the inscription 'FAITH AND TRUTH I WILL
BEAR UNTO YOU' and the dates '1953 – 1993'. (Reverse design: Robert Elderton.)
1993 ....Unc £7; BU £8
— BU in presentation folder £9
— Proof *FDC* (in 1993 set, see PS51)* £10
— Proof in silver *FDC* (Issued: 58,877) £35
— Proof in gold *FDC* (Issued: 2,500)...£2500

* Coins marked thus were originally issued in Royal Mint sets.

L3   L4

L3   **Five pounds.** (Crown.) 70th Birthday of Queen Elizabeth II. O. As L1. R. A
representation of Windsor Castle with five flag poles, two holding forked pennants
with anniversary dates '1926' and '1996', the other flags are Royal Arms, the Union
flag and Our Personal flag. Edge inscription: 'VIVAT REGINA ELIZABETHA'.
(Reverse design: Avril Vaughan.)

1996 ....Unc £7; BU £8
—   BU in presentation folder (issued: 73,311) £10
—   Proof *FDC* (in 1996 set, See PS57)* £10
—   Proof in silver *FDC* (Issued: 39,336) £35
—   Proof in gold *FDC* (Issued: 2,127) £2500

L4   **Five pounds.** (Crown.) Golden Wedding of Queen Elizabeth II and Prince Philip.
O. Conjoint portraits of The Queen and Prince Philip. R. A pair of shields, chevronwise,
on the left, Our Royal Arms, on the right, the shield of Prince Philip, above a Royal
Crown separating the dates '1947' and '1997' with the date '20 NOVEMBER', below an
anchor cabled with the denomination 'FIVE POUNDS'. (Obverse design: Philip Nathan,
reverse design: Leslie Durbin.)

1997 ....Unc £7; BU £8
—   BU in presentation folder £10
—   Proof *FDC* (in 1997 set, See PS59)* £10
—   Proof in silver *FDC* (Issued: 33,689) £35
—   Proof in gold *FDC* (Issued: 2,574) £2500

Obverse portrait by Ian Rank-Broadley

L5

L5   **Five pounds.** (Crown.) Prince Charles' 50th Birthday. R. A portrait of Prince
Charles and in the background words relating to the work of The Prince's Trust. A
circumscription of 'FIFTIETH BIRTHDAY OF HRH THE PRINCE OF WALES'
and below 'FIVE POUNDS' flanked by the anniversary dates '1948' and '1998'.
(Reverse design: Michael Noakes/Robert Elderton.)

1998 ....Unc £8; BU £9
— BU in presentation folder £10
— Proof *FDC* (in 1998 set, see PS61)* £15
— Proof in silver *FDC* (Issued: 13,379) £50
— Proof in gold *FDC* (Issued: 773)...£3000

L6   L7   L7A

L6   **Five pounds.** (Crown.) Diana, Princess of Wales Memorial. O. As L5.
R. A portrait of Diana, Princess of Wales with the dates '1961' and '1997', and the
circumscription 'IN MEMORY OF DIANA PRINCESS OF WALES' with the value
'FIVE POUNDS'. (Reverse design: David Cornell.)
1999 ....Unc £7; BU £9
— BU in presentation folder £12
— Proof *FDC* (in 1999 set, see PS63)* £15
— Proof in silver *FDC* (Issued: 49,545) £60
— Proof in gold *FDC* (Issued: 7,500)...£4000

L7   **Five pounds.** (Crown.) Millennium commemorative. O. As L5. R. A representation
of the dial of a clock with hands set at 12 o'clock with a map of the British Isles and
the dates '1999' and '2000' and the words 'ANNO DOMINI' and the value 'FIVE
POUNDS'. Edge inscription 'WHAT'S PAST IS PROLOGUE' in serif or sans serif
font.
(Reverse design: Jeffrey Matthews.)
1999 ....Unc £6; BU £7
— BU in presentation folder £10
— Proof in silver *FDC* (Issued: 49,057) £35
— Proof in gold *FDC* (Issued: 2,500)...£2300
2000 BU £12
— BU in presentation folder (Issued: 27,546) £20
— Proof *FDC* (in 2000 set, see PS65)* £15
— Proof in gold *FDC* (Issued: 1,487)..£2300

L7A   2000
— BU in presentation folder with Dome mint mark £25
(See illustration above ← the mintmark is located within the shaded area at 3 o'clock).

L7B   2000
— Proof in 0.999 silver *FDC* (Issued: 1,487 plus 13,180 in set PSS16) £50
(The reverse design is the same as the 1999 issue but with the British Isles highlighted with
22 ct. gold.)

L8   L9

L8   **Five pounds.** (Crown.) Queen Mother's 100th Birthday. O. As L5. R. A portrait of the Queen Mother flanked by groups of people with the circumscription 'QUEEN ELIZABETH THE QUEEN MOTHER' the anniversary dates '1900' and '2000' below, and the denomination 'FIVE POUNDS'. Below the portrait a representation of her signature. (Reverse design: Ian Rank-Broadley.)

2000 ....Unc £6; BU £7
—   BU in presentation folder (Issued: 241,261) £10
—   Proof in silver *FDC* (Issued: 31,316) £35
—   Proof piedfort in silver *FDC* (Issued: 14,850) £50
—   Proof in gold *FDC* (Issued: 3,000)...£2300

L9   **Five pounds.** (Crown.) Victorian Anniversary. O. As L5. R. A classic portrait of the young Queen Victoria based on the Penny Black postage stamp with a V representing Victoria, and taking the form of railway lines and in the background the iron framework of the Crystal Palace, and the denomination '5 POUNDS' and the dates '1901' and '2001'. (Reverse design: Mary Milner-Dickens.)

2001 ....Unc £6; BU £7
—   BU in presentation folder £10
—   Proof *FDC* (in 2001 set, see PS68)* £12
—   Proof in silver *FDC* (Issued: 19,216) £45
—   Proof in silver *FDC* with 'reverse frosting' giving matt appearance (Issued:596) (Crown issued with sovereigns of 1901 and 2001)* £200
—   Proof in gold *FDC* (Issued: 2,098)..£2500
—   Proof in gold *FDC* with 'reverse frosting' giving matt appearance.(Issued:733) (Crown issued with four different type sovereigns of Queen Victoria, - Young Head with shield, and Young Head with St.George reverse, Jubilee Head and Old Head.)* £2500

L10

L10   **Five pounds.** (Crown.) Golden Jubilee commemorative 2002. O. Equestrian portrait of The Queen with the inscription 'ELIZABETH II DEI GRA REGINA FID DEF' around the circumference and 'AMOR POPULI PRAESIDIUM REG' within, and the date '2002' below separated by the central element of the Royal Arms. R. New portrait of

The Queen with the denomination 'FIVE POUNDS'. (Obverse and reverse designs: Ian
Rank-Broadley.)
2002 ....Unc £6; BU £9
— BU in presentation folder £12
— Proof *FDC* (in 2002 set, see PS72)* £14
— Proof in silver *FDC* (Issued: 54,012) £40
— Proof in gold *FDC* (Issued: 3,500)...£2750

L11

L11   **Five pounds.** (Crown.) Queen Mother Memorial 2002. ℞. Three quarter portrait of
the Queen Mother within a wreath with the inscription 'QUEEN ELIZABETH THE
QUEEN MOTHER' and the dates '1900' and '2002'. Edge inscription 'STRENGTH,
DIGNITY AND LAUGHTER'. (Reverse design: Avril Vaughan.)
2002 ....Unc £7; BU £8
— BU in presentation folder £10
— Proof in silver *FDC* (Issued: 16,117) £40
— Proof in gold *FDC* (Issued: 2,086)...£2300

L12

L12   **Five pounds.** (Crown.) 50th Anniversary of the Coronation. O. Profile portrait of The
Queen in linear form facing right with the inscription 'ELIZABETH II DEI GRATIA
REGINA F D'. ℞. In the centre the inscription 'GOD SAVE THE QUEEN' surrounded
by the inscription 'CORONATION JUBILEE' the denomination 'FIVE POUNDS' and
the date '2003'. (Obverse and reverse designs: Tom Phillips.)
2003 ....Unc £7; BU £8
— BU in presentation folder (Issued: 100,481) £10
— Proof *FDC* (in 2003 set, see PS78)* £15
— Proof in silver *FDC* (Issued: 28,758) £45
— Proof in gold *FDC* (Issued: 1,896)...£2500

PSS19 - 2002/3 £5 (L10 and L12) silver proofs (2) £100

* *Coins marked thus were originally issued in Royal Mint sets.*

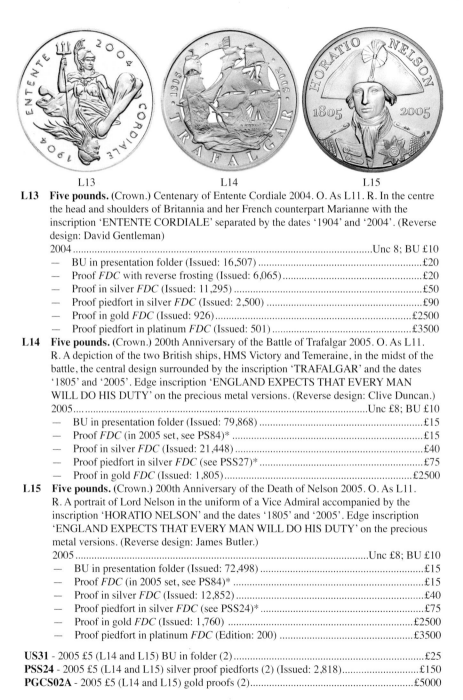

L13   L14   L15

L13   **Five pounds.** (Crown.) Centenary of Entente Cordiale 2004. O. As L11. ℟. In the centre the head and shoulders of Britannia and her French counterpart Marianne with the inscription 'ENTENTE CORDIALE' separated by the dates '1904' and '2004'. (Reverse design: David Gentleman)

2004 ....Unc 8; BU £10
—   BU in presentation folder (Issued: 16,507) £20
—   Proof *FDC* with reverse frosting (Issued: 6,065) £20
—   Proof in silver *FDC* (Issued: 11,295) £50
—   Proof piedfort in silver *FDC* (Issued: 2,500) £90
—   Proof in gold *FDC* (Issued: 926) £2500
—   Proof piedfort in platinum *FDC* (Issued: 501) £3500

L14   **Five pounds.** (Crown.) 200th Anniversary of the Battle of Trafalgar 2005. O. As L11. ℟. A depiction of the two British ships, HMS Victory and Temeraine, in the midst of the battle, the central design surrounded by the inscription 'TRAFALGAR' and the dates '1805' and '2005'. Edge inscription 'ENGLAND EXPECTS THAT EVERY MAN WILL DO HIS DUTY' on the precious metal versions. (Reverse design: Clive Duncan.)

2005 ....Unc £8; BU £10
—   BU in presentation folder (Issued: 79,868) £15
—   Proof *FDC* (in 2005 set, see PS84)* £15
—   Proof in silver *FDC* (Issued: 21,448) £40
—   Proof piedfort in silver *FDC* (see PSS27)* £75
—   Proof in gold *FDC* (Issued: 1,805) £2500

L15   **Five pounds.** (Crown.) 200th Anniversary of the Death of Nelson 2005. O. As L11. ℟. A portrait of Lord Nelson in the uniform of a Vice Admiral accompanied by the inscription 'HORATIO NELSON' and the dates '1805' and '2005'. Edge inscription 'ENGLAND EXPECTS THAT EVERY MAN WILL DO HIS DUTY' on the precious metal versions. (Reverse design: James Butler.)

2005 ....Unc £8; BU £10
—   BU in presentation folder (Issued: 72,498) £15
—   Proof *FDC* (in 2005 set, see PS84)* £15
—   Proof in silver *FDC* (Issued: 12,852) £40
—   Proof piedfort in silver *FDC* (see PSS24)* £75
—   Proof in gold *FDC* (Issued: 1,760) £2500
—   Proof piedfort in platinum *FDC* (Edition: 200) £3500

US31 - 2005 £5 (L14 and L15) BU in folder (2) £25
PSS24 - 2005 £5 (L14 and L15) silver proof piedforts (2) (Issued: 2,818)............................£150
PGCS02A - 2005 £5 (L14 and L15) gold proofs (2)...£5000

* Coins marked thus were originally issued in Royal Mint sets.

L16

L16   **Five pounds.** (Crown.) 80th Birthday of Her Majesty Queen Elizabeth II. O. As L11. Ɍ.
A fanfare of regal trumpets with the inscription 'VIVAT REGINA' and the dates '1926' and
'2006'. Edge inscription 'DUTY SERVICE FAITH'. (Reverse design: Danuta Solowiej-
Wedderburn.)

2006...Unc £8; BU £10
—   BU in presentation folder (Issued: 330,790 ....£12
—   Proof *FDC* (in 2006 set, see PS87)* £15
—   Proof in silver *FDC* (Issued: 20,790)..£45
—   Proof in gold *FDC* (Issued: 2,750)..£2500
—   Proof piedfort in platinum *FDC* (Issued: 250)....................................£3500

L16A —   Proof piedfort in silver with selected gold plating *FDC* (Issued: 5,000).................£70

L17

L17   **Five pounds.** (Crown.) Diamond Wedding Anniversary of Her Majesty Queen Elizabeth
II and The Duke of Edinburgh. O. Conjoint portrait of The Queen and Prince Philip.
Ɍ. The Rose window of Westminster Abbey with the inscription 'TVEATVR VNITA
DEVS', the dates '1947' and '2007', the denomination 'FIVE POUNDS'. Edge
inscription 'MY STRENGTH AND STAY'. (Obverse design: Ian Rank-Broadley,
reverse design: Emma Noble.)

2007..Unc £8; BU £10
—   BU in presentation folder (Issued: 260,856) £12
—   Proof *FDC* (in 2007 set, see PS90)* £15
—   Proof in silver *FDC* (Issued: 15,186)..£45
—   Proof piedfort in silver *FDC* (Issued: 2,000) £70
—   Proof in gold *FDC* (Issued: 2,380)..£2500
—   Proof piedfort in platinum *FDC* (Issued: 250)....................................£3500

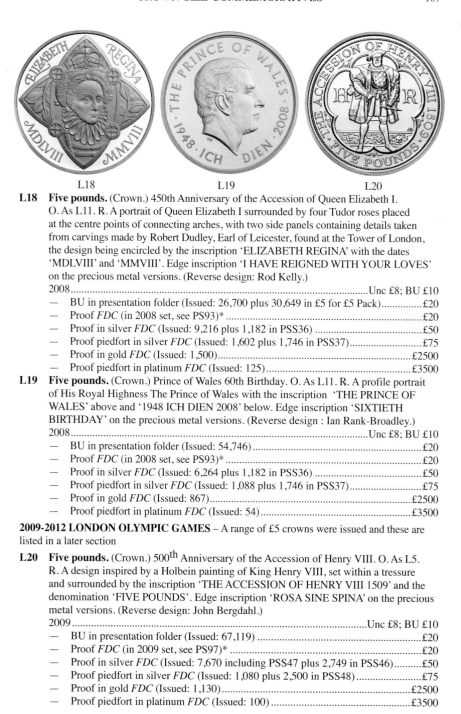

L18　　　　　　　L19　　　　　　　L20

L18　**Five pounds.** (Crown.) 450th Anniversary of the Accession of Queen Elizabeth I.
O. As L11. R. A portrait of Queen Elizabeth I surrounded by four Tudor roses placed
at the centre points of connecting arches, with two side panels containing details taken
from carvings made by Robert Dudley, Earl of Leicester, found at the Tower of London,
the design being encircled by the inscription 'ELIZABETH REGINA' with the dates
'MDLVIII' and 'MMVIII'. Edge inscription 'I HAVE REIGNED WITH YOUR LOVES'
on the precious metal versions. (Reverse design: Rod Kelly.)
2008..Unc £8; BU £10
　—　BU in presentation folder (Issued: 26,700 plus 30,649 in £5 for £5 Pack)...............£20
　—　Proof *FDC* (in 2008 set, see PS93)*...£20
　—　Proof in silver *FDC* (Issued: 9,216 plus 1,182 in PSS36) £50
　—　Proof piedfort in silver *FDC* (Issued: 1,602 plus 1,746 in PSS37)..........................£75
　—　Proof in gold *FDC* (Issued: 1,500)..£2500
　—　Proof piedfort in platinum *FDC* (Issued: 125)..£3500

L19　**Five pounds.** (Crown.) Prince of Wales 60th Birthday. O. As L11. R. A profile portrait
of His Royal Highness The Prince of Wales with the inscription 'THE PRINCE OF
WALES' above and '1948 ICH DIEN 2008' below. Edge inscription 'SIXTIETH
BIRTHDAY' on the precious metal versions. (Reverse design : Ian Rank-Broadley.)
2008..Unc £8; BU £10
　—　BU in presentation folder (Issued: 54,746)...£20
　—　Proof *FDC* (in 2008 set, see PS93)*...£20
　—　Proof in silver *FDC* (Issued: 6,264 plus 1,182 in PSS36) £50
　—　Proof piedfort in silver *FDC* (Issued: 1,088 plus 1,746 in PSS37)..........................£75
　—　Proof in gold *FDC* (Issued: 867)...£2500
　—　Proof piedfort in platinum *FDC* (Issued: 54)...£3500

2009-2012 LONDON OLYMPIC GAMES – A range of £5 crowns were issued and these are
listed in a later section

L20　**Five pounds.** (Crown.) 500th Anniversary of the Accession of Henry VIII. O. As L5.
R. A design inspired by a Holbein painting of King Henry VIII, set within a tressure
and surrounded by the inscription 'THE ACCESSION OF HENRY VIII 1509' and the
denomination 'FIVE POUNDS'. Edge inscription 'ROSA SINE SPINA' on the precious
metal versions. (Reverse design: John Bergdahl.)
2009..Unc £8; BU £10
　—　BU in presentation folder (Issued: 67,119) £20
　—　Proof *FDC* (in 2009 set, see PS97)*...£20
　—　Proof in silver *FDC* (Issued: 7,670 including PSS47 plus 2,749 in PSS46)..........£50
　—　Proof piedfort in silver *FDC* (Issued: 1,080 plus 2,500 in PSS48)......................£75
　—　Proof in gold *FDC* (Issued: 1,130)..£2500
　—　Proof piedfort in platinum *FDC* (Issued: 100) £3500

* Coins marked thus were originally issued in Royal Mint sets.

L21

L21 **Five pounds.** (Crown.) 350th Anniversary of the Restoration of the Monarchy.
O. As L5. R. A design featuring a crown, a spray of oak leaves, interlinked 'C's,
the date '1660', the inscription 'RESTORATION OF THE MONARCHY' and the
denomination 'FIVE POUNDS'. Edge inscription 'A QUIET AND PEACEFUL
POSSESSION' on the precious metal versions. (Reverse design: David Cornell.)
2010 ....Unc £8; BU £10
— BU on presentation card (Issued: combined with below) £20
— BU in presentation folder (Issued: 30,247) £20
— Proof *FDC* (in 2010 set, see PS101)* £20
— Proof in silver *FDC* (Issued: 5,277 including PSS51 plus 1,241 in PSS50)..........£50
— Proof piedfort in silver *FDC* (Issued: 2,854 plus 1,581 in PSS52).......................£80
— Proof in gold *FDC* (Issued: 1,182)..£2500
— Proof piedfort in platinum *FDC* (Edition: 100) £3500

No £5 cupro-nickel crowns have been issued at face value by banks or post offices since 2010.

L22

L22 **Five pounds.** (Crown.) Royal Wedding commemorative. R.A design featuring facing
portraits of His Royal Highness Prince William and Miss Catherine Middleton with the
inscription 'WILLIAM AND CATHERINE' above and the date '29 APRIL 2011' below.
(Reverse design: Mark Richards.)
2011
— BU in presentation folder (Issued: 250,000) £18
— Proof in silver *FDC* (Issued: 26,069) £50
— Proof in silver with gold plating *FDC* (Issued: 7,451) £65
— Proof piedfort in silver *FDC* (Issued: 2,991)..£90
— Proof in gold *FDC* (Issued: 2,066) £2500
— Proof piedfort in platinum *FDC* (Issued: 133) £3500

* Coins marked thus were originally issued in Royal Mint sets.

L23

L23 **Five pounds.** (Crown.) 90th Birthday of Prince Philip. R. A profile portrait of His Royal
Highness The Duke of Edinburgh with the inscription 'PRINCE PHILIP 90TH BIRTHDAY'
and the denomination 'FIVE POUNDS' and the date '2011'. (Reverse design: Mark Richards.)
2011
- — BU in presentation folder (Issued: 18,370) £40
- — Proof *FDC* (in 2011 set, see PS104)* £40
- — Proof in silver *FDC* (Issued: 4,599 inlcuding coins in PSS53 & 54).....................£60
- — Proof piedfort in silver *FDC* (Issued: 2,659 including coins in PSS55) £90
- — Proof in gold *FDC* (Issued: 636) £2500
- — Proof piedfort in platinum *FDC* (Issued: 49) £3500

L24

L24 **Five pounds.** (Crown.) Diamond Jubilee commemorative 2012. O. Our Effigy, inspired
by the sculpture mounted in the entrance to the Supreme Court building on Parliament
Square, with the inscription 'ELIZABETH. II. D. G. REG. F. D. FIVE POUNDS'.
R. Our Effigy first used on United Kingdom coins from 1953, with an olive branch
and ribbon below, the date '2012' to the left and the inscription 'DIRIGE DEVS
GRESSVS MEOS' to the right. Edge inscription 'A VOW MADE GOOD' on the
precious metal coins. (Obverse and reverse designs: Ian Rank-Broadley)
2012
- — BU in presentation folder (Issued: 484,775) £12
- — BU in PNC (Issued: 18,948) £12
- — Proof *FDC* (in 2012 set, see PS107)* £15
- — Proof in silver *FDC* (Issued: 16,820 including coins in sets) £50
- — Proof in silver with gold plating *FDC* (Issued: 12,112).....................................£70
- — Proof piedfort in silver *FDC* (Issued: 3,187) £85
- — Proof in gold *FDC* (Issued: 1,112)..£3000
- — Proof piedfort in platinum *FDC* (Issued: 20) £4000

* Coins marked thus were originally issued in Royal Mint sets.

L25   L26   L27

L25 **Five pounds.** (Crown.) 60th Anniversary of the Coronation. O. As L22. R. In the centre
The Imperial State Crown with the inscription 'TO REIGN AND SERVE' and 'A VOW
MADE GOOD'. (Reverse design: Emma Noble.)

2013 BU* £10
— BU in presentation folder £15
— Proof *FDC* (in 2013 set, see PS109)* £15
— Proof in silver *FDC* (Issued: 7,166 plus 985 coins in PSS58) £60
— Proof in silver with gold plating *FDC* (Issued: 2,547)...................................... £80
— Proof piedfort in silver *FDC* (Issued: 2,686 plus 486 coins in PSS59) £95
— Proof in gold *FDC* (Issued: 458 plus 59 coins in PGCS13)............................ £3000
— Proof piedfort in platinum *FDC* (Issued: 106) £3500

L26 **Five pounds.** (Crown.) Birth of Prince George of Cambridge. O. As L11. R. A depiction
of St. George armed, sitting on horseback, attacking the dragon with a sword, and a
broken spear upon the ground, and the date of the year. (Reverse design: Benedetto
Pistrucci.)

2013 Proof in silver *FDC* (Issued: 7,460) £100
— Proof piedfort in platinum *FDC* (Issued: 25) £4000

L27 **Five pounds.** (Crown.) The Christening of Prince George of Cambridge. O. As L11.
R. A deconstructed silver lily font incorporating cherubs and roses, with a Baroque-style
cartouche with the inscription 'DIEU ET MON DROIT' and 'TO CELEBRATE THE
CHRISTENING OF PRINCE GEORGE OF CAMBRIDGE 2013' in the centre of the
coin. (Reverse design: John Bergdahl.)

2013 BU in presentation folder £20
— Proof in silver *FDC* (Issued: 7,264).. £80
— Proof piedfort in silver *FDC* (Issued: 2,251) £140
— Proof in gold *FDC* (Issued: 486)... £3000
— Proof piedfort in platinum *FDC* (Issued: 38).. £4000

* Coins marked thus were originally issued in Royal Mint sets.

L28   L29

L30   L31

L28-L31 Five pounds. (Crown.) The Queen's Portraits. Obverse design depicts the Royal Arms with the date '2013' below. (Obverse design: James Butler.)

2013

  — **L28 R.** The portrait of The Queen by Mary Gillick with the inscription 'ELIZABETH II DEI GRATIA REGINA F.D.' and the denomination 'FIVE POUNDS' below.

  — **L29 R.** The portrait of The Queen by Arnold Machin with the inscription 'ELIZABETH II D: G: REG: F:D: FIVE POUNDS'.

  — **L30 R.** The portrait of The Queen by Raphael Maklouf with the inscription 'ELIZABETH II DEI. GRATIA. REGINA. F.D.' and the denomination 'FIVE POUNDS' below.

  — **L31 R.** The portrait of The Queen by Ian Rank-Broadley with the inscription 'ELIZABETH II D. G. REG. F.D. and the denomination 'FIVE POUNDS' below.

PSS60 - 2013 £5 (L28-L31) silver proofs (4) (Issued: 1465)... £350
PSS61 - 2013 £5 (L28-L31) silver proofs piedforts (4) (Issued: 697) £600
PGCS15 - 2013 £5 (L28-L31) gold proofs (4) (Issued: 148)... £12000

L32 L33

L32 **Five pounds.** (Crown.) Queen Anne commemorative. O. As L22. ℞. The effigy of Queen Anne enclosed by baroque decoration including the Royal Arms from the reign of Queen Anne and surrounded by the inscription 'QUEEN ANNE DEI GRATIA 1665-1714'. (Reverse design: Mark Edwards.)

2014 BU* £60
— BU in presentation folder (Issued: 12,181) £65
— Proof *FDC* (in 2014 set, see PS112)* £70
— Proof in silver *FDC* (Issued: 2212 plus 368 coins in PSS66 & 283 in PSS67) .. £100
— Proof in silver with gold plating *FDC* (Issued: 627) £120
— Proof piedfort in silver *FDC* (Issued: 636 plus 487 coins in PSS68) £160
— Proof in gold *FDC* (Issued: 271 plus 75 coins in PGCS17) £3000

L33 **Five pounds.** (Crown.) The first birthday of Prince George of Cambridge. O. As L11. ℞. The four Quarterings of Our Royal Arms each contained in a shield and arranged in saltire with, in the intervening spaces, a Rose, a Thistle, both slipped and leaved, a sprig of shamrock and a Leek, in the centre the Crown and in the base the date of the year. (Reverse design: Edgar Fuller.)

2014
— Proof in silver *FDC* (Issued: 7,451) £90

2014-2018 WORLD WAR I CENTENARY– A range of £5 crowns were issued and these are listed in a later section

* Coins marked thus were originally issued in Royal Mint sets.

L34   L35

L36   L37

L34-L37 **Five pounds.** (Crown.) Celebrating British Landmarks I. O. As L22.
2014
— **L34** R. The head of one of the lions in Trafalger Square with Nelson's column in the background and the inscription 'FIVE POUNDS'.
— **L35** R. A view of the Elizabeth Tower and the inscription 'FIVE POUNDS'.
— **L36** R. Tower Bridge and the inscription 'FIVE POUNDS'.
— **L37** R. The Victoria Memorial with Buckingham Palace in the background and the inscription 'FIVE POUNDS'.
(All reverse designs: Glyn Davies and Laura Clancy)

PSS69 - 2014 £5 (L34-L37) silver proofs with colour (4) (Issued: 1,299) £325

For coins with similar designs, see NB3-6 and NG1-3.

L38

L38   Five pounds. (Crown.) 50th Anniversary of the Death of Winston Churchill. O. As L22.
R. A portrait of Winston Churchill with the inscription 'CHURCHILL'. Edge inscription
on the precious metal versions 'NEVER FLINCH, NEVER WEARY, NEVER DESPAIR'.
(Reverse design: Mark Richards.)

2015 BU* £15
— BU in presentation pack £20
— BU in case with 1965 5/- (Issued: 4,987) £22
— BU in PNC (Issued: 9,896) £20
— Proof *FDC* (in 2015 set, see PS115)* £25
— Proof in silver *FDC* (Issued: 4,238 plus 298 coins in PSS70 & 366 in PSS71).......£70
— Proof piedfort in silver *FDC* (Issued: 1,800 plus 434 coins in PSS72) £135
— Proof in gold *FDC* (Issued: 325 plus 99 coins in PGCS20) £2500
— Proof piedfort in platinum *FDC* (Issued: 90)...£3500

L39

L39   Five pounds. (Crown.) Bicentenary of the Battle of Waterloo. O. As L22. R. A depiction
of the Duke of Wellington greeting the Prussian General Gebhard Leberecht von Blucher
after the Battle of Waterloo with the inscription 'THE BATTLE OF WATERLOO
1815'with the edge inscription on the precious metal versions 'THE NEAREST RUN
THING YOU EVER SAW' (Reverse design: David Lawrence).

2015 BU* £15
— BU in presentation pack (Issued: 24,554)..£20
— BU in PNC (Issued: 8,576) £20
— Proof *FDC* (in 2015 set, see PS117)* £20
— Proof in silver *FDC* (Issued: 664, only in sets)* £70
— Proof piedfort in silver *FDC* (Issued: 434, only in sets)*.....................................£130
— Proof in gold *FDC* (Issued: 99, only in sets)* £3000

* Coins marked thus were originally issued in Royal Mint sets.

Obverse portrait by Jody Clark

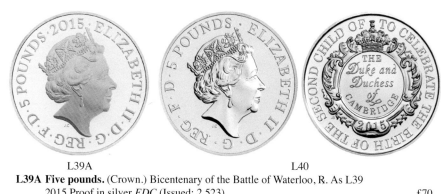

| L39A | L40 |

L39A **Five pounds.** (Crown.) Bicentenary of the Battle of Waterloo, R̫. As L39
2015 Proof in silver *FDC* (Issued: 2,523) £70
— Proof piedfort in silver *FDC* (Issued: 896) £120
— Proof in gold *FDC* (Issued: 273) £2500

L40 **Five pounds.** (Crown.) The Second Child of The Duke and Duchess of Cambridge.
R̫. An ornamental cartouche in the centre featuring the inscription 'THE DUKE AND
DUCHESS OF CAMBRIDGE 2015' surrounded by the inscription 'TO CELEBRATE
THE BIRTH OF THE SECOND CHILD OF'. (Reverse design: John Bergdahl.)
2015 BU in presentation pack £25
— Proof in silver *FDC* (Edition: 9,500) £70
— Proof in gold *FDC* (Edition: 350) £3000

| L41 | L42 |

L41 **Five pounds.** (Crown.) The Christening of Princess Charlotte of Cambridge. O. As L40.
R̫. A design depicting a deconstructed silver lily font incorporating cherubs, with a
Baroque - Style cartouche and 'DIEU ET – MON DROIT' below and in the centre the
inscription 'TO CELEBRATE THE CHRISTENING OF PRINCESS CHARLOTTE
ELIZABETH DIANA OF CAMBRIDGE 2015' (Reverse design: John Bergdahl).
2015 Proof in silver *FDC* (Issued: 4,842) £90
— Proof in gold *FDC* (Issued: 350) £3000

L42 **Five pounds.** (Crown.) Prince George's Second Birthday. O. As L40. R̫. A design
depicting St George slaying the dragon and the date '2015'. (Reverse design:
Christopher Le Brun).
2015 Proof in silver *FDC* (Issued: 4,009) £90

Obverse portrait by James Butler

L43

L43 **Five pounds.** (Crown.) The Longest Serving Monarch. R. St Edwards crown in the centre
and the date '1952'and '2015' above and 'ONE CROWN' below. Edge inscription on the
precious metal versions 'LONG TO REIGN OVER US'.
(Obverse and reverse designs: James Butler).
2015 BU in presentation pack (Issued: 48,848)...£15
— Proof in silver *FDC* (Issued:10,249)..£60
— Proof piedfort in silver *FDC* (Issued: 3,171) £90
— Proof in gold *FDC* (Issued: 899) £2500
— Proof piedfort in platinum *FDC* (Issued: 88)..£3500

Obverse portrait by Jody Clark

L44

L44 **Five pounds.** (Crown.) 90th Birthday of Her Majesty Queen Elizabeth II. O. As L39A.
R. A crowned Royal Cypher above the number '90' encircled by roses. Edge inscription
'FULL OF HONOUR AND YEARS' on the precious metal versions. (Reverse design:
Christopher Hobbs.)
2016 BU (Issued: 10,181) £10
— BU in presentation folder (Issued: 74,195)..£15
— Proof *FDC* (in 2016 set, see PS119)* £20
— Proof in silver *FDC* (Issued: 9,988 plus 1,041 in PSS75 & 76) £60
— Proof piedfort in silver *FDC* (Issued: 3,555, plus 456 in PSS77)...........................£90
— Proof in gold *FDC* ((Issued: 988 plus 82 in PGCS23) £2500
— Proof piedfort in platinum *FDC* (Issued: 87)..£3500

* Coins marked thus were originally issued in Royal Mint sets.

L45   L46

L47   L48

L45-L48 Five pounds. (Crown.) Celebrating British Landmarks II. O. As L39A.
    2016

           L45 R. The White Cliffs of Dover.
           L46 R. The Giant's Causeway.
           L47 R. The Lake District.
           L48 R. Snowdonia.
           (All reverse designs: Glyn Davies and Laura Clancy.)

PSS78 - 2016 £5 (L45-L48) silver proofs with colour (4) (Issued: 1,098) £325

L49

L49 Five pounds. (Crown.) 100th Anniversary of the House of Windsor. R. A depiction
    of the crowned badge of the House of Windsor surrounded by a garland of oak leaves
    accompanied by the inscription ' CENTENARY OF THE HOUSE OF WINDSOR
    2017'. Edge inscription 'THE CHRISTENING OF A DYNASTY' on the precious metal
    versions. (Reverse design: Timothy Noads.)
    2017

— BU in presentation folder (Issued: 30,344) £15
— BU in presentation folder to mark the engagement of Prince Harry and
   Meghan Markle (Issued: 4,972) £20
— Proof *FDC* (in 2017 set, see PS122)* £15
— Proof in silver *FDC* (Issued: 3,701 plus 615 coins in PSS79 & 342 in PSS80) ... £60
— Proof piedfort in silver *FDC* (Issued: 1,480 plus 364 coins in PSS81) £90
— Proof in gold *FDC* (440 plus 24 coins in PGCS25 & 89 in PGCS26) £2500

L50   L51

L50 **Five pounds.** (Crown.) 1000th Anniversary of the Coronation of King Canute.
O. As L49. R. Stylised portrait of Canute accompanied by the inscription '1017 KING
CANUTE 2017'. Edge inscription 'TIME AND TIDE WAIT FOR NO MAN' on the
precious metal versions. (Reverse design: Lee R. Jones.)
2017
— BU in presentation folder (Issued: 26,950) £15
— Proof *FDC* (in 2017 set, see PS122)* £15
— Proof in silver *FDC* (Issued: 2,953 plus 615 coins in PSS79 & 342 in PSS80) ... £60
— Proof piedfort in silver *FDC* (Issued: 1,071 plus 364 coins in PSS81) £95
— Proof in gold *FDC* (Issued: 150 plus 34 coins in PCGS25 & 99 in PGCS26) . £3000

L51 **Five pounds.** (Crown.) Sapphire Jubilee of Her Majesty Queen Elizabeth II.
O. As L49. R. A depiction of the Imperial State Crown accompanied by the inscription
'MY WHOLE LIFE, WHETHER IT BE LONG OR SHORT, DEVOTED TO YOUR
SERVICE' and surrounded by the inscription 'SAPPHIRE JUBILEE' along with the
dates '1952-2017'. Edge inscription 'SHINE THROUGH THE AGES' on the precious
metal versions. (Reverse design: Glyn Davies.)
2017
— BU in presentation folder (Issued: 75,440 .... £15
— BU in PNC (Issued: 9,961) £15
— Proof in silver *FDC* (Issued: 7,794) £60
— Proof in silver *FDC* in PNC (Issued: 499) £80
— Proof piedfort in silver *FDC* (Issued: 2,579) £130
— Proof in gold *FDC* (Issued: 650) £2500
— Proof in gold *FDC* in PNC (Issued: 49) £2500

* Coins marked thus were originally issued in Royal Mint sets.

L52   L53

L54   L55

L52-L55 Five pounds. (Crown.) Celebrating British Landmarks III. O. As L39A.
2017
    L52 R. The door of 10 Downing Street.
    L53 R. Hampton Court Palace.
    L54 R. Edinburgh Castle.
    L55 R. Westminster Abbey.
    (All reverse designs: Glyn Davies and Laura Clancy.)

PSS82 - 2017 £5 (L52-L55) silver proofs with colour (4) (Issued: 1,144) £325

L56

L56   Five pounds. (Crown.) Prince Philip Celebrating a Life of Public Service. O. As L39A.
R. A portrait of His Royal Highness Prince Philip, The Duke of Edinburgh accompanied
by the inscription 'HIS ROYAL HIGHNESS THE DUKE OF EDINBURGH' and 'NON
SIBI SED PATRIAE'. (Reverse design: Humphrey Paget.)
2017
—   BU in presentation folder (Issued: 29,384 .... £20
—   Proof in silver *FDC* (Issued: 2,547)... £75
—   Proof piedfort in silver *FDC* (Issued: 1,199) £140
—   Proof in gold *FDC* (Issued: 299)... £2500

L57

L57   Five pounds. (Crown.) Celebrating the Platinum Wedding Anniversary of HM The
Queen and HRH Prince Philip. O. Portrait of Queen Eliabeth II conjoined with His Royal
Highness Prince Philip, The Duke of Edinburgh with the inscription 'ELIZABETH II D
G REG F D – PHILIP PRINCEPS' and the denomination 'FIVE POUNDS'. R. Queen
Eliabeth II and His Royal Highness Prince Philip, The Duke of Edinburgh on horseback
with the inscription 'WEDDED LOVE HAS JOINED THEM IN HAPPINESS' with the
dates '1947-2017'. Edge inscription 'FELICES JUNXIT CONUBIALIS AMOUR' on
precious metal versions. (Obverse design: Etienne Milner, reverse design:
John Bergdahl.)
2017
—   BU in presentation folder (Issued: 43,608) £15
—   BU in PNC (Issued: 2,492) £13
—   Proof in silver *FDC* (Issued: 6,955)... £75
—   Proof in silver *FDC* in PNC (Issued: 128) £80
—   Proof piedfort in silver *FDC* (Issued: 2,319) £140
—   Proof in gold *FDC* (Issued: 724)... £2500
—   Proof in gold *FDC* in PNC (Issued: 14) £2500

L58   L59

L58   **Five pounds.** (Crown.) Celebrating the Platinum Wedding Anniversary of HM The
Queen and HRH Prince Philip. O. Portrait of Queen Eliabeth II conjoined with His Royal
Highness Prince Philip, The Duke of Edinburgh with the inscription 'ELIZABETH II
D G REG F D – PHILIP PRINCEPS' and the denomination 'FIVE POUNDS'. Ṛ. The
Royal Arms and those of His Royal Highness Prince Philip, The Duke of Edinburgh
above the inscription '70 YEARS OF MARRIAGE 2017'. Edge inscription 'FELICES
JUNXIT CONUBIALIS AMOUR'. (Obverse design: Etienne Milner, reverse design:
John Bergdahl.)
2017
— Proof Platinum Piedfort *FDC* (Issued: 110)...£3500
— Proof Platinum Piedfort in PNC (Issued: 5)...£3500

L59   **Five pounds.** (Crown.) Christmas 2017. O. As L49. Ṛ. A depiction of a decorated
Christmas tree accompanied by the inscription 'CHRISTMAS TREE 2017'. (Reverse
design: Edwina Ellis.)
2017 BU in presentation folder (Issued: 39,413) £20

L60

L60   **Five pounds.** (Crown.) Remembrance Day. O. As L39A. Ṛ. Five poppies with petals
highlighted in red with the inscription 'SILENCE SPEAKS WHEN WORDS CAN
NOT'. (Reverse design: Stephen Taylor).
2017 BU (Issued: 10,771) £12
— BU with colour in presentation folder (Issued: 7,471).........................£20
— Proof in silver *FDC* with colour (Issued: 3,483)................................£75
— Proof piedfort in silver *FDC* with colour (Issued: 1,319) £130

L61   L62

L61   **Five pounds.** (Crown.)The Lion of England. R. A lion accompanied by a shield
depicting The Royal Arms with the inscription '2017 LION OF ENGLAND'.
(Reverse design: Jody Clark.)
2017 BU in presentation folder (Issued: 32,429) £20
2018 BU in presentation folder £20
2019 BU in presentation card (Issued: 6,845) £20

*The 2019 date was issued in a Pride of England pack to commemorate the England victory in
the Cricket World Cup final.*

L62   **Five pounds.** (Crown.) The Unicorn of Scotland. R. A rearing unicorn accompanied
by a shield depicting a lion rampant with the inscription '2017 LION OF SCOTLAND'.
(Reverse design: Jody Clark.)
2017 BU in presentation folder (Issued: 32,700) £20

L63

L63 Five pounds. (Crown.) Sapphire Coronation. O. As L49. R. A garlanded depiction of the
Royal Arms below a depiction of Our Royal Cypher, accompanied by the inscription
'SAPPHIRE ANNIVERSARY 1953 - 2018. Edge inscription 'SHINE THROUGH THE
AGES' on the precious metal versions. (Reverse design: Stephen Taylor.)
2018 BU (Issued: 6,349) £10
—   BU in presentation folder (Issued: 11,947) £15
—   Proof in silver *FDC* (Issued: 3,910)... £75
—   Proof piedfort in silver *FDC* (Issued: 1,635) £140
—   Proof in gold *FDC* (Issued: 475)) £2500

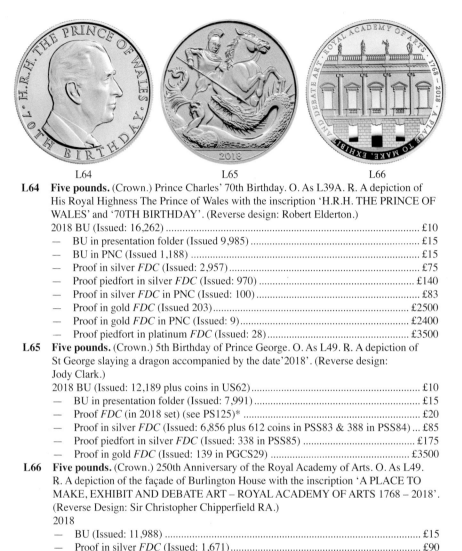

| L64 | L65 | L66 |

L64 **Five pounds.** (Crown.) Prince Charles' 70th Birthday. O. As L39A. R. A depiction of
His Royal Highness The Prince of Wales with the inscription 'H.R.H. THE PRINCE OF
WALES' and '70TH BIRTHDAY'. (Reverse design: Robert Elderton.)
2018 BU (Issued: 16,262) £10
— BU in presentation folder (Issued 9,985) £15
— BU in PNC (Issued 1,188) £15
— Proof in silver *FDC* (Issued: 2,957) £75
— Proof piedfort in silver *FDC* (Issued: 970) £140
— Proof in silver *FDC* in PNC (Issued: 100) £83
— Proof in gold *FDC* (Issued 203) £2500
— Proof in gold *FDC* in PNC (Issued: 9) £2400
— Proof piedfort in platinum *FDC* (Issued: 28) £3500

L65 **Five pounds.** (Crown.) 5th Birthday of Prince George. O. As L49. R. A depiction of
St George slaying a dragon accompanied by the date '2018'. (Reverse design:
Jody Clark.)
2018 BU (Issued: 12,189 plus coins in US62) £10
— BU in presentation folder (Issued: 7,991) £15
— Proof *FDC* (in 2018 set) (see PS125)* £20
— Proof in silver *FDC* (Issued: 6,856 plus 612 coins in PSS83 & 388 in PSS84) ... £85
— Proof piedfort in silver *FDC* (Issued: 338 in PSS85) £175
— Proof in gold *FDC* (Issued: 139 in PGCS29) £3500

L66 **Five pounds.** (Crown.) 250th Anniversary of the Royal Academy of Arts. O. As L49.
R. A depiction of the façade of Burlington House with the inscription 'A PLACE TO
MAKE, EXHIBIT AND DEBATE ART – ROYAL ACADEMY OF ARTS 1768 – 2018'.
(Reverse Design: Sir Christopher Chipperfield RA.)
2018
— BU (Issued: 11,988) £15
— Proof in silver *FDC* (Issued: 1,671) £90

* Coins marked thus were originally issued in Royal Mint sets.

L67

L67   **Five pounds.** (Crown.) Royal Wedding of Prince Harry and Meghan Markle. O. As L49.
R̶. A depiction of His Royal Highness Prince Henry of Wales and Rachel Meghan Markle
with the inscription 'ROYAL WEDDING – 19 MAY 2018' and 'HARRY & MEGHAN'.
(Reverse design: Jody Clark).

2018 BU (Issued: 21,567) £10
—   BU in presentation folder (Issued: 39,132) £15
—   BU in PNC (Issued: 2,056) £15
—   Proof in silver *FDC* (Issued: 5,702) £60
—   Proof in silver *FDC* in PNC (Issued: 181) £60
—   Proof piedfort in silver *FDC* (Issued: 1,353) £100
—   Proof in gold *FDC* (Issued: 355) £2500
—   Proof in gold *FDC* in PNC (Issued: 22) £2500

L68   L69

L68   **Five pounds.** (Crown.) The Red Dragon of Wales. R̶. A depiction of a rearing dragon
accompanied by the Coat of Arms of Llywelyn the Great with the inscription '2018
RED DRAGON OF WALES'. (Reverse design: Jody Clark.)

2018 BU (Issued: 10,998) £12
—   BU in presentation folder (Issued: 14,755) £20

L69   **Five pounds.** (Crown.) The Black Bull of Clarence. R̶. A depiction of the Black Bull
of Clarence supporting the arms used by all the Sovereigns of the Houses of Lancaster
and Stuart with the inscription '2018 BLACK BULL OF CLARENCE'.
 (Reverse design: Jody Clark.)

2018 BU (Issued: 6,500) £12
—   BU in presentation folder (Issued: 11,263) £20

I.70   L71

I.72   L73

L70-L73 Five pounds. (Crown.) Celebrating British Landmarks IV. O. As L39A.
   2018
               L70 R. Tenby Harbour.
               L71 R. Blackpool Tower.
               L72 R. Brighton Pier.
               L73 R. Southwold Beach
               (All reverse designs: Glyn Davies and Laura Clancy.)

PSS86 - 2018 £5 (L70-L73) silver proofs with colour (4) (Issued: 780) £325

L74   L75   L76

L74 Five pounds. (Crown.) Celebrating Four Generations of the Royal Family. O. As L49.
R̴. A depiction of Our initial accompanied by those of His Royal Highness The Prince of
Wales, His Royal Highness The Duke of Cambridge and His Royal Highness Prince George of
Cambridge, royally crowned, above an oak garland with the inscription 'FOUR GENERATIONS
OF THE ROYAL FAMILY' and the date 2018. (Reverse design: Timothy Noad.)
2018 BU (Issued: 8,482) £10
—   BU in presentation folder (Issued: 13,911) £15
—   Proof in silver *FDC* (Issued: 3,275).. £80
—   Proof piedfort in silver *FDC* (Issued: 1,189) £130
—   Proof in gold *FDC* (Issued: 340)... £2500

L75 Five pounds. (Crown.) Remembrance Day. . O. As L39A. R̴. A section of a poppy
accompanied by the inscription 'REMEMBRANCE'. (Reverse design: Laura Clancy.)
2018 BU (Issued: 5,498) £10
—   BU with colour in folder (Issued: 10,443) £20
—   Proof in silver *FDC* with colour (Issued:2,992).. £80
—   Proof piedfort in silver *FDC* with colour (Issued: 846).................................... £140

L76   Five pounds. (Crown.) Christmas 2018. O. As L49. R̴. Four toy soldiers and ballet
dancers, characters from Tchaikovsky's Nutcracker Suite with the inscription
'CHRISTMAS 2018' and 'THE NUTCRACKER'. (Reverse design: Harry Brockway.)
2018 BU (Issued 10,498) £10
BU in greetings card (Issued: 26,900 plus 1,939 in an Advent calendar)..................... £20

 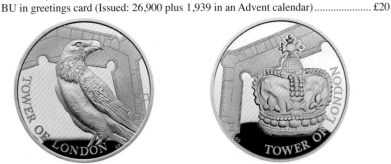

L77   L78

L77   Five pounds. (Crown.) Tower of London. O. As L39A. R̴. A depiction of a raven
and a section of a plan of Mint Street accompanied by the inscription 'TOWER OF
LONDON'. Edge inscription 'ON INTO TWILIGHT WITHIN WALLS OF STONE'.
(Reverse design: Glyn Davies.)
2019 BU (Issued: 5,500) £11
—   BU in folder (Issued: 14,699)... £15
—   Proof in silver *FDC* (Issued: 2,864) £75
—   Proof piedfort in silver *FDC* (Issued:741) £130
—   Proof in gold *FDC* (Issued: 200)... £2500

L79 L80

L78 **Five pounds.** (Crown.) Tower of London. O. As L39A. R. A depiction of the crown of Mary of Modena and a section of a plan of Mint Street accompanied by the inscription 'TOWER OF LONDON'. Edge inscription 'ON INTO TWILIGHT WITHIN WALLS OF STONE'. (Reverse design: Glyn Davies.)

2019 BU (Issued: 5,748) £11
— BU in folder (Issued: 13,238).. £15
— Proof in silver *FDC* (Issued: 2,389)... £75
— Proof piedfort in silver *FDC* (Issued:712) £130
— Proof in gold *FDC* (Issued: 181).. £2500

L79 **Five pounds.** (Crown.) Tower of London. O. As L39A. R. A depiction of a Yeoman Warder and a section of a plan of Mint Street accompanied by the inscription 'TOWER OF LONDON'. Edge inscription 'ON INTO TWILIGHT WITHIN WALLS OF STONE'. (Reverse design: Glyn Davies.)

2019 BU (Issued: 5,500) £11
— BU in folder (Issued: 11,645).. £15
— Proof in silver *FDC* (Issued: 2,222)... £75
— Proof piedfort in silver *FDC* (Issued:601) £130
— Proof in gold *FDC* (Issued: 150).. £2500

L80 **Five pounds.** (Crown.) Tower of London. O. As L39A. R. A depiction of Queen Elizabeth's keys and a lamp and a section of a plan of Mint Street accompanied by the inscription 'TOWER OF LONDON'. Edge inscription 'ON INTO TWILIGHT WITHIN WALLS OF STONE'. (Reverse design: Glyn Davies.)

2019 BU (Issued: 5,498) £11
— BU in folder (Issued: 10,977).. £15
— Proof in silver (Issued: 2,134).. £75
— Proof piedfort in silver *FDC* (Issued:548) £130
— Proof in gold *FDC* (Issued: 145).. £2500

L81

L81 **Five pounds.** (Crown.) 200th Anniversary of the Birth of Queen Victoria. O. As L39A.
R̩. A depiction of Queen Victoria surrounded by gears enclosing scenes portraying
achievements of the Victorian age and the inscription 'VICTORIA 1819 – 2019' and
'5 POUNDS'. Edge inscription: WORKSHOP OF THE WORLD on the precious metal
versions. (Reverse design: John Bergdahl.)

2019 BU* £12
—   BU in folder... £15
—   BU in PNC (Issued: 1,365) £15
—   Proof *FDC* (in 2019 set, see PS128)* £20
—   Proof in silver *FDC* (Issued: 3,854 plus 406 in PSS88) £83
—   Proof in silver *FDC* in PNC (Issued: 154)... £83
—   Proof piedfort in silver *FDC* (Issued: 1,236 plus 282 in PSS89)....................... £155
—   Proof in gold *FDC* (Issued: 583 plus 88 in PGCS36)..................................... £3000
—   Proof in gold *FDC* in PNC (Issued: 11)... £3000

L82   L83

L82 **Five pounds.** (Crown.) The Falcon of the Plantagenets. R̩. A depiction of the Falcon of
the Plantagenets above the personal badge of Edward IV with the inscription '2019
FALCON OF THE PLANTAGENETS'. (Reverse design: Jody Clark.)

2019 BU (Issued 6,653)... £12
—   BU in presentation folder (Issued: 13,041) £20

L83 **Five pounds.** (Crown.) Yale of Beaufort. R̩ A depiction of the Yale of Beaufort
supporting a shield portraying a portcullis surmounted by a royal crown with the
inscription '2019 YALE OF BEAUFORT'. (Reverse design: Jody Clark.)

2019 BU (Issued 6,217)... £12
—   BU in presentation folder (Issued: 11,220)... £20

L84   L85

L84 **Five pounds.** (Crown.) Centenary of Remembrance Day. O. As L49. ℞. A depiction of
a poppy with the inscription 'WE WILL REMEMBER THEM' and the dates, '1919'
and '2019'. (Reverse design: Harry Brockway.)

2019 BU with colour (Issued: 17,199) £13
—   BU with colour in folder (Issued: 10,721) £20
—   BU with colour in PNC (Issued: 641) £20
—   Proof in silver *FDC* with colour (Issued: 2,847)... £90
—   Proof in silver *FDC* with colour in PNC (Issued: 145)...................................... £90
—   Proof piedfort in silver *FDC* with colour (Issued: 775) £160
—   Proof in gold *FDC* (Issued: 119)... £2500
—   Proof in gold *FDC* in PNC (Issued: 11) £2500

L85 **Five pounds.** (Crown.) 200th Anniversary of the death of King George III. O. As L39A.
℞. A portrait of George III in a crowned cartouche accompanied by the floral emblems
of the United Kingdom, His Royal cypher and scenes associated with his life. Edge
inscription 'I GLORY IN THE NAME OF BRITON' on the precious metal versions.
(Reverse design: Dominique Evans.)

2020 BU* £10
—   BU in folder.. £15
—   Proof *FDC*... £20
—   Proof in silver *FDC* (Edition: 2,500 plus coins in sets) £85
—   Proof piedfort in silver *FDC* (Edition: 550 plus coins in sets) £155
—   Proof in gold *FDC* (Edition: 250 plus coins in sets)...................................... £3500

L86   L87

L86 **Five pounds.** (Crown.) Year of the Rat. ℞. A depiction of an agile and inquisitive rat
crouching against a backdrop of peonies with the inscription 'YEAR OF THE RAT 2020'
and the Chinese symbol for Rat. (Reverse design: P J Lynch.)

2020 BU in presentation folder £13

L87   **Five pounds.** (Crown.) Music Legends I – Queen. ℞. Piano keyboard with opening notes of Bohemian Rhapsody pressed down, the group's logo and singer's signature mic stick in centre and below 'Red Special' guitar, Fender Precision Bass and Ludwig bass drum decorated with the Queen crest. (Reverse design: Chris Facey.)

2020 BU in presentation folder £13
—   BU in presentation folder with artwork from Hot Space. (Edition: 25,000)..............£15
—   BU in presentation folder with artwork from A Kind of Magic. (Edition: 25,000)......£15
—   BU in presentation folder with artwork from Live. (Edition: 25,000) £15

         L88   L89

L88   **Five pounds.** (Crown.) 250th Anniversary of the birth of William Wordsworth. O. As L39A. ℞. A mountainous landscape and lakes as a backdrop to the words "Nature never did betray the heart that loved her" taken from the Wordsworth poem 'Lines Written a few miles above Tintern Abbey'. Edge inscription 'I WANDERED LONELY AS A CLOUD' on the precious metal versions. (Reverse design: David Lawrence.)

2020 BU £10
—   BU in folder.. £15
—   Proof in silver *FDC* (Edition: 3,000) £85
—   Proof in gold *FDC* (Edition: 300) £2500

L89   **Five pounds.** (Crown.) Tower of London II. The White Tower. O. As L39A. ℞. The Iconic Mace of Office carried by the Chief Yeoman Warder, with edge inscription 'THE WHITE TOWER' on the precious metal versions. (Reverse design: Timothy Noad.)

2020 BU £10
—   BU in folder.. £15
—   Proof in silver *FDC* (Edition: 2,510) £75
—   Proof piedfort in silver *FDC* (Edition: 460)... £130
—   Proof in gold *FDC* (Edition: 135) £2800

L90 L91

L90 **Five pounds.** (Crown.) Tower of London II. The Royal Menagerie. O. As L39A.
R. Three lions set against a Norman arched window from the White Tower. Edge
inscription 'THE ROYAL MENAGERIE'. (Reverse design: Timothy Noad.)
2020 BU £10
— BU in folder.. £15
— Proof in silver *FDC* (Edition: 1,510) £75
— Proof piedfort in silver *FDC* (Edition: 410).. £130
— Proof in gold *FDC* (Edition: 135) £2800

L91 **Five pounds.** (Crown.) Tower of London II. The Royal Mint. O. As L39A. R. Edward
I penny set against a Norman Arched Window from the White Tower. Edge inscription
'THE ROYAL MINT' on the precious metal versions. (Reverse design: Timothy Noad.)
2020 BU £10
— BU in folder.. £15
— Proof in silver *FDC* (Edition: 1,510) £75
— Proof piedfort in silver *FDC* (Edition: 410).. £130
— Proof in gold *FDC* (Edition: 135) £2800

L92

L92 **Five pounds.** (Crown.) Tower of London II. The Infamous Prison. O. As L39A.
R. A section of the wall of the Beauchamp Tower showing the inscription 'MY
LIBERTIE DENIED'. Edge inscription 'THE INFAMOUS PRISON' on the precious
metal versions. (Reverse design: Timothy Noad.)
2020 BU £10
— BU in folder.. £15
— Proof in silver *FDC* (Edition: 1,510) £75
— Proof piedfort in silver *FDC* (Edition: 410).. £130
— Proof in gold *FDC* (Edition: 135) £2800

L93

L93 **Five pounds.** (Crown.) 150th Anniversary of the British Red Cross. O. As L49.
R. Map of UK with cross (in red on the c/n and silver versions) in the centre with
inscription '1870 BRITISH RED CROSS 2020' and 'THE POWER OF KINDNESS'.
Edge inscription 'PER HUMANITATEM AD PACEM' on the precious metal versions.
(Reverse design: Henry Gray.)
2020 BU £10
—   BU in folder.. £17
—   Proof in silver *FDC* (Edition: 4,000) £90
—   Proof piedfort in silver *FDC* (Edition: 1,150)....................................£140
—   Proof in gold *FDC* (Edition: 250) £2800

L94   L95

L94 **Five pounds.** (Crown.) White Lion of Mortimer. R A depiction of the White Lion
of Mortimer supporting a shield portraying a white rose en soleil with the inscription
'2020 WHITE LION OF MORTIMER'. (Reverse design: Jody Clark.)
2020 BU in presentation folder £13

L95   **Five pounds.** (Crown.) White Horse of Hanover. R. A rearing white horse above
shield with royal arms of George I with the inscription '2020 WHITE HORSE OF
HANOVER'. (Reverse design: Jody Clark.)
2020 BU in presentation folder £13

L96   L97

L96 **Five pounds.** (Crown.) 75th Anniversary of the End of the Second World War.
O. As L49. ℞. The words 'WAR' and 'PEACE' typographically intersected to
capture the sense of the conflict abating and the dawn of a new era. Edge inscription
'THROUGH COURAGE AND ENDURANCE' on the precious metal versions.
(Reverse design: Matt Dent and Christian Davies.)
2020 BU £10
— BU in folder.. £15
— Proof in silver *FDC* (Edition: 2,575) £80
— Proof piedfort in silver *FDC* (Edition: 565)... £140
— Proof in gold *FDC* (Edition: 225) £2800

L97 **Five pounds.** (Crown.) Remembrance Day. O. As L39A. ℞. Silhouette of a sombre soldier
with head hung low in reflection with a sea of poppies in the background with the inscription
'LEST WE FORGET 11 NOVEMBER 2020'. (Reverse design: Natasha Preece.)
2020 BU with colour in folder £20
— Proof in silver *FDC* with colour (Edition: 2,020) £90
— Proof piedfort in silver *FDC* with colour (Edition: 710) £175

*This coin also commemorates the Centenary of the ceremonial burial of the Unknown Warrior
in Westminster Abbey and 100 of the silver proof coins have been issued in a set with eight
1920 dated currency coins obtained from the secondary market.*

L98

L98 **Five pounds.** (Crown.) Music Legends II – Elton John. ℞. Musical notes creating an
image of glasses and a straw boater's hat with the inscription 'ELTON JOHN' and below
his signature bow tie against a Union flag background. (Reverse design:
Bradley Morgan Johnson.).
2020 BU in presentation folder with artwork from Rocket Man £13
— BU in presentation folder with artwork from Dodgers Stadium. (Edition: 15,000)......£15
— BU in presentation folder with artwork from Illustration. (Edition: 15,000) £15
— BU in presentation folder with artwork from The Very Best Of. (Edition: 15,000)......£15

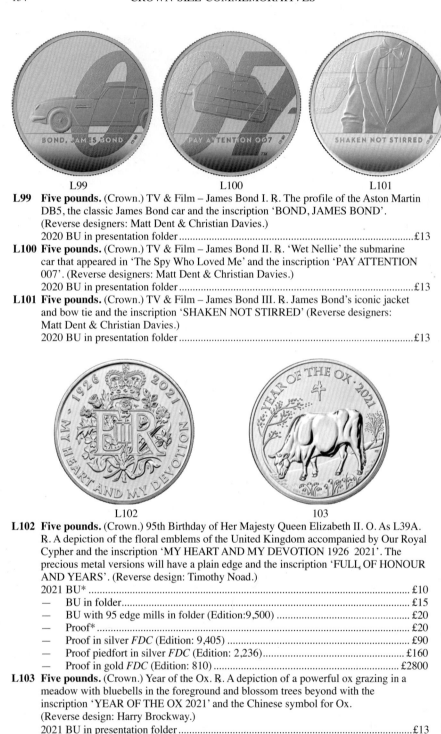

L99   L100   L101

L99   **Five pounds.** (Crown.) TV & Film – James Bond I. R. The profile of the Aston Martin DB5, the classic James Bond car and the inscription 'BOND, JAMES BOND'. (Reverse designers: Matt Dent & Christian Davies.)
2020 BU in presentation folder £13

L100 **Five pounds.** (Crown.) TV & Film – James Bond II. R. 'Wet Nellie' the submarine car that appeared in 'The Spy Who Loved Me' and the inscription 'PAY ATTENTION 007'. (Reverse designers: Matt Dent & Christian Davies.)
2020 BU in presentation folder £13

L101 **Five pounds.** (Crown.) TV & Film – James Bond III. R. James Bond's iconic jacket and bow tie and the inscription 'SHAKEN NOT STIRRED' (Reverse designers: Matt Dent & Christian Davies.)
2020 BU in presentation folder £13

L102   103

L102 **Five pounds.** (Crown.) 95th Birthday of Her Majesty Queen Elizabeth II. O. As L39A. R. A depiction of the floral emblems of the United Kingdom accompanied by Our Royal Cypher and the inscription 'MY HEART AND MY DEVOTION 1926 2021'. The precious metal versions will have a plain edge and the inscription 'FULL OF HONOUR AND YEARS'. (Reverse design: Timothy Noad.)
2021 BU* £10
—   BU in folder.. £15
—   BU with 95 edge mills in folder (Edition:9,500) £20
—   Proof* £20
—   Proof in silver *FDC* (Edition: 9,405) £90
—   Proof piedfort in silver *FDC* (Edition: 2,236).. £160
—   Proof in gold *FDC* (Edition: 810) £2800

L103 **Five pounds.** (Crown.) Year of the Ox. R. A depiction of a powerful ox grazing in a meadow with bluebells in the foreground and blossom trees beyond the inscription 'YEAR OF THE OX 2021' and the Chinese symbol for Ox. (Reverse design: Harry Brockway.)
2021 BU in presentation folder £13

L104

L105

L104 Five pounds. (Crown.) 150th Anniversary of the Royal Albert Hall. O. As L39A.
R. A depiction of the Royal Albert Hall with the inscription 'ROYAL • ALBERT •
HALL' and the dates '1871-2021'. The precious metal versions will have a plain edge
and the inscription 'INSPIRING ARTS AND SCIENCES'. (Reverse design:
Anne Desmet.)

2021 BU	£10
— BU in folder	£15
— Proof in silver *FDC* (Edition: 1,660)	£90
— Proof piedfort in silver *FDC* (Edition: 1,010)	£168
— Proof in gold *FDC* (Edition: 180)	£2800

L104A Five pounds. (Crown.) 150th Anniversary of the Royal Albert Hall. O. As L39A.
R. As L89 with domed reverse and no edge inscription.

2021 Proof in silver *FDC* (Edition: 3,510)	£125
— Proof in gold *FDC* (Edition: 210)	£3000

L105 Five pounds. (Crown) 1150th Anniversary of Alfred the Great's Accession as King of
the West Saxons. O. As L39A. R. A depiction of Alfred the Great with the inscription
'ALFRED THE GREAT' and the dates '871 2021'. The precious metal versions will
have a plain edge and the inscription 'AELFRED MEC HEHT GEWYRCAN'.
(Reverse design: John Bergdahl.)

2021 BU	£10
— BU in folder	£15
— Proof in silver *FDC* (Edition: 2,260)	£90
— Proof piedfort in silver *FDC* (Edition: 910)	£170
— Proof in gold *FDC* (Edition: 170)	£3500

* Coins marked thus were originally issued in Royal Mint sets.

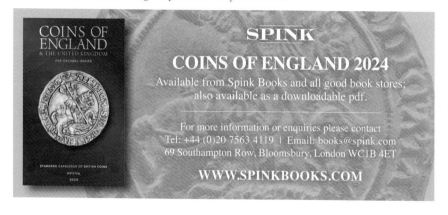

L106   L107

L106   **Five pounds.** (Crown.) White Greyhound of Richmond. ℟. A reimagined greyhound conveying its strength and power above shield depicting the symbol of the Tudor family and the inscription '2021 WHITE GREYHOUND OF RICHMOND'. (Reverse design: Jody Clark.)
2021 BU in presentation folder... £13

L107   **Five pounds.** (Crown.) Mr Men Little Miss I – Mr Happy. ℟. A depiction of the children's character Mr Happy with the inscription 'MR MEN 50 YEARS' and the signature of the author Roger Hargreaves. (Reverse design: Adam Hargreaves.)
2021 BU in folder... £13
2021 BU with colour in folder (Edition: 15,050).. £23

L108   L109

L108   **Five pounds.** (Crown.) Mr Men Little Miss II – Mr Strong & Little Miss Giggles. ℟. A depiction of the children's characters Mr Strong and Little Miss Giggles with the inscription 'MR MEN LITTLE MISS 50 YEARS' and the signature of the author Roger Hargreaves. (Reverse design: Adam Hargreaves.)
2021 BU in folder... £13
2021 BU with colour in folder (Edition: 15,050).. £23

L109   **Five pounds.** (Crown.) Mr Men Little Miss III – Little Miss Sunshine. ℟. A depiction of the children's character Little Miss Sunshine with the inscription 'LITTLE MISS 50 YEARS' and the signature of the author Roger Hargreaves. (Reverse design: Adam Hargreaves.)
2021 BU in folder... £13
2021 BU with colour in folder (Edition: 15,050).. £23

L110   L111

L110 **Five pounds.** (Crown.) The Griffin of Edward III. ℞. A depiction of a griffin with the
heraldic badge of the Royal House of Windsor accompanied by the inscription '2021
GRIFFIN OF EDWARD III'. (Reverse design: Jody Clark.)
2021 BU in presentation folder...£13

L111 **Five pounds.** (Crown.) Music Legends III – David Bowie. ℞. A depiction of David
Bowie with the inscription 'BOWIE'. (Reverse design: Jody Clark.)
2020 BU in presentation folder £13
—   BU in presentation folder with Starman slipcase cover (Edition: 15,000) £15
—   BU in presentation folder with Life on Mars slipcase cover (Edition: 15,000).. £15
—   BU in presentation folder with Space Oddity slipcase cover (Edition: 15,000). £15

L112   L113

L112 **Five pounds.** (Crown.) Peter Rabbit. O. As L39A. ℞. A depiction of Peter Rabbit,
Mrs Rabbit and three other rabbits accompanied by the inscription 'NOW RUN
ALONG, AND DON'T GET INTO MISCHIEF. I AM GOING OUT.'
(Reverse design: Ffion Gwillim.)
2021 BU in presentation pack..£15
*For other coins with the same design see **NB11** & **OB2**.*

L113 **Five pounds.** (Crown.) Prince Philip Memorial 2021. O. As L39A. ℞. A depiction
of Prince Philip with the inscription 'HRH THE PRINCE PHILIP' and 'DUKE OF
EDINBURGH 1921 2021'. (Reverse design: Ian Rank-Broadley.)
2021 BU...£10
—   BU in folder £15
—   Proof in silver *FDC* (Edition: 7,255) £90
—   Proof piedfort in silver *FDC* (Edition: 1,760) £160
—   Proof in gold *FDC* (Edition: 560)..£2800

L114

L114   Five pounds. (Crown.) Remembrance Day. O. As L39A. Ɍ. Four poppies accompanied by the inscription 'AT THE GOING DOWN OF THE SUN & IN THE MORNING WE WILL REMEMBER THEM'. (Reverse design: Gary Breeze.)

2021 BU with colour in folder £20

—   Proof in silver *FDC* with colour (Edition: 2,031) £100

—   Proof piedfort in silver *FDC* with colour (Edition: 610) £180

L115   L116

L115   Five pounds. (Crown.) Music Legends IV – The Who. Ɍ. A depiction of a guitar shaped pinball machine accompanied by the inscription 'THE WHO'. (Reverse design: Henry Gray.)

2021 BU in presentation folder £13

—   BU with colour in presentation folder (Edition: 10,000) £23

L116   Five pounds. (Crown.) The completer coin. Ɍ. A depiction of ten heraldic beasts encircling a portrait of Queen Elizabeth II with the inscription 'THE QUEEN'S BEASTS' and the date of the year. (Reverse design: Jody Clark.)

2021 BU in presentation folder £13

L117   L118

L117 **Five pounds.** (Crown.) Alice's Adventures in Wonderland. R. A depiction of
Alice and the Cheshire cat sat in a tree accompanied by the inscription 'ALICE'S
ADVENTURES IN WONDERLAND'. (Reverse design: Ffion Gwillim.)
2021 BU in folder £13
2021 BU with colour in folder (Edition: 15,000) £20

L118 **Five pounds.** (Crown.) Alice through the Looking Glass. R. A depiction of Alice and
the characters Tweedledee and Tweedledum and the inscription 'THROUGH THE
LOOKING GLASS'. (Reverse design: Ffion Gwillim.)
2021 BU in folder £13
2021 BU with colour in folder (Edition: 15,000) £20

L119   L120

L119 **Five pounds.** (Crown.) The life and legacy of Mahatma Gandhi. O. As L39A.
R. A depiction of a lotus flower with the inscription 'MY LIFE IS MY MESSAGE •
MAHATMA GANDHI'. (Reverse design: Heena Glover.)
2021 BU in folder £15

L120 **Five pounds.** (Crown.) Platinum Jubilee Commemorative 2022. O. Her Majesty the
Queen on horseback with the inscription 'ELIZABETH II • D • G • REG • F • D • 5
POUNDS' accompanied by the Garter Belt with the inscription 'HONI • SOIT • QUI
• MAL • Y• PENSE •' and the date of the year. R. A crowned depiction of the Royal
Arms accompanied by the dates '• 1952 2022 •'. The precious metal versions will
have a plain edge with the inscription 'SERVE YOU ALL THE DAYS OF MY LIFE'.
(Reverse design: John Bergdahl.)
2022 BU... £8
—   BU in folder £10
—   BU with edge inscription in folder (Edition: 10,010)....................................... £18
—   Proof in silver *FDC* (Edition: 6,905)... £93
—   Proof piedfort in silver *FDC* (Edition: 2,162) :... £173
—   Proof in gold *FDC* (Edition: 550).. £3000
—   Proof in platinum *FDC* (Edition: 82)... £5500

L120A Five pounds. (Crown.) Platinum Jubilee Commemorative 2022. O. As L49.
R. As L120.
2022 BU (see US72/3)* £10
— Proof (see PS136/7)* £20
— Proof in silver *FDC* (see PSS98) (Edition: 550)* £93
— Proof piedfort in silver *FDC* (see PSS99) (Edition: 370)* £173
— Proof in gold *FDC* (Edition: 100)* £3000
— Proof in platinum *FDC* (Edition: 30)* £5500

All versions of the above coin are only available in the year sets.

L121

L121   **Five pounds.** (Crown.) Year of the Tiger. R. A tiger with the inscription 'YEAR OF
THE TIGER 2022' and the Chinese symbol for Tiger. (Reverse design:
David Lawrence.)
2022 BU in presentation folder £13

L122   L123

L122 Five pounds. (Crown.) Peter Rabbit. O. As L39A. R. A depiction of the children's
character, Peter Rabbit, with the inscription '120 YEARS' and 'THE TALE OF PETER
RABBIT'. (Reverse design: Ffion Gwillim.)
2022 BU in folder...£13
— BU in folder with colour (Edition: 8,610)...£17

L123 Five pounds. (Crown.) The 40th Birthday of Prince William. O. As L39A. R. A portrait
of HRH The Duke of Cambridge accompanied by his Cypher and age. The precious
metal versions will have edge inscription 'HRH THE DUKE OF CAMBRIDGE'.
(Reverse design: Thomas T. Docherty.)
2022 BU £10
— BU in folder...£13
— Proof in silver *FDC* (Edition: 3,760) £93
— Proof piedfort in silver *FDC* (Edition: 1,510)....................................£175
— Proof in gold *FDC* (Edition: 310) £2800

L124   L125

L124   **Five pounds.** (Crown.) Seymour Panther. ℞. A depiction of the Seymour Panther statue with Duke of Beaufort's coat of arms with inscription 'SEYMOUR PANTHER 2022'. (Reverse design: David Lawrence.)
2022 BU in folder £13

L125   **Five pounds.** (Crown.) Music Legends V – The Rolling Stones. ℞. Silhouettes of the band The Rolling Stones accompanied by the inscription "THE ROLLING STONES" and the dates "'62-'22". (Reverse design: Hannah Philacklea.)
2022 BU in presentation folder £15

L126   L127

L126   **Five pounds.** (Crown.) The Queen's Reign I – The Bestowing of Honours. O. As L39A. ℞. The Queen's signature set against a background of medals accompanied by the inscription 'THE BESTOWING OF HER HONOURS'. The precious metal versions will have edge inscription 'DEVOTED TO YOUR SERVICE'. (Reverse design: P J Lynch.)
2022 BU £10
—   BU in folder £13
—   Proof in silver *FDC* (Edition: 4,160) £93
—   Proof piedfort in silver *FDC* (Edition: 1,510) £175
—   Proof in gold *FDC* (Edition: 268)..£2800

L127   **Five pounds.** (Crown.) The Queen's Reign II – Charity and Patronage. O. As L39A. ℞. The Queen's signature set against a background of Maundy money accompanied by the inscription 'HER CHARITY AND HER PATRONAGE'. The precious metal versions will have edge inscription 'DEVOTED TO YOUR SERVICE'. (Reverse design: P J Lynch.)
2022 BU £10
—   BU in folder £13
—   Proof in silver *FDC* (Edition: 4,160) £93
—   Proof piedfort in silver *FDC* (Edition: 1,510) £175
—   Proof in gold *FDC* (Edition: 268)..£2800

L28   L29

L128   **Five pounds.** (Crown.) The Queen's Reign III – The Commonwealth of Nations.
O. As L39A. ℞. The Queen's signature set against a background of Commonwealth
flags accompanied by the inscription 'HER COMMONWEALTH OF NATIONS'. The
precious metal versions will have edge inscription 'DEVOTED TO YOUR SERVICE'.
2022 BU £10
— BU in folder £13
— Proof in silver *FDC* (Edition: 4,160) £93
— Proof piedfort in silver *FDC* (Edition: 1,510) £175
— Proof in gold *FDC* (Edition: 268) £2800

L129   **Five pounds.** (Crown.) Lion of England. R. A depiction of the Lion of England statue
with impaled Coat of Arms of Henry VIII and Jane Seymour with inscription 'LION
OF ENGLAND 2022'. (Reverse design: David Lawrence.)
2022 BU in folder £13

L130

L130   **Five pounds.** (Crown.) Centenary of Discovery of Tutankhamun's Tomb. O. As L39A.
℞. A depiction of the mask of King Tutankhamun with the inscription 'DISCOVERY
OF TUTANKHAMUN'S TOMB'. The precious metal versions will have edge
inscription 'THE VALLEY OF THE KINGS'. (Reverse design: Laura Clancy)
2022 BU £10
— BU in presentation folder.. £15
— BU in PNC (Edition: 10,000) £18
— Proof in silver FDC (Edition: 1,932) £95
— Proof in silver FDC in PNC (Edition: 750) £95
— Proof piedfort in silver FDC (Edition: 810) £180
— Proof in gold FDC (Edition: 210).. £2800
— Proof in gold FDC in PNC (Edition: 50) £2800

L131   L132

L131   **Five pounds.** (Crown.) Year of the Rabbit. R. A Rabbit with the inscription
'YEAR OF THE RABBIT 2023' and the Chinese symbol for Rabbit.
(Reverse design: Louie Maryon.)
2023 BU in presentation folder..£13

L132   **Five pounds.** (Crown.) Yale of Beaufort. R. A depiction of the Yale of Beaufort
with inscription 'YALE OF BEAUFORT 2023'. (Reverse design: David Lawrence.
2023 BU in folder £13

Other £5 crowns may be found listed in the following later sections:

London Olympic Games 2009-2012.
World War One 2014-2018.

MAUNDY COINS

The Maundy coins continue to be presented each year in the traditional ceremony on Maundy Thursday, with the old denominations being retained as 'new pence'. In the early years of the present reign the ceremony tended to alternate between Westminster Abbey and a cathedral, usually close to London. In more recent years the Queen has travelled to cathedrals right across the country thus bringing this ancient ceremony to the people and increasing the awareness of these coins steeped, as they are, in great British heritage. Latterly St. George's Chapel, Windsor Castle has hosted this event.

Maundy money is given to the same number of men and women as the Monarch's age and each person receives coins to a total value in pence of the Monarch's age. The tradition dates back at least to the thirteenth century, though the origins of the ceremony are to be found in the Last Supper when Jesus washed the feet of His disciples.

The number of sets issued ranges from just over 1000 in 1971 gradually increasing each year to 1,940 in 2016 although in 2000 and 2006 where there were an additional 13,180 & 6,394 respectively in the 13 coin silver proof sets (See PSS8 & PSS17).

The Maundy coins issued from 1977 onwards are frosted proofs. In 2000 and 2006, a 13 coin set was issued from £5 to 1p which included that year's Maundy coins which resulted in the Maundy coins for those years having a higher mintage. The prices below for these two years are for the cased coins out of the 13 coin set. Coins in the traditional Maundy cases would be priced similarly to those of the adjoining period. In 2002 the first Elizabethan Maundy coins in gold were issued, again in a 13 coin set as part of the Golden Jubilee celebrations.

MC1	One penny. Maundy	
	1971-2021 proof in silver *FDC*	*from* 75
	2002 proof in gold *FDC*	350
MC2	Two pence. Maundy	
	1971-2021 proof in silver *FDC*	*from* 50
	2002 proof in gold *FDC*	400
MC3	Three pence. Maundy	
	1971-2021 proof in silver *FDC*	*from* 50
	2002 proof in gold *FDC*	500
MC4	Four pence. Maundy	
	1971-2021 proof in silver *FDC*	*from* 50
	2002 proof in gold *FDC*	800

MS (date) Maundy set of four.	£
1971 *Tewkesbury Abbey*	225
1972 *York Minster*	225
1973 *Westminster Abbey*	225
1974 *Salisbury Cathedral*	225
1975 *Peterborough Cathedral*	225
1976 *Hereford Cathedral*	225
1977 *Westminster Abbey*	225
1978 *Carlisle Cathedral*	225
1979 *Winchester Cathedral*	225
1980 *Worcester Cathedral*	225

1981 *Westminster Abbey* 225
1982 *St. Davids Cathedral* 225
1983 *Exeter Cathedral* 225
1984 *Southwell Minster* 225
1985 *Ripon Cathedral* 225
1986 *Chichester Cathedral* 225
1987 *Ely Cathedral* 225
1988 *Lichfield Cathedral* 225
1989 *Birmingham Cathedral* 225
1990 *Newcastle Cathedral* 225
1991 *Westminster Abbey* 225
1992 *Chester Cathedral* 225
1993 *Wells Cathedral* 225
1994 *Truro Cathedral* 225
1995 *Coventry Cathedral* 225
1996 *Norwich Cathedral* 225
1997 *Bradford Cathedral* 225
1998 *Portsmouth Cathedral* 225
1999 *Bristol Cathedral* 225
2000 *Lincoln Cathedral (inc. in PSS16)* 185
2001 *Westminster Abbey* 225
2002 *Canterbury Cathedral* 225
2002 *Proof in gold from set* (see PCGS1)* 2000
2003 *Gloucester Cathedral* 225
2004 *Liverpool Cathedral* 225
2005 *Wakefield Cathedral* 225
2006 *Guildford Cathedral (inc. in PSS26)* 185
2007 *Manchester Cathedral* 225
2008 *St Patrick's Cathedral, Armagh* 375
2009 *Bury St Edmunds Cathedral* 375
2010 *Derby Cathedral* 375
2011 *Westminster Abbey* 375
2012 *York Minster* 375
2013 *Christ Church Cathedral Oxford* 500
2014 *Blackburn Cathedral* 450
2015 *Sheffield Cathedral* 500
2016 *St George's Chapel Windsor Castle* 500
2017 *Leicester Cathedral* 550
2018 *St George's Chapel Windsor Castle* 650
2019 *St George's Chapel Windsor Castle* 700
2020 *St George's Chapel Windsor Castle* 750
2021 *Westminster Abbey* 750
2022 *St George's Chapel Windsor Castle* 500

The place of distribution is shown after each date although owing to the Coronavirus the coins in 2020 and 2021 were mailed to the chosen recipients.

Prior to decimalisation, the Royal Mint had issued proof sets mainly at the start of a new reign or for significant Royal events and details of these may be found in our companion volume *Coins of England & the United Kingdom Pre-Decimal Issues*. A final proof set of the £sd coinage was issued in 1970 and the proof sets listed in this catalogue follow on from the catalogue number of that set. To enable the public to be familiar with the new decimal coins, a blue wallet containing the 10p down to the $^1/2$p was issued from June 1968 with the bronze coins dated 1971

In 1982 the Royal Mint issued its first uncirculated set and from 1984 onwards the coins in these sets had a superior finish to coins issued for circulation which the Mint called brilliant uncirculated. Loose coins from such sets are listed as BU.

Some coins previously listed here as sets but comprising usually just two coins of the same denomination have now been listed immediately following the corresponding single coins and we hope that users of this catalogue will find this more convenient.

In addition to the annual sets of proof and uncirculated coins sold by the Royal Mint to collectors and dealers, the Mint has produced specially packaged sets and single coins for companies. No details have been made available of these issues and therefore no attempt has been made to include them in the listings although the most well-known of such sets are the 1983 uncirculated sets produced for the Martini and Heinz companies some of which contained the 2p mule (see C2A). The Mint also sells 'Wedding' and 'Christening' sets in distinctive packaging but the numbers circulating in the market are relatively modest and of limited appeal after the year of issue.

Some sets (usually comprising just two coins & often with different year dates) have been released not as part of the annual year set plans. Coins in these sets are always taken from the mintages of single coins and no separate sales figures are ever announced. Also in more recent years the Mint has offered sets that include coins obtained from the secondary market. It is considered that these sets are beyond the scope of this catalogue.

The sets that immediately follow are sets containing currency type coins. Sets comprising gold sovereign coins, Britannia gold and silver and other special series are listed later after the relevant section.

Uncirculated Sets

			£
US00–**MD**	10p,5p,2p,1p,$^1/2$p in blue wallet	(5)	1
US01–**1982**	Uncirculated (specimen) set in Royal Mint folder, 50p to ½p, new reverse type, including 20 pence (Issued: 205,000)	(7)	10
US02–**1983**	'U.K.' £1 to ½p (Issued: 637,100)	(8)	12
US03–**1984**	'Scottish' £1 to ½p (Issued: 158,820)	(8)	12
US04–**1985**	'Welsh' £1 to 1p, new portrait of The Queen (Issued: 178,375)	(7)	12
US05–**1986**	'Commonwealth Games' £2 plus 'Northern Irish' £1 to 1p, (Issued: 167,224)	(8)	17
US06–**1987**	'English' £1 to 1p, (Issued: 172,425)	(7)	14
US07–**1988**	'Arms' £1 to 1p, (Issued: 134,067)	(7)	14
US08–**1989**	'Scottish' £1 to 1p, (Issued: 77,569)	(7)	16
US09–**1989**	£2 (K2 and K3) BU in folder	(2)	40
US10–**1990**	'Welsh' £1 to 1p plus new smaller 5p, (Issued: 102,606)	(8)	12
US11–**1991**	'Northern Irish' £1 to 1p, (Issued: 74,975)	(7)	12
US12–**1992**	'English' £1, 'European Community' 50p and 'Britannia' 50p, 20p to 1p plus new smaller 10p (Issued: 78,421)	(9)	80
US13-**1992**	50p (H4 and H5) BU in folder	(2)	75
US14–**1993**	'UK' £1, 'European Community' 50p and 'Britannia' 50p, 20p to 1p (Issued: 56,945)	(8)	80
US15–**1994**	'Bank of England' £2, 'Scottish' £1 and 'D-Day' 50p to 1p, (Issued: 177,971)	(8)	20
US16–**1995**	'Peace' £2 and 'Welsh' £1 to 1p (Issued: 105, 647)	(8)	20
US17–**1996**	'Football' £2 and 'Northern Irish' £1 to 1p (Issued: 86,501)	(8)	20
US18–**1997**	'Bimetallic' £2, 'English' £1 (4340) to 1p plus new smaller 50p (Issued: 109,557)	(9)	15
US19–**1998**	'Bimetallic' £2, 'UK' £1 and 'EU' 50 pence to1 pence (Issued: 96,192)	(9)	25

US22

		£
US20–**1998**	50p (H8 and H9) BU in folder.. (2)	12
US21–**1999**	'Bimetallic' 'Rugby' £2, 'Scottish' £1 to 1p (Issued: 136,696)...................... (8)	25
US22–**2000**	'Bimetallic' £2, 'Welsh' £1 to 1p plus 'Library' 50 pence (Issued: 117,750) . (9)	20
US22A-**2000**	'Millennium' £5, 'Bimetallic' £2, 'Welsh' £1, 50p to 1p in Time Capsule tin. (9)	30
US23–**2001**	'Bimetallic' £2, 'Bimetallic' 'Marconi' £2, 'Irish' £1 to 1p (Issued: 57,741) . (9)	20
US24–**2002**	'Bimetallic' £2, 'English' £1 to 1p (Issued: 60,539) .... (8)	20
US25–**2002**	£2 (K12-K15) BU in folder .... (4)	80
US26–**2003**	'Bimetallic' 'DNA' £2, 'Bimetallic' £2, 'UK' £1,'Suffragette' 50 pence and 'Britannia' 50 pence to 1p.(Issued: 62,741) ....(10)	30
US27–**2004**	'Bimetallic' 'Penydarren engine' £2, 'Bimetallic' £2, 'Forth Rail Bridge' £1, 'Sub four-minute mile' 50 pence and 'Britannia'50 pence to1p (Issued: 46,032)(10)	26
US28–**2004**	'Bimetallic' 'Penydarren engine' £2, 'Forth Rail Bridge' £1,'Sub four-minute mile' 50 pence (Issued: 14,391) .... (3)	10
US29–**2005**	'Bimetallic' 'Gunpowder Plot' £2, 'Bimetallic' £2, 'Menai Straits Bridge' £1, 'Samuel Johnson's Dictionary' 50 pence and'Britannia' 50 pence to 1p. (Issued: 51,776)..(10)	26
US30–**2005**	'Bimetallic' 'Gunpowder Plot' £2, 'Menai Straits Bridge' £1, 'Samuel Johnson's Dictionary' 50 pence .... (3)	10
US31–**2005**	£5 (L14 and L15) BU in folder .... (2)	25
US32–**2006**	'Bimetallic' 'Isambard Brunel' £2, 'Bimetallic' 'Paddington Station' £2, 'MacNeill's Egyptian Arch' £1, 'Victoria Cross' 50 pence,'Wounded soldier' 50 pence, 20p to 1p (Issued: 74,231)..(10)	30
US33–**2006**	£2 (K20 and K21) BU in folder .... (2)	24
US34–**2006**	50p (H15 and H16) BU in folder .... (2)	15
US35–**2007**	'Bimetallic' 'Act of Union' £2, 'Bimetallic' 'Abolition of Slave Trade' £2, 'Gateshead Millennium Bridge' £1, 'Scouting Movement' 50 pence, 20p to 1p (Issued: 91,878) .... (9)	30
US36–**2008**	'Bimetallic' 'London Olympics Centenary' £2, 'Bimetallic' £2, 'UK' £1, 'Britannia' 50 pence, to 1p (Issued: 79,118) .... (9)	30
US37–**2008**	'Emblems of Britain', 'UK' £1, 'Britannia' 50 pence, and 20 pence to 1 p (Issued: 57,126) .... (7)	15
US38–**2008**	'The Royal Shield of Arms', 'Royal Shield' £1 to1p (Issued: 100,000) .... (7)	16
US39–**2009**	'Bimetallic' 'Charles Darwin' £2, Bimetallic 'Robert Burns' £2 'Bimetallic' £2, 'Royal Shield' £1, 50 pence 'Kew Gardens' 50 pence, 20 pence, 10 pence, 5 pence, 2 pence (4691) and 1 pence (Issued: 81,613)...(11)	295
US40- **2009**	'Bimetallic'£2, 'Royal Shield' £1, 50 pence, 20 pence, 10 pence, 5 pence, 2 pence and 1 pence .... (8)	45
US41- **2009**	'Royal Shield' £1, 50 pence, 20 pence, 10 pence, 5 pence, 2 pence and 1 pence (Issued: 24,561).. (7)	40
US42–**2010**	'Bimetallic 'Florence Nightingale' £2, 'Bimetallic'£2, 'London' £1, 'Belfast' £1, 'Royal Shield '£1, 50 pence 'Girl Guiding', 50 pence, 20 pence, 10 pence, 5 pence, 2 pence and 1 pence (Edition: 50,000).........(12)	75

US48

£

US61–**2017**	Bimetallic £2 'Britannia' 'Bimetallic' £1, 50 pence to 1 pence (Issued: 13,547)	(8)	30
US62–**2018**	5th Birthday Prince George £5, 'Bimetallic' £2 ' Royal Air Force Badge', 'Bimetallic' £2 'Frankenstein', 'Bimetallic' £2 ' Armistice' ...Bimetallic' £2 'Britannia', 'Bimetallic' £1, 50 pence 'Representation of People Act', 50 pence to 1 pence (Issued: 18,900).	(13)	110
US63–**2018**	Bimetallic £2 'Britannia' 'Bimetallic' £1, 50 pence to 1 pence (Issued: 5,855)....	(8)	30
US63A–**2018**	10p Alphabet A-Z (Issued: 37,992)	(26)	50
US64–**2019**	200th Anniversary of the birth of Queen Victoria £5, 'Bimetallic' £2 '75th Anniversary of D-Day', 'Bimetallic' £2 'Wedgwood', 'Bimetallic' £2 'Samuel Pepys' Bimetallic' £2 'Britannia', 'Bimetallic' £1, 50 pence 'Sherlock Holmes', 50 pence to 1 pence (Issued: 23,326)	(13)	80
US65–**2019**	Bimetallic £2 'Britannia' 'Bimetallic' £1, 50 pence to 1 pence (Issued: 6,772)...	(8)	30
US66–**2019**	British Culture Set of five different 50 pence designs of the past to mark the 50th Anniversary of the introduction of the 50 pence coin in 1969 (Issued: 31,250)	(5)	45
US67–**2019**	Military Set of five different 50 pence designs of the past to mark the 50th Anniversary of the introduction of the 50 pence coin in 1969 (Issued: 9,902)..	(5)	45
US67A–**2019**	10p Alphabet A-Z (Issued: 15,660).	(26)	75
US68–**2020**	George III £5, 'Bimetallic' £2 'VE Day', 'Bimetallic' £2 'Mayflower', 'Bimetallic' £2 'Agatha Christie', 'Bimetallic' £2 'Britannia', 'Bimetallic' £1, 50 pence 'Team GB', 50 pence to 1 pence.	(13)	75
US69–**2020**	'Bimetallic' £2 'Britannia', 'Bimetallic' £1, 50 pence to 1 pence.	(8)	30
US70–**2021**	Queen's Birthday £5, 'Bimetallic' £2 'Scott', 'Bimetallic' £2 'Wells', 'Bimetallic' £2 'Britannia', 'Bimetallic' £1, 50p 'Decimal Day', 50p 'Baird', 50p to 1p.	(13)	55
US71–**2021**	'Bimetallic' £2 'Britannia', 'Bimetallic' £1, 50p to 1p.	(8)	30
US72–**2022**	Platinum Jubilee £5, 'Bimetallic' £2 'Vera Lynn', 'Bimetallic' £2 'Bell', 'Bimetallic' £2 'Britannia', 'Bimetallic' £1, 50p 'Platinum Jubilee', 50p 'Commonwealth Games', 50p to 1p.	(13)	60
US73 –**2022**	'Bimetallic' £2 'Britannia', 'Bimetallic' £1, 50p to 1p.	(8)	30
US74 –**2022**	Queen Elizabeth II memorial set. £2 to 1p with privy mark displaying Her Majesty's birth year and the year of her passing, together with King Charles III 50p and £5 crown	(10)	75

Proof Sets in Base Metal

PS21–**1971**	Decimal coinage set, 50 new pence 'Britannia' to ½ new pence, in sealed plastic case with card wrapper (Issued: 350,000)	(6)	22
PS22–**1972**	Proof 'Silver Wedding' Crown struck in c/n plus 50p to ½p (Issued: 150,000) ...	(7)	25
PS23–**1973**	'EEC' 50p plus 10p to ½p, (Issued: 100,000)	(6)	20
PS24–**1974**	'Britannia' 50p to ½p, as 1971 (Issued: 100,000)	(6)	20
PS25–**1975**	'Britannia'50p to ½p (as 1974), (Issued: 100,000)	(6)	19
PS26–**1976**	'Britannia' 50p to ½p, as 1975, (Issued: 100,000)	(6)	15
PS27–**1977**	Proof 'Silver Jubilee' Crown struck in c/n plus 50p to ½p (Issued: 193,000)	(7)	12
PS28–**1978**	'Britannia' 50p to ½p, as 1976, (Issued: 86,100)	(6)	14
PS29–**1979**	'Britannia' 50p to ½p, as 1978, (Issued: 81,000)	(6)	14
PS30–**1980**	'Britannia' 50p to ½p, as 1979, (Issued: 143,000)	(6)	15
PS31–**1981**	'Britannia' 50p to ½p, as 1980, (Issued: 100,300)	(6)	15
PS32–**1982**	'Britannia' 50p to ½p including 20 pence (Issued: 106,800)	(7)	15
PS33–**1983**	'U.K.' £1 to ½p in new packaging (Issued: 107,800)	(8)	18
PS34–**1984**	'Scottish' £1 to ½p, (Issued: 106,520)	(8)	20

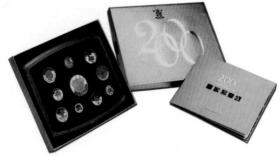

PS62   PS65

				£
PS35–**1985**	'Welsh' £1 to 1p, (Issued: 102,015)		(7)	20
PS36–**1985**	As last but packed in deluxe red leather case (Included above)		(7)	20
PS37–**1986**	'Commonwealth Games' £2 plus 'Northern Irish' £1 to 1p, (Issued: 104,597)		(8)	20
PS38–**1986**	As last but packed in deluxe red leather case (Included above)		(8)	23
PS39–**1987**	'English' £1 to 1p, (Issued: 88,659)		(7)	20
PS40–**1987**	As last but packed in deluxe leather case (Included above)		(7)	23
PS41–**1988**	'Arms' £1 to 1p, (Issued: 79,314)		(7)	20
PS42–**1988**	As last but packed in deluxe leather case (Included above)		(7)	24
PS43–**1989**	'Bill of Rights' and 'Claim of Right' £2s, 'Scottish' £1 to 1p (Issued: 85,704)		(9)	50
PS44–**1989**	As last but packed in red leather case, (Included above)		(9)	50
PS45–**1990**	'Welsh' £1 to 1p plus new smaller 5p, (Issued: 79,052)		(8)	20
PS46–**1990**	As last but packed in red leather case (Included above)		(8)	24
PS47–**1991**	'Northern Irish' £1 to 1p, (Issued: 55,144)		(7)	20
PS48–**1991**	As last but packed in red leather case (Included above)		(7)	24
PS49–**1992**	'English' £1 , 'European Community' 50p and 'Britannia' 50p, 20p to 1p plus new smaller 10p, (Issued: 44,337)		(9)	85
PS50–**1992**	As last but packed in red leather case (Issued: 17,989)		(9)	85
PS51–**1993**	Proof 'Coronation Anniversary' £5 struck in c/n (4302), 'U.K.' £1, 50p to 1p, (Issued: 43,509)		(8)	30
PS52–**1993**	As last but packed in red leather case (Issued: 22,571)		(8)	35
PS53–**1994**	'Bank' £2, 'Scottish' £1, 'D-Day' 50p to 1p, (Issued: 44,643)		(8)	32
PS54–**1994**	As last but packed in red leather case (Issued: 22,078)		(8)	35
PS55–**1995**	'Peace' £2, 'Welsh' £1 to 1p, (Issued: 42,842)		(8)	32
PS56–**1995**	As last but packed in red leather case (Issued: 17,797)		(8)	35
PS57–**1996**	Proof '70th Birthday' £5 struck in c/n, 'Football' £2, 'Northern Irish' £1 to 1p, (Issued: 46,295)		(9)	32
PS58–**1996**	As last but packed in red leather case (Issued: 21,286)		(9)	35
PS59–**1997**	Proof 'Golden Wedding' £5 struck in c/n, 'Bimetallic' £2, 'English' £1 to 1p plus new smaller 50p (Issued: 48,761)		(10)	30
PS60–**1997**	As last but packed in red leather case (Issued: 31,987)		(10)	33
PS61–**1998**	Proof 'Prince of Wales 50th Birthday' £5 struck in c/n, 'Bimetallic' £2 'UK' £1, 'EU' 50 pence to 1p. (Issued: 36,907)		(10)	35
PS62–**1998**	As last, but packed in red leather case. (Issued: 26,763)		(10)	38
PS63–**1999**	Proof 'Diana, Princess of Wales' £5 struck in c/n, 'Bimetallic' 'Rugby' £2, 'Scottish' £1 to 1p. (Issued: 40,317)		(9)	40

		£
PS64–**1999**	As last, but packed in red leather case. (Issued: 39,827)...................................... (9)	40
PS65–**2000**	Proof 'Millennium' £5 struck in c/n, 'Bimetallic' £2, 'Welsh' £1 'Library' 50 pence and 'Britannia' 50 pence to 1p.Standard Set, (Issued: 41,379).........(10)	30
PS66–**2000**	As last, but Deluxe set (Issued: 21,573 above) ....(10)	40
PS67–**2000**	As last, but Executive set (Issued: 9,517) ....(10)	40
PS68–**2001**	Proof 'Victoria' £5 struck in c/n, 'Bimetallic' £2, 'Bimetallic' 'Marconi' £2, 'Irish' £1 to 1p. Standard Set. (Issued: 28,244)..(10)	30
PS69–**2001**	As last, but Gift Set (Issued: 1,351) ....(10)	28
PS70–**2001**	As last, but packed in red leather case (Issued: 16,022)..................................(10)	33
PS71–**2001**	As last, but Executive set (Issued: 3,755) ....(10)	35
PS72–**2002**	Proof 'Golden Jubilee' £5 struck in c/n, 'Bimetallic' £2, 'English' £1 to 1p. Standard set. (Issued: 30,884) .... (9)	30
PS73–**2002**	As last, but Gift Set (Issued: 1,544) .... (9)	30
PS74–**2002**	As last, but packed in red leather case (Issued: 23,342)............................... (9)	33
PS75–**2002**	As last, but Executive set (Issued: 5,000) .... (9)	40
PS76–**2002**	£2 (K12-K15) proofs (Issued: 3358) .... (4)	150
PS77–**2002**	£2 (K12-K15) proofs in display type case (Issued: 673)............................... (4)	150
PS78–**2003**	Proof 'Coronation'£5 struck in c/n, 'Bimetallic' 'DNA' £2, 'Bimetallic' £2, 'UK' £1, 'Suffragette' 50 pence and 'Britannia' 50 pence to 1p. Standard set. (Issued: 23,650) ....(11)	35
PS79–**2003**	As last, but packed in red leather case (Issued: 14,863)...............................(11)	38
PS80–**2003**	As last, but Executive set (Issued: 5,000)..(11)	40
PS81–**2004**	'Bimetallic' 'Penydarren engine' £2, 'Bimetallic' £2, 'Forth Rail Bridge' £1, 'Sub four-minute mile' 50 pence and 'Britannia' 50 pence to 1p. Standard set. (Issued: 17,951) ....(10)	30
PS82–**2004**	As last, but packed in red leather case (Issued: 12,968)................................(10)	33
PS83–**2004**	As last, but Executive set (Issued: 4,101) ....(10)	40
PS84–**2005**	Proof 'Trafalgar'£5 struck in c/n, Proof 'Nelson'£5 struck in c/n 'Bimetallic' 'Gunpowder Plot' £2, 'Bimetallic' £2, 'Menai Straits Bridge' £1, 'Samuel Johnson's Dictionary' 50 pence and 'Britannia' 50 pence to 1p. (Issued: 21,374). (12)	55
PS85–**2005**	As last, but packed in red leather case (Issued: 14,899)................................(12)	55
PS86–**2005**	As last, but Executive set (Issued: 4,290) ....(12)	55
PS87–**2006**	Proof '80th Birthday'£5 struck in c/n, 'Bimetallic' 'Isambard Brunel' £2, 'Bimetallic' 'Paddington Station' £2, 'Bimetallic' £2, 'MacNeill's Egyptian Arch' £1, 'Victoria Cross' 50 pence, 'Heroic Act' 50 pence and 'Britannia' 50 pence to 1p (Issued: 17,689)...(13)	45
PS88 –**2006**	As last, but packed in red leather case (Issued: 15,000)................................(13)	50
PS89 –**2006**	As last, but Executive set (Issued: 5,000) ....(13)	50
PS90 –**2007**	Proof 'Diamond Wedding'£5 struck in c/n, 'Bimetallic' 'Act of Union' £2, 'Bimetallic' 'Abolition of Slave Trade' £2, 'Gateshead Millennium Bridge' £1, 'Scouting Movement' 50 pence, and 'Britannia' 50p to 1p (Issued: 18,215)..(12)	45
PS91 –**2007**	As last, but packed in red leather case (Issued: 15,000)................................(12)	50
PS92 –**2007**	As last, but Executive set (Issued: 5,000) ....(12)	50
PS93 –**2008**	Proof 'Prince Charles 60th Birthday' £5 struck in c/n, Proof 'Elizabeth I Anniversary' struck in c/n, 'Bimetallic' 'London Olympics Centenary' £2, 'Bimetallic' £2 'UK' £1, and 'Britannia' 50p to 1p (Issued: 17,719).............(11)	50
PS94 – **2008**	As last, but packed in black leather case (Issued: 13,614) ....(11)	55
PS95 – **2008**	As last, but Executive set (Issued: 5,000) ....(11)	60
PS96 – **2008**	'The Royal Shield of Arms', 'Royal Shield' £1 to 1p (Issued: 20,000) .... (7)	35
PS97 – **2009**	Proof 'Henry VIII' £5 struck in c/n, 'Bimetallic' 'Charles Darwin' £2 'Bimetallic' 'Robert Burns' £2 'Bimetallic' £2, 'Royal Shield' £1, 'Kew Gardens' 50p, 50 pence, 50 pence to 1 pence (Issued: 19,002) ....(12)	340
PS98 – **2009**	As last, but packed in black leather case (Issued: 12,337)..............................(12)	340

PS110

		£
PS99 – 2009	As last, but Executive set (Issued: 3,918) ....(12)	340
PS100–2009	50p set with reverse designs 1973-2009 c/n proofs (Issued: 1,039) ....(16)	240
PS101–2010	Proof 'Restoration of the Monarchy' £5 struck in c/n, 'Bimetallic' 'Florence Nightingale' £2, 'Bimetallic'£2, 'London' £1, 'Belfast' £1, Royal Shield £1, 'Girl Guiding' 50 pence, and 50 pence to 1 pence (Issued: 30,844 including PS102 and PS103) ....(13)	80
PS102–2010	As last, but packed in black leather case ....(13)	85
PS103–2010	As last, but Executive set ....(13)	85
PS104–2011	Proof 'Prince Philip 90th Birthday' £5 struck in c/n,'Bimetallic' 'Mary Rose' £2, 'Bimetallic' King James Bible'£2, 'Bimetallic' £2 'Edinburgh' £1, 'Cardiff' £1, 'Royal Shield '£1, 50 pence, 'WWF', 50 pence to 1 pence (Edition: 20,000) (Issued: 28,974 including PS105 & 106)......................(14)	110
PS105–2011	As last, but packed in black leather case (Edition: 15,000)..........................(14)	115
PS106–2011	As last, but Executive set (Edition: 5,000)...............................……..….(14)	125
PS107–2012	Collector Proof set, Diamond Jubilee £5, struck in c/n, 'Bimetallic' 'Charles Dickens' £2 'Bimetallic' £2 'Royal Shield '£1 50 pence to 1 pence (Issued: 21,614)...(10)	55
PS108–2012	Premium Proof set, Proof Diamond Jubilee £5, struck in c/n, 'Bimetallic' 'Charles Dickens' £2, 'Bimetallic' £2 'Royal Shield '£1, 50 pence to 1 pence and Mint medal (Issued:.3,463) ....(10)	65

The last base metal Executive set was issued in 2011 but see PSS56A for a 2012 mixed metal Executive set.

PS109–2013	Premium Proof set, Coronation £5, struck in c/n, 'Bimetallic' 'Guinea' £2 'Bimetallic' 'Roundel' £2, 'Bimetallic' 'Train' £2,'Bimetallic' £2 'Royal Shield' £1, 'England' £1, 'Wales' £1 50 pence 'Ironside', 50 pence to 1 pence (Issued:3,965) ....(15)	170
PS110–2013	Collector Proof set, Coronation £5, struck in c/n, 'Bimetallic' 'Guinea' £2 'Bimetallic' 'Roundel' £2, 'Bimetallic' 'Train' £2, 'Bimetallic' £2 'Royal Shield' £1, 'England' £1, 'Wales' £1, 50 pence 'Ironside', 50 pence to 1 pence (Issued:8,493)..(15)	160
PS111–2013	Commemorative Proof set, Coronation £5, struck in c/n, 'Bimetallic' 'Guinea' £2 'Bimetallic' 'Roundel' £2, 'Bimetallic' 'Train'£2, 'England' £1, 'Wales' £1 and 50 pence 'Ironside' (Issued: 6,121) ....(7)	130
PS112–2014	Premium Proof set, Queen Anne £5, struck in c/n, 'Bimetallic''Trinity House' £2, 'Bimetallic' 'World War I' £2, 'Bimetallic' £2 'Royal Shield' £1, 'Northern Ireland' £1, 'Scotland' £1(.), 50 pence 'Commonwealth Games', 50 pence to 1 pence (Issued: 3,405)...(14)	195

£

PS113–**2014**   Collector Proof set, Queen Anne £5, struck in c/n, 'Bimetallic' 'Trinity House' £2,
'Bimetallic' 'World War I' £2, 'Bimetallic' £2 'Royal Shield' £1, 'Northern
Ireland' £1, 'Scotland'£1, 50 pence 'Commonwealth Games', 50 pence to
1 pence (Issued: 6,956) .... (14)   180

PS114–**2014**   Commemorative Proof set, Queen Anne £5, struck in c/n, 'Bimetallic'
'Trinity House' £2, Bimetallic 'World War I' £2, 'Northern Ireland' £1,
'Scotland' £1, and 50 pence 'Commonwealth Games', (Issued: 3,763) ....   (6)   130

PS115–**2015**   Fourth Portrait 'Bimetallic' £2 'Royal Shield', £1, 50 pence to 1 pence
(Issued: 13,206)..   (8)   60

PS116–**2015**   Fifth Portrait 'Bimetallic' £2 'Royal Shield', £1, 50 pence to 1 pence
(Issued: 22,080)..   (8)   60

PS117–**2015**   Premium Proof set, Churchill £5, struck in c/n, Waterloo £5, struck in c/n 'Bimetallic'
'Magna Carta' £2, 'Bimetallic' 'Royal Navy' £2, 'Bimetallic' £2 'Royal
Shield' £1, 50 pence 'Battle of Britain' 50 pence to 1 pence (Issued: 3,559) ...... (13)   155

PS118–**2015**   Collector Proof set, Churchill £5, struck in c/n, Waterloo £5, struck in c/n
'Bimetallic' 'Magna Carta' £2, 'Bimetallic' 'Royal Navy' £2, 'Bimetallic'
£2 'Royal Shield' £1, 50 pence 'Battle of Britain', 50 pence to 1 pence
(Issued: 7,895).. (13)   140

PS118–**2015**   Commemorative Proof set, Churchill £5, struck in c/n, Waterloo £5, struck in
c/n 'Bimetallic' 'Magna Carta' £2, 'Bimetallic' 'Royal Navy' £2, 50 pence
'Battle of Britain' (Issued: 4,467) ....   (5)   65

PS119–**2016**   Premium Proof set, Queen's Birthday £5, struck in c/n, 'Bimetallic' £2
'Comedy', 'Bimetallic' £2 'History', 'Bimetallic' £2 'Tragedy', 'Bimetallic'
£2 'The Army', 'Bimetallic' £2 'Great Fire','Bimetallic' £2, Royal Shield' £1,
Royal Arms £1, 50 pence 'Battle of Hastings', 50 pence to 1 pence
(Issued: 3,409).. (16)   250

PS120–**2016**   Collector Proof set, Queen's Birthday £5, struck in c/n, 'Bimetallic' £2
'Comedy', 'Bimetallic' £2 'History', 'Bimetallic' £2 'Tragedy', 'Bimetallic'
£2 'The Army' 'Bimetallic' £2 'Great Fire' 'Bimetallic' £2, Royal Shield' £1,
Royal Arms £1, 50 pence 'Battle of Hastings', 50 pence to 1 pence
(Issued: 6,919).. (16)   240

PS121–**2016**   Commemorative Proof set, Queen's Birthday £5, struck in c/n, 'Bimetallic'
£2 'Comedy', 'Bimetallic' £2 'History', 'Bimetallic' £2 'Tragedy', 'Bimetallic'
£2 ' The Army' 'Bimetallic' £2 'Great Fire' Royal Arms £1, 50 pence 'Battle
of Hastings' (Issued: 3,161) ....   (8)   95

PS122–**2017**   Premium Proof set, House of Windsor £5, struck in c/n , King Canute £5,
struck in c/n , 'Bimetallic' £2 'First World War Aviation', 'Bimetallic' £2
'Jane Austen', Bimetallic' £2 'Britannia', 'Bimetallic' £1, 50 pence 'Sir Isaac
Newton', 50 pence to 1 pence (Issued: 3,755).. (13)   180

PS123–**2017**   Collector Proof set, House of Windsor £5, struck in c/n , King Canute £5,
struck in c/n , 'Bimetallic' £2 'First World War Aviation', 'Bimetallic' £2
'Jane Austen',   Bimetallic' £2 'Britannia', 'Bimetallic' £1, 50 pence 'Sir Isaac
Newton', 50 pence to 1 pence (Issued: 7,701) ....(13)   160

PS124–**2017**   Commemorative Proof set, House of Windsor £5, struck in c/n , King Canute
£5, struck in c/n , 'Bimetallic' £2 'First World War Aviation', 'Bimetallic' £2
'Jane Austen', 50 pence 'Sir Isaac Newton', (Issued: 2,788) ....   (5)   95

PS125–**2018**   Premium Proof set, 5th Birthday Prince George £5, struck in c/n ,'Bimetallic'
£2 ' Royal Air Force Badge', 'Bimetallic' £2 'Frankenstein', 'Bimetallic'
£2 ' Armistice' Bimetallic' £2 'Britannia', 'Bimetallic' £1, 50 pence
'Representation of People Act', 50 pence to 1 pence (Issued: 2,544) .... (13)   195

PS126–**2018**   Collector Proof set, 5th Birthday Prince George £5, struck in c/n , 'Bimetallic'
£2 ' Royal Air Force Badge', 'Bimetallic' £2 'Frankenstein', 'Bimetallic'
£2 ' Armistice' Bimetallic' £2 'Britannia', 'Bimetallic' £1, 50 pence
'Representation of People Act', 50 pence to 1 pence (Issued: 5,788) .... (13)   175

£

PS127–**2018** Commemorative Proof set, 5th Birthday Prince George £5, struck in c/n ,
'Bimetallic' £2 ' Royal Air Force Badge', 'Bimetallic' £2 'Frankenstein',
'Bimetallic' £2 ' Armistice' 50 pence 'Representation of People Act',
(Issued: 3,177).. (5) 95

PS128–**2019** Premium Proof set, 200th Anniversary of the birth of Queen Victoria £5, .
struck in c/n , 'Bimetallic' £2 '75th Anniversary of D-Day', 'Bimetallic' £2
'Wedgwood', 'Bimetallic' £2 'Samuel Pepys' Bimetallic' £2 'Britannia',
'Bimetallic' £1, 50 pence 'Sherlock Holmes', 50 pence to 1 pence
(Issued::2,053) .... (13) 210

PS129–**2019** Collector Proof set, 200th Anniversary of the birth of Queen Victoria £5, struck
in c/n , 'Bimetallic' £2 '75th Anniversary of D-Day', 'Bimetallic' £2 'Wedgwood',
'Bimetallic' £2 ' Samuel Pepys' Bimetallic' £2 'Britannia', 'Bimetallic' £1,
50 pence 'Sherlock Holmes', 50 pence to 1 pence (Issued: 6,055) .... (13) 155

PS130–**2019** British Culture Set of five different 50 pence designs of the past to mark the 50th
Anniversary of the introduction of the 50 pence coin in 1969. (Issued: 3,500) ... (5) 90

PS131–**2019** Military Set of five different 50 pence designs of the past to mark the 50th
Anniversary of the introduction of the 50 pence coin in 1969, (Issued: 3,144) (5) 90

PS132–**2020** Premium proof set, George III £5, 'Bimetallic' £2 'VE Day', 'Bimetallic' £2
'Mayflower', 'Bimetallic' £2 'Agatha Christie', 'Bimetallic' £2 'Britannia',
'Bimetallic' £1, 50 pence 'Team GB', 50 pence to 1 pence. (Edition: 2,500) (13) 210

PS133–**2020** Collector Proof set. George III £5, 'Bimetallic' £2 'VE Day', 'Bimetallic' £2
'Mayflower', 'Bimetallic' £2 'Agatha Christie', 'Bimetallic' £2 'Britannia',
'Bimetallic' £1, 50 pence 'Team GB', 50 pence to 1 pence. (Edition: 7,000) (13) 155

PS134–**2021** Premium proof set, Queen's Birthday £5, 'Bimetallic' £2 'Scott', 'Bimetallic' £2
'Wells', 'Bimetallic' £2 'Britannia', 'Bimetallic' £1, 50p 'Decimal Day', 50p
'Baird', 50p to 1p. (Edition: 2,500) .... (13) 210

PS135–**2021** Collector Proof set, Queen's Birthday £5, 'Bimetallic' £2 'Scott', 'Bimetallic' £2
'Wells', 'Bimetallic' £2 'Britannia', 'Bimetallic' £1, 50p 'Decimal Day', 50p
'Baird', 50p to 1p. (Edition: 7,000) .... (13) 155

PS136–**2022** Premium proof set. Platinum Jubilee £5, 'Bimetallic' £2 'Vera Lynn',
'Bimetallic' £2 'Bell', 'Bimetallic' £2 'Britannia', 'Bimetallic' £1, 50p
'Platinum Jubilee', 50p 'Commonwealth Games', 50p to 1p. (Edition: 2,500)... (13) 210

PS137–**2022** Collector proof set. Platinum Jubilee £5, 'Bimetallic' £2 'Vera Lynn',
'Bimetallic' £2 'Bell', 'Bimetallic' £2 'Britannia', 'Bimetallic' £1, 50p
'Platinum Jubilee', 50p 'Commonwealth Games', 50p to 1p. (Edition: 7,000) ... (13) 155

Proofs Sets in Silver

PSS01–**1989** £2 (K2 and K3) silver piedfort proofs (Issued: 10,000) .... (2) 85
PSS02–**1989** £2 (K2 and K3) silver proofs.. (2) 65
PSS03–**1990** 5p (D3 and D4) silver proofs (Issued: 35,000)... (2) 25
PSS04–**1992** 'England' £1, 'EEC 50p', 10p (F3 and F4) silver proofs (Edition: 1,000 from
mintage of singles) .... (4) 130
PSS05–**1992** 10p (F3 and F4) silver proofs…... (2) 30
PSS06–**1993** Family silver set 'Coronation' £5, 'Arms' £1, 'EEC 50p' silver proofs
(Edition: 1,000 from mintage of singles) .... (3) 135
PSS07–**1995** Family silver set 'Peace' £2, 'United Nations' £2, 'Wales' £1 silver proofs
(Edition: 1,000 from mintage of singles)... (3) 95
PSS08–**1996** Family silver set '70th Birthday' £5, 'Football' £2, 'Northern Ireland' £1 silver
proofs (Edition: 1,000 from mintage of singles)... (3) 85
PSS09–**1996** 25th Anniversary of Decimal Currency £1 to 1p silver proof (Edition: 15,000) (7) 125
PSS10–**1997** Family silver set, 'Golden Wedding' £5, 'Britannia' £2, 'England' £1, 50p
small silver proofs (Edition: 500 from mintages of singles) .... (4) 280
PSS11–**1997** 50p (H4 and H7) silver proofs (Issued: 10,304).. (2) 45

£

PSS12–**1998**	Family silver set 'Prince of Wales 50th Birthday' £5, 'Britannia' £2, 'Bimetallic' £2, 'UK' £1, 'EU' 50p, 'NHS' 50p (Edition: 500 from mintages of singles).........	(6)	240
PSS13–**1998**	£2 (K8 and K9) silver proofs.........	(2)	60
PSS14–**1998**	50p (H9 and H10) silver proofs.........	(2)	60
PSS15–**1999**	Family silver set 'Diana' £5, 'Millennium' £5, 'Rugby' £2, 'Scotland' £1 silver proofs (Edition: 500 from mintages of singles).........	(4)	140
PSS16–**2000**	'Millennium' £5, 'Bimetallic' £2, 'Welsh' £1, 50p to 1p, and Maundy coins, 4p-1p, in silver proof (Issued: 13,180).........	(13)	300
PSS17–**2002**	£2 (K12-K15) silver proofs (Issued: 2553).........	(4)	180
PSS18–**2002**	£2 (K12A-K15A) silver proof piedfort (Issued: 3497).........	(4)	300
PSS19–**2002/3**	£5 (L10 and L12) silver proofs.........	(2)	100
PSS20–**2003**	'Coronation' £5, 'Britannia' £2, 'Bimetallic' 'DNA' £2, 'UK' £1 and 'Suffragette' 50 pence silver proofs (Edition:).........	(5)	165
PSS21–**2003**	'Bimetallic' 'DNA' £2, 'UK' £1, 'Suffragettes' 50p silver piedfort proofs.........	(3)	150
PSS22–**2004**	'Entente Cordiale' £5, 'Britannia' £2, 'Bimetallic' 'Penydarren engine' £2 'Forth Rail Bridge' £1 and 'Sub four-minute mile' 50 pence silver proofs (Edition:).........	(5)	165
PSS23–**2004**	'Bimetallic' 'Penydarren engine' £2, 'Forth Rail Bridge' £1, 'Sub four-minute mile' 50 pence silver piedfort proofs.........	(3)	145
PSS24–**2005**	£5 (L14 and L15) silver proof piedforts (Issued: 2,818).........	(2)	150
PSS25–**2005**	'Bimetallic' 'Gunpowder Plot' £2, Bimetallic 'World War II' £2, 'Menai Straits Bridge' £1, 'Samuel Johnson's Dictionary' 50 pence Silver piedfort proofs ...	(4)	190
PSS26–**2006**	'H M The Queen's 80th Birthday' £5, 'Bimetallic' £2, 'Northern Ireland' £1, 50p to 1p and Maundy Coins, 4p – 1p, in silver proof (Issued: 6,394).........	(13)	300
PSS27–**2006**	'80th Birthday' £5, 'Bimetallic' 'Isambard Brunel' £2 and 'Bimetallic' 'Paddington Station' £2, 'MacNeill's Egyptian Arch' £1, 'Victoria Cross' 50 pence, 'Wounded soldier' 50 pence silver piedforts (Edition: taken from individual coin limits)	(6)	325
PSS28–**2006**	£2 (K20 and K21) silver proofs.........	(2)	70
PSS29–**2006**	£2 (K20 and K21) silver piedfort proofs.........	(2)	130
PSS30–**2006**	50p (H15 and H16) silver proofs.........	(2)	65
PSS31–**2006**	50p (H15 and H16) silver piedfort proofs.........	(2)	115
PSS32–**2007**	'Diamond Wedding' £5, Britannia £2, 'Bimetallic' 'Act of Union' £2, 'Bimetallic' 'Abolition of Slavery' £2, 'Millennium Bridge' £1 and 'Scout Movement'50p in silver proof (Edition: taken from individual coin limits)	(6)	200
PSS33–**2007**	'Diamond Wedding' £5, 'Bimetallic' 'Act of Union'£2, 'Bimetallic' 'Abolition of Slavery' £2, 'Millennium Bridge' £1 and 'Scout Movement'50p in silver piedfort (Edition: taken from individual coin limits	(5)	250
PSS34–**2004/7**	£1 (J18-J21) silver proofs.........	(4)	115
PSS35–**2004/7**	£1 (J18-J21) silver proof piedforts.........	(4)	200
PSS36–**2008**	'Prince Charles 60th Birthday' £5, 'Elizabeth I Anniversary' £5, Britannia £2, 'London Olympic Centenary' £2 and 'UK' £1 silver proofs (Issued: 1,182)...	(5)	180
PSS37–**2008**	'Prince Charles 60th Birthday' £5, 'Elizabeth I Anniversary' £5, 'London Olympic Centenary' £2 and 'Royal Shield' £1 silver piedforts (Issued: 1,746)	(4)	250
PSS38–**2008**	'Emblems of Britain', 'UK' £1, 'Britannia' 50 pence , 20 pence to 1p silver proofs (Issued: 8,168).........	(7)	125
PSS39–**2008**	'The Royal Shield of Arms', 'Royal Shield' £1 to 1p silver proof (Issued: 10,000)	(7)	150
PSS40–**2008**	As above but silver piedforts (Issued: 3,000).........	(7)	225
PSS41–**2008**	£1 with reverse designs 1983-2007 and with selected gold plating silver proofs (Issued: 2,005).........	(14)	395
PSS42–**2008**	Set of 3 £1 Regional designs for Scotland with selected gold plating to the reverse designs (Edition: 750, taken from above).........	(3)	95

PSS43–**2008**	Set of 3 £1 Regional designs for Wales with selected gold plating to the reverse designs (Edition: 750, taken from above)	(3)	95
PSS44–**2008**	Set of 3 £1 Regional designs for Northern Ireland with selected gold plating to the reverse designs (Edition: 750, taken from above)	(3)	95
PSS45–**2008**	Set of 3 £1 Regional designs for England with selected gold plating to the reverse designs (Edition: 750, taken from above)	(3)	95
PSS46–**2009**	'Henry VIII' £5, 'Bimetallic' 'Charles Darwin' £2, Bimetallic 'Robert Burns' £2 'Bimetallic'£2, 'Royal Shield' £1, 'Kew Gardens' 50 pence, 50 pence, 20 pence, 10 pence, 5 pence, 2 pence and 1 pence silver proofs (Issued: 2,749)	(12)	400
PSS47–**2009**	'Henry VIII' £5, Britannia £2, 'Charles Darwin' £2, 'Robert Burns' £2, 'Royal Shield' £1 and 50 pence 'Kew Gardens' silver proofs (Edition; 1,500)	(6)	275
			£
PSS48–**2009**	'Henry VIII' £5, 'Charles Darwin' £2, 'Robert Burns' £2 and 50 pence 'Kew Gardens' silver piedforts (Issued: 2,500)	(4)	255
PSS49–**2009**	50p Set with reverse designs 1973-2009 silver proofs (Issued: 1,163)	(16)	425
PSS50–**2010**	'Restoration of the Monarchy' £5, 'Bimetallic 'Florence Nightingale' £2, 'Bimetallic'£2, 'London' £1, 'Belfast' £1, Royal Shield £1, 'Girl Guiding' 50 pence, and 50 pence to 1p silver proofs (Issued: 1,241)	(13)	300
PSS51–2010	'Restoration of the Monarchy' £5, 'Bimetallic 'Florence Nightingale' £2, 'London' £1, 'Belfast' £1, and 'Girl Guiding' 50 pence silver proofs (Edition: 2,500)	(5)	175
PSS52–**2010**	'Restoration of the Monarchy'£5, 'Bimetallic 'Florence Nightingale' £2 'London' £1, 'Belfast' £1, and 'Girl Guiding' 50 pence silver piedforts (Issued: 1,581)	(5)	275
PSS53-**2011**	Proof 'Prince Philip 90th Birthday' £5,'Bimetallic' 'Mary Rose' £2, 'Bimetallic' King James Bible'£2,'Bimetallic' £2 'Edinburgh' £1, 'Cardiff' £1, 'Royal Shield '£1, 50 pence,' WWF', 50 pence to 1 pence silver proofs (Edition: 2,500)	(14)	425
PSS54-**2011**	Proof 'Prince Philip 90th Birthday' £5 ,'Bimetallic' 'Mary Rose' £2, 'Bimetallic' King James Bible'£2, 'Edinburgh' £1, 'Cardiff' £1, 50 pence,' 'WWF', silver proofs (Edition: 1,500)	(6)	275
PSS55-**2011**	Proof 'Prince Philip 90th Birthday' £5,'Bimetallic' 'Mary Rose' £2, 'Bimetallic' King James Bible'£2, 'Edinburgh' £1, 'Cardiff' £1, 'WWF', silver piedforts (Edition: 2,000)	(6)	450
PSS56–**2012**	Proof Diamond Jubilee £5, 50 pence to 1 pence silver proofs (Issued: 587) .	(7)	200
PSS56A–**2012**	Executive set Diamond Jubilee £5 silver proof, 'Bimetallic' £2, 'Royal Shield' £1, 50p to 1p in base metal. (Edition: 2,012)	(9)	70
PSS57–**2012**	Proof Diamond Jubilee £5, 'Bimetallic' 'Charles Dickens' £2, 'Bimetallic' £2 'Royal Shield '£1 50 pence to 1 pence silver proofs, £1 to 1 pence with selected gold plating (Edition: 2,012)	(10)	350
PSS58–**2013**	Proof 'Coronation' £5, 'Bimetallic' 'Guinea' £2 'Bimetallic' 'Roundel', 'Bimetallic' 'Train' £2,'Bimetallic' £2 'Royal Shield' £1, 'England' £1, 'Wales' £1, 50 pence 'Ironside', 50 pence to 1 pence silver proofs (Issued: 985)	(15)	550
PSS59–**2013**	Proof 'Coronation' £5, 'Bimetallic' 'Guinea' £2 'Bimetallic' 'Roundel' £2, ' Bimetallic' 'Train'£2, 'England' £1, 'Wales' £1 and 50 pence 'Ironside' silver piedfort (Issued: 486)	(7)	650
PSS60–**2013**	£5 (L28-L31) silver proofs (Issued: 1465)	(4)	350
PSS61–**2013**	£5 (L28-L31) silver proofs piedforts (Issued: 697)	(4)	600
PSS62–**2013**	£2 (K31 and K32) silver proofs (Issued: 2204)	(2)	100
PSS63–**2013**	£2 (K31 and K32) silver proof piedforts	(2)	200
PSS64–**2013**	£1 (J32 and J33) silver proofs (Issued: 1,476)	(2)	100
PSS65–**2013**	£1 (J13, J26, J27) silver proofs (Issued: 1,311)	(3)	150

£

PSS66–**2014** Proof 'Queen Anne' £5, 'Bimetallic' 'Trinity House' £2, 'Bimetallic' 'World
War I' £2, 'Bimetallic' £2 'Royal Shield' £1, 'Northern Ireland' £1, 'Scotland'
£1, 50 pence 'Commonwealth Games', 50 pence to 1 pence silver proofs
(Issued: 368) .... (14) 560

PSS67–**2014** Proof 'Queen Anne' £5, 'Bimetallic' 'Trinity House' £2, 'Bimetallic' 'World
War I' £2, 'Bimetallic' £2 'Royal Shield' £1, 'Northern Ireland' £1, 'Scotland'
£1, and 50 pence 'Commonwealth Games', silver proofs (Issued: 283)....... (6) 300

PSS68–**2014** Proof 'Queen Anne' £5, 'Bimetallic' 'Trinity House' £2, 'Bimetallic' 'World
War I' £2, 'Bimetallic' £2 'Royal Shield'£1, 'Northern Ireland' £1, 'Scotland'
£1, and 50 pence 'Commonwealth Games', silver piedforts (Issued: 487).... (6) 570

PSS69–**2014** £5 (L34-L37) silver proofs with colour (Issued: 1,299) .... (4) 325

PSS70–**2015** Churchill £5, Waterloo £5, 'Bimetallic' 'Magna Carta' £2, 'Bimetallic'
'Royal Navy' £2, 'Bimetallic' £2 'Royal Shield' £1, 50 pence 'Battle of
Britain' 50 pence to 1 pence silver proofs (Issued: 298) ....(13) 500

PSS71–**2015** Churchill £5, Waterloo £5, 'Bimetallic' 'Magna Carta' £2, 'Bimetallic'
'Royal Navy' £2, 50 pence 'Battle of Britain' , silver proofs (Issued: 366)... (5) 275

PSS72–**2015** Churchill £5, Waterloo £5, 'Bimetallic' 'Magna Carta' £2, 'Bimetallic'
'Royal Navy' £2, 50 pence 'Battle of Britain', silver piedforts (Issued: 434)....... (5) 550

PSS73–**2015** Fourth Portrait 'Bimetallic' £2 'Royal Shield', £1, 50 pence to 1 pence,
silver proofs, (Issued: 1,241) .... (8) 240

PSS74–**2015** Fifth Portrait 'Bimetallic' £2 'Royal Shield', £1, 50 pence to 1 pence,
silver proofs, (Issued: 1,876) .... (8) 240

PSS75–**2016** Collector Proof set, Queen's Birthday £5, 'Bimetallic' £2 'Comedy''Bimetallic'
£2 'History', 'Bimetallic' £2 'Tragedy', 'Bimetallic' £2 'The Army' 'Bimetallic'
£2 'Great Fire' 'Bimetallic' £2, Royal Shield' £1, Royal Arms £1, 50 pence
'Battle of Hastings' 50 pence to 1 pence silver proofs (Issued: 383).............(16) 600

PSS76–**2016** Commemorative Proof set, Queen's Birthday £5, 'Bimetallic' £2 'Comedy',
'Bimetallic' £2 'History', 'Bimetallic' £2 'Tragedy', 'Bimetallic' £2 'The
Army' 'Bimetallic' £2 'Great Fire' Royal Arms £1, 50 pence 'Battle of
Hastings' silver proofs (Issued: 658).. (8) 400

PSS77–**2016** Commemorative Proof set, Queen's Birthday £5, 'Bimetallic' £2 'Comedy',
'Bimetallic' £2 'History', 'Bimetallic' £2 'Tragedy', 'Bimetallic' £2 'The
Army', 'Bimetallic' £2 'Great Fire', Royal Arms £1, 50 pence 'Battle of
Hastings' silver piedforts (Issued: 456).. (8) 650

PSS78–**2016** £5 (L45-L48) silver proofs with colour (Issued: 1,098)............................... (4) 325

PSS79–**2017** Collector Proof set, House of Windsor £5, King Canute £5, 'Bimetallic' £2
'First World War Aviation', 'Bimetallic' £2 'Jane Austen', Bimetallic' £2
'Britannia', 'Bimetallic' £1, 50 pence 'Sir Isaac Newton', 50 pence to 1 pence
silver proofs (Issued: 615) ....(13) 575

PSS80–**2017** Commemorative Proof set, House of Windsor £5, King Canute £5,
'Bimetallic' £2 'First World War Aviation', 'Bimetallic' £2 'Jane Austen',
50 pence 'Sir Isaac Newton', silver proofs (Issued:342) .... (5) 300

PSS81–**2017** Commemorative Proof set, House of Windsor £5, King Canute £5,
'Bimetallic' £2 'First World War Aviation', 'Bimetallic' £2 'Jane Austen',
50 pence 'Sir Isaac Newton', silver piedforts (Issued:364) .... (5) 475

PSS82–**2017** £5 (L52-L55) silver proofs with colour (Edition: 2017) .... (4) 325

PSS83–**2018** Collector Proof set, 5th Birthday Prince George £5, 'Bimetallic' £2 'Royal
Air Force Badge', 'Bimetallic' £2 'Frankenstein', 'Bimetallic' £2 'Armistice'
Bimetallic' £2 'Britannia', 'Bimetallic' £1, 50 pence 'Representation of
People Act', 50 pence to 1 pence Silver proofs (Issued: 612)......................(13) 575

PSS84–**2018** Commemorative Proof set, 5th Birthday Prince George £5, 'Bimetallic' £2
'Royal Air Force Badge', 'Bimetallic' £2 'Frankenstein', 'Bimetallic' £2
'Armistice' 50 pence 'Representation of People Act' silver proofs
(Issued: 388) .... (5) 310

£

PSS85–**2018**	Commemorative Proof set, 5th Birthday Prince George £5, 'Bimetallic' £2 'Royal Air Force Badge', 'Bimetallic' £2 'Frankenstein', 'Bimetallic' 'Armistice' 50 pence 'Representation of People Act' silver piedforts (Issued: 338)	(5)	550
PSS86–**2018**	£5 (L66-L69) British Landmarks IV silver proofs with colour (Issued: 780)	(4)	325
PSS87–**2018**	10p Alphabet A-Z silver proofs (Issued: 200)	(26)	900
PSS88–**2019**	Collector Proof set, 200th Anniversary of the birth of Queen Victoria £5, 'Bimetallic' £2 '75th Anniversary of D-Day', 'Bimetallic' '£2 'Wedgwood', 'Bimetallic' £2 'Samuel Pepys' Bimetallic' £2 'Britannia', 'Bimetallic' £1, 50 pence 'Sherlock Holmes', 50 pence to 1 pence. silver proofs (Issued: 406)	(13)	575
PSS89–**2019**	Commemorative Proof set, 200th Anniversary of the birth of Queen Victoria £5, 'Bimetallic' £2 '75th Anniversary of D-Day', 'Bimetallic' '£2 'Wedgwood', 'Bimetallic' £2 'Samuel Pepys' 50 pence 'Sherlock Holmes' silver piedforts (Issued: 282)	(5)	550
PSS90–**2019**	British Culture 50p (H62-H66) silver proofs (Issued 1,933)	(5)	250
PSS91–**2019**	British Culture 50p (H62-H66) silver piedfort proofs (Issued 569)	(5)	350
PSS92–**2019**	Military 50p (H67-H71) silver proofs (Issued 1,934)	(5)	250
PSS93–**2019**	Military Culture 50p (H67-H71) silver piedfort proofs (Issued 333)	(5)	350
PSS94–**2020**	Collector proof set, George III £5, 'Bimetallic' £2 'VE Day', 'Bimetallic' £2 'Mayflower', 'Bimetallic' £2 'Agatha Christie', 'Bimetallic' £2 'Britannia', 'Bimetallic' £1, 50 pence 'Team GB', 50 pence to 1 pence silver proofs. (Edition: 500)	(13)	600
PSS95–**2020**	Commemorative Proof set. George III £5, 'Bimetallic' £2 'VE Day', 'Bimetallic' £2 'Mayflower', 'Bimetallic' £2 'Agatha Christie', 50 pence 'Team GB' silver piedfort proofs. (Edition: 300)	(5)	600
PSS96–**2021**	Collector proof set, Queen's Birthday £5, 'Bimetallic' £2 'Scott', 'Bimetallic' £2 'Wells', 'Bimetallic' £2 'Britannia', 'Bimetallic' £1, 50p 'Decimal Day', 50p 'Baird', 50p to 1p. (Edition: 550)	(13)	550
PSS97–**2021**	Commemorative Proof set. Queen's Birthday £5, 'Bimetallic' £2 'Scott', 'Bimetallic' £2 'Wells', 50p 'Decimal Day', 50p 'Baird' silver piedforts (Edition: 300)	(5)	550
PSS98–**2022**	Collector proof set. Platinum Jubilee £5, 'Bimetallic' £2 'Vera Lynn', 'Bimetallic' £2 'Bell', 'Bimetallic' £2 'Britannia', 'Bimetallic' £1, 50p 'Platinum Jubilee', 50p 'Commonwealth Games', 50p to 1p silver proofs. (Edition: 550)	(13)	600
PSS99–**2022**	Commemorative Proof set. Platinum Jubilee £5, 'Bimetallic' £2 'Vera Lynn', 'Bimetallic' £2 'Bell', 50p 'Platinum Jubilee', 50p 'Commonwealth Games' silver proof piedforts. (Edition: 370)	(5)	600
PSS100–**2022**	Queen Elizabeth II memorial set. £2 to 1p with privy mark displaying Her Majesty's birth year and the year of her passing, together with King Charles III 50p and £5 crown silver proofs. (Edition: 1,500)	10)	465

Proof Sets in Gold

PGCS01–**2002**	£2 (K12-K15) gold proofs (Issued: 315)	(4)	4000
PGCS02–**2002**	'Golden Jubilee' £5, 'Bimetallic' £2, 'English' £1, 50p to 1p and Maundy coins, 4p-1p, in gold proof (Issued: 2,002)	(13)	12000
PGCS02A–**2005**	£5 (L14 and L15) gold proofs	(2)	5000
PGCS03–**2006**	£2 (K20 and K21) gold proofs	(2)	2000
PGCS04–**2006**	50p (H15 and H16) gold proofs	(2)	1800
PGCS05–**2004/7**	£1 (J18-J21) gold proofs (Edition: 300 taken from individual coin limits)	(4)	3750
PGCS06–**2008**	'Emblems of Britain', 'UK' £1, 'Britannia' 50 pence, 20 pence to 1p gold proofs (Issued: 780)	(7)	3800

£

PGCS07–**2008**	'The Royal Shield of Arms', 'Royal Shield' £1 to 1p gold proof (Issued: 886)	(7) 3800
PGCS08–**2008**	£1 with reverse designs 1983-2007 gold proofs (Issued: 150)......	(14)13500
PGCS09–**2009**	50p Set with reverse designs 1973-2009 gold proofs (Issued: 70)......	(16)15000
PGCS10–**2009**	50p Set with reverse designs 1973-2009 gold proofs piedfort (Issued: 40)	(16)30000
PGCS11–**2012**	Diamond Jubilee £5, 'Bimetallic' 'Charles Dickens' £2, 'Bimetallic' £2 'Royal Shield '£1, 50 pence to 1 pence gold proofs (Edition: 150)	(10) 8000
PGCS12–**2012**	Diamond Jubilee £5, and £2 (Sovereign design) set of two (Issued: 60, taken from individual coins limits)......	(2) 4000
PGCS13–**2013**	'Coronation' £5, 'Bimetallic' 'Guinea' £2, 'Bimetallic' 'Roundel' £2, 'Bimetallic' 'Train' £2, 'Bimetallic' £2, 'Royal Shield' £1, 'England' £1, 'Wales' £1, 50 pence 'Ironside', 50 pence to 1 pence gold proofs (Issued: 59)	(15)14000
PGCS14–**2013**	£2 (K31 and K32) gold proofs (Issued: 111)......	(2) 3000
PGCS15–**2013**	£5 (L28-L31) gold proofs (Issued: 148)......	(4)12000
PGCS16–**2013**	£1 (J13, J26, J27) gold proofs (Issued: 17)......	(3) 3600
PGCS17–**2014**	'Queen Anne' £5, 'Bimetallic' 'Trinity House' £2, 'Bimetallic' 'World War I' £2, 'Northern Ireland' £1, 'Scotland' £1, and 50 pence ' Commonwealth Games', gold proofs (Issued: 75)......	(6) 8000
PGCS18–**2015**	Fourth Portrait 'Bimetallic' £2 'Royal Shield', £1, 50 pence to 1 pence gold proofs (Issued: 209)......	(8) 4500
PGCS19–**2015**	Fifth Portrait 'Bimetallic' £2 'Royal Shield', £1 50 pence to 1 pence gold proofs (Issued: 245)......	(8) 4500
PGCS20–**2015**	Churchill £5, Waterloo £5, 'Bimetallic' 'Magna Carta' £2, 'Bimetallic' 'Royal Navy' £2, 50 pence 'Battle of Britain', gold proofs (Issued: 99) ..	(5) 8000
PGCS23–**2016**	Commemorative Proof set, Queen's Birthday £5, 'Bimetallic' £2 'Comedy', 'Bimetallic' £2 'History', 'Bimetallic' £2 'Tragedy', 'Bimetallic' £2 'The Army', 'Bimetallic' £2 'Great Fire', Royal Arms £1, 50 pence 'Battle of Hastings' gold proofs (Issued: 82)......	(8) 8500
PGCS25–**2017**	Collector Proof set. House of Windsor £5, King Canute £5, 'Bimetallic' £2 'First World War Aviation', 'Bimetallic' £2 'Jane Austen', 'Bimetallic' £2 'Britannia', 'Bimetallic' £1, 50 pence 'Sir Isaac Newton', 50 pence to 1 pence gold proofs (Issued: 34)......(13) 12500	
PGCS26–**2017**	Commemorative Proof set, House of Windsor £5,,King Canute £5, 'Bimetallic' £2 'First World War Aviation', 'Bimetallic' £2 'Jane Austen', 50 pence 'Sir Isaac Newton', gold proofs (Issued: 99)	(5) 7500
PGCS28–**MD**	£1 (J38 and J39) gold proofs (Issued: 100)......	(2) 2150
PGCS29–**2018**	Commemorative Proof set, 5th Birthday Prince George £5, 'Bimetallic' £2 'Royal Air Force Badge', 'Bimetallic' £2 'Frankenstein', 'Bimetallic' £2 'Armistice' 50 pence 'Representation of People Act', gold proofs (Issued: 139)	(5) 6500
PGCS32–**2019**	British Culture 50p (H62-H66) gold proofs (Issued: 71)	(5) 6000
PGCS33–**2019**	British Culture 50p (H62-H66) gold piedfort proofs (Issued: 50)......	(5) 9000
PGCS34–**2019**	Military 50p (H67-H71) gold proofs (Issued: 75)	(5) 5500
PGCS35–**2019**	Military 50p (H67-H71) gold piedfort proofs (Issued: 44)......	(5) 9000
PGCS36–**2019**	Commemorative Proof set, 200th Anniversary of the birth of Queen Victoria £5, 'Bimetallic' £2 '75th Anniversary of D-Day', 'Bimetallic' '£2 'Wedgwood', 'Bimetallic' £2 'Samuel Pepys' 50 pence 'Sherlock Holmes' gold proofs (Issued: 88)	.(5) 6500
PGCS37–**2020**	Commemorative Proof set. George III £5, 'Bimetallic' £2 'VE Day', 'Bimetallic' £2 'Mayflower', 'Bimetallic' £2 'Agatha Christie', 50 pence 'Team GB' gold proofs. (Edition: 75)......	(5) 8000

£

PGCS37A–MD	£2 Captain Cook (2018-K47) (2019-K58) (2020-K62) gold proofs (Edition: ??)...	(3)	3500
PGCS38–**2021**	Commemorative Proof set. Queen's Birthday £5, 'Bimetallic' £2 'Scott', 'Bimetallic' £2 'Wells', 50p 'Decimal Day', 50p 'Baird'. (Edition: 95).....	(5)	7500
PGCS39–**2022**	Commemorative Proof set. Platinum Jubilee £5, 'Bimetallic' £2 'Vera Lynn', 'Bimetallic' £2 'Bell', 50p 'Platinum Jubilee', 50p 'Commonwealth Games' gold proofs. (Edition: 100)..	(5)	·7500
PGCS40–**2022**	50p Platinum Jubilee (H103 & H103A) gold proofs (Edition: 70)..............	(2)	2500
PGCS41–**2022**	Queen Elizabeth II memorial set. £2 to 1p with privy mark displaying Her Majesty's birth year and the year of her passing, together with King Charles III 50p and £5 crown gold proofs. (Edition: 200)	(10)	10715

Proof Sets in Platinum

PPLS1–**2008**	'Emblems of Britain', 'UK' £1, 'Britannia' 50 pence and 20 pence to 1p (Issued: 250)...	(7)	3000
PPLS2–**2008**	'The Royal Shield of Arms', 'Royal Shield' £1 to 1p (Issued: 184)............	(7)	3000
PPLS3–**2015**	Two portraits set, 2 x £2-1p (Issued: 10)	(14)	14000
PPLS4–**2022**	Commemorative Proof set. Platinum Jubilee £5, 'Bimetallic' £2 'Vera Lynn', 'Bimetallic' £2 'Bell', 50p 'Platinum Jubilee', 50p 'Commonwealth Games 'platinum proofs. (Edition: 30)	(5)	10000
PPLS5–**2022**	Queen Elizabeth II memorial set. £2 to 1p with privy mark displaying Her Majesty's birth year and the year of her passing, together with King Charles III 50p and £5 crown platinum proofs. (Edition: 96).............	(10)	13645

Arnold Machin portrait

	½p.	1p	2p	5p	10p	20p	50p	£1.00
1968				98,868,250	336,143,250			
1969				120,270,000	314,008,000		188,400,000	
1970				225,948,525	133,571,000		19,461,500	
1971	1,394,188,250	1,521,666,250	1,454,856,250	81,783,475	63,205,000			
1972	No coins were issued into circulation with 1972 date							
1973	365,680,000	280,196,000			152,174,000			
1974	365,448,000	330,892,000			92,741,000			
1975	197,600,000	221,604,000	145,545,000	141,539,000	181,559,000			
1976	412,172,000	300,160,000	181,379,000		228,220,000		43,746,500	
1977	66,368,000	285,430,000	109,281,000	24,308,000	59,323,000		49,536,000	
1978	59,532,000	292,770,000	189,658,000	61,094,000			72,005,500	
1979	219,132,000	459,000,000	260,200,000	155,456,000	115,457,000		58,680,000	
1980	202,788,000	416,304,000	408,527,000	220,566,000	88,650,000		89,086,000	
1981	46,748,000	301,800,000	353,191,000		3,487,000		74,002,000	
1982	190,752,000	100,292,000				740,815,000	51,312,000	
1983	7,600,000	243,002,000				158,463,000	62,824,904	443,053,510
1984	#	154,759,625				65,350,965		146,256,501

Raphael Maklouf portrait

	1p	2p	5p	10p	20p	50p	£1.00	£2.00
1985	200,605,245	107,113,000			74,273,699	682,103	228,430,749	
1986	369,989,130	168,967,500					10,409,501	
1987	499,946,000	218,100,750	48,220,000		137,450,000		39,298,502	
1988	793,492,000	419,889,000	120,744,610		38,038,344		7,118,825	
1989	658,142,000	359,226,000	101,406,000		132,013,890		70,580,501	
1990	529,047,500	204,499,700	1,634,976,005		88,097,500		97,269,302	
1991	206,457,600	86,625,250	724,979,000		35,901,250		38,443,575	
1992	253,867,000	102,247,000	453,173,500	1,413,455,170	31,205,000		36,320,487	
1993	602,590,000	235,674,000			123,123,750		114,744,500	
1994	843,834,000	531,628,000	93,602,000		67,131,250		29,752,525	
1995	303,314,000	124,482,000	183,384,000	43,259,000	102,005,000		34,503,501	
1996	723,840,060	296,278,000	302,902,000	118,738,000	83,163,750		89,886,000	
1997	396,874,000	496,116,000	236,596,000	99,196,000	89,518,750	456,364,100	57,117,450	13,734,625

Numbers exclude coins issued in sets.

 # An unknown quantity of 1984 ½p coins were issued to the Royal Mint's then USA sales agent and many of these subsequently returned to the UK trade.

Ian Rank-Broadley portrait

	1p	2p	5p	10p	20p	50p	£1.00	£2.00
1998	739,770,000	98,676,000	217,376,000		76,965,000	64,306,500		91,110,375
cps		115,154,000						
1999	891,392,000	353,816,000	195,490,000		73,478,750	24,905,000		33,719,000
2000	1,060,420,000	536,659,000	388,512,000	134,733,000	136,428,750	27,915,500	109,496,500	25,770,000
2001	928,698,000	551,880,000	337,930,000	129,281,000	148,122,500	84,998,500	63,968,065	34,984,750
2002	601,446,000	168,556,000	219,258,000	80,934,000	93,360,000	23,907,500	77,818,000	13,024,750
2003	539,436,000	260,225,000	333,230,000	88,118,000	153,383,750	23,583,000	61,596,500	17,531,250
2004	739,764,000	356,396,000	271,810,000	99,602,000	120,212,500	35,315,500	39,162,000	11,981,500
2005	536,318,000	280,396,000	236,212,000	69,604,000	124,488,750	25,363,500	99,429,500	3,837,250
2006	524,605,000	170,637,000	317,697,000	118,803,000	114,800,000	24,567,000	38,038,000	16,715,000
2007	548,002,000	254,500,000	246,720,000	72,720,000	117,075,000	11,200,000	26,180,160	10,270,000
2008	180,600,000	10,600,000	92,880,000	9,720,000	11,900,000	3,500,000	3,910,000	30,107,000

Matthew Dent reverses

	1p	2p	5p	10p	20p	50p	£1.00	£2.00
2008	507,952,000	241,679,000	165,172,000	71,447,000	115,022,000	22,747,000	43,827,300	
2009	556,412,800	150,500,500	132,960,300	84,360,000	121,625,300		27,625,600	8,775,000
2010	609,603,000	99,600,000	396,245,500	96,600,500	112,875,500		57,120,000	6,890,000
2011	431,004,000	144,300,000	50,400,000	59,603,850	191,625,000		25,415,000	24,375,030
2012	227,201,000	67,800,000	339,802,350	11,600,030	69,650,030	32,300,030	35,700,030	3,900,000
2013	260,800,000	40,600,000	378,800,750	320,200,750	66,325,000	10,301,000	13,090,500	15,860,250
2014	464,801,520	247,600,020	885,004,520	490,202,020	173,775,000	49,001,000	79,305,200	18,200,000
2015	154,600,000	85,900,000	163,000,000	119,000,000	63,175,000	20,101,000	29,580,000	35,360,058

Jody Clark portrait

	1p	2p	5p	10p	20p	50p	£1.00	£2.00
2015	418,201,016	139,200,000	536,600,000	91,900,000	131,250,000	39,300,000	129,616,985	650,000
2016	368,482,000	185,600,000	305,740,000	135,380,000	212,625,000		648,936,536	2,925,000
2017	240,990,600	16,600,000	220,515,000	33,300,000		1,800,000	749,616,200	
2018							130,560,000	
2019			92,800,000		125,125,000	122,000,000	138,635,000	
2020	88,071,910		49,200,000	45,347,846	32,725,000	46,540,375	55,840,169	
2021	56,000,000	117,700,000	28,000,000	71,200,000	19,600,000		21,760,000	6,045,000
2022	30,000,000		42,800,000	38,000,000	42,875,000	9,500,000	7,735,000	4,030,000

Numbers exclude coins issued in sets.

25p (Crown)

Cat. No.	Year	Description	Qty. Issued	Cat. No.	Year	Description	Qty. Issued
LL1	1972	Silver Wedding	7,452,100	LL3	1980	Queen Mother	9,306,000
LL2	1977	Silver Jubilee	37,061,160	LL4	1981	Royal Wedding	26,773,600

50p

Cat. No.	Year	Description	Qty. Issued	Cat. No.	Year	Description	Qty. Issued
H2	1973	EEC	89,775,000	LO20	2011	Sailing	1,749,500
H5	1992	EC Presidency	109,000	LO21	2011	Shooting	1,656,500
H6	1994	D-Day Landings	6,705,520	LO22	2011	Table tennis	1,737,500
H9	1998	EU	5,043,000	LO23	2011	Taekwondo	1,664,000
H10	1998	NHS	5,001,000	LO24	2011	Tennis	1,454,000
H11	2000	Library	11,263,000	LO25	2011	Triathlon	1,163,500
H12	2003	Suffragettes	3,124,030	LO26	2011	Volleyball	2,133,500
H13	2004	R Bannister	9,032,500	LO27	2011	Weightlifting	1,879,500
H14	2005	Johnson's Dictionary	17,649,000	LO28	2011	Wheelchair rugby	1,765,500
H15	2006	VC - The Award	12,087,000	LO29	2011	Wrestling	1,129,500
H16	2006	VC - Heroic Acts	10,000,500	H35	2011	WWF	3,400,000
H17	2007	Scouting	7,710,750	H36	2013	Ironside	7,000,000
H19	2009	Kew Gardens	210,000	H37	2013	Benjamin Britten	5,300,000
H34	2010	Girl Guides	7,410,090	H38	2014	Commonwealth Games	6,500,000
LO1	2011	Athletics	2,224,000	H39A	2015	Battle of Britain	5,900,000
LO2	2011	Aquatics	2,179,000	H41	2016	Battle of Hastings	6,700,000
LO3	2011	Archery	3,345,500	H42	2016	Beatrix Potter	6,900,000
LO4	2011	Badminton	2,133,500	H43	2016	Peter Rabbit	9,700,000
LO5	2011	Basketball	1,748,000	H44	2016	Jemima Puddle Duck	2,100,000
LO6	2011	Boccia	2,166,000	H45	2016	Squirrel Nutkin	5,000,000
LO7	2011	Boxing	2,148,500	H46	2016	Miss Tiggie Winkle	8,800,000
LO8	2011	Canoeing	2,166,500	H47	2016	Team GB	6,400,000
LO9	2011	Cycling	2,090,500	H48	2017	Isaac Newton	1,801,500
LO10	2011	Equestrian	2,142,500	H49	2017	Benjamin Bunny	25,000,000
LO11	2011	Fencing	2,115,500	H50	2017	Jeremy Fisher	9,900,000
LO12	2011	Football	1,125,500	H51	2017	Tom Kitten	9,500,000
LO13	2011	Goalball	1,615,500	H52	2017	Peter Rabbit	19,900,000
LO14	2011	Gymnastics	1,720,813	H53	2018	Peter Rabbit	1,400,000
LO15	2011	Handball	1,676,500	H54	2018	Flopsy Bunny	1,400,000
LO16	2011	Hockey	1,773,500	H55	2018	Miss Tittlemouse	1,700,000
LO17	2011	Judo	1,161,500	H56	2018	Tailor of Gloucester	3,900,000
LO18	2011	Modern Pentathlon	1,689,500	H57	2018	Representation of People	9,000,000
LO19	2011	Rowing	1,717,300				

50p (continued)

Cat. No.	Year	Description	Qty. Issued	Cat. No.	Year	Description	Qty. Issued
H58	2018	Paddington at Station	5,001,000	H76	2019	Paddington at St Paul's	9,001,000
H59	2018	Paddington at Palace	5,901,000	H81	2020	Brexit	10,001,000
H61	2019	Sherlock Holmes	8,602,000	H90	2020	Diversity	10,300,000
H75	2019	Paddington at Tower	9,001,000	H103A	2022	Platinum Jubilee	5,000,070
H76	2019	Paddington at St Paul's	9,001,000	H107	2022	Pride	5,000,000

£1

Cat. No.	Year	Description	No. Issue	Cat. No.	Year	Description	No. Issue
J28	2010	London	2,635,000	J32	2013	England	5,270,000
J29	2010	Belfast	6,205,000	J33	2013	Wales	5,270,000
J30	2011	Edinburgh	935,000	J34	2014	N Ireland	5,780,000
J31	2011	Cardiff	1,615,000	J35	2014	Scotland	5,185,000

£2

Cat. No.	Year	Description	No. Issue	Cat. No.	Year	Description	No. Issue
K1	1986	Commonwealth Games	8,212,184	LO31	2008	Olympic Flag Handover	918,000
K2	1989	Bill of Rights	4,392,825	K24	2009	Burns	3,253,000
K3	1989	Claim of Right	381,400	K25	2009	Darwin	3,903,000
K4	1994	Bank of England	1,443,116	K26	2010	Florence Nightingale	6,175,000
K5	1995	Peace	4,394,566	K27	2011	Mary Rose	1,040,000
K6	1995	United Nations	1,668,575	K28	2011	King James Bible	975,000
K7	1996	Euro Football	5,141,350	K29	2012	Charles Dickens	8,190,000
K10	1999	Rugby Football	4,933,000	LO32	2012	Rio Handover	845,000
K11	2001	Marconi	4,558,000	K30	2013	Guinea	2,990,000
K12	2002	Games-England	650,500	K31	2013	Tube-roundel	1,560,000
K13	2002	Games - N Ireland	485,500	K32	2013	Tube-train	1,690,000
K14	2002	Games - Scotland	771,750	K33	2014	Trinity House	3,705,000
K15	2002	Games - Wales	588,500	K34	2014	WWI-Kitchener	5,720,000
K16	2003	DNA	4,299,000	K35	2015	WWI-Navy	650,000
K17	2004	Steam locomotive	5,004,500	K36	2015	Magna Carta	1,495,000
K18	2005	Gunpowder Plot	5,140,500	K38	2016	Shakespeare-Comedies	4,355,000
K19	2005	60th Anniv. End of WWII	10,191,000	K39	2016	Shakespeare - Histories	5,655,000
K20	2006	Brunel - The Man	7,928,250	K40	2016	Shakespeare-Tragedies	4,615,000
K21	2006	Brunel - Achievements	7,452,250	K41	2016	WWI-Army	9,500,000
K22	2007	Act of Union	7,545,000	K42	2016	Great Fire of London	1,625,000
K23	2007	Slavery	8,445,000				
LO30	2008	Centenary 1908 Olympics	910,000				

No £2 commemoratives have been issued for circulation since 2016.

£5

Cat. No.	Year	Description	No. Issue
L1	1990	Queen Mother	2,761,431
L2	1993	Coronation Anniversary	1,834,655
L3	1996	Queen's 70th Birthday	2,396,100
L4	1997	Golden Wedding	1,733,000
L5	1998	Prince Charles	1,407,300
L6	1999	Princess Diana)	5,396,300
L7	1999	Millennium }	3,147,092
	2000	Millennium }	
L8	2000	Queen Mother)	
L9	2001	Queen Victoria	851,491
L10	2002	Golden Jubilee)	3,469,243
L11	2002	Queen Mother)	

Cat. No.	Year	Description	No. Issue
L12	2003	Coronation Anniversary	1,307,147
L13	2004	Entende Cordiale	1,205,594
L14	2005	Trafalgar)	1,075,516
L15	2005	Nelson)	
L16	2006	Queen's 80th Birthday	52,267
L17	2007	Diamond Wedding	30,561
L18	2008	Elizabeth I	20,047
L19	2008	Prince Charles	14,088
L20	2009	Henry VIII	
L21	2010	Restoration of the Monarchy	

No £5 commemoratives have been issued for circulation since 2010.

The gold sovereign with a denomination of £1 in its present specification dates back to 1817 and so is the oldest UK coin still being issued with a heritage dating back to 1489. The outbreak of WWI in 1914 saw the sovereign and the half sovereign disappear from daily use, being replaced by banknotes. Since then these coins have become mainly bullion pieces trading at small premiums over their gold content although there are some interesting variations and some scarcer dates. Benedetto Pistrucci's famous St. George slaying the dragon reverse design first introduced in 1817 has been continued on almost all coins in this series although there are some modern interpretations of this design on the 2005 and 2012 issues. The 500th anniversary of the sovereign was commemorated in 1989 with designs reminiscent of the 1489 originals.

Following decimalisation, sovereigns for bullion use were issued between 1974 and 1982 with a half sovereign appearing in 1982. The first proof in the decimal series was issued in 1979 and half sovereigns were added to the range in 1980, the same year as the first four coin proof set containing a £5, £2, £1 and £1/2 sovereign. In 2000 the Royal Mint recommenced annual issues of bullion sovereigns and halves with the first ever quarter sovereign released in 2009. Prices for cased sets can now be found immediately after the £5 (five sovereign) listings.

In more recent years limited issues of BU sovereigns have been struck on the day of a particular event or anniversary and some of these have added privy marks or other notable differences from the basic type thus making the gold sovereign issues a much more interesting and collectable series. For clarity we have provided full details of the Struck-on-the-Day sovereigns with SSD numbers following the listing of the cased sets. There were also half sovereigns and £2 pieces "struck on the day" in 2012 & 2013 in sets and these appear at the end of the sets listing.

The earlier non-proof coins issued as bullion coins are UNC standard but in 2013 following the opening by the Royal Mint of a separate bullion department which continued to issue UNC coins, the mint also issued some coins in brilliant uncirculated condition referred to as BU and some of these coins have quite low mintages.

Prices for single proof coins relate to coins in original case with Royal Mint certificate. Single coins just in capsules from split up sets can usually be found in the market at lower prices.

Mintages: Numbers issued for coins sold individually are shown alongside each coin. Many coins were also sold within sets, some of which will have subsequently been broken up. A table showing details of these can be found at the end of this section. There are some gaps in these figures which we hope to update as more information becomes available from the Royal Mint. There are a few instances where the sales figures announced by the Royal Mint slightly exceed the authorised mintage! We will endeavour to check the accuracy of these numbers. There are also a number of instances in recent years where the Royal Mint has announced a sell-out and yet later published sales figures have fallen slightly short of the maximum mintage.

Gold Sovereign Series Specifications

Denomination	Metal	Weight	Diameter
¼ Sovereign	0.9166 Gold	1.997 g	13.50 mm
½ Sovereign	0.9166 Gold	3.99 g	19.30 mm
Sovereign	0.9166 Gold	7.98 g	22.05 mm
£2	0.9166 Gold	15.976 g	28.40 mm
£5	0.9166 Gold	39.94 g	36.02 mm

QUARTER SOVEREIGN

Obverse portrait by Ian Rank-Broadley

SA1   SA2

SA1   Quarter sovereign. R. The image of St George armed, sitting on horseback, attacking the dragon with a sword, and a broken spear upon the ground, and the date of the year in the exergue. (Reverse design: Benedetto Pistrucci.)

2009 Unc (Edition: 50,000) £130
—   Proof in gold *FDC* (Issued: 11,745 plus coins in sets) £150
2010 Unc (Issued: 8,985)...£130
—   Proof in gold *FDC* (Issued: 4,546 plus coins in sets)...........................£150
2011 Unc (Edition: 50,000) £130
—   Proof in gold *FDC* (Issued: 6,736 plus coins in sets)...........................£150
2013 BU (Issued:1,729)...£180
—   Proof in gold *FDC* (Issued: 1,696 plus coins in sets)...........................£200
2014 Proof in gold *FDC* (Issued: 1,886 plus coins in sets)..............................£200
2015 Proof in gold *FDC* (Issued: 1,808 plus coins in sets)..............................£200

SA2   Quarter sovereign. R. The image of St George on horseback, attacking the dragon with a lance, with date of the year to the left. (Reverse design: Paul Day.)

2012 Unc £150
—   BU (Issued: 137) £180
—   Proof in gold *FDC* (Issued: 7,579 plus coins in sets)...........................£250

Obverse portrait by Jody Clark

SA3

SA3   Quarter sovereign. R. St George and dragon as SA1.

2015 Proof in gold *FDC* (Issued: 550 plus coins in sets) £200
2019 Proof in gold *FDC* (Issued: 1,312 plus coins in sets) £200

SA3A Quarter sovereign. R. As SA3 but with commemorative privy mark '65'.

2018 Proof in gold *FDC* (Issued: 1,321 plus coins in sets) £200

SA3B Quarter sovereign. R. As SA3 but with George III Royal Cypher on the reverse.

2020 Proof in gold *FDC* * £200

SA3C Quarter Sovereign. R. As SA3 but with '95'crown privy mark on the reverse.

2021 Proof in gold *FDC* *...£200

Obverse portrait by James Butler

SA4

SA4   Quarter sovereign. R. St George and dragon as SA1.

2016 Proof in gold *FDC* (Issued: 1,727 plus coins in sets)............................£250

* Coins marked thus were originally issued in Royal Mint sets.

Obverse portrait by Jody Clark

SA5   SA6

SA5 **Quarter sovereign.** R. The image of St George armed, sitting on horseback, attacking the
dragon with a broken spear surrounded by the inscription 'HONI SOIT QUI MAL Y PENSE'.
2017 Proof in gold *FDC* (Issued: 2,495 plus coins in sets)..£300
SA6 **Quarter Sovereign.** R. As SC12.
2022 Unc £140
—   Proof in gold FDC * £250

HALF SOVEREIGN

Obverse portrait by Arnold Machin

SB1

SB1 **Half sovereign.** R. The image of St George armed, sitting on horseback, attacking the
dragon with a sword, and a broken spear upon the ground, and the date of the year.
(Reverse design: Benedetto Pistrucci.)
1980 Proof in gold *FDC* (Issued: 76,700 plus coins in sets) £300
1982 Unc £250
—   Proof in gold *FDC* (Issued: 19,090 plus coins in sets) £300
1983 Proof in gold *FDC* (Issued: 19,710)**..£300
1984 Proof in gold *FDC* (Issued: 12,410 plus coins in sets) £300

Obverse portrait by Raphael Maklouf

SB2

SB2 **Half sovereign.** R. St. George and dragon as SB1.
1985 Proof in gold *FDC* (Issued: 9,951 plus coins in sets) £300
1986 Proof in gold *FDC* (Issued: 4,575 plus coins in sets) £300
1987 Proof in gold *FDC* (Issued: 8,187 plus coins in sets) £300
1988 Proof in gold *FDC* (Issued: 7,074 plus coins in sets) £300
1990 Proof in gold *FDC* (Issued: 4,231 plus coins in sets) £350
1991 Proof in gold *FDC* (Issued: 3,588 plus coins in sets) £350
1992 Proof in gold *FDC* (Issued: 3,783 plus coins in sets) £400
1993 Proof in gold *FDC* (Issued: 2,910 plus coins in sets) £400
1994 Proof in gold *FDC* (Issued: 5,000 plus coins in sets) £350
1995 Proof in gold *FDC* (Issued: 4,900 plus coins in sets) £350
1996 Proof in gold *FDC* (Issued: 5,730 plus coins in sets) £350
1997 Proof in gold *FDC* (Issued: 7,500 plus coins in sets) £350

*** Numbers include coins sold in sets.*

SB3

SB3 **Half sovereign.** 500th Anniversary of Sovereign.O. Her Majesty Queen Elizabeth II at her Coronation, seated in King Edward's Chair and having received the Sceptre with the Cross and the Rod with the Dove, all within the circumscription 'ELIZABETH. II.DEI.GRA. REG.FID.DEF'. R. A Shield of the Royal Arms ensigned by an open Royal Crown, the whole superimposed upon a double Rose, with the circumscription 'ANNIVERSARY OF THE GOLD SOVEREIGN 1489-1989'. (Designs: Bernald Sindall.)
1989 Proof in gold *FDC* (Issued: 8,888 plus coins in sets) £750

Obverse portrait by Ian Rank-Broadley

SB4   SB5   SB6

SB4 **Half sovereign.** R. St.George and dragon as SB1.
1998 Proof in gold *FDC* (Issued: 6,147 plus coins in sets) £350
1999 Proof in gold *FDC* (Issued: 7,500 plus coins in sets) £350
2000 Unc (Issued: 146,822) £240
— Proof in gold *FDC* (Issued: 7,458 plus coins in sets) £300
2001 Unc (Issued: 94,763)..£240
— Proof in gold *FDC* (Issued: 4,596 plus coins in sets) £300
2003 Unc (Issued: 47,818) £240
— Proof in gold *FDC* (Issued: 4,868 plus coins in sets) £300
2004 Unc (Issued: 34,924) £240
— Proof in gold *FDC* (Issued: 4,446 plus coins in sets) £300
2006 Unc £240
— Proof in gold *FDC* (Issued: 4,173 plus coins in sets) £300
2007 Unc (Edition: 75,000)..£240
— Proof in gold *FDC* (Issued: 2,442 plus coins in sets) £300
2008 Unc (Edition: 75,000)...£240
— Proof in gold *FDC* (Issued: 2,465 plus coins in sets) £300

SB5 **Half sovereign** R. The Shield of Arms of The United Kingdom of Great Britain and Northern Ireland within an open wreath of laurel and ensigned by The Royal Crown and beneath the date of the year. (Reverse design: Timothy Noad.)
2002 Unc (Issued: 61,347) £275
— Proof in gold *FDC* (Issued: 10,000 plus coins in sets) £400

SB6 **Half sovereign.** R. A depiction of St George, carrying a shield and a sword, slaying the dragon, with the date '2005' beneath the wing of the dragon. (Reverse design: Timothy Noad.)
2005 Unc (Issued: 30,299) £275
— Proof in gold *FDC* (Issued: 5,011 plus coins in sets) £400

SB7   SB8

SB7 **Half sovereign.** R. St George. Based on the original design of 1893 with reduced
ground below design and larger exergue with no BP initials
2009 Unc (Edition: 50,000)...£240
— Proof in gold *FDC* (Issued: 2,996 plus coins in sets)...£300
2010 Unc (Issued: 16,485) £240
— Proof in gold *FDC* (Issued: 3,351 plus coins in sets)...£300
SB7A Half sovereign. R. As SB7 but with BP initials.
2011 Unc (Edition: 50,000)...£240
— Proof in gold *FDC* (Issued 4,259 plus coins in sets)..£300
2013 BU (Issued: 1,051 plus coins in sets) £325
— Proof in gold *FDC* (Issued: 1,863 plus coins in sets)...£400
2014 BU (Issued: 672) £325
— Proof in gold *FDC* (Issued: 1,367 plus coins in sets)...£400
2015 BU (Issued: 500) £325
— Proof in gold *FDC* (Issued: 1,704 plus coins in sets)...£400
SB7B Half sovereign. R. St George as SB7A above but with 'I' mint mark on reverse for coins
struck in India.
2014 BU (Issued: 62,000)..£450
SB8 **Half sovereign.** R. The image of St George on horseback, attacking the dragon with
a lance, with date of the year to the left. (Reverse design: Paul Day.)
2012 Unc £300
— BU (Issued: 2,137 plus coins in sets) £350
— Proof in gold *FDC* (Issued: 2,303 plus coins in sets)...£750

Obverse portrait by Jody Clark

SB9 **Half Sovereign.** R. St George and dragon as SB7A.
2015 Proof in gold *FDC** £400
2016 Unc £240
— BU (Issued: 472) £325
2018 Unc £240
2019 Unc £240
— Proof in gold *FDC* (Issued: 1,523 plus coins in sets)...£300
2020 Unc £240
2021 Unc £240
SB9A Half Sovereign. As SB9 but with 200th Anniversary privy mark on the reverse.
2017 Unc £275
SB9B Half sovereign. R. As SB9 but with commemorative privy mark '65'.
2018 Proof in gold *FDC* (Issued: 1,878 plus coins in sets)..£350
SB9C Half sovereign. R. As SB9 but with George III Royal Cypher on the reverse.
2020 Proof in gold *FDC* (Edition: 2,500 plus coins in sets) £350
SB9D Half Sovereign. R. As SB9 but with '95'crown privy mark on the reverse.
2021 Proof in gold *FDC* (Edition: 1,500 plus coins in sets) £350

* *Coins marked thus were originally issued in Royal Mint sets.*

Obverse portrait by James Butler

SB10

SB10 Half sovereign. ℞. St George and dragon.
2016 Proof in gold *FDC* (Issued: 1,995 plus coins in sets)...£550

Obverse portrait by Jody Clark

SB11   SB12

SB11 Half sovereign. ℞. The image of St George armed, sitting on horseback, attacking the
dragon with a sword surrounded by the inscription 'HONI SOIT QUI MAL Y PENSE'.
2017 Proof in gold *FDC* (Issued: 2,492 plus coins in sets)..£550
SB12 Half Sovereign. ℞. As SC12.
2022 Unc £225
— Proof in gold *FDC* (Edition: 2,000 plus coins in sets) £500

SOVEREIGN

Obverse portrait by Arnold Machin

SC1

SC1 Sovereign. ℞. The image of St George armed, sitting on horseback, attacking the
dragon with a sword, and a broken spear upon the ground, and the date of the year.
(Reverse design: Benedetto Pistrucci.)
1974 Unc £400
1976 Unc £400
1976 VIP Proof in gold *FDC* ....*Extremely rare*
1978 Unc £400
1979 Unc £400
— Proof in gold *FDC* (Issued: 50,000)..£500
1980 Unc £400
— Proof in gold *FDC* (Issued: 81,200 plus coins in sets) £450
1981 Unc £400
— Proof in gold *FDC* (Issued: 32,960 plus coins in sets) £450
1982 Unc £400
— Proof in gold *FDC* (Issued: 20,000 plus coins in sets) £450
1983 Proof in gold *FDC* (Issued: 21,250)**..£500
1984 Proof in gold *FDC* (Issued: 12,880 plus coins in sets) £500

*** Numbers include coins sold in sets.*

Obverse portrait by Raphael Maklouf

SC2   SC3

SC2 Sovereign. R. St. George and dragon as SC1.
1985 Proof in gold *FDC* (Issued: 11,393 plus coins in sets)......................................£650
1986 Proof in gold *FDC* (Issued: 5,079 plus coins in sets)...£650
1987 Proof in gold *FDC* (Issued: 9,979 plus coins in sets)...£650
1988 Proof in gold *FDC* (Issued: 7,670 plus coins in sets)...£650
1990 Proof in gold *FDC* (Issued: 4,767 plus coins in sets)...£700
1991 Proof in gold *FDC* (Issued: 4,713 plus coins in sets)...£700
1992 Proof in gold *FDC* (Issued: 4,722 plus coins in sets)...£800
1993 Proof in gold *FDC* (Issued: 4,349 plus coins in sets)...£800
1994 Proof in gold *FDC* (Issued: 4,998 plus coins in sets)...£700
1995 Proof in gold *FDC* (Issued: 7,500 plus coins in sets)...£700
1996 Proof in gold *FDC* (Issued: 7,500 plus coins in sets)...£700
1997 Proof in gold *FDC* (Issued: 7,500 plus coins in sets)...£700

SC3 Sovereign. 500th Anniversary of Sovereign. O. Her Majesty Queen Elizabeth II at her
Coronation, seated in King Edward's Chair and having received the Sceptre with
the Cross and the Rod with the Dove, all within the circumscription 'ELIZABETH.II.
DEI.GRA.REG.FID.DEF'. R. A Shield of the Royal Arms ensigned by an open Royal
Crown, the whole superimposed upon a double Rose, with the circumscription
'ANNIVERSARY OF THE GOLD SOVEREIGN 1489-1989'. (Designs: Bernald Sindall.)
1989 Proof in gold *FDC* (Issued: 10,535 plus coins in sets) £2000

Obverse portrait by Ian Rank-Broadley

SC4

SC4 Sovereign. R. St.George and dragon as SC1.
1998 Proof in gold *FDC* (Issued: 10,000 plus coins in sets)......................................£600
1999 Proof in gold *FDC* (Issued: 10,000 plus coins in sets)......................................£550
2000 Unc (Issued: 129,069) £420
—   Proof in gold *FDC* (Issued: 9,909 plus coins in sets)......................................£500
2001 Unc (Issued: 49,462) £420
—   Proof in gold *FDC* (Issued: 8,915 plus coins in sets)......................................£500
2003 Unc (Issued: 43,230) £420
—   Proof in gold *FDC* (Issued: 12,433 plus coins in sets)....................................£500
2004 Unc (Issued: 30,688) £420
—   Proof in gold *FDC* (Issued: 10,175 plus coins in sets)....................................£500
2006 Unc £420
—   Proof in gold *FDC* (Issued: 9,195 plus coins in sets)......................................£500

2007 Unc (Edition: 75,000)..£420
—   Proof in gold *FDC* (Issued: 8,199 plus coins in sets)...........................£500
2008 Unc (Edition: 75,000)..£420
—   Proof in gold *FDC* (Issued: 7,735 plus coins in sets)...........................£500

SC5   SC6

SC5 **Sovereign** R. The Shield of Arms of The United Kingdom of Great Britain and Northern Ireland within an open wreath of laurel and ensigned by The Royal Crown and beneath the date of the year. (Reverse design: Timothy Noad.)
2002 Unc (Issued: 75,264) £500
—   Proof in gold *FDC* (Issued: 12,500 plus coins in sets).........................£800
SC6 **Sovereign** R. A depiction of St George, carrying a shield and a sword, slaying the dragon, with the date '2005' beneath the wing of the dragon. (Reverse design: Timothy Noad.)
2005 Unc (Issued: 45,542) £500
—   Proof in gold *FDC* (Issued: 12,500 plus coins in sets).........................£750

SC7

SC7 **Sovereign.** R. St George, based on the design of 1821 with the plumed helmet without its streamer.
2009 Unc (Edition: 75,000)..£420
—   Proof in gold *FDC* (Issued: 7,354 plus coins in sets)...........................£500
2010 Unc (Issued: 243,986) £420
—   Proof in gold *FDC* (Issued: 6,809 plus coins in sets)...........................£500
2011 Unc (Edition: 250,000)..£420
—   Proof in gold *FDC* (Issued: 7,181 plus coins in sets)...........................£500
2013 Unc £420
—   BU (Issued: 2,695 plus coins in sets & SSD2 & 3)...............................£450
—   Proof in gold *FDC* (Issued: 8,243 plus coins in sets)...........................£500
2014 Unc £420
—   BU (Issued: 1,000 plus SSD4) £500
—   Proof in gold *FDC* (Issued: 3,263 plus coins in sets)...........................£700
2015 Unc £420
—   BU (Issued: 890 plus SSD5) £500
—   Proof in gold *FDC* (Issued: 4,546 plus coins in sets)...........................£600

The BU coins issued from 2014 onwards have much sharper detail and (except for the matt finish pieces) most have a prooflike reverse compared with the bullion unc versions.

SC7A Sovereign. As SC7 but with 'I' mint mark on reverse for coins struck in India.
2013 BU(Issued: 94,790) £550
2014 BU (Issued: 60,471) £550
2015 BU (Issued: 64,500) £600
For further details of SSD 'Struck on the Day' coins, see after the listing of the sets.

SC8

SC8   Sovereign. R. The image of St George on horseback attacking the dragon with a lance, with date of the year to the left. (Reverse design: Paul Day.)

2012 Unc £450

— BU (Issued: 4,559 plus coins in sets & SSD1) £450

— Proof in gold *FDC* (Issued: 5,501 plus coins in sets) £1500

Obverse portrait by Jody Clark

SC9

SC9   Sovereign. R. St George and dragon as SC7.

2015 BU (see SSD6) £700

— Proof in gold *FDC* (Issued: 7,494 plus coins in sets)...£600

2016 Unc £425

— BU (Issued: 1,251 plus SSD7) £450

2017 BU (See SSD8 & 10) £425

2018 Unc £420

2019 Unc £420

— BU matt (Issued: 1,514) £450

— Proof in gold *FDC* (Issued: 9,538 plus coins in sets)..£550

— Proof in gold piedfort *FDC* (Issued: 656) £1050

2020 Unc £420

2021 Unc £420

SC9A Sovereign. As SC9 but with 'I' mint mark on reverse for coins struck in India.

2016 (Issued: 45,000) £600

2017 BU £600

2018 BU £550

2019 BU £550

2020 BU £550

SC9B Sovereign. As SC9 but with 200th Anniversary privy mark on the reverse.

2017 Unc £450

SC9C Sovereign. As SC9 but with plain edge.

2018 BU (See SSD12)...£750

SC9D Sovereign. As SC9 but with commemorative privy mark 65 on the reverse.

2018 Proof in gold *FDC* (Issued: 10,633 plus coins in sets).....................................£600

— Proof in gold piedfort *FDC* (Issued: 1,930) £1100

SC9E Sovereign. As SC9 but with commemorative privy mark 65 on the reverse and plain edge.

2018 BU (See SSD11)...£750

For further details of SSD 'Struck on the Day' coins, see after the listing of the sets.

SC9F Sovereign. As SC9 but with commemorative privy mark VR on the reverse and plain edge.
  2019 BU Matt (Issued: 649) (See SSD13) £900
SC9G Sovereign. As SC9 but with commemorative privy mark VA on the reverse and
  plain edge.
  2019 BU Matt (Issued: 647) (See SSD14) £800
SC9H Sovereign. As SC9 but with George III Royal Cypher on reverse.
  2020 BU matt (Edition: 12,000)...£450
  —   Proof in gold *FDC* (Edition 7,995 plus coins in sets) £600
SC9J Sovereign. As SC9 but with Crowned Portcullis privy mark 65 on the reverse
  and plain edge.
  2020 BU matt (See SSD15) £900
SC9K Sovereign. As SC9 but with commemorative privy mark VE75 on the reverse
  and plain edge.
  2020 BU matt (See SSD16) £800
SC9L Sovereign. As SC9 but with commemorative privy mark VJ75 on the reverse
  and plain edge.
  2020 BU matt (See SSD17) £800
SC9M Sovereign. As SC9 but with '95'crown privy mark on the reverse. The BU has
  plain edge and the proof has coarser milling of 95 mills on edge to symbolise each year
  of Her Majesty's life.
  2021 BU matt (Edition: 1,295) (See SSD18)...£650
  2021 Proof in gold *FDC* (Edition: 7,995 plus coins in sets) £650

*The Royal Mint issued 100 pieces of the BU coin in a case with a 1926 and 1957 bullion
sovereign.*

Obverse portrait by James Butler

SC10
SC10 Sovereign. R. As SC7.
  2016 Proof in gold *FDC* (Issued: 7,995 plus coins in sets) £1200

Obverse portrait by Jody Clark

SC11   SC12
SC11 Sovereign. R. The image of St George armed, sitting on horseback, attacking the dragon
with a broken spear surrounded by the inscription 'HONI SOIT QUI MAL Y PENSE'.
  2017 Proof in gold *FDC* (Issued: 10,493 plus coins in sets)....................................£1200
  —   Proof in gold piedfort *FDC* (Issued: 3,484) £1750

For further details of SSD 'Struck on the Day' coins, see after the listing of the sets.

SC11ASovereign. ℞. As SC11 but with plain edge
    2017 BU (See SSD9).. £1000
SC12 Sovereign. ℞. A depiction of the Royal Coat of Arms and the date of the year.
    (Reverse design: Timothy Noad.)
    2022 Unc £450
    —   Proof in gold *FDC* (Edition: 10,500 plus coins in sets) £900
    —   Proof piedfort in gold *FDC* (Edition: 3,360)................................... £1250
SC12A Sovereign. ℞. As SC12 but with plain edge.
    —   BU Matt (Edition: 1,200) (See SSD19) £800

TWO POUNDS (DOUBLE SOVEREIGN)

Obverse portrait by Arnold Machin

SD1

SD1   **Two pounds** ℞. The image of St George armed, sitting on horseback, attacking the
    dragon with a sword, and a broken spear upon the ground, and the date of the year.
    (Reverse design: Benedetto Pistrucci.)
    1980 Proof in gold *FDC** £1000
    1982 Proof in gold *FDC**..£1250
    1983 Proof in gold *FDC* (Issued: 12,500) ** £900

Obverse portrait by Raphael Maklouf

SD2

SD2   **Two pounds.** ℞. St. George and dragon as SD1.
    1985 Proof in gold *FDC**..£900
    1987 Proof in gold *FDC* (Issued: 1,801 plus coins in sets)........................£900
    1988 Proof in gold *FDC* (Issued: 1,551 plus coins in sets)........................£900
    1990 Proof in gold *FDC* (Issued: 716 plus coins in sets)...........................£900
    1991 Proof in gold *FDC* (Issued: 620 plus coins in sets)...........................£900
    1992 Proof in gold *FDC* (Issued: 476 plus coins in sets)...........................£900
    1993 Proof in gold *FDC* (Issued: 414 plus coins in sets)...........................£900
    1996 Proof in gold *FDC**..£900

For further details of SSD 'Struck on the Day' coins, see after the listing of the sets.
* Coins marked thus were originally issued in Royal Mint sets.
** Numbers include coins sold in sets

SD3

SD3 **Two pounds.** 500th Anniversary of Sovereign. O. Her Majesty Queen Elizabeth II at her Coronation, seated in King Edward's Chair and having received the Sceptre with the Cross and the Rod with the Dove, all within the circumscription 'ELIZABETH. II.DEI.GRA.REG.FID.DEF'. R. A Shield of the Royal Arms ensigned by an open Royal Crown, the whole superimposed upon a double Rose, with the circumscription 'ANNIVERSARY OF THE GOLD SOVEREIGN 1489-1989' (Designs: Bernald Sindall.)
1989 Proof in gold *FDC* (Issued: 2,000 plus coins in sets).......................................£1750

Obverse portrait by Ian Rank-Broadley

| SD4 | SD5 | SD6 |

SD4 **Two pounds.** R. St. George and dragon as SD1.
1998 Proof in gold *FDC** £1000
2000 Proof in gold *FDC** £900
2003 Proof in gold *FDC** £900
2004 Proof in gold *FDC** £900
2006 Proof in gold *FDC** £900
2007 Proof in gold *FDC** £900
2008 Proof in gold *FDC** £900

SD5 **Two pounds.** R. The Shield of Arms of The United Kingdom of Great Britain and Northern Ireland within an open wreath of laurel and ensigned by The Royal Crown and beneath the date of the year. (Reverse design: Timothy Noad.)
2002 Proof in gold *FDC** £1250
— thin milling (*reported in a number of 3 coin sets*) £1500

SD6 **Two pounds.** R. A depiction of St George, carrying a shield and a sword, slaying the dragon, with the date '2005' beneath the wing of the dragon. (Reverse design: Timothy Noad).
2005 Proof in gold *FDC** £1250

* Coins marked thus were originally issued in Royal Mint sets.

SD7 SD8

SD7 Two pounds. R. St George. Based on the original design of 1820 with greater detail on the dragon.

2009 Proof in gold *FDC** £900
2010 Proof in gold *FDC** £900
2011 Proof in gold *FDC** £900
2013 BU* £900
  — Proof in gold *FDC** £900
2014 BU (Issued: 835) £900
  — Proof in gold *FDC** £900
2015 Proof in gold *FDC** £900

The 2014 £2 BU was issued to celebrate the 1st Birthday of Prince George.

SD8 Two pounds. R. The image of St George on horseback, attacking the dragon with a lance, with date of the year to the left. (Reverse design: Paul Day.)

2012 BU*...£1250
  — Proof in gold *FDC** £1500

Obverse portrait by Jody Clark

SD9 Two pounds. R. St George and dragon as SD7.

2015 Proof in gold *FDC** £1200
2019 Proof in gold *FDC** £900
2020 Unc £900
2021 Unc £900

SD9A Two pounds. R. As SD9 but with commemorative privy mark '65'.

2018 Proof in gold *FDC** £1000

SD9B Two pounds. R. As SD9 but with George III Royal Cypher on the reverse.

2020 Proof in gold *FDC** £1000

SD9C Two pounds. R. As SD9 but with '95' crown privy mark on the reverse.

2021 Proof in gold FDC* £1000

Obverse portrait by James Butler

SD10

SD10 Two pounds. R. St George and dragon.

2016 Proof in gold *FDC**...£1500

* Coins marked thus were originally issued in Royal Mint sets.

Obverse portrait by Jody Clark

SD11 SD12

SD11 Two pounds. ℞. The image of St George armed, sitting on horseback, attacking the dragon with a broken spear surrounded by the inscription 'HONI SOIT QUI MAL Y PENSE'.

2017 Proof in gold *FDC** £1750

SD12 Two pounds. ℞. A depiction of the Royal Coat of Arms and the date of the year.

2022 Unc £900

— Proof in gold *FDC** £1500

FIVE POUNDS (FIVE SOVEREIGN)

Obverse portrait by Arnold Machin

SE1 SE2

SE1 Five pounds. ℞. The image of St George armed, sitting on horseback, attacking the dragon with a sword, and a broken spear upon the ground, and the date of the year. (Reverse design: Benedetto Pistrucci.)

1980 Proof in gold *FDC** £2400

1981 Proof in gold *FDC* (Issued: 3,320 plus coins in sets).................................... £2400

1982 Proof in gold *FDC** £3500

1984 Proof in gold *FDC* (Issued: 905 plus coins in sets)....................................... £2400

SE2 As SE1 but, 'U' in a circle to left of date

1984 BU (Issued: 15,104) £2100

* Coins marked thus were originally issued in Royal Mint sets.

Obverse portrait by Raphael Maklouf

SE3

SE3   **Five pounds.** R. St. George and dragon as SE1.

1985 Proof in gold *FDC* (Issued: 281 plus coins in sets)* £2500
1990 Proof in gold *FDC*...£2500
1991 Proof in gold *FDC*...£2500
1992 Proof in gold *FDC*...£2500
1993 Proof in gold *FDC*...£2500
1994 Proof in gold *FDC*...£2500
1995 Proof in gold *FDC*...£2500
1996 Proof in gold *FDC*...£2500
1997 Proof in gold *FDC*...£2500

SE4   **Five pounds** R. As SE3 but with 'U' in a circle to left of date. (See SE2.)

1985 BU (Issued: 13,626) £2100
1986 BU (Issued: 7,723) £2100
1990 BU (Issued: 1,226) £2100
1991 BU (Issued: 976) £2200
1992 BU (Issued: 797) £2200
1993 BU (Issued: 906) £2200
1994 BU (Issued: 1,000) £2200
1995 BU (Issued: 1,000) £2200
1996 BU (Issued: 901) £2200
1997 BU (Issued: 802) £2200

SE5

SE5   **Five pounds** Uncouped portrait of Queen Elizabeth II. R. St. George,
'U' in a circle to left of date.

1987 BU (Issued: 5,694) £2100
1988 BU (Issued: 3,315) £2100

* Coins marked thus were originally issued in Royal Mint sets.

SE6

SE6 **Five pounds** 500th Anniversary of Sovereign. O. Her Majesty Queen Elizabeth II at her Coronation, seated in King Edward's Chair and having received the Sceptre with the Cross and the Rod with the Dove, all within the circumscription 'ELIZABETH.II.DEI.GRA. REG.FID.DEF'. ℞. A Shield of the Royal Arms ensigned by an open Royal Crown, the whole superimposed upon a double Rose, and with the circumscription 'ANNIVERSARY OF THE GOLD SOVEREIGN 1489-1989' (Designs: Bernald Sindall.)

1989 Proof in gold *FDC**...£4000

SE6A **Five pounds.** As SE6, but with 'U' under the throne on the obverse.

1989 BU (Issued: 2,937) £2800

Obverse portrait by Ian Rank-Broadley

SE7

SE7 **Five pounds.** ℞. St.George and dragon as SE1.

1998 Proof in gold *FDC**	£2500
1999 Proof in gold *FDC**	£2500
2000 Unc (Issued: 4,177)	£2000
— Proof in gold *FDC**	£2400
2001 Proof in gold *FDC**	£2400
2003 BU (Issued: 812)	£2100
— Proof in gold *FDC**	£2400
2004 BU (Issued: 1,000)	£2100
— Proof in gold *FDC**	£2400
2006 BU (Issued: 731)	£2100
— Proof in gold *FDC**	£2400
2007 BU (Issued: 768)	£2100
— Proof in gold *FDC**	£2400
2008 BU (Issued: 750)	£2100
— Proof in gold *FDC**	£2400

* *Coins marked thus were originally issued in Royal Mint sets.*

SE8   **Five pounds.** R. As SE7 but with 'U' in a circle to left of date

     1998 BU (Issued: 825) £2200

     1999 BU (Issued: 970) £2200

     2000 BU (Issued: 994) £2200

     2001 BU (Issued: 1,000) £2200

        SE9   SE10   SE11

SE9   **Five pounds.** R. The Shield of Arms of The United Kingdom of Great Britain and
Northern Ireland within an open wreath of laurel and ensigned by The Royal Crown
and beneath the date of the year. (Reverse design: Timothy Noad.)

     2002 BU (Issued: 1,370) £2500

     —   Proof in gold *FDC**..£3000

SE10 **Five pounds.** R. A depiction of St George, carrying a shield and a sword, slaying
the dragon, with the date '2005' beneath the wing of the dragon.(Reverse design:
Timothy Noad.)

     2005 BU (Issued: 936) £2500

     —   Proof in gold *FDC**..£3000

SE11 **Five pounds.** R. St George and dragon. Based on the original pattern piece of 1820
with the designer's name, 'PISTRUCCI', shown in full in the exergue, and with a
broader rim.

     2009 BU (Issued: 1,000)..£2200

     —   Proof in gold *FDC**..£2400

     2010 BU (Issued: 1,000)..£2200

     —   Proof in gold *FDC**..£2400

     2011 BU (Issued: 657)..£2200

     —   Proof in gold *FDC**..£2400

     2013 BU (Issued: 262)..£2400

     —   Proof in gold *FDC**..£2500

     2014 BU (Issued 605)..£2200

     —   Proof in gold *FDC**..£2500

     2015 Proof in gold *FDC** £2500

* *Coins marked thus were originally issued in Royal Mint sets.*

SE12

SE12 Five pounds. R. The image of St George on horseback, attacking the dragon with a lance, with date of the year to the left. (Reverse design: Paul Day.)

    2012 BU (Issued: 496) £3000
    — Proof in gold *FDC**...£5000

Obverse portrait by Jody Clark

SE13 Five pounds. R. St George and dragon as SE11

    2015 BU (Issued: 609) £2300
    — Proof in gold *FDC**...£2500
    2016 BU (Issued: 498) £2300
    2019 BU Matt (Issued: 400)..£2400
    — Proof in gold *FDC**...£2500
SE13A Five pounds. R. As SE13 but with commemorative privy mark '65'.
    2018 BU (Issued: 459) £2300
    — Proof in gold *FDC**...£2500
SE13B Five pounds. R. As SE13 but with George III Royal Cypher on the reverse.
    2020 BU Matt (Edition: 355) £2400
    — Proof in gold *FDC**...£2500
SE13C Five Pounds. R. As SE13 but with '95'crown privy mark on the reverse.
    2021 BU Matt (Edition: 410) £2400
    — Proof in gold *FDC**...£2500

Obverse portrait by James Butler

SE14

SE14 Five pounds. R. St George and Dragon.
    2016 Proof in gold *FDC**...£4000

* Coins marked thus were originally issued in Royal Mint sets.

Obverse portrait by Jody Clark

SE15

SE15 Five pounds. R. The image of St George armed, sitting on horseback, attacking the dragon with a broken spear surrounded by the inscription 'HONI SOIT QUI MAL Y PENSE'.

2017 BU (Issued: 992) £3000
—   Proof in gold *FDC** £4500

SE16

SE16 Five Pounds. R. A depiction of the Royal Coat of Arms and the date of the year.

2022 BU Matt (Edition: 810) £2500
—   Proof in gold *FDC* * £4000

* Coins marked thus were originally issued in Royal Mint sets.

PGS06

Many of the gold sovereign range of coins were issued as single pieces but most were also included in sets and others, especially a majority of the £5 pieces, only appear in cased sets.

Some sets contain a £2 commemorative of the year instead of the usual St. George & Dragon design and these are noted.

Proof Gold Sovereign Sets £

PGS01–**1980**	Gold £5 to half-sovereign (Issued: 10,000)	(4)	4250
PGS02–**1981**	U.K. Proof coin Commemorative collection. (Consists of £5, sovereign, 'Royal Wedding' Crown in silver, plus base metal proofs 50p to ½p), (Issued: 2080)	(9)	2900
PGS02A-**1981**	Gold sovereign and Royal Wedding silver proof crown (Issued: 2,107)	(2)	500
PGS03–**1982**	Gold £5 to half-sovereign (Issued: 2,500)	(4)	5500
PGS04–**1983**	Gold £2, sovereign and half-sovereign, (Not known)	(3)	1700
PGS05–**1984**	Gold £5, sovereign and half-sovereign, (Issued: 7,095)	(3)	3000
PGS06–**1985**	Gold £5 to half-sovereign (Issued: 5,849)	(4)	4250
PGS07–**1986**	Gold Commonwealth Games £2, sovereign and half-sovereign (Issued: 12,500)	(3)	1800
PGS08–**1987**	Gold £2, sovereign and half-sovereign (Issued: 12,500)	(3)	1800
PGS09–**1988**	Gold £2 to half-sovereign (Issued: 11,192)	(3)	1800
PGS10–**1989**	Sovereign Anniversary Gold £5 to half-sovereign (Issued: 5,000)	(4)	8000
PGS11–**1989**	Sovereign Anniversary Gold £2 to half-sovereign (Issued: 7,936)	(3)	4000
PGS12–**1990**	Gold £5 to half-sovereign (Issued: 1,721)	(4)	4250
PGS13–**1990**	Gold £2 to half-sovereign (Issued: 1,937)	(3)	1900
PGS14–**1991**	Gold £5 to half-sovereign (Issued: 1,336)	(4)	4250
PGS15–**1991**	Gold £2 to half-sovereign (Issued: 1,152)	(3)	1900
PGS16–**1992**	Gold £5 to half-sovereign (Issued: 1,165)	(4)	4500
PGS17–**1992**	Gold £2 to half-sovereign (Issued: 967)	(3)	2000
PGS18–**1993**	Gold £5 to half-sovereign with silver Pistrucci medal in case (Issued: 1,078)	(5)	4500
PGS19–**1993**	Gold £2 to half-sovereign (Issued: 663)	(3)	2000
PGS20–**1994**	Gold £5, Bank of England £2, sovereign and half-sovereign (Issued: 918)	(4)	4500
PGS21–**1994**	Gold Bank of England £2, sovereign and half-sovereign (Issued: 1,249)	(3)	2000
PGS22–**1995**	Gold £5, Dove of Peace £2, sovereign and half-sovereign (Issued: 718)	(4)	4000
PGS23–**1995**	Gold Dove of Peace £2, sovereign and half-sovereign (Issued: 1,112)	(3)	1800
PGS24–**1996**	Gold £5 to half-sovereign (Issued: 742)	(4)	4250
PGS25–**1996**	Gold £2 to half-sovereign (Issued: 868)	(3)	1800
PGS26–**1997**	Gold £5, Industry £2, sovereign and half-sovereign (Issued: 860)	(4)	4250
PGS27–**1997**	Gold Industry £2 to half-sovereign (Issued: 817)	(3)	1800
PGS28–**1998**	Gold £5 to half sovereign (Issued: 789)	(4)	4000
PGS29–**1998**	Gold £2 to half sovereign (Issued: 560)	(3)	1800
PGS30–**1999**	Gold £5, Rugby World Cup £2, sovereign and half sovereign (Issued: 991)	(4)	4000

£

PGS31–**1999**	Gold Rugby World Cup £2, sovereign and half sovereign (Issued: 912).........	(3)	1800
PGS32–**2000**	Gold £5 to half-sovereign (Issued: 1,000)...	(4)	4000
PGS33–**2000**	Gold £2 to half-sovereign (Issued: 1,250)...	(3)	1650
PGS34–**2001**	Gold £5, Marconi £2, sovereign and half sovereign (Issued: 1,000)	(4)	4000
PGS35–**2001**	Gold Marconi £2, sovereign and half sovereign (Issued: 891)	(3)	1650
PGS36–**2002**	Gold £5 to half sovereign (Issued: 3,000)	(4)	5000
PGS37–**2002**	Gold £2 to half sovereign (Issued: 3,947)..	(3)	2000
PGS38–**2003**	Gold £5 to half sovereign (Issued: 2,050)..	(4)	3800
PGS39–**2003**	Gold DNA £2, sovereign and half sovereign (Issued: 1,737)	(3)	1650
PGS40–**2004**	Gold £5 to half sovereign (Issued: 1,749)..	(4)	3800
PGS41–**2004**	Gold Locomotive £2, sovereign and half sovereign (Issued: 761)..................	(3)	1650
PGS42–**2005**	Gold £5 to half sovereign (Issued: 2,161)..	(4)	4800
PGS43–**2005**	Gold £2 to half sovereign (Issued: 797)	(3)	1850
PGS44–**2006**	Gold £5 to half sovereign (Issued: 1,750)..	(4)	3800
PGS45–**2006**	Gold £2 to half sovereign (Issued: 540)	(3)	1650
PGS46–**2007**	Gold £5 to half sovereign (Issued: 1,750)..	(4)	3800
PGS47–**2007**	Gold £2 to half sovereign (Issued: 651)...	(3)	1650
PGS48–**2007**	Gold sovereign and half sovereign (Issued: 818)	(2)	800
PGS49–**2008**	Gold £5 to half sovereign (Issued: 1,750)..	(4)	3800
PGS50–**2008**	Gold £2 to half sovereign (Issued: 583)...	(3)	1650
PGS51–**2008**	Gold sovereign and half sovereign (Issued: 804)	(2)	800
PGS52–**2009**	Gold £5, £2, sovereign, half sovereign, and quarter sovereign (Issued: 1,750)	(5)	3900
PGS53–**2009**	Gold £2, sovereign and half sovereign (Issued: 666)	(3)	1650
PGS54–**2009**	Gold sovereign and half sovereign (Edition: 1,000)....................................	(2)	800
PGS55–**2010**	Gold £5 to quarter sovereign (Issued: 1,461)	(5)	3900
PGS56–**2010**	Gold £2 to half sovereign (Issued: 558)...	(3)	1650
PGS57–**2010**	Gold sovereign, half sovereign and quarter sovereign (Edition: 1,500)........	(3)	800
PGS58–**2011**	Gold £5 to quarter sovereign (Issued: 1,028)	(5)	3900
PGS59–**2011**	Gold £2 to quarter sovereign (Edition: 200)...	(4)	1800
PGS60–**2011**	Gold £2 to half sovereign (Edition: 750)...	(3)	1650
PGS61–**2011**	Gold sovereign, half sovereign and quarter sovereign (Edition: 1,000)........	(3)	800
PGS62–**2012**	Gold £5, £2, sovereign, half sovereign and quarter sovereign (Issued: 956)	(5)	8000
PGS63–**2012**	Gold £2 to quarter sovereign (Issued: 605)	(4)	3600
PGS64–**2012**	Gold £2 to half sovereign (Issued: 335)...	(3)	3250
PGS65–**2012**	Gold sovereign, half sovereign and quarter sovereign (Issued: 701)	(3)	2200
PGS66–**2013**	Gold £5, £2, sovereign, half sovereign and quarter sovereign (Issued: 388)	(5)	4200
PGS67–**2013**	Gold £2 to quarter sovereign (Issued: 495)	(4)	1900
PGS68–**2013**	Gold £2 to half sovereign (Issued: 380)...	(3)	1800
PGS69–**2013**	Gold sovereign, half sovereign and quarter sovereign (Issued: 652)	(3)	1000
PGS70–**2014**	Gold £5, £2, sovereign, half sovereign and quarter sovereign (Issued: 375)	(5)	4200
PGS71–**2014**	Gold £2 to half sovereign (Issued: 306)...	(3)	1800
PGS72–**2014**	Gold sovereign, half sovereign and quarter sovereign (Issued: 669)	(3)	1100
PGS73–**2015**	Gold £5, £2, sovereign, half sovereign and quarter sovereign (Issued: 507)	(5)	4500
PGS74–**2015**	Gold £2 to half sovereign (Issued: 328)...	(3)	1700
PGS75–**2015**	Gold sovereign, half sovereign and quarter sovereign (Issued: 664)	(3)	1100
PGS76–**2015**	Gold £5, £2, sovereign, half sovereign and quarter sovereign (Issued: 598)	(5)	5500
PGS77–**2015**	Gold £2 to half sovereign (Issued: 448)...	(3)	2000
PGS78–**2016**	Gold £5 to quarter sovereign (Issued: 573)	(5)	7000
PGS79–**2016**	Gold £2 to half sovereign (Issued: 348)...	(3)	3000
PGS80–**2016**	Gold sovereign, half sovereign and quarter sovereign (Issued: 745).............	(3)	1750
PGS81–**2017**	Gold £5 to quarter sovereign (Issued: 749)...	(5)	7500
PGS82–**2017**	Gold £2 to half sovereign (Issued: 449)...	(3)	3000

£

PGS83–**2017** Gold sovereign, half sovereign and quarter sovereign (Issued: 997)............ (3) 1750

PGS84–**2018** Gold £5, £2, sovereign, half sovereign and quarter sovereign with '65th
Anniversary Mint mark on the reverses (Issued: 748)................................ (5) 4500

PGS85–**2018** Gold £2, sovereign, half sovereign and quarter sovereign with '65th'
Anniversary Mint Mark (Issued: 229)....................... (4) 2000

PGS86–**2018** Gold £2, sovereign and half sovereign with '65th' Anniversary Mint Mark
(Issued: 432) .... (3) 1800

PGS87–**2018** Gold sovereign, half sovereign and quarter sovereign with '65th' Anniversary
Mint Mark (Issued: 986) .... (3) 1000

PGS88–**2019** Gold £5, £2, sovereign, half sovereign and quarter sovereign (Edition: 750) (5) 4250

PGS89–**2019** Gold £2, sovereign, half sovereign and quarter sovereign (Edition: 300)..... (4) 1750

PGS90–**2019** Gold £2, sovereign and half sovereign (Edition: 450)................................ (3) 1600

PGS91–**2019** Gold sovereign, half sovereign and quarter sovereign (Edition: 1,000)........ (3) 1000

PGS92–**2020** Gold £5, £2, sovereign, half sovereign and quarter sovereign all with
'George III Royal Cypher' on the reverses (Edition: 500) .... (5) 4500

PGS93–**2020** Gold £2, sovereign, half sovereign and quarter sovereign all with
'George III Royal Cypher' on the reverses (Edition: 650) .... (4) 1900

PGS94–**2020** Gold sovereign, half sovereign and quarter sovereign all with 'George III
Royal Cypher' on the reverses (Edition: 750) .... (3) 1000

PGS95-**2021** Gold £5, £2, sovereign, half sovereign and quarter sovereign all with '95'
crown privy mark on the reverses (Edition: 500) .... (5) 4600

PGS96-**2021** Gold £2, sovereign, half sovereign and quarter sovereign all with '95'
crown privy mark on the reverses (Edition: 450) .... (4) 2000

PGS97-**2021** Gold sovereign, half sovereign and quarter sovereign all with '95' crown
privy mark on the reverses (Edition: 750) .... (3) 1100

PGS98-**2022** Gold £5, £2, sovereign, half sovereign and quarter sovereign (Edition: 700) (5) 7000

PGS99-**2022** Gold £2, sovereign, half sovereign and quarter sovereign (Edition: 500)..... (4) 2750

PGS100-**2022** Gold sovereign, half sovereign and quarter sovereign (Edition: 1,000)........ (3) 1500

The Royal Mint issued 70 piedfort sets of PGS98 but as there was no legislation for such set, they
called it a pattern set. However a pattern set would need to be hallmarked and these sets were not. the
Royal Mint subsequently realised their error and requested sets to be returned for hallmarking. It is
suspected that many sets were not returned which means there are legal hallmarked sets in the market
and also illegal non-hallmarked sets.

Struck on the Day – A number of BU sovereigns were struck on significant dates and sold by the Royal Mint in a limited issue with appropriate certificate. The catalogue numbers, dates and associated event are as follows. Prices are for coins in original case with certificate. SSD1-5 & 7 also exist as regular coins so will generally be available at lower prices if uncased.

SSD	Cat No.	Date	Event	Privy Mark	Edge	BU or Matt	Edition	Issued	£
1	SC8	2 /6/2012	Diamond Jubilee Celebration Day	None	Milled	BU	2012	1990	500
2	SC7	2 /6/2013	60th Anniversary of the Coronation	None	Milled	BU	2013	900	500
3	SC7	22/7/2013	Birth of Prince George	None	Milled	BU	2013	2013	600
4*	SC7	22/7/2014	First Birthday of Prince George	None	Milled	BU	400	398	700
5	SC7	2/5/2015	Birth of Princess Charlotte	None	Milled	BU	750	743	600
6	SC9	22/7/2015	Second Birthday of Prince George	None	Milled	BU	400	301	700
7	SC9	11/6/2016	Queen's 90th Birthday	None	Milled	BU	500	499	550
8	SC9	6/2/2017	65th Anniversary of the Accession	None	Milled	BU	750	750	550
9	SC11A	1/7/2017	200th Anniversary of 1817 Sovereign	None	Plain	BU	1817	1786	1000
10	SC9	20/11/2017	Platinum Wedding	None	Milled	BU	750	744	550
11	SC9E	2/6/2018	65th Anniversary of the Coronation	65	Plain	BU	650	650	750
12	SC9C	22/7/2018	Fifth Birthday of Prince George	None	Plain	BU	750	485	750
13	SC9F	24/5/2019	200th Anniversary of Birth of Queen Victoria	VR	Plain	Matt	650	649	900
14	SC9G	26/8/2019	200th Anniversary of Birth of Prince Albert	VA	Plain	Matt	650	647	800
15	SC9J	31/1/2020	Brexit Day	Crowned Portcullis	Plain	Matt	1500	—	900
16	SC9K	8/5/2020	75th Anniversary of VE Day	VE75	Plain	Matt	750	—	800
17	SC9L	15/8/2020	75th Anniversary of End of World War II.	VJ75	Plain	Matt	750	—	800
18	SC9M	12/6/2021	Queen's 95th Birthday**	95 crown	Plain	Matt	1295	—	650
19	SC12A	6/2/2022	Queen's Platinum Jubilee	None	Plain	Matt	1200	—	800

* SSD4 has a prooflike reverse.
** Owing to the death of HRH The Duke of Edinburgh the issue was postponed from the Queen's actual birthday of 21st April to her Official birthday of 12th June.

Many of the gold sovereign coins were sold as both singles and in sets. The sales figures in the preceding text indicate the sales of coins sold singly in presentation cases. The numbers below show the total sales of each denomination year by year. There are some years where the Royal Mint has not published fully detailed sales figures and other years where the coins sold in sets came out of the authorised mintage for the single coin. In addition to the numbers sold we have listed the announced authorised mintage and as indicated in the introduction to this section there are just a few instances where the published numbers sold are in excess of the authorised. We will endeavour to keep this information updated.

Proof Gold Sets

1980	½ Sov.	Sov.	£2	£5	SET		Authorised
PS01	10000	10000	10000	10000	10000	(4)	10000
SC1		81200					100000
SB1	76700						100000
	86700	91200	10000	10000			

1981	½ Sov.	Sov.	£2	£5	SET		Authorised
PGS02		2080		2080			5000
PGS02A		2107			2107	(2)	
SE1				3320			10000
SC1		32960					50000
		37147		5400			

1982	½ Sov.	Sov.	£2	£5	SET		Authorised
PGS03	2500	2500	2500	2500	2500	(4)	2500
SC1		20000					20000
SB1	19090						20000
	21590	22500	2500	2500			

1983	½ Sov.	Sov.	£2	£5	SET		Authorised
PGS04	(figures below include coins in this set)					(3)	
SD1			12500				12500
SC1		21250					22500
SB1	19710						22500
	19710	21250	12500				

1984	½ Sov.	Sov.	£2	£5	SET		Authorised
PGS05	7095	7095		7095	7095	(3)	
SE1				905			8000
SC1		12880					22500
SB1	12410						22500
	19505	19975		8000			

1985	½ Sov.	Sov.	£2	£5	SET		Authorised
PGS06	5849	5849	5849	5849	5849	(4)	12500
SE3				281			
SC2		11393					12500
SB2	9951						12500
	15800	17242	5849	6130			

1986	½ Sov.	Sov.	£2 is K1	£5	SET		Authorised
PGS07	12500	12500	12500		12500	(3)	12500
K1			3277				5000
SC2		5079					12500
SB2	4575						12500
	17075	17579	15777				

1987	½ Sov.	Sov.	£2	£5	SET		Authorised
PGS08	12500	12500	12500		12500	(3)	12500
SD2			1801				2500
SC2		9979					10000
SB2	8187						10000
	20687	22479	14301				

1988	½ Sov.	Sov.	£2	£5	SET		Authorised
PGS09	11192	11192	11192		11192	(3)	12500
SD2			1551				2500
SC2		7670					12500
SB2	7074						10000
	18266	18862	12743				

1989	½ Sov.	Sov.	£2	£5	SET		Authorised
PGS10	5000	5000	5000	5000	5000	(4)	5000
PGS11	7936	7936	7936		7936	(3)	10000
SD3			2000				2000
SC3		10535					12500
SB3	8888						10000
	21824	23471	14936	5000			

1990	½ Sov.	Sov.	£2	£5	SET		Authorised
PGS12	1721	1721	1721	1721	1721	(4)	2500
PGS13	1937	1937	1937		1937	(3)	7500
SD2			716				2000
SC2		4767					10000
SB2	4231						10000
	7889	8425	4374	1721			

1991	½ Sov.	Sov.	£2	£5	SET		Authorised
PGS14	1336	1336	1336	1336	1336	(4)	1500
PGS15	1152	1152	1152		1152	(3)	2500
SD2			620				1000
SC2		4713					5000
SB2	3588						5000
	6076	7201	3108	1336			

1992	½ Sov.	Sov.	£2	£5	SET		Authorised
PGS16	1165	1165	1165	1165	1165	(4)	1250
PGS17	967	967	967		967	(3)	1250
SD2			476				500
SC2		4772					5000
SB2	3783						5000
	5915	6904	2608	1165			

1993	½ Sov.	Sov.	£2	£5	SET		Authorised
PGS18	1078	1078	1078	1078	1078	(4)	1250
PGS19	663	663	663		663	(3)	1250
SD2			414				500
SC2		4349					5000
SB2	2910						5000
	4651	6090	2155	1078			

1994	½ Sov.	Sov.	£2 is K4	£5	SET		Authorised
PGS20	918	918	918	918	918	(4)	1250
PGS21	1249	1249	1249		1249	(3)	1250
K4			1000				1000
SC2		4998					5000
SB2	5000						5000
	7167	7165	3167	918			

1995	½ Sov.	Sov.	£2 is K5	£5	SET		Authorised
PGS22	718	718	718	718	718	(4)	1250
PGS23	1112	1112	1112		1112	(3)	1250
K5			2500				2500
SC2		7500					7500
SB2	4900						5000
	6730	9330	4330	718			

1996	½ Sov.	Sov.	£2	£5	SET		Authorised
PGS24	742	742	742	742	742	(4)	1250
PGS25	868	868	868		868	(3)	1250
SC2		7500					7500
SB2	5730						7500
	7340	9110	1610	742			

1997	½ Sov.	Sov.	£2 is K8	£5	SET		Authorised
PGS26	860	860	860	860	860	(4)	1000
PGS27	817	817	817		817	(3)	1250
K8			2482				2500
SC2		7500					7500
SB2	7500						7500
	9177	9177	4159	860			

1998	½ Sov.	Sov.	£2	£5	SET		Authorised
PGS28	789	789	789	789	789	(4)	1500
PGS29	560	560	560		560	(3)	2000
SC4		10000					10000
SB4	6147						7500
	7496	11349	1349	789			

1999	½ Sov.	Sov.	£2 is K10	£5	SET		Authorised
PGS30	991	991	991	991	991	(4)	1000
PGS31	912	912	912		912	(3)	1250
K10			311				3250
SC4		10000					10000
SB4	7500						7500
	9403	11903	2214	991			

2000	½ Sov.	Sov.	£2	£5	SET		Authorised
PGS32	1000	1000	1000	1000	1000	(4)	1000
PGS33	1250	1250	1250		1250	(3)	1250
SC4		9909					10000
SB4	7458						7500
	9708	12159	2250	1000			

2001	½ Sov.	Sov.	£2 is K11	£5	SET		Authorised
PGS34	1000	1000	1000	1000	1000	(4)	1000
PGS35	891	891	891		891	(3)	1500
K11			1658				2500
SC4		8915					12500
SB4	4596						7500
	6487	10806	3549	1000			

2002	½ Sov.	Sov.	£2	£5	SET		Authorised
PGS36	3000	3000	3000	3000	3000	(4)	3000
PGS37	3947	3947	3947		3947	(3)	5000
SC5		12500					12500
SB5	10000						10000
	16947	19447	6947	3000			

2003	½ Sov.	Sov.	£2	£5	SET		Authorised
PGS38	2050	2050	2050	2050	2050	(4)	2250
PGS39	1737	1737	†		1737	(3)	2500
SC4		12433					15000
SB4	4868						10000
	8655	16220	2050	2050			

†[£2 in 3 coin set is K16]

2004	½ Sov.	Sov.	£2	£5	SET		Authorised
PGS40	1749	1749	1749	1749	1749	(4)	2250
PGS41	761	761	†		761	(3)	2500
SC4		10175					15000
SB4	4446						10000
	6956	12685	1749	1749			

†[£2 in 3 coin set is K17]

2005	½ Sov.	Sov.	£2	£5	SET		Authorised
PGS42	2161	2161	2161	2161	2161	(4)	2500
PGS43	797	797	797		797	(3)	2500
SC6		12500					12500
SB6	5011						7500
	7969	15458	2958	2161			

2006	½ Sov.	Sov.	£2	£5	SET		Authorised
PGS44	1750	1750	1750	1750	1750	(4)	1750
PGS45	540	540	540		540	(3)	1750
SC4		9195					12500
SB4	4173						5000
	6463	11485	2290	1750			

2007	½ Sov.	Sov.	£2	£5	SET		Authorised
PGS46	1750	1750	1750	1750	1750	(4)	1750
PGS47	651	651	651		651	(3)	750
PGS48	818	818			818	(2)	
SC4		8199					10000
SB4	2442						5000
	5661	11418	2401	1750			

2008	½ Sov.	Sov.	£2	£5	SET		Authorised
PGS49	1750	1750	1750	1750	1750	(4)	1750
PGS50	583	583	583		583	(3)	750
PGS51	804	804			804	(2)	
SC4		7735					12500
SB4	2465						5000
	5602	10872	2333	1750			

2009	¼ Sov.	½ Sov.	Sov.	£2	£5	SET		Authorised
PGS52	1750	1750	1750	1750	1750	1750	(5)	1750
PGS53		666	666	666		666	(3)	750
PGS54	*(figures below include coins in this set)*						(2)	1000
SC7			7354					12500
SB7		2996						2500
SA1	11745							21500
	13495	5412	9770	2416	1750			

2010	¼ Sov.	½ Sov.	Sov.	£2	£5	SET		Authorised
PGS55	1461	1461	1461	1461	1461	1461	(5)	1750
PGS56		558	558	558		558	(3)	750
PGS57	*(figures below include coins in this set)*						(3)	1500
SC7			6809					7500
SB7		3351						2500
SA1	4546							14000
	6007	5370	8828	2019	1461			

2011	¼ Sov.	½ Sov.	Sov.	£2	£5	SET		Authorised
PGS58	1028	1028	1028	1028	1028	1028	(5)	1500
PGS59	*(figures below include coins in this set)*						(4)	200
PGS60	*(figures below include coins in this set)*						(3)	750
PGS61	*(figures below include coins in this set)*						(3)	1000
SC7			7181					7500
SB7A		4259						2500
SA1	6736							5000
	7764	5287	8209	2149	1028			

2012	¼ Sov.	½ Sov.	Sov.	£2	£5	SET		Authorised
PGS62	956	956	956	956	956	956	(5)	999
PGS63	605	605	605	605		605	(4)	295
PGS64		335	335	335		335	(3)	750
PGS65	701	701	701			701	(3)	700
PGCS12				60				60
SC8			5501					5500
SB8		2303						2250
SA2	7579							6500
	9841	4900	8098	1956	956			

2013	¼ Sov.	½ Sov.	Sov.	£2	£5	SET		Authorised
PGS66	388	388	388	388	388	388	(5)	1000
PGS67	495	495	495	495		495	(4)	295
PGS68		380	380	380		380	(3)	400
PGS69	652	652	652			652	(3)	650
SC7			8243					7500
SB7A		1863						2250
SA1	1696							3500
	3231	3778	10158	1263	388			

2014	¼ Sov.	½ Sov.	Sov.	£2	£5	SET		Authorised
PGS70	375	375	375	375	375	375	(5)	750
PGS71		306	306	306		306	(3)	500
PGS72	669	669	669			669	(3)	750
SC7			3263					7500
SB7A		1367						2000
SA1	1886							3000
	2930	2717	4613	681	375			

2015	¼ Sov.	½ Sov.	Sov.	£2	£5	SET		Authorised
PGS73	407	407	407	407	407	407	(5)	500
	100	100	100	100	100	100	(5) Ω	100
PGS74		328	328	328		328	(3)	500
PGS75	664	664	664			664	(3)	1000
SC7			4346					7500
SC7			200				Ω	200
SB7A		1704						2500
SA1	1808							3000
	2979	3203	6045	835	507			

2015 New Portrait	¼ Sov.	½ Sov.	Sov.	£2	£5	SET		Authorised
PGS76	348	348	348	348	348	348	(5)	350
	250	250	250	250	250	250	(5) Ω	250
PGS77		448	448	448		448	(3)	500
SC9			6994					7000
SC9			500				Ω	500
SA3	550						Ω	550
	1148	1046	8540	1046	598			

2016	¼ Sov.	½ Sov.	Sov.	£2	£5	SET		Authorised
PGS78	498	498	498	498	498	498	(5)	500
	75	75	75	75	75	75	(5) Ω	75
PGS79		348	348	348		348	(3)	350
PGS80	745	745	745			745	(3)	750
SC10			7495					7500
SC10			500				Ω	500
SB10		1995						2000
SA4	1727							1750
	3045	3661	9661	921	573			

2017	¼ Sov.	½ Sov.	Sov.	£2	£5	SET		Authorised
PGS81	749	749	749	749	749	749	(5)	750
PGS82		449	449	449		449	(3)	450
PGS83	1000	1000	1000			1000	(3)	1000
SC11			10493					10500
SB11		2492						2500
SA5	2495							2500
	4244	4690	12691	1198	749			

2018	¼ Sov.	½ Sov.	Sov.	£2	£5	SET		Authorised
PGS84	749	749	749	749	749	749	(5)	750
	100	100	100	100	100	100	(5) Ω	100
PGS85	299	299	299	299		299	[4]	300
PGS86		432	432	432		432	(3)	450
PGS87	986	986	986			986	(3)	1000
SC9D			10483					10500
SC9D			150				Ω	
SB9A		1878						2500
SA3A	1321							2500
	3455	4444	13199	1580	849			

Ω Coins sold to the US market and not in standard Royal Mint cases.
Mintages not yet known

2019	¼ Sov.	½ Sov.	Sov.	£2	£5	SET		Authorised
PGS88	618	618	618	618	618	618	(5)	750
PGS89	299	299	299	299		299	[4]	300
PGS90		346	346	346		346	(3)	450
PGS91	840	840	840			840	(3)	1000
SC9			9538					10500
SB9		1523						2500
SA3	1312							2500
	2451	3626	11641	1263	618			

2020	¼ Sov.	½ Sov.	Sov.	£2	£5	SET		Authorised
PGS92	#	#	#	#	#	#	(5)	500
PGS93	#	#	#	#		#	(4)	600
PGS94	#	#	#			#	(3)	750
SC9H			#					7995
SB9B		#						2000

2021	¼ Sov.	½ Sov.	Sov.	£2	£5	SET		Authorised
PGS95	#	#	#	#	#	#	(5)	500
PGS96	#	#	#	#		#	(4)	450
PGS97	#	#	#			#	(3)	750
SC9M			#					7995
SB9D		#						1500

2022	¼ Sov.	½ Sov.	Sov.	£2	£5	SET		Authorised
PGS98	#	#	#	#	#	#	(5)	700
PGS99	#	#	#	#		#	(4)	500
PGS100	#	#	#			#	(3)	1000
SC12			#					10500
SB12		#						2000

Uncirculated Gold Sovereign Sets

UGS01–**2012** (Formerly PGS66) £2 to half sovereign BU (Issued: 119) .... (3) 2000
This set was struck on the day of the commencement of the Diamond Jubilee
Celebrations, 2nd June 2012.

UGS02–**2013** (Formerly PGS70) £2 to half sovereign BU (Issued: 124) .... (3) 1600
This set was struck on the day of the Diamond Jubilee of the Coronation,
2nd June 2013

Uncirculated Gold Sets

2012	½ Sov.	Sov.	£2	SET		Authorised
UGS01	119	119	119	119	(3)	125
SC8		4559				
SSD1		1990				2012
SB8	2137					
	2256	6668	119			

2013	½ Sov.	Sov.	£2	SET		Authorised
UGS02	124	124	124	124	(3)	125
SC7		2695				
SSD2		900				2013
SSD3		2013				2013
SB7A	1051					
	1175	5732	124			

Ω Coins sold to the US market and not in standard Royal Mint cases.
Mintages not yet known

Bullion Sovereign Issues

Bullion Sovereigns Issued

1974	5,002,566	2001	49,462	2009	60,292
1976	4,150,000	2002	75,264	2010	243,986
1978	6,550,000	2003	43,230	2011	253,773
1979	9,100,000	2004	30,688	2012	432,925
1980	5,100,000	2005	45,542	2013	261,581
1981	5,000,000	2006	33,012	2014	261,216
1982	2,950,000	2007	27,628	2015	113,177
2000	129,069	2008	58,894		

Bullion Half Sovereigns Issued

1982	2,500,000	2002	61,347	2005	30,299
2000	146,822	2003	47,818	2010	16,485
2001	94,763	2004	34,924		
2002	61,347				

Bullion Quarter Sovereigns Issued

2010	8985

Numbers issued for later bullion coins have not yet been announced.

This page, effectively, marks the start of the second part of this catalogue because none of the coins that are listed in this Britannia section or the various sections that follow from here onwards had versions issued for circulation other than the 50p & £2 Olympic coins and they are sometimes referred to as NCLT issues (non-circulating legal tender) – an expression that was coined in the USA way back in the early 1970s.

In 1987 the Mint decided to enter the market for bullion coins and launched a series of four gold coins depicting Britannia with weights that corresponded to those already issued by a number of gold producing countries such as Australia, Canada, China and South Africa. The plan was to sell bullion quality coins in quantity to trade customers and investors at modest premiums over the ruling gold market price, and also to sell proof versions in limited editions to collectors.

Until 2013 the gold coins were struck in 22 carat gold (.9166), the standard for UK gold coins. From 1990 silver was included with copper which made the coins more yellow and more acceptable in the Far East market. From 2013 onwards the gold coins were struck in .999 gold.

To mark the 10th anniversary of the first design, silver Britannia coins struck in Britannia silver (0.958) were introduced in the same four weights in 1997 although only the £2 (one ounce) was issued in quantity as a bullion coin. The silver fineness was increased to .999 in 2013 and smaller denominations were introduced as proofs in 2013 & 2014.

There are some attractive and different interpretations of Britannia with the gold and silver issues sharing the same designs as they are changed, but by and large the bullion coins have retained the designs from the first series so as to make them more recognisable across the world as UK bullion coins.

Most of the fraction coins are only issued within sets but some along with the 1oz versions were issued individually. Prices given relate to cased coins with certificates; uncased coins from split sets can often be found at lower prices. Sets of silver and gold Britannia coins are now listed immediately after the listing of the individual coins.

Since 2012 a wide range of other commemorative coins with both bullion and collector versions have been issued with specifications based on the ounce or, for higher denomination coins, the kilo and they are recorded in the sections that follow the Britannia listings. As all the coins listed in the various sections that follow this Britannia section have specifications based on the Britannia range, except for the 50p & £2 Olympic coins and a number of £5 (crown) coins which have traditional currency specifications, the tables of specifications below cover all these coins.

Silver Coins Specifications

Denomination	Metal	Weight		Diameter
5p - from 2014	0.999 silver	$^1/_{40}$ ounce	0.80 g	8.00 mm
10p - from 2013	0.999 silver	$^1/_{20}$ ounce	1.58 g	12.00 mm
20p 1997-2002	0.958 silver	$^1/_{10}$ ounce	3.24 g	16.50 mm
- from 2013	0.999 silver	$^1/_{10}$ ounce	3.15 g	16.50 mm
50p 1997-2012	0.958 silver	$^1/_4$ ounce	8.11 g	22.00 mm
- from 2013	0.999 silver	$^1/_4$ ounce	7.86 g	22.00 mm
£1 1997-2012	0.958 silver	$^1/_2$ ounce	16.22 g	27.00 mm
- from 2013	0.999 silver	$^1/_2$ ounce	15.71 g	27.00 mm
£2 1997-2012	0.958 silver	1 ounce	32.45 g	40.00 mm
- from 2013	0.999 silver	1 ounce	31.21 g	38.61 mm
£5	0.999 silver	2 ounce	62.42 g	40.00 mm
£10	0.999 silver	5 ounce	156.30 g	65.00 mm

Silver Coins Specification continued

£10	0.999 silver	10 ounce	311.03 g	89.00 mm
£50	0.999 silver	1 kilo	1005 g	100.00 mm
£250	0.999 silver	20 ounce	625.20 g	100.00 mm
£500	0.999 silver	1 kilo	1005 g	100.00 mm
£1000	0.999 silver	2 kilo	2020 g	150.00 mm

Gold Coins Specifications

Denomination	Metal	Weight		Diameter
50p from 2014	0.999 gold	$^1/_{40}$ ounce	0.80 g	8.00 mm
£1 from 2013	0.999 gold	$^1/_{20}$ ounce	1.58 g	12.00 mm
£10 1987-2012	0.916 gold	$^1/_{10}$ ounce	3.41 g	16.50 mm
- from 2013	0.999 gold	$^1/_{10}$ ounce	3.13 g	16.50 mm
£10	0.999 gold	5 ounce	156.30 g	50.00 mm†
£25 1987-2012	0.916 gold	¼ ounce	8.51 g	22.00 mm
- from 2013	0.999 gold	¼ ounce	7.80 g	22.00 mm
£50 1987-2012	0.916 gold	½ ounce	17.03 g	27.00 mm
- from 2013	0.999 gold	½ ounce	15.60 g	27.00 mm
£100 1987-2012	0.916 gold	1 ounce	34.05 g	32.69 mm
-2013	0.999 gold	1 ounce	31.11 g	38.61 mm
- from 2014	0.999 gold	1 ounce	31.11 g	32.69 mm
£200	0.999 gold	2 ounce	62.42 g	40.00 mm
£500	0.999 gold	5 ounce	156.30 g	50.00 mm
£800	0.999 gold	30 ounce	933.2 g	100.00 mm
£1000	0.999 gold	1 kilo	1005 g	100.00 mm
£2000	0.999 gold	2 kilo	2010 g	150.00 mm
£3000	0.999 gold	3 kilo	3010 g	165.00 mm
£5000	0.999 gold	5 kilo	5020 g	175.00 mm
£7000	0.999 gold	7 kilo	7035 g	185.00 mm
£8000	0.999 gold	8 kilo	8040 g	185.00 mm
£9500	0.999 gold	9.5 kilo	9525 g	195.00 mm
£10000	0.999 gold	10 kilo	100025 g	200.00 mm

† M1, M2, M18 – 65mm

Platinum Coins Specifications

Denomination	Metal	Weight		Diameter
£10	0.995 platinum	$^1/_{10}$ ounce	3.14 g	2007-2008 - 15.00 mm *from* 2018 - 16.50 mm
£25	0.995 platinum	¼ ounce	7.85 g	20.00 mm
£50	0.995 platinum	½ ounce	15.69 g	25.00 mm
£100	0.995 platinum	1 ounce	31.39 g	32.69 mm

FIVE PENCE

Obverse portrait by Ian Rank-Broadley
BSA1 **Britannia Five Pence.** (1/40 oz of fine silver.) R. As BSF13 with the inscription
'BRITANNIA 999 1/40 OZ FINE SILVER 2014'.
2014 Proof in silver *FDC** £15

Obverse portrait by Jody Clark
BSA2 **Britannia Five Pence.** (1/40 oz of fine silver.) R. As BSF14 with the inscription
'BRITANNIA 1/40 OZ FINE SILVER 999 2015'.
2015 Proof in silver *FDC** £15
BSA3 **Britannia Five Pence.** (1/40 oz of fine silver.) R. As BSF16 with the inscription
'BRITANNIA 1/40 OZ FINE SILVER 999 2016'.
2016 Proof in silver *FDC** £15
BSA4 **Britannia Five Pence.** (1/40 oz of fine silver.) R. As BSF17 with the inscription
'BRITANNIA 1/40 OZ FINE SILVER 999 2017' and with Trident mint mark to
mark the 20th Anniversary of the first Britannia silver issue.
2017 Proof in silver *FDC** £15
BSA5 **Britannia Five Pence.** (1/40 oz of fine silver.) R. As BSF18 with the inscription
'BRITANNIA 1/40 OZ FINE SILVER 999 2018'.
2018 Proof in silver *FDC** £15
BSA6 **Britannia Five Pence.** (1/40 oz of fine silver.) R. As BSF21 with the inscription
'BRITANNIA 1/40 OZ FINE SILVER 999 2019'.
2019 Proof in silver *FDC** £15
BSA7 **Britannia Five Pence.** (1/40 oz of fine silver.) R. As BSF22 with the inscription
'BRITANNIA 1/40 OZ FINE SILVER 999 2020'.
2020 Proof in silver *FDC** £15
BSA8 **Britannia Five Pence.** (1/40oz of fine silver.) R. As BSF24 with the inscription
'BRITANNIA 1/40 OZ 999 FINE SILVER 2021'.
2021 Proof in silver *FDC* (Edition: 1,100)* £15
BSA9 **Britannia Five Pence.** (1/40oz of fine silver) R. As BSF26 with the inscription '1/40
OZ 999 BRITANNIA FINE SILVER 2022'.
2022 Proof in silver *FDC* (Edition: 1,310)* £15

TEN PENCE

Obverse portrait by Ian Rank-Broadley
BSB1 **Britannia Ten Pence.** (1/20 oz of fine silver.) R. As BSF11 with the inscription
'BRITANNIA 999 1/20 OUNCE FINE SILVER 2013'.
2013 Proof in silver *FDC** £15
BSB2 **Britannia Ten Pence.** (1/20 oz of fine silver.) R. As BSF13 with the inscription
'BRITANNIA 999 1/20 OZ FINE SILVER 2014'.
2014 Proof in silver *FDC** £15

Obverse portrait by Jody Clark
BSB3 **Britannia Ten Pence.** (1/20 oz of fine silver.) R. As BSF14 with the inscription
'BRITANNIA 1/20 OZ FINE SILVER 999 2015'.
2015 Proof in silver *FDC** £20
BSB4 **Britannia Ten Pence.** (1/20 oz of fine silver.) R. As BSF16 with the inscription
'BRITANNIA 1/20 OZ FINE SILVER 999 2016'.
2016 Proof in silver *FDC** £20

* Coins marked thus were originally issued in Royal Mint sets.
For coin specifications please see table at the beginning of this section.

BSB5 **Britannia Ten Pence.** (1/20 oz of fine silver.) R. As BSF17 with the inscription 'BRITANNIA 1/20 OZ FINE SILVER 999 2017' and with Trident mint mark to mark the 20th Anniversary of the first Britannia silver issue.
2017 Proof in silver *FDC** £20

BSB6 **Britannia Ten Pence.** (1/20 oz of fine silver.) R. As BSF18 with the inscription 'BRITANNIA 1/20 OZ FINE SILVER 999 2018'.
2018 Proof in silver *FDC** £20

BSB7 **Britannia Ten Pence.** (1/20 oz of fine silver.) R. As BSF21 with the inscription 'BRITANNIA 1/20 OZ FINE SILVER 999 2019'.
2019 Proof in silver *FDC** £20

BSB8 **Britannia Ten Pence.** (1/20 oz of fine silver.) R. As BSF22 with the inscription 'BRITANNIA 1/20 OZ FINE SILVER 999 2020'.
2020 Proof in silver *FDC** £20

BSB9 **Britannia Ten Pence.** (1/20oz of fine silver.) R. As BSF24 with the inscription 'BRITANNIA 1/20 OZ 999 FINE SILVER 2021'.
2021 Proof in silver *FDC* (Edition: 1,100)* £20

BSB10 **Britannia Ten Pence.** (1/20oz of fine silver) R. As BSF26 with the inscription '1/20 OZ 999 BRITANNIA FINE SILVER 2022'.
2022 Proof in silver *FDC* (Edition: 1,310)* £20

TWENTY PENCE

Obverse portrait by Raphael Maklouf

BSC1 **Britannia Twenty Pence.** (1/10 oz of fine silver.) R. As BSF1 with the inscription 'BRITANNIA TENTH OUNCE FINE SILVER 1997'.
1997 Proof in silver *FDC* (Issued: 8,686 plus coins in sets) £20

Obverse portrait by Ian Rank-Broadley

BSC2 **Britannia Twenty Pence.** (1/10 oz of fine silver.) R. As BSF2 with the inscription 'BRITANNIA 1/10 OUNCE FINE SILVER' and the date of the year.
1998 Proof in silver *FDC* (Issued: 2,724 plus coins in sets) £20
2006 BU £20
2012 Proof in silver *FDC** £20

BSC3 **Britannia Twenty Pence.** (1/10 oz of fine silver.) R. As BSF4 with the inscription 'BRITANNIA TENTH OUNCE FINE SILVER 2001'.
2001 Proof in silver *FDC* (Issued: 826 plus coins in sets) £20

BSC4 **Britannia Twenty Pence.** (1/10 oz of fine silver.) R. As BSF5 with the inscription 'BRITANNIA TENTH OUNCE FINE SILVER 2003' .
2003 Proof in silver *FDC* (Issued: 1,179 plus coins in sets) £20

BSC5 **Britannia Twenty Pence.** (1/10 oz of fine silver.) R. As BSF6 with the inscription 'BRITANNIA TENTH OUNCE FINE SILVER 2005'.
2005 Proof in silver *FDC* (Issued: 913 plus coins in sets) £20

BSC6 **Britannia Twenty Pence.** (1/10 oz of fine silver.) R. As BSF7 with the inscription 'BRITANNIA TENTH OUNCE FINE SILVER 2007'.
2007 Proof in silver *FDC* (Issued: 901 plus coins in sets) £20

BSC7 **Britannia Twenty Pence.** (1/10 oz of fine silver.) R. As BSF8 with the inscription 'BRITANNIA TENTH OUNCE FINE SILVER 2008'.
2008 Proof in silver *FDC* (Issued: 725 plus coins in sets) £20

BSC8 **Britannia Twenty Pence.** (1/10 oz of fine silver.) R. As BSF 3 with the inscription 'BRITANNIA TENTH OUNCE FINE SILVER 2009'.
2009 Proof in silver *FDC* (Issued: 1,000 plus coins in sets) £20

* *Coins marked thus were originally issued in Royal Mint sets.*
For coin specifications please see table at the beginning of this section.

BSC9 **Britannia Twenty Pence.** (1/10 oz of fine silver.) Ṛ. As BSF9 with the inscription 'BRITANNIA TENTH OUNCE FINE SILVER 2010'.
2010 Proof in silver *FDC* (Issued: 989 plus coins in sets)......................................£20

BSC10 **Britannia Twenty Pence.** (1/10 oz of fine silver.) Ṛ. As BSF10 with the inscription 'BRITANNIA TENTH OUNCE FINE SILVER 2011'.
2011 Proof in silver *FDC** £20

BSC11 **Britannia Twenty Pence.** (1/10 oz of fine silver.) Ṛ. As BSF11 with the inscription 'BRITANNIA 1/10 OUNCE FINE SILVER 2013'.
2013 Proof in silver *FDC** £20

BSC12 **Britannia Twenty Pence.** (1/10 oz of fine silver.) Ṛ. As BSF13 with the inscription 'BRITANNIA 999 1/10 OZ FINE SILVER 2014'.
2014 Proof in silver *FDC** £25

Obverse portrait by Jody Clark
BSC13 **Britannia Twenty Pence.** (1/10 oz of fine silver.) Ṛ. As BSF14 with the inscription 'BRITANNIA 1/10 OZ FINE SILVER 999 2015'.
2015 Proof in silver *FDC** £25

BSC14 **Britannia Twenty Pence.** (1/10 oz of fine silver.) Ṛ. As BSF16 with the inscription 'BRITANNIA 1/10 OZ FINE SILVER 999 2016'.
2016 Proof in silver *FDC** £25

BSC15 **Britannia Twenty Pence.** (1/10 oz of fine silver.) Ṛ. As BSF17 with the inscription 'BRITANNIA 1/10 OZ FINE SILVER 999 2017' and with Trident mint mark to mark the 20th Anniversary of the first Britannia silver issue.
2017 Proof in silver *FDC** £25

BSC16 **Britannia Twenty Pence.** (1/10 oz of fine silver.) Ṛ. As BSF18 with the inscription 'BRITANNIA 1/10 OZ FINE SILVER 999 2018'.
2018 Proof in silver *FDC** £25

BSC17 **Britannia Twenty Pence.** (1/10 oz of fine silver.) Ṛ. As BSF21 with the inscription 'BRITANNIA 1/10 OZ FINE SILVER 999 2019'.
2019 Proof in silver *FDC** £25

BSC18 **Britannia Twenty pence.** (1/10oz of fine silver.) Ṛ. As BSF15F with the inscription 'BRITANNIA' the date of the year '1/10OZ 999 FINE SILVER'.
2019 Unc £15
2020 Unc £15
2021 Unc £15

BSC19 **Britannia Twenty Pence.** (1/10 oz of fine silver.) Ṛ. As BSF22 with the inscription 'BRITANNIA 1/10 OZ FINE SILVER 999 2020'.
2020 Proof in silver *FDC** £25

BSC20 **Britannia Twenty Pence.** (1/10oz of fine silver.) Ṛ. As BSF24 with the inscription 'BRITANNIA 1/10 OZ 999 FINE SILVER 2021'.
2021 Proof in silver *FDC** (Edition: 1,100) £25

BSC21 **Britannia Twenty Pence.** (1/10oz of fine silver) Ṛ. As BSF26 with the inscription '1/10 OZ 999 BRITANNIA FINE SILVER 2022'.
2022 Proof in silver *FDC* (Edition: 1,310)* £25

FIFTY PENCE

Obverse portrait by Raphael Maklouf
BSD1 **Britannia Fifty Pence.** (1/4 oz of fine silver.) Ṛ. As BSF1 with the inscription 'BRITANNIA QUARTER OUNCE FINE SILVER 1997'.
1997 Proof in silver *FDC** £25

* Coins marked thus were originally issued in Royal Mint sets.
For coin specifications please see table at the beginning of this section.
Obverse portrait by Ian Rank-Broadley
BSD2 **Britannia Fifty Pence.** (1/4 oz of fine silver.) Ṛ. As BSF2 with the inscription

'BRITANNIA 1/4 OUNCE FINE SILVER' and the date of the year.

1998 Proof in silver *FDC**...£25

2012 Proof in silver *FDC**...£25

BSD3 **Britannia Fifty Pence.** (1/4 oz of fine silver.) R. As BSF4 with the inscription 'BRITANNIA QUARTER OUNCE FINE SILVER 2001'.

2001 Proof in silver *FDC**...£25

BSD4 **Britannia Fifty Pence.** (1/4 oz of fine silver.) R. As BSF5 with the inscription 'BRITANNIA QUARTER OUNCE FINE SILVER 2003'.

2003 Proof in silver *FDC**...£25

BSD5 **Britannia Fifty Pence.** (1/4 oz of fine silver.) R. As BSF6 with the inscription 'BRITANNIA 1/4 OUNCE FINE SILVER 2005'.

2005 Proof in silver *FDC**...£25

BSD6 **Britannia Fifty Pence.** (1/4 oz of fine silver.) R. As BSF7 with the inscription 'BRITANNIA QUARTER OUNCE FINE SILVER 2007'.

2007 Proof in silver *FDC**...£25

BSD7 **Britannia Fifty Pence.** (1/4 oz of fine silver.) R. As BSF8 with the inscription 'BRITANNIA 1/4 OUNCE FINE SILVER 2008'.

2008 Proof in silver *FDC**...£25

BSD8 **Britannia Fifty Pence.** (1/4 oz of fine silver.) R. As BSF3 with the inscription 'BRITANNIA 1/4 OUNCE FINE SILVER 2009'.

2009 Proof in silver *FDC**...£25

BSD9 **Britannia Fifty Pence.** (1/4 oz of fine silver.) R. As BSF9 with the inscription 'BRITANNIA 1/4 OUNCE FINE SILVER 2010'.

2010 Proof in silver *FDC**...£25

BSD10 **Britannia Fifty Pence.** (1/4 oz of fine silver.) R. As BSF10 with the inscription 'BRITANNIA 1/4 OUNCE FINE SILVER 2011'.

2011 Proof in silver *FDC**...£25

BSD11 **Britannia Fifty Pence.** (1/4 oz of fine silver.) R. As BSF11 with the inscription 'BRITANNIA 1/4 OUNCE FINE SILVER 2013'.

2013 Proof in silver *FDC**...£25

BSD12 **Britannia Fifty Pence.** (1/4oz of fine silver.) R. As BSD2 but with edge inscription 'SS GAIRSOPPA'.

2013 BU £12

The silver for this coin & BSD13A was salvaged from the wreck of the SS 'Gairsoppa' sunk in 1941.

BSD13 **Britannia Fifty Pence.** (1/4 oz of fine silver.) R. As BSF13 with the inscription 'BRITANNIA 999 1/4 OZ FINE SILVER 2014'.

2014 Proof in silver *FDC**...£30

BSD14 **Britannia Fifty pence.** (1/4oz of fine silver.) R. As BSF12 with the inscription 'BRITANNIA 2014 ¼ OZ 999 FINE SILVER'

2014 Unc (Edition: Sold in a case with a 2014 bullion sovereign).......................£30

It is not known whether this coin exists in any other presentation.

BSD14A Britannia Fifty Pence. (1/4oz of fine silver.) R. As BSD13 but with edge inscription 'SS GAIRSOPPA'.

2014 BU in pack (Issued: 19,214)..£25

BSD15 **Britannia Fifty Pence.** (1/4 oz of fine silver.) R. As BSD2 with revised inscription '1/4OZ 999 FINE SILVER' the date '2015' and textured background on the obverse and reverse.

2015 Unc (Edition: 100 in a case with a 2015 bullion sovereign) £25

It is not known whether this coin exists in any other presentation.

* *Coins marked thus were originally issued in Royal Mint sets.*
For coin specifications please see table at the beginning of this section.

Obverse portrait by Jody Clark
BSD16 Britannia Fifty Pence. (1/4 oz of fine silver.) R̩. As BSF14 with the inscription
'BRITANNIA 1/4 OZ FINE SILVER 999 2015'.
2015 Proof in silver *FDC** £30
BSD17 Britannia Fifty Pence. (1/4 oz of fine silver.) R̩. As BSF16 with the inscription
'BRITANNIA 1/4 OZ FINE SILVER 999 2016'.
2016 Proof in silver *FDC** £30
BSD18 Britannia Fifty Pence. (1/4 oz of fine silver.) R̩. As BSF17 with the inscription
'BRITANNIA 1/4 OZ FINE SILVER 999 2017' and with Trident mint mark to mark
the 20th Anniversary of the first Britannia silver issue.
2017 Proof in silver *FDC** £30
BSD19 Britannia Fifty Pence. (1/4 oz of fine silver.) R̩. As BSF18 with the inscription
'BRITANNIA 1/4 OZ FINE SILVER 999 2018'.
2018 Proof in silver *FDC** £30
BSD20 Britannia Fifty Pence. (1/4 oz of fine silver.) R̩. As BSF21 with the inscription
'BRITANNIA 1/4 OZ FINE SILVER 999 2019'.
2019 Proof in silver *FDC** £30
BSD21 Britannia Fifty Pence. (1/4 oz of fine silver.) R̩. As BSF22 with the inscription
'BRITANNIA 1/4 OZ FINE SILVER 999 2020'.
2020 Proof in silver *FDC** £30
BSD22 Britannia Fifty Pence. (1/4oz of fine silver.) R̩. As BSF24 with the inscription
'BRITANNIA 1/4 OZ 999 FINE SILVER 2021'.
2021 Proof in silver *FDC** (Edition: 1,100) £30
BSD23 Britannia Fifty Pence. (1/4oz of fine silver.) R̩. As BSF15F with the inscription
'BRITANNIA' the date of the year '1/4 OZ 999 FINE SILVER'.
2021 Unc £12
2022 Unc £12
BSD24 Britannia Fifty Pence. (1/4oz of fine silver) R̩. As BSF26 with the inscription
'1/4 OZ 999 BRITANNIA FINE SILVER 2022'.
2022 Proof in silver *FDC* (Edition: 1,310)* £30

ONE POUND

Obverse portrait by Raphael Maklouf
BSE1 Britannia. One pound. (1/2 oz of fine silver.) R̩. As BSF1 with the inscription
'BRITANNIA HALF OUNCE FINE SILVER 1997'.
1997 Proof in silver *FDC** £30

Obverse portrait by Ian Rank-Broadley
BSE2 Britannia. One pound. (1/2 oz of fine silver.) R̩. As BSF2 with the inscription
'BRITANNIA 1/2 OUNCE FINE SILVER' and the date of the year.
1998 Proof in silver *FDC** £30
2012 Proof in silver *FDC** £30
BSE2A Britannia. One pound. (1/2 oz of fine silver.) R̩. As BSE2 with satin finish on reverse.
2007 Proof in silver* £30
BSE3 Britannia. One pound. (1/2 oz of fine silver.) R̩. As BSF4 with the inscription
'BRITANNIA HALF OUNCE FINE SILVER' and the date of the year.
2001 Proof in silver *FDC** £30
2012 Proof in silver *FDC** £30
BSE3A Britannia. One pound. (1/2 oz of fine silver.) R̩. As BSE3 with satin finish on reverse.
2007 Proof in silver* £30

* Coins marked thus were originally issued in Royal Mint sets.
For coin specifications please see table at the beginning of this section.

BSE4 **Britannia. One pound.** (1/2 oz of fine silver.) R̟. As BSF5 with the inscription 'BRITANNIA HALF OUNCE FINE SILVER' and the date of the year.
2003 Proof in silver *FDC** £30
2012 Proof in silver *FDC** £30

BSE4A **Britannia. One pound.** (1/2 oz of fine silver.) R̟. As BSE4 with satin finish on reverse.
2007 Proof in silver* £30

BSE5 **Britannia. One pound.** (1/2 oz of fine silver.) R̟. As BSF6 with the inscription 'BRITANNIA 1/2 OUNCE FINE SILVER' and the date of the year.
2005 Proof in silver *FDC** £30
2012 Proof in silver *FDC** £30

BSE5A **Britannia. One pound.** (1/2 oz of fine silver.) R̟. As BSE5 with satin finish on reverse.
2007 Proof in silver* £30

BSE6 **Britannia. One pound.** (1/2 oz of fine silver.) R̟. As BSF7 with the inscription 'BRITANNIA HALF OUNCE FINE SILVER' and the date of the year.
2007 Proof in silver *FDC** £30
2012 Proof in silver *FDC** £30

BSE6A **Britannia. One pound.** (1/2 oz of fine silver.) R̟. As BSE6 with satin finish on reverse.
2007 Proof in silver* £30

BSE6B **Britannia. One pound.** (1/2 oz of fine silver.) R̟. As BSF3 with the inscription 'BRITANNIA HALF OUNCE FINE SILVER' and the date of the year with satin finish on reverse.
2007 Proof in silver* £30

BSE7 **Britannia. One pound.** (1/2 oz of fine silver.) R̟. As BSF8 with the inscription 'BRITANNIA HALF OUNCE FINE SILVER' and the date of the year.
2008 Proof in silver *FDC** £30
2012 Proof in silver *FDC** £30

BSE8 **Britannia. One pound.** (1/2 oz of fine silver.) R̟. As BSF3 with the inscription 'BRITANNIA 1/2 OUNCE FINE SILVER' and the date of the year.
2009 Proof in silver *FDC** £30
2012 Proof in silver *FDC** £30

BSE9 **Britannia. One pound.** (1/2 oz of fine silver.) R̟. As BSF9 with the inscription 'BRITANNIA 1/2 OUNCE FINE SILVER' and the date of the year.
2010 Proof in silver *FDC** £30
2012 Proof in silver *FDC** £30

BSE10 **Britannia. One pound.** (1/2 oz of fine silver.) R̟. As BSF10 with the inscription 'BRITANNIA 1/2 OUNCE FINE SILVER' and the date of the year.
2011 BU (Edition: 5,000) £25
— Proof in silver *FDC** £30
2012 Proof in silver *FDC** £30

BSE11 **Britannia. One pound.** (1/2 oz of fine silver.) R̟. As BSF11 with the inscription 'BRITANNIA 1/2 OUNCE FINE SILVER 2013'.
2013 Proof in silver *FDC** £30

BSE12 **Britannia. One pound.** (1/2 oz of fine silver.) R̟. As BSF13 with the inscription 'BRITANNIA 999 1/2 OZ FINE SILVER 2014'.
2014 Proof in silver *FDC** £40

* Coins marked thus were originally issued in Royal Mint sets.
For coin specifications please see table at the beginning of this section.

Obverse portrait by Jody Clark

BSE13 Britannia. One pound. (1/2 oz of fine silver.) Ŗ. As BSF14 with the inscription 'BRITANNIA 1/2 OZ FINE SILVER 999 2015'.
2015 Proof in silver *FDC** £40

BSE14 Britannia. One pound. (1/2 oz of fine silver.) Ŗ. As BSF16 with the inscription 'BRITANNIA 1/2 OZ FINE SILVER 999 2016'.
2016 Proof in silver *FDC** £40

BSE15 Britannia. One pound. (1/2 oz of fine silver.) Ŗ. As BSF17 with the inscription 'BRITANNIA 1/2 OZ FINE SILVER 999 2017' and wSith Trident mint mark to mark the 20th Anniversary of the first Britannia silver issue.
2017 Proof in silver *FDC** £40

BSE16 Britannia. One pound. (1/2 oz of fine silver.) Ŗ. As BSF18 with the inscription 'BRITANNIA 1/2 OZ FINE SILVER 999 2018'.
2018 Proof in silver *FDC** £40

BSE17 Britannia. One pound. (1/2 oz of fine silver.) Ŗ. As BSF21 with the inscription 'BRITANNIA 1/2 OZ FINE SILVER 999 2019'.
2019 Proof in silver *FDC** £40

BSE18 Britannia. One pound. (1/2 oz of fine silver.) Ŗ. As BSF22 with the inscription 'BRITANNIA 1/2 OZ FINE SILVER 999 2020'.
2020 Proof in silver *FDC** £40

BSE19 Britannia. One pound. (1/2oz of fine silver.) Ŗ. As BSF24 with the inscription 'BRITANNIA 1/2 OZ 999 FINE SILVER 2021'.
2021 Proof in silver *FDC** (Edition: 1,100)* £45

BSE20 Britannia. One pound. (1/2oz of fine silver) Ŗ. As BSF26 with the inscription '1/2 OZ 999 BRITANNIA FINE SILVER 2022'.
2022 Proof in silver *FDC* (Edition: 1,310)* £45

TWO POUNDS

Obverse portrait by Raphael Maklouf

BSF1

BSF1 Britannia. Two pounds. (1 oz of fine silver.) 10th Anniversary of Britannia bullion coins. Ŗ. The figure of Britannia standing in a chariot drawn along the seashore by two horses, with the word 'BRITANNIA', the inscription 'ONE OUNCE FINE SILVER' and the date of the year. (Reverse design: Philip Nathan.)
1997 Proof in silver *FDC* (Issued: 4,173 plus coins in sets)......................................£200

* *Coins marked thus were originally issued in Royal Mint sets.*
For coin specifications please see table at the beginning of this section.

Obverse portrait by Ian Rank-Broadley

BSF2

BSF2   **Britannia. Two pounds**. (1 oz of fine silver.) ℞. The figure of Britannia standing upon
a rock in the sea, her right hand grasping a trident and her left hand resting on a shield
and holding an olive branch, with the word 'BRITANNIA', the date of the year and the
inscription 'ONE OUNCE FINE SILVER'. (Reverse design: Philip Nathan.)

1998 Unc (Issued: 88,909) £40
— Proof in silver *FDC* (Issued: 2,168 plus coins in sets) £80
2000 Unc (Issued: 81,301) £40
2002 Unc (Issued: 36,543) £40
2004 Unc (Edition: 100,000) £40
— Proof in silver *FDC* (Issued: 2,174)...£65
2006 Unc (Edition: 100,000) £40
— Proof in silver *FDC* (Issued: 2,529)...£65
2012 Unc (Edition: 100,0000 ....£40
— Proof in silver *FDC* (Issued: 2,937 plus coins in sets) £75

BSF2A **Britannia. Two pounds.** (1 oz of fine silver.) ℞. As BSF2 with selected gold plating
of obverse and reverse.

2006 Proof in silver *FDC** £70

BSF3

BSF3   **Britannia. Two pounds.** (1 oz of fine silver.) ℞. As BSF1 with the word 'BRITANNIA',
the inscription 'ONE OUNCE FINE SILVER' and the date of the year.

1999 Unc (Issued: 69,394) £40
2009 Unc (Issued: 100,000) £40
— Proof in silver *FDC* (Issued: 4,284 plus coins in sets).......................................£65

BSF3A **Britannia. Two pounds.** (1 oz of fine silver.) ℞. As BSF3 with selected gold plating of
obverse and reverse.

2006 Proof in silver *FDC** £70

* *Coins marked thus were originally issued in Royal Mint sets.*
For coin specifications please see table at the beginning of this section.

BSF4   BSF5

BSF4 **Britannia. Two pounds.** (1 oz of fine silver) ℞. The figure of Britannia, as guardian, with a shield in her left hand and a trident in her right hand, accompanied by a lion and, against the background of a wave motif, the words 'ONE OUNCE FINE SILVER' to the left and 'BRITANNIA' and the date of the year to the right. (Reverse design: Philip Nathan.)

2001 Unc (Issued: 44,816) £40
— Proof *FDC* (Issued: 3,047 plus coins in sets)......................................£65

BSF4A **Britannia. Two pounds.** (1 oz of fine silver.) ℞. As BSF4 with selected gold plating of obverse and reverse.

2006 Proof in silver *FDC** £70

BSF5 **Britannia. Two pounds.** (1 oz fine silver.) ℞. Helmeted head of Britannia with, to the left, the word 'BRITANNIA' and, to the right, the inscription 'ONE OUNCE FINE SILVER' and the date of the year, the whole being overlaid with a wave pattern. (Reverse design: Philip Nathan.)

2003 Unc (Issued: 73,271) £45
— Proof *FDC* (Issued: 2,016 plus coins in sets)......................................£65

BSF5A **Britannia. Two pounds.** (1 oz of fine silver.) ℞. As BSF5 with selected gold plating of obverse and reverse.

2006 Proof in silver *FDC** £70

BSF6   BSF7

BSF6 **Britannia. Two pounds.** (1 oz of fine silver.) ℞. Seated figure of Britannia facing to the left holding a trident with a shield at her side, with the word 'BRITANNIA', the inscription 'ONE OUNCE FINE SILVER' and the date of the year. (Reverse design: Philip Nathan.)

2005 Unc (Edition: 100,000) £45
— Proof *FDC* (Issued: 1,539 plus coins in sets) £65

* Coins marked thus were originally issued in Royal Mint sets.
For coin specifications please see table at the beginning of this section.

BSF6A Britannia. Two pounds. (1 oz of fine silver.) R. As BSF6 with selected gold
plating of obverse and reverse.
2006 Proof in silver *FDC** £70

BSF7   Britannia. Two pounds. (1 oz of fine silver.) R. Seated figure of Britannia facing right
holding a trident in her right hand and a sprig of olive in the left hand with a lion at her
feet with the inscription 'ONE OUNCE FINE SILVER' and the word 'BRITANNIA' and
the date of the year. (Reverse design: Christopher Le Brun.)
2007 Unc (Edition: 100,000) £40
—   Proof *FDC* (Issued: 5,157 plus coins in sets) £65

| BSF8 | BSF9 | BSF10 |

BSF8   Britannia. Two pounds. (1 oz of fine silver) R. A Standing figure of Britannia holding a
trident with a shield at her side, the folds of her dress transforming into a wave, with the
word 'BRITANNIA' and the date of the year and the inscription 'ONE OUNCE FINE
SILVER'.(Reverse design: John Bergdahl)
2008 Unc (Edition: 100,000)   £40
—   Proof *FDC* (Issued: 2,500 plus coins in sets)   £65

BSF9   Britannia. Two pounds. (1 oz of fine silver.) R. A design depicting a profile bust of
Britannia wearing a helmet, accompanied by the name 'BRITANNIA', the inscription
'ONE OUNCE FINE SILVER' and the date '2010'. (Reverse design: Suzie Zamit.)
2010 Unc (Issued: 126,367) £40
—   Proof *FDC* (Issued: 3,042 plus coins in sets)..£75

BSF10 Britannia. Two pounds. (1 oz fine silver.) R. A design depicting a seated figure of
Britannia set against a background of a rippling Union Flag accompanied by the
words 'ONE OUNCE FINE SILVER BRITANNIA' and the date '2011'. (Reverse
design: David Mach.)
2011 Unc (Edition: 500,000) £40
—   Unc Matt £45
—   Proof *FDC* (Issued: 2,490 plus coins in sets) £75

BSF10A Britannia. Two Pounds. (1oz of fine silver.) R. As BSF2 but .999 silver and
38.61mm diameter.
2013 Unc £40

BSF10B Britannia. Two Pounds. (1oz of fine silver.) R. As BSF10A but with incuse
decoration on edge as indicated.
2013 Snake Unc £45

* Coins marked thus were originally issued in Royal Mint sets.
For coin specifications please see table at the beginning of this section..

BSF11

BSF11 Britannia. Two pounds. (1 oz of fine silver.) R. Seated figure of Britannia holding a trident with a shield at her side and an owl upon her knee with the word 'BRITANNIA' and the date of the year above and the inscription 'ONE OUNCE FINE SILVER' below the figure of Britannia. (Reverse design: Robert Hunt.)
2013 BU (Issued: 2,387) £55
—   Proof in silver *FDC* (Issued: 3,468 plus coins in sets)..£75

Obverse portrait by Ian Rank-Broadley

BSF12

BSF12 Britannia. Two pounds. (1 oz of fine silver.) R. As BSF2 with revised inscription '1oz 999 FINE SILVER' and the date of the year.
2014 Unc £40
—   BU(Issued: 1,493) £50
2015 BU (Issued: 2,870) £50
BSF12 Error obverse – known as a mule. See CLBB1A in Chinese Lunar Year series.
BSF12A Britannia. Two pounds. (1 oz of fine silver.) R. As BF12 but with incuse decoration on edge as indicated.
2014 Horse Unc...£45
BSF12B Britannia. Two pounds. (1 oz of fine silver.) R. As BSF12 but with textured background on the obverse and reverse.
2015 Unc £40
BSF12C Britannia. Two pounds. (1oz of fine silver.) R. As BSF12B but with incuse decoration on edge as indicated.
2015 Sheep Unc £45

For coin specifications please see table at the beginning of this section.

BSF13

BSF13 Britannia. Two pounds. (1 oz of fine silver.) ℞. A design of the standing figure of Britannia bearing a trident and shield, with a lion at her feet, set against the backdrop of a globe, and with the inscription 'BRITANNIA 999 1 OZ FINE SILVER 2014'.(Reverse design: Jody Clark.)

2014 — Proof in silver *FDC* (Issued: 2,981 plus coins in sets)................................£150

Obverse portrait by Jody Clark

BSF14

BSF14 Britannia. Two pounds. (1 oz of fine silver.) ℞. A figure of Britannia bearing a trident and shield, set against a backdrop of a sailing ship, cliffs and a lighthouse with the inscription 'BRITANNIA 1 OZ FINE SILVER 999 2015'. (Reverse design: Antony Dufort.)

2015 Proof in silver *FDC* (Issued: 4,240 plus coins in sets)......................................£85

For coin specifications please see table at the beginning of this section.

BSF15 Britannia. Two pounds. (1 oz of fine silver.) R̟. As BSF12.
    2016 BU (Issued: 3,901) £50
    2017 BU (Issued: 4,056) £50
    2018 BU (Issued: 2,940) £50
BSF15A Britannia. Two pounds. (1oz of fine silver.) R̟. As BSF12 but with textured
    background on the obverse and reverse.
    2016 Unc £40
BSF15B Britannia. Two pounds. (1oz of fine silver.) R̟. As BSB15A but with incuse
    decoration on edge as indicated.
    2016 Monkey Unc (Issued 750,000) £45

BSF15C   BSF15E

BSF15C Britannia. Two pounds. (1oz of fine silver.) R̟. As BSF12 but with textured
    background on the obverse and a speckled radial sunburst on the reverse.
    2017 Unc £40
BSF15D Britannia. Two pounds. (1oz of fine silver.) R̟. As BSB15C but with incuse
    decoration on edge as indicated.
    2017 Rooster Unc £45
BSF15E Britannia. Two pounds. (1oz of fine silver.) R̟. As BSF15C but with Trident 20
    mint mark on reverse to mark the 20th anniversary of this Philip Nathan design and
    with guilloché finish to the table area of the obverse.
    2017 Unc (Edition: 120,000) £50
BSF15F Britannia. Two pounds. (1oz of fine silver.) R̟. As BSF12 but with guilloché
    background on the obverse table area and a speckled radial sunburst on the reverse.
    2018 Unc £40
    2019 Unc £40
    2020 Unc £35
BSF15G Britannia. Two pounds. (1oz of fine silver.) R̟. As BSF15F but with incuse
    decoration on edge depicting a lunar year animal as indicated.
    2018 Dog Unc £45
    2019 Pig Unc £75
    2020 Rat Unc £45

BSF16   BSF17

BSF16 Britannia. Two pounds. (1 oz. of fine silver.) R. A standing figure of Britannia
holding in her left hand a trident and in her right hand a shield with a lion in the
background and the inscription 'BRITANNIA 1 OZ FINE SILVER 999 2016'.
(Reverse design: Suzie Zamit.)
2016 Proof in silver *FDC* (Issued: 4,553 plus coins in sets)......................................£85
—   Proof in silver *FDC* with reversed frosting (Edition: 500)* £120

BSF17 Britannia. Two pounds. (1 oz of fine silver.) R. The figure of Britannia, holding
a shield and trident, with her body combined with the United Kingdom and the
inscription 'BRITANNIA 1 OZ FINE SILVER 999 2017' with a Trident mint mark
to mark the 20th Anniversary of the first Britannia silver issue. (Reverse design:
Louis Tamlyn.)
2017 Proof in silver *FDC* (Issued: 5,304 plus coins in sets)......................................£85
—   Proof in silver *FDC* with reversed frosting (Edition: 500)* £120

BSF18 Britannia. Two pounds. (1 oz of fine silver.) R. As BSF1 but with textured
background of speckled radial sunburst on the reverse, plain edge with inscription
'1997-2017' to mark the 20th anniversary of this Philip Nathan design.
2017 Unc £55

BSF19   BSF20

BSF19 Britannia. Two pounds. (1 oz of fine silver.) R. The figure of Britannia wearing a
Corinthian helmet garlanded with the floral symbols of Britain and the inscription
'BRITANNIA 1 OZ FINE SILVER 999 2018'. (Reverse design: David Lawrence.)
2018 Proof in silver *FDC* (Issued: 3,630 plus coins in sets)......................................£85
—   Proof in silver *FDC* with reversed frosting (Issued: 84)* £120

BSF20 Britannia. Two pounds. (1 oz of fine silver.) R. The centre design of Britannia as
BSF12 but with an Oriental Border and the inscription within the centre rather than
around the design.
2018 Unc (Edition: 100,000)..£40
—   Proof in silver *FDC* (Edition: 2,500) £85
2019 Unc (Edition: 50,000)..£40
2020 Unc (Edition: 50,000)..£40

* Coins marked thus were originally issued in Royal Mint sets.

BSF21   BSF22

BSF21 Britannia. Two pounds. (1 oz of fine silver.) Ɍ. Britannia raising trident towards a
new dawn with a lion beside her as a steadfast companion with the word
'BRITANNIA', the date of the year and the inscription '1 OZ FINE SILVER 999'.
(Reverse design: David Lawrence.)
2019 BU (Issued 1,826) £55
—   Proof in silver *FDC* (Issued: 2,995 plus coins in sets).....................................£85
—   Proof in silver *FDC* with reversed frosting (Issued: 539)* £120

BSF22 Britannia. Two pounds. (1 oz of fine silver.) Ɍ. Britannia standing amid a rocky
ocean setting as waves crash around her with the word "BRITANNIA", the date of the
year and the inscription "1 OZ 999 FINE SILVER". (Reverse design: James Tottle.)
2020 BU (Edition: 7,010)...£55
—   Proof in silver *FDC* (Edition: 3,000 plus coins in sets) £85
—   Proof in silver *FDC* with reversed frosting (Edition: 700)* £120

BSF23   BSF24

BSF23 Britannia. Two pounds. (1oz of fine silver.) Ɍ. As BSF12 but with four added
elements; the image of waves behind Britannia, additional details on shield, thin inner
rim with repeated inscription 'DECUS ET TUTAMEN' in microtext, and hologram at
lower left showing alternately a trident and a padlock.
2021 Unc £30
2022 Unc £30
2023 Unc £30

BSF24 Britannia. Two pounds. (1oz of fine silver.) Ɍ. A depiction of the figure of Britannia
aside a seated lion and the inscription 'BRITANNIA 1oz 999 FINE SILVER 2021'.
(Reverse design: P J Lynch.)
2021 Proof in silver *FDC* (Edition: 4,860 including coins in sets)...........................£95
—   Proof in silver *FDC* with reversed frosting (Edition: 500)* £120

BSF25 Britannia. Two pounds. (1oz of fine silver.) Ɍ. As BSG1 but with the inscription
'BRITANNIA 1oz 999 FINE SILVER 2021'.
2021 BU (Edition: 7,510)..£60

* Coins marked thus were originally issued in Royal Mint sets.
For coin specifications please see table at the beginning of this section.

BSF26   BSF27

BSF26 Britannia. Two pounds. (1oz of fine silver.) Ɍ. A depiction of the figure of Britannia
    carrying a trident and shield and the inscription '1oz 999 BRITANNIA FINE SILVER
    2022'. (Reverse design: Dan Thorne.)
    2022 Proof in silver *FDC* (Edition: 3,500 plus coins in sets) £95
    —   Proof in silver *FDC* with reversed frosting (Edition: 500)* £120
BSF27 Britannia. Two pounds. (1oz of fine silver.) Ɍ. A depiction of Britannia at different
    ages of her life and the inscription 'BRITANNIA 2022 1oz 999 FINE SILVER'.
    (Reverse design: Sandra Deiana.)
    2022 BU in silver FDC (Edition: 5,010) £60

FIVE POUNDS

BSG1

BSG1   Britannia. Five pounds. (2oz of fine silver.) Ɍ. A profile of the head of Britannia and
    the inscription 'BRITANNIA 2 OZ 999 FINE SILVER 2021'. (Reverse design:
    P J Lynch.)
    2021 Proof in silver *FDC* (Edition: 550) £195
BSG2   Britannia. Five pounds. (2oz of fine silver.) Ɍ. As BSF24 but with the inscription
    'BRITANNIA 2OZ 999 FINE SILVER 2021'.
    2021 Proof in silver *FDC* (Edition: 860) £195
BSG3   Britannia. Five pounds. (2oz of fine silver.) Ɍ. As BSF26 but with the inscription
    '2 OZ 999 BRITANNIA FINE SILVER 2022'.
    2022 Proof in silver *FDC* (Edition: 760) £185
BSG4   Britannia. Five pounds. (2oz of fine silver.) Ɍ. As BSF27 but with the inscription
    'BRITANNIA 2022 2 OZ 999 FINE SILVER'.
    2022 Proof in silver *FDC* (Edition: 556) £185

* Coins marked thus were originally issued in Royal Mint sets.
For coin specifications please see table at the beginning of this section.

TEN POUNDS

Obverse portrait by Ian Rank-Broadley

BSH1

BSH1   Britannia. Ten pounds. (5 oz of fine silver.) R. Seated figure of Britannia holding
a trident with a shield at her side and an owl upon her knee with the word
'BRITANNIA' and the date of the year above and the inscription '5 OUNCES FINE
SILVER' below the figure of Britannia. (Reverse design: Robert Hunt.)
2013 Proof in silver *FDC* (Issued: 4,054) £450

BSH2

BSH2   Britannia. Ten pounds. (5 oz of fine silver.) R. A design of the standing figure of
Britannia bearing a trident and shield, with a lion at her feet, set against the backdrop
of a globe, and with the inscription 'BRITANNIA 999 5 OZ FINE SILVER 2014'.
(Reverse design: Jody Clark.)
2014 Proof in silver *FDC* (Issued: 1,348) £395

For coin specifications please see table at the beginning of this section.

Obverse portrait by Jody Clark

BSH3

BSH3   **Britannia. Ten pounds.** (5 oz of fine silver.) ℞. A figure of Britannia bearing a trident
and shield, set against a backdrop of a sailing ship, cliffs and a lighthouse with the
inscription 'BRITANNIA 5 OZ FINE SILVER 999 2015'. (Reverse design:
Antony Dufort.)
2015 Proof in silver *FDC* (Issued: 995) £395

BSH4   BSH5

BSH4   **Britannia. Ten pounds.** (5 oz of fine silver.) ℞. A standing figure of Britannia holding
in her left hand a trident and in her right hand a shield with a lion in the background
and the inscription 'BRITANNIA 5 OZ FINE SILVER 999 2016'. (Reverse design:
Suzie Zamit.)
2016 Proof in silver *FDC* (Issued: 783) £395

BSH5   **Britannia. Ten pounds.** (5 oz of fine silver.) ℞. The figure of Britannia, holding a
shield and trident, with her body combined with the United Kingdom and the inscription
'BRITANNIA 5 OZ FINE SILVER 999 2017' with a Trident mint mark to mark the 20th
Anniversary of the first Britannia silver issue. (Reverse design:Louis Tamlyn.)
2017 — Proof in silver *FDC* (Issued: 669) £415

BSH6   **Britannia. Ten pounds.** (5 oz of fine silver.) ℞. The figure of Britannia wearing a
Corinthian helmet garlanded with the floral symbols of Britain and the inscription
'BRITANNIA 5 OZ FINE SILVER 999 2018'. (Reverse design: David Lawrence.)
2018 Proof in silver *FDC* (Issued: 453) £420

BSH7   **Britannia. Ten pounds.** (5 oz of fine silver.) ℞. Britannia raising trident towards a
new dawn with a lion beside her as a steadfast companion with the word
'BRITANNIA', the date of the year and the inscription '5 OZ FINE SILVER 999'.
(Reverse design: David Lawrence.)
2019 Proof in silver *FDC* (Issued: 302) £420

For coin specifications please see table at the beginning of this section.

BSH8 **Britannia. Ten pounds.** (5 oz of fine silver.). R. Britannia standing amid a rocky ocean setting as waves crash around her with the word 'BRITANNIA', the date of the year and the inscription '5 OZ 999 FINE SILVER'. (Reverse design: James Tottle.)
2020 Proof in silver *FDC* (Edition: 250) £420

BSH9 **Britannia. Ten pounds.** (5oz of fine silver.) R. As BSF24 with the inscription 'BRITANNIA 5OZ 999 FINE SILVER 2021'.
2021 Proof in silver *FDC* (Edition: 285) £455

BSH10 **Britannia. Ten pounds.** (5oz of fine silver.) R. As BSF26 with the inscription '5OZ 999 BRITANNIA FINE SILVER 2022'.
2022 Proof in silver *FDC* (Edition: 386) £465

BSJ1 **Britannia. Ten pounds.** (10 oz of fine silver.) R. As BSF2 with the inscription 'BRITANNIA', the date of the year, '10 OZ 999 FINE SILVER'.
2021 Unc £275

BSJ2 **Britannia. Ten pounds.** (10 oz of fine silver.) R. As BSJ1 but with four added elements; the image of waves behind Britannia, additional details on shield, thin inner rim with repeated inscription 'DECUS ET TUTAMEN' in microtext, and hologram at lower left showing alternately a trident and a padlock.
2022 Unc £300

TWO HUNDRED AND FIFTY POUNDS
Obverse portrait by Jody Clark

BSL1 **Britannia. Two hundred and fifty pounds.** (20 oz of fine silver.) R. As BSH5 with revised inscription 'BRITANNIA 20 OZ FINE SILVER 999 2017' with a Trident mint mark to mark the 20th Anniversary of the first Britannia silver issue. (Reverse design: Louis Tamlyn.)
2017 Proof in silver *FDC* (Issued: 103)...£1650

FIVE HUNDRED POUNDS
Obverse portrait by Jody Clark

BSM1

BSM1 **Britannia. Five hundred pounds.** (1 kilo of fine silver.) R. The figure of Britannia wearing a Corinthian helmet garlanded with the floral symbols of Britain and the inscription 'BRITANNIA 1 KILO FINE SILVER 999 2018'. (Reverse design: David Lawrence)
2018 Proof in silver *FDC* (Issued: 235)...£2100

For coin specifications please see table at the beginning of this section.

BSM2   **Britannia. Five hundred pounds.** (1 kilo of fine silver.) ℞. Britannia raising trident towards a new dawn with a lion beside her as a steadfast companion with the word 'BRITANNIA', the date of the year and the inscription '1 KILO FINE SILVER 999'. (Reverse design: David Lawrence.)
2019 Proof in silver *FDC* (Issued: 83) £2100

BSM3   **Britannia. Five hundred pounds.** (1 kilo of fine silver.) ℞ As BSF22.
2020 Proof in silver *FDC* (Edition: 60) £2100

BSM4   **Britannia. Five hundred pounds.** (1 kilo of fine silver.) ℞. As BSG1 with the inscription 'BRITANNIA 1 KILO 999 FINE SILVER'.
2021 Proof in silver *FDC* (Edition: 50) £2445

BSM5   **Britannia. Five hundred pounds.** (1 kilo of fine silver.) ℞. As BSF27 with the inscription 'BRITANNIA 2022 1 KILO 999 FINE SILVER'.
2022 Proof in silver *FDC* (Edition: 43) £2330

ONE THOUSAND POUNDS

Obverse portrait by Jody Clark

BSN1   **Britannia. One thousand pounds.** (2 kilos of fine silver) ℞. As BSF24 with the inscription "BRITANNIA 2 KILO 999 FINE SILVER". .
2021 Proof in silver *FDC* (Edition: 110)...£5000

BSN2   **Britannia. One thousand pounds.** (2 kilos of fine silver) ℞. As BSF26 with the inscription '2 KILO 999 BRITANNIA FINE SILVER'.
2022 Proof in silver *FDC* (Edition: 78) £4995

For coin specifications please see table at the beginning of this section.

Britannia Silver Proof Sets

				£
PBS01–**1997**	£2 – 20p (Issued: 11,832)	(4)	200
PBS02–**1998**	£2 – 20p (Issued: 3,045)	(4)	110
PBS03–**2001**	£2 – 20p (Issued: 4,596)	(4)	110
PBS04–**2003**	£2 – 20p (Issued: 3,669)	(4)	110
PBS06–**2005**	£2 – 20p (Issued: 2,360)	(4)	125
PBS07–**2006**	Britannia set of five different £2 designs with selected gold plating of obverse and reverse (Issued: 3,000)	(5)	350
PBS08–**2007**	£2 - 20p (Issued: 2,500)	(4)	110
PBS09–**2007**	Britannia set of six different proof £1 designs with satin finish on reverse (Issued: 2,000)	(6)	225
PBS10–**2008**	£2 – 20p (Issued: 2,500)	(4)	110
PBS11–**2009**	£2 – 20p (Issued: 2,500)	(4)	110
PBS12–**2010**	£2 – 20p (Issued: 3,497)	(4)	110
PBS13–**2011**	£2 – 20p (Issued: 2,483)	(4)	110
PBS14–**2012**	£2 – 20p (Issued: 2,595)	(4)	125
PBS15–**2012**	Britannia £1 proofs, set of nine different reverse designs (Issued: 1,656)	(9)	400
PBS16–**2013**	£2 – 10p (Issued: 3,087)	(5)	150
PBS17–**2013**	20p and 10p	(2)	35
PBS18–**2014**	£2 – 5p (Issued: 1,735)	(6)	330
PBS19–**2014**	20p – 5p (Issued: 998)	(3)	45
PBS20–**2015**	£2 – 5p (Issued: 1,009)	(6)	200
PBS22–**2016**	£2 – 5p (Issued: 1,050)	(6)	200
PBS23–**2016**	£2 – set of two with one reverse frosted (Edition: 500)	(2)	185
PBS24–**2017**	£2 – 5p (Issued: 1,351)	(6)	215
PBS25–**2017**	£2 – set of two with one reverse frosted (Issued: 500)	(2)	185
PBS26–**2018**	£2 – 5p (Issued: 937)	(6)	215
PBS27–**2018**	£2 – set of two with one reverse frosted (Issued: 84)	(2)	185
PBS28–**2019**	£2 - 5p (Issued: 949)	(6)	215
PBS29–**2019**	£2 – set of two with one reverse frosted (Issued: 539)	(2)	185
PBS30–**2020**	£2 - 5p (Edition: 1,000)	(6)	225
PBS31–**2020**	£2 – set of two with one reverse frosted (Edition: 700)	(2)	185
PBS32–**2021**	£2 – 5p (Edition: 1,100)	(6)	230
PBS33–**2021**	£2 – set of two with one reverse frosted (Edition: 500)	(2)	185
PBS34–**2022**	£2 – 5p (Edition: 1300)	(6)	235
PBS35–**2022**	£2 – set of two with one reverse frosted (Edition: 500)	(2)	190

Note: PBS21 has been deleted as there is no evidence it was issued.

Britannia Silver Uncirculated Set

UBS01–**MD** £2 BSF2 (2002), BSF3 (1999), BSF4 (2001), BSF5 (2003) (Edition: 5,000) (4) 160

1997	20p ($^{1}/_{10}$ oz)	50p (¼ oz)	£1 (½ oz)	£2 (1 oz)	SET		Authorised
PBS01	11832	11832	11832	11832	11832	(4)	15000
BSF1				4173			20000
BSC1	8686						50000
	20518	11832	11832	16005			

1998	20p ($^{1}/_{10}$ oz)	50p (¼ oz)	£1 (½ oz)	£2 (1 oz)	SET		Authorised
PBS02	3045	3045	3045	3045	3045	(4)	10000
BSF2				2168			20000
BSC2	2724						10000
	5769	3045	3045	5213			

2001	20p ($^{1}/_{10}$ oz)	50p (¼ oz)	£1 (½ oz)	£2 (1 oz)	SET		Authorised
PBS03	4596	4596	4596	4596	4596	(4)	5000
BSF4				3047			10000
BSC3	826						10000
	5422	4596	4596	7643			

2003	20p ($^{1}/_{10}$ oz)	50p (¼ oz)	£1 (½ oz)	£2 (1 oz)	SET		Authorised
PBS04	3669	3669	3669	3669	3669	(4)	5000
BSF5				2016			5000
BSC4	1179						5000
	4848	3669	3669	5685			

2005	20p ($^{1}/_{10}$ oz)	50p (¼ oz)	£1 (½ oz)	£2 (1 oz)	SET		Authorised
PBS06	2360	2360	2360	2360	2360	(4)	3500
BSF6				1539			2500
BSC5	913						2500
	3273	2360	2360	3899			

2007	20p ($^{1}/_{10}$ oz)	50p (¼ oz)	£1 (½ oz)	£2 (1 oz)	SET		Authorised
PBS08	2500	2500	2500	2500	2500	(4)	2500
BSF7				5157			7500
BSC6	901						2500
	3401	2500	2500	7657			

2008	20p ($^{1}/_{10}$ oz)	50p (¼ oz)	£1 (½ oz)	£2 (1 oz)	SET		Authorised
PBS10	2500	2500	2500	2500	2500	(4)	2500
BSF8				2500			2500
BSC7	725						2500
	3225	2500	2500	5000			

2009	20p ($^1/_{10}$ oz)	50p (¼ oz)	£1 (½ oz)	£2 (1 oz)	SET		Authorised
PBS11	2500	2500	2500	2500	2500	(4)	2500
BSF3				4284			3000
BSC8	1000						1000
	3500	2500	2500	6784			

2010	20p ($^1/_{10}$ oz)	50p (¼ oz)	£1 (½ oz)	£2 (1 oz)	SET		Authorised
PBS12	3497	3497	3497	3497	3497	(4)	3500
BSF9				3042			4500
BSC9	989						2500
	4486	3497	3497	6539			

2011	20p ($^1/_{10}$ oz)	50p (¼ oz)	£1 (½ oz)	£2 (1 oz)	SET		Authorised
PBS13	2483	2483	2483	2483	2483	(4)	3500
BSF11				2490			2500
	2483	2483	2483	4973			

2012	20p ($^1/_{10}$ oz)	50p (¼ oz)	£1 (½ oz)	£2 (1 oz)	SET		Authorised
PBS14	2595	2595	2595	2595	2595	(4)	2600
PBS15			1656			(9)	2012
BSF2				2937			2450
	2595	2595	4251	5532			

2013	10p ($^1/_{20}$ oz)	20p ($^1/_{10}$ oz)	50p (¼ oz)	£1 (½ oz)	£2 (1 oz)	SET		Authorised
PBS16	3087	3087	3087	3087	3087	3087	(5)	3000
PBS17	#	#				#	(2)	7500
BSF11					3468			2500
	3087	3087	3087	3087	6555			

2014	5p ($^1/_{40}$ oz)	10p ($^1/_{20}$ oz)	20p ($^1/_{10}$ oz)	50p (¼ oz)	£1 (½ oz)	£2 (1 oz)	SET		Authorised
PBS18	1735	1735	1735	1735	1735	1735	1735	(6)	1750
		550	550	550	550	550	550	(5)Ω	550
PBS19	998	998	998				998	(3)	1000
BSF13						2981			2500
	2733	3283	3283	2285	2285	5266			

Ω Coins sold to the US market and not in standard Royal Mint cases.
Mintages not yet known

2015	5p (1/40 oz)	10p (1/20 oz)	20p (1/10 oz)	50p (1/4 oz)	£1 (1/2 oz)	£2 (1 oz)	SET		Authorised
PBS20	1009	1009	1009	1009	1009	1009	1009	(6)	1750
		550	550	550	550	550	550	(5)Ω	550
BSF14						2990			3000
BSF14						1250		Ω	1250
	1009	1559	1559	1559	1559	5799			

2016	5p (1/40 oz)	10p (1/20 oz)	20p (1/10 oz)	50p (1/4 oz)	£1 (1/2 oz)	£2 (1 oz)	SET		Authorised
PBS22	1050	1050	1050	1050	1050	1050	1050	(6)	1100
		250	250	250	250	250	250	(5)Ω	250
PBS23						#			500
BSF16						4553			5900
	1050	1300	1300	1300	1300	5853			

2017	5p (1/40 oz)	10p (1/20 oz)	20p (1/10 oz)	50p (1/4 oz)	£1 (1/2 oz)	£2 (1 oz)	SET		Authorised
PBS24	1351	1351	1351	1351	1351	1351	1351	(6)	2500
PBS25						500	500		500
BSF17						5304			7500
	1351	1351	1351	1351	1351	7155			

2018	5p (1/40 oz)	10p (1/20 oz)	20p (1/10 oz)	50p (1/4 oz)	£1 (1/2 oz)	£2 (1 oz)	SET		Authorised
PBS26	937	937	937	937	937	937	937	(6)	1350
PBS27						84	84		500
BSF19						3630			5800
	937	937	937	937	937	4651			

2019	5p (1/40 oz)	10p (1/20 oz)	20p (1/10 oz)	50p (1/4 oz)	£1 (1/2 oz)	£2 (1 oz)	SET		Authorised
PBS28	949	949	949	949	949	949	949	(6)	950
	50	50	50	50	50	50	50	(6)Ω	
PBS29						539	539		700
BSF21						2995			3390
	999	999	999	999	999	999			

Ω Coins sold to the US market and not in standard Royal Mint cases.
Mintages not yet known

2020	5p (¹/₄₀ oz)	10p (¹/₂₀ oz)	20p (¹/₁₀ oz)	50p (¼ oz)	£1 (½ oz)	£2 (1 oz)	SET		Authorised
PBS30	#	#	#	#	#	#		(6)	1000
PBS31						#			700
BSF22						#			3000

2021	5p (¹/₄₀ oz)	10p (¹/₂₀ oz)	20p (¹/₁₀ oz)	50p (¼ oz)	£1 (½ oz)	£2 (1 oz)	SET		Authorised
PBS32	#	#	#	#	#	#		(6)	1100
PBS33						#		[2]	500
BSF24						#			2900

2022	5p (¹/₄₀ oz)	10p (¹/₂₀ oz)	20p (¹/₁₀ oz)	50p (¼ oz)	£1 (½ oz)	£2 (1 oz)	SET		Authorised
PBS34	#	#	#	#	#	#		(6)	1250
PBS35						#		(2)	500
BSF26						#			3500

\# Mintages not yet known

THE ROYAL MINT®

THE ORIGINAL MAKER

The House of Windsor

Established by George V in 1917, the House of Windsor has produced five monarchs who have reigned over the United Kingdom and has overseen some of the most remarkable events in British royal history. For more than a century, The Royal Mint has struck coins that capture the story of the Royal House, and we continue to do so.

www.royalmint.com/royalty

CELEBRATE | COLLECT | INVEST | SECURE | DISCOVER

Nearly all the ½ oz coins and many of the others are only issued within sets but some coins were issued individually. Prices given relate to cased coins with certificates where these were issued; uncased versions of these coins from split sets can often be found at lower prices.

A table of specifications for the gold coins appears at the beginning of the Britannia section.

FIFTY PENCE

Obverse portrait by Ian Rank-Broadley

BGA1 **Britannia Fifty pence.** (1/40 oz of fine gold.) R. As BGF15 with the inscription 'BRITANNIA 999 1/40 OZ FINE GOLD 2014'.
2014 Proof in gold *FDC* (Issued: 5.521 plus coins in sets)...£50

Obverse portrait by Jody Clark

BGA2 **Britannia Fifty pence.** (1/40 oz of fine gold.) R. As BGF17 with the inscription 'BRITANNIA 1/40 OZ FINE GOLD 999.9 2015'.
2015 Proof in gold *FDC* (Issued: 3,075 plus coins in sets)...£50

BGA3 **Britannia Fifty pence.** (1/40 oz of fine gold.) R. As BGF19 with the inscription 'BRITANNIA 1/40 OZ FINE GOLD 999.9 2016'.
2016 Proof in gold *FDC* (Issued: 1,447 plus coins in sets)...£50

BGA4 **Britannia Fifty pence.** (1/40 oz of fine gold.) R. As BGF20 with the inscription 'BRITANNIA 1/40 OZ FINE GOLD 999.9 2017' and with Trident mint mark to mark the 30th Anniversary of the first Britannia gold issue.
2017 Proof in gold *FDC* (Issued: 888 plus coins in sets)...£50

BGA5 **Britannia Fifty pence.** (1/40 oz of fine gold.) R. As BGF21 with the inscription 'BRITANNIA 1/40 OZ FINE GOLD 999.9 2018'.
2018 Proof in gold *FDC**...£70

BGA6 **Britannia Fifty pence.** (1/40 oz of fine gold.) R. As BGF23 with the inscription 'BRITANNIA 1/40 OZ FINE GOLD 999.9 2019'.
2019 Proof in gold *FDC**...£70

BGA7 **Britannia Fifty pence.** (1/40 oz of fine gold.) R. As BGF24 with the inscription 'BRITANNIA 1/40 OZ FINE GOLD 999.9 2020'.
2020 Proof in gold *FDC**...£70

BGA8 **Britannia Fifty pence.** (1/40 oz of fine gold.) R. As BGG3 with the inscription 'BRITANNIA 1/40 OZ 999.9 FINE GOLD 2021'.
2021 Proof in gold *FDC**...£90

BGA9 **Britannia Fifty pence.** (1/40 oz of fine gold.) R. As BGG5 with the inscription '1/40 OZ 999.9 BRITANNIA FINE GOLD 2022'.
2022 Proof in gold *FDC**...£90

ONE POUND

Obverse portrait by Ian Rank-Broadley

BGB1 **Britannia One pound.** (1/20 oz of fine gold) R. As BGF12 with the inscription 'BRITANNIA 999 1/20 OUNCE FINE GOLD 2013'.
2013 Proof in gold *FDC* (Issued: 2,496 plus coins in sets)...£100

BGB2 **Britannia One pound.** (1/20 oz of fine gold) R. As BGF15 with the inscription 'BRITANNIA 999 1/20 OZ FINE GOLD 2014'.
2014 Proof in gold *FDC* (Issued: 993 plus coins in sets)...£100

* Coins marked thus were originally issued in Royal Mint sets.
For coin specifications please see table at the beginning of this section.

Obverse portrait by Jody Clark

BGB3 **Britannia One pound.** (1/20 oz of fine gold.) R. As BGF17 with the inscription 'BRITANNIA 1/20 OZ FINE GOLD 999.9 2015'.
2015 Proof in gold *FDC**... £100

BGB4 **Britannia One pound.** (1/20 oz of fine gold) R. As BGF19 with the inscription 'BRITANNIA 1/20 OZ FINE GOLD 999.9 2016'.
2016 Proof in gold *FDC**... £100

BGB5 **Britannia One pound.** (1/20 oz of fine gold.) R. As BGF20 with the inscription 'BRITANNIA 1/20 OZ FINE GOLD 999.9 2017' and with Trident mint mark to mark the 30th Anniversary of the first Britannia gold issue.
2017 Proof in gold *FDC**... £100

BGB6 **Britannia One pound.** (1/20 oz of fine gold.) R. As BGF21 with the inscription 'BRITANNIA 1/20 OZ FINE GOLD 999.9 2018'.
2018 Proof in gold *FDC**... £100

BGB7 **Britannia One pound.** (1/20 oz of fine gold.) R. As BGF23 with the inscription 'BRITANNIA 1/20 OZ FINE GOLD 999.9 2019'.
2019 Proof in gold *FDC**... £100

BGB8 **Britannia One pound.** (1/20 oz of fine gold.) R. As BGF24 with the inscription 'BRITANNIA 1/20 OZ FINE GOLD 999.9 2020'.
2020 Proof in gold *FDC**... £100

BGB9 **Britannia One pound.** (1/20 oz of fine gold.) R. As BGG3 with the inscription 'BRITANNIA 1/20 OZ 999.9 FINE GOLD 2021'.
2021 Proof in gold *FDC**... £150

BGB10 **Britannia One pound.** (1/20 oz of fine gold.) R. As BGG5 with the inscription '1/20 OZ 999.9 BRITANNIA FINE GOLD 2022'.
2022 Proof in gold *FDC**... £150

TEN POUNDS

Obverse portrait by Raphael Maklouf

BGC1 **Britannia Ten pounds.** (1/10 oz of fine gold.) R. As BGF1 with the inscription 'BRITANNIA 1/10 OUNCE FINE GOLD' and the date of the year.
1987 Unc £175
— Proof in gold *FDC* (Issued: 3,500 plus coins in sets).................................... £200
1988 Unc £175
— Proof in gold *FDC* (Issued: 2,694 plus coins in sets).................................... £200
1989 Unc £175
— Proof in gold *FDC* (Issued: 1609 plus coins in sets)..................................... £200
1990 Unc £175
— Proof in gold *FDC* (Issued: 1571 plus coins in sets)..................................... £200
1991 Unc £175
— Proof in gold *FDC* (Issued: 954 plus coins in sets)....................................... £200
1992 Unc £175
— Proof in gold *FDC* (Issued: 1,000 plus coins in sets).................................... £200
1993 Unc £175
— Proof in gold *FDC* (Issued: 997 plus coins in sets)....................................... £200
1994 Unc £175
— Proof in gold *FDC* (Issued: 994 plus coins in sets)....................................... £200
1995 Unc £175
— Proof in gold *FDC* (Issued: 1,500 plus coins in sets).................................... £200
1996 Unc £175
— Proof in gold *FDC* (Issued: 2,379 plus coins in sets).................................... £200

* *Coins marked thus were originally issued in Royal Mint sets.*
For coin specifications please see table at the beginning of this section.

BGC2 **Britannia Ten pounds.** (1/10 oz of fine gold.) R. As BGF2 with the inscription 'BRITANNIA TENTH OUNCE FINE GOLD' and the date of the year.
1997 Proof in gold *FDC* (Issued: 1,821 plus coins in sets).. £200

Obverse portrait by Ian Rank-Broadley
BGC3 **Britannia Ten pounds.** (1/10 oz of fine gold.) R. As BGF3 with the inscription 'BRITANNIA 1/10 OUNCE FINE GOLD' and the date of the year.
1998 Proof in gold *FDC* (Issued: 392 plus coins in sets).. £200
1999 Unc £175
— Proof in gold *FDC* (Issued: 1,058 plus coins in sets).. £200
2000 Unc £175
— Proof in gold *FDC* (Issued: 659 plus coins in sets).. £200
2002 Unc £175
— Proof in gold *FDC* (Issued: 1,500 plus coins in sets).. £200
2004 Unc £175
— Proof in gold *FDC* (Issued: 929 plus coins in sets).. £200
2006 Proof in gold *FDC* (Issued: 700 plus coins in sets).. £200
2012 Unc £175
— Proof in gold *FDC* (Issued: 1,249 plus coins in sets).. £200

BGC4 **Britannia Ten pounds.** (1/10 oz of fine gold.) R. As BGF4 with the inscription 'BRITANNIA TENTH OUNCE FINE GOLD 2001'.
2001 unc £175
— Proof in gold *FDC* (Issued: 1,557 plus coins in sets.).. £200

BGC5 **Britannia Ten pounds.** (1/10 oz of fine gold.) R. As BGF5 with the inscription 'BRITANNIA TENTH OUNCE FINE GOLD 2003'.
2003 Unc £175
— Proof in gold *FDC* (Issued: 1,382 plus coins in sets).. £200

BGC6 **Britannia Ten pounds.** (1/10 oz of fine gold.) R. As BGF6 with the inscription 'BRITANNIA TENTH OUNCE FINE GOLD 2005'.
2005 Proof in gold *FDC* (Issued: 1,225 plus coins in sets).. £200

BGC7 **Britannia Ten pounds.** (1/10 oz of fine gold.) R. As BGF7 with the inscription 'BRITANNIA TENTH OUNCE FINE GOLD 2007'.
2007 Unc £175
— Proof in gold *FDC* (Issued: 893 plus coins in sets).. £200

BGC8 **Britannia Ten pounds.** (1/10 oz of fine gold.) R. As BGF8 with the inscription 'BRITANNIA TENTH OUNCE FINE GOLD 2008'.
2008 Proof in gold *FDC* (Issued: 748 plus coins in sets).. £200

BGC9 **Britannia Ten pounds.** (1/10 oz of fine gold.) R. As BGF2 with the inscription 'BRITANNIA TENTH OUNCE FINE GOLD 2009'.
2009 Unc £175
— Proof in gold *FDC* (Issued: 749 plus coins in sets).. £200

BGC10 Britannia Ten pounds. (1/10 oz of fine gold.) R. As BGF10 with the inscription 'BRITANNIA TENTH OUNCE FINE GOLD 2010'.
2010 Unc (Issued: 3,530) £175
— Proof in gold *FDC* (Issued: 1,049 plus coins in sets).. £200

BGC11 Britannia Ten pounds. (1/10 oz of fine gold.) R. As BGF11 with the inscription 'BRITANNIA TENTH OUNCE FINE GOLD 2011'.
2011 Proof in gold *FDC* (Issued: 3,511 including coins in sets) £200

BGC12 Britannia Ten pounds. (1/10 oz of fine gold.) R. As BGF12 with the inscription 'BRITANNIA 1/10 OUNCE FINE GOLD 2013'.
2013 Proof in gold *FDC* (Issued: 1,150 plus coins in sets).. £200

* Coins marked thus were originally issued in Royal Mint sets.
For coin specifications please see table at the beginning of this section.

BGC13 Britannia Ten pounds. (1/10 oz of fine gold.) R. As BGF15 with the inscription 'BRITANNIA 999.9 1/10 OZ FINE GOLD 2014'.
2014 Proof in gold *FDC** £200

BGC14 Britannia Ten pounds. (1/10 oz of fine gold.) R. As BGC3 with the inscription 'BRITANNIA 2014 1/10 OZ 999.9 FINE GOLD'.
2014 Unc £175

BGC15 Britannia Ten pounds. (1/10 oz of fine gold.) R. As BGC3 but with textured background on the obverse and reverse, and with the inscription 'BRITANNIA 2015 1/10 OZ 999.9 FINE GOLD'.
2015 Unc £175

Obverse portrait by Jody Clark

BGC16 Britannia Ten pounds. (1/10 oz of fine gold.) R. As BGF17 with the inscription 'BRITANNIA 1/10 OZ FINE GOLD 999.9 2015'.
2015 Proof in gold *FDC** £200

BGC17 Britannia Ten pounds. (1/10 oz of fine gold.) As BGC14.
2016 Unc £175

BGC17A Britannia Ten pounds. (1/10 oz of fine gold.) As BGC16 but with textured background of a speckled radial sunburst on the reverse.
2017 Unc £175

BGC17B Britannia. Ten pounds. As BGC17A but with guilloché finish to the obverse table area.
2018 Unc £175
2019 Unc £175
2020 Unc £175

BGC18 Britannia Ten pounds. (1/10 oz of fine gold.) R. As BGF19 with the inscription 'BRITANNIA 1/10 OZ FINE GOLD 999 2016'.
2016 Proof in gold *FDC** £200

BGC19 Britannia Ten pounds. (1/10 oz of fine gold.) R. As BGF20 with the inscription 'BRITANNIA 1/10 OZ FINE GOLD 999 2017' and with Trident mint mark to mark the 30th Anniversary of the first Britannia gold issue.
2017 Proof in gold *FDC** £200

BGC20 Britannia Ten pounds. (1/10 oz of fine gold.) R. As BGF21 with the inscription 'BRITANNIA 1/10 OZ FINE GOLD 999 2018'.
2018 Proof in gold *FDC** £200

BGC21 Britannia Ten pounds. (1/10 oz of fine gold.) R. As BGF23 with the inscription 'BRITANNIA 1/10 OZ FINE GOLD 999 2019'.
2019 Proof in gold *FDC** £200

BGC22 Britannia Ten pounds. (1/10 oz of fine gold.) R. As BGF24 with the inscription 'BRITANNIA 1/10 OZ FINE GOLD 999 2020'.
2020 Proof in gold *FDC** £200

BGC23 Britannia. Ten pounds. (1/10 oz of fine gold.) R. As BGF25 with the inscription 'BRITANNIA 1/10 OZ FINE GOLD 999' and the date of the year.
2021 Unc £200
2022 Unc £200
2023 Unc £200

BGC24 Britannia Ten pounds. (1/10 oz of fine gold.) R. As BGG3 with the inscription 'BRITANNIA 1/10 OZ FINE GOLD 999 2021'.
2021 Proof in gold *FDC** £250

BGC25 Britannia Ten pounds. (1/10 oz of fine gold.) R. As BGG5 with the inscription '1/10 OZ 999.9 BRITANNIA FINE GOLD 2022'.
2022 Proof in gold *FDC** £250

* Coins marked thus were originally issued in Royal Mint sets.
For coin specifications please see table at the beginning of this section.

TWENTY FIVE POUNDS

Obverse portrait by Raphael Maklouf

BGD1 **Britannia Twenty five pounds.** (1/4 oz of fine gold.) R. As BGF1 with the inscription '1/4 OUNCE FINE GOLD BRITANNIA' and the date of the year.

1987 Unc	£425
— Proof in gold *FDC* (Issued: 3,500 plus coins in sets)	£500
1988 Unc	£425
— Proof in gold *FDC**	£500
1989 Unc	£425
— Proof in gold *FDC**	£500
1990 Unc	£425
— Proof in gold *FDC**	£500
1991 Unc	£425
— Proof in gold *FDC**	£500
1992 Unc	£425
— Proof in gold *FDC**	£500
1993 Unc	£425
— Proof in gold *FDC**	£500
1994 Unc	£425
— Proof in gold *FDC**	£500
1995 Unc	£425
— Proof in gold *FDC**	£500
1996 Unc	£425
— Proof in gold *FDC**	£500

BGD2 **Britannia Twenty five pounds.** (1/4 oz of fine gold.) R. As BGF2 with the inscription 'BRITANNIA QUARTER OUNCE FINE GOLD' and the date of the year.

1997 Proof in gold *FDC* (Issued: 923 plus coins in sets)	£500

Obverse portrait by Ian Rank-Broadley

BGD3 **Britannia Twenty five pounds.** (1/4 oz of fine gold.) R. As BGF1 with the inscription '1/4 OUNCE FINE GOLD BRITANNIA' and the date of the year.

1998 Proof in gold *FDC* (Issued: 560 plus coins in sets)	£500
1999 Unc	£425
— Proof in gold *FDC* (Issued: 1,000 plus coins in sets)	£500
2000 Unc	£425
— Proof in gold *FDC* (Issued: 500 plus coins in sets)	£500
2002 Proof in gold *FDC* (Issued: 750 plus coins in sets)	£500
2004 Proof in gold *FDC* (Issued: 750 plus coins in sets)	£500
2006 Proof in gold *FDC* (Issued: 728 plus coins in sets)	£500
2012 Proof in gold *FDC* (Issued: 316 plus coins in sets)	£500
2013 Unc	£425

BGD4 **Britannia Twenty five pounds.** (1/4 oz of fine gold.) R. As BGF4 with the inscription 'BRITANNIA QUARTER OUNCE FINE GOLD' and the date of the year.

2001 Unc	£425
— Proof in gold *FDC* (Issued: 500 plus coins in sets)	£500
2006 Proof in gold *FDC**	£500

BGD5 **Britannia Twenty five pounds.** (1/4 oz of fine gold.) R. As BGF5 with the inscription 'BRITANNIA QUARTER OUNCE FINE GOLD' and the date of the year.

2003 Proof in gold *FDC* (Issued 609 plus coins in sets)	£500
2006 Proof in gold *FDC**	£500

* Coins marked thus were originally issued in Royal Mint sets.
For coin specifications please see table at the beginning of this section.

BGD6 **Britannia Twenty five pounds.** (1/4 oz of fine gold.) R̖. As BGF6 with the inscription 'BRITANNIA 1/4 OUNCE FINE GOLD' and the date of the year.
2005 Proof in gold *FDC* (Issued: 750 plus coins in sets) £500
2006 Proof in gold *FDC** £500

BGD7 **Britannia Twenty five pounds.** (1/4 oz of fine gold.) R̖. As BGF2 with the inscription 'BRITANNIA QUARTER OUNCE FINE GOLD' and the date of the year.
2006 Proof in gold *FDC** £500
2009 Proof in gold *FDC** £500

BGD8 **Britannia Twenty five pounds.** (1/4 oz of fine gold.) R̖. As BGF7 with the inscription 'BRITANNIA QUARTER OUNCE FINE GOLD 2007'.
2007 Unc £425
— Proof in gold *FDC* (Issued: 1,000 plus coins in sets) £500

BGD9 **Britannia Twenty five pounds.** (1/4 oz of fine gold.) R̖. As BGF8 with the inscription 'BRITANNIA 1/4 OUNCE FINE GOLD 2008'.
2008 Proof in gold *FDC* (Issued: 1,000 plus coins in sets) £500

BGD10 **Britannia Twenty five pounds.** (1/4 oz of fine gold.) R̖. As BGF10 with the inscription 'BRITANNIA 1/4 OUNCE FINE GOLD 2010'.
2010 Unc (Issued: 1,501) £425
— Proof in gold *FDC* (Issued: 517 plus coins in sets) £500

BGD11 **Britannia Twenty five pounds.** (1/4 oz of fine gold.) R̖. As BGF11 with the inscription 'BRITANNIA 1/4 OUNCE FINE GOLD 2011'.
2011 Proof in gold *FDC* (Issued: 698 including coins in sets) £500

BGD12 **Britannia Twenty five pounds.** (1/4 oz of fine gold.) R̖. As BGF12 with the inscription 'BRITANNIA 1/4 OUNCE FINE GOLD 2013'.
2013 Proof in gold *FDC** £500

BGD13 **Britannia Twenty five pounds.** (1/4 oz of fine gold.) R̖. As BGF15 with the inscription 'BRITANNIA 999.9 1/4 OZ FINE GOLD 2014'.
2014 Proof in gold *FDC** £500

BGD14 **Britannia Twenty five pounds.** (1/4 oz of fine gold.) R̖. As BGD3 with the inscription 'BRITANNIA 2014 1/4 OZ 999.9 FINE GOLD'.
2014 Unc £425

BGD15 **Britannia Twenty five pounds.** (1/4 oz of fine gold.) R̖. As BGD3 with revised inscription '1/4OZ 999.9 FINE GOLD' the date '2015' and textured background on the obverse and reverse.
2015 Unc £425

Obverse portrait by Jody Clark
BGD16 **Britannia Twenty five pounds.** (1/4 oz of fine gold.) R̖. As BGF17 with the inscription 'BRITANNIA 1/4 OZ FINE GOLD 999.9 2015'.
2015 Proof in gold *FDC** £500

BGD17 **Britannia Twenty five pounds.** (1/4 oz of fine gold.) As BGD14.
2016 Unc £425

BGD17A **Britannia Twenty five pounds.** (1/4 oz of fine gold.) As BGD17 but with textured background of a speckled radial sunburst on the reverse.
2017 Unc £425

BGD17B **Britannia. Twenty five pounds.** As BGD17A but with guilloché finish to the obverse table area.
2018 Unc £425
2019 Unc £425
2020 Unc £425

* Coins marked thus were originally issued in Royal Mint sets.
For coin specifications please see table at the beginning of this section.

BGD18 Britannia Twenty five pounds. (1/4 oz of fine gold.) ℞. As BGF19 with the inscription 'BRITANNIA 1/4 OZ FINE GOLD 999.9 2016'.
2016 Proof in gold *FDC* (Issued: 829 plus coins in sets)...................................... £500
BGD19 Britannia Twenty five pounds. (1/4 oz of fine gold.) ℞. As BGF20 with the inscription 'BRITANNIA 1/4 OZ FINE GOLD 999.9 2017' and with Trident mint mark to mark the 30th Anniversary of the first Britannia GOLD issue.
2017 Proof in gold *FDC* (Issued: 712 plus coins in sets)...................................... £500
BGD20 Britannia Twenty five pounds. (1/4 oz of fine gold.) ℞. As BGF21 with the inscription 'BRITANNIA 1/4 OZ FINE GOLD 999.9 2018'.
2018 Proof in gold *FDC* (Issued: 608 plus coins in sets)...................................... £500
BGD21 Britannia Twenty five pounds. (1/4 oz of fine gold.) ℞. As BGF23 with the inscription 'BRITANNIA 1/4 OZ FINE GOLD 999.9 2019'.
2019 Proof in gold *FDC* (Edition: 645 plus coins in sets)..................................... £500
BGD22 Britannia Twenty five pounds. (1/4 oz of fine gold.) ℞. As BGF24 with the inscription 'BRITANNIA 1/4 OZ FINE GOLD 999.9 2020'.
2020 Proof in gold *FDC* (Edition: 700 plus coins in sets)..................................... £600
BGD23 Britannia Twenty five pounds. (1/4oz of fine gold.) ℞. As BGF25 with the inscription 'BRITANNIA 1/4 OZ FINE GOLD 999.9' and the date of the year.
2021 Unc £425
2022 Unc £425
BGD24 Britannia Twenty five pounds. (1/4oz of fine gold.) ℞. As BGG3 with the inscription 'BRITANNIA 1/4 OZ 999.9 FINE GOLD 2021'.
2021 Proof in gold *FDC* (Edition: 1,060 including coins in sets)........................... £600
BGD25 Britannia Twenty five pounds. (1/4oz of fine gold.) ℞. As BGG5 with the inscription '1/4 OZ 999.9 BRITANNIA FINE GOLD 2022'.
2022 Proof in gold *FDC* (Edition: 775 plus coins in sets) £600

FIFTY POUNDS

Obverse portrait by Raphael Maklouf
BGE1 Britannia. Fifty pounds. (1/2 oz of fine gold.) ℞. As BGF1 with the inscription 'BRITANNIA 1/2 OUNCE FINE GOLD' and the date of the year.
1987 Unc £850
— Proof in gold *FDC* (Issued: 2,485 plus coins in sets)...................................... £950
1988 Unc £850
— Proof in gold *FDC**.. £950
1989 Unc £850
— Proof in gold *FDC**.. £950
1990 Unc £850
— Proof in gold *FDC**.. £950
1991 Unc £850
— Proof in gold *FDC**.. £950
1992 Unc £850
— Proof in gold *FDC**.. £950
1993 Unc £850
— Proof in gold *FDC**.. £950
1994 Unc £850
— Proof in gold *FDC**.. £950
1995 Unc £850
— Proof in gold *FDC**.. £950
1996 Unc £850
— Proof in gold *FDC**.. £950

* Coins marked thus were originally issued in Royal Mint sets.
For coin specifications please see table at the beginning of this section.

BGE2 **Britannia. Fifty pounds.** (1/2 oz of fine gold.) R. As BGF2 with the inscription 'BRITANNIA HALF OUNCE FINE GOLD' and the date of the year.
1997 Proof in gold *FDC** £1000

Obverse portrait by Ian Rank-Broadley
BGE3 **Britannia. Fifty pounds.** (1/2 oz of fine gold.) R. As BGF2 with the inscription 'BRITANNIA 1/2 OUNCE FINE GOLD' and the date of the year.
1998 Proof in gold *FDC** £950
1999 Unc £850
— Proof in gold *FDC** £950
2000 Unc £850
— Proof in gold *FDC** £950
2002 Proof in gold *FDC** £950
2004 Proof in gold *FDC** £950
2006 Proof in gold *FDC** £950
2012 Proof in gold *FDC** £950
BGE4 **Britannia. Fifty pounds.** (1/2 oz of fine gold.) R. As BGF4 with the inscription 'BRITANNIA HALF OUNCE FINE GOLD' and the date of the year.
2001 Unc £850
— Proof in gold *FDC** £950
2012 Proof in gold *FDC** £950
BGE5 **Britannia. Fifty pounds.** (1/2 oz of fine gold.) R. As BGF5 with the inscription 'BRITANNIA HALF OUNCE FINE GOLD' and the date of the year.
2003 Unc £850
— Proof in gold *FDC** £950
2012 Proof in gold *FDC** £950
BGE6 **Britannia. Fifty pounds.** (1/2 oz of fine gold.) R. As BGF6 with the inscription 'BRITANNIA HALF OUNCE FINE GOLD' and the date of the year.
2005 Proof in gold *FDC** £950
2012 Proof in gold *FDC** £950
BGE7 **Britannia. Fifty pounds.** (1/2oz of fine gold.) R. As BGF7 with the inscription 'BRITANNIA HALF OUNCE FINE GOLD' and the date of the year.
2007 Unc £850
— Proof in gold *FDC** £950
2012 Proof in gold *FDC** £950
BGE8 **Britannia. Fifty pounds.** (1/2oz of fine gold.) R. As BGF8 with the inscription 'BRITANNIA 1/2 OUNCE FI NE GOLD' and the date of the year.
2008 Proof in gold *FDC** £950
2012 Proof in gold *FDC** £950
BGE9 **Britannia. Fifty pounds.** (1/2 oz of fine gold.) R. As BGF9 with the inscription 'BRITANNIA HALF OUNCE FINE GOLD' and the date of the year.
2009 Unc £850
— Proof in gold *FDC** £950
2012 Proof in gold *FDC** £950
BGE10 **Britannia. Fifty pounds.** (1/2 oz of fine gold.) R. As BGF10 with the inscription 'BRITANNIA 1/2 OUNCE FINE GOLD' and the date of the year.
2010 Unc (Issued: 1,301) £850
— Proof in gold *FDC** £950
2012 Proof in gold *FDC** £950

* Coins marked thus were originally issued in Royal Mint sets.
For coin specifications please see table at the beginning of this section.

BGE11 Britannia. Fifty pounds. (1/2 oz of fine gold.) R. As BGF11 with the inscription 'BRITANNIA 1/2 OUNCE FINE GOLD' and the date of the year.
2011 Proof in gold *FDC* (Issued: 847 including coins in sets) £950
2012 Proof in gold *FDC** £950
BGE12 Britannia. Fifty pounds. (1/2 oz of fine gold.) R. As BGF12 with the inscription 'BRITANNIA 1/2 OUNCE FINE GOLD 2013'.
2013 Proof in gold *FDC** £950
BGE13 Britannia. Fifty pounds. (1/2 oz of fine gold.) R. As BGF15 with the inscription 'BRITANNIA 999.9 1/2 OZ FINE GOLD 2014'.
2014 Proof in gold *FDC** £950
BGE14 Britannia Fifty pounds. (1/2 oz of fine gold.) R. As BGE3 with the inscription 'BRITANNIA 2014 1/2 OZ 999.9 FINE GOLD'.
2014 Unc £850
BGE15 Britannia. Fifty pounds. (1/2 oz of fine gold.) R. As BGE3 with revised inscription '1/2 OZ 999.9 FINE GOLD' the date '2015' and textured background on the obverse and reverse.
2015 Unc £850

Obverse portrait by Jody Clark
BGE16 Britannia. Fifty pounds. (1/2 oz of fine gold.) R. As BGF17 with the inscription 'BRITANNIA 1/2 OZ FINE GOLD 999.9 2015'.
2015 Proof in gold *FDC** £950
BGE17 Britannia. Fifty pounds. (1/2 oz of fine gold.) R. As BGE14.
2016 Unc £850
BGE17A Britannia. Fifty pounds. (1/2 oz of fine gold.) R. As BGE14 but with textured background of a speckled radial sunburst on the reverse.
2017 Unc £800
BGE17B Britannia. Fifty pounds. As BGE17A but with guilloché finish to the obverse table area.
2018 Unc £850
2019 Unc £850
2020 Unc £850
BGE18 Britannia. Fifty pounds. (1/2 oz of fine gold.) R. As BGF19 with the inscription 'BRITANNIA 1/2 OZ FINE GOLD 999.9 2016'.
2016 Proof in gold *FDC** £950

BGE19 Britannia. Fifty pounds. (1/2 oz of fine gold.) R. As BGF20 with the inscription 'BRITANNIA 1/2 OZ FINE GOLD 999.9 2017' and with Trident mint mark to mark the 30th Anniversary of the first Britannia gold issue.
2017 Proof in gold *FDC** £950
BGE20 Britannia. Fifty pounds. (1/2 oz of fine gold.) R. As BGF21 with the inscription 'BRITANNIA 1/2 OZ FINE GOLD 999.9 2018'.
2018 Proof in gold *FDC** £950
BGE21 Britannia. Fifty pounds. (1/2 oz of fine gold.) R. As BGF23 with the inscription 'BRITANNIA 1/2 OZ FINE GOLD 999.9 2019'.
2019 Proof in gold *FDC** £950
BGE22 Britannia. Fifty pounds. (1/2 oz of fine gold.) R. As BGF24 with the inscription 'BRITANNIA 1/2 OZ FINE GOLD 999.9 2020'.
2020 Proof in gold *FDC** £950

* Coins marked thus were originally issued in Royal Mint sets.
For coin specifications please see table at the beginning of this section.

BGE23 Britannia. Fifty pounds. (1/2oz of fine gold.) R. As BGF25 with the inscription 'BRITANNIA 1/2 OZ FINE GOLD 999.9' and the date of the year.

2021 Unc £850
2022 Unc £850

BGE24 Britannia. Fifty pounds. (1/2oz of fine gold.) R. As BGG3 with the inscription 'BRITANNIA 1/2 OZ 999.9 FINE GOLD 2021'.

2021 Proof in gold *FDC** £1100

BGE25 Britannia. Fifty pounds. (1/2oz of fine gold.) R. As BGG5 with the inscription '1/2 OZ 999.9 BRITANNIA FINE GOLD 2022'.

2022 Proof in gold *FDC** £1100

ONE HUNDRED POUNDS
Obverse portrait by Raphael Maklouf

BGF1

BGF1 Britannia. One hundred pounds. (1 oz of fine gold.) R. The figure of Britannia standing upon a rock in the sea, her right hand grasping a trident and her left hand resting on a shield and holding an olive branch, with the inscription 'ONE OUNCE FINE GOLD BRITANNIA' and the year of the date. (Reverse design: Philip Nathan.)

1987 Unc £1650
— Proof in gold *FDC* (Issued: 2,486 plus coins in sets)....................................£1800
1988 Unc £1650
— Proof in gold *FDC* (Issued: 626 plus coins in sets).......................................£1800
1989 Unc £1650
— Proof in gold *FDC* (Issued: 338 plus coins in sets).......................................£1800
1990 Unc £1650
— Proof in gold *FDC* (Issued: 262 plus coins in sets).......................................£1800
1991 Unc £1650
— Proof in gold *FDC* (Issued: 143 plus coins in sets).......................................£1800
1992 Unc £1650
— Proof in gold *FDC** £1800
1993 Unc £1650
— Proof in gold *FDC** £1800
1994 Unc £1650
— Proof in gold *FDC** £1800
1995 Unc £1650
— Proof in gold *FDC** £1800
1996 Unc £1650
— Proof in gold *FDC** £1800

* Coins marked thus were originally issued in Royal Mint sets.
For coin specifications please see table at the beginning of this section.

BGF2

BGF2   Britannia. One Hundred pounds. (1 oz of fine gold, alloyed with silver.) 10th
Anniversary of Britannia issue. ℞. The figure of Britannia standing in a chariot drawn
along the seashore by two horses, with the word 'BRITANNIA', the inscription. 'ONE
OUNCE FINE GOLD' and the date of the year. (Reverse design: Philip Nathan.)
1997..£1650
—   Proof in gold *FDC* (Issued: 164 plus coins in sets) £1850

Obverse portrait by Ian Rank-Broadley

BGF3   BGF4

BGF3 Britannia. One Hundred pounds. (1 oz of fine gold.) ℞. The figure of Britannia standing
upon a rock in the sea, her right hand grasping a trident and her left hand resting on a shield and
holding an olive branch, with the word 'BRITANNIA', the date of the year, and the inscription'
ONE OUNCE FINE GOLD'. (Reverse design: Philip Nathan.)

1998 Proof in gold *FDC**	£1800
1999 Unc	£1650
1999 Proof in gold *FDC**	£1800
2000 Unc	£1650
2000 Proof in gold *FDC**	£1800
2002 Proof in gold *FDC**	£1800
2004 Unc	£1650
2004 Proof in gold *FDC**	£1800
2006 Proof in gold *FDC**	£1800
2012 Unc	£1650
2012 Proof in gold *FDC**	£1800

BGF4   Britannia. One Hundred pounds. (1 oz of fine gold.) ℞. The figure of Britannia, as
guardian, with a shield in her left hand and a trident in her right hand, accompanied by
a lion and, against ....the background of a wave motif, the words 'ONE OUNCE FINE
GOLD' to the left and 'BRITANNIA' and the date of the year to the right.
(Reverse design: Philip Nathan.)

2001	£1650
2001 Proof in gold *FDC**	£1800

* Coins marked thus were originally issued in Royal Mint sets.
For coin specifications please see table at the beginning of this section.

BGF5   BGF6   BGF7

BGF5   **Britannia. One Hundred pounds.** (1 oz of fine gold.) R. Helmeted head of Britannia with, to the left, the word 'BRITANNIA' and, to the right, the inscription 'ONE OUNCE FINE GOLD' and the date of the year, the whole being overlaid with a wave pattern. (Reverse design: Philip Nathan.)

2003..£1650
2003 Proof in gold *FDC**..£1800

BGF6   **Britannia. One Hundred pounds.** (1 oz of fine gold.) R. Seated figure of Britannia facing to the left holding a trident with a shield at her side, with the word 'BRITANNIA', the inscription 'ONE OUNCE FINE GOLD' and the date of the year. (Reverse design: Philip Nathan.)

2005 Proof in gold *FDC**..£1800

BGF7   **Britannia. One Hundred pounds.** (1 oz of fine gold.) R. Seated figure of Britannia facing right holding a trident in her right hand and a sprig of olive in the left hand with a lion at her feet with the inscription 'ONE OUNCE FINE GOLD' and the word 'BRITANNIA' and the date of the year. (Reverse design: Christopher Le Brun.)

2007..£1650
2007 Proof in gold *FDC**..£1800

BGF8   BGF9

BGF8   **Britannia. One Hundred pounds.** (1 oz of fine gold,) R. A Standing figure of Britannia holding a trident with a shield at her side, the folds of her dress transforming into a wave, with the word 'BRITANNIA', the date of the year, and the inscription 'ONE OUNCE FINE GOLD'. (Reverse design: John Bergdahl.)

2008..£1650
2008 Proof in gold *FDC**..£1800

BGF9   **Britannia. One Hundred pounds.** (1 oz of fine gold.) R. Standing figure of Britannia in horse drawn chariot. (Reverse design: Philip Nathan.)

2009..£1650
2009 Proof in gold *FDC**..£1800

* *Coins marked thus were originally issued in Royal Mint sets.*
For coin specifications please see table at the beginning of this section.

BGF10   BGF11

BGF10 Britannia. One Hundred pounds. (1 oz of fine gold alloyed with silver.) R. A design
depicting a profile bust of Britannia wearing a helmet, accompanied by the name
'BRITANNIA', the inscription 'ONE OUNCE FINE GOLD' and the date '2010'.
(Reverse design: Suzie Zamit.)
2010 Unc (Issued: 13,860)..£1650
2010 Proof in gold *FDC**...£1800

BGF11 Britannia. One Hundred pounds. (1 oz of fine gold.) R. A design depicting a seated
figure of Britannia set against a background of a rippling Union Flag accompanied by
the words 'ONE OUNCE FINE GOLD BRITANNIA, and the date '2011'.
(Reverse design: David Mach.)
2011 Proof in gold *FDC** £1800

BGF12   BGF15

BGF12   Britannia. One Hundred pounds. (1 oz of fine gold.) R. Seated figure of Britannia
holding a trident with a shield at her side and an owl upon her knee with the word
'BRITANNIA' and 'ONE OUNCE FINE GOLD' and the date '2013' below the figure
of Britannia. (Reverse design: Robert Hunt.)
2013 — Proof in gold *FDC** £1800

BGF13   Britannia. One Hundred pounds. (1 oz of fine gold.) As BGF3 but .999 gold
and 38.61mm diameter.
2013 Unc £1650

BGF14   Britannia. One Hundred pounds. (1 oz of fine gold) R. As BGF3 but with revised
inscription "BRITANNIA 2014 1OZ 999.9 FINE GOLD".
2014 Unc £1650

BGF14A Britannia. One Hundred pounds. (1oz fine gold.) R. As BGF14 but with plain
edge and incuse decoration as indicated.
2014 Horse Unc £1700

BGF15   Britannia. One Hundred pounds. (1 oz of fine gold.) R. A design of the standing
figure of Britannia bearing a trident and shield, with a lion at her feet, set against the
backdrop of a globe, and with the inscription 'BRITANNIA 999.9 1 OZ FINE GOLD
2014'. (Reverse design: Jody Clark.)
2014 Proof in gold *FDC** £2500

* Coins marked thus were originally issued in Royal Mint sets.
For coin specifications please see table at the beginning of this section.

BGF16

BGF16 Britannia. One Hundred pounds. (1 oz of fine gold.) R. As BGF4 but with textured
background on the obverse and reverse,
2015 Unc £1650

Obverse portrait by Jody Clark

BGF17

BGF17 Britannia. One Hundred pounds. (1 oz of fine gold.) R. A figure of Britannia
bearing a trident and shield, set against a backdrop of a sailing ship, cliffs and a
lighthouse with the inscription 'BRITANNIA 1 OZ FINE GOLD 999.9 2015'.
(Reverse design: Antony Dufort.)
2015 – Proof in gold *FDC** £1800

BGF18

BGF18 Britannia. One Hundred pounds. (1 oz of fine gold.) R. As BGF16.
2016 Unc £1650
BGF18A Britannia. One Hundred pounds. (1oz fine gold.) R. As BGF18 but with
plain edge and incuse decoration as indicated.
2016 Monkey Unc (Issued: 4,470) £1650

* Coins marked thus were originally issued in Royal Mint sets.
For coin specifications please see table at the beginning of this section.

| BGF18B | BGF18C |

BGF18B Britannia. One Hundred pounds. (1 oz of fine gold.) ℞. As BGF16 but with textured background of a speckled radial sunburst on the reverse.

2017 Unc £1650

BGF18C Britannia. One hundred pounds. As BGF18B but with trident 30 mint mark on reverse to mark thirtieth anniversary of first issue of the Nathan reverse design and guilloché finish to the obverse table area.

2017 Unc (Edition: 7,030)..£1650

BGF18D Britannia. One hundred pounds. As BGF18B but with guilloché finish to the obverse table area.

2018 Unc £1650
2019 Unc £1650
2020 Unc £1650

| BGF19 | BGF20 | BGF21 |

BGF19 Britannia. One Hundred pounds. (1 oz of fine gold.) ℞. A standing figure of Britannia holding in her left hand a trident and in her right hand a shield with a lion in the background and the inscription 'BRITANNIA 1 OZ FINE GOLD 999.9 2016'. (Reverse design: Suzie Zamit.)

2016 Proof in gold *FDC** £2000

BGF20 Britannia. One Hundred pounds. (1 oz of fine gold.) ℞. The figure of Britannia, holding a shield and trident, with her body combined with the United Kingdom and the inscription 'BRITANNIA 1 OZ FINE GOLD 999.9 2017'with a trident mintmark to mark the 30th Anniversary of the first Britannia issue. (Reverse design: Louis Tamlyn.)

2017 Proof in gold *FDC** £2000

BGF21 Britannia. One hundred pounds. (1 oz of fine gold.) ℞. The figure of Britannia wearing a Corinthian helmet garlanded with the floral symbols of Britain and the inscription 'BRITANNIA 1 OZ FINE GOLD 999.9 2018'. (Reverse design: David Lawrence.)

2018 Proof in gold *FDC** £2000

* Coins marked thus were originally issued in Royal Mint sets.
For coin specifications please see table at the beginning of this section.

BGF22

BGF22 Britannia. One hundred pounds. (1 oz of fine gold.) R. The centre design of
Britannia as BGF18B but with an Oriental Border and the inscription within the
centre rather than around the design.

2018 Unc (Edition: 5,000)..£1650
—   Proof in gold *FDC* [Edition: 500] £2500
2019 Unc (Edition: 5,000)..£1650
2020 Unc (Edition: 5,000)..£1650

BGF23   BGF24   BGF25

BGF23 Britannia. One hundred pounds. (1 oz of fine gold.) R. Britannia raising trident
towards a new dawn with a lion beside her as a steadfast companion with the word
'BRITANNIA', the date of the year and the inscription '1 OZ FINE GOLD 999,9'.
(Reverse design: David Lawrence.)
2019 Proof in gold *FDC**...£2000

BGF24 Britannia. One hundred pounds. (1 oz of fine gold.) R. Britannia standing amid a
rocky ocean setting as waves crash around her with the word 'BRITANNIA', the date of
the year and the inscription '1 OZ 999.9 FINE GOLD'. (Reverse design: James Tottle.)
2020 Proof in gold *FDC**...£2000

BGF25 Britannia. One Hundred pounds. (1oz fine gold.) R. As BGF18B but with four added
elements; the image of waves behind Britannia, additional details on shield, thin inner
rim with repeated inscription 'DECUS ET TUTAMEN' in microtext, and hologram at
lower left showing alternately a trident and a padlock.
2021 Unc £1650
2022 Unc £1650
2023 Unc £1650

BGF26 Britannia. One hundred pounds. (1oz fine gold.) R. As BGG3 with the inscription
'BRITANNIA 1OZ 999.9 FINE GOLD 2021'. (Reverse design: P J Lynch.)
2021 Proof in gold *FDC**...£2500

BGF27 Britannia. One hundred pounds. (1oz fine gold.) R. As BGG5 with the inscription
'1OZ 999.9 BRITANNIA FINE GOLD 2022'.
2022 Proof in gold *FDC**...£2500

* Coins marked thus were originally issued in Royal Mint sets.
For coin specifications please see table at the beginning of this section.

TWO HUNDRED POUNDS
Obverse portrait by Jody Clark

BGG1   BGG2

BGG1 **Britannia. Two hundred pounds.** (2 oz of fine gold.) ℞. Britannia raising trident
towards a new dawn with a lion beside her as a steadfast companion with the word
'BRITANNIA', the date of the year and the inscription '2 OZ FINE GOLD 999.9'.
(Reverse design: David Lawrence.)
2019 Proof in gold *FDC* (Issued: 100).. £4500

BGG2 **Britannia. Two hundred pounds.** (2 oz of fine gold.) ℞. Britannia standing amid
a rocky ocean setting as waves crash around her with the word 'BRITANNIA', the
date of the year and the inscription '2 OZ 999.9 FINE GOLD'. (Reverse design:
James Tottle.)
2020 Proof in gold *FDC* (Edition: 160) £4500

BGG3   BGG4

BGG3 **Britannia. Two hundred pounds.** (2oz fine gold.) ℞. A depiction of the figure of
Britannia aside a seated lion and the inscription 'BRITANNIA 2OZ 999.9 FINE
GOLD 2021'. (Reverse design: P J Lynch.)
2021 Proof in gold *FDC* (Edition: 103) £5500

BGG4 **Britannia. Two hundred pounds.** (2oz fine gold.) ℞. A profile of the head of
Britannia and the inscription 'BRITANNIA 2OZ 999.9 FINE GOLD 2021'.
(Reverse design: P J Lynch)
2021 Proof in gold *FDC* (Edition: 230) £5000

For coin specifications please see table at the beginning of this section.

BGG5   BGG6

BGG5   Britannia. Two hundred pounds. (2oz fine gold.) R. A depiction of the figure of
Britannia carrying a trident and shield and the inscription '2OZ 999.9 FINE GOLD
BRITANNIA 2022'. (Reverse design: Dan Thorne)

2022 Proof in gold *FDC* (Edition: 106) £4775

BGG6   Britannia. Two hundred pounds. (2oz fine gold.) R. A depiction of Britannia at
different ages and the inscription 'BRITANNIA 2022 2OZ 999.9 FINE GOLD'.
(Reverse design: Sandra Deiana)

2022 Proof in gold *FDC* (Edition: 106) £4775

FIVE HUNDRED POUNDS
Obverse portrait by Ian Rank-Broadley

BGH1   BGH2

BGH1   Britannia. Five Hundred pounds. (5 oz of fine gold.) R. Seated figure of Britannia
holding a trident with a shield at her side and an owl upon her knee with the word
'BRITANNIA' and '5 OUNCES FINE GOLD' and the date '2013' below the figure of
Britannia. (Reverse design: Robert Hunt.)

2013 — Proof in gold *FDC* (Issued: 61)...£14000

BGH2   Britannia. Five Hundred pounds. (5 oz of fine gold.) R A design of the standing
figure of Britannia bearing a trident and shield, with a lion at her feet, set against the
backdrop of a globe, and with the inscription 'BRITANNIA 999.9 5 OZ FINE GOLD
2014'. (Reverse design: Jody Clark.)

2014 — Proof in gold *FDC* (Issued: 75)...£17500

For coin specifications please see table at the beginning of this section.

Obverse portrait by Jody Clark

BGH3

BGH3 **Britannia. Five hundred pounds.** (5 oz of fine gold.) ℞. A figure of Britannia bearing a
trident and shield, set against a backdrop of a sailing ship, cliffs and a lighthouse with the
inscription 'BRITANNIA 5 OZ FINE GOLD 999.9 2015'. (Reverse design:
Anthony Dufort.)
2015 Proof in gold *FDC* (Issued: 60) £14000

BGH4   BGH5   BGH6

BGH4 **Britannia. Five Hundred pounds.** (5 oz of fine gold.) ℞. A standing figure of Britannia
holding in her left hand a trident and in her right hand a shield with a lion in the background
and the inscription 'BRITANNIA 5 OZ FINE GOLD 999.9 2016'. (Reverse design:
Suzie Zamit.)
2016 Proof in gold *FDC* (Issued: 64) £15000

BGH5 **Britannia. Five Hundred pounds.** (5 oz of fine gold.) ℞. The figure of Britannia,
holding a shield and trident, with her body combined with the United Kingdom
and the inscription 'BRITANNIA 5 OZ FINE GOLD 999.9 2017' with a trident
mintmark to mark the 30th Anniversary of the first Britannia issue. (Reverse design:
Louis Tamlyn.)
2017 Proof in gold *FDC* (Issued: 106) £11000

BGH6 **Britannia. Five hundred pounds.** (5 oz of fine gold.) ℞. The figure of Britannia
wearing a Corinthian helmet garlanded with the floral symbols of Britain and the
inscription 'BRITANNIA 5 OZ FINE GOLD 999.9 2018'. (Reverse design:
David Lawrence.)
2018 Proof in gold *FDC* (Issued: 69) £11000

BGH7 **Britannia. Five hundred pounds.** (5 oz of fine gold.) ℞. Britannia raising trident
towards a new dawn with a lion beside her as a steadfast companion with the word
'BRITANNIA', the date of the year and the inscription '5 OZ FINE GOLD 999.9'.
(Reverse design: David Lawrence.)
2019 Proof in gold *FDC* (Issued: 60) £11000

BGH8 **Britannia. Five hundred pounds.** (5 oz of fine gold.) ℞. Britannia standing amid a
rocky ocean setting as waves crash around her with the word 'BRITANNIA', the date
of the year and the inscription '5 OZ 999.9 FINE GOLD'. (Reverse design:
James Tottle.)
2020 Proof in gold *FDC* (Edition: 58) £11000

BGH9 **Britannia. Five hundred pounds.** (5oz fine gold.) ℞. As BGG3 with the inscription
'BRITANNIA 5OZ 999.9 FINE GOLD 2021'.
2021 Proof in gold *FDC* (Edition: 83) £11000

BGH10 **Britannia. Five hundred pounds.** (5oz fine gold.) ℞. As BGG5 with the inscription
'5OZ 999.9 FINE GOLD BRITANNIA 2022'.
2022 Proof in gold *FDC* (Edition: 106) £11000

EIGHT HUNDRED POUNDS

BGJ1 **Britannia. Eight hundred pounds.** (30 oz of fine gold.) ℞. As BGH5 with the
inscription 'BRITANNIA 30 OZ FINE GOLD 999.9 2017' with a trident mintmark to
mark the 30th Anniversary of the first Britannia issue. (Reverse design: Louis Tamlyn.)
2017 Proof in gold *FDC* (Issued: 19) £55000

ONE THOUSAND POUNDS

BGK1 **Britannia. One thousand pounds.** (1 kilo fine gold.) ℞. As BGG4 with the
inscription 'BRITANNIA 1 KILO 999.9 FINE GOLD 2021'.
2021 Proof in gold *FDC* (Edition: 6) £75000

BGK2 **Britannia. One thousand pounds.** (1 kilo fine gold.) ℞. As BGG6 with the inscription
'BRITANNIA 2022 1 KILO 999.9 FINE GOLD'.
2022 Proof in gold *FDC* (Edition: 6) £69500

For coin specifications please see table at the beginning of this section.

Britannia Gold Proof Sets

		£
PBG01–**1987**	£100, £50, £25, £10 (Issued: 10,000) ....(4)	3250
PBG02–**1987**	£25, £10 (Issued: 11,100) ....(2)	600
PBG03–**1988**	£100, £50, £25, £10 (Issued: 3,505) ....(4)	3250
PBG04–**1988**	£25, £10 (Issued: 894) ....(2)	600
PBG05–**1989**	£100, £50, £25, £10 (Issued: 2,268) ....(4)	3250
PBG06–**1989**	£25, £10 (Issued: 451) ....(2)	600
PBG07–**1990**	£100, £50, £25, £10 (Issued: 527) ....(4)	3250
PBG08–**1991**	£100, £50, £25, £10 (Issued: 509) ....(4)	3250
PBG09–**1992**	£100, £50, £25, £10 (Issued: 500) ....(4)	3250
PBG10–**1993**	£100, £50, £25, £10 (Issued: 462) ....(4)	3250
PBG11–**1994**	£100, £50, £25, £10 (Issued: 435) ....(4)	3250
PBG12–**1995**	£100, £50, £25, £10 (Issued: 500) ....(4)	3250
PBG13–**1996**	£100, £50, £25, £10 (Issued: 483) ....(4)	3250
PBG14–**1997**	£100, £50, £25, £10 (Issued: 892) ....(4)	3400
PBG15–**1998**	£100, £50, £25, £10 (Issued: 750) ....(4)	3250
PBG16–**1999**	£100, £50, £25, £10 (Issued: 740) ....(4)	3250
PBG17–**2000**	£100, £50, £25, £10 (Issued: 750) ....(4)	3250
PBG18–**2001**	£100, £50, £25, £10 (Issued: 1,000) ....(4)	3250
PBG19–**2002**	£100, £50, £25, £10 (Issued: 945) ....(4)	3250
PBG20–**2003**	£100, £50, £25, £10 (Issued: 1,250) ....(4)	3250
PBG21–**2003**	£50, £25, £10 (Issued: 825) ....(3)	1550
PBG22–**2004**	£100, £50, £25, £10 (Issued: 973) ....(4)	3250
PBG23–**2004**	£50, £25, £10 (Issued: 223) ....(3)	1550
PBG24–**2005**	£100, £50, £25, £10 (Issued: 1,439) ....(4)	3250
PBG25–**2005**	£50, £25, £10 (Issued: 417) ....(3)	1550
PBG26–**2006**	£100, £50, £25, £10 (Issued: 1,163) ....(4)	3250
PBG27–**2006**	£25 BGE3,4,5,6,7 (Issued: 250) ....(5)	2250
PBG28–**2007**	£100, £50, £25, £10 (Issued: 1,250) ....(4)	3250
PBG29–**2008**	£100, £50, £25, £10 (Issued: 1,250) ....(4)	3250
PBG30–**2009**	£100, £50, £25, £10 (Issued: 797) ....(4)	3250
PBG31–**2010**	£100, £50, £25, £10 (Issued: 867) ....(4)	3250
PBG32–**2010**	£50, £25, £10 (Issued: 186) ....(3)	1550
PBG33–**2011**	£100, £50, £25, £10 (Issued: 1,000) ....(4)	3250
PBG34–**2011**	£50, £25, £10 (Issued: 250) ....(3)	1550
PBG35–**2012**	£100, £50, £25, £10 (Issued: 352) ....(4)	3250
PBG36–**2012**	£50, £25, £10 (Issued: 99) ....(3)	1550
PBG37–**2012**	£50 BGD3,4,5,6,7, 8,9,10,11(Issued: 25)......................................(9)	8000
		£
PBG38–**2013**	£100, £50, £25, £10, £1 (Issued: 261) ....(5)	3400
PBG39–**2013**	£50, £25, £10 (Issued: 90) ....(3)	1650
PBG40–**2013**	£25, £10, £1 (Issued: 136) ....(3)	700
PBG41–**2014**	£100, £50, £25, £10, £1,50p (Issued: 225) ....(6)	4000
PBG42–**2014**	£50, £25, £10 (Issued: 98) ....(3)	1750
PBG43–**2014**	£25, £10, £1 (Issued: 140) ....(3)	700
PBG44–**2015**	£100, £50, £25, £10, £1, 50p (Issued: 138) ....(6)	3500
PBG45–**2015**	£50, £25, £10 (Issued: 99) ....(3)	1650
PBG46–**2015**	£10, £1, 50p (Issued: 176) ....(3)	360
PBG47–**2016**	£100, £50, £25, £10, £1, 50p (Issued: 174) ....(6)	3700
PBG48–**2016**	£50, £25, £10 (Issued: 69) ....(3)	1650
PBG49–**2017**	£100, £50, £25, £10, £1, 50p (Issued: 182) ....(6)	3700
PBG50–**2017**	£50, £25, £10 (Issued: 158) ....(3)	1650

PBG51–**2018**	£100, £50, £25, £10, £1, 50p (Issued: 150)	(6)	3700
PBG52–**2018**	£50, £25, £10 (Issued: 105)	(3)	1650
PBG53–**2019**	£100, £50, £25, £10, £1, 50p (Edition: 150)	(6)	3700
PBG54–**2019**	£50, £25, £10 (Edition 130)	(3)	1650
PBG55–**2020**	£100, £50, £25, £10, £1, 50p (Edition: 150)	(6)	3800
PBG56–**2020**	£50, £25, £10 (Edition: 130)	(3)	1750
PBG57–**2021**	£100, £50, £25, £10, £1, 50p (Edition: 150)	(6)	4300
PBG58–**2021**	£50, £25, £10 (Edition: 115)	(3)	1900
PBG59–**2022**	£100, £50, £25, £10, £1, 50p (Edition: 150)	(6)	4300
PBG60–**2022**	£50, £25, £10 (Edition: 150)	(3)	1900

Britannia gold uncirculated sets

UBG1–**MD**	£100 BGF1 (1987), BGF2 (1997), BGF5 (2001), BGF5 (2003) (Edition 2,500)	(4)	7500

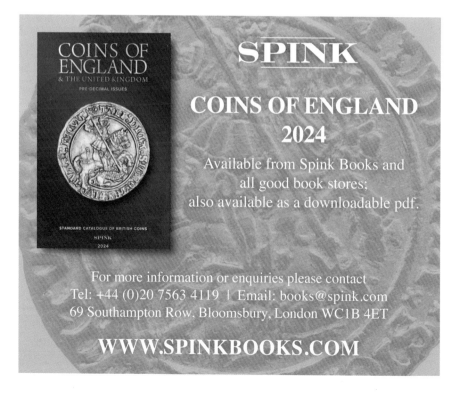

1987	£10 ($^1/_{10}$ oz)	£25 (¼ oz)	£50 (½ oz)	£100 (1 oz)	SET		Authorised
PBG01	10000	10000	10000	10000	10000	(4)	10000
PBG02	11100	11100			11100	(2)	12500
BGF1				2486			2500
BGE1			2485				2500
BGD1		3500					3500
BGC1	3500						3500
	24600	24600	12485	12486			

1988	£10 ($^1/_{10}$ oz)	£25 (¼ oz)	£50 (½ oz)	£100 (1 oz)	SET		Authorised
PBG03	3505	3505	3505	3505	3505	(4)	6500
PBG04	894	894			894	(2)	7500
BGF1				626			2000
BGC1	2694						5000
	7093	4399	3505	4131			

1989	£10 ($^1/_{10}$ oz)	£25 (¼ oz)	£50 (½ oz)	£100 (1 oz)	SET		Authorised
PBG05	2268	2268	2268	2268	2268	(4)	2500
PBG06	451	451			451	(2)	1500
BGF1				338			1000
BGC1	1609						2500
	4328	2719	2268	2606			

1990	£10 ($^1/_{10}$ oz)	£25 (¼ oz)	£50 (½ oz)	£100 (1 oz)	SET		Authorised
PBG07	527	527	527	527	527	(4)	2500
BGF1				262			1000
BGC1	1571						2500
	2098	527	527	789			

1991	£10 ($^1/_{10}$ oz)	£25 (¼ oz)	£50 (½ oz)	£100 (1 oz)	SET		Authorised
PBG08	509	509	509	509	509	(4)	750
BGF1				143			500
BGC1	954						2000
	1463	509	509	652			

1992	£10 ($^1/_{10}$ oz)	£25 (¼ oz)	£50 (½ oz)	£100 (1 oz)	SET		Authorised
PBG09	500	500	500	500	500	(4)	500
BGC1	1000						1000
	1500	500	500	500			

1993	£10 ($^1/_{10}$ oz)	£25 (¼ oz)	£50 (½ oz)	£100 (1 oz)	SET		Authorised
PBG10	462	462	462	462	462	(4)	500
BGC1	997						1000
	1459	462	462	462			

1994	£10 ($^1/_{10}$ oz)	£25 (¼ oz)	£50 (½ oz)	£100 (1 oz)	SET		Authorised
PBG11	435	435	435	435	435	(4)	500
BGC1	994						1000
	1429	435	435	435			

1995	£10 ($^1/_{10}$ oz)	£25 (¼ oz)	£50 (½ oz)	£100 (1 oz)	SET		Authorised
PBG12	500	500	500	500	500	(4)	500
BGC1	1500						1500
	2000	500	500	500			

1996	£10 ($^1/_{10}$ oz)	£25 (¼ oz)	£50 (½ oz)	£100 (1 oz)	SET		Authorised
PBG13	483	483	483	483	483	(4)	500
BGC1	2379						2500
	2862	483	483	483			

1997	£10 ($^1/_{10}$ oz)	£25 (¼ oz)	£50 (½ oz)	£100 (1 oz)	SET		Authorised
PBG14	892	892	892	892	892	(4)	1500
BGF2				164			1000
BGD2		923					2500
BGC2	1821						5000
	2713	1815	892	1056			

1998	£10 ($^1/_{10}$ oz)	£25 (¼ oz)	£50 (½ oz)	£100 (1 oz)	SET		Authorised
PBG15	750	750	750	750	750	(4)	750
BGD3		560					1000
BGC3	392						5000
	1142	1310	750	750			

1999	£10 ($^1/_{10}$ oz)	£25 (¼ oz)	£50 (½ oz)	£100 (1 oz)	SET		Authorised
PBG16	740	740	740	740	740	(4)	750
BGD3		1000					1000
BGC3	1058						5000
	1798	1740	740	740			

2000	£10 ($^1/_{10}$ oz)	£25 (¼ oz)	£50 (½ oz)	£100 (1 oz)	SET		Authorised
PBG17	750	750	750	750	750	(4)	750
BGD3		500					500
BGC3	659						5000
	1409	1250	750	750			

2001	£10 ($^1/_{10}$ oz)	£25 (¼ oz)	£50 (½ oz)	£100 (1 oz)	SET		Authorised
PBG18	1000	1000	1000	1000	1000	(4)	1000
BGD4		500					500
BFC4	1557						2500
	2557	1500	1000	1000			

2002	£10 ($^1/_{10}$ oz)	£25 (¼ oz)	£50 (½ oz)	£100 (1 oz)	SET		Authorised
PBG19	945	945	945	945	945	(4)	1000
BGD3		750					1750
BGC3	1500						2500
	2445	1695	945	945			

2003	£10 ($^1/_{10}$ oz)	£25 (¼ oz)	£50 (½ oz)	£100 (1 oz)	SET		Authorised
PBG20	1250	1250	1250	1250	1250	(4)	1250
PBG21	825	825	825		825	(3)	1500
BGD5		609					750
BGC5	1382						1500
	3457	2684	2075	1250			

2004	£10 ($^1/_{10}$ oz)	£25 (¼ oz)	£50 (½ oz)	£100 (1 oz)	SET		Authorised
PBG22	973	973	973	973	973	(4)	1250
PBG23	223	223	223		223	(3)	1500
BGD3		750					750
BGC3	929						1500
	2125	1946	1196	973			

2005	£10 ($^1/_{10}$ oz)	£25 (¼ oz)	£50 (½ oz)	£100 (1 oz)	SET		Authorised
PBG24	1439	1439	1439	1439	1439	(4)	1500
PBG25	417	417	417		417	(3)	500
BDG6		750					750
BGC6	1225						1500
	3081	2606	1856	1439			

2006	£10 (¹/₁₀ oz)	£25 (¼ oz)	£50 (½ oz)	£100 (1 oz)	SET		Authorised
PBG26	1163	1163	1163	1163	1163	(4)	1250
PBG27		250				(5)	
BGD3		728					1000
BGC3	700						1500
	1863	2141	1163	1163			

2007	£10 (¹/₁₀ oz)	£25 (¼ oz)	£50 (½ oz)	£100 (1 oz)	SET		Authorised
PBG28	1250	1250	1250	1250	1250	(4)	1250
BGD7		1000					1000
BGC7	893						1500
	2143	2250	1250	1250			

2008	£10 (¹/₁₀ oz)	£25 (¼ oz)	£50 (½ oz)	£100 (1 oz)	SET		Authorised
PBG29	1250	1250	1250	1250	1250	(4)	1250
BGD8		1000					1000
BGC8	748						1000
	1998	2250	1250	1250			

2009	£10 (¹/₁₀ oz)	£25 (¼ oz)	£50 (½ oz)	£100 (1 oz)	SET		Authorised
PBG30	797	797	797	797	797	(4)	1250
BGD9		770					2250
BGC9	749						2000
	1546	1567	797	797			

2010	£10 (¹/₁₀ oz)	£25 (¼ oz)	£50 (½ oz)	£100 (1 oz)	SET		Authorised
PBG31	867	867	867	867	867	(4)	1250
PBG32	186	186	186		186	(3)	500
BGD10		617					1250
BGC10	1049						1250
	2102	1670	1053	867			

2011	£10 (¹/₁₀ oz)	£25 (¼ oz)	£50 (½ oz)	£100 (1 oz)	SET		Authorised
PBG33	#	#	#	#		(4)	1000
PBG34	#	#	#			(3)	250
BGD11		#					5250
BGC11	#						1000
	3511	698	847	5735			

2012	£10 ($^1/_{10}$ oz)	£25 (¼ oz)	£50 (½ oz)	£100 (1 oz)	SET		Authorised
PBG35	365	365	365	365	365	(4)	550
PBG36	99	99	99		99	(3)	100
PBG37			25			(9)	
BGD3		316					620
BGC3	1249						750
	1713	780	489	365			

2013	£1 ($^1/_{20}$ oz)	£10 ($^1/_{10}$ oz)	£25 (¼ oz)	£50 (½ oz)	£100 (1 oz)	SET		Authorised
PBG38	261	261	261	261	261	261	(5)	250
PBG39		90	90	90		90	(3)	125
PBG40	136	136	136			136	(3)	350
BGC12		1150						1125
BGB1	2496							1000
	2893	1637	487	351	261			

2014	50p ($^1/_{40}$ oz)	£1 ($^1/_{20}$ oz)	£10 ($^1/_{10}$ oz)	£25 (¼ oz)	£50 (½ oz)	£100 (1 oz)	SET		Authorised
PBG41	225	225	225	225	225	225	225	(6)	250
		150	150	150	150	150	150	(5) Ω	150
PBG42			98	98	98		98	(3)	100
PBG43		140	140	140			140	(3)	150
	100	100					100	(2) Ω	100
BGB2		993							1000
BGA1	5521								9650
	5846	1608	613	613	473	475			

2015	50p ($^1/_{40}$ oz)	£1 ($^1/_{20}$ oz)	£10 ($^1/_{10}$ oz)	£25 (¼ oz)	£50 (½ oz)	£100 (1 oz)	SET		Authorised
PBG44	138	138	138	138	138	138	138	(6)	250
		96	96	96	96	96	96	(5) Ω	
PBG45			99	99	99		99	(3)	100
PBG46		176	176	176			176	(3)	250
BGA2	3075								7500
	3213	410	509	509	333	234			

2016	50p ($^1/_{40}$ oz)	£1 ($^1/_{20}$ oz)	£10 ($^1/_{10}$ oz)	£25 (¼ oz)	£50 (½ oz)	£100 (1 oz)	SET		Authorised
PBG47	174	174	174	174	174	174	174	(6)	175
		50	50	50	50	50	50	(5) Ω	50
PBG48			69	69	69		69	(3)	70
BGD17				729					730
BGD17				100				Ω	100
BGA3	1447								2250
	1621	224	293	1122	293	224			

Ω Coins sold to the US market and not in standard Royal Mint cases.

2017	50p (¹/₄₀ oz)	£1 (¹/₂₀ oz)	£10 (¹/₁₀ oz)	£25 (¹/₄ oz)	£50 (¹/₂ oz)	£100 (1 oz)	SET		Authorised
PBG49	182	182	182	182	182	182	182	(6)	250
		82	82	82	82	82	82	(5) Ω	
PBG50			158	158	158		158	(3)	200
BGD18				712					2500
BGA4	888								1500
	1070	264	422	1934	422	264			

2018	50p (¹/₄₀ oz)	£1 (¹/₂₀ oz)	£10 (¹/₁₀ oz)	£25 (¹/₄ oz)	£50 (¹/₂ oz)	£100 (1 oz)	SET		Authorised
PBG51	150	150	150	150	150	150	150	(6)	220
	30	30	30	30	30	30	30	(6) Ω	30
PBG52			103	103	103		103	(3)	170
BGD19				608					1080
	180	180	283	891	283	180			

2019	50p (¹/₄₀ oz)	£1 (¹/₂₀ oz)	£10 (¹/₁₀ oz)	£25 (¹/₄ oz)	£50 (¹/₂ oz)	£100 (1 oz)	SET		Authorised
PBG53	150	150	150	150	150	150	150	(6)	150
	15	15	15	15	15	15	15	(6) Ω	
PBG54			116	116	116		116	(3)	130
BGD20				644					645
				150				Ω	
	165	165	281	1075	281	165			

2020	50p (¹/₄₀ oz)	£1 (¹/₂₀ oz)	£10 (¹/₁₀ oz)	£25 (¹/₄ oz)	£50 (¹/₂ oz)	£100 (1 oz)	SET		Authorised
PBG55	#	#	#	#	#	#		(6)	150
PBG56			#	#	#			(3)	130
BGD21				#					700
	0	0	0	0	0	0			

2021	50p (¹/₄₀ oz)	£1 (¹/₂₀ oz)	£10 (¹/₁₀ oz)	£25 (¹/₄ oz)	£50 (¹/₂ oz)	£100 (1 oz)	SET		Authorised
PBG57	#	#	#	#	#	#		(6)	150
PBG58			#	#	#			(3)	115
BGD23				#					775
	0	0	0	0	0	0			

2022	50p (¹/₄₀ oz)	£1 (¹/₂₀ oz)	£10 (¹/₁₀ oz)	£25 (¹/₄ oz)	£50 (¹/₂ oz)	£100 (1 oz)	SET		Authorised
PBG59	#	#	#	#	#	#		(6)	150
PBG60			#	#	#			(3)	150
BGD25				#					775

Ω Coins sold to the US market and not in standard Royal Mint cases.
Mintages not yet known

TEN POUNDS

Obverse portrait by Ian Rank-Broadley

BPA1   **Britannia. Ten pounds.** (1/10 oz platinum.) R. As BGF7 with the inscription
'TENTH OUNCE PLATINUM BRITANNIA 2007'.
2007 Proof *FDC* (Issued: 691 plus coins in sets.)..£200

BPA2   **Britannia. Ten pounds.** (1/10 oz platinum.) R. As BGF8 with the inscription
'BRITANNIA 2008 1/10 OUNCE 999.5 PLATINUM'.
2008 Proof *FDC* (Issued: 268 plus coins in sets.)..£250

Obverse portrait by Jody Clark

BPA3   **Britannia. Ten pounds.** (1/10 oz platinum.) R. As BGF18C with the inscription
'BRITANNIA', the date of the year, '1/10 OZ 999.5 PLATINUM'.
2018 Unc £125
2019 Unc £125
2020 Unc £125
2021 Unc £125

BPA4   **Britannia. Ten pounds.** (1/10 oz platinum.) R. As BGF1 but with four added elements;
the image of waves behind Britannia, additional details on shield, thin
inner rim with repeated inscription 'DECUS ET TUTAMEN' in microtext, and
hologram at lower left showing alternately a trident and a padlock.
2022 Unc £125

TWENTY FIVE POUNDS

Obverse portrait by Ian Rank-Broadley

BPB1   **Britannia. Twenty five pounds.** (1/4 oz platinum.) R. As BGF7 with the inscription
'QUARTER OUNCE PLATINUM BRITANNIA 2007'.
2007 Proof *FDC* (Issued: 210 plus coins in sets)..£400

BPB2   **Britannia. Twenty five pounds.** (1/4 oz platinum.) R. As BGF8 with the inscription
'BRITANNIA 2008 1/4 OUNCE 999 .5 PLATINUM'.
2008 Proof *FDC* (Issued: 100 plus coins in sets)..£450

Obverse portrait by Jody Clark

BPB3   **Britannia. Twenty five pounds.** (1/4 oz platinum.) R. As BGF20 with the inscription
'BRITANNIA 1/4 OUNCE PLATINUM 999.5 2017'.
2017 Proof *FDC* (Issued: 558) £450

BPB4   **Britannia. Twenty five pounds.** (1/4 oz platinum.) R. As BGF23 with the inscription
'BRITANNIA 1/4 OUNCE PLATINU M 999.5 2018'.
2018 Proof *FDC* (Issued: 370) £450

BPB5   **Britannia. Twenty five pounds.** (1/4 oz platinum.) R. As BGF25 with the inscription
'BRITANNIA 1/4 OUNCE PLATINUM 999.5 2019'.
2019 Proof *FDC* (Issued: 168) £500

BPB6   **Britannia. Twenty five pounds.** (1/4 oz platinum.) R. As BGF26 with the inscription
'BRITANNIA 1/4 OUNCE PLATINUM 999.5 2020'.
2020 Proof *FDC* (Edition: 150) £525

BPB7   **Britannia. Twenty five pounds.** (1/4oz platinum.) R. As BGG3 with the inscription
'BRITANNIA 1/4 OUNCE 999.5 PLATINUM 2021'.
2021 Proof *FDC* (Edition: 160) £550

BPB8   **Britannia. Twenty five pounds.** (1/4oz platinum.) R. As BGG5 with the inscription
'1/4 OUNCE 999.5 BRITANNIA PLATINUM 2022'.
2022 Proof *FDC* (Edition: 160) £600

FIFTY POUNDS

Obverse portrait by Ian Rank-Broadley

BPC1   **Britannia. Fifty pounds.** (1/2 oz platinum.) R. As BGF7 with the inscription
'HALF OUNCE PLATINUM BRITANNIA 2007'.
2007 Proof *FDC** £800

* *Coins marked thus were originally issued in Royal Mint sets.*

BPC2 **Britannia. Fifty pounds.** (1/2 oz platinum.) ℞. As BGF8 with the inscription 'BRITANNIA 2008 1/2 OUNCE 999.5 PLATINUM'.
2008 Proof *FDC** £900

ONE HUNDRED POUNDS

Obverse portrait by Ian Rank-Broadley
BPD1 **Britannia. One hundred pounds.** (1 oz platinum.) ℞. As BGF7 with the inscription 'ONE OUNCE PLATINUM BRITANNIA 2007'.
2007 Proof *FDC** £1600
BPD2 **Britannia. One hundred pounds.** (1 oz platinum.) ℞. As BGF8 with the inscription 'BRITANNIA 2008 ONE OUNCE 999.5 PLATINUM'.
2008 Proof *FDC** £1800

Obverse portrait by Jody Clark
BPD3 **Britannia. One hundred pounds.** (1 oz platinum.) ℞. As BGF18C with the inscription 'BRITANNIA 1 OZ 999.5 PLATINUM' and the date of the year.
2018 Unc £1100
2019 Unc £1100
2020 Unc £1100
2021 Unc £1100
BPD4 **Britannia. One hundred pounds.** (1oz platinum.) ℞. As BGG4 with the inscription 'BRITANNIA 1 OZ 999.5 PLATINUM 2021'.
2021 Proof *FDC* (Edition: 275) £1600
BPD5 **Britannia. One hundred pounds.** (1 oz platinum.) ℞. As BGF1 but with four added elements; the image of waves behind Britannia, additional details on shield, thin inner rim with repeated inscription 'DECUS ET TUTAMEN' in microtext, and hologram at lower left showing alternately a trident and a padlock.
2022 Unc £1100
BPD6 **Britannia. One hundred pounds.** (1oz platinum.) ℞. As BGG5 with the inscription '1 OZ 999.5 BRITANNIA PLATINUM 2022'.
2022 Proof *FDC* £1600

* *Coins marked thus were originally issued in Royal Mint sets.*

Britannia Platinum Proof Sets

		£
PBP1-2007	£100, £50, £25, £10 (Issued: 250)	3000
PBP2-2008	£100, £50, £25, £10 (Issued: 150)	3250

Britannia Platinum Proof Coin Sales

2007	£10 (*1/10 oz*)	£25 (*¼ oz*)	£50 (*½ oz*)	£100 (*1 oz*)	SET	*	Authorised
PBP1	250	250	250	250	250	(4)	250
BPB1		210					1000
BPA1	691						1000
	941	460	250	250			

2008	£10 (*1/10 oz*)	£25 (*¼ oz*)	£50 (*½ oz*)	£100 (*1 oz*)	SET		Authorised
PBP2	150	150	150	150	150	(4)	250
BPB2		100					500
BPA2	268						750
	418	250	150	150			

2012 saw two major events in the UK – the Diamond Jubilee of the reign of Queen Elizabeth II and the Olympic Games, the first in the UK since 1948. The Royal Mint decided this was the time to introduce new denominations and sizes and therefore 5 ounce and 1 kilo coins were issued in both silver and gold – two sizes which had become popular with collectors all over the world following similar issues from other countries. The new UK coins also proved popular and so the range has grown in the years since with other sizes and denominations added including some coins struck in platinum. Most of the £10 5oz coins were struck in silver and gold versions whereas the higher denomination coins were only issued in one metal. This short section just covers the £10 5oz coins and the following section lists other commemoratives in denomination order but with metals separated and this includes other 5oz coins but with higher denominations. The coin specifications may be found at the beginning of the Britannia section.

TEN POUNDS

Obverse portrait by Ian Rank Broadley

M1

M1 **Ten pounds.** (Five ounce.) Diamond Jubilee commemorative 2012. O. Portrait of Queen Elizabeth II, inspired by the sculpture mounted in the entrance to the Supreme Court building on Parliament Square, with the inscription 'ELIZABETH. II. D. G. REG. F. D. TEN POUNDS'. R. An enthroned representation of the Queen surrounded by the inscription 'DILECTA REGNO MCMLII – MMXII'. (Obverse and reverse design: Ian Rank-Broadley)

2012 Proof in silver *FDC* (Issued: 1,933) £350
— Proof in gold *FDC* (Issued: 140) £11500

For coin specifications please see table at beginning of the Britannia section.

M2

M2   Ten pounds. (Five ounce.) 60th Anniversary of the Coronation. ℞. In the foreground
the Orb and Sceptre resting upon the Coronation Robe with the arches of Westminster
Abbey in the background with the inscription 'HER MAJESTY QUEEN ELIZABETH II
CORONATION ANNIVERSARY'. (Reverse design: Jonathan Olliffe.)
2013 Proof in silver *FDC* (Issued: 1,604) £450
—   Proof in gold *FDC* (Issued: 74) £12500

M3

M3   Ten pounds. (Five ounce.) The Christening of Prince George of Cambridge. ℞. A
deconstructed silver lily font incorporating cherubs and roses, with a Baroque-style
cartouche with the inscription 'DIEU ET MON DROIT' and 'TO CELEBRATE THE
CHRISTENING OF PRINCE GEORGE OF CAMBRIDGE 2013' in the centre of the
coin. (Reverse design: John Bergdahl.)
2013 Proof in silver *FDC* (Issued: 912) £450
—   Proof in gold *FDC* (Issued: 48) £12500

For coin specifications please see table at beginning of the Britannia section.

M4

M4   **Ten pounds.** (Five ounce.) 50th Anniversary of the Death of Winston Churchill.
R. A depiction of Sir Winston Churchill with the inscription 'CHURCHILL' at the base
of the coin. (Reverse design: Etienne Millner.)
2015 Proof on silver *FDC* (Issued: 855) £425
—   Proof in gold *FDC* (Issued: 58)..£12500

Obverse portrait by Jody Clark

M5

M5   **Ten pounds.** (5 oz fine silver.) The Christening of Princess Charlotte of Cambridge.
R. A design depicting a deconstructed silver lily font incorporating cherubs, with a
Baroque-Style cartouche and 'DIEU ET – MON DROIT' below and in the centre the
inscription 'TO CELEBRATE THE CHRISTENING OF PRINCESS CHARLOTTE
ELIZABETH DIANA OF CAMBRIDGE 2015'. (Reverse design: John Bergdahl.)
2015 Proof in silver *FDC* (Edition: 500) £400

See OD1 for 5oz coin in gold.

For coin specifications please see table at beginning of the Britannia section.

Obverse portrait by James Butler

M6

M6 **Ten pounds.** (Five ounce.) The Longest Serving Monarch. R. A design depicting
The Royal Cypher below five definitive coinage portraits and the inscription 'THE
LONGEST REIGN'. (Reverse design: Stephen Taylor.)
2015 Proof in silver *FDC* (Issued: 1,499) £400
—   Proof in gold *FDC* (Issued: 180)..£12500

Obverse portrait by Jody Clark

M7

M7 **Ten pounds.** (Five ounce.) 400th Anniversary of the Death of William Shakespeare.
R. In the centre a depiction of William Shakespeare accompanied with the inscription
'OTHELLO ACT 1 SC 3' surrounded by the inscription 'PUT MONEY IN THY PURSE'
2016'. (Reverse design: Tom Phillips.)
2016 Proof in silver *FDC* (Issued: 343)...£450
—   Proof in gold *FDC* (Issued: 50)...£12500

For coin specifications please see table at beginning of the Britannia section.

M8

M8 **Ten pounds.** (Five ounce.) 90th Birthday of Her Majesty Queen Elizabeth II.
R. A crowned Royal Cypher above the number '90' encircled by roses.
(Reverse design: Christopher Hobbs.)
2016 Proof in silver *FDC* (Issued: 1,727) £400
— Proof in gold *FDC* (Issued: 170) £11500

M9

M9 **Ten pounds.** (Five ounce.) Sapphire Jubilee of Her Majesty Queen Elizabeth II.
O. As M5. R. A crowned depiction of the Royal Arms above the number '65' surrounded
by sprigs of oak and olive leaves, accompanied by the inscription 'HER MAJESTY
THE QUEEN'S SAPPHIRE JUBILEE 1952-2017'. (Reverse design: Gregory Cameron.)
2017 Proof in silver *FDC* (Issued: 1,446) £400
— Proof in gold *FDC* (Issued: 110) £11500

For coin specifications please see table at beginning of the Britannia section.

M10

M10 Ten pounds. (Five ounce.) Celebrating the Platinum Wedding Anniversary of HM The Queen and HRH Prince Philip. O. Portrait of Queen Elizabeth II conjoined with His Royal Highness Prince Philip, The Duke of Edinburgh with the inscription 'ELIZABETH 11 D G REG F D – PHILIP PRINCEPS' and the denomination 'TEN POUNDS'. R. A depiction of the royal arms and those of His Royal Highness Prince Philip, The Duke of Edinburgh above the inscription '70 YEARS OF MARRIAGE 2017'. (Obverse design: Etienne Milner; reverse: John Bergdahl.)

2017 Proof in silver *FDC* (Issued: 1,057)...£400
—   Proof in gold *FDC* (Issued: 115)..£11500

M11

M11 Ten pounds. (Five ounce.) Sapphire Coronation. R. A portrait of Queen Elizabeth II taken from the Coronation and accompanied by the dates '1953' and '2018'. (Reverse design: Dominique Evans.)

2018 Proof in silver *FDC* (Issued: 591)..£420
—   Proof in gold *FDC* (Issued: 87)..£12000

M12 Ten pounds. (Five ounce.) Celebrating Four Generations of the Royal Family. R. As L70

2018 Proof in silver *FDC* (Issued: 399)..£420
—   Proof in gold *FDC* (Issued: 67)..£12000

For coin specifications please see table at beginning of the Britannia section.

M13 Ten pounds. (Five ounce.) Tower of London - A Raven. ℞. as L73
2019 Proof in silver *FDC* (Issued: 234) £420
— Proof in gold *FDC* (Issued: 21) £11500

M14 Ten pounds. (Five ounce.) Tower of London - Crown of Mary of Modena. ℞. as L74
2019 Proof in silver *FDC* (Issued: 138) £420
— Proof in gold *FDC* (Issued: 33) £11500

M15 Ten pounds. (Five ounce.) Tower of London - A Yeoman Warder. ℞. as L75
2019 Proof in silver *FDC* (Issued: 97) £420
— Proof in gold *FDC* (Issued: 23) £11500

M16 Ten pounds. (Five ounce.) Tower of London - Queen Elizabeth's Keys. ℞. as L76
2019 Proof in silver *FDC* (Issued: 89) £420
— Proof in gold *FDC* (Issued: 29) £11500

M17

M17 Ten pounds. (Five ounce.) 200th Anniversary of the Birth of Queen Victoria. ℞. A
conjoined portrait of Queen Victoria and Prince Albert with the inscription 'VICTORIA
REGINA + ALBERTUS PRINCEPS CONJUX' and the date 'MDCCCXIX'. (Reverse
design: William Wyon.)
2019 Proof in silver *FDC* (Issued: 498) £420
— Proof in gold *FDC* (Issued: 70) £13000
*The reverse design revives a design first created by William Wyon for a Council medal for
the Great Exhibition of 1851*

M18 Ten pounds. (5oz of fine silver.) 75th Anniversary of the End of the Second World War.
℞. As L86.
2020 Proof in silver *FDC* (Edition: 285) £420
See OD2 for 5oz coin in gold.

M19 Ten pounds. (5 oz of fine gold.) 200th Anniversary of the Death of King George III.
℞. As L79.
2020 Proof in gold *FDC* (Edition: 45) £15000

For coin specifications please see table at beginning of the Britannia section.

M20   M21

M20 **Ten pounds.** (Five ounce.) 95th Birthday of Her Majesty Queen Elizabeth II. R. A depiction of intertwined flowers accompanied by the Royal Cypher and the inscription 'MY HEART AND MY DEVOTION 1926 2021'. (Reverse design: Gary Breeze.)
2021 Proof in silver *FDC* (Edition: 960) £500
— Proof in gold *FDC* (Edition: 160) £11500

M21 **Ten pounds.** (5oz fine silver.) Prince Philip Memorial 2021. R. A depiction of Prince Philip with the inscription 'HRH THE PRINCE PHILIP' and 'DUKE OF EDINBURGH 1921 2021'. (Reverse design: Ian Rank-Broadley.)
2021 Proof in silver *FDC* (Edition: 756) £500
— Proof piedfort in silver FDC (Edition: 156) £900
See OD3 for 5oz coin in gold.

M22   M23

M22 **Ten pounds.** (5oz fine silver.) Platinum Jubilee Commemorative 2022. O. Her Majesty the Queen on horseback with the inscription 'ELIZABETH II • D • G • REG • F• D • 10 POUNDS' accompanied by the Garter Belt with the inscription 'HONI • SOIT • QUI • MAL • Y• PENSE •' and the date of the year. R. A crowned depiction of the Royal Cypher surrounded by the floral emblems of the United Kingdom and the dates '1952 - 2022'. (Reverse design: John Bergdahl.)
2022 Proof in silver *FDC* (Edition: 1,006) £465
— Proof piedfort in silver *FDC* (Edition: 156)..£885

M23 **Ten pounds.** (5oz fine silver.) The life and legacy of Dame Vera Lynn. R. A portrait of Dame Vera Lynn with the inscription 'DAME VERA LYNN 1917-2020'.
2022 Proof in silver *FDC* (Edition: 246) £465

For coin specifications please see table at beginning of the Britannia section.

At one time all precious metal commemorative coins were versions of currency coins with traditional specifications but in more recent years a growing number of commemoratives have been issued with Britannia specifications. A few of these have been supplied to other mints who have then marketed them with a similar commemorative of their country with the result that single pieces are not easy to locate. Our listing of these coins may not be complete as there are not always any press details issued by the Royal Mint.

Higher denomination coins have also been issued with specifications based on the ounce or kilo and this range is still growing with the largest in this section being a 15 kg gold piece for the Queen's Platinum Jubilee in 2022.

Specifications for all the coins in this section may be found at the start of the Britannia listings except for the following silver coins:

Denomination	Metal	Weight		Diameter
£20	0.999 silver	$^1/_2$ ounce	15.71 g	27 mm
£50	0.999 silver	1 ounce	31.43 g	34 mm
£100	0.999 silver	2 ounce	62.86 g	40 mm

SILVER

ONE POUND
Obverse portrait by Jody Clark.

NA1

NA1   **One pound.** (1/2 oz of fine silver.) 75th Anniversary of VE Day. ℞. A group of people with rays echoing anti-aircraft searchlights but becoming rays of hope.
(Reverse design: Dominique Evans.)
2020 Proof in silver *FDC* (Edition: 2,000) £50

The above was issued in a set with a Canada & Netherlands coin.

For coin specifications please see table at beginning of the Britannia section.

TWO POUNDS

Obverse portrait by Jody Clark.

NB1 **Two pounds.** (1 oz of fine silver.) Bi-centenary of the Battle of Waterloo. R. As L39A.
2015 Proof in silver FDC (Edition: 1,250)... £80
This coin was supplied either to the Dutch Mint or another Netherlands based company.

NB2 **Two pounds.** (1 oz of fine silver.) 400th Anniversary of the Death of William
Shakespeare. R. As M7.
2016 Proof in silver *FDC* matt reverse (Edition: 999)...£60

NB3   NB5   NB7

NB3 **Two pounds.** (1 oz of fine silver.) Elizabeth Tower. R. As L35 with inscription 'BIG
BEN 2017'.
2017 Proof in silver *FDC* (Edition: 800)* £80
— Proof in silver *FDC* with reverse frosting (Edition: 800)* £80

NB4 **Two pounds.** (1 oz of fine silver.) 400th Anniversary of "The Mayflower" voyage to
the New World. R. "The Mayflower" bursting out of the frame as it sails through the
rough seas with inscription '1620 MAYFLOWER 2020'. (Reverse design:
Chris Costello.)
2020 Proof in silver *FDC* (Edition: 5,000) £75
*The above was issued in a set with a USA silver medal. A further 5.000 coins were supplied to
the US Mint which they marketed in their own case with the silver medal.*

NB5 **Two pounds.** (1 oz of fine silver.) 80th Anniversary of the Battle of Britain. R. As H31.
2020 Proof in silver *FDC* (Edition: 2,000) £80
This coin was issued in a set with a Czech coin and marketed by the Czech Mint.

NB6 **Two pounds.** (1 oz of fine silver.) 95th Birthday of Her Majesty Queen Elizabeth II.
R. As L88.
2021 Proof in silver *FDC* (Edition: 6,500) £100
This coin was issued in a case with a Canada $20 silver proof coin.

NB7 **Two pounds.** (1 oz of fine silver.) Peter Rabbit. R. A depiction of Peter Rabbit, Mrs
Rabbit and three other rabbits accompanied by the inscription 'NOW RUN ALONG,
AND DON'T GET INTO MISCHIEF. I AM GOING OUT.' (Reverse design: Ffion
Gwillim.)
2021 Proof in silver *FDC* (Edition: 5,010) £95
For other coins with the same design see L91.

For coin specifications please see table at beginning of the Britannia section.

NB8   Two pounds. (1oz of fine silver.) The life and legacy of Mahatma Gandhi. R. A depiction of a lotus flower with the inscription 'MY LIFE IS MY MESSAGE • MAHATMA GANDHI'. (Reverse design: Heena Glover.)
2021 Proof in silver *FDC* (Edition: 2,510) £90

NB9   Two pounds. (1 oz of fine silver.) Platinum Jubilee Commemorative 2022. O. & R. As L95.
2022 Proof in silver *FDC* (Edition: 5,500) £95
This coin was issued in a case with a Canada $20 silver proof coin.

NB10 Two pounds. (1 oz of fine silver.) Peter Rabbit. R. A depiction of the children's character, Peter Rabbit, with the inscription '120 YEARS' and 'THE TALE OF PETER RABBIT'. (Reverse design: Ffion Gwillim.)
2022 Proof in silver *FDC* (Edition: 3,510) £100

FIVE POUNDS

NC1   Five pounds. (2 oz of fine silver.) 95th Birthday of Her Majesty Queen Elizabeth II. R. As L88.
2021 Proof in silver FDC (Edition: 995)..£200

NC2   Five pounds. (2 oz of fine silver.) Prince Philip Memorial 2021. R. A depiction of Prince Philip with the inscription 'HRH THE PRINCE PHILIP' and 'DUKE OF EDINBURGH 1921 2021'. (Reverse design: Ian Rank-Broadley.)
2021 Proof in silver *FDC* (Edition: 1,006) £250

NC3   Five pounds. (2 oz of fine silver.) Platinum Jubilee Commemorative 2022. O. & R. As L95.
2022 Proof in silver *FDC* (Edition: 1,006) £185

TWENTY POUNDS

£20, £50 and £100 silver coins containing respectively 1/2 oz 1 oz and 2 oz fine silver were issued by the Royal Mint at face value and the Royal Proclamation, as is customary for all coins, states that 'The said silver coin shall be legal tender for payment of any amount in any part of Our United Kingdom'. In spite of this, it soon became apparent that these could not be spent nor redeemed at any bank so they had no effective legal tender status with the result that pieces are often traded at below their alleged face value.

Obverse portrait by Ian Rank-Broadley

NE1

NE1   Twenty pounds. (1/2 oz of fine silver.) R. A depiction of St. George armed, sitting on horseback, attacking the dragon with a sword, and a broken spear upon the ground and the date of the year. (Reverse design: Benedetto Pistrucci.)
2013 Silver BU (Issued: 250,000)..£20

For coin specifications please see table at beginning of the Britannia section.

NE2   NE3

NE2 **Twenty pounds.** (1/2 oz of fine silver.) World War I. R. A depiction of a lion behind the figure of Britannia holding a shield and a trident, watching over departing ships from a cliff top, with the inscription 'THE FIRST WORLD WAR 1914 1918' and the date at the base of the coin. (Reverse design: John Bergdahl.)

2014 BU (Issued: 141,751) £20

NE3 **Twenty pounds.** (1/2 oz of fine silver.) 50th Anniversary of the Death of Winston Churchill. R. A depiction of Sir Winston Churchill with the inscription 'CHURCHILL' at the base of the coin. (Reverse design: Etienne Millner.)

2015 BU (Issued: 132,142)...£20

Obverse portrait by Jody Clark

NE4   NE5

NE4 **Twenty pounds.** (1/2 oz of fine silver.) The Longest Serving Monarch. R. A design depicting the Royal Cypher below the five definitive coinage portraits and the inscription 'THE LONGEST REIGN'. (Reverse design: Stephen Taylor.)

2015 BU (Issued: 149,282)...£20

NE5 **Twenty pounds.** (1/2 oz of fine silver.) 90th Birthday of Her Majesty Queen Elizabeth II. R. A crowned Royal Cypher above the number '90' encircled by roses. (Reverse design: Christopher Hobbs.)

2016 BU (Issued: 116,354) £20

For coin specificaitons please see table at the beginning of this section.

NE6

NE6 **Twenty pounds.** (1/2 oz of fine silver.) R. A dragon with the inscription 'TWENTY
POUNDS'. (Reverse design: Norman Sillman.)

2016 BU (Edition: 150,000)..£20
2017 BU (Edition: 2,329)...£24
2018 BU (Edition: 1,607)...£24
2019 BU (Issued: 1,020) £24
—   BU in 'Pride of Wales' pack for Wales Rugby Grand Slam victory
       (Issued: 2,175)..£30
2020 BU (Edition: 714)..£24

*The 2016 & 2019 Pride of Wales coins were on general sale but the others were only available
for purchase at the Royal Mint Experience.*

NE7   NE8

NE7 **Twenty pounds.** (1/2 oz of fine silver.) Christmas. R. A depiction of Mary and the
baby Jesus receiving gifts from the Magi, with the inscription 'THE NATIVITY:
CHRISTMAS 2016'. (Reverse design: Gregory Cameron.)

2016 BU (Issued: 29,929) £25

NE8 **Twenty pounds.** (1/2 oz of fine silver.) Celebrating the Platinum Wedding Anniversary
of HM The Queen and HRH Prince Philip. O. Portrait of Queen Elizabeth II conjoined
with his Royal Highness Prince Philip, The Duke of Edinburgh with the inscription
'ELIZABETH II D G REG F D – PHILIP PRINCEPS' and the denomination. R. A
depiction of the Queen and that of his Royal Highness Prince Philip, The Duke of
Edinburgh on horseback with the inscription 'WEDDED LOVE HAS JOINED THEM
IN HAPPINESS' with the dates '1947-2017'. (Obverse design: Etienne Milne, reverse:
John Bergdahl.)

2017 BU (issued: 24,363)..£20

For coin specificaitons please see table at the beginning of this section

FIFTY POUNDS

Obverse portrait by Jody Clark

NF1

NF1   **Fifty pounds.** (1 oz of fine silver.) Britannia. R. A design of the standing figure of
Britannia bearing a trident and a shield, with a lion at her feet, set against the
backdrop of a globe, and the inscription 'BRITANNIA 50 POUNDS' and the date'
2015' below. (Reverse design: Jody Clark.)
2015 BU (Issued: 78,644) £50

NF2

NF2   **Fifty pounds.** (1 oz of fine silver.) 400th Anniversary of the Death of William
Shakespeare. R. A design depicting a mask of tragedy and comedy with inscription
'WILLIAM SHAKESPEARE 2016' (Reverse design: John Bergdahl.)
2016 BU (Issued: 14,948) £50

For coin specifications please see table at beginning of this section.

ONE HUNDRED POUNDS

Obverse portrait by Ian Rank-Broadley

NG1

NG1 One hundred pounds. (2 oz of fine silver.) Elizabeth Tower. (Reverse design:
Glyn Davies and Laura Clancy.)
2015 BU (Issued: 49,147) £100

Obverse portrait by Jody Clark

NG2   NG3

NG2 One hundred pounds. (2 oz of fine silver.) Buckingham Palace. R. A design of the
Victoria Memorial with Buckingham Palace in the background. (Reverse design:
Glyn Davies and Laura Clancy.)
2015 BU (Issued: 47,851) £100
NG3 One hundred pounds. (2 oz of fine silver.) Trafalgar Square. R. A view of Trafalgar
Square with the head of a lion in the foreground and Nelson Column in the background.
(Reverse design: Laura Clancy and Glyn Davies.)
2016 BU (Issued: 14,878) £100

For coins with similar designs, see L34-37, NB3, QB2-3 & QB5.
See note above NE1.

For coin specifications please see table at beginning of the Britannia section.

FIVE HUNDRED POUNDS

Obverse portrait by Ian Rank-Broadley

NH1

NH1   Five hundred pounds. (1 kilo of fine silver.) Diamond Jubilee commemorative 2012.
O. Portrait of Queen Elizabeth II inspired by the sculpture mounted in the entrance to
the Supreme Court building on Parliament Square, with the inscription 'ELIZABETH. II.
D. G. REG. F. D. 500 POUNDS'. R. A full achievement of the Royal Arms based on
those mounted on the front gates of Buckingham Palace with the date '2012' below.
(Obverse and reverse design: Ian Rank-Broadley.)
2012 Proof in silver *FDC* (Issued: 206) £1500

NH2   Five hundred pounds. (1 kilo of fine silver.) R. 60th Anniversary of the Coronation.
R. In the foreground the Orb and Sceptre with the St. Edward's Crown behind
surrounded by flowers representing the constituent parts of the United Kingdom and in
the background a ribbon showing the '2nd JUNE 1953' with the inscription 'QUEEN
ELIZABETH II' and 'THE 60TH ANNIVERSARY OF THE CORONATION'.
(Reverse design: John Bergdahl.)
2013 Proof in silver *FDC* (Issued: 301)) £1500

NH3

NH3   Five hundred pounds. (1 kilo of fine silver.) The Christening of Prince George of
Cambridge. R. A deconstructed silver lily font incorporating cherubs and roses, with
a Baroque-style cartouche with the inscription 'DIEU ET MON DROIT' and 'TO
CELEBRATE THE CHRISTENING OF PRINCE GEORGE OF CAMBRIDGE 2013'
in the centre of the coin. (Reverse design: John Bergdahl.)
2013 Proof in silver *FDC* (Issued: 194) £1500

For coin specifications please see table at beginning of the Britannia section.

Obverse portrait by James Butler

NH4

NH4 Five hundred pounds. (1 kilo of fine silver.) The Longest Serving Monarch.
R. A design depicting the Royal Cypher below the five definitive coinage portraits
and the inscription 'THE LONGEST REIGN'. (Reverse design: Stephen Taylor.)
2015 Proof in silver *FDC* (Issued: 278) £1500

Obverse portrait by Ian Rank-Broadley

NH5 Five hundred pounds. (1 kilo of fine silver.) 50th Anniversary of the Death of
Winston Churchill. R. As M4.
2015 Proof in silver *FDC* (Issued: 117) £1500

Obverse portrait by Jody Clark

NH6

NH6 Five hundred pounds. (1 kilo of fine silver.) 90th Birthday of Her Majesty Queen
Elizabeth II. R. A crowned Royal Cypher above the number '90' encircled by
roses with the inscription 'FULL OF HONOUR AND YEARS'. (Reverse design:
Christopher Hobbs.)
2016 Proof in silver *FDC* (Issued: 447) £1500

For coin specifications please see table at beginning of the Britannia section.

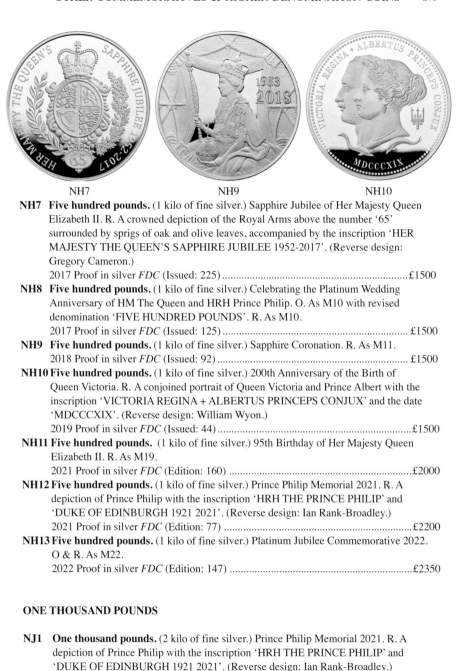

NH7   NH9   NH10

NH7 **Five hundred pounds.** (1 kilo of fine silver.) Sapphire Jubilee of Her Majesty Queen Elizabeth II. R̟. A crowned depiction of the Royal Arms above the number '65' surrounded by sprigs of oak and olive leaves, accompanied by the inscription 'HER MAJESTY THE QUEEN'S SAPPHIRE JUBILEE 1952-2017'. (Reverse design: Gregory Cameron.)
2017 Proof in silver *FDC* (Issued: 225) £1500

NH8 **Five hundred pounds.** (1 kilo of fine silver.) Celebrating the Platinum Wedding Anniversary of HM The Queen and HRH Prince Philip. O. As M10 with revised denomination 'FIVE HUNDRED POUNDS'. R̟. As M10.
2017 Proof in silver *FDC* (Issued: 125) £1500

NH9 **Five hundred pounds.** (1 kilo of fine silver.) Sapphire Coronation. R̟. As M11.
2018 Proof in silver *FDC* (Issued: 92) £1500

NH10 **Five hundred pounds.** (1 kilo of fine silver.) 200th Anniversary of the Birth of Queen Victoria. R̟. A conjoined portrait of Queen Victoria and Prince Albert with the inscription 'VICTORIA REGINA + ALBERTUS PRINCEPS CONJUX' and the date 'MDCCCXIX'. (Reverse design: William Wyon.)
2019 Proof in silver *FDC* (Issued: 44) £1500

NH11 **Five hundred pounds.** (1 kilo of fine silver.) 95th Birthday of Her Majesty Queen Elizabeth II. R̟. As M19.
2021 Proof in silver *FDC* (Edition: 160) £2000

NH12 **Five hundred pounds.** (1 kilo of fine silver.) Prince Philip Memorial 2021. R̟. A depiction of Prince Philip with the inscription 'HRH THE PRINCE PHILIP' and 'DUKE OF EDINBURGH 1921 2021'. (Reverse design: Ian Rank-Broadley.)
2021 Proof in silver *FDC* (Edition: 77) £2200

NH13 **Five hundred pounds.** (1 kilo of fine silver.) Platinum Jubilee Commemorative 2022. O & R̟. As M22.
2022 Proof in silver *FDC* (Edition: 147) £2350

ONE THOUSAND POUNDS

NJ1 **One thousand pounds.** (2 kilo of fine silver.) Prince Philip Memorial 2021. R̟. A depiction of Prince Philip with the inscription 'HRH THE PRINCE PHILIP' and 'DUKE OF EDINBURGH 1921 2021'. (Reverse design: Ian Rank-Broadley.)
2021 Proof in silver FDC (Edition: 51)..£5000

For coin specifications please see table at beginning of the Britannia section.

GOLD

TWENTY FIVE POUNDS

Obverse portrait by Ian Rank-Broadley

OA1   Twenty five pounds. (1/4 oz of fine gold.) 50th Anniversary of the Death of Winston Churchill. R. As NE3.
2015 Proof in gold *FDC* (Issued: 500)*..£ 550

This coin was marketed by a Continental company in a set containing a gold coin from France, Russia and USA to commemorate the 70th Anniversary of the end of World War II.

Obverse portrait by Jody Clark

OA2   OA10

OA2   Twenty five pounds. (1/4 oz of fine gold.) 150th Anniversary of the Birth of Beatrix Potter. R. A portrait of Peter Rabbit with the incription 'PETER RABBIT'. (Reverse design: Emma Noble.)
2016 Proof in gold *FDC* (Issued: 500) £700

OA3   Twenty five pounds. (1/4 oz of fine gold.) 400th Anniversary of the Death of William Shakespeare. R. As M7.
2016 Proof in gold *FDC* (Issued: 350) £550

OA4   Twenty five pounds. (1/4 oz of fine gold.) Celebrating Four Generations of the Royal Family. R. as L70.
2018 Proof in gold *FDC* (Issued: 736) £550

OA5   Twenty five pounds. (1/4 oz of fine gold.) 100th Anniversary of the Royal Air Force. R. As K50
2018 Proof in gold *FDC* (Issued: 270)...£600

This coin was issued in a set with a USA $10 gold proof coin.

OA6   Twenty five pounds. (1/4 oz of fine gold.) Tower of London - A Raven. R. as L73.
2019 Proof in gold *FDC* (Issued: 335) £550

OA7   Twenty five pounds. (¼ oz of fine gold.) Tower of London - Crown of Mary of Modena. R. as L74.
2019 Proof in gold *FDC* (Issued: 168) £550

OA8   Twenty five pounds. (1/4 oz fine gold.) Tower of London - A Yeoman Warder. R. as L75.
2019 Proof in gold *FDC* (Issued: 146) £550

OA9   Twenty five pounds. (1/4 oz fine gold.) Tower of London - Queen Elizabeth's Keys. R. as L76.
2019 Proof in gold *FDC* (Issued: 110)...£550

OA10 Twenty five pounds. (1/4 oz fine gold.) 400th Anniversary of "The Mayflower" voyage to the New World. R. "The Mayflower" bursting out of the frame as it sails through the rough seas with inscription '1620 MAYFLOWER 2020'. (Reverse design: Chris Costello.)
2020 Proof in gold *FDC* (Edition: 500) £550

The above was issued in a set with a USA $10 gold proof coin. A further 4,500 coins were supplied to the US Mint which they marketed in their own case with the $10 gold coin.

For coin specifications please see table at beginning of the Britannia section.

OA11 Twenty five pounds. (1/4 oz of fine gold) 80th Anniversary of the Battle of Britain. Ṙ. As H31.
2020 Proof in gold *FDC* (Edition: 300) £600
This coin was issued in a set with a Czech coin and marketed by the Czech Mint.

OA12 Twenty five pounds. (1/4 oz of fine gold) 75th Anniversary of the End of the Second World War. Ṙ. As L86 but with no edge inscription.
2020 Proof in gold *FDC* (Edition: 300) £600

OA13 Twenty five pounds. (1/4 oz of fine gold) 95th Birthday of Her Majesty Queen Elizabeth II. Ṙ. As L88.
2021 Proof in gold *FDC* (Edition: 950) £650

OA14 Twenty five pounds. (1/4 oz of fine gold.) Prince Philip Memorial 2021. Ṙ. A depiction of Prince Philip with the inscription 'HRH THE PRINCE PHILIP' and 'DUKE OF EDINBURGH 1921 2021'. (Reverse design: Ian Rank-Broadley.)
2021 Proof in gold *FDC* (Edition: 760) £650

OA15 Twenty five pounds. (1/4oz of fine gold.) Platinum Jubilee Commemorative 2022. O. & Ṙ. As OC5.
2022 Proof in gold *FDC* (Edition: 1110) £670

OA16 Twenty five pounds. (1/4oz of fine gold.) The life and legacy of Dame Vera Lynn. Ṙ. As OD6.
2022 Proof in gold *FDC* (Edition: 400) £650
This coin was only sold in a case with a 1917 sovereign.

OA17 Twenty five pounds. (1/4oz of fine gold.) The 40th Birthday of Prince William. O. & Ṙ. As OC6.
2022 Proof in gold *FDC* (Edition: 510 plus 100 in set with 1982 sovereign) £670

OA18 Twenty five pounds. (1/4oz of fine gold.) The Queen's Reign I – The Bestowing of Honours. O. & Ṙ. As L98.
2022 Proof in gold *FDC* (Edition: 510) £700

OA19 Twenty five pounds. (1/4oz of fine gold.) The Queen's Reign II – Charity and Patronage. O. & Ṙ. As L99.
2022 Proof in gold *FDC* (Edition: 510) £700

OA20 Twenty five pounds. (1/4oz of fine gold.) The Queen's Reign III – The Commonwealth of Nations. O. & Ṙ. As L100.
2022 Proof in gold *FDC* (Edition: 510) £700

ONE HUNDRED POUNDS

OB1 One hundred pounds. (1 oz of fine gold.) 400th Anniversary of "The Mayflower" voyage to the New World. Ṙ. As OA10 but with edge inscription 'UNDERTAKEN FOR THE GLORY OF GOD' and with obverse reverse frosted.
2020 Proof in gold *FDC* (Edition: 500) £2750

OB2 One hundred pounds. (1 oz of fine gold.) Peter Rabbit. Ṙ. A depiction of Peter Rabbit, Mrs Rabbit and three other rabbits accompanied by the inscription 'NOW RUN ALONG, AND DON'T GET INTO MISCHIEF. I AM GOING OUT.' (Reverse design: Ffion Gwillim.)
2021 Proof in gold *FDC* (Edition: 260) £2400

OB3 One hundred pounds. (1oz of fine gold.) The life and legacy of Mahatma Gandhi. Ṙ. A depiction of a lotus flower with the inscription 'MY LIFE IS MY MESSAGE • MAHATMA GANDHI'. (Reverse design: Heena Glover.)
2021 Proof in gold *FDC* (Edition: 185) £2500

OB4 One hundred pounds. (1 oz of fine gold.) Peter Rabbit. Ṙ. A depiction of the children's character, Peter Rabbit, with the inscription '120 YEARS' and 'THE TALE OF PETER RABBIT'. (Reverse design: Ffion Gwillim.)
2022 Proof in gold *FDC* (Edition: 130) £2500

For coin specifications please see table at beginning of the Britannia section.

TWO HUNDRED POUNDS

OC1 **Two hundred pounds.** (2 oz of fine gold.) 200th Anniversary of the death of King George III. ℞. As L79.
2020 Proof in gold *FDC* (Edition: 125) £7000

OC2 **Two hundred pounds.** (2 oz of fine gold.) 95th Birthday of Her Majesty Queen Elizabeth II. ℞. As L88 but with no edge inscription.
2021 Proof in gold *FDC* (Edition: 200) £6000

OC3 **Two hundred pounds.** (2 oz of fine gold.) Prince Philip Memorial 2021. ℞. A depiction of Prince Philip with the inscription 'HRH THE PRINCE PHILIP' and 'DUKE OF EDINBURGH 1921 2021'. (Reverse design: Ian Rank-Broadley.)
2021 Proof in gold *FDC* (Edition: 306) £6000

OC4 **Two hundred pounds.** (2 oz of fine gold.) 1150th Anniversary of Alfred the Great's Accession as King of the West Saxons. ℞. A depiction of Alfred the Great with the inscription 'ALFRED THE GREAT' and the dates '871 2021'. (Reverse design: John Bergdahl.)
2021 Proof in gold *FDC* (Edition: 125) £7000

OC5 **Two hundred pounds.** (2oz of fine gold.) Platinum Jubilee Commemorative 2022. O. Her Majesty the Queen on horseback with the inscription 'ELIZABETH II • D • G • REG • F• D • 200 POUNDS' accompanied by the Garter Belt with the inscription 'HONI • SOIT • QUI • MAL • Y• PENSE •' and the date of the year. ℞. A crowned depiction of the Royal Arms accompanied by the dates '• 1952 2022 •'. (Reverse design: John Bergdahl.)
2022 Proof in gold *FDC* (Edition: 206) £5500

OC6 **Two hundred pounds.** (2oz of fine gold.) The 40th Birthday of Prince William. O. As L39A. ℞. A portrait of HRH The Duke of Cambridge accompanied by his Cypher and age. The precious metal versions will have edge inscription 'HRH THE DUKE OF CAMBRIDGE'. (Reverse design: Thomas T. Docherty.)
2022 Proof in gold *FDC* (Edition: 106) £5000

FIVE HUNDRED POUNDS

OD1

OD1 **Five hundred pounds.** (5 oz of fine gold.) The Christening of Princess Charlotte of Cambridge. ℞. A design depicting a deconstructed silver lily font incorporating cherubs, with a Baroque Style cartouche and 'DIEU ET – MON DROIT' below and in the centre the inscription 'TO CELEBRATE THE CHRISTENING OF PRINCESS CHARLOTTE ELIZABETH DIANA OF CAMBRIDGE 2015'.
(Reverse design: John Bergdahl.)
2015 Proof in gold *FDC* £12500

For coin specifications please see table at beginning of the Britannia section.

OD2 Five hundred pounds. (5 oz of fine gold.) 75th Anniversary of the End of the
Second World War. Ŗ. As L86.
2020 Proof in gold *FDC* (Edition: 85) £12000

OD3 Five hundred pounds. (5 oz of fine gold.) Prince Philip Memorial 2021. Ŗ. A
depiction of Prince Philip with the inscription 'HRH THE PRINCE PHILIP' and
'DUKE OF EDINBURGH 1921 2021'. (Reverse design: Ian Rank-Broadley.)
2021 Proof in gold *FDC* (Edition: 156) £12000
—   Proof piedfort in gold *FDC* (Editon: 56) £22000

OD4 Five hundred pounds. (5 oz of fine gold.) 1150th Anniversary of Alfred the
Great's Accession as King of the West Saxons. Ŗ. A depiction of Alfred the Great
with the inscription 'ALFRED THE GREAT' and the dates '871 2021'. (Reverse
design: John Bergdahl.)
2021 Proof in gold *FDC* (Edition: 45) £15000

OD5 Five hundred pounds. (5 oz of fine gold.) Platinum Jubilee Commemorative 2022.
O. Her Majesty the Queen on horseback with the inscription 'ELIZABETH II • D •
G • REG • F• D • 500 POUNDS' accompanied by the Garter Belt with the inscription
'HONI • SOIT • QUI • MAL • Y• PENSE •' and the date of the year. Ŗ. A crowned
depiction of the Royal Cypher surrounded by the floral emblems of the United
Kingdom and the dates '1952 - 2022'. (Reverse design: John Bergdahl.)
2022 Proof in gold *FDC* (Edition: 136) £12000

OD5AFive hundred pounds. (10 oz of fine gold.) Platinum Jubilee Commemorative 2022.
O. & Ŗ. As OD5.
2022 Proof in gold *FDC* (Edition: 56) £24000

*The above coin was described in the legislation as a Piedfort but as it has a diameter of 65mm
it cannot be regarded as a piedfort of the £500 50mm 5oz version.*

OD6 Five hundred pounds. (5 oz of fine gold.) The life and legacy of Dame Vera Lynn.
Ŗ. A portrait of Dame Vera Lynn with the inscription 'DAME VERA LYNN 1917-2020.
2022 Proof in gold *FDC* (Edition: 41) £12000

OD7 Five hundred pounds. (5oz of fine gold.) The 40th Birthday of Prince William.
O. & Ŗ. As OC6.
2022 Proof in gold *FDC* (Edition: 46) £12000

ONE THOUSAND POUNDS
Obverse portrait by Ian Rank-Broadley

OE1

OE1 One thousand pounds. (1 kilo of fine gold.) Diamond Jubilee commemorative 2012.
O. Portrait of Queen Elizabeth II inspired by the sculpture mounted in the entrance to the
Supreme Court building on Parliament Square, with the inscription 'ELIZABETH. II. D.
G. REG. F. D. 1000 POUNDS'. Ŗ. A full achievement of the Royal Arms based on those
mounted on the front gates of Buckingham Palace with the date '2012' below.
(Obverse and reverse design: Ian Rank Broadley.)
2012 Proof in gold *FDC* (Issued: 21) £75000

OE2　One thousand pounds. (1 kilo of fine gold.) 60th Anniversary of the Coronation.
R. In the foreground the Orb and Sceptre with the St. Edward's Crown behind
surrounding by flowers representing the constituent parts of the United Kingdom
and in the background a ribbon showing the '2nd JUNE 1953' with the inscription
'QUEEN ELIZABETH II' and 'THE 60TH ANNIVERSARY OF THE CORONATION'.
(Reverse design: John Bergdahl.)
2013 Proof in gold *FDC* (Issued: 13)...£75000

OE3

OE3　One thousand pounds. (1 kilo of fine gold.) The Christening of Prince George of
Cambridge. R. A deconstructed silver lily font incorporating cherubs and roses, with
a Baroque-style cartouche with the inscription 'DIEU ET MON DROIT' and 'TO
CELEBRATE THE CHRISTENING OF PRINCE GEORGE OF CAMBRIDGE 2013'in
the centre of the coin. (Reverse design: John Bergdahl.)
2013 Proof in gold *FDC* (Issued: 19)...£70000

OE4　One thousand pounds. (1 kilo of fine gold.) 50th Anniversary of the Death of Winston
Churchill. R. A depiction of Sir Winston Churchill with the inscription 'CHURCHILL'
at the base of the coin. (Reverse design: Etienne Millner.)
2015 Proof in gold *FDC* (Issued: 9)... £70000

Obverse portrait by James Butler

OE5

OE5　One thousand pounds. (1 kilo of fine gold.) The Longest Serving Monarch.
R. A design depicting the Royal Cypher below the five definitive coinage portraits
and the inscription 'THE LONGEST REIGN'. (Reverse design: Stephen Taylor.)
2015 Proof in gold *FDC* (Issued: 15)...£75000

For coin specifications please see table at beginning of the Britannia section.

Obverse portrait by Jody Clark

OE6

OE6 One thousand pounds. (1 kilo of fine gold.) 90th Birthday of Her Majesty Queen
Elizabeth II. R. A crowned Royal Cypher above the number '90' encircled by roses
with the inscription 'FULL OF HONOUR AND YEARS'. (Reverse design:
Christopher Hobbs.)
2016 Proof in gold *FDC* (Issued: 15) £75000

OE7

OE7 One thousand pounds. (1 kilo of fine gold.) Sapphire Jubilee of Her Majesty Queen
Elizabeth II. R. A crowned depiction of the Royal Arms above the number '65'
surrounded by sprigs of oak and olive leaves, accompanied by the inscription 'HER
MAJESTY THE QUEEN'S SAPPHIRE JUBILEE 1952-2017'. (Reverse design:
Gregory Cameron.)
2017 Proof in gold *FDC* (Issued: 19).. £70000

OE8 One thousand pounds. (1 kilo of fine gold.) Celebrating the Platinum Wedding
Anniversary of HM The Queen and HRH Prince Philip. O. As M10 with revised
denomination 'FIVE HUNDRED POUNDS'. R. As M10.
2017 Proof in gold *FDC* (Issued: 21)..£75000

OE9 One thousand pounds. (1 kilo of fine gold.) Sapphire Coronation. R. O. As OE7.
R. As M11.
2018 Proof in gold *FDC* (Issued: 15)..£70000

OE10 One thousand pounds. (1 kilo of fine gold.) 200th Aniversary of the Birth of Queen
Victoria. R. A conjoined portrait of Queen Victoria and Prince Albert with the
inscription 'VICTORIA REGINA + ALBERTUS PRINCEPS CONJUX' and the date
'MDCCCXIX'. (Reverse design: William Wyon.)
2019 Proof in gold *FDC* (Issued: 12)...£70000

For coin specifications please see table at beginning of the Britannia section.

OE11 One thousand pounds. (1 kilo of fine gold.) 95th Birthday of Her Majesty Queen
Elizabeth II. ℞. As M20.
2021 Proof in gold *FDC* (Edition: 18) £70000
OE12 One thousand pounds. (1 kilo of fine gold.) Prince Philip Memorial 2021.
℞. A depiction of Prince Philip with the inscription 'HRH THE PRINCE PHILIP'
and 'DUKE OF EDINBURGH 1921 2021'. (Reverse design: Ian Rank-Broadley.)
2021 Proof in gold *FDC* (Edition: 12) £70000
OE13 One thousand pounds. (1 kilo of fine gold.) Platinum Jubilee Commemorative 2022.
O. & ℞. As OD5.
2022 Proof in gold *FDC* (Edition: 17) £70000

TWO THOUSAND POUNDS

OF1 Two thousand pounds. (2 kilos of fine gold.) Prince Philip Memorial 2021.
℞. A depiction of Prince Philip with the inscription 'HRH THE PRINCE PHILIP'
and 'DUKE OF EDINBURGH 1921 2021'. (Reverse design: Ian Rank-Broadley.)
2021 Proof in gold *FDC* (Edition: 6) £150000
OF2 Two thousand pounds. (2 kilos of fine gold.) Platinum Jubilee Commemorative
2022. O. & ℞. As OD5.
2022 Proof in gold *FDC* (Edition: 8) £150000

FIVE THOUSAND POUNDS

OG1 Five thousand pounds. (5 kilos of fine gold.) Prince Philip Memorial 2021.
℞. A depiction of Prince Philip with the inscription 'HRH THE PRINCE PHILIP'
and 'DUKE OF EDINBURGH 1921 2021'. (Reverse design: Ian Rank-Broadley.)
2021 Proof in gold *FDC* (Edition: 1) £400000
OG2 Five thousand pounds. (5 kilos of fine gold.) Platinum Jubilee Commemorative
2022. O. & ℞. As OD5.
2022 Proof in gold *FDC* (Edition: 2) £400000

SEVEN THOUSAND POUNDS

OH1 Seven thousand pounds. (7 kilos of fine gold.) Platinum Jubilee Commemorative
2022. O. & ℞. As OD5.
2022 Proof in gold *FDC* (Edition: 1) £500000

NINE THOUSAND FIVE HUNDRED POUNDS

OJ1 Nine thousand five hundred pounds. (9½ kilos of fine gold.) 95th Birthday of Her
Majesty Queen Elizabeth II. ℞. As M19 but with leaf patterned edge.
2021 Proof in gold *FDC* (Edition: 1) £750000

FIFTEEN THOUSAND POUNDS

OK1 Fifteen thousand pounds. (15 kilos of fine gold.) Platinum Jubilee Commemorative
2022. O. & ℞. As OD5.
2022 Proof in gold *FDC* (Edition: 1) £1250000

For coin specifications please see table at beginning of the Britannia section.

PLATINUM

TWENTY FIVE POUNDS

PA1 **Twenty five pounds**. (1/4 oz platinum.) The Platinum Wedding Anniversary of HM
The Queen and HRH Prince Philip. O. Portrait of Queen Elizabeth II conjoined
with His Royal Highness Prince Philip, The Duke of Edinburgh with the inscription
'ELIZABETH II D G REG F D – PHILIP PRINCEPS' and the denomination
'TWENTY FIVE POUNDS'. R. A depiction of the royal arms and those of His Royal
Highness Prince Philip, The Duke of Edinburgh above the inscription '70 YEARS OF
MARRIAGE 2017'. (Obverse design: Etienne Milner, reverse: John Bergdahl.)
2017 Proof in platinum (Issued: 898)...£450

PA2

PA2 **Twenty five pounds**. (1/4 oz platinum.) The 70th Birthday of HRH the Prince of
Wales. (Reverse design: Robert Elderton.)
2018 Proof in platinum *FDC* (Issued: 202)..£500

ONE HUNDRED POUNDS

PB1 **One hundred pounds.** (1oz platinum.) Platinum Jubilee Commemorative 2022.
O. & R. As OC5.
2022 Proof in platinum *FDC* (Edition: 180)..£2200

Although the main UK bullion coins are the Britannia range, a number of other bullion coins have been issued based on Britannia specifications. Some of these have been supplied only to overseas based bullion dealers so are not always easy to locate in the UK.

SILVER

TWO POUNDS

Obverse portrait by Jody Clark

QB1 QB2

QB1 **Two pounds.** (1oz of fine silver.) Elizabeth Tower. O. As NB3. R. Elizabeth Tower with inscription 'BIG BEN 2017 1OZ '999' FINE SILVER'.
2017..£30

QB2 **Two pounds.** (1 oz of fine silver.) Trafalgar Square. R. As L34 but with inscription 'TRAFALGAR SQUARE 2018 1OZ '999' FINE SILVER'.
2018 (Edition: 50,000) £30

QB3 **Two pounds.** (1oz of fine silver.) Tower Bridge. R. As L36 but with inscription 'TOWER BRIDGE 2018 1OZ '999' FINE SILVER'.
2018..£30

QB4 QB6

QB4 **Two pounds.** (1 oz of fine silver.) Two Dragons. R. Two Dragons with inscription 'TWO DRAGONS' and 'ONE OUNCE FINE SILVER 999 • 2018'
2018 ....£30
— Proof in silver *FDC* £80

QB5 **Two pounds.** (1 oz of fine silver.) Buckingham Palace. R. As L37 but with inscription 'BUCKINGHAM PALACE 2019 1OZ '999' FINE SILVER'.
2019 (Edition: 50,000) £30

QB6 **Two pounds.** (1 oz of fine silver.) The Valiant. R. St George and the dragon with the inscription '1 OZ FINE SILVER 999.9' and the date of the year. (Reverse design: Etienne Millner.)
2019..£30
2020..£30
2021..£30

For coin specifications please see table at beginning of the Britannia section.

QB7   QB8

QB7   **Two pounds.** (1 oz of fine silver.) The Royal Arms. ℞. The Lion of England and the Unicorn of Scotland supporting the shield with the inscription '1 OZ FINE SILVER 999' and the date of the year. (Reverse design: Timothy Noad.)

2019..£30
2020..£30
2021..£30
2022..£30

QB8   **Two pounds.** (1oz of fine silver.) ℞. A depiction of Franklin Roosevelt and Winston Churchill in front of the flags of the United States of America and the United Kingdom with the inscription 'UNITED STATES – UNITED KINGDOM' and 'A SPECIAL RELATIONSHIP' the date of the year '1OZ FINE SILVER 999'. (Reverse design: David Lawrence.)

2021 ....£35
2022..£35

The 2021 issue was sold to a USA distributor.

QB9   QB10   QB11

QB9   **Two pounds.** (1 oz of fine silver.) Robin Hood I. ℞. A depiction of Robin Hood with the inscription 'ROBIN HOOD • 1OZ • FINE SILVER• 999' and the date of the year. (Reverse design: Jody Clark)

2021 Unc...£35

QB10 **Two pounds.** (1oz of fine silver.) Robin Hood II. ℞. A depiction of Maid Marian with the inscription 'MAID MARIAN • 1OZ • FINE SILVER• 999' and the date of the year. (Reverse design: Jody Clark)

2022 Unc...£35

QB11 **Two pounds.** (1oz of fine silver.) Robin Hood III. ℞. A depiction of Little John with the inscription 'LITTLE JOHN • 1OZ • FINE SILVER• 999' and the date of the year. (Reverse design: Jody Clark)

2022 Unc...£35

QB12   QB13

QB12 **Two pounds.** (1oz of fine silver.) King Arthur. ℞. A depiction of King Arthur clasping his legendary sword, Excalibur, with the inscription 'KING ARTHUR 1OZ FINE SILVER 999 2023'. (Reverse design: David Lawrence.)

2023 ....£35

QB13 **Two pounds.** (1oz of fine silver.) ℞. A depiction of the Mayflower in rough seas with the inscriptions 'THE MAYFLOWER' and 'PLYMOUTH', 'CAPE COD' the date of the year and '1OZ FINE SILVER 999'. (Reverse design: John Bergdahl.)

2023 ....£35

TEN POUNDS

QD1

QD1 **Ten pounds.** (10 oz of fine silver.) The Valiant. ℞. St George and the dragon with the inscription '10 OZ FINE SILVER 999.9' and the date of the year. (Reverse design: Etienne Millner.)

2018..£320

QD2 **Ten pounds.** (10 oz of fine silver.) The Royal Arms. ℞. As QB7 but with the inscription '10 OZ FINE SILVER 999'.

2018..£320

2020..£320

2021..£320

2022..£290

QD3 **Ten pounds.** (10 oz of fine silver.) The Valiant. ℞. As QB6 but with the inscription '10 OZ FINE SILVER 999.9'.

2019..£320

2020..£320

2021..£320

QD4 **Ten pounds.** (10oz of fine silver.) Robin Hood I. ℞. As QB9 but with the inscription 'ROBIN HOOD • 10OZ • FINE SILVER• 999.9'

2023 Unc £275

For coin specifications please see table at beginning of the Britannia section.

GOLD

TEN POUNDS

RA1

RA1 **Ten pounds.** (1/10 oz of fine gold.) The Royal Arms. ℞. As QB7 with the inscription
'1/10 OZ FINE GOLD 999.9'.
2020 Unc £200
2022 Unc £200
RA2 **Ten pounds.** (1/10 oz of fine gold.) The Gold Standard. ℞. As RD3 but with inscription
'1/10 OZ FINE GOLD 999.9'.
2022 Unc £200

TWENTY FIVE POUNDS

RB2	RB3	RB4

RB1 **Twenty five pounds.** (1/4 oz of fine gold.) 200th Anniversary of the Adoption of the
Gold Standard in the 1816 Coinage Act. ℞. Set of Scales with inscription '1816 2016'
and '1/4 OZ FINE GOLD 999.9'. (Reverse design: Dominique Evans.)
2016 Unc £450
RB2 **Twenty five pounds.** (1/4 oz fine gold.) ℞. As RB1 but with revised reverse inscription
'THE GOLD STANDARD', date of year, '1/4 OZ FINE GOLD 999.9'. (Reverse design:
Dominique Evans.)
2018 Unc £450
2019 Unc £450
2020 Unc £450
2021 Proof in gold FDC (Edition: 910) £600
2022 Unc £450
The 2021 proof was issued to commemorate the 200th Anniversary of the UK formalising the
Gold Standard. 300 coins were issued in a case with a 1931 sovereign.

RB3 **Twenty five pounds.** (1/4 oz of fine gold.) R. A depiction of Franklin Roosevelt and
Winston Churchill in front of the flags of the United States of America and the United
Kingdom with the inscription 'UNITED STATES – UNITED KINGDOM' and 'A
SPECIAL RELATIONSHIP' the date of the year '1/4OZ FINE GOLD 999.9'.
2021..£475
2022..£475
The 2021 issue was sold to a USA distributor.
RB4 **Twenty five pounds.** (1/4 oz of fine gold.) R. A depiction of the Mayflower in rough
seas with the inscriptions 'THE MAYFLOWER' and 'PLYMOUTH', 'CAPE COD' the
date of the year and '1/4OZ FINE GOLD 999.9'. (Reverse design: John Bergdahl.)
2023..£475

FIFTY POUNDS

RC1   Fifty pounds. (1/2 oz of fine gold.) The Gold Standard. ℞. As RD3 but with inscription
'1/2 OZ FINE GOLD 999.9'.
2022 Unc £800

For coin specifications please see table at beginning of the Britannia section.

ONE HUNDRED POUNDS

RD1   RD2

RD1   One hundred pounds. (1 oz of fine gold.) Two Dragons. ℞. Two Dragons with
inscription 'TWO DRAGONS' and 'ONE OUNCE FINE GOLD 999.9 • 2018'
2018 BU £1600
—   Proof in gold *FDC* (Edition: 500) £2400
RD2   One hundred pounds. (1 oz of fine gold.) The Royal Arms. ℞. As QB7 with the
inscription "1 OZ FINE GOLD 999.9".
2019 Unc £1600
2020 Unc £1600
2021 Unc £1600
2022 Unc £1600

RD3

RD3   One hundred pounds. (1 oz of fine gold.) ℞. A beam balance set against a decorative
background with the inscription 'THE GOLD STANDARD' and '1 OZ FINE GOLD •
999.9' and the date of the year. (Reverse design: Dominique Evans.)
2020..£1600
2021 ....£1600
—   Proof in gold *FDC* (Edition: 260) £2500
2022 ....£1600

*The 2021 proof was issued to commemorate the 200th Anniversary of the UK formalising the
Gold Standard.*

RD4   RD5

RD4 **One hundred pounds.** (1 oz of fine gold.) Robin Hood I. ℞. A depiction of Robin
Hood with the inscription 'ROBIN HOOD • 1OZ • FINE GOLD • 999.9' and the
date of the year.
2021 Unc.. £1800

RD5 **One hundred pounds.** (1 oz of fine gold.) Robin Hood II. ℞. A depiction of Maid
Marian with the inscription 'MAID MARIAN • 1OZ • FINE GOLD • 999.9' and
the date of the year.
2022 Unc.. £1800

RD6   RD7

RD6 **One hundred pounds.** (1oz of fine gold.) Robin Hood III. ℞. A depiction of Little John
with the inscription 'LITTLE JOHN • 1OZ • FINE GOLD • 999.9' and the date of the
year. (Reverse design: Jody Clark)
2022 Unc.. £1800

RD7 **One hundred pounds.** (1oz of fine gold.) King Arthur. R. A depiction of King Arthur
clasping his legendary sword, Excalibur, with the inscription 'KING ARTHUR 1OZ
FINE GOLD 999.9 2023'. (Reverse design: David Lawrence.)
2023 Unc.. £1600

PLATINUM

ONE HUNDRED POUNDS

TA1 **One hundred pounds.** (1 oz platinum.) The Royal Arms. ℞. As QB7 with the inscription
'1 OZ PLATINUM 999.5'.
2020 BU £900

TA2 **One hundred pounds.** (1oz of platinum.) Robin Hood I. ℞. As RD4 but with
inscription 'ROBIN HOOD 1OZ FINE PLATINUM 999.5'.
2023 Unc.. £1000

Other bullion coins may be found in the second sections of the Chinese Lunar, Queen's Beasts
and Tudor Beasts listings and also within the Music Legends listings: Queen QN2A, QN7A;
Elton John EJ2A, EJ7A; David Bowie DB2A, DB7A; The Who WH2A, WH7A.

As the Royal Mint issued a considerable number of coins to mark the London 2012 Olympic and Paralympic Games, it was decided that it would be easier for collectors if these coins were grouped together rather than be included with other coins of the same denomination. As a consequence the £2 coins issued in 2008 have been renumbered and are now listed within this section.

The Olympic series commenced in 2008 with the issue of two £2 coins – one for the centenary of the first London Olympic Games and the other for the handover of the Olympic flag from Beijing to London following the end of the Beijing Olympics that year. 2009 saw the first of an annual issue of £5 crown coins marking the Countdown to 2012 followed by the first of 29 50p coins depicting the range of sports to be seen at the games. Also in 2009 the first six silver crowns from a set of 18 celebrating the Best of Britain were issued depicting the Mind of Britain. The final coin in this series depicted Olaudah Equiano, the first person from a slave background to feature on a British coin. Gold coins were issued from 2010 depicting the legendary gods associated with the ancient Greek games, and finally in 2012 the UK's first 5oz and kilo coins were issued. A third £2 coin was issued late in 2012 to mark the passing of the Olympic flag from London to Rio de Janeiro the host for the 2016 games.

Specifications of the coins from 50p to £5 are the same as those in the specification table in the introduction and for the £10 and higher gold and silver coins, readers may refer to the tables at the head of the Britannia section.

Numbers issued are quoted where these are available but there are still some gaps where we are waiting for figures from the Royal Mint.

FIFTY PENCE

LO1

LO1   **Fifty pence. Athletics.** To commemorate the London 2012 Olympic and Paralympic Games. O. As H8. R. A design which depicts an athlete clearing a high jump bar, with the London 2012 logo above and the denomination '50 pence' below. (Reverse design: Florence Jackson.)

2009 BU on presentation card (Issued: 19,722) £95
— Gold *FDC* – presented to the artist
2011 Unc (Issued: 2,224,000) £2
— BU in card (3/29) (Issued: 194,257)...£3
— BU in presentation folder signed by Daley Thompson (Issued: 490) £50
— BU in presentation folder signed by Dame Kelly Holmes (Issued: 485)................£50
— BU in presentation folder signed by Lord Sebastian Coe (Issued: 376) £50
— Silver BU (Issued: 7,640)..£25
2012 Proof piedfort in gold *FDC* (Issued: 11 plus 15 coins in sets)............................£4500

LO2   LO2A   LO3

LO2   **Fifty pence. Aquatics.** To commemorate the London 2012 Olympic and Paralympic
Games. R. A design which depicts a swimmer submerged in water, with the London
Olympic logo above and the denomination '50 PENCE' below. (Reverse design:
Jonathan Olliffe.)
2011 Unc (Issued: 2,179,600) £2
— BU in card (1/29) (Issued: 183,749)..£3
— Silver BU (Issued: 6,600)..£25
— Gold *FDC* – presented to the artist

LO2A **Fifty pence.** As LO2 but with lines over face.
2011 ....£900

LO3   **Fifty pence. Archery.** To commemorate the London 2012 Olympic and Paralympic
Games. R. A design which depicts a bow being drawn, with the London Olympic logo
above and the denomination '50 PENCE' below. (Reverse design: Piotr Powaga.)
2011 Unc (Issued: 3,345,500) £2
— BU in card (2/29) (Issued: 165,954)..£3
— Silver BU (Issued: 5,205)..£25
— Gold *FDC* – presented to the artist

LO4   LO5

LO4   **Fifty pence. Badminton.** To commemorate the London 2012 Olympic and Paralympic
Games. R. A design which depicts a shuttlecock and a diagram of badminton actions, with
the London Olympic logo above and the denomination '50 PENCE' below.
(Reverse design: Emma Kelly.)
2011 Unc (Issued: 2,133,500)..£2
— BU in card (4/29) (Issued: 149,996)..£3
— Silver BU (Issued: 5,257) £25
— Gold *FDC* – presented to the artist

LO5   **Fifty pence. Basketball.** To commemorate the London 2012 Olympic and Paralympic
Games. R. A design which depicts basketball players against a textured background
of a large basketball, with the London Olympic logo above and the denomination '50
PENCE' below. (Reverse design: Sarah Payne.)
2011 Unc (Issued: 1,748,000)..£2
— BU in card (5/29) (Issued:162,916) £3
— Silver BU (Issued: 11,445) £25
— Gold *FDC* – presented to the artist

LO6   LO7

LO6   **Fifty pence. Boccia.** To commemorate the London 2012 Olympic and Paralympic
Games. ℞. A design which depicts a boccia player in a wheelchair throwing a ball,
with the London Olympic logo above and the denomination '50 PENCE' below.
(Reverse design: Justin Chung.)

2011 Unc (Issued: 2,166,000) £2
—   BU in card (6/29) (Issued: 152,421)...£3
—   Silver BU (Issued: 5,229)..£25
—   Gold *FDC* – presented to the artist

LO7   **Fifty pence. Boxing.** To commemorate the London 2012 Olympic and Paralympic
Games. ℞. A design which depicts a pair of boxing gloves against the background of a
boxing ring, with the London Olympic logo above and the denomination '50 PENCE'
below. (Reverse design: Shane Abery.)

2011 Unc (Issued: 2,148,500) £2
—   BU in card (7/29) (Issued: 167,910)..£3
—   Silver BU (Issued: 5,872)..£25
—   Gold *FDC* – presented to the artist

2012 Proof piedfort in gold *FDC* (Issued: 3 plus 15 coins in sets) £4500

LO8   LO9

LO8   **Fifty pence. Canoeing.** To commemorate the London 2012 Olympic and Paralympic Games.
℞. A design which depicts a figure in a canoe on a slalom course, with the London Olympic
logo above and the denomination '50 PENCE' below. (Reverse design: Timothy Lees.)

2011 Unc (Issued: 2,166,500) £2
—   BU in card (8/29) (Issued: 141,873 ....£3
—   Silver BU (Issued: 8,498)..£25
—   Gold *FDC* – presented to the artist

2012 Proof piedfort in gold *FDC* (Issued: 2 plus 15 coins in sets) £4500

LO9   **Fifty pence. Cycling.** To commemorate the London 2012 Olympic and Paralympic
Games. ℞. A design which depicts a cyclist in a velodrome, with the London Olympic logo
above and the denomination '50 PENCE' below. (Reverse design: Theo Crutchley- Mack.)

2010
—   Gold *FDC* – presented to the artist

2011 Unc (Issued: 2,090,500) £2
—   BU in card (9/29) (Issued: 182,631)..£3
—   Silver BU (Issued: 16,379)..£25

2012 Proof piedfort in gold *FDC* (Issued: 13 plus 13 coins in sets) £4500

LO10   LO11

LO10 **Fifty pence. Equestrian.** To commemorate the London 2012 Olympic and Paralympic Games. R. A design which depicts a horse and rider jumping over a fence, with the London Olympic logo above and the denomination '50 PENCE' below. (Reverse design: Thomas Babbage.)

2011 Unc (Issued: 2,142,500) £2
— BU in card (10/29) (Issued: 170,881)..£3
— Silver BU (Issued: 5,382)...£25
— Gold *FDC* – presented to the artist
2012 Proof piedfort in gold *FDC* (Issued: 7 plus 15 coins in sets).........................£4500

LO11 **Fifty pence. Fencing.** To commemorate the London 2012 Olympic and Paralympic Games. R. A design which depicts two figures fencing, with the London Olympic logo above and the denomination "50 PENCE" below. (Reverse design: Ruth Summerfield.)

2011 Unc (Issued: 2,115,500)..£2
— BU in card (11/29) (Issued: 156,574)..£3
— Silver BU (Issued: 7,183)...£25
— Gold *FDC* – presented to the artist

LO12   LO13

LO12 **Fifty pence. Football.** To commemorate the London 2012 Olympic and Paralympic Games. R. A diagrammatic explanation of the offside rule in football, with the London Olympic logo above and the denomination '50 PENCE' below. (Reverse design: Neil Wolfson.)

2011 Unc (Issued: 1,125,500) £10
— BU in card (12/29) (Issued: 214,021)...£12
— Silver BU (Issued: 6,688)...£25
— Gold *FDC* – presented to the artist

LO13 **Fifty pence. Goalball.** To commemorate the London 2012 Olympic and Paralympic Games. R. A design which depicts a goalball player throwing a ball, with the London Olympic logo above and the denomination '50 PENCE' below. (Reverse design: Jonathan Wren.)

2011 Unc (Issued: 1,615,500) £2
— BU in card (13/29) (Issued: 140,093)...£3
— Silver BU (Issued: 5,131)...£25
— Gold *FDC* – presented to the artist

LO14   LO15

LO14   **Fifty pence. Gymnastics.** To commemorate the London 2012 Olympic and Paralympic
Games. R. A design which depicts a gymnast with a ribbon, with the London Olympic
logo above and the denomination '50 PENCE' below. (Reverse design: Jonathan Olliffe.)
2011 Unc (Issued: 1,720,813) £2
—   BU in card (14/29) (Issued: 171,654)...£3
—   Silver BU (Issued: 7,083)..£25
—   Gold *FDC* – presented to the artist

LO15   **Fifty pence. Handball.** To commemorate the London 2012 Olympic and Paralympic
Games. R. A design which depicts a handball player throwing a ball against a
background of a handball court, with the London Olympic logo above and the
denomination '50 PENCE' below. (Reverse design: Natasha Ratcliffe.)
2011 Unc (Issued: 1,676,500) £2
—   BU in card (15/29) (Issued: 143,325)...£3
—   Silver BU (Issued: 5,593)..£25
—   Gold *FDC* – presented to the artist

LO16   LO17

LO16   **Fifty pence. Hockey.** To commemorate the London 2012 Olympic and Paralympic
Games. R. A design which depicts two hockey players challenging for the ball, with
the London Olympic logo above and the denomination '50 PENCE' below. (Reverse
design: Robert Evans.)
2011 Unc (Issued: 1,773,500) £2
—   BU in card (16/29) (Issued:156,572)...£3
—   Silver BU (Issued: 5,642)..£25
—   Gold *FDC* – presented to the artist

LO17   **Fifty pence. Judo.** To commemorate the London 2012 Olympic and Paralympic
Games. R. A depiction of a judo throw, with the London Olympic logo above and the
denomination '50 PENCE' below. (Reverse design: David Cornell.)
2011 Unc (Issued: 1,161,500) £2
—   BU in card (17/29) (Issued: 154,201)...£3
—   Silver BU (Issued: 5,624)..£25
—   Gold *FDC* – presented to the artist

LO18 LO19

LO18 Fifty pence. Modern Pentathlon. To commemorate the London 2012 Olympic and Paralympic Games. ℞. A montage of the five sports which form the modern pentathlon, with the London Olympic logo above and the denomination '50 PENCE' below. (Reverse design: Daniel Brittain.)

2011 Unc (Issued: 1,689,500) £2
— BU in card (18/29) (Issued: 149,116 ....£3
— Silver BU (Issued: 5,889)..£25
— Gold *FDC* – presented to the artist

LO19 Fifty pence. Rowing. To commemorate the London 2012 Olympic and Paralympic Games. ℞. A design which depicts a rowing boat accompanied by a number of words associated with the Olympic movement, with the London Olympic logo above and the denomination '50 PENCE' below. (Reverse design: David Podmore.)

2011 Unc (Issued: 1,717,300) £2
— BU in card (19/29) (Issued 166,736)...£3
— BU in presentation folder signed by Sir Steve Redgrave (Issued: 486).............£50
— Silver BU (Issued: 9,043)...£25
— Gold *FDC* – presented to the artist
2012 Proof piedfort in gold FDC (Issued: 11 plus 15 coins in sets) £4500

LO20 LO21

LO20 Fifty pence. Sailing. To commemorate the London 2012 Olympic and Paralympic Games. ℞. A design which depicts three sailing boats accompanied by a map of the coast of Weymouth, with the London Olympic logo above and the denomination '50 PENCE' below. (Reverse design: Bruce Rushin.)

2011 Unc (Issued: 1,749,500) £2
— BU in card (20/29) (Issued: 164,294)..£3
— Silver BU (Issued: 7,267)...£25
— Gold *FDC* – presented to the artist
2012 Proof piedfort in gold *FDC* (Issued: 2 plus 15 coins in sets) £4500

LO21 Fifty pence. Shooting. To commemorate the London 2012 Olympic and Paralympic Games. ℞. A design which depicts a figure shooting, with the London Olympic logo above and the denomination '50 PENCE' below. (Reverse design: Pravin Dewdhory.)

2011 Unc (Issued: 1,656,500) £2
— BU in card (21/29) (Issued: 151,157)...£3
— Silver BU (Issued: 5,358)...£25
— Gold *FDC* – presented to the artist
2012 Proof piedfort in gold *FDC* (Issued: 2 plus 15 coins in sets) £4500

LO22   LO23

LO22 **Fifty pence. Table Tennis.** To commemorate the London 2012 Olympic and
Paralympic Games. ℞. A design which depicts two table tennis bats against the
background of a table and net, with the London Olympic logo above and the
denomination '50 PENCE' below. (Reverse design: Alan Linsdell.)
2011 Unc (Issued: 1,737,500) £2
— BU in card (22/29) (Issued: 148,954)...£3
— Silver BU (Issued: 5,797)..£25
— Gold *FDC* – presented to the artist

LO23 **Fifty pence. Taekwondo.** To commemorate the London 2012 Olympic and Paralympic
Games. ℞. A design which depicts two athletes engaged in Taekwondo, with the London
Olympic logo above and the denomination '50 PENCE' below. (Reverse design:
David Gibbons.)
2011 Unc (Issued: 1,664,000) £2
— BU in card (23/29) (Issued: 145,969)...£3
— Silver BU (Issued: 5,305)..£25
— Gold *FDC* – presented to the artist
2012 Proof piedfort in gold *FDC* (Issued: 15) £4500

LO24   LO25

LO24 **Fifty pence. Tennis.** To commemorate the London 2012 Olympic and Paralympic
Games. ℞. A design which depicts a tennis net and tennis ball, with the London Olympic
logo above and the denomination '50 PENCE' below. (Reverse design: Tracy Baines.)
2011 Unc (Issued: 1,454,000) £2
— BU in card (24/29) (Issued: 170,294)...£3
— Silver BU (Issued: 6,137)..£25
— Gold *FDC* – presented to the artist
2012 Proof piedfort in gold *FDC* (Issued: 10 plus 15 coins in sets) £4500

LO25 **Fifty pence. Triathlon.** To commemorate the London 2012 Olympic and Paralympic
Games. ℞. A montage of the three sports which form the triathlon, with the London
Olympic logo above and the denomination '50 ' below. (Reverse design: Sarah
Harvey.)
2011 Unc (Issued: 1,163,500) £3
— BU in card (25/29) (Issued: 172,113)...£3
— Silver BU (Issued: 7,247)..£25
— Gold *FDC* – presented to the artist
2012 Proof piedfort in gold *FDC* (Issued: 7 plus 15 coins in sets) £4500

LO26   LO27

LO26 **Fifty pence. Volleyball.** To commemorate the London 2012 Olympic and Paralympic Games. ℞. A design which depicts three figures playing beach volleyball, with the London Olympic logo above and the denomination '50 PENCE' below. (Reverse design: Daniela Boothman.)

2011 (Issued: 2,133,500) £2
— BU in card (26/29) (Issued: 149,874)..£3
— Silver BU (Issued: 5,870)...£25
— Gold *FDC* – presented to the artist

LO27 **Fifty pence. Weight Lifting.** To commemorate the London 2012 Olympic and Paralympic Games. ℞. A design which depicts the outline of a weightlifter starting a lift, with the London Olympic logo above and the denomination '50 PENCE' below. (Reverse design:Rob Shakespeare.)

2011 (Issued: 1,879,500) £2
— BU in card (27/29) (Issued: 147,537)..£3
— Silver BU (Issued: 5,500)...£25
— Gold *FDC* – presented to the artist

LO28   LO29

LO28 **Fifty pence. Wheelchair Rugby.** To commemorate the London 2012 Olympic and Paralympic Games. ℞. A design which depicts a wheelchair rugby player in action, with the London Olympic logo above and the denomination '50 PENCE' below. (Reverse design: Natasha Ratcliffe.)

2011 (Issued: 1,765,500) £2
— BU in card (28/29) (Issued: 146,934)..£3
— Silver BU (Issued: 5,956)...£25
— Gold *FDC* – presented to the artist

LO29 **Fifty pence. Wrestling.** To commemorate the London 2012 Olympic and Paralympic Games. ℞. A design which depicts two figures wrestling in a stadium, with the London Olympic logo above and the denomination '50 PENCE' below. (Reverse design: Roderick Enriquez.)

2011 (Issued: 1,129,500) £3
— BU in card (29/29) (Issued: 153,038)..£3
— Silver BU (Issued: 5,727)...£25
— Gold *FDC* – presented to the artist

TWO POUNDS

LO30   LO31   LO32

LO30 **Two pounds.** Centenary of the Olympic Games of 1908 held in London. O. As K9.
R. A running track on which is superimposed the date '1908' accompanied by the
denomination 'TWO POUNDS' and the date '2008', the whole design being encircled
by the inscription 'LONDON OLYMPIC CENTENARY' with the edge inscription
'THE 4TH OLYMPIAD LONDON'. (Reverse design: Thomas T Docherty.)
2008 (Issued: 910,000) ....Unc £6; BU £10
— BU in presentation folder (Issued: 29,594) £15
— Proof *FDC* (in 2008 set, see PS93/95)* £18
— Proof in silver *FDC* (Issued: 6,481 plus 1182 in set PSS35) £35
— Proof piedfort in silver *FDC* (Issued: 1,619 plus 1746 in set PSS36) £55
— Proof in gold *FDC* (Issued: 1,908 including coins in set LOGS1) £950

LO31 **Two pounds.** London Olympic Handover Ceremony. O. As K23. R. The Olympic
flag being passed from one hand to another, encircled by the inscription 'BEIJING
2008 LONDON 2012' and with the London 2012 logo below with the edge
inscription 'I CALL UPON THE YOUTH OF THE WORLD'. (Reverse design:
Royal Mint Engraving Department.)
2008 (Issued: 918,000) ....Unc £5; BU £12
— BU in presentation folder (Issued: 47,765) £20
— Proof in silver *FDC* (Issued: 30,000) £38
— Proof piedfort in silver *FDC* (Issued: 3,000) £60
— Proof in gold *FDC* (Issued: 3,250 including coins in set LOGS1) £950

LO32 **Two pounds.** London to Rio Olympic Handover coin. O. As K29. R. A design which
depicts a baton being passed from one hand to another, accompanied by the conjoined
Union and Brazilian Flags, and set against the background of a running track motif,
with the London 2012 logo above and the surrounding inscription 'LONDON 2012
RIO 2016', with the edge inscription 'I CALL UPON THE YOUTH OF
THE WORLD'. (Reverse design: Jonathan Olliffe.)
2012 (Issued: 845,000) ....Unc £8; BU £12
— BU in presentation card (Issued: 28,356)...£25
— Proof in silver *FDC* (Issued: 3,781) £60
— Proof piedfort in silver *FDC* (Issued: 2,000) £105
— Proof in gold *FDC* (Issued: 771)..£1000

* *Coins marked thus were originally issued in Royal Mint sets.*

FIVE POUNDS

2009-2012 THE COUNTDOWN TO THE OLYMPICS

LO33   LO34

LO33   **Five pounds.** (Crown.) UK countdown to 2012 Olympic Games. O. As L11.
R. In the centre a depiction of two swimmers as faceted figures accompanied by the
number '3' with a section of a clock face to the right and the London 2012 logo to
the left printed in coloured ink on the precious metal versions and surrounded by a
plan view of the main Olympic Stadium incorporating the date '2009' with the words
'COUNTDOWN' above and the inscription 'XXX OLYMPIAD' below. (Reverse
design: Claire Aldridge.)
2009 BU in presentation card (Issued: combined with below) £10
—   BU in presentation folder (Issued: 184,921) £15
—   Proof in silver *FDC* (Issued: 26,645) £50
—   Proof piedfort in silver *FDC* (Issued: 4,874) £80
—   Proof in gold *FDC* (Issued: 1,860)..£2300

LO34   **Five pounds.** (Crown.) UK countdown to 2012 Olympic Games. O. As L11.
R. In the centre a depiction of two runners as faceted figures accompanied by the
number '2' with a section of a clock face to the right and the London 2012 logo to
the left printed in coloured ink on the precious metal versions and surrounded by a
plan view of the main Olympic Stadium incorporating the date '2010' with the words
'COUNTDOWN' above and the inscription 'XXX OLYMPIAD' below. (Reverse
design: Claire Aldridge.)
2010 BU in presentation card (Issued: combined with below) £10
—   BU in presentation folder (Issued: 153,080) £15
—   Proof in silver *FDC* (Issued: 20,159) £50
—   Proof piedfort in silver *FDC* (Issued: 2,197) £100
—   Proof in gold *FDC* (Issued: 1,562)..£2300

LO35   LO36

LO35   **Five pounds.** (Crown.) UK countdown to 2012 Olympic Games. O. As L11.
R. In the centre a depiction of a cyclist as a faceted figure, accompanied by the
number '1' with a section of a clock face to the right, below and to the left, and the
London 2012 logo to the right printed in coloured ink on the precious metal versions
and surrounded by a plan view of the main Olympic Stadium incorporating the date
'2011' with the words 'COUNTDOWN' above and the inscription 'XXX OLYMPIAD'
below. (Reverse design: Claire Aldridge.)
2011 BU in presentation card (Issued: combined with below) £10
—   BU in presentation folder (Issued: 163,235) £15
—   Proof in silver *FDC* (Issued: 25,877) £50
—   Proof piedfort in silver *FDC* (Issued: 4,000) £80
—   Proof in gold *FDC* (Issued: 1,300)..£2300

LO36   **Five pounds.** (Crown.) UK countdown to 2012 Olympic Games. O. As L11.
R. A depiction of three athletes as faceted figures standing on a victory podium,
with a section of a clock-face to the right, to the left and above, and the London 2012
logo to the right. The reverse design is surrounded by a plan view of the main Olympic
Stadium, incorporating the date '2012' at the top, and the word 'COUNTDOWN'
above and the inscription 'XXX OLYMPIAD' below. (Reverse design:
Claire Aldridge.)
2012 BU in presentation card (Edition: combined with below)................................£12
—   BU in presentation folder (Edition: 250,000)..£15
—   BU in PNC (Issued: 13,014) £15
—   Proof in silver *FDC* (Issued: 12,670) £60
—   Proof piedfort in silver *FDC* (Issued: 2,324) £90
—   Proof in gold *FDC* (Issued: 1,007)..£2500

2009-2010 THE CELEBRATION OF BRITAIN
Eighteen silver proof coins were issued in three cased series of 6 and also in an 18 piece case.

LO37

LO37 **Five pounds.** (Crown.) The Mind of Britain. ℞. A depiction of the clock-face of
the Palace of Westminster accompanied by the London 2012 logo, printed in
coloured ink on the silver coin and a quotation From Walter Bagehot, 'NATIONS
TOUCH AT THEIR SUMMITS'. (Reverse design: Shane Greeves and the Royal
Mint Engraving Department.)
2009 Proof *FDC* (Edition: 100,000; Issued: 9,681) £20
—   Proof in silver *FDC* (Issued: 26,630) £60

*The authorised mintage of the 18 coins LO37-LO49 is 95,000 each. The numbers sold indicated
against each coin include the numbers sold in various sets as listed at the end of this Olympic
section but the numbers may not yet be complete. Even at this late stage we hope for more
information from the Royal Mint.*

LO38   LO39

LO38 **Five pounds.** (Crown.) The Mind of Britain. ℞. A depiction of Stonehenge
accompanied by the London 2012 logo, printed in coloured ink and a quotation from
William Blake 'GREAT THINGS ARE DONE WHEN MEN AND MOUNTAINS
MEET'. (Reverse design: Shane Greeves and the Royal Mint Engraving Department.)
2009 Proof in silver *FDC* (Issued: 26,824) £60
LO39 **Five pounds.** (Crown.) The Mind of Britain. ℞. A depiction of the Angel of the
North accompanied by the London 2012 logo printed in coloured ink and a quotation
from William Shakespeare 'I HAVE TOUCHED THE HIGHEST POINT OF MY
GREATNESS'. (Reverse design: Shane Greeves and the Royal Mint Engraving
Department.)
2009 Proof in silver *FDC* (Issued: 24,700) £60

LO40   LO41

LO40   **Five pounds.** (Crown.) The Mind of Britain. R. A depiction of the Flying Scotsman accompanied by the London 2012 logo printed in coloured ink and a quotation from William Shakespeare 'TRUE HOPE IS SWIFT'. (Reverse design: Shane Greeves and the Royal Mint Engraving Department.)
2009 Proof in silver *FDC* (Issued: 24,700)...£60

LO41   **Five pounds.** (Crown.) The Mind of Britain. R. A depiction of Eduardo Paolozzi's sculpture of Isaac Newton accompanied by the London 2012 logo printed in coloured ink and a quotation from William Shakespeare 'MAKE NOT YOUR THOUGHTS YOUR PRISONS'. (Reverse design: Shane Greeves and the Royal Mint Engraving Department).
2009 Proof in silver *FDC* (Issued: 24,734)...£60

LO42   LO43

LO42   **Five pounds.** (Crown.) The Mind of Britain. R. A depiction of the Globe Theatre accompanied by the London 2012 logo printed in coloured ink and a quotation from William Shakespeare 'WE ARE SUCH STUFF AS DREAMS ARE MADE ON'. (Reverse design: Shane Greeves and the Royal Mint Engraving Department.)
2009 Proof in silver *FDC* (Issued: 24,708)...£60

LO43   **Five pounds.** (Crown.) The Body of Britain. R. A depiction of Rhossili Bay accompanied by the London 2012 logo printed in coloured ink, and a quotation from William Blake 'TO SEE A WORLD IN A GRAIN OF SAND'. (Reverse design: Shane Greeves and the Royal Mint Engraving Department.)
2010 Proof in silver *FDC* (Issued: 4,311)...£70

LO44   LO45

LO44   **Five pounds.** (Crown.) The Body of Britain R̶. A depiction of Giant's Causeway
accompanied by the London 2012 logo printed in coloured ink, and a quotation
from Alice Oswald 'WHEN THE STONE BEGAN TO DREAM'. (Reverse design:
Shane Greeves and the Royal Mint Engraving Department.)
2010 Proof in silver *FDC* (Issued: 4,310) £70

LO45   **Five pounds.** (Crown.) The Body of Britain R̶. A depiction of the River Thames
accompanied by the London 2012 logo printed in coloured ink, and a quotation from
Percy Bysshe Shelley, 'TAMELESS, AND SWIFT AND PROUD'. (Reverse design:
Shane Greeves and the Royal Mint Engraving Department.)
2010 Proof in silver *FDC* (Issued: 6,209) £70

LO46   LO47

LO46   **Five pounds.** (Crown.) The Body of Britain. R̶. A depiction of a barn owl accompanied
by the London 2012 logo printed in coloured ink, and a quotation from Samuel Johnson
'THE NATURAL FLIGHTS OF THE HUMAN MIND'. (Reverse design: Shane
Greeves and the Royal Mint Engraving Department.)
2010 Proof in silver *FDC* (Issued: 4,341) £70

LO47   **Five pounds.** (Crown.) The Body of Britain. R̶. A depiction of oak leaves and an
acorn accompanied by the London 2012 logo printed in coloured ink, and a quotation
from Alfred, Lord Tennyson, 'TO STRIVE, TO SEEK . . . AND NOT TO YIELD'.
(Reverse design: Shane Greeves and the Royal Mint Engraving Department.)
2010 Proof in silver *FDC* (Issued: 4,313) £70

LO48   LO49

LO48 **Five pounds.** (Crown.) The Body of Britain. ℞. A depiction of a weather-vane accompanied by the London 2012 logo printed in coloured ink, and a quotation from Charlotte Bronte, NEVER MAY A CLOUD COME O'ER THE SUNSHINE OF YOUR MIND'. (Reverse design: Shane Greeves and the Royal Mint Engraving Department.)
2010 Proof in silver *FDC* (Issued: 4,341)..£70

LO49 **Five pounds.** (Crown.) The Spirit of Britain. ℞. A depiction of the intertwined national emblems of England, Scotland, Wales and Northern Ireland accompanied by the London 2012 logo, printed in coloured ink, and a quotation from John Lennon, 'AND THE WORLD WILL BE ONE'. (Reverse design: Shane Greeves and the Royal Mint Engraving Department.)
2010 Proof in silver *FDC* (Issued: 5,019)...£75

LO50   LO51

LO50 **Five pounds.** (Crown.) The Spirit of Britain. ℞. A depiction of the White Rabbit from Lewis Carroll's *Alice in Wonderland* accompanied by the London 2012 logo, printed in coloured ink, and a quotation from T S Eliot, 'ALL TOUCHED BY A COMMON GENIUS'. (Reverse design: Shane Greeves and the Royal Mint Engraving Department.)
2010 Proof in silver *FDC* (Issued: 5,048)...£75

LO51 **Five pounds.** (Crown.) The Spirit of Britain. ℞. A view down the Mall of cheering crowds accompanied by the London 2012 logo, printed in coloured ink on the silver coins, and a quotation from Alfred, Lord Tennyson, 'KIND HEARTS ARE MORE THAN CORONETS'. (Reverse design: Shane Greeves and the Royal Mint Engraving Department.)
2010 Proof *FDC* (Edition; 100,000; Issued: 8,986) £20
—   Proof in silver *FDC* (Issued: 6,949) £75

LO52   LO53

LO52   **Five pounds.** (Crown.) The Spirit of Britain. ℞. A depiction of the statue of
Winston Churchill in Parliament Square accompanied by the London 2012 logo,
printed in coloured ink on the silver coins, and a quotation from Anita Roddick,
'BE DARING, BE FIRST, BE DIFFERENT, BE JUST'. (Reverse design:
Shane Greeves and the Royal Mint
Engraving Department.)
2010 Proof *FDC* (Edition; 100,000; Issued: 14,930) £20
—   Proof in silver *FDC* (Issued: 7,103) £75

LO53   **Five pounds.** (Crown.) The Spirit of Britain. ℞. An arrangement of musical
instruments based on a well known sculpture accompanied by the London 2012 logo,
printed in coloured ink, and a quotation from John Lennon and Paul McCartney,
'ALL YOU NEED IS LOVE'. (Reverse design: Shane Greeves and the Royal Mint
Engraving Department.)
2010 Proof in silver *FDC* (issued: 7,047)* £75

LO54

LO54   **Five pounds.** (Crown.) The Spirit of Britain. ℞. An image of the nineteenth-century
anti-slavery campaigner Equiano accompanied by the London 2012 logo, printed in
coloured ink, and a quotation from William Shakespeare, 'TO THINE OWN SELF
BE TRUE'. (Reverse design: Shane Greeves and the Royal Mint Engraving
Department.)
2010 Proof in silver *FDC* (Issued: 5,005) £100

2012 THE OLYMPICS & PARALYMPICS

LO55   LO56

LO55 **Five pounds.** (Crown.) The London 2012 Olympic Games. O. As LO37. R. An image of the skyline of some of the most well-known landmarks and buildings in London reflected in the River Thames, with the inscription 'LONDON 2012' above. Surrounding the skyline image is a selection of sports from the London 2012 Games with the London 2012 logo at the top. (Reverse design: Saiman Miah.)

2012 BU in presentation folder (Issued: 267,449) £15
— BU in PNC (Issued: 13,959) £15
— BU in folder with L24 (2012 Diamond Jubilee) (Issued: 2,115) £35
— Proof in silver *FDC* (Edition: 100,000) (Issued: 20,810) £70
— Proof in silver with gold plating *FDC* (Issued: 8,180)..£80
— Proof piedfort in silver *FDC* (Edition: 7,000) (Issued: 5,946).........................£100
— Proof in gold *FDC* (Edition: 5,000) (Issued: 1,045) £2500

LO56 **Five pounds.** (Crown.) The London 2012 Paralympic Games. O. As LO37. R. A design showing segments of a target, a spoked wheel, a stopwatch and the clock face of the Palace of Westminster. The inscription 'LONDON 2012' appears on the target and the London 2012 Paralympic logo appears on the stopwatch. On the gold and silver coins the London Paralympic logo is printed in coloured ink, while on the cupro-nickel coin the logo is struck into the surface. (Reverse design: Pippa Anderson.)

2012 BU in presentation folder (Edition: 250,000; Issued: 50,387)..........................£15
— Proof in silver *FDC* (Edition: 10,000) £75
— Proof in silver with gold plating *FDC* (Edition: 3,000)....................................£85
— Proof piedfort in silver *FDC* (Edition: 2,012) £120
— Proof in gold *FDC* (Edition: 2,012)..£2500

TEN POUNDS

LO57

LO57 **Ten pounds.** (Five ounce.) R. A design of the winged horse Pegasus rearing on its hind legs surrounded by the inscription 'LONDON OLYMPIC GAMES', and the London 2012 logo and the date '2012'. (Reverse design: Christopher Le Brun.)

2012 Proof in silver *FDC* (Issued: 5,056) £400
— Proof in gold *FDC* (Issued: 193) .:...£12500

TWENTY FIVE POUNDS

LO58   LO59   LO60

LO58 **Twenty five pounds.** (1/4 oz of fine gold.) **Faster.** R. An image of Diana accompanied by a depiction of the sport of cycling, specifically pursuit racing ,with Olympic Rings above, the name 'DIANA' to the left, the Latin word for faster 'CITIUS', to the right, and the inscription 'LONDON 2012' below. (Reverse design: John Bergdahl.)
2010 Proof in gold *FDC* (Issued: 7,275)..£500

LO59 **Twenty five pounds.** (1/4 oz of fine gold.) **Faster.** R. An image of Mercury accompanied by a depiction of the sport of running, with Olympic Rings above, the name 'MERCURY' to the left, the Latin word for faster 'CITIUS', to the right, and the inscription 'LONDON 2012' below. (Reverse design: John Bergdahl.)
2010 Proof in gold *FDC* (Issued: 7,230)..£500

LO60 **Twenty five pounds.** (1/4 oz of fine gold.) **Higher.** R. An image of Apollo accompanied by a depiction of the sport of rhythmic gymnastics, with Olympic Rings above, the name 'APOLLO'to the left, the Latin word for higher 'ALTIUS', to the right, and the inscription 'LONDON 2012' below. (Reverse design: John Bergdahl.)
2011 Proof in gold *FDC* (Issued: 3,152)..£500

LO61   LO62   LO63

LO61 **Twenty five pounds.** (1/4 oz of fine gold.) **Higher.** R. An image of Juno accompanied by a depiction of the sport of pole vaulting, with Olympic Rings above, the name 'JUNO' to the left, the Latin word for higher 'ALTIUS', to the right, and the inscription 'LONDON 2012' below. (Reverse design: John Bergdahl.)
2011 Proof in gold *FDC* (Issued: 3,257)..£500

LO62 **Twenty five pounds.** (1/4 oz of fine gold.) **Stronger.** R. An image of Vulcan accompanied by a depiction of the sport of hammer throwing, with the Olympic Rings above, the name 'VULCAN' to the left, and the Latin word for stronger 'FORTIUS', to the right, and the inscription 'LONDON 2012' below. (Reverse design: John Bergdahl.)
2012 Proof in gold *FDC* (Issued 2,500)..£500

LO63 **Twenty five pounds.** (1/4 oz of fine gold.) **Stronger.** R. An image of Minerva accompanied by a depiction Of the sport of javelin throwing, with the Olympic Rings above, the name 'MINERVA' to the left , the Latin word for stronger, 'FORTIUS', to the right, and the inscription 'LONDON 2012' below. (Reverse design: John Bergdahl.)
2012 Proof in gold *FDC* (Issued: 2,268)..£500

For specifications please see table at the beginning of the Britannia section.

ONE HUNDRED POUNDS

LO64   LO65

LO64   **One hundred pounds.** (1 oz of fine gold.) **Faster.** R. An image of Neptune, accompanied
by a depiction of the sport of sailing, with the Olympic Rings above, the name
'NEPTUNE' to the left, the Latin word for faster 'CITIUS' to the right, and the inscription
'LONDON 2012' below. (Reverse design: John Bergdahl.)
2010 Proof in gold *FDC* (Issued: 3,178)..£1750

LO65   **One hundred pounds.** (1 oz of fine gold.) **Higher.** R. An image of Jupiter, accompanied
by a depiction of the sport of diving, with the Olympic Rings above, the name
'JUPITER' to the left, the Latin word for higher 'ALTIUS' to the right, and the
inscription 'LONDON 2012' below. (Reverse design: John Bergdahl.)
2011 Proof in gold *FDC* (Issued: 1,858)..£1750
—   Proof in gold *FDC* with 'IRB' below portrait. £2000

*The designer's initials, IRB, usually appear on all coins bearing the Ian Rank Broadley portrait
but for reasons unknown the 2011 Olympic £100 gold were issued with and without the initials.
As the Royal Mint's publicity image depicted the coin without the initials we are regarding the
coin with the initials as the rarer piece at the moment.*

LO66

LO66   **One hundred pounds.** (1 oz of fine gold.) **Stronger.** R. An image of Mars
accompanied by a depiction of the sport of boxing, with the Olympic Rings above, the
name 'MARS' to the left, the Latin word for stronger, 'FORTIUS', to the right, and the
inscription 'LONDON 2012' below. (Reverse design: John Bergdahl.)
2012 Proof in gold *FDC* (Issued 1,514) £1750

For specifications please see table at the beginning of the Britannia section.

FIVE HUNDRED POUNDS

LO67

LO67 **Five hundred pounds.** (1 kilo of fine silver.) Ŗ. A design consisting of celebratory
pennants and the inscription 'XXX OLYMPIAD' surrounded by the epigram 'UNITE
OUR DREAMS TO MAKE THE WORLD A TEAM OF TEAMS'. (Reverse design:
Tom Phillips.)
2012 Proof in silver (Issued: 910) £3000

ONE THOUSAND POUNDS

LO68

LO68 **One thousand pounds.** (1 kilo of fine gold.) Ŗ. A design depicting individual
pieces of sporting equipment encircled by a laurel of victory. (Reverse design:
Sir Anthony Caro)
2012 Proof in gold (Issued: 20) £80000

For specifications please see table at the beginning of the Britannia section.

Uncirculated coin sets

£

LOCS1–**2011**   Set of 29 50 pence coins in individual card packs .... (29)   90
LOCS2–**2011**   Set of 29 50 pence coins in folder with Completer medallion
         (Issued: 25,759) .... (30)   125
LOCS3–**MD**   Gold Medal Winners set of 50 pence Cuni and £5 Olympic 2012 £5,
         (Athletics, Boxing, Canoeing, Cycling, Equestrian, Rowing, Sailing,
         Shooting, Taekwondo, Tennis, Triathlon, and £5) (Edition: 2,012) .... (12)   45
LOCS4–**MD**   Five pounds.(crowns). Set of the four Countdown issues and the
         Olympic and Paralympic £5 cuni coins (Edition: 2,012; Issued 244) ...... (6)   70
LOCS5–**MD**   Five pounds. (crowns). Set of four Countdown folders in box .... (4)   50
LOCS6–**2011**   50p Aquatics (LO2), 50p Cycling (LO9), 50p Rowing (LO19), 50p Sailing
         (LO20), 50p Triathlon (LO25) in presentation folder .... (5)   15

Silver coin sets

LOSS1–**2009**.   The Mind of Britain. Set of six £5 silver proofs (Issued: 1,480) .... (6)   350
LOSS2–**2010**   The Body of Britain. Set of six £5 silver proofs (Issued: 854) .... (6)   400
LOSS3–**2010**   The Spirit of Britain. Set of six £5 silver proofs (Issued: 1,564) .... (6)   425
LOSS4–**MD**   Great British Icons. Set of six £5 silver proofs (LO37,38,45,49,50,52)
         (Issued: 1,830).. (6)   425
LOSS5–**MD**   'Countdown to London'. Set of four £5 silver proof coins......................... (4)   200
LOSS6–**2011**   'Countdown to London'. Set of four £5 silver proof piedfort coins .... (4)   325
LOSS7–**MD**   The Mind, Body and Spirit of Britain. Set of 18 £5 silver proofs
         (Issued: 3,407) .... (18)   1200
LOSS8–**2011**   Set of 29 50 pence silver brilliant uncirculated coins (Issued: 384).......... (29)   700
LOSS9–**2011**   Gold Medal Winners set of 50 pence silver brilliant uncirculated coins
         and £5 Olympic 2012 silver proof, (Athletics, Boxing, Canoeing, Cycling,
         Equestrian, Rowing, Sailing, Shooting, Taekwondo, Triathlon, and £5)
         (Edition: 999 but coins taken from individual issue limits) .... (12)   350
LOSS10–**2011**   Accuracy. Set of six 50 pence silver brilliant uncirculated coins depicting
         various sports (Badminton, Basketball, Fencing, ..Football, Hockey, and
         Tennis) (Edition: 2,012 but taken from individual issue limits;
         Issued: 40)... (6)   150
LOSS11–**2011**   Agility. Set of six 50 pence silver brilliant uncirculated coins depicting
         various sports (Boxing, Equestrian, Gymnastics, Judo, Sailing, and
         Taekwondo) (Edition: 2,012 but taken from individual issue limits;
         Issued: 19)... (6)   150
LOSS12–**2011**   Speed. Set of six 50 pence silver brilliant uncirculated coins depicting
         various sports (Athletics, Aquatics, Canoeing, Cycling, Rowing, Triathlon)
         (Edition: 2,012 but taken from individual issue limits; Issued: 41) .... (6)   150
LOSS13–**MD**   Five pounds.(crowns). Set of the four Countdown issues and the Official
         Olympic and Paralympic £5 proof silver coins   (Edition: 800 taken from
         individual issue limits; Issued: 224) .... (6)   400

Gold coin sets

LOGS1–**2008**   'Bimetallic' 'Centenary of Olympic Games of 1908' £2 and 'Bimetallic'
         'United Kingdom Olympic Handover Ceremony' £2 gold proofs
         (Edition: 250) .... (2)   1800
LOGS2–**2010**   'Faster' 2-coin proof set, two £25 (Issued: 246)..................................... (2)   1000
LOGS3–**2010**   'Faster' 3-coin proof set, £100, and two £25 (Issued: 1079)..................... (3)   2800
LOGS4–**2011**   'Higher' 2-coin proof set, two £25 (Issued: 229) .... (2)   1000
LOGS5–**2011**   'Higher' 3-coin proof set, £100, and two £25 (Issued: 381) .... (3)   2800

£

LOGS6–**2012**   'Stronger' 2-coin proof set, two £25 (Issued: 156) .... (2) 1000
LOGS7–**2012**   'Stronger' 3-coin proof set, £100, and two £25 (Issued: 243) .... (3) 2800
LOGS8–**MD**   'Faster', 'Higher' and 'Stronger' set of three £100 and six £25 (Issued: 477) (9) 8500
LOGS9–**MD**   'Countdown to London'. Set of four £5 gold proof coins .... (4) 9000
LOGS10–**2012**   Set of £5 proof London Olympic Games and Paralympic Games
(Edition: taken from individual coin limits) .... (2) 5000
LOGS11–**2012**   Set of eleven different 50 pence gold piedfort proofs depicting designs of
sports where there were United Kingdom gold medals winners.
(Issued: 15) .... (11) 45000

Celebration of Britain Silver Coin Sales

	LOSS1	*LOSS2*	*LOSS3*	*LOSS4*	*LOSS7*	*Singles*	*Totals*
SETS	**1480**	**854**	**1564**	**1830**	**3407**		
LO37	1480			1830	3407	19913	26630
LO38	1480			1830	3407	20107	26824
LO39	1480				3407	19813	24700
LO40	1480				3407	19813	24700
LO41	1480				3407	19847	24734
LO42	1480				3407	19821	24708
LO43		854			3407	49	4310
LO44		854			3407	52	4313
LO45		854		1830	3407	118	6209
LO46		854			3407	80	4341
LO47		854			3407	50	4311
LO48		854			3407	80	4341
LO49			1564	1830	3407	302	7103
LO50			1564	1830	3407	148	6949
LO51			1564		3407	48	5019
LO52			1564	1830	3407	246	7047
LO53			1564		3407	77	5048
LO54			1564		3407	34	5005

The sales figures for the coins sold as singles may not be complete.

Gold Coin Sales

2010	£25.00	£25.00	£100.00	SET		Authorised
LOGS2	1079	1079	1079	1079	(3)	
LOGS3	246	246		246	(2)	
LOGS8	477	477	477	477	(9)	
LO64			1622			7500
LO58	5473					20000
LO59		5428				20000
	7275	7230	3178			

2011	£25.00	£25.00	£100.00	SET		Authorised
LOGS4	555	555	555	555	(3)	
LOGS5	125	125		125	(2)	
LOGS8	477	477	477	477	(9)	
LO65			826			7500
LO60	1995					20000
LO61		2100				20000
	3152	3257	1858			

2012	£25.00	£25.00	£100.00	SET		Authorised
LOGS6	243	243	243	243	(3)	
LOGS7	156	156		90	(2)	
LOGS8	477	477	477	477	(9)	
LO66			794			7500
LO62	1624					20000
LO63		1392				20000
	2500	2268	1514			

In 2014 the Royal Mint launched a five year series of coins marking the journey from the outbreak of World War One in 1914 to the armistice in 1918. There are 36 proof crowns in silver and gold issued as six sets of 6 and a number of higher denomination coins which are all listed in this separate section. The first coin in the series was a £2 bi-metal piece depicting the famous recruitment image of Lord Kitchener and as this is a currency coin it can be found as K34 in the currency section. Other World War One related coins may be found under K35, K41, K44, K49 and NE2.

FIVE POUNDS

Obverse portrait by Ian Rank-Broadley

2014 - CENTENARY OF THE OUTBREAK 1914

WW1   WW2

WW1   **Five pounds.** (Crown.) R. A design depicting British troops waving to crowds as they embark on a ship with the inscription '1914 THE FIRST WORLD WAR 1918. BEF' with the edge inscription 'SALUTE THE OLD CONTEMPTIBLES'. (Reverse design: John Bergdahl)

WW2   **Five pounds.** (Crown.) R. A design depicting three Howitzers with the inscription '1914 THE FIRST WORLD WAR 1918' and the edge inscription 'NEW AND FURIOUS BOMBARDMENT' (Reverse design: Edwina Ellis.)

WW3   WW4

WW3   **Five pounds.** (Crown.) ℞. A design depicting an effigy of Walter Tull in uniform with soldiers walking out over no man's land and the inscription '1914 THE FIRST WORLD WAR 1918' and 'WALTER TULL' around the coin, separated by poppy flowers with barbed wire with the edge inscription 'A HERO ON AND OFF THE FIELD'. (Reverse design: David Cornell.)

WW4   **Five pounds.** (Crown.) ℞. A design depicting a naval gun being loaded on board the deck of a battleship with the inscription '1914 THE FIRST WORLD WAR 1918. NAVY' and the edge inscription 'THE KING'S SHIPS WERE AT SEA'. (Reverse design: David Rowlands)

WW5   WW6

WW5   **Five pounds.** (Crown.) ℞. A design depicting a man putting up propaganda posters onto a brick wall with the inscription '1914 THE FIRST WORLD WAR 1918' and the edge inscription 'FOLLOW ME! YOUR COUNTRY NEEDS YOU'. (Reverse design: David Lawrence.)

WW6   **Five pounds.** (Crown.) ℞. A design depicting a woman working fields with a plough with the inscription '1914 THE FIRST WORLD WAR 1918. HOMEFRONT' and the edge inscription 'SPEED THE PLOUGH AND THE WOMAN WHO DRIVES IT'. (Reverse design: David Rowlands.)

WWSS1-2014 £5 (WW1-6) silver proofs (6) (Issued: 839) £395
WWGS1-2014 £5 (WW1-6) gold proofs (6) (Issued: 20) £18000

2015 - A WORLD IN THE GRIP OF CONFLICT 1915

Obverse portrait by Jody Clark

WW7   WW8

WW7   **Five pounds.** (Crown.) R. A design of troops landing on the beaches below a map
showing the Gallipoli landings with the inscription '1914 THE FIRST WORLD
WAR 1918 – GALLIPOLI' with the edge inscription 'HEROES THAT SHED
THEIR BLOOD'. (Reverse design : John Bergdahl.)

WW7A Five pounds. (Crown.) As WW7 but with obverse portrait by Ian Rank-Broadley.
2015 Proof in silver *FDC* (Edition: 2,500) £80

This coin was only issued in a set with an Australia, New Zealand and Turkey coin.

WW8   **Five pounds.** (Crown.) R. An effigy of Edith Cavell together with a nurse
tending a patient and the inscription '1914 THE FIRST WORLD WAR 1918'
and 'EDITH CAVELL' around the coin, separated by poppy flowers attached
with barbed wire and the edge inscription 'SHE FACED THEM GENTLE
AND BOLD'. (Reverse design: David Cornell.)
2015 Proof in silver *FDC* (Edition: 500 plus 807 issued in sets)............................£120

WW9   WW10

WW9   **Five pounds.** (Crown.) R. An effigy of Albert Ball with First World War
fighter planes and the inscription '1914 THE FIRST WORLD WAR 1918' and
'ALBERT BALL VC' around the coin , separated by poppy flowers attached
with barbed wire and with the edge inscription 'BY FAR THE BEST ENGLISH
FLYING MAN'. (Reverse design: David Cornell.)

WW10 **Five pounds.** (Crown.) R. A First World War submarine and the inscription '1914
THE FIRST WORLD WAR 1918'and the edge inscription 'IN LITTLE BOXES
MADE OF TIN'. (Reverse design: Edwina Ellis.)

WW11   WW12

WW11 **Five pounds.** (Crown.) R. A horse carrying munitions and a howitzer in the background with the inscription '1914 THE FIRST WORLD WAR 1918' with the edge inscription ' PATIENT EYES COURAGEOUS HEARTS'. (Reverse design: David Lawrence.)

WW12 **Five pounds.** (Crown.) R. A sailor standing on deck below a red ensign with a ship in the background and the inscription '1914 THE FIRST WORLD WAR 1918 MERCHANT NAVY' and the edge inscription 'SEPULCHRED IN THE HARBOUR OF THE DEEP'. (Reverse design: David Rowlands.)

WWSS2-2015 £5 (WW7-12) silver proofs (6) (Issued: 807) £395
WWGS2-2015 £5 (WW7-12) gold proofs (6) (Issued: 25) £18000

2016 - RELENTLESS, BRUTAL AND BLOODY 1916

WW13   WW14

WW13 **Five pounds.** (Crown.) R. Troops accompanying a tank across the battle field with the inscription '1914 THE FIRST WORLD WAR 1918 SOMME' around the coin with the edge inscription 'DEAD MEN CAN ADVANCE NO FURTHER'. (Reverse design: John Bergdahl.)
      2016 Proof in silver *FDC* (Issued: 3,678 plus coins in sets).................................... £80

WW14 **Five pounds.** (Crown.) R. An image of Jack Cornwell accompanied by an image of a naval gun and a battleship with the inscription '1914 THE FIRST WORLD WAR 1918' and 'JACK CORNWELL VC' around the coin, separated by poppy flowers attached with barbed wire and the edge inscription 'MOTHER, DON'T WATCH FOR POSTIE'. (Reverse design: David Cornell.)

WW15   WW16

WW15 Five pounds. (Crown.) R. A depiction of battleships under fire and the inscription
'1914 THE FIRST WORLD WAR 1918 JUTLAND' around the coin and the edge
inscription 'OUR CHILDREN SHALL MEASURE THEIR WORTH'
(Reverse design: John Bergdahl.)

WW16 Five pounds. (Crown.) R. A line of troops walking across the battlefield accompanied
by the inscription 'THERE SHALL BE IN THAT RICH EARTH A RICHER DUST
CONCEALED' and the inscription '1914 THE FIRST WORLD WAR 1918' and the
edge inscription 'THE TRUTH UNTOLD, THE PITY OF WAR'. (Reverse design:
David Lawrence.)

2016 — Proof in silver *FDC* (Edition: 4.000 plus coins in sets) £80

WW17   WW18

WW17 Five pounds. (Crown.) R. A group of soldiers sat in a trench and the inscription
'1914 THE FIRST WORLD WAR 1918' 'ARMY' and the edge inscription 'MEN
WHO MARCH AWAY'. (Reverse design: David Rowlands.)

2016 — Proof in silver *FDC* (Issued: 101 plus coins in sets) £80

WW18 Five pounds. (Crown.) R. A depiction of a naval gun on a Dreadnought and the
inscription '1914 THE FIRST WORLD WAR 1918' and the edge inscription
'WATCH-DOGS OF THE NATION'. (Reverse design: Edwina Ellis.)

WWSS3-2016 £5 (WW12-18) silver proofs (6) (Issued: 499) £395
WWGS3-2016 £5 (WW12-18) gold proofs (6) (Issued: 25) £18000

2017 - THE GRUELLING WAR CONTINUES TO TAKE ITS TOLL 1917

WW19　　　　　　　　　　　　　　WW20

WW19 Five pounds. (Crown.) R. A portrait of Noel Chavasse VC accompanied by an image
of him tendingto a wounded soldier with the inscription '1914 THE FIRST WORLD
WAR 1918'and 'NOEL CHAVASSE VC' around the coin, separated by poppy flowers
attached with barbed wire with the edge inscription 'DUTY CALLED AND CALLED
ME TO OBEY'. (Reverse design: David Cornell.)

WW20 Five pounds. (Crown.) R. A depiction of the Battle of Arras, showing howitzers with
planes flying overhead and the inscription '1914 THE FIRST WORLD WAR 1918 -
ARRAS' with the edge inscription 'THE MONSTROUS ANGER OF THE GUNS'.
(Reverse design: John Bergdahl.)

WW21　　　　　　　　　　　　　　WW22

WW21 Five pounds. (Crown.) R A view of a Sopwith Camel shown from directly in front of
the propeller and the inscription '1914 THE FIRST WORLD WAR 1918' with the edge
inscription 'IRRITATUS LACESSIT CRABRO'. (Reverse design: Edwina Ellis.)

WW22 Five pounds. (Crown.) R. An image of a First World War gas mask and the inscription
'1914 THE FIRST WORLD WAR 1918' with the edge inscription 'GUTTERING,
CHOKING, DROWNING'. (Reverse design: Edwina Ellis.)

WW23   WW24

WW23 Five pounds. (Crown.) R.A depiction of a First World War medical station with troops
carrying a stretcher and the inscription '1914 THE FIRST WORLD WAR 1918 -
MEDICAL SERVICES' with the edge inscription 'IN ARDUIS FIDELIS'.
(Reverse design: David Rowlands.)

WW24 Five pounds. (Crown.) R. A design showing a war artist sketching a line of soldiers
who have been gassed and the inscription '1914 THE FIRST WORLD WAR 1918'
with the edge inscription 'WAR AS IT IS'. (Reverse design: David Lawrence).

WWSS4-2017 £5 (WW19-24) silver proofs (6) (Issued: 573) £395
WWGS4-2017 £5 (WW19-24) gold proofs (6) (Issued: 24) £18000

2018 - THE BEGINNING OF THE END 1918

WW25   WW26

WW25 Five pounds. (Crown.) R. A portrait of T.E.Lawrence accompanied by an image of
soldiers on camels with the inscription '1914 THE FIRST WORLD WAR 1918' and
'T.E.LAWRENCE' around the coin, separated by poppy flowers attached with
barbed wire and with the edge inscription 'I WROTE MY WILL ACROSS THE
SKY IN STARS'. (Reverse design: David Cornell.)

WW25 Five pounds. (Crown.) R. A depiction of the aftermath of the Battle of Ypres, showing
soldiers by a grave and the inscription '1914 THE FIRST WORLD WAR – YPRES'
and with the edge inscription ' HERE WAS THE WORLD'S WORST WOUND'.
(Reverse design: John Bergdahl.)

WW27   WW28

WW27 **Five pounds.** (Crown.) R̟. A view of a First World War tank and the inscription
'1914 THE FIRST WORLD WAR 1918' and with the edge inscription 'THE DEVIL
IS COMING'. (Reverse design: Edwina Ellis.)

WW28 **Five pounds.** (Crown.) R̟. A view of a woman working in a factory and the
inscription '1914 THE FIRST WORLD WAR 1918' and with the edge inscription
'ON HER THEIR LIVES DEPEND'. (Reverse design: David Lawrence.)

WW29   WW30

WW29 **Five pounds.** (Crown.) R̟. A depiction of a bi-plane from the First World War and
the inscription '1914 THE FIRST WORLD WAR 1918 – ROYAL AIR FORCE'
and with the edge inscription 'TUMULT IN THE CLOUDS'. (Reverse designs:
David Rowlands.)

WW30 Five pounds. (Crown.) R̟. A design showing a Victory Medal on a letter in front
of a family portrait and the inscription '1914 THE FIRST WORLD WAR 1918'
and with the edge inscription ' THE WATCHES BY LONELY HEARTHS'.
(Reverse design: David Lawrence.)

WWSS5-2018 £5 (WW25-30) silver proofs (6) (Issued: 444) £395
WWGS5-2018 £5 (WW25-30) gold proofs (6) (Issued: 25) £18000

2018 - CENTENARY OF THE ARMISTICE 1918

WW31   WW32

WW31 Five Pounds. (Crown.) Remembrance Day design. R. Poppy wreath with centred inscription '11:00 11 NOVEMBER 1918 LEST WE FORGET 2018'. (Reverse design: David Lawrence.)

2018 Proof in silver *FDC* – (Issued: 156 plus coins in WWSS6) £85
— Proof in gold *FDC* (Issued: 22 plus coins in WWGS6) £2800

WW32 Five pounds. (Crown.) War Memorial design. R. A design showing the Cenotaph centred with the inscription 'THE GLORIOUS DEAD 1914-1918 2018'. (Reverse design: John Bergdahl.)

2018 Proof in silver *FDC* (Issued: 100 plus coins in WWSS6) £85

WW33   WW34

WW33 Five pounds. (Crown.) R. A design with poppies and barbed wire and the inscription 'REMEMBER'. (Reverse design: Edwina Ellis.)

2018 Proof in silver *FDC* (Issued: 961 plus coins in WWSS6) £85

In addition 249 silver proofs were sold in a three coin set with Australia and New Zealand $1 silver coins.

WW34 Five pounds. (Crown.) R. A design representing Imperial War Museums with the inscription 'IMPERIAL WAR MUSEUMS 1918-2018'. (Reverse design: David Rowlands.)

2018 Proof in silver *FDC* (Issued: 100 plus coins in WWSS6) £85

WW35   WW36

WW35 Five pounds. (Crown.) R. A design representing War Graves with the inscription
‘COMMONWEALTH WAR GRAVES COMMISSION 2018’. (Reverse design:
David Cornell.)

    2018 Proof in silver *FDC* (Issued: 100 plus coins in WWSS6) £85

WW36 Five pounds. (Crown.) R. A design showing the Dove of Peace with the incscription
‘PEACE 1918’. (Reverse design: David Lawrence.)

    2018 Proof in silver *FDC* (Issued: 100 plus coins in WWSS6) £85

WWSS6-2018 £5 (WW31-36) silver proofs (6) (Issued: 593) £395
WWGS6-2018 £5 (WW31-36) gold proofs (6) (Issued: 25) £18000

TEN POUNDS

Obverse portrait by Ian Rank Broadley

WW37

WW37 Ten pounds. (Five ounce.) 100th Anniversary of the Outbreak of the First World
War. R. A depiction of a lion behind the figure of Britannia holding a shield and a
trident, watching over departing ships from a cliff top, with the inscription ‘THE
FIRST WORLD WAR 1914 1918’ and the date at the base of the coin.
(Reverse design: John Bergdahl.)

    2014 Proof in silver *FDC* (Issued: 606) £395

  —   Proof in gold *FDC* (Issued: 36).. £12500

Obverse portrait by Jody Clark

WW38

WW38 Ten pounds. (Five ounce.) World War One. R.A depiction of the landscape of the
Western Front with the inscription '1914–1918'. (Reverse design: James Butler.)
2015 Proof on silver *FDC* (Issued: 355) £395
— Proof in gold *FDC* (Issued: 17) £12500

WW39

WW39 Ten pounds. (Five ounce.) R. A line of troops walking across the battlefield
accompanied by the inscription 'THERE SHALL BE IN THAT RICH EARTH A
RICHER DUST CONCEALED' and the inscription '1914 THE FIRST WORLD
WAR 1918' and the edge inscription 'THE TRUTH UNTOLD, THE PITY OF WAR'.
(Reverse design: David Lawrence.)
2016 Proof in silver *FDC* (Edition: 500) £395
— Proof in gold *FDC* (Edition: 30) £12500

WW40   WW41

WW40 Ten pounds. (Five ounce.) R. A soldier from the First World War encircled by a
wreath. (Reverse design: Philip Jackson.)
2017 Proof in silver *FDC* (Issued: 357) £395
— Proof in gold *FDC* (Issued: 28).. £12500

WW41 Ten pounds. (Five ounce.) Centenary of Armistice. R. A design depicting a kneeling
soldier accompanied by the inscription 'ARMISTICE THE GUNS FALL SILENT'.
(Reverse design: Paul Day.)
2018 Proof in silver *FDC* (Issued: 287) £395
— Proof in gold *FDC* (Issued: 13) £12500

ONE HUNDRED POUNDS

Obverse portrait by Ian Rank Broadley

WW42

WW42 One hundred pounds. (1 oz of fine platinum.) World War I. R. A depiction
of Lord Kitchener pointing above the inscription 'YOUR COUNTRY NEEDS
YOU' and the inscription 'THE FIRST WORLD WAR 1914-1918' and the date
'2014' surrounding the design. (Reverse design: John Bergdahl.)
2014 Proof in Platinum *FDC* (Issued: 325) £2000

See K34 for £2 coins with this design.

FIVE HUNDRED POUNDS

WW43

WW43 **Five hundred pounds.** (1 kilo of fine silver.) World War 1. ℞. A design depicting British soldiers marching through no man's land with the figure of a British soldier with rifle and helmet in the foreground and the dates '1914-1918' at the base of the coin. (Reverse design: Michael Sandle.)
2014 Proof in silver *FDC* (Issued: 165) £2000

Obverse portrait by Jody Clark

WW44

WW44 **Five hundred pounds.** (1 kilo of fine silver.) Centenary of Armistice. ℞. A design depicting a kneeling soldier accompanied by the inscription 'ARMISTICE THE GUNS FALL SILENT'. (Reverse design: Paul Day.)
2018 Proof in silver *FDC* (Issued: 40) £2000

ONE THOUSAND POUNDS

Obverse portrait by Ian Rank-Broadley

WW45

WW45 One thousand pounds. (1 kilo of fine gold.) World War 1. R̶. A design depicting
British soldiers marching through no man's land with the figure of a British soldier
with rifle and helmet in the foreground and the dates '1914-1918' at the base of the
coin. (Reverse design: Michael Sandle, Obverse Ian Rank Broadley.)
2014 Proof in gold *FDC* (Issued: 10) £70000

Obverse portrait by Jody Clark
WW46 One thousand pounds. (1 kilo of fine gold.) Centenary of Armistice. R̶. As WW44.
2018 Proof in gold *FDC* (Issued: 1) £70000

World War One Silver Sets   £

WWSS1–**2014**	£5 (WW1-6) silver proofs (6) (Issued: 839)	395
WWSS2–**2015**	£5 (WW7-12) silver proofs (6) (Issued: 807)	395
WWSS3–**2016**	£5 (WW13-18) silver proofs (6) (Issued: 499)	395
WWSS4–**2017**	£5 (WW19-24) silver proofs (6) (Issued: 573)	395
WWSS5–**2018**	£5 (WW25-30) silver proofs (6) (Issued: 444)	395
WWSS6–**2018**	£5 (WW31-36) silver proofs (6) (Issued: 593)	395

World War One Gold Sets   £

WWGS1–**2014**	£5 (WW1-6) gold proofs (6) (Issued: 20)	18000
WWGS2–**2015**	£5 (WW7-12) gold proofs (6) (Issued: 25)	18000
WWGS3–**2016**	£5 (WW13-18) gold proofs (6) (Issued: 25)	18000
WWGS4–**2017**	£5 (WW19-24) gold proofs (6) (Issued: 24)	18000
WWGS5–**2018**	£5 (WW25-30) gold proofs (6) (Issued: 25)	18000
WWGS6–**2018**	£5 (WW31-36) gold proofs (6) (Issued: 25)	18000

For other World War I related Coins, please see: K34, K35, K41, K44, K49 and NE2

In 2014 the Royal Mint launched the first of a series of Chinese Lunar Calendar coins starting with the animal for that year – the horse. Centuries old, the Shengxiao relates each year to one of 12 animals. Proof coins are issued in a range of sizes in gold and silver. Some of these plus one platinum has also been issued as bullion uncirculated coins. These carry an additional inscription stating the coin weight and are listed following the collector series. In 2020 a cupro-nickel £5 crown was added to the range.

Although the 2023 Chinese new year did not commence until 22nd January 2023, the Royal Mint withdrew the 2023 Year of the Sheep issue from sale at 31st December 2022. Unusually there were no bullion pieces minted for this issue.

COLLECTOR ISSUES

The £5 cupro-nickel crowns previously listed here are now listed withing the Crown Size Commemoratives section

SILVER

TWO POUNDS

Obverse portrait by Ian Rank-Broadley

CLCB1

CLCB1   **Two pounds.** (1 oz of fine silver.) Year of the Horse. ℞. Design depicting a horse prancing past the Uffington chalk white horse, with the inscription 'YEAR OF THE HORSE. 2014' and the Chinese symbol for horse. (Reverse design: Wuon-Gean Ho.)
2014 Proof in silver *FDC* (Issued: 8,347)... £83

CLCB2

CLCB2   **Two pounds.** (1 oz of fine silver.) Year of the Sheep. ℞. Design depicting two Swaledale sheep, with the inscription 'YEAR OF THE SHEEP 2015' and the Chinese symbol for sheep. (Reverse design: Wuon-Gean Ho.)
2015 Proof in silver *FDC* (Issued: 4,463) £83
—   Proof in silver *FDC* in PNC (Issued: 788)..£85
—   Proof in silver with gold plating *FDC* (Issued: 1,358) £110

For coin specifications please see the tables at the beginning of the Britannia section.

Obverse portrait by Jody Clark

CLCB3

CLCB3   **Two pounds.** (1 oz of fine silver.) Year of the Monkey. R̸. Design depicting a monkey leaping through the trees with the inscription 'YEAR OF THE MONKEY 2016' and the Chinese symbol for monkeys. (Reverse design: Wuon-Gean Ho.)
2016 Proof in silver *FDC* (Issued: 3,749) £83
—   Proof in silver *FDC* in PNC (Issued: 980)...£85

CLCB4   CLCB5

CLCB4   **Two pounds.** (1 oz of fine silver.) Year of the Rooster. R̸. Design depicting a crowing rooster accompanied by a number of gladiola flowers with the inscription 'YEAR OF THE ROOSTER 2017' and the Chinese symbol for a rooster. (Reverse design: Wuon-Gean Ho.)
2017 Proof in silver *FDC* (Issued: 3,847) £85

CLCB5   **Two pounds.** (1 oz of fine silver.) Year of the Dog. R̸. Design depicting a running dog with the inscription 'YEAR OF THE DOG 2018' and the Chinese lunar symbol for a dog. (Reverse design: Wuon-Gean Ho.)
2018 Proof in silver *FDC* (Issued:3,166) £85

For coin specifications please see the tables at the beginning of the Britannia section.

CLCB6   CLCB7

CLCB6   **Two pounds.** (1 oz of fine silver.) Year of the Pig. ℞. Design depicting a cottage on a hill at night and in the foreground piglets suckling from a sow with the inscription 'YEAR OF THE PIG 2019' and the Chinese symbol for a pig. (Reverse design: Harry Brockway.)

2019 Proof in silver *FDC* (Issued: 2,960) £85

CLCB7   **Two pounds.** (1 oz of fine silver.) Year of the Rat. ℞. Design depicting an agile and inquisitive rat crouching against a backdrop of peonies with the inscription 'YEAR OF THE RAT 2020' and Chinese symbol for a rat. (Reverse design: P J Lynch.)

2020 Proof in silver *FDC* (Edition: 3,898) £85

CLCB8   CLCB9   CLCB10

CLCB8   **Two pounds.** (1 oz of fine silver.) Year of the Ox. ℞. Design depicting a powerful ox grazing in a meadow with bluebells in the foreground and blossom trees beyond with inscription 'YEAR OF THE OX 2021' and Chinese symbol for Ox. (Reverse design: Harry Brockway.)

2021 Proof in silver *FDC* (Edition: 3,998) £85

CLCB9   **Two pounds.** (1oz of fine silver.) Year of the Tiger. ℞. A Tiger with the inscription 'YEAR OF THE TIGER 2022' and Chinese symbol for a Tiger. (Reverse design: David Lawrence.)

2022 Proof in silver *FDC* (Edition: 3,988) £93

CLCB10   **Two pounds.** (1oz of fine silver.) Year of the Rabbit. ℞. A Rabbit with the inscription 'YEAR OF THE RABBIT 2023' and the Chinese lunar symbol for a Rabbit. (Reverse design: Louie Maryon.)

2023 Proof in silver *FDC* (Edition: 3,898) £93

For coin specifications please see the tables at the beginning of the Britannia section.

TEN POUNDS

Obverse portrait by Ian Rank-Broadley

CLCC1 **Ten pounds.** (5 oz of fine silver.) Year of the Horse. R. As CLCB1.
2014 Proof in silver *FDC* (Issued: 799) £450
CLCC2 **Ten pounds.** (5 oz of fine silver.) Year of the Sheep. R. As CLCB2.
2015 Proof in silver *FDC* (Issued: 331) £395

Obverse portrait by Jody Clark

CLCC3 **Ten pounds.** (5 oz of fine silver.) Year of the Monkey. R.As CLCB3.
2016 Proof in silver *FDC* (Issued: 303) £395
CLCC4 **Ten pounds.** (5 oz of fine silver.) Year of the Rooster. R. As CLCB4.
2017 Proof in silver *FDC* (Issued: 380) £420
CLCC5 **Ten pounds.** (5 oz of fine silver.) Year of the Dog. R. As CLCB5.
2018 Proof in silver *FDC* (Issued: 165) £420
CLCC6 **Ten pounds.** (5 oz of fine silver.) Year of the Pig. R. As CLCB6.
2019 Proof in silver *FDC* (Issued: 144) £420
CLCC7 **Ten pounds.** (5 oz of fine silver.) Year of the Rat. R. As CLCB7.
2020 Proof in silver *FDC* (Edition: 198) £420
CLCC8 **Ten pounds.** (5 oz of fine silver.) Year of the Ox. R. As CLCB8.
2021 Proof in silver *FDC* (Edition: 198) £420
CLCC9 **Ten pounds.** (5oz of fine silver.) Year of the Tiger. R. As CLCB9.
2022 Proof in silver *FDC* (Edition: 228) £455
CLCC10 Ten pounds. (5oz of fine silver.) Year of the Rabbit. R. As CLCB10.
2023 Proof in silver *FDC* (Edition: 238) £455

FIVE HUNDRED POUNDS

Obverse portrait by Jody Clark

CLCD1 **Five hundred pounds.** (1 kilo of fine silver.) Year of the Monkey. R. As CLCB3.
2016 Proof in silver *FDC* (Issued: 54) £2000
CLCD2 **Five hundred pounds.** (1 kilo of fine silver.) Year of the Rooster. R. As CLCB4.
2017 Proof in silver *FDC* (Issued: 62) £2000
CLCD3 **Five hundred pounds.** (1 kilo of fine silver.) Year of the Dog. R. As CLCB5.
2018 Proof in silver *FDC* (Issued: 25) £2000
CLCD4 **Five hundred pounds.** (1 kilo of fine silver.) Year of the Pig. R. As CLCB6.
2019 Proof in silver *FDC* (Issued: 23) £2025
CLCD5 **Five hundred pounds.** (1 kilo of fine silver.) Year of the Rat. R. As CLCB7.
2020 Proof in silver *FDC* (Edition: 38) £2025
CLCD6 **Five hundred pounds.** (1 kilo fine silver.) Year of the Ox. R. As CLCB8.
2021 Proof in silver *FDC* (Edition: 38) £2050
CLCD7 **Five hundred pounds.** (1 kilo of fine silver.) Year of the Tiger. R. As CLCB9.
2022 Proof in silver *FDC* (Edition: 38) £2270
CLCD8 **Five hundred pounds.** (1 kilo of fine silver.) Year of the Rabbit. R. As CLCB10.
2023 Proof in silver *FDC* (Edition: 52) £2270

For coin specifications please see the tables at the beginning of the Britannia section.

GOLD

TEN POUNDS

Obverse portrait by Ian Rank-Broadley

CLCE1 **Ten pounds.** (1/10 oz of fine gold.) Year of the Horse. ℞. As CLCG1.
2014 BU (Issued; 1,779) £225
CLCE2 **Ten pounds.** (1/10 oz of fine gold.) Year of the Sheep. ℞. As CLCG2.
2015 BU (Issued: 922) £225

Obverse portrait by Jody Clark

CLCE3 **Ten pounds.** (1/10 oz of fine gold.) Year of the Monkey. ℞. As CLCG3.
2016 BU (Issued: 1,353) £225
CLCE4 **Ten pounds.** (1/10 oz of fine gold.) Year of the Rooster. ℞. As CLCG4.
2017 BU (Issued: 991) £225
CLCE5 **Ten pounds.** (1/10 oz of fine gold.) Year of the Dog. ℞. As CLCG5
2018 BU (Issued: 910) £225
CLCE6 **Ten pounds.** (1/10 oz of fine gold.) Year of the Pig. ℞. As CLCG6.
2019 BU (Issued: 698) £225
CLCE7 **Ten pounds.** (1/10 oz of fine gold.) Year of the Rat. ℞. As CLCG7.
2020 BU (Edition: 1,088) £225

TWENTY FIVE POUNDS

CLCF1 **Twenty five pounds.** (1/4 oz of fine gold.) Year of the Rat. ℞. As CLCG7.
2020 Proof in gold *FDC* (Edition: 398) £600
CLCF2 **Twenty five pounds.** (1/4 oz of fine gold.) Year of the Ox. ℞. As CLCG8.
2021 Proof in gold *FDC* (Edition: 388) £600
CLCF3 **Twenty five pounds.** (1/4 oz of fine gold.) Year of the Tiger. ℞. As CLCG9.
2022 Proof in gold FDC (Edition: 398) £600
CLCF4 **Twenty five pounds.** (1/4 oz of fine gold.) Year of the Rabbit. ℞. As CLCG10.
2023 Proof in gold *FDC* (Edition: 398) £700

For coin specifications please see the tables at the beginning of the Britannia section.

ONE HUNDRED POUNDS

Obverse portrait by Ian Rank-Broadley

CLCG1   CLCG2

CLCG1 **One hundred pounds.** (1 oz of fine gold.) Year of the Horse. ℞. Design depicting
a horse prancing past the Uffington chalk white horse, with the inscription 'YEAR
OF THE HORSE . 2014' and the Chinese symbol for horse. (Reverse design:
Wuon-Gean Ho.)
2014 Proof in gold *FDC* (Issued: 811) £2200

CLCG2 **One hundred pounds.** (1 oz of fine gold.) Year of the Sheep. ℞. Design depicting
two Swaledale sheep, with the inscription 'YEAR OF THE SHEEP 2015' and the
Chinese symbol for sheep. (Reverse design: Wuon-Gean Ho.)
2015 Proof in gold *FDC* (Issued: 548) £2200

Obverse portrait by Jody Clark

CLCG3   CLCG4

CLCG3 **One hundred pounds.** (1 oz of fine gold.) Year of the Monkey. ℞. Design depicting
a monkey leaping through the trees with the inscription 'YEAR OF THE
MONKEY 2016' and the Chinese symbol for monkeys. (Reverse design:
Wuon-Gean Ho.)
2016 Proof in gold *FDC* (Issued: 661) £2200

CLCG4 **One hundred pounds.** (1 oz of fine gold.) Year of the Rooster. ℞. Design depicting
a crowing rooster accompanied by a number of gladiola flowers with the inscription
'YEAR OF THE ROOSTER 2017' and the Chinese symbol for a rooster.
(Reverse design: Wuon-Gean Ho.)
2017 Proof in gold *FDC* (Issued: 636) £2200

For coin specifications please see the tables at the beginning of the Britannia section.

| CLCG5 | CLCG6 | CLCG7 |

CLCG5   **One hundred pounds.** (1 oz of fine gold.) Year of the Dog. ℞. Design depicting a running dog with the inscription 'YEAR OF THE DOG 2018' and the Chinese lunar symbol for a dog. (Reverse design: Wuon-Gean Ho.)

2018 Proof in gold (Issued: 571).. £2200

CLCG6   **One hundred pounds.** (1 oz of fine gold.) Year of the Pig. ℞. Design depicting a cottage on a hill at night and in the foreground piglets suckling from a sow with the inscription 'YEAR OF THE PIG 2019' and Chinese symbol for a pig. (Reverse design: Harry Brockway.)

2019 Proof in gold *FDC* (issued: 728).. £2200

CLCG7   **One hundred pounds.** (1 oz of fine gold.) Year of the Rat. ℞. Design depicting an agile and inquisitive rat crouching against a backdrop of peonies with the inscription 'YEAR OF THE RAT 2020' and Chinese symbol for a rat. (Reverse design: P J Lynch.)

2020 Proof in gold *FDC* (Edition: 898) £2200

| CLCG8 | CLCG9 | CLCG10 |

CLCG8   **One hundred pounds.** (1 oz of fine gold.) Year of the Ox. ℞. Design depicting a powerful ox grazing in a meadow with bluebells in the foreground and blossom trees beyond with inscription 'YEAR OF THE OX 2021' and Chinese symbol for Ox. (Reverse design: Harry Brockway.)

2021 Proof in gold *FDC* (Edition: 898) £2400

CLCG9   **One hundred pounds.** (1oz of fine gold.) Year of the Tiger. ℞. A Tiger with the inscription "YEAR OF THE TIGER 2022" and Chinese symbol for a Tiger. (Reverse design: David Lawrence.)

2022 Proof in gold *FDC* (Edition: 898) £2400

CLCG10   **One hundred pounds**. (1oz of fine gold.) Year of the Rabbit. ℞. A Rabbit with the inscription "YEAR OF THE RABBIT 2023" and the Chinese lunar symbol for a Rabbit. (Reverse design: Louie Maryon.)

2023 Proof in gold *FDC* (Edition: 898) £2500

For coin specifications please see the tables at the beginning of the Britannia section.

FIVE HUNDRED POUNDS

Obverse portrait by Ian Rank-Broadley

CLCH1   **Five hundred pounds.** (5 oz of fine gold.) Year of the Sheep. R. As CLCG2.
2015 Proof in gold *FDC* (Issued: 26) £12000

Obverse portrait by Jody Clark

CLCH2   **Five hundred pounds.** (5 oz of fine gold.) Year of the Monkey. R. As CLCG3.
2016 Proof in gold *FDC* (Issued: 24) £12000

CLCH3   **Five hundred pounds.** (5 oz of fine gold.) Year of the Rooster. R. As CLCG4.
2017 Proof in gold *FDC* (Issued: 35) £12000

CLCH4   **Five hundred pounds.** (5 oz of fine gold.) Year of the Dog. R. As CLCG5.
2018 Proof in gold *FDC* (Issued: 34) £12000

CLCH5   **Five hundred pounds.** (5 oz of fine gold.) Year of the Pig. R. As CLCG6.
2019 Proof in gold *FDC* (Issued: 38) £12000

CLCH6   **Five hundred pounds.** (5 oz of fine gold.) Year of the Rat. R. As CLCG7.
2020 Proof in gold *FDC* (Edition: 30) £12000

CLCH7   **Five hundred pounds.** (5 oz fine gold.) Year of the Ox. R. As CLCG8.
2021 Proof in gold *FDC* (Edition: 38) £12000

CLCH8   **Five hundred pounds.** (5oz of fine gold.) Year of the Tiger. R. As CLCG9.
2022 Proof in gold *FDC* (Edition: 128) £11000

CLCH9   **Five hundred pounds.** (5oz of fine gold.) Year of the Rabbit. R. As CLCG10.
2023 Proof in gold *FDC* (Edition: 138) £12500

ONE THOUSAND POUNDS

Obverse portrait by Jody Clark

CLCJ1   **One thousand pounds.** (1 kilo of fine gold.) Year of the Monkey. R. As CLCG3.
2016 Proof in gold *FDC* (Issued: 8) £70000

CLCJ2   **One thousand pounds.** (1 kilo of fine gold.) Year of the Rooster. R. As CLCG4.
2017 Proof in gold *FDC* (Issued: 8) £70000

CLCJ3   **One thousand pounds.** (1 kilo of fine gold.) Year of the Dog. R. As CLCG5.
2018 Proof in gold *FDC* (Issued: 7) £70000

CLCJ4   **One thousand pounds.** (1 kilo of fine gold.) Year of the Pig. R. As CLCG6.
2019 Proof in gold FDC (Issued: 5) £70000

CLCJ5   **One thousand pounds.** (1 kilo of fine gold.) Year of the Rat. R. As CLCG7.
2020 Proof in gold *FDC* (Edition: 10) £70000

CLCJ6   **One thousand pounds.** (1 kilo of fine gold.) Year of the Ox. R. As CLCG8.
2021 Proof in gold *FDC* (Edition: 10) £70000

CLCJ7   **One thousand pounds.** (1 kilo of fine gold.) Year of the Tiger. R. As CLCG9.
2022 Proof in gold *FDC* (Edition: 10) £70000

CLCJ8   **One thousand pounds.** (1 kilo of fine gold.) Year of the Rabbit. R. As CLCG10.
2023 Proof in gold *FDC* (Edition: 10) £70000

EIGHT THOUSAND POUNDS

CLCK1   **Eight thousand pounds.** (8 kilos of fine gold.) Year of the Tiger. R. As CLCG9.
2022 Proof in gold *FDC* (Edition: 1) £550000

For coin specifications please see the tables at the beginning of the Britannia section.

BULLION ISSUES
SILVER
ONE POUND

Obverse portrait by Jody Clark

CLBA1   **One pound.** (1/2 oz of fine silver.) ℞. As CLBB5 but with the inscription 'YEAR OF THE DOG -2018 ½ OZ FINE SILVER'. (Reverse design: Wuon-Gean Ho.)
2018 Unc £20

TWO POUNDS

Obverse portrait by Ian Rank-Broadley

CLBB1

CLBB1   **Two pounds.** (1 oz of fine silver). Year of the Horse. ℞. As CLCB1 but with the additional inscription '1 OZ FINE SILVER 999'.
2014 Unc £40

CLBB1A   **Two pounds. Error obverse – known as a Mule.** The obverse design of The Queen used for the £2 Silver Britannia uncirculated coin was paired with the reverse design of the Year of the Horse £2 silver coin.
2014 ....£50

Obverse portrait by Jody Clark

CLBB2   CLBB3

CLBB2   **Two pounds.** (1 oz of fine silver.) Year of the Sheep. ℞. As CLCB2 but with the additional inscription '1 OZ FINE SILVER 999'.
2015 Unc £40

CLBB3   **Two pounds.** (1 oz of fine silver.) Year of the Monkey. ℞ As CLCB3 but with the additional inscription '1 OZ FINE SILVER 999'.
2016 Unc (Edition: 138,888) £40

CLBB4 **Two pounds.** (1 oz of fine silver.) Year of the Rooster. R. As CLCB4 but with the additional inscription '1 OZ FINE SILVER 999'. (Reverse design: Wuon-Gean Ho.)
2017 Unc £40

CLBB5 **Two pounds.** (1 oz of fine silver.) Year of the Dog. R. As CLCB4 but with the additional inscription '1 OZ FINE SILVER 999).
2018 Unc £40

CLBB6 **Two pounds.** (1 oz of fine silver.) Year of the Pig. R. As above but with the additional inscription '1 OZ FINE SILVER 999'.
2019 Unc £40

CLBB7 **Two pounds.** (1 oz of fine silver.) Year of the Rat. R. As above but with the additional inscription '1 OZ FINE SILVER 999'.
2020 Unc £36

CLBB8 **Two pounds.** (1 oz of fine silver.) Year of the Ox. R. As above but with the additional inscription '1 OZ FINE SILVER 999'.
2021 Unc £36

CLBB9 **Two pounds.** (1oz of fine silver.) Year of the Tiger. R. As CLCB9 but with the additional inscription '1 OZ FINE SILVER 999'.
2022 Unc £30

GOLD

TEN POUNDS

CLBC1 **Ten pounds.** (1/10oz of fine gold.) Year of the Sheep. R. As CLCE2 but with the additional inscription '1/10 OZ FINE GOLD 999.9'.
2015 Unc £225

CLBC2 **Ten pounds.** (1/10 oz of fine gold.) Year of the Monkey. R. As CLCE3 but with the additional inscription '1 /10 OZ FINE GOLD 999.9'. (Reverse design: Wuon-Gean Ho.)
2016 Unc £225

TWENTY FIVE POUNDS

Obverse protrait by Ian Rank-Broadley

CLBD1 **Twenty five pounds.** (1/4 oz of fine gold.) Year of the Sheep. R. As CLCG2 but with the additional inscription '1/4 OZ FINE GOLD 999.9'.
2015 Unc (Issued: 5,000) £500

Obverse protrait by Jody Clark

CLBD2 **Twenty five pounds.** (1/4 oz of fine gold.) Year of the Monkey. R. As CLCG3 but with the additional inscription '1/4 OZ FINE GOLD 999.9'.
2016 Unc (Issued: 40,000) £500

CLBD3 **Twenty five pounds.** (1/4 oz of fine gold.) Year of the Rooster. R. As CLCG4 but with the additional inscription 1/4 OZ FINE GOLD 999.9'.
2017 Unc £500

CLBD4 **Twenty five pounds.** (1/4 oz fine gold.) Year of the Dog. R. As CLCG5 but with the additional inscription '1/4 OZ FINE GOLD 999.9'.
2018 Unc £500

CLBD5 **Twenty five pounds.** (1/4 oz of fine gold.) Year of the Rat. R. As CLCF1 but with the additional inscription '1/4 OZ FINE GOLD 999.9'.
2020 Unc £500

For coin specifications please see the tables at the beginning of the Britannia section.

ONE HUNDRED POUNDS
Obverse portrait by Ian Rank-Broadley

CLBE1   CLBE2

CLBE1   **One hundred pounds.** (1 oz of fine gold.) Year of the Horse. ℞. As CLCG1
but with the additional inscription '1 OZ FINE GOLD 999.9'.
2014 Unc (Edition: 30,000) £1700
CLBE2   **One hundred pounds.** (1 oz of fine gold.) Year of the Sheep. ℞. As CLCG2
but with the additional inscription '1OZ FINE GOLD 999.9'.
2015 Unc £1700

Obverse portrait by Jody Clark

CLBE3   **One hundred pounds.** (1 oz of fine gold.) Year of the Monkey. ℞. As CLCG3
but with the additional inscription '1OZ FINE GOLD 999.9'.
2016 Unc (Edition: 8,888) £1700
CLBE4   **One hundred pounds.** (1 oz of fine gold.) Year of the Rooster. ℞. As CLCG4
but with the additional inscription '1 OZ FINE GOLD 999.9'.
2017 Unc (Edition: 8,888) £1700
CLBE5   **One hundred pounds.** (1 oz of fine gold.) Year of the Dog. ℞. As CLCG5 but
with the additional inscription '1 OZ FINE GOLD 999.9'.
2018 Unc (Edition: 8,888) £1700
CLBE6   **One hundred pounds.** (1 oz of fine gold.) Year of the Pig. ℞. As CLCG6 but
with the additional inscription '1OZ FINE GOLD 999.9'.
2019 Unc (Edition: 8,888) £1700
CLBE7   **One hundred pounds.** (1 oz of fine gold.) Year of the Rat. ℞. As CLCG7 but
with the additional inscription '1OZ FINE GOLD 999.9'.
2020 Unc (Edition: 8,888) £1700
CLBE8   **One hundred pounds.** (1 oz of fine gold.) Year of the Ox. ℞. As CLCG8 but
with the additional inscription '1OZ FINE GOLD 999.9',
2021 Unc £1700
CLBE9   **One hundred pounds.** (1oz of fine gold.) Year of the Tiger. ℞. As CLCG9 but
with the additional inscription '1 OZ FINE GOLD 999.9'.
2022 Unc £1700

PLATINUM

TWENTY FIVE POUNDS

CLBF1   **Twenty five pounds.** (1/4 oz of fine platinum.) Year of the Dog. ℞. As CLCB5
but with the additional inscription '1/4 OZ FINE PLATINUM 999.5'.
2018 Unc £450

For later coins in this series please see the Charles III section.

For coin specifications please see the tables at the beginning of the Britannia section.

At Her Majesty the Queen's coronation, ten symbolic sculptures named The Queen's Beasts lined her entrance to Westminster Abbey, representing centuries of royal bloodlines. This series will therefore consist of ten different designs plus a completer coin. The proof and bullion designs differ in the reverse arrangement so the proof issues are listed first as Collector Issues with the bullion issues following.

Two extra denominations – 50p & £5 – were added to this range in 2021 and this necessitated a complete revision of the catalogue numbers which now consist of mainly letters.

QB – Queen's Beasts; C or B – Collector or Bullion Series; C, S or G – Cupro-nickel, silver or gold; followed by either a number or letter – A – Z – in denomination order.

Following the completion of the Queen's Beasts series in 2021 with a completer coin, a new series depicting the Tudor Beasts at Hampton Court Palace was commenced in 2022.

Reverse and obverse design by Jody Clark

COLLECTOR ISSUES

The £5 cupro-nickel crowns previously listed here are now listed withing the Crown Size Commemoratives section

SILVER

FIFTY PENCE

QBCSA1   **Fifty pence.** (1/4 oz of fine silver.) Griffin of Edward III. R. As QBCSB10.
2021 Proof in silver reverse frosted *FDC** £40

QBCSA2   **Fifty pence.** (1/4 oz of fine silver.) White Greyhound of Richmond. R. As QBCSB9.
2021 Proof in silver reverse frosted *FDC** £40

QBCSA3   **Fifty pence.** (1/4 oz of fine silver.) White Horse of Hanover. R. As QBCSB8.
2021 Proof in silver reverse frosted *FDC** £40

QBCSA4   **Fifty pence.** (1/4 oz of fine silver.) White Lion of Mortimer. R. As QBCSB7.
2021 Proof in silver reverse frosted *FDC ** £40

QBCSA5   **Fifty pence.** (1/4 oz of fine silver.) Yale of Beaufort. R. As QBCSB6.
2021 Proof in silver reverse frosted *FDC** ....£.40

QBCSA6   **Fifty pence.** (1/4 oz of fine silver.) Black Bull of Clarence. R. As QBCSB4.
2021 Proof in silver reverse frosted *FDC** £40

QBCSA7   **Fifty pence.** (1/4 oz of fine silver.) Falcon of the Plantagenets. R. As QBCSB5.
2021 Proof in silver reverse frosted *FDC ** £40

QBCSA8   **Fifty pence.** (1/4 oz of fine silver.) Red Dragon of Wales. R. As QBCSB3.
2021 Proof in silver reverse frosted *FDC** £40

QBCSA9   **Fifty pence.** (1/4 oz of fine silver.) Unicorn of Scotland. R. As QBCSB2.
2021 Proof in silver reverse frosted *FDC ** £40

QBCSA10   **Fifty pence.** (1/4 oz of fine silver.) Lion of England. R. As QBCSB1.
2021 Proof in silver reverse frosted *FDC ** £40

For coin specifications please see the tables at the beginning of the Britannia section.

TWO POUNDS

QBCSB1

QBCSB1 Two pounds. (1 oz of fine silver.) The Lion of England. ℞. A lion accompanied
by a shield depicting Our Royal Arms with the inscription '2017 LION OF
ENGLAND'.
2017 Proof in silver *FDC* (Issued: 8,430)... £85

QBCSB2   QBCSB3

QBCSB2 Two pounds. (1 oz of fine silver.) The Unicorn of Scotland. ℞. A rearing unicorn
accompanied by a shield depicting a lion rampant with the inscription '2017
UNICORN OF SCOTLAND'.
2017 Proof in silver *FDC* (Issued: 5,970)... £85
QBCSB3 Two pounds. (1 oz of fine silver.)The Red Dragon of Wales. ℞. A depiction of a
rearing dragon accompanied by the Coat of Arms of Llywelyn the Great with the
inscription '2018 RED DRAGON OF WALES'.
2018 Proof in silver *FDC* (Issued: 5,991)... £85

For coin specifications please see the tables at the beginning of the Britannia section.

QBCSB4   QBCSB5

QBCSB4 **Two pounds.** (1 oz of fine silver.) The Black Bull of Clarence. R. A depiction of
the Black Bull of Clarence supporting the arms as used by Edward IV and
Richard III as well as all the Sovereigns of the Houses of Lancaster and Tudor
with the inscription '2018 BLACK BULL OF CLARENCE'.
2018 Proof in silver *FDC* (Issued: 4,860).. £85

QBCSB5 **Two pounds.** (1 oz of fine silver.) The Falcon of the Plantagenets. R. A depiction
of the Falcon of the Plantagenets above the personal badge of Edward IV with the
inscription '2019 FALCON OF THE PLANTAGENETS'.
2019 Proof in silver *FDC* (Issued: 4,831).. £85

QBCSB6   QBCSB7

QBCSB6 **Two pounds.** (1 oz of fine silver.) Yale of Beaufort. R. A depiction of the Yale of
Beaufort supporting a shield portraying a portcullis surmounted by a royal crown
with the inscription '2019 YALE OF BEAUFORT'.
2019 Proof in silver *FDC* (Issued: 4,337).. £85

QBCSB7 **Two pounds.** (1 oz of fine silver). The White Lion of Mortimer. R. A depiction of
the White Lion of Mortimer supporting a shield portraying a white rose en soleil
with the inscription '2020 WHITE LION OF MORTIMER'.
2020 Proof in silver FDC (Edition 4,360).. £85

For coin specifications please see the tables at the beginning of the Britannia section.

QBCSB8   QBCSB9   QBCSB10

QBCSB8 **Two pounds.** (1 oz of fine silver.) White Horse of Hanover. ℞. A rearing white horse above shield with royal arms of George I with the incsription '2020 WHITE HORSE OF HANOVER'.
2020 Proof in silver *FDC* (Edition: 4310) £85

QBCSB9 **Two pounds.** (1 oz of fine silver.) White Greyhound of Richmond. ℞. A reimagined greyhound conveying its strength and power above shield depicting the symbol of the Tudor family and inscription '2021 WHITE GREYHOUND OF RICHMOND'.
2021 Proof in silver *FDC* (Edition: 3,960) £85

QBCSB10 **Two pounds.** (1oz of fine silver.) The Griffin of Edward III. ℞. A depiction of a griffin with the heraldic badge of the Royal House of Windsor accompanied by the inscription '2021 GRIFFIN OF EDWARD III'
2021 Proof in silver *FDC* (Edition:4,400).. £100

QBCSB11 **Two pounds.** (1oz of fine silver.) The completer coin. ℞. As QBCSC11.
2021 Proof in silver *FDC* (Edition: 7,260).. £100

FIVE POUNDS

QBCSC1 **Five pounds.** (2 oz of fine silver.) Griffin of Edward III. ℞. As QBCSB10.
2021 Proof in silver *FDC** £220

QBCSC2 **Five pounds.** (2 oz of fine silver.) White Greyhound of Richmond. ℞. As QBCSB9.
2021 Proof in silver *FDC** £220

QBCSC3 **Five pounds.** (2 oz of fine silver.) White Horse of Hanover. ℞. As QBCSB8.
2021 Proof in silver *FDC** £220

QBCSC4 **Five pounds.** (2 oz of fine silver.) White Lion of Mortimer. ℞. As QBCSB7.
2021 Proof in silver *FDC** £220

QBCSC5 **Five pounds.** (2 oz of fine silver.) Yale of Beaufort. ℞. As QBCSB6.
2021 Proof in silver *FDC** .... £.220

QBCSC6 **Five pounds.** (2 oz of fine silver.) Black Bull of Clarence. ℞. As QBCSB4.
2021 Proof in silver *FDC** £220

QBCSC7 **Five pounds.** (2 oz of fine silver.) Falcon of the Plantagenets. ℞. As QBCSB5.
2021 Proof in silver *FDC** £220

QBCSC8 **Five pounds.** (2 oz of fine silver.) Red Dragon of Wales. ℞. As QBCSB3.
2021 Proof in silver *FDC** £220

QBCSC9 **Five pounds.** (2 oz of fine silver.) Unicorn of Scotland. ℞. As QBCSB2.
2021 Proof in silver *FDC** £220

QBCSC10 **Five pounds.** (2 oz of fine silver.) Lion of England. ℞. As QBCSB1.
2021 Proof in silver *FDC** £220

* These coins are only available in the set QBCSS2.
For coin specifications please see the tables at the beginning of the Britannia section.

QBCSC11

QBCSC11 Five pounds. (2oz of fine silver.) The completer coin. R. A depiction of ten heraldic beasts encircling a portrait of Queen Elizabeth II with the inscription 'THE QUEEN'S BEASTS' and the date of the year.
2021 Proof in silver FDC (Edition: 750) £300

TEN POUNDS

QBCSD1 Ten pounds. (5 oz of fine silver.) The Lion of England. R. As QBCSB1.
2017 Proof in silver *FDC* (Issued: 677) £415
—   Proof piedfort in silver *FDC* (Issued: 686) £795

QBCSD2 Ten pounds. (5 oz of fine silver.) The Unicorn of Scotland. R. As QBCSB2.
2017 Proof in silver *FDC* (Issued: 461) £415
—   Proof piedfort in silver *FDC* (Issued: 345) £795

QBCSD3 Ten pounds. (5 oz of fine silver.) The Red Dragon of Wales. R. As QBCSB3.
2018 Proof in silver *FDC* (Issued: 661) £420
—   Proof piedfort in silver *FDC* (Issued: 313) £795

QBCSD4 Ten pounds. (5 oz of fine silver.) The Black Bull of Clarence. R.As QBCSB4.
2018 Proof in silver *FDC* (Issued: 459) £420
—   Proof piedfort in silver *FDC* (Issued: 269) £795

QBCSD5 Ten pounds. (5 oz of fine silver.) The Falcon of the Plantagenets. R. As QBCSB5.
2019 Proof in silver *FDC* (Issued: 390) £420
—   Proof piedfort in silver *FDC* (Issued: 213) £795

QBCSD6 Ten pounds. (5 oz of fine silver.) Yale of Beaufort. R As QBCSB6
2019 Proof in silver *FDC* (Issued: 324) £420
—   Proof piedfort in silver *FDC* (Issued: 226) £795

QBCSD7 Ten pounds. (5 oz of fine silver.) White Lion of Mortimer. R As QBCSB7
2020 Proof in silver *FDC* (Edition: 335) £420
—   Proof piedfort in silver *FDC* (Edition: 240) £795

QBCSD8 Ten pounds. (5 oz of fine silver.) White Horse of Hanover. R. As QBCSB8.
2020 Proof in silver *FDC* (Edition: 315) £420
—   Proof piedfort in silver *FDC* (Edition: 235) £795

QBCSD9 Ten pounds. (5 oz of fine silver) White Greyhound of Richmond. R. As QBCSB9.
2021 Proof in silver *FDC* (Edition: 370) £420
—   Proof piedfort in silver *FDC* (Edition: 195) £795

QBCSD10 Ten pounds. (5 oz of fine silver) The Griffin of Edward III. R. As QBCSB10.
2021 Proof in silver *FDC* (Edition: 400) £485
—   Proof piedfort in silver *FDC* (Edition: 195) £850

QBCSD11 Ten pounds. (5oz of fine silver.) The completer coin. R. As QBCSC11.
2021 Proof in silver *FDC* (Edition: 435) £600
—   Proof piedfort in silver *FDC* (Edition: 175) £1000

The piedforts listed under QBCSD1-10 were previously listed as separate £10 coins but as the completer coin is described as a piedfort in the legislation all of them are now listed as piedfort versions of the 5oz coin.

FIVE HUNDRED POUNDS

QBCSE1   **Five hundred pounds.** (1 kilo of fine silver.) The Lion of England. ℞. As QBCSB1.
2017 Proof in silver *FDC* (Issued: 116) £2050
QBCSE2   **Five hundred pounds.** (1 kilo of fine silver.) The Unicorn of Scotland.
℞. As QBCSB2.
2017 Proof in silver *FDC* (Issued: 88) £2050
QBCSE3   **Five hundred pounds.** (1 kilo of fine silver.) The Red Dragon of Wales.
℞. As QBCSB3.
2018 Proof in silver *FDC* (Issued: 129) £2050
QBCSE4   **Five hundred pounds.** (1 kilo of fine silver). The Black Bull of Clarence.
℞. As QBCSB4.
2018 Proof in silver *FDC* (Issued: 99) £2050
QBCSE5   **Five hundred pounds.** (1 kilo of fine silver.) The Falcon of the Plantagenets.
℞. As QBCSB5.
2019 Proof in silver *FDC* (Issued: 72) £2050
QBCSE6   **Five hundred pounds.** (1kilo of fine silver.) Yale of Beaufort. ℞ As QBCSB6.
2019 Proof in silver *FDC* (Issued: 89) £2050
QBCSE7   **Five hundred pounds.** (1 kilo of fine silver.) White Lion of Mortimer.
℞ As QBCSB7.
2020 Proof in silver *FDC* (Edition: 120)...£2050
QBCSE8   **Five hundred pounds.** (1 kilo of fine silver.) White Horse of Hanover.
℞. As QBCSB8.
2020 Proof in silver *FDC* (Edition: 115)...£2050
QBCSE9   **Five hundred pounds.** (1 kilo of fine silver.) White Greyhound of Richmond.
℞. As QBCSB9.
2021 Proof in silver *FDC* (Edition: 80)..£2050
QBCSE10 **Five hundred pounds.** (1 kilo of fine silver.) The Griffin of Edward III.
℞. As QBCSB10.
2021 Proof in silver *FDC* (Edition: 105)...£2270
QBCSE11 **Five hundred pounds.** (1 kilo of fine silver.) The completer coin.
℞. As QBCSC11.
2021 Proof in silver *FDC* (Edition: 95) £2500

ONE THOUSAND POUNDS

QBCSF1 **One thousand pounds.** (2 kilos of fine silver.) The completer coin.
℞. As QBCSC11.
2021 Proof in silver FDC (Edition: 50) £5000

Queen's Beasts Silver Proof Sets

QBCSS1–**2021**   50p (QBCSA1-10) (Edition: 1,360) ....(10)   £400
QBCSS2–**2021**   £5 (QBCSC1-10) (Edition: 310)......................................(10)   £2000

For coin specifications please see the tables at the beginning of the Britannia section.

GOLD

TWENTY FIVE POUNDS

QBCGA1   **Twenty five pounds.** (1/4 oz of fine gold.) The Lion of England.
R. As QBCGB1.
2017 Proof in gold *FDC* (Issued: 2,495)...£600
2021 Proof in gold reverse frosted *FDC** £650

QBCGA2   **Twenty five pounds.** (1/4 oz of fine gold.) The Unicorn of Scotland.
R. As QBCGB2.
2017 Proof in gold *FDC* (Issued: 1,499)...£600
2021 Proof in gold reverse frosted *FDC** £650

QBCGA3   **Twenty five pounds.** (1/4 oz of fine gold.) The Red Dragon of Wales.
R. As QBCGB3.
2018 Proof in gold *FDC* (Issued: 1,468)...£600
2021 Proof in gold reverse frosted *FDC** £650

QBCGA4   **Twenty five pounds.** (1/4 oz of fine gold.) The Black Bull of Clarence.
R. As QBCGB4.
2018 Proof in gold *FDC* (Issued: 1,480)...£600
2021 Proof in gold reverse frosted *FDC** £650

QBCGA5   **Twenty five pounds.** (1/4 oz of fine gold.) The Falcon of the Plantagenets.
R. As QBCGB5
2019 Proof in gold *FDC* (Issued: 1,199)...£600
2021 Proof in gold reverse frosted *FDC** £650

QBCGA6   **Twenty five pounds.** (1/4 oz of fine gold.) Yale of Beaufort. R. As QBCGB6.
2019 Proof in gold *FDC* (Issued: 1,000)...£600
2021 Proof in gold reverse frosted *FDC** £650

QBCGA7   **Twenty five pounds.** (1/4 oz of fine gold.) White Lion of Mortimer.
R. As QBCGB7
2020 Proof in gold *FDC* (Edition: 1,000) £600
2021 Proof in gold reverse frosted *FDC** £650

QBCGA8   **Twenty five pounds.** (1/4 oz of fine gold.) White Horse of Hanover.
R. As QBCGB8.
2020 Proof in gold *FDC* (Edition: 1,000) £600
2021 Proof in gold reverse frosted *FDC** £650

QBCGA9   **Twenty five pounds.** (1/4 oz of fine gold.) White Greyhound of Richmond.
R. As QBCGB9.
2021 Proof in gold *FDC* (Edition: 1,010) £600
—   Proof in gold reverse frosted *FDC** £650

QBCGA10 **Twenty five pounds.** (1/4 oz of fine gold.) The Griffin of Edward III.
R. As QBCGB10.
2021 Proof in gold *FDC* (Edition: 1,250) £600
—   Proof in gold reverse frosted *FDC** £650

* These coins are only in QBCGS1.
For coin specifications please see the tables at the beginning of the Britannia section.

ONE HUNDRED POUNDS

Obverse design QBCGB1-QBCGB11

QBCGB1   QBCGB2

QBCGB1 One hundred pounds. (1 oz of fine gold.) The Lion of England. R. A lion
accompanied by a shield depicting Our Royal Arms with the inscription '2017
LION OF ENGLAND'.
2017 Proof in gold *FDC* (Issued: 590) £2500

QBCGB2 One hundred pounds. (1 oz of fine gold.) The Unicorn of Scotland. R. A rearing
unicorn accompanied by a shield depicting a lion rampant with the inscription
'2017 UNICORN OF SCOTLAND'
2017 Proof in gold FDC (Issued: 418) £2500

QBCGB3   QBCGB4   QBCGB5

QBCGB3   One hundred pounds. (1 oz of fine gold.) The Red Dragon of Wales.
R. A depiction of a rearing dragon accompanied by the Coat of Arms of Llywelyn
the Great with the inscription '2018 RED DRAGON OF WALES'.
2018 Proof in gold *FDC* (Issued: 497) £2500

QBCGB4   One hundred pounds. (1 oz of fine gold.) Black Bull of Clarence. R. A depiction
of the Black Bull of Clarence supporting the arms used by Edward IV and
Richard III with the inscription '2018 BLACK BULL OF CLARENCE'.
2018 Proof in gold *FDC* (Issued: 468) £2500

QBCGB5   One hundred pounds. (1 oz of fine gold.) Falcon of the Plantagenets.
R. A depiction of the Falcon of the Plantagenets above the personal badge of
Edward IV and the inscription '2019 FALCON OF THE PLANTAGENETS'.
2019 Proof in gold *FDC* (Issued: 424) £2500

QBCGB6   QBCGB7   QBCGB8

QBCGB6   **One hundred pounds.** (1 oz of fine gold.) Yale of Beaufort. R. A depiction of the Yale of Beaufort supporting a shield portraying a portcullis surmounted by a royal crown with the inscription '2019 YALE OF BEAUFORT'.
2019 Proof in gold *FDC* (Issued: 431) £2500

QBCGB7   **One hundred pounds.** (1 oz of fine gold.) The White Lion of Mortimer. R. A depiction of the White Lion of Mortimer supporting a shield portraying a white rose en soleil with the inscription '2020 WHITE LION OF MORTIMER'
2020 Proof in gold *FDC* (Edition: 445).. £2500

QBCGB8   **One hundred pounds.** (1 oz of fine gold.) White Horse of Hanover. R. A rearing white horse above shield with royal arms of George I and inscription '2020 WHITE HORSE OF HANOVER'.
2020 Proof in gold *FDC* (Edition: 435).. £2500

QBCGB9   QBCGB10   QBCGB11

QBCGB9   **One hundred pounds.** (1 oz of fine gold.) White Greyhound of Richmond. R. A reimagined greyhound conveying its strength and power above royal arms of Henry VII and inscription '2021 WHITE GREYHOUND OF RICHMOND'.
2021 Proof in gold *FDC* (Edition: 425).. £2500

QBCGB10 **One hundred pounds.** (1 oz of fine gold.) The Griffin of Edward III. R. A depiction of a griffin with the heraldic badge of the Royal House of Windsor accompanied by the inscription '2021 GRIFFIN OF EDWARD III'
2021 Proof in gold *FDC* (Edition: 500).. £2500

QBCGB11 **One hundred pounds.** (1 oz of fine gold). The completer coin. R. A depiction of ten heraldic beasts encircling a portrait of Queen Elizabeth II with the inscription 'THE QUEEN'S BEASTS' and the date of the year.
2021 Proof in gold *FDC* (Edition: 690).. £2500

For coin specifications please see the tables at the beginning of the Britannia section.

TWO HUNDRED POUNDS

QBCGC1 **Two hundred pounds.** (2 oz of fine gold.) The completer coin. ℞. As QBCGB11.
2021 Proof in gold FDC (Edition: 100) £6000

FIVE HUNDRED POUNDS

QBCGD1 **Five hundred pounds.** (5 oz of fine gold.) The Lion of England. ℞. As QBCGB1.
2017 Proof in gold *FDC* (Issued: 100) £12000
QBCGD2 **Five hundred pounds.** (5 oz of fine gold.) The Unicorn of Scotland.
℞. As QBCGB2.
2017 Proof in gold *FDC* (Issued: 75) £12000
QBCGD3 **Five hundred pounds.** (5 oz of fine gold.) The Red Dragon of Wales.
℞. As QBCGB3.
2018 Proof in gold *FDC* (Issued: 90) £12000
QBCGD4 **Five hundred pounds.** (5 oz of fine gold.) The Black Bull of Clarence.
℞. As QBCGB4.
2018 Proof in gold *FDC* (Issued: 70) £12000
QBCGD5 **Five hundred pounds.** (5 oz of fine gold.) The Falcon of the Plantagenets.
℞. As QBCGB5.
2019 Proof in gold *FDC* (Issued: 71) £12000
QBCGD6 **Five hundred pounds.** (5 oz of fine gold.) Yale of Beaufort. ℞. As QBCGB6.
2019 Proof in gold *FDC* (Issued: 60) £12000
QBCGD7 **Five hundred pounds.** (5 oz of fine gold.) White Lion of Mortimer.
℞. As QBCGB7.
2020 Proof in gold *FDC* (Edition: 70) £12000
QBCGD8 **Five hundred pounds.** (5 oz of fine gold.) White Horse of Hanover.
℞. As QBCGB8.
2020 Proof in gold *FDC* (Edition: 65) £12000
QBCGD9 **Five hundred pounds.** (5 oz of fine gold.) White Greyhound of Richmond.
℞. As QBCGB9.
2021 Proof in gold *FDC* (Edition: 69) £12000
QBCGD10 **Five hundred pounds.** (5 oz of fine gold.) The Griffin of Edward III.
℞. As QBCGB10.
2021 Proof in gold *FDC* (Edition: 129) £11000
QBCGD11 **Five hundred pounds.** (5 oz of fine gold.) The completer coin. ℞. As QBCGB11.
2021 Proof in gold *FDC* (Edition: 150) £14000
—   Proof piedfort in gold *FDC* (Edition: 30) £24000

ONE THOUSAND POUNDS

QBCGE1 **One thousand pounds.** (1 kilo of fine gold.) The Lion of England.
℞. As QBCGB1.
2017 Proof in gold *FDC* (Issued: 13) £70000
QBCGE2 **One thousand pounds.** (1 kilo of fine gold.) The Unicorn of Scotland.
℞. As QBCGB2.
2017 Proof in gold *FDC* (Issued: 8) £70000
QBCGE3 **One thousand pounds.** (1 kilo of fine gold.) The Red Dragon of Wales.
℞. As QBCGB3.
2018 Proof in gold *FDC* (Issued: 13) £70000

For coin specifications please see the tables at the beginning of the Britannia section.

QBCGE4 **One thousand pounds.** (1 kilo of fine gold.) The Black Bull of Clarence.
R. As QBCGB4.
2018 Proof in gold *FDC* (Issued: 9) £70000
QBCGE5 **One thousand pounds.** (1 kilo of fine gold.) The Falcon of the Plantagenets.
R. As QBCGB5.
2019 Proof in gold *FDC* (Issued: 9) £70000
QBCGE6 **One thousand pounds.** (1 kilo of fine gold.) Yale of Beaufort. R As QBCGB6.
2019 Proof in gold *FDC* (Issued: 6) £70000
QBCGE7 **One thousand pounds.** (1 kilo of fine gold.) White Lion of Mortimer.
R As QBCGB7.
2020 Proof in gold *FDC* (Edition: 10) £70000
QBCGE8 **One thousand pounds.** (1 kilo of fine gold.) White Horse of Hanover.
R. As QBCGB8.
2020 Proof in gold *FDC* (Edition: 13) £70000
QBCGE9 **One thousand pounds.** (1kilo of fine gold.) White Greyhound of Richmond.
R. As QBCGB9.
2021 Proof in gold *FDC* (Edition: 10) £70000
QBCGE10 **One thousand pounds.** (1 kilo of fine gold.) The Griffin of Edward III.
R. As QBCGB10.
2021 Proof in gold *FDC* (Edition: 13) £70000
QBCGE11 **One thousand pounds.** (1 kilo of fine gold.) The completer coin.
R. As QBCGB11.
2021 Proof in gold *FDC* (Edition: 17) £70000

TWO THOUSAND POUNDS

QBCGF1 **Two thousand pounds.** (2 kilos of fine gold.) The completer coin.
R. As QBCGB11.
2021 Proof in gold *FDC* (Edition: 4) £160000

FIVE THOUSAND POUNDS

QBCGG1 **Five thousand pounds.** (5 kilos of fine gold.) The completer coin. R. As
QBCGB11.
2021 Proof in gold *FDC* (Edition:) £400000

TEN THOUSAND POUNDS

QBCGH1 **Ten thousand pounds.** (10 kilos of fine gold.) The completer coin. R. As
QBCGB11.
2021 Proof in gold *FDC* (Edition: 1) £750000

Queen's Beasts Gold Proof Sets

QBCGS1–**2021**   £25 (QBCGA1-10) reverse frosted (Edition: 250) ....(10) £6500

For coin specifications please see the tables at the beginning of the Britannia section.

BULLION ISSUES

Reverse and obverse design by Jody Clark

SILVER

FIVE POUNDS

QBBSA1

QBBSA1 **Five pounds.** (2 oz of fine silver.) The Lion of England. ℞. A lion accompanied
by a shield depicting Our Royal Arms with the inscription 'LION OF ENGLAND
2 OZ FINE SILVER 999.9 2016'.
2016 Unc..£65

QBBSA2   QBBSA3

QBBSA2 **Five pounds.** (2 oz of fine silver.) The Red Dragon of Wales. ℞. A depiction
of a rearing dragon accompanied by the Coat of Arms of Llywelyn the Great
with the inscription 'RED DRAGON OF WALES 2 OZ OF FINE SILVER
999.9 2017'.
2017 Unc..£65

QBBSA3 **Five pounds.** (2 oz of fine silver.) The Griffin of Edward III. ℞. A griffin
accompanied by a shield depicting the badge of the House of Windsor with the
inscription 'GRIFFIN OF EDWARD III 2 OZ FINE SILVER 999.9 2017'.
2017 Unc..£65

For coin specifications please see the tables at the beginning of the Britannia section.

QBBSA4   QBBSA5

QBBSA4 **Five pounds.** (2 oz of fine silver.) The Unicorn of Scotland. ℞. A depiction of a
rearing unicorn accompanied by a shield depicting a lion rampant with the
inscription 'UNICORN OF SCOTLAND 2 OZ FINE SILVER 999.9 2018'.
2018 Unc... £65

QBBSA5 **Five pounds.** (2 oz of fine silver.) Black Bull of Clarence. ℞. A depiction of the
Black Bull of Clarence supporting the arms used by Edward IV and Richard III
with the inscription 'BLACK BULL OF CLARENCE 2 OZ FINE SILVER 999.9 2018'.
2018 Unc... £65

QBBSA6   QBBSA7

QBBSA6 **Five pounds.** (2 oz of fine silver.) Falcon of the Plantagenets. ℞. A depiction of
the Falcon of the Plantagenets above the personal badge of Edward IV and the
inscription 'FALCON OF THE PLANTAGENETS 2 OZ FINE SILVER 999.9 2019'.
2019 Unc... £65

QBBSA7 **Five pounds.** (2 oz of fine silver.) Yale of Beaufort. ℞. A depiction of the Yale of
Beaufort supporting a shield portraying a portcullis surmounted by a royal crown
with the inscription 'YALE OF BEAUFORT 2 OZ FINE SILVER 999.9 2019'.
2019 Unc... £65

For coin specifications please see the tables at the beginning of the Britannia section.

QBBSA8   QBBSA9

QBBSA8   Five pounds. (2 oz of fine silver.) White Lion of Mortimer. ℞. A depiction of the
White Lion of Mortimer supporting a shield portraying a white rose en soleil with
the inscription 'WHITE LION OF MORTIMER 2OZ FINE SILVER 999.9 2020'.
2020 Unc.. £ 65

QBBSA9   Five pounds. (2 oz of fine silver.) White Horse of Hanover. ℞. A rearing white
horse above shield with royal arms of George I and the inscription 'WHITE
HORSE OF HANOVER 2 OZ FINE SILVER 999.9 2020'.
2020 Unc.. £65

QBBSA10

QBBSA10 Five pounds. (2 oz of fine silver.) White Greyhound of Richmond. ℞. A reimagined
greyhound conveying its strength and power above shield depicting the symbol of
the Tudor family and inscription 'WHITE GREYHOUND OF RICHMOND 2 OZ
FINE SILVER 999.9 2021'.
2021 Unc.. £65

QBBSA11 Five pounds. (2 oz of fine silver.) The completer coin. ℞. A depiction of ten
heraldic beasts encircling a portrait of Queen Elizabeth II with the inscription
'THE QUEEN'S BEASTS 2OZ FINE SILVER 999.9 2021'
2021 Unc.. £65

TEN POUNDS

QBBSB1   Ten pounds. (10 oz of fine silver.) The Lion of England. ℞. As QBBSA1 but with
inscription 'LION OF ENGLAND 10 OZ FINE SILVER 999.9 2017'.
2017 Unc...£320

QBBSB2   Ten pounds. (10 oz of fine silver.) The Griffin of Edward III. ℞. As QBBSA3 but
with inscription 'GRIFFIN OF EDWARD III 10 OZ FINE SILVER 2018'.
2018 Unc...£320

QBBSB3   **Ten pounds.** (10 oz of fine silver.) The Red Dragon of Wales. ℞. As QBBSA2 but with inscription 'RED DRAGON OF WALES 10 OZ FINE SILVER 999.9 2018' 2018 Unc..£320

QBBSB4   **Ten pounds.** (10 oz of fine silver.) Black Bull of Clarence. ℞. As QBBSA5 but with inscription 'BLACK BULL OF CLARENCE 10 OZ FINE SILVER 999.9 2019' 2019 Unc..£320

QBBSB5   **Ten pounds.** (10 oz of fine silver.) The Unicorn of Scotland. ℞. As QBBSA4 but with inscription 'UNICORN OF SCOTLAND 10 OZ FINE SILVER 999.9 2019' 2019 Unc..£320

QBBSB6   **Ten pounds.** (10 oz of fine silver.) Falcon of the Plantagenets. ℞. As QBBSA6 but with inscription 'FALCON OF THE PLANTAGENETS 10 OZ FINE SILVER 999.9 2020'. 2020 Unc..£320

QBBSB7   **Ten pounds.** (10 oz of fine silver.) Yale of Beaufort. ℞. As QBBSA7 but with inscription 'YALE OF BEAUFORT 10 OZ FINE SILVER 999.9 2020'. 2020 Unc..£320

QBBSB8   **Ten pounds.** (10 oz of fine silver.) The White Lion of Mortimer. ℞. As QBBSA8 but with inscription 'WHITE LION OF MORTIMER 10 OZ FINE SILVER 999.9 2021' 2021 Unc..£320

QBBSB9   **Ten pounds.** (10 oz of fine silver.) The White Horse of Hanover. ℞. As QBBSA9 but with inscription 'WHITE HORSE OF HANOVER 10 OZ FINE SILVER 999.9 2021' 2021 Unc..£320

QBBSB10   **Ten pounds.** (10 oz of fine silver.) The White Greyhound of Richmond. ℞. As QBBSA10 but with inscription 'WHITE GREYHOUND OF RICHMOND 10 OZ FINE SILVER 999.9 2022' 2022 Unc..£320

QBBSB11   **Ten pounds.** (10 oz of fine silver.)The completer coin. ℞. As QBBSA11 but with the inscription 'THE QUEEN'S BEASTS 10OZ FINE SILVER 999.9 2022'. 2022 Unc..£320

FIVE HUNDRED POUNDS

QBBSC1   **Five hundred pounds.** (1 kilo of fine silver). The completer coin. ℞. As QBBSA11 but with the inscription 'THE QUEEN'S BEASTS 1 KILO FINE SILVER 999.9 2021'. 2021 Unc..£ 750

GOLD

TEN POUNDS

QBBGA1   **Ten pounds.** (1/10th oz of fine gold.) ℞. As QBBGC2 but with the inscription 'RED DRAGON OF WALES 1/10 OZ OF FINE GOLD 999.9 2017'. 2017 Unc..£200

QBBGA2   **Ten pounds.** (1/10th oz of fine gold).℞. As QBBGC3 but with the inscription 'GRIFFIN OF EDWARD III 1/10th OZ FINE GOLD 999.9 2017'. 2017 Unc..£200

For coin specifications please see the tables at the beginning of the Britannia section.

TWENTY FIVE POUNDS

QBBGB1 **Twenty five pounds.** (1/4 oz of fine gold.) The Lion of England. R. As QBBGC1
but with the inscription 'LION OF ENGLAND 1/4 OZ FINE GOLD 999.9 2016'.
2016 Unc £500

QBBGB2 **Twenty five pounds.** (1/4 oz of fine gold.) The Red Dragon of Wales.
R. As QBBGC2 but with inscription 'RED DRAGON OF WALES 1/4OZ FINE
GOLD 999.9 2017'.
2017 Unc £500

QBBGB3 **Twenty five pounds.** (1/4 oz of fine gold) The Griffin of Edward III.
R. As QBBGC3 but with inscription 'GRIFFIN OF EDWARD III 1/4OZ FINE
GOLD 999.9 2017'.
2017 Unc £500

QBBGB4 **Twenty five pounds.** (1/4 oz of fine gold.) The Unicorn of Scotland.
R. As QBBGC4 but with inscription 'UNICORN OF SCOTLAND 1/4OZ FINE
GOLD 999.9 2018'.
2018 Unc £500

QBBGB5 **Twenty five pounds.** (1/4 oz of fine gold.) Black Bull of Clarence.
R. As QBBGC5 but with inscription 'BLACK BULL OF CLARENCE 1/4OZ FINE
GOLD 999.9 2018'.
2018 Unc £500

QBBGB6 **Twenty five pounds.** (1/4 oz of fine gold.) Yale of Beaufort.
R. As QBBGC6 but with inscription 'YALE OF BEAUFORT 1/4OZ FINE GOLD
999.9 2019'.
2019 Unc £500

QBBGB7 **Twenty five pounds.** (1/4 oz of fine gold.) The Falcon of the Plantagenets.
R. As QBBGC7 but with inscription 'FALCON OF THE PLANTAGENETS 1/4OZ
FINE GOLD 999.9 2019'.
2019 Unc £500

QBBGB8 **Twenty five pounds.** (1/4 oz of fine gold.) White Lion of Mortimer.
R. As QBBGC8 but with inscription 'WHITE LION OF MORTIMER 1/4OZ
FINE GOLD 999.9 2020'.
2020 Unc £500

QBBGB9 **Twenty five pounds.** (1/4 oz of fine gold.) White Horse of Hanover.
R. As QBBGC9 but with inscription 'WHITE HORSE OF HANOVER 1/4OZ
FINE GOLD 999.9 2020'.
2020 Unc £500

QBBGB10 **Twenty five pounds.** (1/4 oz of fine gold.) White Greyhound of Richmond.
R. As QBBGC10 but with inscription 'WHITE GREYHOUND OF RICHMOND
1/4OZ FINE GOLD 999.9 2021'.
2021 Unc £500

ONE HUNDRED POUNDS

QBBGC1   QBBGC2

QBBGC1   **One hundred pounds.** (1 oz of fine gold.) The Lion of England. R. A lion
accompanied by a shield depicting Our Royal Arms with the inscription 'LION OF
ENGLAND 1 OZ FINE GOLD 999.9 2016'.
2016 Unc £1800

QBBGC2 One hundred pounds. (1 oz of fine gold.) The Red Dragon of Wales. R. A depiction
of a rearing dragon accompanied by the Coat of Arms of Llywelyn the Great with
the inscription 'RED DRAGON OF WALES 1 OZ OF FINE GOLD 999.9 2017'.
2017 Unc £1800

QBBGC3   QBBGC4   QBBGC5

QBBGC3 One hundred pounds. (1 oz of fine gold.) The Griffin of Edward III. R. A griffin
accompanied by a shield depicting the badge of the House of Windsor with the
inscription 'GRIFFIN OF EDWARD III 1 OZ FINE GOLD 999.9 2017'.
2017 Unc £1800

QBBGC4   **One hundred pounds.** (1 oz of fine gold.) The Unicorn of Scotland. R. A rearing
unicorn accompanied by a shield depicting a lion rampant with the inscription
'UNICORN OF SCOTLAND 1 OZ FINE GOLD 999.9 2018'.
2018 Unc £1800

QBBGC5   **One hundred pounds.** (1 oz of fine gold.) Black Bull of Clarence. R. A depiction
of the Black Bull of Clarence supporting the arms used by Edward IV and Richard
III with the inscription 'BLACK BULL OF CLARENCE 1 OZ FINE GOLD
999.9 2018'.
2018 Unc £1800

For coin specifications please see the tables at the beginning of the Britannia section.

QBBGC6   QBBGC7

QBBGC6   **One hundred pounds.** (1 oz of fine gold.) Yale of Beaufort. ℞. A depiction of the Yale of Beaufort supporting a shield portraying a portcullis surmounted by a royal crown with the inscription 'YALE OF BEAUFORT 1 OZ FINE GOLD 999.9 2019'. 2019 Unc £1800

QBBGC7   **One hundred pounds.** (1 oz of fine gold.) Falcon of the Plantagenets. ℞. A depiction of the Falcon of the Plantagenets above the personal badge of Edward IV with the inscription 'FALCON OF THE PLANTAGENETS 1 OZ FINE GOLD 999.9 2019'. 2019 Unc £1800

QBBGC8   QBBGC9

QBBGC8   **One hundred pounds.** (1 oz of fine gold.) White Lion of Mortimer. ℞. A depiction of the White Lion of Mortimer supporting a shield portraying a white rose en soleil with the inscription 'WHITE LION OF MORTIMER 1 OZ FINE GOLD 999.9 2020'. 2020 Unc £1800

QBBGC9   **One hundred pounds.** (1 oz of fine gold.) White Horse of Hanover. ℞. A rearing white horse above shield with royal arms of George I and the inscription 'WHITE HORSE OF HANOVER 1 OZ FINE GOLD 999.9 2020'. 2020 Unc £1800

QBBGC10

QBBGC10 **One hundred pounds.** (1 oz of fine gold.) White Greyhound of Richmond. ℞. A reimagined greyhound conveying its strength and power above shield depicting the symbol of the Tudor family and inscription 'WHITE GREYHOUND OF RICHMOND 1 OZ FINE GOLD 999.9 2021'. 2021 Unc £1800

QBBGC11

QBBGC11 One hundred pounds. (1 oz of fine gold.) The completer coin. ℞. A depiction of
ten heraldic beasts encircling a portrait of Queen Elizabeth II with the inscription
'THE QUEEN'S BEASTS 1OZ FINE GOLD 999.9 2021'.
2021 Unc £1800

PLATINUM

ONE HUNDRED POUNDS

QBBPA1 One hundred pounds. (1 oz of fine platinum.) The Lion of England. ℞. As
QBBGC1 but with inscription 'LION OF ENGLAND 1OZ FINE PLATINUM
999.5 2017'.
2017 Unc £1000
QBBPA2 One hundred pounds. (1 oz of fine platinum.) The Griffin of Edward III.
℞. As QBBGC3 but with inscription 'GRIFFIN OF EDWARD III 1OZ FINE
PLATINUM 999.5 2018'.
2018 Unc £1000
QBBPA3 One hundred pounds. (1 oz of fine platinum.) The Red Dragon of Wales.
℞. As QBBGC2 but with inscription 'RED DRAGON OF WALES 1OZ FINE
PLATINUM 999.5 2018'.
2018 Unc £1000
QBBPA4 One hundred pounds. (1 oz of fine platinum.) The Unicorn of Scotland.
℞. As QBBGC4 but with inscription 'UNICORN OF SCOTLAND 1OZ FINE
PLATINUM 999.5 2019'.
2019 Unc £1000

QBBPA5

QBBPA5 One hundred pounds. (1 oz of fine platinum.) Black Bull of Clarence.
℞. As above with inscription 'BLACK BULL OF CLARENCE 1OZ FINE
PLATINUM 999.5 2019'.
2019 Unc £1000

For coin specifications please see the tables at the beginning of the Britannia section.

QBBPA6 **One hundred pounds.** (1 oz of fine platinum.) Falcon of the Plantagenets.
R. As QBBGC7 but with inscription 'FALCON OF THE PLANTAGENETS
1OZ FINE PLATINUM 999.5 2020'.
2020 Unc £1000

QBBPA7 **One hundred pounds.** (1 oz of fine platinum.) Yale of Beaufort.
R. As QBBGC6 but with inscription 'YALE OF BEAUFORT 1OZ FINE
PLATINUM 999.5 2020'.
2020 Unc £1000

QBBPA8 **One hundred pounds.** (1 oz of fine platinum.) White Lion of Mortimer.
R. As QBBGC8 with inscription 'WHITE LION OF MORTIMER 1 OZ FINE
PLATINUM 999.9 2020'.
2020 Unc £1000

QBBPA9 One hundred pounds. (1 oz of fine platinum.) White Horse of Hanover.
R. As QBBGC9 but with inscription 'WHITE HORSE OF HANOVER 1OZ
FINE PLATINUM 999.5 2021'.
2021 Unc £1000

QBBPA10 One hundred pounds. (1 oz of fine platinum.) White Greyhound of Richmond.
R. As QBBGC10 but with inscription 'WHITE GREYHOUND OF RICHMOND
1OZ FINE PLATINUM 999.5 2022'.
2022 Unc £1000

QBBPA11 One hundred pounds. (1 oz of fine platinum). The completer coin.
R. As QBBGC11 but with the inscription 'THE QUEEN'S BEASTS 1 OZ FINE
PLATINUM 999.5 2022'.
2022 Unc £1000

For coin specifications please see the tables at the beginning of the Britannia section.

This second series of Royal Beasts depicts the ten stone Royal Beasts that flank the Moat Bridge at Hampton Court Palace, the home of England's Tudor monarchs. The first coin features the panther which Henry VIII gave to Jane Seymour as a celebration of their marriage.

Obverse portrait by Jody Clark; Reverse designs by David Lawrence.

COLLECTOR SERIES

The £5 cupro-nickel crowns previously listed here are now listed withing the Crown Size Commemoratives section

SILVER

TWO POUNDS

TBCSA1

TBCSA1   **Two pounds.** (1 oz of fine silver.) Seymour Panther. R. A depiction of the Seymour Panther statue with Duke of Beaufort's coat of arms with inscription 'SEYMOUR PANTHER 2022' and with edge inscription 'HAMPTON COURT PALACE ROYAL TUDOR BEASTS'.
2022 Proof in silver *FDC* (Edition: 7,010) £95
—   Proof in silver *FDC* with reversed frosting (Edition: 1,000)* £110

TBCSA2

TBCSA2   **Two pounds.** (1 oz of fine silver.) Lion of England. R. A depiction of the Lion of England statue with impaled Coat of Arms of Henry VIII and Jane Seymour with inscription 'LION OF ENGLAND 2022' and with edge inscription 'HAMPTON COURT PALACE ROYAL TUDOR BEASTS'.
2022 Proof in silver *FDC* (Edition: 7,010) £95
—   Proof in silver *FDC* with reversed frosting (Edition: 1,000)* £110

For coin specifications please see the tables at the beginning of the Britannia section.

TBCSA3

TBCSA3 **Two pounds.** (1 oz of fine silver.) Yale of Beaufort. ℞. A depiction of the
Yale of Beaufort with inscription 'YALE OF BEAUFORT 2023' and with edge
inscription 'HAMPTON COURT PALACE ROYAL TUDOR BEASTS'.
2023 Proof in silver *FDC* (Edition: 5.510) £95
—   Proof in silver *FDC* with reversed frosting (Edition: 500)* £110

FIVE POUNDS

TBCSB1 **Five pounds.** (2 oz of fine silver.) Seymour Panther. ℞. As TBCSA1 but with
milled edge.
2022 Proof in silver *FDC* (Edition: 2,006) £185
TBCSB2 **Five pounds.** (2 oz of fine silver.) Lion of England. ℞. As TBCSA2 but with
milled edge.
2022 Proof in silver *FDC* (Edition: 2,006) £185
TBCSB3 **Five pounds.** (2 oz of fine silver.) Yale of Beaufort. ℞. As TBCSA3 but with
milled edge.
2023 Proof in silver *FDC* (Edition: 1.256) £185

TEN POUNDS

TBCSC1 **Ten pounds.** (5oz of fine silver.) Seymour Panther. ℞. As TBCSA1 but with
milled edge.
2022 Proof in silver *FDC* (Edition: 306) £465
—   Proof piedfort in silver *FDC* (Edition: 156)... £885
TBCSC2 **Ten pounds.** (5oz of fine silver.) Lion of England. ℞. As TBCSA2 but with
milled edge.
2022 Proof in silver *FDC* (Edition: 306) £465
—   Proof piedfort in silver *FDC* (Edition: 156)... £885
TBCSC3 **Ten pounds.** (5oz of fine silver.) Yale of Beaufort. ℞. As TBCSA3 but with
milled edge.
2023 Proof in silver *FDC* (Edition: 306) £465
—   Proof piedfort in silver *FDC* (Edition: 106)... £885

For coin specifications please see the tables at the beginning of the Britannia section.

FIVE HUNDRED POUNDS

TBCSD1 **Five hundred pounds.** (1 kilo of fine silver.) Seymour Panther. R. As TBCSA1
but with milled edge.
2022 Proof in silver *FDC* (Edition: 72) £2330

TBCSD2 **Five hundred pounds.** (1 kilo of fine silver.) Lion of England. R. As TBCSA2
but with milled edge.
2022 Proof in silver *FDC* (Edition: 72) £2330

TBCSD3 **Five hundred pounds.** (1 kilo of fine silver.) Yale of Beaufort. R. As TBCSA3
but with milled edge.
2023 Proof in silver *FDC* (Edition: 72) £2330

ONE THOUSAND POUNDS

TBCSE1 **One thousand pounds.** (2 kilos of fine silver.) Seymour Panther. R. As TBCSA1
but with milled edge.
2022 Proof in silver *FDC* (Edition: 56) £4995

TBCSE2 **One thousand pounds.** (2 kilos of fine silver.) Lion of England. R. As TBCSA2
but with milled edge.
2022 Proof in silver *FDC* (Edition: 56) £4995

Royal Tudor Beasts Silver Proof Sets

TBCSS1–**2022**   £2 – Seymour Panther set of two with one reversed frosted
(Edition: 1,000) ....(2)   £210

TBCSS2–**2022**   £2 – Lion of England set of two with one reversed frosted
(Edition: 1,000) ....(2)   £210

TBCSS3–**2023**   £2 – Yale of Beaufort set of two with one reversed frosted
(Edition: 500) ....(2)   £210

GOLD

TWENTY FIVE POUNDS

TBCGA1 **Twenty five pounds.** (1/4oz fine gold.) Seymour Panther. R. As TBCGB1.
2022 Proof in gold *FDC* (Edition: 1,010)..£700

TBCGA2 **Twenty five pounds.** (1/4oz fine gold.) Lion of England. R. As TBCGB2.
2022 Proof in gold *FDC* (Edition: 1,010)..£700

TBCGA3 **Twenty five pounds.** (1/4oz fine gold.) Yale of Beaufort. R. As TBCGB3.
2023 Proof in gold *FDC* (Edition: 760)..£700

For coin specifications please see the tables at the beginning of the Britannia section.

ONE HUNDRED POUNDS

TBCGB1   TBCGB2   TBCGB3

TBCGB1 One hundred pounds. (1oz fine gold.) Seymour Panther. ℞. A depiction of the
Seymour Panther statue with Duke of Beaufort's coat of arms with inscription
'SEYMOUR PANTHER 2022'.
2022 Proof in gold *FDC* (Edition: 560) £2600

TBCGB2 One hundred pounds. (1oz fine gold.) Lion of England. ℞. A depiction of the
Lion of England statue with impaled Coat of Arms of Henry VIII and
Jane Seymour with inscription 'LION OF ENGLAND 2022'.
2022 Proof in gold *FDC* (Edition: 410) £2600

TBCGB3 One hundred pounds. (1oz fine gold.) Yale of Beaufort. ℞. A depiction of the
Yale of Beaufort with inscription 'YALE OF BEAUFORT 2023'.
2023 Proof in gold *FDC* (Edition: 410) £2600

TWO HUNDRED POUNDS

TBCGC1 Two hundred pounds. (2oz fine gold.) Seymour Panther. ℞. As TBCGB1.
2022 Proof in gold *FDC* (Edition: 356) £5000

TBCGC2 Two hundred pounds. (2oz fine gold.) Lion of England. ℞. As TBCGB2.
2022 Proof in gold *FDC* (Edition: 181) £5000

TBCGC3 Two hundred pounds. (2oz fine gold.) Yale of Beaufort. ℞. As TBCGB3.
2023 Proof in gold *FDC* (Edition: 106) £5000

FIVE HUNDRED POUNDS

TBCGD1   **Five hundred pounds.** (5oz fine gold.) Seymour Panther. ℞. As TBCGB1.
2022 Proof in gold *FDC* (Edition: 131) £12000

TBCGD1A Five hundred pounds. (10oz fine gold.) Seymour Panther. ℞. As TBCGB1.
2022 Proof in gold *FDC* (Edition: 31) £23000

TBCGD2   **Five hundred pounds.** (5oz fine gold.) Lion of England. ℞. As TBCGB2.
2022 Proof in gold *FDC* (Edition: 76) £12000

TBCGD2A Five hundred pounds. (10oz fine gold.) Lion of England. ℞. As TBCGB2.
2022 Proof in gold *FDC* (Edition: 11) £23000

*The above 10oz coins were described in the legislation as Piedforts but as they have a diameter
of 65mm they cannot be regarded as piedforts of the £500 50mm 5oz versions.*

TBCGD3   **Five hundred pounds.** (5oz fine gold.) Yale of Beaufort. ℞. As TBCGB3.
2023 Proof in gold *FDC* (Edition: 56) £12000

For coin specifications please see the tables at the beginning of the Britannia section.

ONE THOUSAND POUNDS

TBCGF1 One thousand pounds. (1 kilo fine gold.) Seymour Panther. ℞. As TBCGB1.
2022 Proof in gold *FDC* (Edition: 14) £70000
TBCGF2 One thousand pounds. (1 kilo fine gold.) Lion of England. ℞. As TBCGB2.
2022 Proof in gold *FDC* (Edition: 5) £70000

TWO THOUSAND POUNDS

TBCGG1 Two thousand pounds. (2 kilos fine gold.) Seymour Panther. ℞. As TBCGB1.
2022 Proof in gold *FDC* (Edition: 5) £150000
TBCGG2 Two thousand pounds. (2 kilos fine gold.) Lion of England. ℞. As TBCGB2.
2022 Proof in gold *FDC* (Edition: 2) £150000
TBCGG3 Two thousand pounds. (2 kilos fine gold.) Yale of Beaufort. ℞. As TBCGB3.
2023 Proof in gold *FDC* (Edition: 2) £150000

BULLION ISSUES

SILVER

FIVE POUNDS

TBBSA1   TBBSA2

TBBSA1 Five pounds. (2 oz of fine silver.) Lion of England. ℞. A depiction of the
Lion of England statue with impaled Coat of Arms of Henry VIII and Jane Seymour
with inscription 'LION OF ENGLAND 2OZ FINE SILVER 999.9 2022'.
2022 Unc £65
TBBSA2 Five pounds. (2 oz of fine silver.) Yale of Beaufort. ℞. A depiction of the
Yale of Beaufort with inscription 'YALE OF BEAUFORT 2OZ FINE SILVER
999.9 2023'.
2023 Unc £65

TEN POUNDS

TBBSB1 Ten pounds. (10oz of fine silver.) Lion of England. ℞. As TBBSA1 but with
inscription 'LION OF ENGLAND 10OZ FINE SILVER 999.9 2022'.
2022 Unc £275
TBBSB2 Ten pounds. (10oz of fine silver.) Yale of Beaufort. ℞. As TBBSA3 but with
inscription 'YALE OF BEAUFORT 10OZ FINE SILVER 999.9 2023'.
2023 Unc £275

For coin specifications please see the tables at the beginning of the Britannia section.

GOLD

TWENTY FIVE POUNDS

TBBGA1 Twenty five pounds. (1/4oz fine gold.) Lion of England. R̷. As TBBGB1 but
with inscription 'LION OF ENGLAND 1/4OZ FINE GOLD 999.9 2022'.
2022 Unc £500
TBBGA2 Twenty five pounds. (1/4oz fine gold.) Yale of Beaufort. R̷. As TBBGB3 but
with inscription 'YALE OF BEAUFORT 1/4OZ FINE GOLD 999.9 2023'.
2023 Unc £500

ONE HUNDRED POUNDS

TBBGB1   TBBGB2

TBBGB1 One hundred pounds. (1oz fine gold.) Lion of England. R̷. A depiction of the
Lion of England statue with impaled Coat of Arms of Henry VIII and
Jane Seymour with inscription 'LION OF ENGLAND 1OZ FINE GOLD 999.9
2022'.
2022 Unc £1800
TBBGB2 One hundred pounds. (1oz fine gold.) Yale of Beaufort. R̷. A depiction of the
Yale of Beaufort with inscription 'YALE OF BEAUFORT 1OZ FINE GOLD
999.9 2023'.
2023 Unc £1800

PLATINUM

ONE HUNDRED POUNDS

TBBPA1 One hundred pounds. (1oz fine platinum.) Lion of England. R̷. As TBBGB1 but
with inscription 'LION OF ENGLAND 1OZ FINE PLATINUM 999.5 2022'.
2022 Unc £1000
TBBPA2 One hundred pounds. (1oz fine platinum.) Yale of Beaufort. R̷. As TBBGB3 but
with inscription 'YALE OF BEAUFORT 1OZ FINE PLATINUM 999.5 2023'
2023 Unc £1000

For later coins in this series please see the Charles III section.

For coin specifications please see the tables at the beginning of the Britannia section.

The Great Engravers series celebrates the finest artists who have worked on British coinage, beginning with William Wyon RA. The first coin in this series depicts Una and the Lion taken from the original 1839 die which casts the young Queen Victoria in the role of Una from the poem 'The Fairie Queen' while the lion she guides represents the people of Britain.

Obverse portrait by Jody Clark.

UNA AND THE LION
SILVER

GE1

GE1 **Five pounds.** (2 oz of fine silver.) Great Engravers I – Una and the Lion. ℞. William Wyon's Una & the Lion from 1839 with the inscription 'DIRIGE DEUS GRESSUS MEOS.' (May God Direct My Steps), the date 2019 in Roman numerals 'MMXIX' and 'W. WYON R.A.'.
2019 Proof in silver *FDC* (Issued: 3,000)... £2500

GE2 **One thousand pounds.** (2 kilos of fine silver.) Great Engravers I – Una and the Lion. ℞. As GE1.
2019 Proof in silver *FDC* (Issued: 39)... £15000

GOLD

GE3

GE3 **Two hundred pounds.** (2 oz of fine gold.) Great Engravers I – Una and the Lion. ℞. William Wyon's Una & the Lion from 1839 with the inscription 'DIRIGE DEUS GRESSUS MEOS.' (May God Direct My Steps), the date 2019 in Roman numerals 'MMXIX' and 'W. WYON R.A.'.
2019 Proof in gold *FDC* (Issued: 225) £18000

For coin specifications please see the tables at the beginning of the Britannia section.

GE4   **Five hundred pounds.** (5 oz of fine gold.) Great Engravers I – Una and the Lion.
R. As GE3.
2019 Proof in gold *FDC* (Issued: 65) £28000

GE5   **One thousand pounds.** (1 kilo of fine gold.) Great Engravers I – Una and the
Lion. R. As GE3.
2019 Proof in gold *FDC* (Issued: 12) £130000

GE6   **Two thousand pounds.** (2 kilos of fine gold.) Great Engravers I – Una and the Lion.
R. As GE3.
2019 Proof in gold *FDC* (Issued: 4) £250000

GE7   **Five thousand pounds.** (5 kilos of fine gold.) Great Engravers I – Una and the Lion.
R. As GE3.
2019 Proof in gold *FDC* (Issued: 1) £500000

THE THREE GRACES
SILVER

GE8

GE8   **Five pounds.** (2 oz of fine silver.) Great Engravers II – The Three Graces. R. A
depiction of three female figures representing Britannia, Hibernia and Scotia with the
inscription 'FOEDUS INVIOLABILE'.
2020 Proof in silver *FDC* (Edition: 3,510) £600

GE9   **Ten pounds.** (5 oz of fine silver.) Great Engravers II – The Three Graces. R. As GE8.
2020 Proof in silver *FDC* (Edition: 510) £2500
2021 Proof piedfort in silver *FDC* (Edition: 175) £4000

GE10   **Five hundred pounds.** (1 kilo of fine silver.) Great Engravers II – The Three Graces.
R. As GE8.
2021 Proof in silver *FDC* (Edition: 100) £6000

GE11   **One thousand pounds.** (2 kilos of fine silver.) Great Engravers II – The Three Graces.
R. As GE8.
2020 Proof in silver *FDC* (Edition: 50) £12000

For coin specifications please see the tables at the beginning of the Britannia section.

GOLD

GE12

GE12 **Two hundred pounds.** (2 oz of fine gold.) Great Engravers II – The Three Graces. ℞. A depiction of three female figures representing Britannia, Hibernia and Scotia with the inscription 'FOEDUS INVIOLABILE'.
2020 Proof in gold *FDC* (Edition: 335).. £12000

GE13 **Five hundred pounds.** (5 oz of fine gold.) Great Engravers II – The Three Graces. ℞. As GE12.
2020 Proof in gold *FDC* (Edition: 160).. £25000

GE14 **Five hundred pounds.** (10 oz of fine gold.) Great Engravers II – The Three Graces. ℞. As GE12.
2021 Proof in gold *FDC* (Edition: 50)... £35000

The above coin was described in the legislation as a Piedfort but as it has a diameter of 65mm it cannot be regarded as a piedfort of the £500 50mm 5oz version.

GE15 **One thousand pounds.** (1 kilo of fine gold.) Great Engravers II – The Three Graces. ℞. As GE12.
2020 Proof in gold *FDC* (Edition: 21)...£110000

GE16 **Two thousand pounds.** (2 kilos of fine gold.) Great Engravers II – The Three Graces. ℞. As GE12.
2020 Proof in gold *FDC* (Edition: 9)... £200000

GE17 **Three thousand pounds.** (3 kilos of fine gold.) Great Engravers II – The Three Graces. ℞. As GE12.
2020 Proof in gold *FDC* (Edition: 3)... £300000

GE18 **Five thousand pounds.** (5 kilos of fine gold.) Great Engravers II – The Three Graces. ℞. As GE12.
2020 Proof in gold *FDC* (Edition: 1)... £500000

For coin specifications please see the tables at the beginning of the Britannia section

GOTHIC CROWN REVERSE

SILVER

GE19

GE19 **Five pounds.** (2 oz of fine silver.) Great Engravers III – The Gothic Crown reverse.
R. The crowned shields of England, Scotland and Ireland from the 1847 Gothic
crown accompanied by the inscription 'TUEATUR UNITA DEUS ANNO DOM'
and the date of the year in Roman numerals. (Reverse designer: Thomas Simon.)
2021 Proof in silver *FDC* (Edition: 4006) £500

GE20 **Ten pounds.** (5oz of fine silver.) Great Engravers III – The Gothic Crown reverse.
R. As GE19.
2021 Proof in silver *FDC* (Edition: 506) £1500
—   Proof piedfort in silver *FDC* (Edition: 231) £2500

GE21 **Five hundred pounds.** (1 kilo of fine silver.) Great Engravers III – The Gothic
Crown reverse. R. As GE19.
2021 Proof in silver *FDC* (Edition: 128) £5000

GE22 **One thousand pounds.** (2 kilos of fine silver.) Great Engravers III – The Gothic
Crown reverse. R. As GE19.
2021 Proof in silver *FDC* (Edition: 53) £8000

GOLD

GE23 **Two hundred pounds.** (2 oz of fine gold.) Great Engravers III – The Gothic Crown
reverse. R. The crowned shields of England, Scotland and Ireland from the 1847
Gothic crown accompanied by the inscription 'TUEATUR UNITA DEUS ANNO
DOM' and the date of the year in Roman numerals. (Reverse designer:
Thomas Simon.)
2021 Proof in gold *FDC* (Edition: 411) £8000

GE23A **Two hundred pounds.** (2 oz of fine gold.) R. As GE23 but with plain edge.
2022 Proof in gold *FDC* (Edition: 131)..£10000

GE24 **Five hundred pounds.** (5 oz of fine gold.) Great Engravers III – The Gothic
Crown reverse. R. As GE23.
2021 Proof in gold *FDC* (Edition: 181)..£15000

GE25 **Five hundred pounds.** (10 oz of fine gold.) Great Engravers III – The Gothic
Crown reverse. R. As GE23.
2021 Proof in gold *FDC* (Edition: 56)..£25000

*The above coin was described in the legislation as a Piedfort but as it has a diameter of 65mm
it cannot be regarded as a piedfort of the £500 50mm 5oz version.*

For coin specifications please see the tables at the beginning of the Britannia section

GE26   **One thousand pounds.** (1 kilo of fine gold.) Great Engravers III – The Gothic
           Crown reverse. R. As GE23.
           2021 Proof in gold *FDC* (Edition:22) £85000
GE27   **Two thousand pounds.** (2 kilos of fine gold.) Great Engravers III – The Gothic
           Crown reverse. R. As GE23.
           2021 Proof in gold *FDC* (Edition: 9) £165000
GE28   **Five thousand pounds.** (5 kilos of fine gold.) Great Engravers III – The Gothic
           Crown reverse. R. As GE23.
           2021 Proof in gold *FDC* (Edition: 2) £450000
GE29   **Ten thousand pounds.** (10 kilos of fine gold.) Great Engravers III – The Gothic
           Crown reverse. R. As GE23.
           2021 Proof in gold *FDC* (Edition: 1) £800000

GOTHIC CROWN OBVERSE

SILVER

GE30

GE30   **Five pounds.** (2 oz of fine silver.) Great Engravers III – The Gothic Crown obverse.
           R. Portrait of Queen Victoria from the 1847 Gothic crown with the inscription
           'VICTORIA DEI GRATIA BRITANNIAR : REG : F : D •'. (Reverse designer:
           Thomas Simon.)
           2021 Proof in silver *FDC* (Edition: 4006) £500
GE31   **Ten pounds.** (5oz of fine silver.) Great Engravers III – The Gothic Crown obverse.
           R. As GE30.
           2021 Proof in silver *FDC* (Edition: 506) £1500
  —   Proof piedfort in silver *FDC* (Edition: 231) £2500
GE32   **Five hundred pounds.** (1 kilo of fine silver.) Great Engravers III – The Gothic
           Crown obverse. R. As GE30.
           2021 Proof in silver *FDC* (Edition: 128) £5000
GE33   **One thousand pounds.** (2 kilos of fine silver.) Great Engravers III – The Gothic
           Crown obverse. R. As GE30.
           2021 Proof in silver *FDC* (Edition:53) £8000

For coin specifications please see the tables at the beginning of the Britannia section

GOLD

GE34 **Two hundred pounds.** (2 oz of fine gold.) Great Engravers III – The Gothic Crown obverse. ℞. Portrait of Queen Victoria from the 1847 Gothic crown with the inscription 'VICTORIA DEI GRATIA BRITANNIAR : REG : F : D •'. (Reverse designer: Thomas Simon.)
2021 Proof in gold *FDC* (Edition: 411) £8000

GE34A **Two hundred pounds.** (2 oz of fine gold.) ℞. As GE34 but with plain edge.
2022 Proof in gold *FDC* (Edition: 131) £10000

GE35 **Five hundred pounds.** (5 oz of fine gold.) Great Engravers III – The Gothic Crown obverse. ℞. As GE34.
2021 Proof in gold *FDC* (Edition: 181) £15000

GE36 **Five hundred pounds.** (10 oz of fine gold.) Great Engravers III – The Gothic Crown obverse. ℞. As GE34.
2021 Proof in gold *FDC* (Edition: 56) £25000

The above coin was described in the legislation as a Piedfort but as it has a diameter of 65mm it cannot be regarded as a piedfort of the £500 50mm 5oz version.

GE37 **One thousand pounds.** (1 kilo of fine gold.) Great Engravers III – The Gothic Crown obverse. ℞. As GE34.
2021 Proof in gold *FDC* (Edition: 22) £85000

GE38 **Two thousand pounds.** (2 kilos of fine gold.) Great Engravers III – The Gothic Crown obverse. ℞. As GE34.
2021 Proof in gold *FDC* (Edition: 9) £165000

GE39 **Five thousand pounds.** (5 kilos of fine gold.) Great Engravers III – The Gothic Crown obverse. ℞. As GE34.
2021 Proof in gold *FDC* (Edition: 2) £450000

GE40 **Ten thousand pounds.** (10 kilos of fine gold.) Great Engravers III – The Gothic Crown obverse. ℞. As GE34.
2021 Proof in gold *FDC* (Edition: 1) £800000

For later coins in this series please see the Charles III section.

For coin specifications please see the tables at the beginning of the Britannia section.

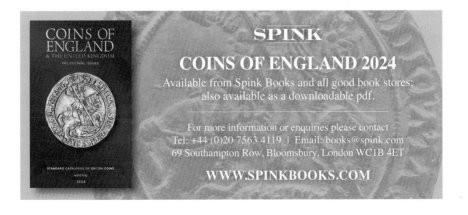

A Music Legends collection celebrating innovation and success of British music was commenced in 2020 with a range of coins celebrating the legacy of one of Britain's most loved bands – Queen. David Bowie, The Who and The Rolling Stones have subsequently been issued.

Obverse portrait by Jody Clark.

QUEEN

QN1 One pound. (1/2 oz of fine silver.) Music Legends I – Queen. ℞. As QN2.
2020 Proof in silver *FDC* (Edition: 20.000) £60

QN2   QN2A

QN2   **Two pounds.** (1 oz of fine silver.) Music Legends I – Queen. ℞. Piano keyboard with opening notes of Bohemian Rhapsody pressed down, the group's logo and singer's signature mic stick in centre and below 'Red Special' guitar, Fender Precision Bass and Ludwig bass drum decorated with the Queen crest. Edge lettering MERCURY • MAY • TAYLOR • DEACON •. (Reverse design: Chris Facey)
2020 Proof in silver *FDC* with colour (Edition: 10.000).......................................£100

QN2A   **Two pounds.** (1 oz of fine silver.) Music Legends I – Queen. ℞. As QN2 with added thin inner rim with repeated inscription '1OZ FINE SILVER 999 2020' in microtext, and no edge lettering.
2020 Unc..£40

QN3   **Five pounds.** (2 oz of fine silver.) Music Legends I – Queen. ℞. As QN2.
2020 Proof in silver FDC (Edition: 500) £400

QN4   *The £5 cupro-nickel crowns previously listed here are now listed within the Crown Size Commemoratives section.*

QN5   **Ten pounds.** (5 oz of fine silver.) Music Legends I – Queen. ℞. As QN2.
2020 Proof in silver *FDC* (Edition: 750) £600

QN6   **Twenty five pounds.** (1/4 oz of fine gold.) Music Legends I – Queen. ℞. As QN6.
2020 Proof in gold *FDC* (Edition: 1,350)..£650

For coin specifications please see the tables at the beginning of the Britannia section.

QN7   QN7A

QN7   **One hundred pounds.** (1 oz of fine gold.) Music Legends I – Queen. ℞. Piano keyboard with opening notes of Bohemian Rhapsody pressed down, the group's logo and singer's signature mic stick in centre and below 'Red Special' guitar, Fender Precision Bass and Ludwig bass drum decorated with the Queen crest. (Reverse design: Chris Facey.)
2020 Proof in gold *FDC* (Edition: 350) £2800

QN7A   **One hundred pounds.** (1 oz of fine gold.). Music Legends I – Queen. ℞. As QN7 with added thin inner rim with repeated inscription '1OZ FINE GOLD 999.9 2020' in microtext.
2020 Unc (Edition: 2,500) £1800

QN8   **Two hundred pounds.** (2 oz of fine gold.) Music Legends I – Queen. ℞. As QN7.
2020 Proof in gold *FDC* (Edition: 53) £7000

QN9   **Five hundred pounds.** (5 oz of fine gold.) Music Legends I – Queen. ℞. As QN7.
2020 Proof in gold FDC (Edition: 50) £14000

QN10   **One thousand pounds.** (1 kilo of fine gold.) Music Legends I – Queen. ℞. As QN7.
2020 Proof in gold *FDC* (Edition: 6) £75000

ELTON JOHN

EJ1   **One pound.** (1/2 oz of fine silver.) Music Legends II – Elton John. ℞. As EJ2.
2020 Proof in silver *FDC* (Edition: 15,000) £60

EJ2   EJ2A

EJ2   **Two pounds.** (1 oz of fine silver.) Music Legends II – Elton John. ℞. Musical notes creating an image of glasses and a straw boater's hat with inscription 'ELTON JOHN' and below his signature bow tie against a Union flag background. With edge lettering 'ELTON JOHN' only on this coin. (Reverse design: Bradley Morgan Johnson.)
2020 Proof in silver *FDC* with colour (Edition: 10.000) £100

EJ2A   **Two Pounds.** (1 oz of fine silver.) Music Legends II – Elton John. ℞. As EJ2 with added thin inner rim with repeated inscription '1OZ FINE SILVER 999 2021' in microtext, and no edge lettering.
2021 Unc £30

For coin specifications please see the tables at the beginning of the Britannia section

EJ3 **Five pounds.** (2 oz of fine silver.) Music Legends II – Elton John. ℞. As EJ2 but with high relief on the hat, glasses and bow tie, and with pulsating star pattern in the lenses of the glasses.

2020 Proof in silver *FDC* (Edition: 500).. £350

EJ4 *The £5 cupro-nickel crowns previously listed here are now listed within the Crown Size Commemoratives section.*

EJ5 **Ten pounds.** (5 oz of fine silver.) Music Legends II – Elton John. ℞. As EJ2 but with high relief on the hat, glasses and bow tie, and with pulsating star pattern in the lenses of the glasses.

2020 Proof in silver *FDC* (Edition: 425)..£600

EJ6 **Twenty five pounds.** (1/4 oz fine gold.) Music Legends II – Elton John. ℞. As EJ7.

2020 Proof in gold *FDC* (Edition: 1100)..£650

EJ7

EJ7 **One hundred pounds.** (1 oz of fine gold.) Music Legends II – Elton John.
℞. Musical notes creating an image of glasses and a straw boater's hat with inscription 'ELTON JOHN' and below his signature bow tie against a Union flag background. (Reverse design: Bradley Morgan Johnson.)

2020 Proof in gold *FDC* (Edition: 300)..£2800

EJ7A **One hundred pounds.** (1 oz of fine gold.) Music Legends II – Elton John. ℞. As EJ7 with added thin inner rim with repeated inscription '1OZ FINE GOLD 999.9 2021' in microtext.

2021 Unc (Edition: 2,500) £1800

EJ8

EJ8 **Two hundred pounds.** (2 oz of fine gold.) Music Legends II – Elton John.
℞. As EJ7 but with high relief on the hat, glasses and bow tie, and with pulsating star pattern in the lenses of the glasses.

2020 Proof in gold *FDC* (Edition: 50)..£7000

For coin specifications please see the tables at the beginning of the Britannia section

EJ9 **Five hundred pounds.** (5 oz of fine gold.) Music Legends II – Elton John.
℞. As EJ7 but with high relief on the hat, glasses and bow tie, and with pulsating
star pattern in the lenses of the glasses.
2020 Proof in gold *FDC* (Edition: 50)..£15000

EJ10 **One thousand pounds.** (1 kilo of fine gold.) Music Legends II – Elton John.
℞. As EJ7 but with high relief on the hat, glasses and bow tie, and with pulsating
star pattern in the lenses of the glasses. and with piano patterned edge.
2020 Proof in gold *FDC* (Edition: 4)...£75000

DAVID BOWIE

DB1 **One pound.** (1/2 oz fine silver.) Music Legends III – David Bowie. ℞. As DB2.
2020 Proof in silver *FDC* (Edition: 13,500)..£65

DB2

DB2 **Two pounds.** (1 oz of fine silver.) Music Legends III – David Bowie. ℞. A depiction
of David Bowie and the inscription 'BOWIE' and with edge inscription 'THE STARS
ARE NEVER FAR AWAY'. (Reverse design: Jody Clark.)
2020 Proof in silver *FDC* with colour (Edition: 8,100) £100

DB2A **Two pounds.** (1 oz of fine silver.) Music Legends III – David Bowie. ℞. As DB2 with
added thin inner rim with repeated inscription '1OZ FINE SILVER 999 2021'
in microtext.
2021 Unc £40

DB3 **Five pounds.** (2 oz of fine silver.) Music Legends III – David Bowie. ℞. As DB2,
with no edge inscription but with high relief 'Stardust' on bolt.
2020 Proof in silver *FDC* (Edition: 550)..£300

DB4 *The £5 cupro-nickel crowns previously listed here are now listed within the Crown Size
Commemoratives section.*

DB5 **Ten pounds.** (5 oz of fine silver.) Music Legends III – David Bowie. ℞. As DB2,
with no edge inscription but with high relief 'Stardust' on bolt.
2020 Proof in silver *FDC* (Edition: 500)..£550

DB6 **Twenty five pounds.** (1/4 oz of fine gold.) Music Legends III – David Bowie. ℞. As DB7
2020 Proof in gold *FDC* (Edition: 1,400)...£650

For coin specifications please see the tables at the beginning of the Britannia section

DB7

DB7   One hundred pounds. (1 oz of fine gold.) Music Legends III – David Bowie. Ŗ. A depiction of David Bowie and the inscription 'BOWIE'. (Reverse design: Jody Clark)
2020 Proof in gold *FDC* (Edition: 400)...£2800
DB7A One hundred pounds. (1 oz of fine gold.) Music Legends III – David Bowie. Ŗ. As DB7 with added thin inner rim with repeated inscription '1OZ FINE GOLD 999.9 2021' in microtext.
2021 Unc (Edition: 2,500) £1800
DB8   Two hundred pounds. (2 oz of fine gold.) Music Legends III – David Bowie. Ŗ. As DB7 and with high relief 'Stardust' on bolt.
2020 Proof in gold *FDC* (Edition: 100)..£7000
DB9   Five hundred pounds. (5 oz of fine gold.) Music Legends III – David Bowie. Ŗ. As DB7 and with high relief 'Stardust' on bolt.
2020 Proof in gold *FDC* (Edition: 60)..£15000
DB10 One thousand pounds. (1 kilo of fine gold.) Music Legends III – David Bowie. Ŗ. As DB7 but with high relief 'Stardust' on bolt and with decorative patterned edge.
2020 Proof in gold *FDC* (Edition: 11)...£75000

THE WHO

WH1 One pounds. (1/2 oz fine silver.) Music Legends IV – The Who. R. As WH2.
2021 Proof in silver FDC (Edition: 10,010) £65

WH2

WH2 Two pounds. (1 oz of fine silver.) Music Legends IV – The Who. Ŗ. A depiction of a guitar shaped pinball machine accompanied by the inscription 'THE WHO' and with edge inscription 'PINBALL WIZARD'. (Reverse design: Henry Gray.)
2021 Proof in silver *FDC* with colour (Edition: 8,110)..£100

For coin specifications please see the tables at the beginning of the Britannia section

WH2A Two pounds. (1oz of fine silver.) Music Legends IV – The Who. R. As WH2 with added thin inner rim with repeated inscription '2021 1OZ FINE SILVER 999' in microtext.
2021 Unc £35

WH3 Five pounds. (2 oz of fine silver.) Music Legends IV – The Who. R. As WH2, with no edge inscription but with 'shockwave' effect radiating from the speaker.
2021 Proof in silver *FDC* (Edition: 550)..£260

WH4 *The £5 cupro-nickel crowns previously listed here are now listed within the Crown Size Commemoratives section.*

WH5 Ten pounds. (5 oz of fine silver.) Music Legends IV – The Who. R. As WH2, with no edge inscription but with 'shockwave' effect radiating from the speaker.
2021 Proof in silver *FDC* (Edition: 500)..£550

WH6 Twenty five pounds. (1/4oz of fine gold.) Music Legends IV – The Who. R. As WH7
2021 Proof in gold *FDC* (Edition: 1,010)..£650

WH7

WH7 One hundred pounds. (1 oz of fine gold.) Music Legends IV – The Who. R. A depiction of a guitar shaped pinball machine accompanied by the inscription 'THE WHO'. (Reverse design: Henry Gray.)
2021 Proof in gold *FDC* (Edition: 360)..£2800

WH7A One hundred pounds. (1 oz of fine gold.) Music Legends IV – The Who.
R. As WH7 with added thin inner rim with repeated inscription '2021 1OZ FINE GOLD 999.9' in microtext.
2021 Unc (Edition: 2,500) £1800

WH8 Two hundred pounds. (2 oz of fine gold.) Music Legends IV – The Who.
R. As WH7 but with 'shockwave' effect radiating from the speaker.
2021 Proof in gold *FDC* (Edition: 150)..£5500

WH9 Five hundred pounds. (5 oz of fine gold.) Music Legends IV – The Who.
R. As WH7 but with 'shockwave' effect radiating from the speaker.
2021 Proof in gold *FDC* (Edition: 64)..£14000

WH10 One thousand pounds. (1 kilo of fine gold.) Music Legends IV – The Who.
R. As WH7 but with 'shockwave' effect radiating from the speaker and plain edge with incuse symbols representing The Who.
2021 Proof in gold *FDC* (Edition: 12)..£75000

For coin specifications please see the tables at the beginning of the Britannia section

THE ROLLING STONES

RS1 RS6

RS1 **Two pounds.** (1oz of fine silver.) Music Legends V – The Rolling Stones.
R. Silhouettes of the band The Rolling Stones accompanied by the inscription 'THE
ROLLING STONES' and the dates "62-'22'. (Reverse design: Hannah Philacklea.)
2022 Proof in silver *FDC* with colour (Edition: 8,010) £100

RS1A **Two pounds.** (1oz of fine silver.) Music Legends V – The Rolling Stones.
R. As RS1 and, in microtext, '2022' with '1OZ FINE SILVER 999'.
2022 Unc (Edition: 50,000) £35

RS2 **Five pounds.** (2oz of fine silver.) Music Legends V – The Rolling Stones.
R. As RS1.
2022 Proof in silver *FDC* (Edition: 556)..£200

RS3 *The £5 cupro-nickel crowns previously listed here are now listed within the Crown Size
Commemoratives section.*

RS4 **Ten pounds.** (5oz of fine silver.) Music Legends V – The Rolling Stones.
R. As RS1.
2022 Proof in silver *FDC* with colour (Edition: 606) £480

RS5 **Twenty five pounds.** (1/4oz of fine gold.) Music Legends V – The Rolling Stones.
R. As RS6.
2022 Proof in gold *FDC* (Edition: 1,010)..£650

RS6 **One hundred pounds.** (1oz of fine gold.) Music Legends V – The Rolling Stones.
R. Silhouettes of the band The Rolling Stones accompanied by the inscription 'THE
ROLLING STONES' and the dates "62-'22'. (Reverse design: Hannah Philacklea.)
2022 Proof in gold *FDC* (Edition: 360)..£2700

RS6A **One hundred pounds.** (1oz of fine gold.) Music Legends V – The Rolling Stones.
R. As RS6 and, in microtext, '2022' with '1OZ FINE GOLD 999.9'.
2022 Unc (Edition: 5,000) £1700

RS7 **Two hundred pounds.** (2oz of fine gold.) Music Legends V – The Rolling Stones.
R. As RS6.
2022 Proof in gold *FDC* (Edition: 156)..£5200

RS8 **Five hundred pounds.** (5oz of fine gold.) Music Legends V – The Rolling Stones.
R. As RS6.
2022 Proof in gold *FDC* (Edition: 36)..£12500

For other Music coins see H37 and LO53

For coin specifications please see the tables at the beginning of the Britannia section

There are many coins depicting famous scions of British literature with the earliest being the 50p issued in 2005 for the 250th anniversary of Samuel Johnson's dictionary, but as this is a currency coin it may be located under **H14** in the currency section earlier in this catalogue. Quite a number of other similarly themed currency coins have also been issued since and a reference table listing these appears at the end of this section. In 2020 an extensive series of coins commemorating James Bond was issued and as none of these had any versions issued for circulation, it was decided to group them together in a TV and Film section. Following this, coins depicting the Mr Men and Robin Hood issued in 2021, again with no pieces destined for circulation, has resulted in the revised heading for this section.

Obverse portrait by Jody Clark.

JAMES BOND

The first group of coins in this new section launched in 2020 features James Bond, the world famous, quintessentially British spy who has been thrilling audiences for decades, ahead of the release of the 25th James Bond film 'No Time To Die'. The coins were issued in three groups:

I **Bond, James Bond** – The Aston Martin DB5, the classic Bond car.
II **Pay Attention, 007** – 'Wet Nellie' the submarine car that appeared in 'The Spy who loved me'.
III **Shaken not Stirred** – James Bond's iconic jacket and bow tie.

JB1 **One pounds.** (1/2 oz of fine silver.) TV & Film – James Bond I. ℞. As JB4.
2020 Proof in silver *FDC* (Edition: 15,017)..£65
JB2 **One pounds.** (1/2 oz of fine silver.) TV & Film – James Bond II. ℞. As JB5.
2020 Proof in silver *FDC* (Edition: 15,017)..£65
JB3 **One pounds.** (1/2 oz of fine silver.) TV & Film – James Bond III. ℞. As JB6.
2020 Proof in silver *FDC* (Edition: 15,017)..£65

JB4   JB5

JB4 **Two pounds.** (1 oz of fine silver.) TV & Film – James Bond I. ℞. The profile of the Aston Martin DB5, the classic Bond car and the inscription 'BOND, JAMES BOND'. (Reverse designers: Matt Dent & Christian Davies.)
2020 Proof in silver *FDC* with colour (Edition: 8,517) £90
JB5 **Two pounds.** (1 oz of fine silver.) TV & Film – James Bond II. ℞. 'Wet Nellie' the submarine car that appeared in 'The Spy who loved me' and the inscription 'PAY ATTENTION 007'. (Reverse designers: Matt Dent & Christian Davies.)
2020 Proof in silver *FDC* with colour (Edition: 8,517) £90

For coin specifications please see the tables at the beginning of the Britannia section

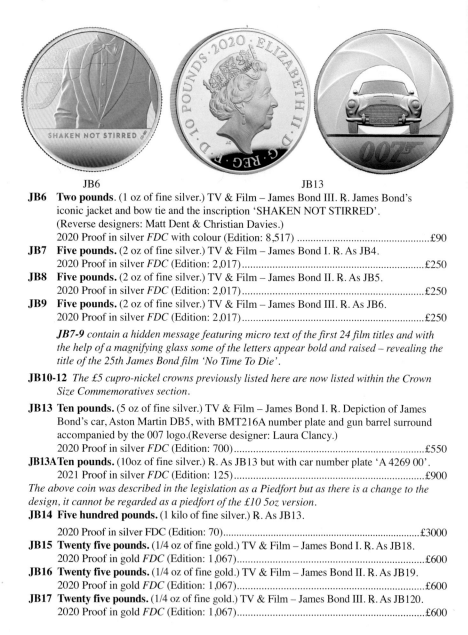

JB6   JB13

JB6 **Two pounds**. (1 oz of fine silver.) TV & Film – James Bond III. Ŗ. James Bond's
iconic jacket and bow tie and the inscription 'SHAKEN NOT STIRRED'.
(Reverse designers: Matt Dent & Christian Davies.)
2020 Proof in silver *FDC* with colour (Edition: 8,517) £90

JB7 **Five pounds**. (2 oz of fine silver.) TV & Film – James Bond I. Ŗ. As JB4.
2020 Proof in silver *FDC* (Edition: 2,017)..£250

JB8 **Five pounds**. (2 oz of fine silver.) TV & Film – James Bond II. Ŗ. As JB5.
2020 Proof in silver *FDC* (Edition: 2,017)..£250

JB9 **Five pounds**. (2 oz of fine silver.) TV & Film – James Bond III. Ŗ. As JB6.
2020 Proof in silver *FDC* (Edition: 2,017)..£250

*JB7-9 contain a hidden message featuring micro text of the first 24 film titles and with
the help of a magnifying glass some of the letters appear bold and raised – revealing the
title of the 25th James Bond film 'No Time To Die'.*

JB10-12 *The £5 cupro-nickel crowns previously listed here are now listed within the Crown
Size Commemoratives section.*

JB13 **Ten pounds**. (5 oz of fine silver.) TV & Film – James Bond I. Ŗ. Depiction of James
Bond's car, Aston Martin DB5, with BMT216A number plate and gun barrel surround
accompanied by the 007 logo.(Reverse designer: Laura Clancy.)
2020 Proof in silver *FDC* (Edition: 700)..£550

JB13A **Ten pounds**. (10oz of fine silver.) Ŗ. As JB13 but with car number plate 'A 4269 00'.
2021 Proof in silver *FDC* (Edition: 125)...£900

*The above coin was described in the legislation as a Piedfort but as there is a change to the
design, it cannot be regarded as a piedfort of the £10 5oz version.*

JB14 **Five hundred pounds**. (1 kilo of fine silver.) Ŗ. As JB13.

2020 Proof in silver FDC (Edition: 70)..£3000

JB15 **Twenty five pounds**. (1/4 oz of fine gold.) TV & Film – James Bond I. Ŗ. As JB18.
2020 Proof in gold *FDC* (Edition: 1,067)...£600

JB16 **Twenty five pounds**. (1/4 oz of fine gold.) TV & Film – James Bond II. Ŗ. As JB19.
2020 Proof in gold *FDC* (Edition: 1,067)...£600

JB17 **Twenty five pounds**. (1/4 oz of fine gold.) TV & Film – James Bond III. Ŗ. As JB120.
2020 Proof in gold *FDC* (Edition: 1,067)...£600

For coin specifications please see the tables at the beginning of the Britannia section

JB18   JB19   JB20

JB18 **One hundred pounds.** (1 oz of fine gold.) TV & Film – James Bond I. R. The profile of the Aston Martin DB5, the classic Bond car and the inscription 'BOND, JAMES BOND'. (Reverse designers: Matt Dent & Christian Davies)
2020 Proof in gold *FDC* (Edition: 360)...£2600

JB19 **One hundred pounds.** (1 oz of fine gold.) TV & Film – James Bond II. R. 'Wet Nellie' the submarine car that appeared in 'The Spy who loved me' and the inscription 'PAY ATTENTION 007'. (Reverse designers: Matt Dent & Christian Davies)
2020 Proof in gold *FDC* (Edition: 360)...£2600

JB20 **One hundred pounds.** (1 oz of fine gold.) TV & Film – James Bond III. R. James Bond's iconic jacket and bow tie and the inscription 'SHAKEN NOT STIRRED'. (Reverse designers: Matt Dent & Christian Davies)
2020 Proof in gold *FDC* (Edition: 360)...£2600

JB21 **Two hundred pounds.** (2 oz of fine gold.) TV & Film – James Bond I. R. As JB18.
2020 Proof in gold *FDC* (Edition: 260)...£4500

JB22 **Two hundred pounds.** (2 oz of fine gold.) TV & Film – James Bond II. R. As JB19.
2020 Proof in gold *FDC* (Edition: 260)...£4500

JB23 **Two hundred pounds.** (2 oz of fine gold.) TV & Film – James Bond III. R. As JB20.
2020 Proof in gold *FDC* (Edition: 260)...£4500

JB21-23 contain a hidden message featuring micro text of the first 24 film titles and with the help of a magnifying glass some of the letters appear bold and raised – revealing the title of the 25th James Bond film 'No Time To Die'.

JB24

JB24 **Five hundred pounds.** (5 oz of fine gold.) TV & Film – James Bond I. R. Depiction of James Bond's car, Aston Martin DB5, with BMT216A number plate and gun barrel surround accompanied by the 007 logo. (Reverse designer: Laura Clancy.)
2020 Proof in gold *FDC* (Edition: 64)...£14000

For coin specifications please see the tables at the beginning of the Britannia section

JB24A Five hundred pounds. (10oz of fine gold.) Ŗ. As JB24 but with car number plate
'A 4269 00'.
2021 Proof in gold *FDC* (Edition: 50)..£25000
The above coin was described in the legislation as a Piedfort but as there is a change to the
design and also the coin has a diameter of 65mm it cannot be regarded as a piedfort of the
£500 50mm 5oz version.

JB25 One thousand pounds. (1 kilo of fine gold.) TV & Film – James Bond I.
Ŗ. As JB24.
2020 Proof in gold *FDC* (Edition: 20)...£65000

JB26 Two thousand pounds. (2 kilos of fine gold.) TV & Film – James Bond I.
Ŗ. As JB24.
2020 Proof in gold *FDC* (Edition: 10)...£150000

JB27 Five thousand pounds. (5 kilos of fine gold.) TV & Film – James Bond I.
Ŗ. As JB24.
2021 Proof in gold *FDC* (Edition: 2)...£400000

JB28 Seven thousand pounds. (7 kilos of fine gold.) TV & Film – James Bond I.
Ŗ. As JB24.
2020 Proof in gold *FDC* (Edition: 1)...£550000

MR MEN LITTLE MISS

A series of three designs commemorating the 50th Anniversary of the Mr Men Little Miss
characters.

MM1 One pound. (1/2 oz of fine silver.) Mr Men Little Miss I – Mr Happy. Ŗ. As MM4.
2021 proof in silver *FDC* (Edition: 9,010)... £65

MM2 One pound. (1/2 oz of fine silver.) Mr Men Little Miss II – Mr Strong &
Little Miss Giggles. Ŗ. As MM5.
2021 proof in silver *FDC* (Edition: 9,010)... £65

MM3 One pound. (1/2 oz of fine silver.) Mr Men Little Miss III – Little Miss Sunshine.
Ŗ. As MM6.
2021 proof in silver *FDC* (Edition: 9,010)... £65

MM4

MM4 Two pounds. (1 oz of fine silver.) Mr Men Little Miss I – Mr Happy. Ŗ. A depiction
of the children's character Mr Happy with the inscription 'MR MEN 50 YEARS' and
the signature of the author Roger Hargreaves. (Reverse design: Adam Hargreaves.)
2021 proof in silver *FDC* with colour (Edition: 6,510) £80

For coin specifications please see the tables at the beginning of the Britannia section

MM5 MM6

MM5 **Two pounds.** (1 oz of fine silver.) Mr Men Little Miss II – Mr Strong & Little Miss Giggles. ℞. A depiction of the children's characters Mr Strong and Little Miss Giggles with the inscription 'MR MEN LITTLE MISS 50 YEARS' and the signature of the author Roger Hargreaves. (Reverse design: Adam Hargreaves.)
2021 proof in silver *FDC* with colour (Edition: 6,510) £80

MM6 **Two pounds.** (1 oz of fine silver.) Mr Men Little Miss III – Little Miss Sunshine. ℞. A depiction of the children's character Little Miss Sunshine with the inscription 'LITTLE MISS 50 YEARS' and the signature of the author Roger Hargreaves. (Reverse design: Adam Hargreaves.)
2021 proof in silver *FDC* with colour (Edition: 6,510) £80

MM7-9 *The £5 cupro-nickel crowns previously listed here are now listed within the Crown Size Commemoratives section.*

MM10 **Twenty five pounds.** (1/4 oz of fine gold.) Mr Men Little Miss I – Mr Happy. ℞. As MM13.
2021 proof in gold FDC (Edition: 760)... £550

MM11 **Twenty five pounds.** (1/4 oz of fine gold.) Mr Men Little Miss II – Mr Strong & Little Miss Giggles. ℞. As MM14.
2021 proof in gold FDC (Edition: 760)... £550

MM12 **Twenty five pounds.** (1/4 oz of fine gold.) Mr Men Little Miss III – Little Miss Sunshine. ℞. As MM15.
2021 proof in gold FDC (Edition: 760)... £550

MM13 MM14 MM15

MM13 **One hundred pounds.** (1 oz of fine gold.) Mr Men Little Miss I – Mr Happy. ℞. A depiction of the children's character Mr Happy with the inscription 'MR MEN 50 YEARS' and the signature of the author Roger Hargreaves. (Reverse design: Adam Hargreaves.)
2021 proof in gold *FDC* (Edition: 280) £2500

For coin specifications please see the tables at the beginning of the Britannia section.

MM14 **One hundred pounds.** (1 oz of fine gold.) Mr Men Little Miss II – Mr Strong & Little Miss Giggles. ℞. A depiction of the children's characters Mr Strong and Little Miss Giggles with the inscription 'MR MEN LITTLE MISS 50 YEARS' and the signature of the author Roger Hargreaves. (Reverse design: Adam Hargreaves.)
2021 proof in gold *FDC* (Edition: 280) £2500

MM15 **One hundred pounds.** (1 oz of fine gold.) Mr Men Little Miss III – Little Miss Sunshine. ℞. A depiction of the children's character Little Miss Sunshine with the inscription 'LITTLE MISS 50 YEARS' and the signature of the author Roger Hargreaves. (Reverse design: Adam Hargreaves.)
2021 proof in gold *FDC* (Edition: 280) £2500

ROBIN HOOD

The Robin Hood series previously listed here has been moved to the 'Other Bullion Coins' section.

LEWIS CARROLL'S ALICE

These coins commemorate the 150th Anniversary of '*Through the Looking Glass*'.

AW1 **One pound.** (1/2 oz of fine silver.) Alice's Adventures in Wonderland.
℞. As AW3 but with milled edge.
2021 proof in silver *FDC* (Edition: 5,510) £65

AW2 **One pound**. (1/2 oz of fine silver.) Alice through the Looking Glass.
℞. As AW4 but with milled edge.
2021 proof in silver *FDC* (Edition: 5.510) £65

AW3   AW4

AW3 **Two pounds.** (1 oz of fine silver.) Alice's Adventures in Wonderland, ℞. A depiction of Alice and the Cheshire cat sat in a tree accompanied by the inscription 'ALICE'S ADVENTURES IN WONDERLAND' with a plain edge and the inscription 'CURIOUSER AND CURIOUSER'. (Reverse design: Ffion Gwillim.)
2021 proof in silver *FDC* with colour (Edition: 3,510).. £100

AW4 **Two pounds.** (1 oz of fine silver.) Alice through the Looking Glass. ℞. A depiction of Alice and the characters Tweedledee and Tweedledum and the inscription 'THROUGH THE LOOKING~GLASS' with a plain edge and the inscription 'FOUR TIMES ROUND IS ENOUGH FOR ONE DANCE. (Reverse design: Ffion Gwillim.)
2021 proof in silver *FDC* with colour (Edition: 3,510).. £100

AW5-6 *The £5 cupro-nickel crowns previously listed here are now listed within the Crown Size Commemoratives section.*

For coin specifications please see the tables at the beginning of the Britannia section.

AW7 **Twenty five pounds.** (1/4 oz of fine gold.) Alice's Adventures in Wonderland.
℞. As AW9.
2021 proof in gold *FDC* (Edition: 510) £600
AW8 **Twenty five pounds.** (1/4 oz of fine gold.) Alice through the Looking Glass.
℞. As AW10.
2021 proof in gold *FDC* (Edition: 510) £600

AW9   AW10

AW9 **One hundred pounds.** (1 oz of fine gold.) Alice's Adventures in Wonderland.
℞. A depiction of Alice and the Cheshire cat sat in a tree accompanied by the
inscription 'ALICE'S ADVENTURES IN WONDERLAND'. (Reverse design:
Ffion Gwillim.)
2021 proof in gold *FDC* (Edition: 160) £2500
AW10 **One hundred pounds.** (1 oz of fine gold.) Alice through the Looking Glass.
℞. A depiction of Alice and the characters Tweedledee and Tweedledum and the
inscription 'THROUGH THE LOOKING-GLASS'. (Reverse design:
Ffion Gwillim.)
2021 proof in gold *FDC* (Edition: 160) £2500

HARRY POTTER

A series of coins commemorating the 25th Anniversary since the launch of the Harry Potter
series of books. There are also 50p coins which are listed as H112-H113 in the currency section.

Obverse portrait by Jody Clark

TWO POUNDS

HP1

HP1 **Two pounds.** (1 oz of fine silver.) Harry Potter I. O. As H39A. ℞. A depiction of
Harry Potter with the inscription 'HARRY POTTER 25 YEARS OF MAGIC' with a
latent feature that displays a lightning bolt and the number '25' and with edge inscription
of 'HARRY POTTER – THE BOY WHO LIVED!' (Reverse design: Ffion Gwillim from
illustration by Jim Kay.)
2022 Proof in silver *FDC* (Edition: 15,010) £100

HP2   **Two pounds.** (1 oz of fine silver.) Harry Potter II. O. As H39A. Ɍ. A depiction of the Hogwarts Express and the figure of Harry Potter with the inscription 'HOGWARTS EXPRESS 25 YEARS OF MAGIC' with a latent feature that displays a lightning bolt and the number '25' and with edge inscription of 'PLATFORM NINE AND THREE-QUARTERS'. (Reverse design: Ffion Gwillim from illustration by Jim Kay.)
2022 Proof in silver *FDC* (Edition: 15,010) £95

FIVE POUNDS

HP5   **Five pounds.** (2 oz of fine silver.) Harry Potter I. Ɍ. As HP1 but with milled edge and no edge inscription.
2022 Proof in silver *FDC* (Edition: 760) £190

HP6   **Five pounds.** (2 oz of fine silver.) Harry Potter II. Ɍ. As HP2 but with milled edge and no edge inscription.
2022 Proof in silver *FDC* (Edition: 760) £185

TEN POUNDS

HP9   **Ten pounds.** (5oz of fine silver.) Harry Potter I. Ɍ. As HP1 but with milled edge and no edge inscription.
2022 Proof in silver *FDC* (Edition: 310) £480

HP10   **Ten pounds.** (5oz of fine silver.) Harry Potter II. Ɍ. As HP2 but with milled edge and no edge inscription
2022 Proof in silver *FDC* (Edition: 310) £465

TWENTY FIVE POUNDS

HP13   **Twenty five pounds.** (1/4oz fine gold.) Harry Potter I. Ɍ. As HP17 but with no latent feature.
2022 Proof in gold *FDC* (Edition: 660) £725

HP14   **Twenty five pounds.** (1/4oz fine gold.) Harry Potter II. Ɍ. As HP18.
2022 Proof in gold *FDC* (Edition: 660) £670

TWO HUNDRED POUNDS

HP17   **Two hundred pounds.** (2oz fine gold.) Harry Potter I. Ɍ. A depiction of Harry Potter with the inscription 'HARRY POTTER 25 YEARS OF MAGIC'. (Reverse design: Ffion Gwillim.)
2022 Proof in gold *FDC* (Edition: 110) £5200

HP18   **Two hundred pounds.** (2oz fine gold.) Harry Potter II. Ɍ. A depiction of the Hogwarts Express and the figure of Harry Potter with the inscription 'HOGWARTS EXPRESS 25 YEARS OF MAGIC'.
2022 Proof in gold *FDC* (Edition: 110) £5000

For later coins in this series please see the Charles III section.

For coin specifications please see the tables at the beginning of the Britannia section.

Other coins with topics covered by this section are:

Jane Austen	£2	K45
Robert Burns	£2	K24
Agatha Christie	£2	K61
Charles Dickens	£2	K29
Sir Arthur Conan Doyle	50p	H61
Johnson's Dictionary	50p	H14
A A Milne	50p	H87-89, H97, H100, H102, H105, H106, H109
Samuel Pepys	£2	K57
Beatrix Potter	50p	H42-46, H49-56, H74, H85, L96, NB7, OA2, OB2, OB4
Sir Walter Scott	£2	K64
William Shakespeare	£2	K38-K40
Mary Shelley	£2	K47
H G Wells	£2	K63
William Wordsworth	£5	L88
Alice in Wonderland	£5	LO50
James Bond	10p	F10
Paddington Bear	50p	H58-59, H75-76
Gruffalo	50p	H72, H77
Snowman	50p	H60, H79, H91, H101, H111
Wallace & Gromit	50p	H78

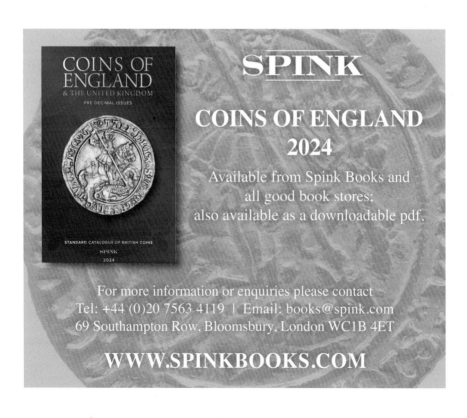

A 21 coin series celebrating some of the kings and queens from the last 500 years. Reverses depict historic coinage portraits of the monarchs recreated by Gordon Summers.

BMSA1

BMSA1   **Two pounds.** (1oz of fine silver.) British Monarchs I – Henry VII. R. Portrait of Henry VII with the inscription 'HENRIC VII DI GRA REX AGL Z'. (Reverse design: Alexander of Bruchsal.)
2022 Proof in silver *FDC* (Edition: 1,260) £95

<table>
<tr><td>BMSA2</td><td>BMSA3</td><td>BMSA4</td></tr>
</table>

BMSA2   **Two pounds.** (1oz of fine silver.) British Monarchs II – James I. R. Portrait of James I with the inscription 'JACOBVS D: G: MAG: BRIT: FRAN: ET HIB: REX'.
2022 Proof in silver *FDC* (Edition: 1,260) £95

BMSA3   **Two pounds.** (1oz of fine silver.) British Monarchs III –George I. R. Portrait of George I with the inscription 'GEORGIVS DG M BR FR ET HIB REX F D'. (Reverse design: John Croker.)
2022 Proof in silver *FDC* (Edition: 1,360) £95

BMSA4   **Two pounds.** (1oz of fine silver.) British Monarchs IV –Edward VII. R. Portrait of Edward VII with the inscription 'EDWARDVS VII DEI GRA: BRITT: OMN: REX FID: DEF: IND: IMP'.
2022 Proof in silver *FDC* (Edition: 1,360) £95

BMSB1   **Five pounds.** (2oz of fine silver.) British Monarchs I – Henry VII. R. As BMSA1.
2022 Proof in silver *FDC* (Edition: 710) £185

BMSB2   **Five pounds.** (2oz of fine silver.) British Monarchs II –James I. R. As BMSA2.
2022 Proof in silver *FDC* (Edition: 856) £185

BMSB3   **Five pounds.** (2oz of fine silver.) British Monarchs III–George I. R. As BMSA3.
2022 Proof in silver *FDC* (Edition: 756) £185

BMSB4   **Five pounds.** (2oz of fine silver.) British Monarchs IV–Edward VII. R. As BMSA4.
2022 Proof in silver *FDC* (Edition: 756) £185

BMSC1   **Ten pounds.** (5oz of fine silver.) British Monarchs I – Henry VII. ℞. As BMSA1.
2022 Proof in silver *FDC* (Edition: 281) £465
—   Proof piedfort in silver *FDC* (Edition: 156)... £885
BMSC2   **Ten pounds.** (5oz of fine silver.) British Monarchs II –James I. ℞. As BMSA2.
2022 Proof in silver *FDC* (Edition: 281) £465
—   Proof piedfort in silver *FDC* (Edition: 156)... £885
BMSC3   **Ten pounds.** (5oz of fine silver.) British Monarchs III –George I. ℞. As BMSA3.
2022 Proof in silver *FDC* (Edition: 281) £465
—   Proof piedfort in silver *FDC* (Edition: 156)... £885
BMSC4   **Ten pounds.** (5oz of fine silver.) British Monarchs IV –Edward VII. ℞. As BMSA4.
2022 Proof in silver *FDC* (Edition: 281) £465
—   Proof piedfort in silver *FDC* (Edition: 156)... £885

BMGA1

BMGA2   BMGA3   BMGA4

BMGA1   **One hundred pounds.** (1oz of fine gold.) British Monarchs I – Henry VII.
℞. Portrait of Henry VII with the inscription 'HENRIC VII DI GRA REX AGL Z'.
(Reverse design: Alexander of Bruchsal.)
2022 Proof in gold *FDC* (Edition: 610) £2500
BMGA2   **One hundred pounds.** (1oz of fine gold.) British Monarchs II –James I.
℞. Portrait of James I with the inscription 'JACOBVS D: G: MAG: BRIT: FRAN:
ET HIB: REX'.
2022 Proof in gold *FDC* (Edition: 610) £2500
BMGA3   **One hundred pounds.** (1oz of fine gold.) British Monarchs III –George I.
℞. Portrait of George I with the inscription 'GEORGIVS DG M BR FR ET HIB
REX F D'. (Reverse design: John Croker.)
2022 Proof in gold *FDC* (Edition: 610) £2500
BMGA4   **One hundred pounds.** (1oz of fine gold.) British Monarchs IV –Edward VII.
℞. Portrait of Edward VII with the inscription 'EDWARDVS VII DEI GRA:
BRITT: OMN: REX FID: DEF: IND: IMP'.
2022 Proof in gold *FDC* (Edition: 610) £2500

For coin specifications please see the tables at the beginning of the Britannia section

BMGB1 **Two hundred pounds.** (2oz of fine gold.) British Monarchs I – Henry VII.
R. As BMGA1.
2022 Proof in gold *FDC* (Edition: 195) £4800

BMGB2 **Two hundred pounds.** (2oz of fine gold.) British Monarchs II –James I.
R. As BMGA2.
2022 Proof in gold *FDC* (Edition: 221) £4800

BMGB3 **Two hundred pounds.** (2oz of fine gold.) British Monarchs III –George I.
R. As BMGA3.
2022 Proof in gold *FDC* (Edition: 126) £4800

BMGB4 **Two hundred pounds.** (2oz of fine gold.) British Monarchs IV –Edward VII.
R. As BMGA4.
2022 Proof in gold *FDC* (Edition: 106) £4800

BMGC1 **Five hundred pounds.** (5oz of fine gold.) British Monarchs I – Henry VII.
R. As BMGA1.
2022 Proof in gold *FDC* (Edition: 81) £11500

BMGC2 **Five hundred pounds.** (5oz of fine gold.) British Monarchs II –James I.
R. As BMGA2.
2022 Proof in gold *FDC* (Edition: 81) £11500

BMGC3 **Five hundred pounds.** (5oz of fine gold.) British Monarchs III –George I.
R. As BMGA3.
2022 Proof in gold *FDC* (Edition: 56) £11500

BMGC4 **Five hundred pounds.** (5oz of fine gold.) British Monarchs IV –Edward VII.
R. As BMGA4.
2022 Proof in gold *FDC* (Edition: 56) £11500

For later coins in this section please see the Charles III section.

For coin specifications please see the tables at the beginning of the Britannia section

City Views is a new series that celebrates breath-taking views of iconic urban landmarks around the world renowned as cultural marvels. The first coin — for London – features the Tower of London, the imposing stone fortress built by William the Conqueror that has dominated the city's skyline for almost a thousand years. The design has been skilfully adapted from a work by the Bohemian artist Wenceslaus Hollar.

LONDON

CV1

CV1 **Two pounds.** (1oz of fine silver.) City Views I – London. Ṛ. The Tower of London. (Reverse design: Royal Mint Design Dept.)
2022 Proof in silver *FDC* (Edition: 3,010) £100

CV2 **Five pounds.** (2oz of fine silver.) City Views I - London. Ṛ. As CV1.
2022 Proof in silver *FDC* (Edition: 1,506) £220

CV3 **Ten pounds.** (5oz of fine silver.) City Views I - London. Ṛ. As CV1.
2022 Proof in silver *FDC* (Edition: 256) £550

CV4 **Five hundred pounds.** (1 kilo of fine silver.) City Views I - London. Ṛ. As CV1.
2022 Proof in silver *FDC* (Edition: 52) £2500

CV5

CV5 **One hundred pounds.** (1oz of fine gold.) City Views I - London. Ṛ. The Tower of London.(Reverse design: Royal Mint Design Dept.)
2022 Proof in gold *FDC* (Edition: 310) £2600

CV6 **Two hundred pounds.** (2oz of fine gold.) City Views I - London. Ṛ. As CV5.
2022 Proof in gold *FDC* (Edition: 256) £5500

CV7 **Five hundred pounds.** (5oz of fine gold.) City Views I - London. Ṛ. As CV5.
2022 Proof in gold *FDC* (Edition: 56) £12500

CV8 **One thousand pounds.** (1 kilo of fine gold.) City Views I - London. Ṛ. As CV5.
2022 Proof in gold *FDC* (Edition: 6) £68000

For coin specifications please see the tables at the beginning of the Britannia section

ROME

CV9

CV9   **Two pounds.** (1oz of fine silver.) City Views II - Rome. ℞. A historic view of Rome. (Reverse design: Royal Mint Design Dept.)
2022 Proof in silver *FDC* (Edition: 2,010) £95

CV10   **Five pounds.** (2oz of fine silver.) City Views II - Rome. ℞. As CV9.
2022 Proof in silver *FDC* (Edition: 1,006) £185

CV11   **Ten pounds.** (5oz of fine silver.) City Views II - Rome. ℞. As CV9.
2022 Proof in silver *FDC* (Edition: 206) £465

CV13

CV13   **One hundred pounds.** (1oz of fine gold.) City Views II - Rome. ℞. A historic view of Rome. (Reverse design: Royal Mint Design Dept.)
2022 Proof in gold *FDC* (Edition: 210) £2600

CV14   **Two hundred pounds.** (2oz of fine gold.) City Views II - Rome. ℞. As CV13.
2022 Proof in gold *FDC* (Edition: 156) £5000

CV15   **Five hundred pounds.** (5oz of fine gold.) City Views II - Rome. ℞. As CV13.
2022 Proof in gold *FDC* (Edition: 31) £12000

CV16   **One thousand pounds.** (1 kilo of fine gold.) City Views II - Rome. ℞. As CV13.
2022 Proof in gold *FDC* (Edition: 4) £65000

For later coins in this section please see the Charles III section.

For coin specifications please see the tables at the beginning of the Britannia section

List of amended catalogue numbers from previous volume.

Previous	New
CROWNS	
L61	L63
L62	L64
L63	L65
L64	L66
L65	L67
L66	L70
L67	L71
L68	L72
L69	L73
L70	L74
L71	L75
L72	L76
L73	L77
L74	L78
L75	L79
L76	L80
L77	L81
L78	L84
L79	L85
L80	L88
L81	L89
L82	L90
L83	L91
L84	L92
L85	L93
L86	L96
L87	L97
L88	L102
L89	L104
L89A	L104A
L90	L105
L91	L112
L92	L113
L93	L114
L94	L119
L95	L120
L95A	L120A
L96	L122

Previous	New
L97	L123
L98	L126
L99	L127
L100	L128
L101	L130

Previous	New
BRITANNIA SILVER	
BSC21	BSC20
BSC22	BSC21
BSF2B	BSF10B

Previous	New
CHINESE LUNAR	
CLCA1	L86
CLCA2	L103
CLCA3	L121
CLCA4	L131

Previous	New
QUEEN'S BEASTS	
QBCC1	L61
QBCC2	L62
QBCC3	L68
QBCC4	L69
QBCC5	L82
QBCC6	L83
QBCC7	L94
QBCC8	L95
QBCC9	L106
QBCC10	L110
QBCC11	L116

Previous	New
TUDOR BEASTS	
TBCCA1	L124
TBCCA2	L129
TBCCA3	L132
TBCCA4	DELETED
TBCSA4	DELETED

Previous	New
TBCSB4	DELETED
TBCSC4	DELETED
TBCSD4	DELETED
TBCSS4	DELETED
TBCGA4	DELETED
TBCGB4	DELETED
TBCGC4	DELETED
TBCGD4	DELETED
TBCGG4	DELETED

Previous	New
MUSIC LEGENDS	
QN4	L87
EJ4	L98
DB4	L111
WH4	L115
TRS3	L125

Previous	New
BOOKS, FILM & TV	
JB10	LL99
JB11	L100
JB12	L101
MM7	L107
MM8	L108
MM9	L109
RH1	QB9
RH2	QB10
RH3	QB11
RH4	QD4
RH7	RD4
RH8	RD5
RH9	RD6
RH10	TA2
RH11	DELETED
RH12	DELETED
AW5	L117
AW6	L118

CONSIGN NOW

THE GLOBAL COLLECTABLES AUCTION HOUSE

LONDON | NEW YORK | HONG KONG | SINGAPORE | SWITZERLAND

SPINK

Where History Is Valued

WWW.SPINK.COM

King Charles III

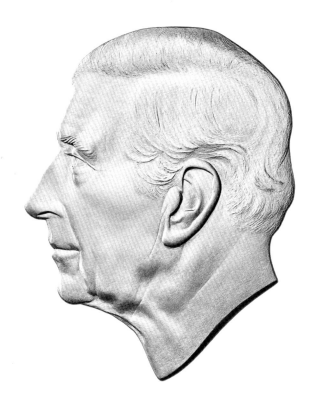

King Charles III was proclaimed king on 10th September 2022 following the death of Her Majesty Queen Elizabeth II on 8th September. The first coins of the new reign commemorate the life and legacy of Her Majesty Queen Elizabeth II, and these comprise a currency 50p and £5 plus a range of silver, gold and platinum coins.

Following the new king's coronation in May 2023, a 50p but with uncrowned portrait entered into circulation although the number issued was so small that few people will have seen it. A new set of 8 definitive designs inspired by flora and fauna found across Britain and reflecting King Charles III's passion for conservation and the natural world was launched in October 2023. All eight coins will be issued into circulation but as Queen Elizabeth II coins will remain in circulation for probably some decades, the new designs will only appear once banks need new supplies and with the current movement away from using cash it may be some months maybe even years before all eight new designs are regularly seen in change. It is not known whether the circulation coins will carry the Tudor Crown privy mark on the obverse.

CURRENCY COINS

ONE PENCE

B11

B11   **One penny.** O. As H123. R. A depiction of a dormouse with the inscription '1 PENNY' set against a background of three interlocking C's repeated. (Reverse design: The Royal Mint.)

     2023 BU*..£5

     —   Proof in silver *FDC** £25

     —   Proof in gold *FDC** £350

B12

B12   **One penny.** O. As E2. R. A depiction of a portcullis with chains royally crowned, being the badge of King Henry VII and His successors, accompanied by the inscription 'ONE PENNY' and the date of the year.

     2023 silver BU £20

* These coins were only available in the year sets.

TWO PENCE

C9

C9   **Two pence.** O. As H123. ℞. A depiction of a red squirrel with the inscription
         '2 PENCE' set against a background of three interlocking C's repeated.
         (Reverse design: The Royal Mint.)
         2023 BU*...£4
         —   Proof in silver *FDC** £25
         —   Proof in gold *FDC** £700

FIVE PENCE

D10

D10   **Five pence.** O. As H123. ℞. A depiction of a sprig of oak with the inscription
         '5 PENCE' set against a background of three interlocking C's repeated.
         (Reverse design: The Royal Mint.)
         2023 BU*...£4
         —   Proof in silver *FDC** £20
         —   Proof in gold *FDC** £325

SIXPENCE

E2

E2   **Six pence.** ℞. A depiction of the Royal Cypher surrounded by a floral motif with the
         inscription 'SIXPENCE' and the date of the year. (Reverse design: John Bergdahl.)
         2024 BU in silver..£20
         —   Proof in gold *FDC* £530

* These coins were only available in the year sets.

TEN PENCE

F36

F36   **Ten pence.** O. As H123. Ŗ. A depiction of a capercaillie with the inscription
'10 PENCE' set against a background of three interlocking C's repeated.
(Reverse design: The Royal Mint.)
2023 BU*..£4
—   Proof in silver *FDC** £25
—   Proof in gold *FDC** £650

TWENTY PENCE

G7

G7   **Twenty pence.** O. As H123. Ŗ. A depiction of a puffin with the inscription "20
PENCE" set against a background of three interlocking C's repeated. (Reverse design:
The Royal Mint.)
2023 BU*..£4
—   Proof in silver *FDC** £30
—   Proof in gold *FDC** £500

* These coins were only available in the year sets

Obverse portrait by Martin Jennings
FIFTY PENCE

H114

H114   **Fifty pence**. O. Portrait of King Charles III. R. As L33 but with date '2022'.

2022 .... £1
— BU in presentation folder (Issued: 194,080)....................................£11
— BU in PNC (Issued: 1,870) £18
— Proof in silver *FDC* (Issued: 22,932) £60
— Proof in silver *FDC* in PNC (Issued: 199) £60
— Proof piedfort in silver *FDC* (Issued: 4,600) £110
— Proof in gold *FDC* (Issued: 1,261)...£1250
— Proof in gold *FDC* in PNC (Issued: 13).......................................£1250
— Proof piedfort in gold *FDC* (Issued: 86) £2500
— Proof piedfort in platinum *FDC* (Issued: 168) £1750
— Proof piedfort in platinum in PNC (Issued: 2) £1750

The number of the precious metal coins issued was equal to the number ordered by
31st December 2022.

H115   H116

H115   **Fifty pence.** Harry Potter – III. R. A depiction of Albus Dumbledore and the
inscription 'ALBUS DUMBLEDORE 25 YEARS OF MAGIC' with a latent feature
that displays a lightning bolt and the number '25'. (Reverse design: Ffion Gwillim from
illustration by Jim Kay.)

2023 BU £6
— BU in presentation folder...£11
— BU with colour in presentation folder £20
— Proof in silver *FDC* (Edition: 15,010) £70
— Proof in gold *FDC* (Edition: 310)..£1250

H116   **Fifty pence.** Harry Potter – IV. O. As H115. R. A depiction of Hogwarts School and the
inscription 'HOGWARTS 25 YEARS OF MAGIC' with a latent feature that displays a
lightning bolt and the number '25'. (Reverse design: Ffion Gwillim from illustration by
Jim Kay.)

2023 BU.. £6
— BU in presentation folder £11
— BU with colour in presentation folder £20
— Proof in silver *FDC* (Edition: 15,010)... £70
— Proof in gold *FDC* (Edition: 310).. £1250

H117

H117 **Fifty pence.** Coronation of King Charles III. O. King Charles with Tudor Crown.
R. The Royal Cypher set against a depiction of a section of the exterior of Westminster
Abbey. (Reverse design: Natasha Jenkins.)
2023 BU £6
—   BU in presentation folder £11
—   BU in PNC (Edition: 20,000) £12
—   Proof in silver *FDC* (Edition: 14,910) £60
—   Proof in silver *FDC* in PNC (Edition: 1,250) £60
—   Proof piedfort in silver *FDC* (Edition: 3,260) £110
—   Proof in gold *FDC* (Edition: 635) £1500

H117A **Fifty pence.** Coronation of King Charles III. O. As H115. R. The Royal Cypher set
against a depiction of a section of the exterior of Westminster Abbey. (Reverse design:
Natasha Jenkins.)
2023 Unc £1

H118   H119

H118 **Fifty pence.** 75th Anniversary of the National Health Service. O. As H115. R. The
inscription 'NATIONAL HEALTH SERVICE 75' surrounded by words describing
qualities associated with the NHS. (Reverse design: Alice Lediard.)
2023 BU £6
—   BU in presentation folder £11
—   Proof in silver *FDC* (Edition: 4,260) £60
—   Proof piedfort in silver *FDC* (Edition: 400)* £125
—   Proof in gold *FDC* (Edition: 410) £1250
—   Proof in platinum *FDC* (Edition: 30)* £2000

H119 **Fifty pence.** 75 Years of the Windrush Generation. O. As H115. R. A depiction of a
man and a woman set against a Union flag accompanied by the number 75 and the
inscription 'WINDRUSH GENERATIONS'. (Reverse design: Valda Jackson.)
2023 BU £6
—   BU in presentation folder £11
—   BU in PNC (Edition: 10,000) £11
—   BU with colour in presentation folder (Edition: 10,000) £15
—   Proof in silver *FDC* (Edition: 650)* £60
—   Proof in silver *FDC* with colour (Edition: 2,808) £70
—   Proof in silver *FDC* with colour in PNC (Edition: 750) £70

— Proof piedfort in silver *FDC* (Edition: 400) * £125
— Proof piedfort in silver *FDC* with colour (Edition: 1260) £135
— Proof in gold *FDC* (Edition: 285) £1250
— Proof in gold *FDC* in PNC (Edition: 60) £1250
— Proof in platinum *FDC* (Edition: 30)* £2000

H120   H121

H120 **Fifty pence.** Star Wars - I. O. As H115. R. A depiction of R2-D2 and C-3PO with the
inscription 'STAR WARS' with special lenticular feature depicting Tatooine and the
Rebel Alliance Starbird. (Reverse design: Lucasfilm Ltd.)
2023 BU £6
— BU in presentation folder £11
— BU with colour in presentation folder (Edition: 20,010) £20
— Proof in silver *FDC* with colour (Edition: 12,510) £70
— Proof in gold *FDC* (Edition: 210) £1225

H121 **Fifty pence.** Star Wars - II. O. As H115. R. A depiction of Darth Vader and Emperor
Palpatine with the inscription 'STAR WARS'. (Reverse design: Lucasfilm Ltd.)
2023 BU £6
— BU in presentation folder £11
— BU with colour in presentation folder (Edition: 20,010) £20
— Proof in silver *FDC* with colour (Edition: 12,510) £70
— Proof in gold *FDC* (Edition: 210) £1225

H122

H122 **Fifty pence.** The Lion, Witch and Wardrobe. O. As H115. R. A depiction of the
characters Mr Tumnus and Lucy from the book with the inscription 'THE LION,
THE WITCH AND THE WARDROBE'. (Reverse design: Ffion Gwillim.)
2023 BU £6
— BU in presentation folder £11
— BU with colour in presentation folder (Edition: 10,000) £20
— Proof in silver *FDC* with colour (Edition: 5,010) £70
— Proof in gold *FDC* (Edition: 110) £1220

H123 **Fifty pence**. O. Portrait of King Charles III with Tudor Crown coronation privy mark.
R. A depiction of an Atlantic salmon with the inscription '50 PENCE' set against a
background of three interlocking C's repeated. (Reverse design: The Royal Mint.)
2023 BU*...£8
— Proof in silver *FDC** £55
— Proof in gold *FDC** £1000

H124   H125

H124 **Fifty pence**. The Snowman. O. As H115. R. A depiction of the Snowman and the
boy from the book The Snowman. (Reverse design: Robin Shaw)
2023 BU...£6
— BU in presentation folder £11
— BU with colour in presentation folder (Edition: 10,000)...................£20
— Proof in silver with *FDC* with colour (Edition: 5,010) £70
— Proof in gold *FDC* (Edition: 110)..£1225
H125 **Fifty pence**. Star Wars - III. O. As H115. R. A depiction of Luke Skywalker and
Princess Leia with the inscription 'STAR WARS'. (Reverse design: Lucasfilm Ltd.)
2023 BU...£6
— BU in presentation folder £11
— BU with colour in presentation folder (Edition:)...............................£20
— Proof in silver *FDC* with colour (Edition:) £60
— Proof in gold *FDC* (Edition:)..£1225

Forthcoming 50p coins:

Star Wars IV

Royal National Lifeboat Institution

Team GB Athletes

Tyrannosaurus Rex

Stegosaurus

Diplodocus

ONE POUND

J41

J41   **One pound.** O. As H123. R. A depiction of two bees with the inscription
'1 POUND' set against a background of three interlocking C's repeated.
(Reverse design: The Royal Mint.)
2023 BU* £8
— Proof in silver *FDC** £60
— Proof in gold *FDC** £1250

TWO POUNDS

K69

K69   **Two pounds.** 200th Anniversary of the Death of Edward Jenner. R. An abstract
depiction of a smallpox cell accompanied by a representation of the people who have
benefitted from vaccination with the inscription 'EDWARD JENNER A VACCINE
TO END SMALLPOX' with the edge inscription 'INNOVATION IN SCIENCE •
JENNER. (Reverse design: Henry Gray.)
2023 BU £6
— BU in presentation folder £12
— Proof in silver *FDC* (Edition: 2,510) £75
— Proof piedfort in silver *FDC* (Edition: 1,260)................................£125
— Proof in gold *FDC* (Edition: 160) £1250

K70   K71

K70   **Two pounds.** The Centenary of The Flying Scotsman. O. As K69. R. A depiction of the
Flying Scotsman with the inscriptions 'FLYING SCOTSMAN LNER 4472' and '1923-2023'
with the edge inscription 'LIVE FOR THE JOURNEY'. (Reverse design: John Bergdahl.)
2023 BU...£6
—   BU in presentation folder £12
—   BU with colour in presentation folder £21
—   BU with colour in PNC (Edition: 10,000) £22
—   Proof in silver *FDC* (Edition: 650)*..£90
—   Proof in silver *FDC* with colour (Edition: 4,482) £85
—   Proof in silver *FDC* with colour in PNC (Edition: 1,200)...........................£90
—   Proof piedfort in silver *FDC* (Edition: 400)*...£150
—   Proof piedfort in silver *FDC* with colour (Edition: 1,933)...........................£135
—   Proof in gold *FDC* (Edition: 560)..£1500
—   Proof in gold *FDC* in PNC (Edition: 100)...£1235
—   Proof in platinum *FDC* (Edition: 30)* £2000

100 gold proofs were marketed in a set with a 1923 sovereign

K71   **Two pounds.** Ada Lovelace. O. As K69. R. A depiction of computer punch cards
accompanied by the inscription 'ADA LOVELACE COMPUTER VISIONARY 1815-1852
A DISCOVERER OF THE HIDDEN REALITIES OF NATURE' with the edge inscription
'INNOVATION IN SCIENCE • LOVELACE'. (Reverse design: Osborne Ross.)
2023 BU...£6
—   BU in presentation folder £12
—   Proof in silver *FDC* (Edition: 1,760)...£90
—   Proof piedfort in silver *FDC* (Edition: 760) £150
—   Proof in gold *FDC* (Edition: 85)...£1225

K72

K72   **Two pounds.** 50th Anniversary of the death of J R R Tolkien. O. As K69.
R. A depiction of Tolkien's monogram with the inscription '1892 JRR TOLKIEN 1973
WRITER • POET • SCHOLAR' with the edge inscription NOT ALL THOSE WHO
WANDER ARE LOST'. (Reverse design: David Lawrence.)
2023 BU...£6
—   BU in presentation folder £12
—   Proof in silver *FDC* (Edition: 5,160)*..£90
—   Proof piedfort in silver *FDC* (Edition: 2,410)* £150
—   Proof in gold *FDC* (Edition: 385)..£1250
—   Proof in platinum *FDC* (Edition: 30)* £2000

K73

K73 **Two pounds.** O. As H123. R. A depiction of the floral symbol of the United
Kingdom; thistle, rose, daffodil and clover, with the inscription '2 POUNDS' with
a background of three interlocking C's repeated, and an edge inscription in incuse
letters 'IN SERVITIO OMNIUM' (Reverse design: The Royal Mint.)
2023 BU* £10
— Proof in silver *FDC** £70
— Proof in gold *FDC** £1500

FIVE POUNDS

L132

L132 **Five pounds.** (Crown.) O. Portrait of King Charles III. R. Two portraits of Queen
Elizabeth II. (Reverse design: John Bergdahl.)
2022 BU in presentation pack (Issued: 161,539) £15
— BU in PNC (Issued: 3,192) £20
— Proof in silver *FDC* (Issued: 23,701) £95
— Proof in silver *FDC* in PNC (Issued: 320) £95
— Proof piedfort in silver *FDC* (Issued: 4,964) £180
— Proof in gold *FDC* (Issued: 1,245)... £3000
— Proof in gold in PNC (Issued: 13) £3000
— Proof piedfort in platinum *FDC* (Issued: 88)............................... £5800

*The number of the precious metal coins issued was equal to the number ordered by
31st December 2022.*

* These coins were only available in the year sets.

L133   L134   L135

L133 **Five pounds.** (Crown.) Myths & Legends - King Arthur. O. As L132. ℞. A depiction
of King Arthur clasping his legendary sword, Excalibur, with the inscription 'KING
ARTHUR MYTHS AND LEGENDS • 2023'. (Reverse design: David Lawrence.)
2023 BU in presentation folder £15

L134 **Five pounds.** (Crown.) Tudor Beasts – Bull of Clarence. O. As L132. ℞. A depiction
of the Bull of Clarence with the inscription 'BULL OF CLARENCE 2023'. (Reverse
design: David Lawrence.)
2023 BU in presentation folder £15

L135 **Five pounds.** (Crown.) Myths & Legends – Merlin. O. As L132. ℞. A depiction
of Merlin holding a magic staff with an owl perched upon his shoulder against a
background of Avalon with the inscription 'MERLIN • MYTHS AND LEGENDS •
2023'. (Reverse design: David Lawrence.)
2023 BU in presentation folder £15

L136

L136 **Five pounds.** (Crown.) Coronation of King Charles III. O. King Charles with
Tudor Crown. ℞. A depiction of St Edward's Crown accompanied by the sovereign's
sceptre with dove and the sovereign's sceptre with cross with the inscription 'THE
CORONATION OF KING CHARLES III 6 MAY 2023' with the edge inscription
'GOD SAVE OUR GRACIOUS KING' on the precious metal versions. (Reverse
design: Timothy Noad.)
2023 BU...£10
—   BU in presentation folder £15
—   BU in PNC (Edition: 20,000) £16
—   Proof in silver *FDC* (Edition: 16,860) £95
—   Proof in silver *FDC* in PNC (edition: 1,500)...£95
—   Proof piedfort in silver *FDC* (Edition: 3,260)..£180
—   Proof in gold *FDC* (Edition: 735) £3250
—   Proof in gold *FDC* in PNC (Edition: 100)..£3250

L137   L138

L137 Five pounds. (Crown.) England. O. As L132. ℞. A depiction of three lions passant
guardant, being that quartering of The Royal Arms known heraldically as England and
the inscription 'FIVE POUNDS'. (Reverse design: Norman Sillman.)
2023 BU in presentation folder £15
—   Proof in silver *FDC* (Edition:)* £95
*The number of the silver proof coins to be issued will be equal to the number ordered by 31st
August 2023.*

*The reverse design was previously issued on the 1997 £1 circulation coin and this £5 coin
celebrates the European Championship victory in 2022 of the England Lionesses.*

L138 Five pounds. (Crown.) Myths & Legends – Morgan Le Fay. O. As L132. ℞. A
depiction of Morgan Le Fay wearing a winged headpiece and poised to use magic
against her enemies with the inscription 'MORGAN LE FAY • MYTHS AND
LEGENDS •' and the date of the year. (Reverse design: David Lawrence.)
2023 BU in presentation folder £15

L139   L140

L139 Five pounds. (Crown.) Shirley Bassey. O. As L132. ℞. A depiction of the silhouette
of Dame Shirley Bassey accompanied by the inscription 'DAME SHIRLEY BASSEY'
and the song titles 'GOLDFINGER', 'MOONRAKER' and 'DIAMONDS ARE
FOREVER'. (Reverse design: Sue Aperghis.)
2023 BU in presentation folder £15
—   BU with colour in presentation folder (Edition: 5,000)....................................£24

L140 Five pounds. (Crown.) The Police. O. As L132. ℞. A depiction of the silhouettes of
the three members of The Police accompanied by the inscription 'THE POLICE'.
(Reverse design: Heena Glover.)
2023 BU in presentation folder £15
—   BU with colour in presentation folder (Edition: 7,500)....................................£24

L141

L141   **Five pounds.** (Crown.) Mary Seacole. O. As L132. R, A depiction of Mary Seacole
set against a background of the Union flag and the inscription 'MARY SEACOLE'
and with edge inscription 'THE ONE WHO NURSED HER SICK' on the precious
metal versions. (Reverse design: Sandra Deiana.)
2023 BU..£10
— BU in presentation folder £12
— Proof in silver *FDC* (Edition: 1,510)...£90
— Proof piedfort in silver *FDC* (Edition: 760) £150
— Proof in gold *FDC* (Edition: 135)..£3250

L142

L142   **Five pounds.** (Crown.) 75th Birthday of King Charles III. O. As L132. R. A
depiction of a floral arrangement surrounding the Royal Cypher, the number 75 and
accompanied by the inscription 'HIS MAJESTY KING CHARLES III 1948 2023' with
the edge inscription 'RESTORING HARMONY WITH NATURE' on the precious
metal versions. (Reverse design; Dan Thorne.)
2023 BU..£10
— BU in presentation folder £12
— Proof in silver *FDC* (Edition: 4,510)...£90
— Proof piedfort in silver *FDC* (Edition: 1,410) £150
— Proof in gold *FDC* (Edition: 435)..£3250
— Proof in platinum *FDC* (Edition: 30)* £5000

L143   **Five pounds.** (Crown.) James Bond. O. As L132. R. A depiction of James Bond
flying a microlight set against a background of James Bond titles and the
inscription '007'.
2023 BU in presentation folder £15

L144   **Five pounds.** (Crown.) Robin Hood. O. As L132. R. A depiction of Robin Hood with
the inscription 'ROBIN HOOD • MYTHS AND LEGENDS' and the date of the year.
2023 BU in presentation folder £15

* *These coins were only available in the year sets.*

L145

L145 **Five pounds.** (Crown.) Year of the Dragon. O. As L132. R. A depiction of a dragon with the inscription 'YEAR OF THE DRAGON • 2024' and the Chinese lunar symbol for a dragon. (Reverse design: William Webb.)
2024 BU in presentation folder £15

L146

L146 **Five pounds.** (Crown.) Seymour Unicorn. O. As L132. R. A depiction of the Seymour Unicorn accompanied by the inscription 'SEYMOUR UNICORN' and the date of the year. (Reverse design: David Lawrence.)
2024 BU in presentation folder £15

Forthcoming £5 coins:

Scotland Lion

Tudor Dragon

The Maundy coins will continue to be presented each year in the traditional ceremony on
Maundy Thursday.

MC5	**One penny.** Maundy	
	2023 proof in silver *FDC*	£400
MC6	**Two pence.** Maundy	
	2023 proof in silver *FDC*	£350
MC7	**Three pence.** Maundy	
	2023 proof in silver *FDC*	£350
MC8	**Four pence.** Maundy	
	2023 proof in silver *FDC*	£350
MS *(date)* Maundy set of four		
	2023 *York Minster*	£ 1250

The place of distribution is shown after each date.

UNCIRCULATED AND PROOF CURRENCY SETS

**2023 Commemorative sets - £5 King Charles 75th Birthday, £2 Flying Scotsman,
£2 J R R Tolkien, 50p National Health Service, 50p Windrush.**

BU set	(5)	£50
Premium proof set (Edition: 2,750)	(5)	£150
Proof set (Edition: 7,500)	(5)	£110
Silver proof set (Edition: 650)	(5)	£325
Silver piedfort proof set (Edition: 400)	(5)	£625
Gold proof set (Edition: 150)	(5)	£7500
Platinum proof set (Edition: 30)	(5)	£10000

2023 Definitive sets - £2, £1, 50p, 20p, 10p, 5p, 2p, 1p.

BU set	(8)	£33
BU First & Last set to include QEII £2-1p	(16)	£66
Proof set (Edition: 12,023)	(8)	£100
Silver proof set (Edition: 3,000)	(8)	£370
Silver proof set including 50p & £5 Coronation (Edition: 300)	(10)	£550
Gold proof set (Edition: 125)	(8)	£7725
Gold proof set including 50p & £5 Coronation (Edition: 30)	(10)	£12000

The first coins in the sovereign series depicting the obverse portrait of King Charles III were issued late in 2022 as a memorial issue to Queen Elizabeth II. The reverse design is the coat of arms quite similar to that used for the Platinum Jubilee series earlier in 2022 but the date is very small and not easy to identify. Following the Coronation, 2023 dated coins have been issued and these depict the traditional St George and Dragon on the reverse. The obverse depicts the crowned king but this will be used only for this year's series.

SA7   **Quarter sovereign.** Memorial issue. O & R. As SC13.
     2022 Unc.. £150
     —   Proof in gold *FDC* (Issued: 2,701 plus coins in sets)..................... £250
SA8   **Quarter sovereign.** Coronation issue. O & R. As SC14.
     2023 Unc.. £150
     —   Proof in gold *FDC* (Edition: 1,750 plus coins in sets) £250
SA9   **Quarter sovereign.** O. As SC13. R. As SC14.
     2024 Unc.. £150
     —   Proof in gold *FDC** £250
SB13   **Half sovereign.** Memorial issue. O & R. As SC13.
     2022 Unc.. £250
     —   Proof in gold *FDC* (Issued: 2,866 plus coins in sets)..................... £400
SB14   **Half sovereign.** Coronation issue. O & R. As SC14.
     2023 Unc.. £250
     —   Proof in gold *FDC* (Edition: 2,500 plus coins in sets) £400
SB15   **Half sovereign.** O. As SC13. R. As SC14.
     2024 Unc.. £250
     —   Proof in gold *FDC* (Edition: 1,250 plus coins in sets) £400

SC13

SC13   **Sovereign.** Memorial issue. R. A depiction of the Royal Coat of Arms and the date of the year. (Reverse design: Jody Clark.)
     2022 Unc.. £450
     —   Proof in gold *FDC* (Issued: 17,271 plus coins in sets)................... £750
     —   Proof piedfort in gold *FDC* (Issued: 1,915) £1400

SC14

SC14   **Sovereign.** Coronation issue. O. King Charles with Tudor crown. R. A depiction of St George armed, sitting on horseback, attacking a dragon with a sword, and a broken spear upon the ground, and the date of the year. (Reverse design: Benedetto Pistrucci.)
     2023 Unc.. £430
     —   Proof in gold *FDC* (Edition: 15,000 plus coins in sets) £750
     —   Proof piedfort in gold *FDC* (Edition: 1,260)................................ £1400

SC14A Sovereign. Coronation issue. R̩. As SC14 but with plain edge.
2023 BU Matt (Edition: 1,260).. £1200
These coins were struck on 6th May 2023, the day of the Coronation.
SC15   **Sovereign. O.** As SC13. R̩. As SC14.
2023 BU (Edition: 860) £600
This coin was struck on the King's 75th birthday 14th November, 2023.
SC16   **Sovereign. O.** As SC13. R̩. As SC14.
2024 Unc... £400
—   Proof in gold *FDC* (Edition: 7,500 plus coins in sets) £750
SD13   **Two pounds.** Memorial issue. O & R̩. As SC13.
2022 Unc... £900
—   Proof in gold *FDC** £1500
SD14   **Two pounds.** Coronation issue. O & R̩. As SC14.
2023 Unc... £900
—   Proof in gold *FDC** £1500
SD15   **Two pounds. O.** As SC13. R̩. As SC14.
2024 Proof in gold *FDC** £1500
SE17   **Five pounds.** Memorial issue. O & R̩. As SC13.
2022 Unc (issued: 661)... £3000
—   Proof in gold *FDC** £4000
SE18   **Five pounds.** Coronation issue. O & R̩. As SC14.
2023 Unc (Edition: 660) £3000
—   Proof in gold *FDC** £4000
SE19   **Five pounds. O.** As SC13. R̩. As SC14.
2024 Proof in gold *FDC** £4000

GOLD SOVEREIGN PROOF SETS

PGS101–2022 Memorial issue. Gold £5, £2, sovereign, half sovereign, quarter
sovereign (Issued: 1,113) ....(5)   £6000
PGS102–2022 Memorial issue. Gold £2, sovereign, half sovereign, quarter
sovereign (Issued: 674)...(4)   £2500
PGS103–2022 Memorial issue. Gold Sovereign, half sovereign, quarter sovereign
(Issued: 1,340) ....(3)   £1150
PGS104–2023 Coronation issue. Gold £5, £2, sovereign, half sovereign, quarter
sovereign (Edition: 1,050) ....(5)   £6000
PGS105–2023 Coronation issue. Gold £2, sovereign, half sovereign, quarter
sovereign (Edition: 575) ....(4)   £2500
PGS106–2023 Coronation issue. Gold Sovereign, half sovereign, quarter
sovereign (Edition: 1,250) ....(3)   £1150
PGS107–2024 Gold £5, £2, sovereign, half sovereign, quarter sovereign (Edition: 450) .(5)   £6000
PGS108–2024 Gold £2, sovereign, half sovereign, quarter sovereign (Edition: 350) ... (4)   £2500
PGS109–2024 Gold Sovereign, half sovereign, quarter sovereign (Edition: 650).. (3)   £1150

Gold Sovereign Sales Figures

2022	¼ Sov.	½ Sov.	Sov.	£2	£5	Set	Authorised
PGS101	1,113	1,113	1,113	1,113	1,113	1,113	1,200
PGS102	674	674	674	674		674	750
PGS103	1,340	1,340	1,340			1,340	1,500
SC13			17,271				17,500
SB13		2,866					3,000
SA7	2,701						3,000
	5,828	5,993	20,398	1,787	1,113		

SILVER COINS

2022 The Life and Legacy of Queen Elizabeth II

£2 silver proof (Issued: 24,947)* £100
£10 silver proof (Issued: 2,603) £575
£10 silver proof piedfort (Issued: 854) £1050
£1000 silver proof (Issued: 259) £2600

The number of coins issued was equal to the number ordered by 31st December 2022.

2023 Monarchy series – Henry VIII

£2 silver proof (Edition: 1,361)..................£100
£5 silver proof (Edition: 607).....................£190
£10 silver proof (Edition: 257)...................£480
£10 silver proof piedfort (Edition: 107).....£910

2023 Myths & Legends - King Arthur

£2 silver proof (Edition: 2,510)..................£100
£5 silver proof (Edition: 510)....................£190

2023 Tudor Beasts – Bull of Clarence

£2 silver proof (Edition: 5,510)....................£95
£2 silver proof reverse frosted (Edition: 500)*
£5 silver proof (Edition: 1,256)..................£185
£10 silver proof (Edition: 256)...................£465
£10 silver proof piedfort (Edition: 106).....£885

* £2 set of two with one reversed frosted
   (Edition:500)...£210

2023 Harry Potter III - Dumbledore

£2 silver proof (Edition: 5,010).................£100
£5 silver proof (Edition: 510)....................£185
£10 silver proof (Edition: 310)..................£480

For coin specifications please see the tables at the beginning of the Britannia section

2023 Britannia
5p   silver proof (Edition: 1,010)*
—   reverse frosted (Edition: 1,560)*
10p silver proof (Edition: 1,010)*
—   reverse frosted (Edition: 1,560)*
20p silver proof (Edition: 1,010)*
50p silver proof (Edition: 1,010)*
—   reverse frosted (Edition: 1,560)*
£1   silver proof (Edition: 1,010)*
£2   silver proof (Edition: 5,210) £100
—   reverse frosted (Edition: 2,260)*
£5   silver proof (Edition: 1,010) £190
£10 silver proof (Edition: 470) £480
• Silver proof set (6) (Edition: 1,010) £245
• Silver proof set reverse frosted (4)
   (Edition: 1,560) £165
• Silver proof set (2 x £2) (Edition: 700) ... £195

2023 Monarchy series – Charles I
£2 silver proof (Edition: 1,360).................. £100
£5 silver proof (Edition: 606)..................... £190
£10 silver proof (Edition: 256).................... £480
£10 silver proof piedfort (Edition: 106)..... £910

2023 Great Engravers – Petition Crown Obverse
£5 silver proof (Edition: 3,260)...........................
£10 silver proof (Edition: 506)...........................
£10 silver proof piedfort (Edition: 156)..............

2023 Great Engravers – Petition Crown Reverse
£5 silver proof (Edition: 3,260)................. £560
£10 silver proof (Edition: 506)................. £1190
£10 silver proof piedfort (Edition: 156)... £2375
The above two coins were sold in sets of 2 so the prices shown are for sets.

2023 Harry Potter IV – Hogwarts School
£2 silver proof (Edition: 5,010)................. £100
£5 silver proof (Edition: 510)..................... £185
£10 silver proof (Edition: 310).................. £480

For coin specifications please see the tables at the beginning of the Britannia section

2023 Myths & Legends - Merlin
£2 silver proof (Edition: 2,510)..................£100
£5 silver proof (Edition: 510).....................£190

2023 Myths & Legends – Morgan le Fay
£2 silver proof (Edition: 2,510)..................£100
£5 silver proof (Edition: 510).....................£190

2023 Coronation of King Charles III.
£2 silver proof (Edition: 18,660)................£100
£5 silver proof (Edition: 1,006)..................£190
— reverse frosted (Edition: 1,006) £190
£10 silver proof (Edition: 1,536)................£480
£500 silver proof (Edition: 202)...............£2390

2023 Shirley Bassey
£2 silver proof (Edition: 3.260)..................£100
£5 silver proof (Edition: 360).....................£190

2023 Star Wars I
£2 silver proof (Edition: 3,010)..................£100
£5 silver proof (Edition: 760).....................£190
£10 silver proof (Edition: 360)..................£485

2023 Monarchy series – Charles II
£2 silver proof (Edition: 1,360)..................£100
£5 silver proof (Edition: 606).....................£190
£10 silver proof (Edition: 256)...................£480
£10 silver proof piedfort (Edition: 106).....£910

For coin specifications please see the tables at the beginning of the Britannia section

2023 The Police
£2 silver proof (Edition: 6,010) £100
£5 silver proof (Edition: 706) £190
£10 silver proof (Edition: 306) £485

2023 King Charles III 75th Birthday
£1 silver proof (Edition: 5,010) £55

2023 Star Wars III
£2 silver proof (Edition: 3,010) £100
£5 silver proof (Edition: 760) £190
£10 silver proof (Edition: 360) £485

2023 Monarchy series – George II
£2 silver proof (Edition: 1,360) £100
£5 silver proof (Edition: 606) £190
£10 silver proof (Edition: 256) £480
£10 silver proof piedfort (Edition: 106).. £950

2023 James Bond I
£2 silver proof (Edition:) £100
£5 silver proof (Edition:) £190
£10 silver proof (Edition:) £485

2023 Robin Hood.
£2 silver proof (Edition:) £100
£5 silver proof (Edition:) £190

2023 Star Wars II
£2 silver proof (Edition: 3,010) £100
£5 silver proof (Edition: 760) £190
£10 silver proof (Edition: 360) £485

For coin specifications please see the tables at the beginning of the Britannia section

2024 Year of the Dragon
£2 silver proof (Edition: 5,008) £100
£10 silver proof (Edition: 298) £485
£500 silver proof (Edition: 52) £2425

2024 Tudor Beasts – Seymour Unicorn
£2 silver proof (Edition: 5,510) £95
£2 silver proof reverse frosted (Edition: 750)*
£5 silver proof (Edition: 1,256) £185
£10 silver proof (Edition: 256) £465
£10 silver proof piedfort (Edition: 106).. £885

*£2 set of two with one reversed frosted
(Edition: 750) £210

GOLD COINS

2022 The Life and Legacy of Queen Elizabeth II
£25 gold proof (Issued: 3,411)* £750
£100 gold proof (Issued: 1,263)* £2800
£200 gold proof (Issued: 563) £5500
£500 gold proof (Issued: 204) £13000
£500 gold proof (Issued: 38) £27500
£1000 gold proof (Issued: 20) £85000
£2000 gold proof (Issued: 1) £165000
£5000 gold proof (Issued: 1) £425000
£7000 gold proof (Edition: 1) £600000
£15000 gold proof (Issued: 1) £1500000

The number of coins issued was equal to the number ordered by 31st December 2022.

For coin specifications please see the tables at the beginning of the Britannia section

2023 Monarchy series – Henry VIII
£100 gold proof (Edition: 261) £2800
£200 gold proof (Edition: 77) £5500
£500 gold proof (Edition: 27) £12500

2023 Harry Potter III - Dumbledore
£25 gold proof (Edition: 510) £750
£200 gold proof (Edition: 60) £6000

2023 Myths & Legends - King Arthur
£25 gold proof (Edition: 610) £750
£100 gold proof (Edition: 210) £2850

2023 Tudor Beasts – Bull of Clarence
£25 gold proof (Edition: 660) £750
£100 gold proof (Edition: 310) £3000
£200 gold proof (Edition: 66) £5000
£500 gold proof (Edition: 26) £12500

2023 Britannia
50p gold proof (Edition: 195)*
— reverse frosted (Edition: 260)*
£1 gold proof (Edition: 195)*
— reverse frosted (Edition: 260)*
£10 gold proof (Edition: 345)*
£25 gold proof (Edition: 1,345)................£725
— reverse frosted (Edition: 260)*
£50 gold proof (Edition: 345)*
£100 gold proof (Edition: 195)*
— reverse frosted (Edition: 260)*
£200 gold proof (Edition: 135)................£5500
£500 gold proof (Edition: 90)................£12,500
• Gold proof set(6) (Edition: 195) £5000
• Gold proof set(3) (Edition: 150) £2200
• Gold proof set reverse frosted (4)
 (Edition: 260) £3500

2023 Monarchy series – Charles I
£100 gold proof (Edition: 260) £3000
£200 gold proof (Edition: 56) £5500
£500 gold proof (Edition: 26) £12500

For coin specifications please see the tables at the beginning of the Britannia section

2023 Great Engravers – Petition Crown Obverse
£200 gold proof (Edition: 310) ....
£500 gold proof (Edition: 131) ....
£1000 gold proof (Edition: 8) ....
£5000 gold proof (Edition: 1) ....

2023 Great Engravers – Petition Crown Reverse
£200 gold proof (Edition: 310) £12500
£500 gold proof (Edition: 131) £30000
£1000 gold proof (Edition: 8) £180000
£5000 gold proof (Edition: 1)

The above two coins were sold in sets of 2 so the prices shown are for sets.

2023 Harry Potter IV – Hogwarts School
£25 gold proof (Edition: 510) £750
£200 gold proof (Edition: 60) £6000

2023 Myths & Legends - Merlin
£25 gold proof (Edition: 610) £750
£100 gold proof (Edition: 210) £2850

2023 Coronation of King Charles III
50p gold proof (Edition: 3,033) £125
£25 gold proof (Edition: 1,360) £750
£100 gold proof (Edition: 685) £3000
--- reverse frosted (Edition: 210)............. £3500
£200 gold proof (Edition: 306) £5500
£500 gold proof (Edition: 106) £12750
£1000 gold proof (Edition: 17) £80000

2023 Monarchy series – Charles II
£100 gold proof (Edition: 261) £3000
£200 gold proof (Edition: 56) £5500
£500 gold proof (Edition: 26) £12500

2023 Myths & Legends – Morgan le Fay
£25 gold proof (Edition: 260) £750
£100 gold proof (Edition: 210) £2850

For coin specifications please see the tables at the beginning of the Britannia section

2023 Shirley Bassey
£25 gold proof (Edition: 410) £750
£100 gold proof (Edition: 160) £2770
£200 gold proof (Edition: 80) £5300

2023 Star Wars I
£25 gold proof (Edition: 510) £750
£100 gold proof (Edition: 260) £2770

2023 The Police
£25 gold proof (Edition: 510) £750
£100 gold proof (Edition: 310) £2770
£200 gold proof (Edition: 150) £5300

2023 Monarchy series – George II
£100 gold proof (Edition: 261) £2770
£200 gold proof (Edition: 77) £5300

2023 Star Wars II
£25 gold proof (Edition: 510) £750
£100 gold proof (Edition: 260) £2770

2023 King Charles III 75th Birthday
50p gold proof (Edition: 2,033) £80
£25 gold proof (Edition: 585) £750
£200 gold proof (Edition: 81) £5500

2023 Star Wars III
£25 gold proof (Edition: 510) £750
£100 gold proof (Edition: 260) £2770

2023 James Bond I
£25 gold proof (Edition:) £750
£100 gold proof (Edition:) £2770
£200 gold proof (Edition:) £5300

2023 Robin Hood.
£100 gold proof (Edition:) £2770

For coin specifications please see the tables at the beginning of the Britannia section

2024 Year of the Dragon
£25 gold proof (Edition: 398) £750
£100 gold proof (Edition: 898) £2770
£500 gold proof (Edition: 138) £12725
£1000 gold proof (Edition: 10) £77500

2024 Tudor Beasts – Seymour Unicorn
£25 gold proof (Edition: 660) £750
£100 gold proof (Edition: 260) £3000
£200 gold proof (Edition: 56) £5000
£500 gold proof (Edition: 26) £12500

PLATINUM COINS

2022 The Life and Legacy of Queen Elizabeth II
£100 platinum proof (Issued: 117)* £2500

2023 Britannia
£25 platinum proof (Edition: 210) £450

Forthcoming Commemorative coins:

Star Wars IV

Harry Potter

Lion and Eagle

Paris

Royal National Lifeboat Institution

Edward VI

Athens

Tudor Dragon

For coin specifications please see the tables at the beginning of the Britannia section

The Bullion range of coins are uncirculated pieces sold by the Royal Mint at a small premium over the metal content so their cost can fluctuate daily in line with world wide metal prices.

SILVER COINS

2023 Britannia

20p silver	£5
50p silver	£8
£2 silver	£30
£500 silver	£950

2023 Myths & Legends - Merlin

£2 silver	£30

2023 Coronation

£2 silver	£30

For coin specifications please see the tables at the beginning of the Britannia section

2023 Britannia Coronation
20p silver £5
50p silver £8
£2 silver £30
£500 silver £950

2023 Myths & Legends – Maid Marian
£10 silver £300
Shown here at reduced size. Original coin
89mm diameter.

2023 Bull of Clarence
£2 silver £30
£10 silver £300

2023 Roosevelt & Churchill
£2 silver... £30

2024 Britannia.
£2 silver... £30

2023 Royal Arms
£2 silver £30
£10 silver £300

For coin specifications please see the tables at the beginning of the Britannia section

GOLD COINS

2023 Britannia
£10 gold £180
£25 gold £475
£50 gold £900
£100 gold £1750

2023 Myths & Legends - Merlin
£100 gold £1750

2023 Coronation
£10 gold £180
£25 gold £475
£100 gold £1750

2023 Britannia Coronation
£10 gold £180
£25 gold £475
£50 gold £900
£100 gold £1750

For coin specifications please see the tables at the beginning of the Britannia section

2023 Royal Arms
£10 gold £180
£100 gold £1750

2023 Bull of Clarence
£25 gold £475
£100 gold £1750

2023 Gold Standard
£25 gold £475
£100 gold £1750

2023 Roosevelt & Churchill
£25 gold £475

2024 Britannia.
£10 gold £180
£25 gold £475
£50 gold £900
£100 gold £1750

PLATINUM COINS

2023 Britannia
£10 platinum £125
£100 platinum £950

2023 Bull of Clarence
£100 platinum £950

Forthcoming Bullion coins:
Seymour Unicorn

Beowolf & Grendel

CONSIGN NOW

THE GLOBAL COLLECTABLES AUCTION HOUSE

LONDON | NEW YORK | HONG KONG | SINGAPORE | SWITZERLAND

SPINK

Where History is Valued

WWW.SPINK.COM